Five Thousand Years of Monarchy

Five Thousand Years of Monarchy

Dr. Michael Arnheim

WILEY Blackwell

Library of Congress Cataloging-in-Publication Data

Names: Arnheim, M. T. W. (Michael T. W.) author
Title: Five thousand years of monarchy / Dr. Michael Arnheim.
Other titles: 5000 years of monarchy
Description: First edition. | Hoboken, New Jersey : Wiley-Blackwell, 2026.
  | Includes bibliographical references and index.
Identifiers: LCCN 2025021739 (print) | LCCN 2025021740 (ebook) | ISBN
  9781394154418 paperback | ISBN 9781394154425 pdf | ISBN 9781394154432
  epub
Subjects: LCSH: Monarchy–History
Classification: LCC JC375 .A764 2025 (print) | LCC JC375 (ebook) | DDC
  321/.609–dc23/eng/20250701
LC record available at https://lccn.loc.gov/2025021739
LC ebook record available at https://lccn.loc.gov/2025021740

Set in 11.5/14 pt STIXTwoText by Straive, Pondicherry, India

POSUI DEUM ADIUTOREM MEUM

To the Sacred Memory of My Beloved Parents

Dr Wilhelm Arnheim (1901–75)
A wise medical doctor and true polymath, with the driest sense of humor
And
Mrs Vicky Arnheim (1905–90)
A brilliant musician, gifted teacher, dedicated social organizer,
Great cook, and loving mother
And
To the sacred memory of my beloved grandmother, "Oma"
Mrs Martha Arnheim (1875–1965)
An eternally cheerful and optimistic, courageous spirit
Who taught me German, and whose wonderful humorous tales
Of the old Germany will remain with me always.

Contents

PART VI: CONCLUSION   397

PART VII: ROUND-UP   403

List of Illustrations

About the Author

Dr Michael Arnheim (commonly known as "Doctor Mike") is a practising London barrister, sometime Fellow of St John's College, Cambridge, and author of 25 published books to date, this being the 25th.

Born in Johannesburg, South Africa, to a German father and South African mother, he attended the prestigious King Edward VII School. As a 14-year-old schoolboy he was picked to join the "Quiz Kids" team of five capped and gowned teenagers appearing every Friday evening on South Africa's Springbok Radio, of which he became a stalwart member, "retiring" at the age of eighteen.

He entered Johannesburg's University of the Witwatersrand at the age of 16, taking a first-class BA in History and Classics at the age of 19, first-class Honors in Classics at 20 and an MA with distinction at the age of 21.

Michael Arnheim then went up to St John's College, Cambridge, on a National Scholarship (later converted to a St John's College scholarship supplemented by a Strathcone Travel Exhibition). He was awarded a Cambridge PhD in 1969 in record time, and in 1972 his doctoral dissertation was published by the Oxford University Press under the title *The Senatorial Aristocracy in the Later Roman Empire*. In the meantime he was elected into a Fellowship of St John's College, Cambridge, where he combined research with a great deal of teaching for a number of colleges in Classics and Ancient History.

At the age of 31, Michael Arnheim was invited to take up the position of full Professor and Head of the Department of Classics back at his old university in South Africa. During his time in that position, he devised a new system of learning Latin and also taught his students Spanish under the title of "Modern Latin," using etymological links with English.

Despondent about the future of South Africa, Dr Arnheim returned to Britain, where he was called to the Bar by Lincoln's Inn in 1988, combining his practice of law with the writing of books, a combination that is still continuing.

For further information on Michael Arnheim, you may consult the Wikipedia article on him at en.wikipedia.org/wiki/Michael_Arnheim. You are also welcome to contact him by email (at Counsel@arnheim-law.com).

Preface

Unlike most other academic subjects, history lacks its own technical theory or arcane terminology, and is therefore accessible to the "general reader." But that does not mean that a historical work should just be an account of "one damned fact after another." Instead, it is important for a historian to make sense of history, for it to become, in the words of the great Greek historian Thucydides, "a possession for all time."

As an undergraduate in the 1960s I came across various elitist theories which posited an "iron law of oligarchy" according to which every society, regardless of its label, is ruled by an elite minority. To my utter surprise, Oxford's Professor Sir Ronald Syme, one of the biggest names among twentieth-century historians, was a member of this one-size-fits-all "oligarchy club": "In all ages, whatever the form and name of government, be it monarchy, republic, or democracy, an oligarchy lurks behind the façade." This was written in 1939, and Syme was still unrepentant 50 years later, describing Augustus's regime as "autocratic government" but at the same time insisting that "Oligarchy is imposed as the guiding theme, the link from age to age whatever be the form and name of government." Syme knew full well that the regime instituted by the Roman Emperor Augustus was a monarchy, but he sought to square the circle by stating baldly: "A monarchy rules through an oligarchy"—a contradiction in terms.

I first embarked on an analysis of power structure with my *Senatorial Aristocracy in the Later Roman Empire* (a revised version of my 1969 Cambridge doctoral dissertation) published by the Oxford University Press (Arnheim 1972), followed by my *Aristocracy in Greek Society* (Arnheim 1977). The result of expanding my power structure analysis to encompass a number of societies was my *Two Models of Government* (Arnheim 2017), in which I concluded that oligarchy was only one half of the picture, the other half being monarchy. I found that every society which I analyzed was ruled either by an oligarchy made up of a privileged elite minority or by a monarch. Those findings were corroborated in my *Why Rome Fell: Decline and Fall, or Drift and Change?* (Arnheim 2022).

The present work is the result of greatly expanding the scope of that analysis, which has confirmed my conclusion that, since the beginning of recorded time, there have been, regardless of label, essentially only two forms of government: monarchy and oligarchy. Modern Britain, supposedly a monarchy par excellence, is in fact an oligarchy, while the People's Republic of China is a monarchy. What about democracy? The "direct democracy" of ancient Athens was actually a populist monarchy, while the modern indirect or representative "democracies" are mostly oligarchies, or in the case of the United States, a hybrid between monarchy and oligarchy.

Classifying governments in terms of power structure is not just an exercise in bottling and labelling. This study goes on to investigate the relationship, if any, between the power structure of a regime and its stability, the degree of liberty and equality within it, its foreign policy, and its social and political ethos.

The people whose help and assistance I have received are too numerous to name. But I cannot omit to mention my former student and long-time friend Tom Malnati of Florida, to whom I owe a debt of gratitude for proofreading the whole book. All errors remaining are my own responsibility alone. And there have been many fruitful discussions with colleagues and former students over the years.

I am delighted to say that I have had a long and happy association with Wiley, starting with my *U.S. Constitution for Dummies,* the first edition of which came out in 2009, and the second in 2018, and then *Why Rome Fell: Decline and Fall, or Drift and Change?* (Arnheim 2022). I owe a debt of gratitude to the Wiley team with whom I have been working on this book: commissioning editor Will Croft and managing editor Pascal Raj Francois.

Any reader of this book is welcome to contact me with queries or comments at: Counsel@arnheim-law.com

Dr. Michael Arnheim

28 February 2025

Glossary

Definitions

Monarchy: Rule by one person, or a state under such rule. From the Greek *monos* ("alone") + *archein* ("to rule"). The term "monarch" without qualification is used in this book to refer to someone exercising real power, regardless of title. Besides the numerous individuals discussed in the body of the book, the "Round-up" in Part VII lists many more, classified as follows:

A—An actual or true monarch exercising absolute, autocratic, or at least real power, regardless of title, but without specific popular support. Examples: Hammurabi of Babylon, Charlemagne, Henry VIII of England, Shogun Tokugawa Ieyasu of Japan, Francisco Franco of Spain, Xi Jinping of China.

A*—An actual or true monarch, regardless of title, exercising absolute, autocratic, or at least real power, ruling against the interests of the elite with active or passive popular support. Examples: Sumerian Urukagina, Cyrus the Great of Persia, Pericles of Athens, Alexander the Great, Roman Emperor Augustus, Juan Perón of Argentina.

H—Hybrid: monarch sharing power with an elite. Examples: Phraates of Parthia, Shapur I of the Persian Sasanian Empire, French President François Mitterand, US President Franklin D. Roosevelt, King Hussein of Jordan.

C—Constitutional monarch: head of state with little or no actual power. Examples: All doges of Venice between 1268 and 1797, all British monarchs since George I, all Danish monarchs since 1849, all Japanese emperors since 1947, all presidents of the German Federal Republic since 1949.

Oligarchy: Rule by an elite minority; also, the members of such an elite. From the Greek *oligoi* ("the few") + *archein* ("to rule"). Note that minority rule can always be referred to as an oligarchy, regardless of whether or not that oligarchy is hereditary. Where the oligarchy is hereditary, it can be termed an "aristocracy." So, all ruling aristocracies are oligarchies, but not all ruling oligarchies are aristocracies.

Aristocracy: Rule by a hereditary elite, a hereditary oligarchy; also, the members of such an elite. From the Greek *aristos* ("best") + *kratos* ("power, rule"), so, literally "rule of the best."

Noble, nobility: In this book, the terms *noble* and *nobility* are used to refer to any member of an aristocracy by birth or origin. Therefore, in reference to people (as against reference to forms of government), "nobility" is used as a synonym for "aristocracy."

Elite: A privileged minority, whether based on birth, wealth, race, nationality, or religion, and whether or not exercising dominant political power. A French term, *élite,* deriving from Latin *electus,* "chosen, selected."

"Heretic": In reference to Christianity, a devotee of any deviant belief condemned and anathematized by a dominant Christian denomination. In this book, this is always encased in quotation marks to indicate that the author does not accept, endorse, or condemn beliefs on either side of these religious disputes.

"Pagan," "paganism": The adherent of any religion other than Judaism, Christianity, or Islam, first used as a pejorative term by Christians in the fourth century CE. Because of its negative connotations, in this book it is always encased in quotation marks. It is sometimes now replaced by "polytheist" and "polytheism," referring, literally, to the worship of "many gods," as distinct from the monotheism of Judaism, Christianity, and Islam. However, polytheism is hardly less pejorative than pagan, and not all pagans worshipped multiple gods in any case. So, in this book, "pagan" and "paganism" continue to be used, but without any negative connotations.

"Barbarians": The English word "barbarian" comes from Greek *barbaros,* via Latin *barbarus,* a pejorative term used by the Romans to refer to anyone who was neither Greek nor Roman, and whose unintelligible speech sounded to the Romans like a babble of *bar-bar-bar-bar.* However, the term "barbarian" is used in this book without any pejorative connotations.

Introduction

This book is the result of a long study analyzing the power structure of a number of societies over the past five thousand years, and geographically from China in the east to the United States in the west, and from Scandinavia in the north down to Egypt in the south. My findings are as follows:

- There are, and have been, essentially only two models of government: monarchy and oligarchy.
- Since the beginning of recorded time, society has always been divided into two main elements: a privileged elite and the ordinary people.
- There has always been a certain tension or antagonism between these two elements.
- Where the elite are in control, the government is an oligarchy, a subdivision of which—where the oligarchy is hereditary—is aristocracy.
- The only other pure type of government is monarchy.
- There is popular monarchy, when a strong leader rules with broad popular support.
- Then there is actual, absolute, or autocratic monarchy without specific popular support.
- What is commonly referred to as constitutional monarchy, where the supposed monarch has little or no actual power, is not really monarchy at all but oligarchy in disguise.

It is important to realize that the term "monarchy" as used in this book includes any regime where power is concentrated in the hands of a single individual, regardless of title. So, while Fidel Castro, the leader of the Republic of Cuba, was in fact a monarch, his contemporary, the "constitutional monarch" King

Baudouin of the Belgians, was, in reality, merely a non-executive titular head of state. Is it possible for power to be shared between a monarch and an oligarchic elite? The question to ask is: Who has the whip hand? True shared power in a hybrid form of government is rare. More often, what appears as shared power will turn out to be either a disguised monarchy or a disguised oligarchy.

Just as oligarchies (and aristocracies), in which power is shared by an elite group, have a visceral fear of monarchy, so, by the same token, monarchies should recognize the serious danger to their position from an ambitious power elite that threatens to take power away from them and share it among themselves.

Ancient Mesopotamia

Though this threat has existed since time immemorial, not all monarchs have been conscious of it. The Mesopotamian *lugal* (king) Urukagina of Lagash in the twenty-fourth century BCE is one of the earliest examples we know of where someone, with popular support, evidently overthrew a priestly aristocracy and ruled in the interests of the lower classes. This can also be seen from his legal code, probably the earliest such document known to history (see Chapter 16).

China, Ancient and Modern

The Chinese emperors were particularly conscious of the aristocratic threat to the monarchy, and it was to counter this threat that the famous Chinese competitive civil service examination system was instituted, which lasted for close on two thousand years, starting during the Han dynasty (206 BCE– 220 CE) and being abolished only in 1905, just before the imperial system as a whole was swept away. The expense of the tuition involved gave the wealthier classes an advantage in the examinations, but the rank of scholar-official was not hereditary. Though these highly educated and intelligent officials enjoyed great status and prestige, they never posed a threat to imperial power. The eunuchs formed another important bastion of imperial power against the aristocracy from at least around 146 CE until the end of the Qing (Manchu) dynasty in 1912. Some eunuchs exercised great power, which was facilitated by their closeness to the emperor. The reason they were entrusted with such responsibility was that, as they could not have children and start a dynasty, they would not be tempted to seize the throne, and they could easily be demoted or disposed of. The eunuchs were also a useful counterweight to the scholar-officials, with whom they were always in competition for influence with the emperor (see Chapter 19).

The French Revolution

By contrast, let us take the French Revolution as an example picked almost at random, a cataclysmic event in world history on which there is no shortage of evidence and a plethora of historical studies, hardly any of which show the slightest awareness of the significance—or even the existence—of the power structure (see Chapters 17 and 19).

The wise and wily Louis XV (r. 1715–74) was well aware of the longstanding threat to the French crown posed by the aristocracy, particularly in the shape of the *Parlement de Paris*—not a legislature but a court that had arrogated to itself the right to "register" (and therefore to veto) any royal decree. By 1771 the king's able chief minister, René de Maupeou, had finally defeated the *Parlement de Paris* and replaced it with a royal court, and then took similar action against the provincial *parlements*. These were intended as merely the first steps in a wholesale reform of the judicial system, but the whole enterprise was abruptly cut short by Louis XV's death and Maupeou's dismissal by the new king, Louis XV's grandson, Louis XVI, a callow 19-year-old, who did not understand that, far from being his allies, the aristocracy were actually hostile at once to royal power and to the interests of the mass of the population. "I had won for the King a case that has dragged on for three hundred years," lamented Maupeou. "He wishes to lose it again. It is his decision."

More interested in tinkering with locks in his workshop than with affairs of state, Louis XVI never got to understand the true nature of power, a failing which was to prove fatal for himself and the *ancien régime*. The brilliant eccentric royalist revolutionary Mirabeau (1749–91) desperately tried to make Louis recognize and develop the bond between the monarchy and the ordinary people of France: "The indivisibility of monarch and people is in the heart of every Frenchman. It is necessary for it to exist in action and in power." Ignoring this sound advice, Louis made a frantic run to the frontier to link up with France's enemies. Recognized (ironically, from his embossed profile on the *assignat*, the new revolutionary paper money), he was arrested and ignominiously dragged back to Paris as a prisoner. From there it was but a short step to deposition, trial, and execution.

But that was not quite the end of the story. Napoleon Bonaparte, who saw himself as the heir to the Revolution, subsequently reinvented himself as a monarch under the style of emperor, a title deliberately chosen for its Roman populist associations. It is no accident that Maupeou's right-hand man, Charles-François Lebrun (1739–1824), was picked by Napoleon to serve as Third Consul under himself in 1799 to take a leading role in the reorganization of the national finances and of the administration—both pet projects of Maupeou's aborted by the death of Louis XV in 1774. Casting his mind back 30 years, Lebrun also cautioned Napoleon against recreating a hereditary aristocracy.

Augustus

One of the few dates that most people recognize is the assassination of Julius Caesar on the Ides of March 44 BCE. But, besides the drama and gore surrounding that date, of which Hollywood has taken full advantage, it also marks an important historical watershed. The Roman Republic, an oligarchy with a visceral fear of one-man rule, had come into existence in 509 BCE. But when the populist Caesar was named *dictator perpetuo* ("dictator for life"), the Republic was effectively dead. His senatorial assassins, brandishing the deceptive watchword "liberty" (which really meant "freedom" for the privileged elite alone), desperately wanted to revive the oligarchy that was the Republic, and made a failed last-ditch stand in a bloody civil war to do so. When the dust settled after a further round of civil war, Caesar's great-nephew, adoptive son, and heir found himself presiding as sole ruler over the whole Roman world. Carefully trying to avoid offending the surviving senatorial oligarchs, he eschewed the title of "king" or "dictator" in favor of the innocuous designation of *princeps,* or "first citizen". In 27 BCE he reinvented himself under the style *Imperator Caesar Augustus*: 'Caesar' being the key to his inherited popular support; "Imperator", the ovation given to a victorious general, but used as a forename; and "Augustus" meaning "the sublime one", an honorific awarded him by the Senate. He was in addition *pontifex maximus,* or chief priest of the Roman state religion, and *pater patriae,* "father of the fatherland", a benign title with connotations of fatherly love without any harsh overtones.

As the first Roman emperor, Augustus ushered in a golden age of two centuries (27 BCE–180 CE) of a "Principate" of strong monarchy with popular support while placating the senatorial elite; followed by a "Dominate" of autocratic monarchy without specific popular support from 284 to 395; and, in the Eastern half of the Empire, a further thousand years of Caesaropapism, until 1453, of what is now known as the Byzantine Empire; while in the West there was a recrudescence of the Roman Empire with a more northerly centre of gravity, the Holy Roman Empire, which lasted from 962 until 1806.

Most of the Western half of the Roman Empire still speaks a Romance language, a latter-day version of Latin: Italian, Spanish, Catalan, Portuguese, French, and Romanian. Rome never imposed its language, culture, or religion on anyone, and in fact Rome was always a bilingual empire, with Latin in the West (and in the army) and Greek (a legacy from Alexander the Great) in the East. And it is no accident that the European states where Romance languages are spoken now form part of the European Union, the latest attempt to create a united Europe on the Roman model.

It was by conquest that Rome grew from a small Italian city-state to encompass the whole Mediterranean basin. There was some initial resistance to Roman rule. Rebel names that stand out include Vercingetorix in Gaul and Boudicca in Britain. But, before long the benefits of Roman rule became apparent. Roman citizenship with all its concomitant benefits was prized, and in 212 the Emperor Caracalla granted Roman citizenship to all free male inhabitants of the empire, though that resulted in citizens being divided into two broad classes, *honestiores* ("more honorable") and *humiliores* ("more lowly"), with the latter gradually losing many of the privileges of citizenship. Starting under the Emperor Claudius (r. 41–54), senatorial status was opened up to provincials, and, with Trajan (r. 98–117), even emperors were drawn from the ranks of provincials. Though Trajan was born in Spain, his family was originally from Italy. But from Septimius Severus (r. 193–211), who was born in Leptis (or Lepcis) Magna in modern Libya, most emperors were of provincial stock.

Until the "crisis of the third century" (235–284) and the death-throes of the Western Empire in the fifth century, the Roman Empire enjoyed general domestic peace coupled with great stability—all the more remarkable when it is realized that, outside of the environs of the City of Rome itself, there was no police force, and army units had to be used to keep order when necessary.

The chief exception to the general domestic order in the Roman Empire was Judaea. Though (unusually for a conquered nation) the Jews had been granted autonomy under their own kings, after several risings, the province was placed under a Roman governor, which was followed by the First Jewish Revolt of 66–70, resulting in the destruction of the Temple in Jerusalem, and the Bar-Kokhba Revolt of 132–136.

Until 312 CE the Roman emperor was the head of a system, not just of religious toleration, but of freedom of worship, welcoming numerous "oriental cults" alongside the polytheistic "pagan" Roman state religion, which included the "imperial cult", which, in the West at least, did not involve worship of a living emperor but only of his *genius,* or life spirit. The myth of Roman pagan persecution of Christianity has been powerfully exploded by Candida Moss: "We are talking about fewer than ten years out of nearly three hundred during which Christians were executed as the result of imperial initiatives" (Moss 2013, p. 127)—and then for political, not religious, reasons.

Communal religions, of which the Roman state religion was one, lacked any "creed" or set of beliefs, and the concepts of "conversion" and "heresy" were unknown. This all changed with Emperor Theodosius I's Edict of Thessalonica of 380, making Nicene Christianity, a creed religion, the official religion of the empire. From then on, persecution became the order of the day of all forms of "paganism", Judaism, and "heresy", defined as even the slightest deviation from the Nicene creed (as formulated by the 325 Council of Nicaea and amended by the Council of Constantinople of 381) (see Chapter 6).

So What?

As mentioned earlier, classifying governments in terms of power structure is not just a bottling and labeling process. Power structure is also relevant to other features of the societies concerned, such as stability, liberty, equality, and foreign policy, as well as to the social and political ethos of those societies.

Very few historians have taken any interest in power structure, and the majority of those who have done so have managed to get hold of the wrong end of the stick:

- **Syme:** While describing the Roman Emperor Augustus as an 'autocrat', Oxford Professor Sir Ronald Syme asserted that the Roman Empire, and all governments at all times regardless of label, have been "oligarchies": "A monarchy rules through an oligarchy". This makes no sense. Monarchy and oligarchy are polar opposites (see Chapter 10).
- **Andrewes:** Though the author of a book on the Greek Tyrants, Oxford Professor Antony Andrewes failed to recognize that there was a common thread running through them, namely popular anti-aristocratic monarchy (see Chapter 10).
- **Brown:** Peter Brown of "Late Antiquity" failed to notice the marked shift in power structure with Constantine's support of the senatorial aristocracy in the West. And: "Precisely because correct religion was the glory of the empire, it had to be imposed in a manner that reflected the overwhelming dignity of the imperial power." How can it ever be justifiable to "impose" a particular religion on people, and how, in any case, can it be imposed with "dignity"? (See Chapter 10.)
- **Finley:** In the face of mounting archeological and linguistic evidence of the Homeric epics as a valuable source of information about Mycenaean Greek government, Professor Sir Moses Finley of Cambridge stuck doggedly to his assertion, first made in 1954, that the poems were "a collection of fictions from beginning to end". Finley's left-wing credentials became evident in his adulation of Athenian "democracy", which was actually a form of popular monarchy. Finley did at least recognize the important truth that Pericles and the tyrant Peisistratus were both "champions of the people" against the rich and noble (see Chapter 10).
- **Millar:** Flying in the face of detailed prosopographical evidence, Professor Fergus Millar of Oxford opined that "neither an aristocracy nor an oligarchy ever existed in Republican Rome" and that the Republic was essentially a direct democracy. He even went so far as to claim, contrary to all evidence, that the Augustan principate was a form of direct democracy (see Chapter 10).
- **Beard:** Under the heading "The First Emperor", Professor Mary Beard suggested that neither Augustus nor Julius Caesar but Caesar's adversary

Pompey "has a good claim to be called the first Roman emperor". An analysis of the power structure of the time shows this to be as baseless as the same writer's claim that Caesar's assassin Marcus Brutus was aiming at "autocratic power" (see Arnheim 2022, pp. 58, 26).

- **Schama:** Simon Schama has suggested that "Benign torpor should perhaps have been on the list of recommended virtues for successful princes", citing England's James I and France's Louis XV as examples of "benign torpor" and their successors, Charles I and Louis XVI, respectively, together with Augustus, Constantine, and Alfred the Great, as examples of the opposite. Yet, were Augustus, Constantine, and Alfred not "successful"—except perhaps for Alfred's fabled burning of the cakes? (See Arnheim 2022, p. 285.)
- **Jewish history:** The main reason the Jews are so widely misunderstood is that they form a "communal religion" in a world dominated by Christianity and Islam, "creed religions" (both terms coined by myself). The destruction of the Second Temple in 70 CE transferred power from a hereditary priestly aristocracy (*kohanim*) to generations of rabbis with belief in a supposedly divine "Oral Torah" devised by themselves. This crucial change, which I have not found discussed in any book on Jewish history, resulted in giving the Jewish religion the worst feature of a creed religion—intolerance—piled on top of the worst feature of a communal religion, namely exclusivism, resulting in the parlous state in which Israel finds itself today.
- **Scandinavian School:** Members of a contemporary "Scandinavian School" of historians are obsessed with the idea that primogeniture produced stable monarchy and reduced the incidence of regicide. Of far greater relevance is power structure, which these historians completely ignore (see Chapter 12).
- **Skinner:** Professor Quentin Skinner, a vaunted authority on Machiavelli, completely fails to notice Machiavelli's practical advice to rulers that the way to become a strong ruler is with popular support against the elite. Of all the historians, past and present, that I have read, Machiavelli is the only one to share my view of the "two models of government" (see Chapter 11).

Part I
The Framework

Chapter 1
When Is a Monarchy not a Monarchy?

The usual classification of states as either "monarchies" or "republics" is superficial and misleading. For example, the United Kingdom and Japan are both found in the "monarchy" column, while Russia (the Russian Federation) and the People's Republic of China are labeled "republics." From a power-structure vantage point this makes no sense. Instead, both Russia and China should be classified as monarchies, while the United Kingdom and Japan should be classified as oligarchies. No state, past or present, can properly be labeled a democracy.

A leitmotif of this book is power structure, in particular the relationship between monarchy and oligarchy—the importance of which is not often recognized, even by historians—and, beyond that, the relationship between the power structure of a society and other features, such as stability, liberty, equality, foreign policy, and ethos.

The term "oligarchy" (literally, "rule of the few") covers any ruling minority and any regime controlled by such a minority. If a ruling minority is hereditary, it is still an oligarchy but can be termed an "aristocracy" (literally "rule of the best"), as can a government controlled by them. The terms "noble" and "nobility" are synonyms for "aristocrat" and "aristocracy." And, to add to the confusion, "nobility" and "aristocracy" can also refer to a titled minority that does not have political power.

Monarchy exerts a certain fascination on the human mind. It is hard to imagine what it was like to be a regular person in some past age. Evidence tends to be scarce and unreliable, and the subject matter may well turn out to be mind-numbing. The swashbuckling and flamboyant, or scandalous and dissolute, antics of rulers, on the other hand—and especially of those who "bestride the narrow world like a Colossus" (Shakespeare's description of Julius Caesar)—are

Five Thousand Years of Monarchy, First Edition. Michael Arnheim.
© 2026 John Wiley & Sons, Inc. Published 2026 by John Wiley & Sons, Inc.

the stuff, not only of popular entertainment, but also of the majority of historical writing, ancient and modern alike.

Governmental titles are many and varied—and extremely misleading. For example, the title of king, emperor, or president may indicate the possession of genuine power, or may represent a titular or nominal headship with purely ceremonial functions. It is virtually impossible for one person to wield total, or absolute, power. Even the most autocratic or absolute monarch is likely to have to delegate power to others to some extent. The test must be: Who has the whip hand?

The formal division among modern Western states into "monarchies" and "republics" has no real significance, as monarchy in the modern West is not real monarchy at all. The royal heads of state of "constitutional monarchies" have no more power than the presidents of republics such as Germany, Portugal, Greece, or India. Present-day China is supposedly a "people's republic," while Japan is classified as a monarchy. In reality, China under Xi Jinping is a monarchy and Japan is an oligarchy.

Just as modern Western monarchies are generally oligarchies in disguise, so the nominally republican governments of Vladimir Putin's Russia, Xi Jinping's China, Viktor Orbán's Hungary, or Turkey under Recep Tayyip Erdogan can probably be labeled as essentially "populist" monarchical regimes.

In every society, past and present, it is possible to identify an elite (or group of elites)—whether labeled aristocracy, aristocrats, nobles, nobility, oligarchs, oligarchy, power elite, or simply elite (or élite), whether hereditary or not, and whether based on birth, wealth, status or office, or a combination of two or more of these factors. This elite (or combination of elites) is normally dominant socially and economically, and often politically as well in the form of an oligarchy, or, if hereditary, an aristocracy. This "power elite," intent on preserving and perpetuating its own group dominance, tends to have a deep-seated fear of one-person or monarchical rule.

At the same time there is a natural antipathy inherent in the lower classes toward any oligarchy or aristocracy. This tends to impel the common people to give their support to a strong leader as their champion against the privileged classes, which may lead to the establishment of a form of popular, or "populist," monarchy or dictatorship.

There are essentially only two forms of government: on the one hand, oligarchy, morphing into aristocracy, and, on the other, monarchy. True monarchy, properly so called (from the Greek *monarchia,* "the rule of one person"), is a form of government where power is concentrated in the hands of a single individual, whether a hereditary crowned head, a dictator, or an elected politician. Genuine monarchical power is essentially anti-aristocratic, and generally, though not invariably, depends on lower-class support—a form of what tends now to be labeled as "populism."

Although true monarchy and oligarchy/aristocracy are the only pure forms of government, hybrid forms are possible, combining populist monarchy with elitist, oligarchical, or aristocratic features. Among these are the current or recent regimes of Narendra Modi in India, Boyko Borisov in Bulgaria, Andrej Babiš in the Czech Republic (Czechia), Evo Morales in Bolivia, Daniel Ortega in Nicaragua, Rodrigo Duterte in the Philippines, and Donald Trump's presidency of the United States.

What, then, about democracy? According to my analysis, Athenian "direct democracy" under Pericles and his successors was in reality a form of populist monarchy, and modern "representative democracies" are in reality oligarchies (see later).

But why, you may well ask, does power structure matter in any event? The answer is that the whereabouts of power reveals who benefits from a particular regime. The power structure in a society goes to the very heart of that society, relates to its stability, impacts directly on the degree of social mobility and equality in that society, and is related, directly or indirectly, to the ethos of the society concerned.

"Five Kings"

King Farouk of Egypt (r. 1936–52) is reputed to have predicted that there would soon be only five kings left in the world: the king of England, the king of spades, the king of clubs, the king of hearts and the king of diamonds. A list of current "monarchies" at the time of this writing would appear to belie this prediction, showing as it does no fewer than 43 sovereign states with a monarch at their head, though only a few of these are absolute, autocratic, or true monarchs. In terms of power structure, regardless of labels, "constitutional monarchies" are in fact oligarchies. The (usually hereditary) monarch occupies a position somewhere between a purely ceremonial head of state and one with certain very limited prerogative or reserve powers, and with actual power in the hands of an elected legislature and executive government, generally under a prime minister. A key feature of a constitutional monarchy is separation between head of state and head of government, which is also found in many modern republics. The chief difference between, say, the king of Sweden and the president of Germany is that the king is there for life and his position is hereditary.

In the West, at least, monarchy usually began with a ruler who combined in his own person executive, legislative, and usually judicial power. The monarch would be likely to surround himself with advisers in one or more of these spheres. The monarch would need to raise money, whether to finance wars, to keep law and order, or simply to administer his domain. For these purposes he would have to raise taxes, for which he would require the consent of the aristocracy, who would want some redress of grievances in return. Sooner or later some form of consultation would be extended to the propertied classes below the aristocracy, generally through their elected representatives. Most European monarchies have ended up as "constitutional" monarchies. The monarchs have been largely or essentially reduced to ceremonial heads of state. They reign but do not rule.

Venetian Republic

A classic example of this is the Republic of Venice, which existed for a millennium before being dissolved under pressure from Napoleon in 1797. The Venetian head of state, known as the *doge* (derive from Latin *dux*), was a byword for a powerless monarch. Elected for life in a complex process combining election and sortition, he was drawn from one of the inner circle of Venetian aristocratic houses and there were safeguards in place to prevent hereditary succession, although the same family names do recur from time to time on the list of doges. Instead of receiving payment for his service, on his election a doge was required to lay out a large sum of money as a bounty to his subjects when coins were thrown to the crowd thronging his coronation. Treated with the utmost dignity and respect both in Venice itself and internationally, the doge nevertheless had essentially a ceremonial role. Between 742 and 1423, real power resided in the *Concio*, or "assembly," and from 1423 until 1797 in the *Signoria*, or "Senate."

"A Republic... If You Can Keep It"

As he was leaving the Philadelphia Convention, which had just concluded its deliberations on the United States Constitution in 1787, Benjamin Franklin was accosted by a Philadelphia matron. "Well, doctor, what have we got," she enquired, "a republic or a monarchy?" "A republic," came the reply, "if you can keep it."

The implicit warning in this succinct reply was that a republic was so delicate as to require tireless vigilance to prevent supreme power from being usurped by a single autocratic ruler. Living three thousand miles from the seat of the British Government, the American "Founding Fathers" were under the false impression that King George III was an autocratic monarch, and they therefore aimed their barbed attacks at him personally. In fact, the British Crown had lost most of its power in the so-called "Glorious Revolution" of 1689, over 70 years before George III's accession in 1760.

Yet the American Declaration of Independence, drafted by Thomas Jefferson in 1776, accused the king of having established "an absolute Tyranny over these states." The rest of the Declaration consists of a long series of accusations directed against King George personally. The American Founding Fathers were educated men who would have been familiar with the standard exposition of English law, Blackstone's *Commentaries on the Laws of England*, which included such statements as: "Besides the attribute of sovereignty, the law also ascribes to the king, in his political capacity, absolute perfection. The king can do no wrong" (Blackstone 1765, Chapter 7). Blackstone does go on to set out certain limitations to this absolute power, but the general impression that he presents is one of overweening royal supremacy.

Besides overestimating the degree of control exercised by George III on policy, the American Founding Fathers, who were steeped in the Classics, also felt an exaggerated admiration for the Roman Republic, an oligarchy, whose watchword was "liberty," meaning opposition to one-man rule, which was successfully resisted for 450 years, and whose constitution of checks and balances formed the basis of the US Constitution in certain important respects. It was also no accident that the upper legislative chamber created by the US Constitution should have been called the Senate, a name drawn directly from the Roman Republic.

"Liberty" was also a slogan of the American Revolution. It is no accident that the American Founders should have had this affinity with the Roman Republic. For both, "liberty" meant opposition to and freedom from one-man rule, but it certainly did not mean democracy, the prospect of which instilled fear into

Figure 1   President Donald Trump swearing-in ceremony, 20 January 2017.
SOURCE: The White House / Wikimedia Commons / Public domain.

the hearts of the Founders. John Adams, who was to become the second US president, warned: "Democracy will soon degenerate into an anarchy, such an anarchy that every man will do what is right in his own eyes and no man's life or property or reputation or liberty will be secure."

The US Constitution guaranteed "a Republican Form of Government," not "democracy," a word that does not appear anywhere in the Constitution. James Madison, the "father of the Constitution" and future president, did not mince his words on the dangers of democracy: "Democracy is the most vile form of government – democracies have ever been spectacles of turbulence and contention: have ever been found incompatible with personal security or the rights of property: and have in general been as short in their lives as they have been violent in their deaths."

The fallacious identification of "republic" with "democracy" dates from the French Revolution of 1789 and persists to the present day. The "People's Republic of China," the "Democratic People's Republic of Korea" (North Korea), and the "Republic of Cuba" (since 1959) are in fact autocratic monarchies. The former "socialist" (commonly called "communist") states describing themselves as "democratic republics," "people's republics," "democratic people's republics," or "socialist republics" were either autocratic monarchies or oligarchies. The former Soviet Union (properly, the Union of Soviet Socialist Republics) was an autocratic monarchy under Stalin (1924–53), as is the Russian Federation (since 2012), and the rest of the time an oligarchy.

Other states that claim the democratic label are "constitutional monarchies," sometimes termed "crowned republics," such as Denmark, Norway, Sweden, the Netherlands, Belgium, Spain, Japan, Thailand, the United Kingdom, Canada, Australia, and New Zealand, all of which are in fact oligarchies.

The V-Dem ("Varieties of Democracy") Institute, founded by Political Science Professor Staffan Lindberg of Sweden's University of Gothenburg, modestly ranked Sweden as the eighth most democratic state in the world in 2023, reserving the top spot for its neighbor, Denmark, despite that country's rocky relationship with Greenland, an autonomous territory under the Danish Crown. Although over 70% of Greenlanders opposed entry into the European Economic Community, Greenland found itself part of the Community on Denmark's accession in 1973. Opposition to this in Greenland resulted in Greenland's withdrawal from the Community in 1985 (while Denmark remained a member). On the basis of a referendum in which 75% of Greenland voters approved greater autonomy, Greenland was granted self-rule in 2009 and the official language was changed from Danish to Greenlandic, an Eskimo-Aleut language, closely related to the other Inuit languages spoken in Canada and Alaska.

This aside, there is a much more general problem with vaunted democratic systems of government. The type of "democracy" that we are dealing with is parliamentary, representative, or indirect democracy, the only type claimed by any modern state.

Rousseau

The French philosophe Jean-Jacques Rousseau famously remarked: "The English people believe themselves to be free; they are gravely mistaken; they are free only during election of Members of Parliament; as soon as the Members are elected, the people are enslaved." This was written in 1762, long before there was universal adult franchise, which was only introduced in 1918 (at the age of 21 for men and 30 for women). It even predates the so-called Great Reform Bill of 1832, at a time when the electorate amounted to only about 10% of the adult male population.

Yet Rousseau's stricture remains true today, as election results by no means always reflect majority opinion. Even in the general election of 2024, widely proclaimed a Labour Party "landslide victory," that party actually obtained only 33.7% of the vote, which, however, gave them 63.2% of the seats in the House of Commons, an absolute majority entitling them to form a government with their leader, Sir Keir Starmer, as prime minister. In the previous general election, held in 2019, Labour's share of the vote had not been very different, 32.1%, but on that occasion they won only 31.1% of the seats, while the Conservatives, with 43.6% of the vote, got a majority of 56.2% of the seats, on the basis of which they formed the government under their then leader, Boris Johnson.

How democratic was either of these outcomes? What it really means is that in neither election did the elected government have the support of the majority of the participating voters. Rousseau is actually doubly right. Not only do the voters lose all say between elections on who their representatives should be, but the elected representatives themselves have no obligation to take their constituents' views into account. They are not *delegates*, bound by a mandate given to them by those they represent, but *representatives*, who are free to adopt whatever position they choose. This was explained in Edmund Burke's famous 1774 Speech to the Electors of Bristol, whom he represented in the House of Commons from 1774 to 1780: "Your representative owes you, not his industry only, but his judgment; and he betrays, instead of serving you, if he sacrifices it to your opinion.... You choose a member indeed; but when you have chosen him, he is not member of Bristol, but he is a member of *parliament*" (*The Founders' Constitution*, Vol. 1, Chapter 13, Document 7; Kurland and Lerner 1987).

But even that is not the whole story. There are broadly two types of electoral systems: those based on some form of proportional representation, on the one hand, and, on the other, systems commonly referred to as "first past the post" or "winner take all." The chief advantage of a first-past-the-post electoral system is that it tends to result in a two-party system in which one or other party generally ends up with a majority of seats. This is particularly important in a country like the United Kingdom, in which the right to form a government goes to the party with a majority in the House of Commons, the Lower House of Parliament. But it is far from being democratic, however defined.

In a parliamentary, first-past-the-post electoral system, the country is divided into constituencies or voting districts, commonly referred to as "parliamentary seats." To win a seat costs a good deal of money, so candidates generally band together in "parties," which finance election campaigns for their candidates. But that gives them a deciding voice both in the selection of the candidates in the first place and over the successful candidates once elected. In Britain there is strong party discipline, enforced by aptly named "whips," who make sure their members toe the party line, especially on any important issues, for which there is what is termed a "three-line whip." Rebellious members of parliament may have the whip removed from them, which sounds liberating and cuts them loose from party discipline and in that sense does gives them more independence, but it also means that they will not be selected by that party at the next election. So, unless they can "cross the floor" to an opposing party that can offer them a home and a winnable seat in the next election, their political career is likely to be over. It is even possible to cross the floor twice, first in one direction and then back again. To my knowledge, the only British politician to have achieved this feat successfully was Winston Churchill (1874–1965), who, with characteristic mock modesty, opined: "Anyone can rat, but it takes a certain amount of ingenuity to re-rat."

With its command of a majority in the House of Commons the British Government can pass virtually any legislation it likes. This highly undemocratic feature was identified and stigmatized as "elective dictatorship" by Lord Hailsham, Lord Chancellor under Edward Heath and Margaret Thatcher in a BBC lecture in 1976, and again in a book in 1979 (*Elective Dictatorship,* Richard Dimbleby Lectures, BBC, 1976; Hailsham 1979). The only (slight) check on this power is the even more undemocratic House of Lords, the unelected Upper House of Parliament, made up of life peers (political nominees of the various parties) plus (at the time of writing) 90 hereditary peers, who, strangely enough, actually *are* elected, though only by other hereditaries, but who are about to be excluded from membership of the House of Lords altogether.

So much for British "democracy," not to mention the privileges accorded to special interest groups favored by "politically correct" policies. Other states with a first-past-the-post electoral system share some, but not all, of the undemocratic features of the British system. But what about those with proportional representation?

The basis of all the various proportional representation electoral systems is that every party will have approximately the same proportion of seats in the legislature as their proportion of the vote. This sounds democratic and fair, but there are some serious drawbacks. What is labeled a "hung parliament" in a first-past-the-post system like that in Britain is the norm in proportional systems, because it hardly ever happens that one party wins a majority of seats in parliament. Proportional systems generally tend to result in a proliferation and fragmentation of parties, which in turn makes coalition government almost inevitable. All coalition partners have to compromise, so that none of them can carry out their policies. Coalitions are also notoriously fragile and short-lived, making for instability, ineffectual government and periods of interregnum during which a *formateur*, or sometimes the constitutional monarch, attempts to broker a deal amongst the various parties with a view to reaching agreement on a new coalition and a new prime minister.

All vaunted "democracies" in existence at the time of this writing are essentially indirect, representative electoral systems, a means to electing a government with popular support. As we have seen, these "democracies" do not succeed in achieving this objective. But in fact many adulators of democracy go much further and identify democracy with some definite ethical and political values. Here is one commentator's self-contradictory take on the subject: "For people in the West, democracy means 'liberal democracy': a political system marked not only by free and fair elections but also by the rule of law, a separation of powers, and the protection of basic liberties of speech, assembly, religion and property. But this bundle of freedoms—what might be termed 'constitutional liberalism'—has nothing intrinsically to do with democracy and the two have not always gone together, even in the West. After all, Adolf Hitler became chancellor of Germany via free elections" (Zakaria 2003, p. 17).

Direct "Democracy"

Up to now we have been dealing solely with indirect, representative democracy. What about direct democracy? There is much adulation expressed by politicians, academics, and "liberal-minded" people generally for the supposed direct democracy epitomized particularly by ancient Athens, a topic to which I shall be returning in a later chapter, but I shall summarize my views here. It is worth quoting the authoritative judgment on Athenian democracy by the highly trustworthy contemporary historian Thucydides (c. 460–400 BCE): "What was in name a democracy became in Pericles's hands government by the first citizen. With his successors it was different. More on a level with one another, and each grasping at supremacy, they ended by committing even the conduct of state affairs to the whims of the multitude" (Thuc. 2:65.9–10). According to this, Athenian "democracy" was an autocratic monarchy under Pericles and then degenerated to ochlocracy, or mob rule, neither of which is "democracy" *tout court*.

To put it in a nutshell, therefore, neither direct nor indirect "democracy" actually exists. So what? How important is the power structure in any given state? Or, in other words, what difference does it make how a state's form of government is classified? Isn't this just an exercise in bottling and labeling? The answer is decidedly "no." As will be seen in future chapters, there is some correlation between the power structure of a state and its stability, the degree of liberty and equality prevalent there, as well as its foreign policy and its overall ethos.

In United States presidential elections, on five occasions, most recently in 2016, the winner lost the popular vote. This is in a complicated "electoral college" system, where each state is allocated a certain number of electoral votes and (except in two states) the winner of the popular vote in each state (even by a margin of one vote) carries all the electoral votes for that state.

Chapter 2
Two Models of Government

In every society in the past five thousand years that I have studied, there has been a built-in antagonism between the elite and the ordinary people. Where the elite are in control, the government is an oligarchy, or, if hereditary, an aristocracy. The only other pure type of government is monarchy, of which there are several varieties: popular monarchy, where a strong leader rules with the support of the masses; rarely, where the ruler has popular support plus aristocratic acquiescence (as in the Roman Principate established by Augustus); and where an autocrat rules without the specific support of any class. Oligarchy and aristocracy, being systems of shared power, have a visceral fear of monarchy (the Roman Republic is a good example of this). By the same token, monarchs tend to fear an elite that threatens to take power away from them and share it among themselves. The "tall poppy syndrome," exemplified by the ancient Greek tyrants, epitomizes this (see Chapter 15). Is it possible for power to be shared between a monarch and an elite? The question to ask is: Who has the whip hand? True shared power in a hybrid form of government is rare. More often, what appears as shared power will turn out to be either a disguised monarchy (as in the case of Periclean Athens) or a disguised oligarchy (as in the "constitutional monarchies" found today in Britain and Western Europe).

Most writings on government and politics, whether by historians, lawyers, political scientists, or theorists, tend to be fixated on constitutions, institutions, elections, parties, and other features which are really just externals. Hence the fallacious argument that, because the main debates in Britain take place in the House of Commons, this is where power lies. In spite of the vaunted bedrock constitutional principle of the sovereignty of Parliament, in reality the House of Commons is largely controlled by the executive government (essentially the prime minister and Cabinet) rather than the other way round.

Five Thousand Years of Monarchy, First Edition. Michael Arnheim.
© 2026 John Wiley & Sons, Inc. Published 2026 by John Wiley & Sons, Inc.

Figure 2   Amenhotep III.
SOURCE: A. Parrot / Wikimedia Commons / Public domain.

But that is not the end of the story, because the executive government is itself constrained by other forces, above all by the judiciary, which has arrogated to itself the right to override both the executive and Parliament—which is why I classify the United Kingdom as a composite oligarchy made up of several disparate elements. This is not a "conspiracy theory." I am not suggesting for a minute that the disparate groups that make up the composite oligarchy meet together in secret conclave to co-ordinate policy. Indeed, my view is that these disparate groups do not actually co-operate with one another at all and may well pull in different directions from time to time.

Question: *So how does the judiciary, for example, exercise power?*
Answer: Simply by means of decisions handed down in individual lawsuits.
Question: *In what sense does this amount to exercising power?*
Answer: By stopping the government from doing certain things and simply by laying down the law, which it all too often makes up as it goes along.
Question: *But, if power is diffused like this, why can Britain not be regarded as a democracy?*
Answer: Because the one element that has no power is the mass of the citizenry.
Question: *But does not the citizen body have at least indirect input through the ballot box, opinion polls, and the like?*
Answer: Only very occasionally and marginally (see Chapter 1). The "poll tax riots" of 1990 are probably the only example in modern times when public

opinion had a direct impact on government policy, but even that was really achieved by the violence of a small minority rather than by the sounding of broad opinion. A peaceful protest of "up to 70,000 people" in London on 31 March 1990, according to David Meynell, deputy assistant Metropolitan Police commissioner, was "completely overshadowed by the actions of about 3,000–3,500 people in minority groups," who launched "a ferocious and sustained attack on the police," resulting in 340 people being arrested and 113 (including 45 police officers) being injured, in addition to 20 police horses.[1] This is a far cry from any kind of democratic input, being more in the nature of "ochlocracy," or mob rule.

Two Fallacies

The two main fallacies that my binary model is intended to counter are:

- **The oligarchic fallacy:** which maintains that all governments, regardless of name or form, are in reality oligarchies. Leading members of the "oligarchy club," as I call it, include Gaetano Mosca, Vilfredo Pareto, and Robert Michels, and, surprisingly, even Sir Ronald Syme, a leading historian of ancient Rome, who asserted that oligarchy lurks behind every kind of government regardless of label or outward appearance, and goes so far as to opine that, "A monarchy rules through an oligarchy," which is a meaningless contradiction in terms (see Chapter 10).
- **The democratic fallacy:** which is a tendency to be unduly impressed by most regimes that describe themselves as democracies. Many modern "liberal" academics are devotees of this cult. Although generally realistic enough to see through the "democracy" label of the former Soviet Union, its satellite states, and other "communist" countries, they tend to be less critical of the democratic claims of western Europe and North America, and positively adulate the ancient Athenian vaunted "direct democracy," which I, in agreement with the ancient sources, show (in Chapter 13) to be a form of monarchy; and some modern academics even go so far as to claim the Roman Republic, that prime case of oligarchy, as another example of "direct democracy" (see Chapter 6).

"Democracy" Plus "Equality"

The widespread belief in the existence of representative "democracy" plus belief in the attainability and desirability of "equality" is a dangerously explosive combination. An extreme example of this belief is Thomas Piketty's best-selling book *Capital in the Twenty-First Century* (2013), which argues that inequality has

---

[1] [Online: http://news.bbc.co.uk/onthisday/hi/dates/stories/march/31/newsid_2530000/2530763.stm].

increased since 1975 in Europe and the United States and that without government intervention to reverse this growing trend, "democracy" will be threatened. Piketty's "solution" is the imposition of a "progressive annual global wealth tax of up to 2%," together with a progressive income tax with a top rate of 80%!

Four Fallacies

This is based on four main fallacies:

a. that democracy is attainable;
b. that democracy actually exists in Europe and America;
c. that equality is a desirable objective; and
d. that government intervention can produce equality, or at least reduce inequality.

Let me take these points one by one.

(a) Is Democracy Attainable?

There are supposedly two types of democracy, direct and indirect, neither of which has ever existed in practice (see Chapter 13).

Direct democracy supposedly existed in ancient Athens. But, as is shown in Chapter 13, the putative Athenian "democracy" was not a democracy at all but a form of monarchy. It is naïve to be unduly impressed, as all too many modern academics are, by the spectacle of an assembly of citizens voting on resolutions, as if that proved that the assembly concerned was a genuine deliberative body. (Even the British House of Commons, which has a far better claim than the Athenian Assembly to be regarded as a deliberative body, has very little power).

Thucydides famously described Athens under Pericles (495–429 BCE) as, "In name a democracy but in reality rule by the first citizen" (Thuc. 2:65), and there is no shortage of other evidence pointing in the same direction (see Arnheim, 1977). But the desire to believe in the reality of "direct democracy" is so strong as to blind many writers to the true reality of Athenian "democracy." Such is the fascination exerted by the sight of a popular assembly in session that there are some academics who opine that even the Roman Republic was essentially a "direct democracy"— which not even the Romans themselves believed (see Chapter 6).

Two Illusions of Indirect "Democracy"

There are two types of putative indirect, representative democracy: one based on a head-count of votes and the other on "democratic values." In the first group are those regimes that are deemed to be democratic simply because there is universal suffrage, meaning that all adults have the right to elect representatives who form either the (whole or part of the) legislature or the executive, or both. The second group, offering an alternative criterion for "indirect democracy" or "representative democracy," identifies "democracy" with a set of values, which may or may not be shared with the electorate, who have no direct input into policy. In most western "democracies" today, these values tend to be "liberal" or "politically correct" dogmas and policies, which are equated with "democracy" and enforced by the courts. Therefore, what the two types of supposed indirect or representative democracy have in common is that in neither do the voters have any real say over policy. Neither, therefore, constitutes genuine democracy.

(b) Does Democracy Exist?

What passes for "democracy," particularly in present-day Britain and western Europe, is actually a form of composite oligarchy, made up of several disparate groupings (see Chapter 1).

So much, then, for the first two fallacies relating to "democracy." What about the latter two concerned with equality?

(c) Is Equality a Desirable Objective?

It is now generally taken for granted that equality is a "good thing" and a goal worth pursuing. Before that assumption can be tested, however, we have to examine its underpinnings. The underlying basis of this assumption is the modern belief in the inherent equality of all people, that "all men are created equal" (US Declaration of Independence, 1776). These words were penned by Thomas Jefferson (1743–1826), the future third president of the United States, at a time when he owned 187 slaves. Purportedly an opponent of slavery, Jefferson never owned fewer than 130 slaves at any one time and 600 over his whole lifetime, though his purchases were sometimes in order to unite families. In his book on the state of Virginia, written in 1785, Jefferson passed some pretty negative judgments on black people: "Comparing them by their faculties of memory, reason, and imagination, it appears to me, that in memory they are equal to the whites; in reason much inferior, as I think one could scarcely be found capable of tracing and comprehending the investigations of Euclid; and that in imagination they are dull, tasteless, and anomalous." But he added: "In music they are more generally gifted than the whites with accurate ears for tune and time, and they have been found capable of imagining a small catch" (Jefferson 1785, p. 266). But Jefferson then backtracks slightly: "The opinion that they are inferior in the faculties of reason and imagination, must be hazarded with great diffidence" (ibid., p. 269).

More than two centuries later it is still commonly believed that intelligence is at least partially race-based. Many studies have been published both in favor and against that proposition, none of which have aroused more of a furor than

The Bell Curve by Richard J. Herrnstein and Charles A. Murray (Hernstein and Murray 1994) in the wake of which the Board of Scientific Affairs of the American Psychological Association (APA) set up a task force of 11 experts who in 1995 issued a report titled *Intelligence: Knowns and Unknowns*, which concluded that "[N]o adequate explanation of the differential between the IQ means of Blacks and Whites is presently available" (APA 1995). This inconclusive assessment does at least concede that there is a "differential between the IQ means" of the two ethnic groups.

Where does this leave us in regard to the question whether equality is a desirable objective? If, as it appears, people are *not* all equal, at least in terms of intelligence, then trying to *make* them equal, or more equal, would actually be unfair—in Plato's famous words, "distributing a kind of equality indiscriminately to equals and unequals alike" (Plato, *Republic VIII*. 558c).

(d) Can Government Intervention Produce Equality, or at least Reduce Inequality?

Before we can answer this question, we have to identify what we mean by "equality," of which there are at least four types:

(i) **Equality of opportunity**: which really means "equality to become unequal." This type of "non-equality equality" is indeed desirable if one wishes to develop a society with open elites, high social mobility, or a meritocracy, all of which mean more or less the same thing. One of the commonest ways that this goal is usually tackled is by means of educational policy, like desegregation busing of schoolchildren in the United States in the 1970s and 1980s. In 1992, Harvard Professor Gary Orfield, a supporter of busing, found that black and Hispanic students lacked "even modest overall improvement" as a result of court-ordered busing (Orfield 1992).

(ii) **Equality before the law**: which is undoubtedly desirable and which all states that regard themselves as democratic pride themselves on possessing. However, as Lord Chief Justice Hewart (1870–1943) famously remarked: "The courts are open to all, just like the Ritz Hotel"—in other words, equality before the law is a sham. This observation is probably even truer today than when it was first made.

(iii) **Political equality**: "one man, one vote" or "one person, one vote" is a slogan used in campaigns for universal suffrage and also for redistricting voting districts to ensure that no one person's vote counts for more than another's (see the US Supreme Court majority decision in *Reynolds v.*

Sims, 1964). But this is a superficial, and essentially meaningless, view of political equality, because genuine political equality is belied by the non-existence of genuine democracy, as a result of which some people, in reality, have far more political clout than others.

(iv) Economic equality: it is this type of equality which has become the main focus of recent discussion, aroused, among others, by Thomas Piketty's *Capitalism in the Twenty-First Century*. One of the most important and topical questions is: Do social-welfare programs help to reduce poverty? The conventional view, supported by Lane Kenworthy's 1998 study (published in 1999), is "yes." However, in Kenworthy's words:

> Yet a growing number of critics assert that such programs in fact fail to do so, because too small a share of transfers actually reaches the poor, or because such programs create a welfare/poverty trap, or because they weaken the economy. (Kenworthy, 1999.)

Among these critics is the co-author of the much-debated *The Bell Curve*, Charles Murray, who also wrote an even more influential book, entitled *Losing Ground*, which concluded "that social-welfare programs, far from relieving poverty, increase it and should be stopped." "For the first time in American history," wrote Murray, referring to the period starting in 1965, "it became socially acceptable within poor communities to be unemployed. . . . When working no longer provides either income or status, the last reason for working has truly vanished. The man who keeps working is, in fact, a chump" (Murray 1984). Even the liberal *New York Times* admitted that "there's surely something to Mr Murray's belief that welfare creates disincentives to work" ("Losing More Ground," *New York Times*, 3 February 1985).

If welfare is a disincentive to work, the same appears to apply to equalized or low wages. With the introduction of equal wages for all in the early days of the Soviet Union, the famous Russian opera singer Feodor Chaliapin is reputed to have declared that if he was going to be paid the same as a stage-hand, he would give up singing and just move the props around, which as a very large muscular man he would have found less stressful than performing on stage. Subsequently, policies were introduced to give workers an incentive to work, notably the "Stakhanovite" system, which rewarded and honored productive workers and over-achievers (see Chapter 8). However, by the 1980s, with full employment and overmanning, Soviet productivity was poor, which was a factor leading to the collapse of the Soviet system. The Russian economist Grigory Yavlinsky, a leading adviser to Mikhail Gorbachev (General Secretary of the Communist Party of the Soviet Union 1985–91), explained it like this: "The Soviet system is not working because the workers are not working" (online: "The Economic Collapse of the Soviet Union," San José State University, `http://www.sjsu.edu/faculty/watkins/sovietcollapse.htm`).

Piketty, of course, is not satisfied with welfare programs. His much more radical "solution," as mentioned earlier, is the imposition of a "progressive annual global wealth tax of up to 2%," together with a progressive income tax with a top rate of 80%. In fact, Western "democracies" already have progressive income tax systems. Even in the United States, in fact, the top 1% of earners, whose income accounts for 17% of the total, pay 46% of total tax revenues, and 84% of tax revenues comes from the top 20% of earners (Barone 2015).

Swingeing tax rates like that suggested by Piketty are nothing new—but they have never had the desired effect. In the United Kingdom during and shortly after World War II, top earnings were hit by a 99.25% "super tax," which was reduced to around 90% throughout the 1950s and 1960s. In 1974 the top rate of tax on earned income was 83% and, with investment income surcharge, the top rate on investment income went to 98%, which was paid by about seven hundred and fifty thousand taxpayers.

All these rates have come down with the recognition that less is more—or, in other words, more tax revenue is collected when tax rates are reasonable than when they are high. "Lower tax rates can produce more revenue than higher tax rates for the same reason that Wal-Mart, with its lower prices, makes more money than Tiffany & Co." (Rotunda 2014). For example, since 2003, when the US reduced the capital gains tax rate from 39.6% to 15%, the amount of capital gains tax collected has increased by 79%. This effect has been explained by the so-called "Laffer curve."

Naïve

For Piketty to pick on such a creaking old "solution" as swingeing taxes is simply naïve. High tax rates are a disincentive to wealthy individuals and businesses to earn above the threshold of the highest rate—and a positive incentive for them to find ways around paying it, by resorting to tax havens, by transferring their businesses to other countries, or by hiring smart tax accountants and lawyers to find loopholes in the tax code.

Even if soaking the rich were to succeed in raising large amounts of revenue to alleviate poverty with a view to creating greater equality, it would be most unlikely to achieve its objective, because you cannot make people more equal simply by giving them handouts. Unless the recipients of welfare payments use the money constructively to work and further improve their position, the whole social welfare policy will be a flop. Because, as even the *New York Times* has conceded, "welfare creates disincentives to work" (see earlier).

From Rights to Privileges

Rights given to supposed victims of discrimination by "progressive" government programs tend to become privileges, which discriminate by means of quotas or other means against the former supposedly favored group.

The first step from rights to privileges is "affirmative action," positive discrimination or reverse discrimination. In the wake of the landmark 1954 US Supreme Court decision in *Brown v. Board of Education* outlawing racial segregation in public schools, school busing and other forms of affirmative action were implemented. However, after several twists and turns, in 2023 the US Supreme Court ruled by 6-3 that race-based college admissions programs were unconstitutional as they violated the Equal Protection Clause of the Fourteenth Amendment to the US Constitution. In the words of Justice Clarence Thomas's concurring opinion: "It is not even theoretically possible to "help" a certain racial group without causing harm to members of other racial groups" (*Students for Fair Admissions v. Harvard*, 2023).

To sum up my conclusions on the four fallacies identified above:

a. Is democracy an attainable goal? *No.*
b. Does democracy now exist in Europe or America? *No.*
c. Is equality a desirable objective? *No.*
d. Can government intervention produce equality, or at least reduce inequality? *No.*

Chapter 3
Charismatic Leadership

"The history of the world is but the biography of great men." Thus declared the well-known and controversial Scottish historian Thomas Carlyle (1795–1881). This "great man" theory is a gross exaggeration of the truth. But charismatic leadership does go some way toward explaining the rise of strong monarchical figures such as Cyrus the Great, Pericles, Alexander the Great, Qin Shi Huang of China, Julius Caesar, Augustus, Constantine, Frederick the Great, Adolf Hitler, Franklin Roosevelt, Mao Zedong, and Fidel Castro.

It will be noted that some of these individuals were kings who ascended a hereditary throne, while others came to power as elected heads of government or by force of arms. Some are commonly classified as "right wing" and others as "left wing." My own view is that these classifications do not matter. What does matter is the power structure in the various societies concerned, and that all the men listed, among many others, are examples of true monarchy, in the sense of wielding supreme power, as defined in Chapters 1 and 2. It is, of course, true that no one person can singlehandedly control a whole society without assistance. Even the Prince of Liechtenstein, who has power over all three branches of government in a state with a population of just forty thousand, is assisted by a prime minister and council of four. The question must always be: Who has the whip hand? In the case of Liechtenstein the answer since 2003 has undoubtedly been "the Prince." The national motto is: *Für Gott, Fürst und Vaterland* ("For God, Prince and Fatherland")—not a million miles from the German slogan under Adolf Hitler: *Ein Volk, Ein Reich, Ein Führer* ("one nation, one state, one leader"). Hitler had a number of associates—notably Göring, Goebbels, Himmler, and Bormann—to whom he delegated a good deal of authority and whom he liked to play off one against another in the interests of his own power. But there could never be any doubt that it was Hitler himself who had the whip

Five Thousand Years of Monarchy, First Edition. Michael Arnheim.
© 2026 John Wiley & Sons, Inc. Published 2026 by John Wiley & Sons, Inc.

Figure 3   Adolf Hitler and Benito Mussolini, Munich 1937.
SOURCE: The United States Holocaust Memorial Museum / Wikkimedia Commons / Public Domain.

hand. The similarity in the power structure of present-day Liechtenstein and Nazi Germany should not blind us to the huge differences between the two, notably in the use to which the ruler put his power. There is certainly no suggestion that Prince Hans-Adam of Liechtenstein has ever used his power for any nefarious purpose.

Hitler's *Führerprinzip* ("leader principle") applied not only at central government level but also at every level in government, administration, industry, education, and sport, to mention a few relevant areas. At each level the superior (who was appointed, not elected) exercised complete authority over each of his subordinates, and it was the duty of the subordinates to give complete and unconditional personal loyalty to their superior. This was used as the basis of the defense used repeatedly in the Nuremberg trials of Nazis held after World War II: "I was just following orders."

Charismatic leadership is an important aspect of the popular appeal of strong rulers, but by no means do all strong leaders have that appeal. Adolf Hitler undoubtedly possessed that sort of appeal, as can be seen from the hysterical enthusiasm with which he was greeted by crowds, especially in the early years of his dictatorship. Hermann Göring seems to have exuded a certain amount of charisma, but Goebbels, Himmler, and Bormann did not show any signs of having done so, thus diminishing their ability to command respect. Charisma is more likely to be an innate quality, though it can be developed artificially by means of rhetoric and showmanship. The well-known 1930 sequence of film clips showing Hitler rehearsing a speech for the camera with exaggerated hand gestures is an example, though the same poses could be used to ridicule him and turn him into a figure of fun, as was successfully achieved in Charlie Chaplin's 1940 film, *The Great Dictator*.

Another way of developing charisma is by a leader's showing an interest, whether feigned or real, in their subjects. This was successfully achieved by the Prussian King Frederick the Great (r. 1740–86), who on his annual inspection of his troops made a point of talking to individual soldiers. The story goes that, on one such occasion, a young Polish recruit to the Prussian army who spoke no German was reassured by his comrades in arms that the king always asked the same questions. The Polish recruit was accordingly coached on how to answer the questions in German. But, unfortunately for him, Frederick reversed the usual order of his questions. So, when asked, "How old are you?" the nervous recruit replied "Six months, Your Majesty." And to the question, "How long have you been in my army?" the young soldier replied, "Eighteen years." But, luckily for the young Pole, Frederick had a good sense of humor.

Max Weber

Charismatic leadership was first identified under that name by the German sociologist and historian Max Weber (1864–1920). There is now a welter of different definitions of charismatic leadership, but this definition by Professor Ronald E. Riggio is perhaps a useful starting point: "Charismatic leaders are essentially very skilled communicators—individuals who are both verbally eloquent, but also able to communicate to followers on a deep, emotional level. They are able to articulate a compelling or captivating vision, and are able to arouse strong emotions in followers" (*Psychology Today*, 7 October 2012—online: www.psychology today.com).

Arising out of this is charismatic authority, which has been usefully defined as: "[P]ower legitimized on the basis of a leader's exceptional personal qualities or the demonstration of extraordinary insight and accomplishment, which inspire loyalty and obedience from followers" (Kendall et al. 2000, pp. 438–439).

Pericles and Alcibiades

In "democratic" Athens of the fifth century BCE, Pericles, Cleon, and Alcibiades were clearly charismatic leaders with the broad support of the lower-class majority in the assembly, with whom they had a reciprocal, almost symbiotic relationship (see Chapter 13). In their different ways, all three were elected Athenian generals at different times. Pericles and Alcibiades were of aristocratic lineage, while Cleon supposedly had a commercial background. "The Athenian people," remarked A.H.M. Jones, "were rather snobbish in their choice of leaders." Pericles deliberately made a point of no longer associating with his friends and others of his class, to show that he was now the people's friend. Pericles was actually Alcibiades's guardian, but, unlike Pericles, Alcibiades preferred to retain his aristocratic *hauteur,* which did him no good in the end. In the *Memorabilia of Socrates* by Xenophon (430–354 BCE) we come across this charming little vignette purporting to represent an exchange between Pericles and the 19-year-old Alcibiades:

> "Tell me, Pericles," he said, "can you teach me what a law is?"
>
> "Certainly," he replied.
>
> "Then pray teach me. For whenever I hear men praised for keeping the laws, it occurs to me that no one can really deserve that praise who does not know what a law is."
>
> "Well, Alcibiades, there is no great difficulty about what you desire. You wish to know what a law is. Laws are all the rules approved and enacted by the majority in assembly, whereby they declare what ought and what ought not to be done."
>
> "Do they suppose it is right to do good or evil."
>
> "Good, of course, young man---not evil."
>
> "But if, as happens under an oligarchy, not the majority, but a minority meet and enact rules of conduct, what are these?"
>
> "Whatsoever the sovereign power in the State, after deliberation, enacts and directs to be done is known as a law."
>
> "If, then, a tyrant, being the sovereign power, enacts what the citizens are to do, are his orders also a law?"
>
> "Yes, whatever a tyrant as ruler enacts is also known as a law."
>
> "But force, the negation of law, what is that, Pericles? Is it not the action of the stronger when he constrains the weaker to do whatever he chooses, not by persuasion, but by force?"
>
> "That is my opinion."
>
> "Then whatever a tyrant by enactment constrains the citizens to do without persuasion, is the negation of law?"
>
> "I think so: and I withdraw my answer that whatever a tyrant enacts without persuasion is a law."
>
> "And when the minority passes enactments, not by persuading the majority but through using its power, are we to call that force or not?"
>
> "Everything, I think, that men constrain others to do without persuasion, whether by enactment or not, is not law but force."
>
> "It follows, then, that whatever the assembled majority, though using its power over the owners of property, enacts without persuasion is not law but force?"

"Alcibiades," said Pericles, "at your age, I can tell you, I too was very clever at this sort of thing."

"Ah, Pericles," cried Alcibiades, "if only I had known you when you were at your cleverest in these things!" (Xenophon, *Memorabilia*, 42–47).

Alcibiades's cynicism about Athenian "democracy" comes out clearly. Had he lived more recently, he might have agreed with the Liberal statesman William Gladstone that "Decision by majorities is as much an expedient as lighting by gas" (from a House of Commons speech, 1858). The point is that expedients are only a provisional solution until something better comes along—and lighting by gas is, of course, now obsolete. Elected an Athenian general, Alcibiades held the Assembly in the palm of his hand when he advocated for the aggressive Sicilian Expedition, which failed dismally. When charged with sacrilege (for mutilating the "herms," plinths with the head of the god Hermes on top and a phallus in the appropriate position lower down), he fled to Sparta, supervising several campaigns against Athens, and then defected to Persia, finally returning to Athens and serving as general for a few more years before being exiled again and assassinated in Persia.

Moses Finley

Max Weber classified the Greek *polis* in general, and Athenian "democracy" in particular, as belonging to the model of charismatic *Herrschaft,* which roughly translates as "institutionalized authority." M.I. Finley predictably dismissed the whole idea of the applicability to Athens of charismatic leadership, rejecting the "mystical faith" that he charged Weber with stressing and favoring instead an "instrumental view of politics" (whatever that is supposed to mean), locating the explanation for the workings of Athenian leadership "in the area of programs and politics"; and pouting: "To dismiss the Greek *polis* in general and Athens in particular as irrational does not advance our understanding" (Finley 2010, p. 93). Josiah Ober, himself a strong admirer of Athenian "democracy," comments: "Finley is certainly correct to attack as simplistic and misleading a purely charismatic view of Athenian leadership and to point out the overemphasis of the ancient critics on demagogic appeals to base emotions. But Finley himself seems to go too far in the other direction. His eagerness to debunk the critics of the democracy leads him to overrationalize the nature of the Athenian orator's appeal to his audience" (Ober 2009, p. 124). Ober suggests seeking "a middle ground between Weber's charismatic emotionalism and Finley's instrumental rationalism. And the middle ground can be sought in what I have described as ideology."

Not for the first time, Finley has got hold of the wrong end of the stick, but (to switch metaphors) Ober seems to have fallen between two stools.

Max Weber's original portrayal of charismatic authority was undoubtedly ground-breaking at the time, but Weber has been dead since 1920, over a century ago, and his concept of charismatic authority has been greatly refined since then. It is tilting against windmills to attack Weber's original formulation. But characterizing the government of "democratic" Athens as charismatic does not necessarily involve any "mystical faith."

What about irrationality? Charismatic authority *does* generally involve a certain amount of irrationality, especially when applied to a mass assemblage, which is precisely what we find in fifth-century Athens. And it would be difficult to characterize some of the most important decisions taken by Athens in this period as anything but irrational or even delusional. As for Ober's "middle ground" of a democratic ideology common to most Athenians, there is simply no evidence of any such thing. Quite the reverse, in fact: an aristocratic ethos pervades the whole of society.

Julian on Augustus and Diocletian

In his satirical sketch, *De Caesaribus* ("The Caesars"), penned in December 361, the Emperor Julian (r. 361–63), Constantine's nephew, draws a marked contrast between Augustus (r. 31 BCE–14 CE) and Diocletian (r. 284–305). Here, first, is his portrait of Augustus, whom he calls Octavian, presumably because "Augustus" would have been confusing, as it was a standard title borne by emperors from the time of the original Augustus down to his own day—and by Julian himself:

> Octavian entered, changing color continually, like a chameleon, turning now pale, now red; one moment his expression was gloomy, sombre, and overcast, the next he unbent and showed all the charms of Aphrodite and the Graces. Moreover, in the glances of his eyes he was fain to resemble mighty Helios, for he preferred that none who approached should be able to meet his gaze. 'Good Heavens!' exclaimed Silenus, 'what a changeable monster is this! What mischief will he do us?' 'Cease trifling,' said Apollo, 'after I have handed him over to Zeno here, I shall transform him for you straightaway to gold without alloy. Come, Zeno,' he cried, 'take charge of my nursling.' Zeno obeyed, and thereupon, by reciting over Octavian a few of his doctrines, in the fashion of those who mutter the incantations of Zamolxis, he made him wise and temperate. (Julian *Caes.* 307, tr. W.C. Wright, 1913, http://attalus.org/translate/caesars.html)

After mocking Augustus for his apparently shifting identities as a young man, Julian, a noted philosopher in his own right, concluded by praising him unstintingly as "wise and temperate" through his supposed conversion to Stoicism (Zeno of Citium being the founder of the Stoic school of philosophy).

Julian's portrait of Diocletian was rather different, coupling his pomp with the collegiate nature of the tetrarchy that he established:

> Next Diocletian advancing in pomp, bringing with him the two Maximians and my grandfather Constantius. These latter held one another by the hand and did not walk alongside of Diocletian, but formed a sort of chorus round him. And when they wished to run before him as a bodyguard he prevented them, since he did not think himself entitled to more privileges than they. But when he realized that he was growing weary he gave over to them all the burdens that he carried on his shoulders, and admired their unanimity and permitted them to sit far in front of many of their predecessors. (Julian, *Caes.* 315, ibid.)

In the interests of humor, Julian fails to do justice to either of his great predecessors. That Augustus was a great dissembler is not in doubt, pretending to have restored the Republic while keeping a tight grasp on power. But Julian missed the opportunity to demonstrate Augustus's *pietas* as *pontifex maximus,* the chief priest of the infinitely tolerant Roman state religion, which in his brief reign was essentially what Julian himself was trying to emulate, even going so far as to issue an edict guaranteeing freedom of religion. But, above all, Julian fails to recognize Augustus's charisma and popularity with the ordinary people of the empire—just what Julian himself sought in vain. Julian exaggerates Diocletian's concern with his "tetrarchy" and ignores his lack of charisma and failure to seek popular support in his attack on the senatorial aristocracy.

Chapter 4
Divine Right

"The State of Monarchie is the supremest thing upon earth: For Kings are not only God's Lieutenants upon earth, and sit upon God's throne, but even by God himself they are called Gods."—James I of England

This is an extreme version of the "divine right of kings" as formulated by King James I of England (r. 1603–25) in an address to the English Parliament in 1610 (quoted by Burgess 1992).

According to John Neville Figgis, the doctrine of the divine right of kings was "necessary as a transition stage between medieval and modern politics, because it served as the popular form of expression for the theory of sovereignty" (Figgis 1922, p. 258). Following John Austin, Figgis defined sovereignty as the doctrine "that there must be some ultimate authority, which because it can make laws is above the law" (ibid, p. 13). Figgis concluded: "Monarchy is pure, the sovereignty being entirely vested in the king, whose power is incapable of legal limitation. All law is a mere concession to his will, and all constitutional forms and assemblies exist entirely at his pleasure.... A mixed or limited monarchy is a contradiction in terms" (ibid., 5f).

Though not himself wedded to the idea of absolute monarchy, Jean Bodin (1530–96), a leading exponent of the theory of sovereignty, held that "the principal point of Sovereign majesty and absolute power ... [lies] in giving laws unto the subjects in general, without their consent." In a well-ordered state, he believed, sovereign power should be exercised subject to the principles of natural and divine law, including the subjects' rights of liberty and property. However, even where these limits are not respected, he held that the subjects, whose duty it is to obey their ruler, did not have the right to resist (Bodin 1576). This type of thinking posed a serious problem for Calvinists and other Reformers who believed in predestination, like John Knox (1514–72), the fiery Calvinist theologian who founded the Church of Scotland and clashed with the staunchly Catholic Mary, Queen of Scots (1542–87). When Mary asked Knox whether he believed that subjects had a right to resist their ruler, he replied that subjects did indeed have the right to resist even by force, if their ruler exceeded their lawful limits. His argument ran something like this, on the premise that everything is divinely preordained: (a) Rulers owe their position to God. (b) If you have a bad ruler, that is God's will. (c) But, if you rise up in revolt against that bad ruler, that too is divinely ordained.

In sixteenth- and seventeenth-century Europe the doctrine of divine right was fused with the theory of absolute monarchy, but this was not necessarily the case. In England, for example, there was a different tradition, as represented by the English jurist Henry de Bracton (c. 1210–68), who declared: *"Quod rex non debet esse sub homine sed sub Deo et lege"* ("Because the king ought not to be under man but under God and law"). According to this, the king was not above the law but under it—a far cry from the position in Roman law as pronounced by the Roman jurist Ulpian (c. 170–223 or 228): *"Princeps legibus solutus est,"* ("The emperor is not bound by the laws", *Dig.* I.2.31) and: *"Quod principi placuit legis habet vigorem"* ("What pleases the emperor has the force of law", *Digest* I.4.10). The first Roman emperor, Augustus, would certainly not have admitted to being above the law, though in practice he probably was. He would not even have admitted to being more than *princeps,* or "first citizen," which was part of his general masquerade (see Chapter 6 for more on this).

History of Divine Right

The theory of divine right can be traced back to ancient Egypt, Israel, China, and Mesopotamia. In China it was adumbrated by the Zhou dynasty (1046–256 BCE) as "The Mandate of Heaven," on which see Chapter 19. Ardashir I (180–242 CE), founder of the Sasanian Persian Empire, was a noted exponent of divine right, which survives to this day in attenuated form in the designation *Dei Gratia* ("By the Grace of God") still found on British coinage (but dropped in Australia and in most other modern monarchies) (see Chapter 5).

Ancient Egypt

In ancient Egypt, from around 3150 BCE, the ruler, known as "pharaoh," was believed to be the incarnation of the god Horus, the son of Isis and Osiris. (There is a possibility that this "holy family" was the origin of the Christian doctrine of the Trinity.) After the expulsion of the foreign Hyksos rulers from the Nile Delta by Ahmose in about 1550 BCE, the god Amun, or, in fusion with the sun god, Amun-Ra or Amun-Re, became the chief god of the Egyptian pantheon, as indicated by the theophoric names of pharaohs such as Amenhotep ("Amen is satisfied") and Tutankhamun ("living image of Amun"). The long-reigning Amenhotep III (r. c. 1390–52 BCE) claimed Amun as his true father. Because of his long reign, he celebrated three spectacular "Sed festivals" to mark his first 30 years on the throne and then regnal years 34 and 37, which he used to transition from being semi-divine to full divine status. He initiated a huge building program, including temples to several gods, but chiefly to Amun, whose name was erased by his reforming son, who changed his name from Amenhotep IV to Akhenaten, meaning "effective for the Aten," the Aten being the radiant disc of the sun, with which the pharaoh sought to replace Amun and all the other traditional gods and convert Egypt to some form of monotheism by decreeing after a few years that the Aten was the only god to be worshipped. Though the pharaoh showed all the signs of a true believer, and indeed a militant zealot, in pursuit of his new religion, there may well have been a political side to it, as promoting the Aten at the expense of Amun also meant that the priests of Amun lost their revenue and with it their tremendous political power. So it could be seen as a move to make the pharaoh rather than the priests the main focus of public loyalty and thereby increase the power of the pharaoh. A pointer in this direction is the increase in popularity of sun worship even before the Amarna period, as it is called, of Akhenaten. The female pharaoh Hatshepsut (r. 1479–58 BCE), for example, is described in an inscription as "the female Re shining like the sun disc." Amenhotep III was described as "he who rises over every foreign land, Nebmare, the dazzling disc." And a hymn to the sun also became popular at this time. Could there be a link between that and Akhenaten's new religion? It is hard to tell, but the new religion did not catch on, and Amun was completely restored after the death of Akhenaten. So his eventual successor, the boy pharaoh Tutankhaten, reverted to the name Tutankhamun, meaning "living image of Amun".

The divinity of the pharaoh was perpetuated for centuries and even adopted by its Persian conquerors, so that Darius the Great (r. 522–486 BCE) appears as a living god in Egyptian temple inscriptions. And, always quick to go native, the conqueror of the Persian Empire, Alexander the Great, after making sacrifices to the gods at Memphis, made a special trip to the oracle at the remote Siwa Oasis in the Libyan desert, where he was pronounced the son of Amun-Ra. The lesson was well learned by his successors, the Ptolemies, who ruled Egypt for 300 years until the death of Cleopatra VII in 30 BCE.

Ancient Rome

The "pagan" religions of the ancient world, including the old Roman state religion, were normally tolerant of one another. They were "communal" religions, a term coined by myself in my books *Is Christianity True?* (1984), *The God*

Book (2015), and *God Without Religion* (2016). Unlike Christianity, which is a "creed" religion (another term coined by myself), communal religions mostly had no definite beliefs, only ceremonial and rituals. It was taken for granted that every nation had its own religion and its own gods, so one would respect foreign religions. Rome was exceptional in being (by ancient standards) a huge cosmopolis that attracted people from all over the empire and beyond. These people brought their religions with them, so there were numerous foreign cults with their own gods, priests and temples active in Rome. On the communal principle, these were generally tolerated. Even though a number of them had long been separated from their polytheistic roots and were simply what are sometimes described by modern writers as "oriental mystery cults." The bond between monarchy and religion is particularly close in states with a communal religion as distinct from a creed religion.

"Oh Dear, I Think I'm Becoming a God"

On his deathbed the Roman Emperor Vespasian (r. 69–79 CE) is reputed to have remarked: "Oh dear, I think I'm becoming a god" (Suet., *Vespasian* 23.4n). This was a light-hearted reference to the Roman practice of deifying emperors after their death. This practice can be traced back to the origins of the imperial Augustan regime, which arose out of the aftermath to the assassination of the dictator Julius Caesar on the Ides of March, 44 BCE. It is wrong to regard Julius Caesar himself as the first emperor. That honor must go to his great-nephew, adoptive son and heir, Augustus (63 BCE–14 CE), who had his adoptive father, Julius Caesar, deified as *divus Julius* (the divine Julius), allowing Augustus eventually to style himself Imperator Caesar *divi filius* ("son of a god") Augustus.

The Roman Republic (509–49 BCE) had excoriated the concept of one-man power and with it the worship of a living person as a god. Julius Caesar's flirting with accepting such honors cost him his life, and his heir Augustus was careful not to make the same mistake. Augustus followed in his adoptive father's feet by accepting a lifetime appointment as *pontifex maximus*, chief priest of the Roman state religion, an appointment that was held by all subsequent Roman emperors until relinquished by the Christian Emperor Gratian (r. 367–83).

Augustus declined all requests from the Western provinces for a cult dedicated to himself, the only type of worship being allowed (and only to non-Romans) being to the Goddess Roma in conjunction with Augustus: *Roma et Augustus*.

The Eastern provinces were a completely different proposition. In pre-Roman Egypt, Greece, and Asia, worship of living rulers as gods was well established. The Roman emperors simply had to step into the shoes of those earlier monarchs, sometimes literally, as in Egypt, where Augustus and his successors were portrayed in the full costume, attire, and pose of an Egyptian pharaoh, complete with double crown. It was in the East, too, that the cult of Antinous flourished. The premature death and deification of the young favorite and lover of the Emperor Hadrian (r. 117–138 CE) gave rise to a surprisingly popular cult in East and West alike that was still thriving even in the fourth century.

The Roman Imperial Cult

Sacrificial offerings were believed to propitiate the gods, and deified emperors were honored in the same way as the more established gods. The great majority of the population of the Roman Empire were not offended by the imperial cult, which actually served to consolidate loyalty to the Roman state and emperor. In the Eastern areas there was a long tradition of worshipping even living rulers, going back well beyond their incorporation into the Roman Empire. So the imperial cult formed a natural and integral part of the state religion.

In the West, and particularly in Italy, to avoid worshipping the living emperor, the emperor's *genius* was worshiped instead. Every Roman *paterfamilias* was believed to have his own *genius,* which was not the same thing as his soul, but rather his "attendant spirit." As all *genii* were divine, they were a proper object of worship, sidestepping the worship of a living person.

Japan

When Emperor Hirohito's World War II surrender speech was broadcast on radio and public loudspeakers throughout Japan at noon on 15 August 1945, people fell silent, bowed their heads, and muttered prayers. This was the first time that the ordinary people of Japan had ever heard the voice of their emperor. Couched in formal, archaic language, the speech was not easy for ordinary people to understand, and the emperor carefully eschewed the word "surrender," though he did allude to the atomic bomb and effectively admitted that it was because of that that Japan had to give up the fight:

> The enemy has begun to employ a new and most cruel bomb, the power of which to do damage is, indeed, incalculable, taking the toll of many innocent lives. Should we continue to fight, not only would it result in an ultimate collapse and obliteration of the Japanese nation, but also it would lead to the total extinction of human civilization.

While Prime Minister General Hideki Tojo and other leading figures in wartime Japan were tried and executed in the war crimes trials held after World War II, neither the emperor nor any of his relatives were indicted, though imperial power was severely curtailed in the new 1947 US-inspired Japanese constitution, which is still in force today and under which the emperor does not have any "reserve powers" at all. The emperor has no say as far as legislation is concerned, but only the duty of "promulgating" or publishing it. The emperor is still widely adulated as the head of the state religion, in which he is believed to be a direct descendant of the sun goddess Amaterasu, though under American pressure Hirohito formally renounced his divine status in a declaration dated 1 January 1946:

> The ties between Us and Our people have always stood upon mutual trust and affection. They do not depend upon mere legends and myths. They are not predicated on the false conception that the Emperor is divine, and that the Japanese people are superior to other races and fated to rule the world (Wetzler 1998 p. 3).

The interpretation of this statement has been contested, with the emperor himself and the prime minister of the day playing down the "renunciation of divinity" and stressing instead the claim that Japan had been democratic since the "Meiji Restoration" of 1868, which was not in fact the case (see below).

General Douglas MacArthur, the head of the US army of occupation in Japan, pleaded with General Dwight Eisenhower, the US Chief of Staff (and future president) not to put the emperor on trial. Here's what MacArthur wrote to Eisenhower on 25 January 1946:

> [The Emperor's] indictment will unquestionably cause a tremendous convulsion among the Japanese people, the repercussions of which cannot be overestimated. He is a symbol which unites all Japanese. Destroy him and the nation will disintegrate. Practically all Japanese venerate him as the social head of state. . ... [If the Emperor is indicted,] It would be absolutely essential to greatly increase the occupational forces. It is quite possible that a minimum of a million troops would be required which would have to be maintained for an indefinite number of years (`https://history.state.gov/historicaldocuments/frus1946v08/d308`)

MacArthur's assessment of the role of the emperor turned out to be correct. And it is in no small measure to his credit that Japan has remained one of America's staunchest allies from that day to this—that baseball is its most popular sport, outranking Japan's national sport of Sumo wrestling, and that Coca-Cola is Japan's favorite soft drink (albeit sold as a colorless liquid!). Hirohito's involvement in all the major decisions of the war, including the unprovoked attack on Pearl Harbor, has become increasingly apparent as the years have passed. But he never made any admissions, let alone an apology of any kind. When asked directly in an interview in 1975 about the "responsibility for the war," Hirohito gave an evasive answer: "I can't comment on that figure of speech because I've never done research in literature."

Figure 4   Puyi (last emperor of China) with Japanese Emperor Hirohito, 1940.
SOURCE: Unknown author / Wikimedia Commons / Public Domain.

Those arguing against Hirohito's involvement in war crimes point out that his whole reign (1926–89) fell under the Meiji Constitution, so called after the "Meiji Revolution" or "Meiji Restoration" of 1868, which is something of a misnomer. Supposedly a restoration of the power of the Emperor after 700 years of shogunate, during which the emperor was merely a figurehead, the truth is that the Meiji Revolution merely used the Emperor's name to replace the shogunate with an oligarchy, sometimes referred to as the "Meiji Oligarchy," which abolished the old fourfold class division of *samurai*, farmer, artisan and merchant, and replaced it with a new hereditary peerage (*Kazoku*) formed by a merger of the *daimyo* ("feudal lords") with the court nobility *(kuge),* and the transmogrification of the *samurai* into gentry, with the rest of the population being lumped together as commoners. Power was largely in the hands of the new *Kazoku,* not the Emperor. The Meiji Constitution of 1889 declared the Emperor "sacred and inviolable" with sovereignty vested in the person of the Emperor, who (nominally) united in himself all three branches of government (executive, legislative and judicial), though legislation and the budget required the consent of the legislature, known as the Imperial Diet.

Modeled on Germany's "Bismarck Constitution" of 1871 and touted as a "constitutional monarchy," the Meiji Restoration was actually a hybrid between monarchy and oligarchy. Unlike the current 1947 Constitution, which vests sovereignty in the people, the Meiji Constitution vests sovereignty in the emperor:

- **Art 1:** "The Empire of Japan shall be reigned over and governed by a line of Emperors unbroken for ages eternal." According to the traditional order of succession this made the Meiji Emperor (r. 1867–1912), number 122, though Emperor Kinmei (r. 540–71), number 29 on the list, is the first historically verifiable emperor and all subsequent emperors (and a few empresses regnant) were directly descended from him. "Reigned over and governed" means that the emperor did not only reign but also ruled. This at least is what the constitution *claimed*.
- **Art 3:** "The Emperor is sacred and inviolable." Here we are in the presence of a living god.
- **Art 5:** "The Emperor exercises the legislative power with the consent of the Imperial Diet." The Diet, or parliament, was elective, though initially there was a substantial property qualification meaning that only about 1% of the population had the right to vote. Universal manhood suffrage for all males over 25 was introduced in 1925.
- **Art 6:** "The Emperor gives sanction to laws, and orders them to be promulgated and executed." Nothing is said about whether the emperor had the right to withhold his "sanction," or assent.
- **Art 11:** "The Emperor has the supreme command of the Army and the Navy."
- **Art 13:** "The Emperor declares war, makes peace, and concludes treaties."

Despite all this, it is not for nothing that the period between 1868 and 1940 is sometimes referred to as the Meiji Oligarchy, because, lurking behind the emperor was a small group of highly influential unofficial, informal and extra-constitutional advisers, later known as the *genrō*. Appointed by the emperor himself, there were only nine of them throughout the whole period of 72 years, and they advised him on the most important matters. They collectively advised the emperor on peace and war and foreign policy generally. They selected and nominated prime ministers, and most members of the *genrō* themselves served in that capacity at some point.

Yamagata Aritomo (1838–1922), the longest serving member of the *genrō*, was responsible for writing the *Gunjin Chokuyu* ("*Imperial Rescript to Soldiers and Sailors*") the official code of ethics for military personnel, issued in 1882. which was considered the most important document in the development of the Japanese armed forces. The *Rescript* stressed absolute loyalty to the emperor, but a clause making it clear that the military was ultimately subordinate to civilian authority was deleted from the final version of the document. In keeping with his reputation (among modern writers) as father of Japanese militarism, in 1912 Yamagata forced the resignation of the Cabinet of Prime Minister Salonji Kinmochi (another member of the *genrō*) when the government refused to do the bidding of the military.

This was all part of the so-called Taisho political crisis that was precipitated by the death of Emperor Meiji (r. 1867–1912), Taisho being the "era" name of his son and successor, known in his lifetime as Emperor Yoshihito (r. 1912–26). Katsura Taro, yet another member of the *genrō*, who succeeded Salonji as prime minister, tried to cut the Gordian knot by going directly to the new emperor. But, despite the strong stance taken by Admiral Yamamoto Gonnohyoe, who served briefly as prime minister from 1923 to 1924, the problem of military domination over the civilian government continued to plague Japan until the end of World War II.

The "Meiji Revolution" or "Meiji Restoration" marked a major break with the past after a long period of shogunate (1192–1868), during which the emperor played second fiddle to a shogun. The word *shōgun* essentially means military commander-in-chief, and the first shogun was appointed by the emperor at some point in the eighth century CE to head up campaigns against the *Emishi*. Described as "hairy people," the Emishi were evidently a non-Japonic tribe akin to the present-day Ainu people of northern Japan. Between 794 and 1185 the Fujiwara clan dominated Japanese politics as either regents (*sessho*) or *kampaku* (chief adviser) to the emperor, consolidating their position by marrying off their daughters to members of the imperial family. The Emperor Shomu (r. 724–49) was the first of many so-called "cloistered emperors," so called because they abdicated and became Buddhist monks, exercising power from behind the scenes. No fewer than 23 cloistered "retired" emperors are known, the last being Emperor Satohito (posthumously honored as Reigen), who, after a reign of 24 years (1663–87), abdicated in favor of his son Higashiyama and began to rule as a cloistered emperor, though he did not actually take the tonsure until 1713, dying in 1732.

Though the emperor of Japan is no longer believed to be divine, and though his political power has been cut almost to nothing, his position in Shinto ensures not only the continuation of the Japanese monarchy but also the stability of Japan as a state and society.

Chapter 5
Ceremonial, Titulature, and Trappings

Monarchy has always been associated with religion, which is particularly evident in coronations, court ceremonial, costume, and titulature. Ceremonial is of less real significance in the case of a modern constitutional monarch than, for example, in Solomon's consecration as king of Israel, or to that of other strong monarchs throughout history. Charlemagne's coronation by the Pope has echoed down the ages. And Napoleon was fully conscious of its importance when he sidelined the expectant Pope and placed the crown on his own head.

Fidei Defensor

The king of the United Kingdom is "Supreme Governor of the Church of England." Unlike the emperor of Japan, the British monarch is not regarded as a priest. He is a constitutional head of state with very little actual power, but is also designated, even on the humble penny piece, as *Dei Gratia* ("By the Grace of God") and *Fidei Defensor* ("Defender of the Faith"). The description "By the Grace of God" is also used by the king of Denmark, who heads up the "Danish People's Church" jointly with the *folketing* ("parliament"). The king of the Netherlands is the only other European monarch to use the formula "By the Grace of God".

While Prince of Wales, the occupant of the British throne at the time of this writing, King Charles III, was occasionally quoted as saying that when he became king he would like to be known as "Defender of Faith" rather than as "Defender of the Faith," to indicate that his protection extended to *all* religious faiths. In the event, since his accession in 2022 there has been no murmur of

Five Thousand Years of Monarchy, First Edition. Michael Arnheim.
© 2026 John Wiley & Sons, Inc. Published 2026 by John Wiley & Sons, Inc.

this suggestion, though, as Latin has neither a definite nor an indefinite article (that is, no word for "a" or "the"), *Fidei Defensor* can be translated as "Defender of Faith" just as well as "Defender of *the* Faith". The origin of the title goes back to 1521, when it was awarded by Pope Leo X to Henry VIII in recognition of a theological treatise attacking the recently published ideas of Martin Luther and the Protestant Reformation.

The title *Fidei Defensor* was clearly meant to refer to Henry's defense of the Roman Catholic Church against the Reformation, which Henry, in common with the Pope, excoriated as a serious heresy. When Henry himself broke with the Roman Catholic Church in 1534 and had himself declared head of a breakaway Church of England, he was stripped of the title and excommunicated by the then Pope Paul III. In 1543, however, the English Parliament cheekily invested Henry with it again, this time in English, where it became clear that it meant Defender of the specific faith of the Church of England, and this title became part of the official style and title of all his successors (except Mary I), including Charles III, who ascended the throne in 2022.

Protestant Succession

England is therefore still in the anomalous position of having an established religion with a state church, the Church of England, of which the king is "Supreme Governor," while at the same time allowing freedom of belief and worship. By a further twist, between 1701 and 2013, marriage to a Roman Catholic disqualified anyone from occupying the throne or from being in the line of succession to the throne. By the Succession to the Crown Act 2013, that disqualification was removed, but the monarch himself or herself is still prohibited from being a Roman Catholic.

Scotland

Scotland has had its own crown, probably at least since the reign of Robert the Bruce (r. 1306–29), and he is depicted on coins wearing an open crown, to which arches were added, to give it its present form, for James V in 1540. It was then used at every Scottish coronation until Charles II's daring coronation challenging Oliver Cromwell in 1651. Since the Act of Union of 1707, Scotland has not been a separate kingdom, so its crown was mothballed until, with "devolution" in 1999, Scotland was granted a new (subsidiary) Parliament, at each opening ceremony of which the Scottish crown is displayed.

On 10 September 2022, shortly after his accession, King Charles took a special oath to "inviolably maintain and preserve" the independent (Presbyterian)

Church of Scotland, and, in a tradition going back to 1689, the Moderator of the General Assembly of the Church of Scotland presents the king with a Bible at the coronation.

The most curious Scottish association with the coronation is the Stone of Scone or Stone of Destiny, which was seized and brought to England by Edward I in 1296. It had previously been used by Scottish kings for centuries, to sit on when they were crowned, and from at least 1399 it served the same purpose in England, housed in the Coronation Chair commissioned by Edward I in 1297. Until the seventeenth century, when a wooden platform was added to the Chair, the king would sit directly on the Stone. With the creation of a devolved Scottish Parliament in 1999, the Stone was returned to Scotland on condition that it is returned to Westminster Abbey for coronations.

In a further anomaly, the position in Scotland is different from that in England. Scotland has its own national church, the Church of Scotland, or the Kirk, which is Presbyterian in church government and Calvinist in doctrine. When in Scotland, the monarch is a member of the Church of Scotland, but not its head, and to this day every new monarch has to take an oath to "maintain and preserve" the Church of Scotland, even though it is the much smaller Scottish Episcopal Church that is linked to the Church of England. The Church of Scotland is the biggest Scottish church, with the Roman Catholic Church hot on its heels, and the Scottish Episcopal Church trailing way behind in third position.

Coronation

European coronations go back to Roman times, though there was no formal coronation ceremony until the Byzantine Emperor Leo I was crowned by the Patriarch of Constantinople in 457. Prior to that, Roman emperors would be shown wearing either the radiate crown of the sun or a jeweled diadem. Charlemagne's coronation in 800 (see later) established the tradition of European coronations to which the English/British coronation belongs, with a gold crown set with jewels placed on the head of the monarch by a bishop in a religious ceremony.

Britain is the only European monarchy to have kept the tradition of a coronation. It is no coincidence that coronations in Europe have disappeared at a time when monarchs have been stripped of most of their powers and reduced to largely ceremonial status. By contrast with this reality—which applies in Britain as much as in most other European monarchies—a coronation gives the false impression of great monarchical power and divine grace.

The form of the British—or, rather, the English—coronation has remained substantially the same for over a thousand years, since before the Norman Conquest, with the coronation of the Anglo-Saxon King Edgar in the year 973 by Dunstan, the then archbishop of Canterbury. The order of service devised by Dunstan is a skillful blend of different traditions. First, there is acclamation followed by an oath, derived from the old Germanic tradition of an elective monarchy. Then comes anointment with oil, considered the most sacred part of the service, which is based on the anointing of the kings of Ancient Israel. And thirdly there is the crowning itself, which goes back to ancient Egypt, when the pharaoh was crowned with the hedjet (the white crown of Upper Egypt) and the deshret (the red crown of Lower Egypt). In modern Britain, too, though for a very different reason, the monarch actually wears two separate crowns during the coronation ceremony. The coronation itself is performed by the Archbishop of Canterbury's placing of St Edward's Crown on the monarch's head, but the crown worn as the monarch leaves the Abbey is the lighter so-called Imperial State Crown.

When the monarch is male, the queen consort is crowned as well as the king, usually with a crown specially commissioned for the occasion, the main exception being Anne Boleyn's coronation in 1533 as Henry VIII's consort with the St Edward's Crown. When there is a queen regnant, her male consort is not given the title of king. The one exception was the future King Philip II of Spain, who on his marriage to Mary I in 1554 became a king regnant equal in every respect to Mary, including appearing on the coinage, but who was not crowned as, by the time the marriage took place, Mary had already been crowned. William III and Mary II, who were joint monarchs, were crowned together in 1689. Whereas Prince Philip, Duke of Edinburgh, consort to Queen Elizabeth II, had no role at her coronation in 1953 other than to pledge his loyalty to her, Camilla, consort to King Charles III, was not only given the title of "queen" but was also crowned by the archbishop of Canterbury at Charles's coronation.

The Two Crowns

The St Edward's Crown was supposedly first worn by King Edward the Confessor, who reigned from 1042 to 1066 (and who was later canonized, hence the title of the crown), but, even if the crown does not go back as far as that, a closed or arched crown (which is what this is) referred to as St Edward's Crown is recorded as being used in the coronation of Henry III in 1220. After the abolition of the monarchy and execution of Charles I in 1649, this crown was valued at £248 10s 0d and possibly melted down, though that is now disputed. On the Restoration of Charles II in 1660, a new St Edward's Crown was commissioned, which is still in use today. This crown is worn by the monarch only in the coronation service itself. The crown worn by the monarch in the procession leaving the Abbey after the service and on any major ceremonial occasion thereafter, like the opening of Parliament, is the so-called Imperial State Crown, of which there have been many versions since the fifteenth century, the current one dating only from the coronation of George VI in 1937.

Figure 5   The Imperial Crown of India made for George V 1911. Creative Commons. Royalty free. Full resolution.
SOURCE: Pietro & Silvia / Wikimedia Commons / CC BY 2.0

But why is it called the *Imperial* State Crown"? British rulers had the title of emperor or empress only between 1877 and 1947, in reference to India: otherwise they were just king or queen. But the use of the term "imperial" for the state crown has nothing to do with this. It goes all the way back to Roman times, as discussed below.

Coronation Service

The king is led into Westminster Abbey by two bishops, the Bishop of Durham and the Bishop of Bath & Wells, who flank him throughout the ceremony. After the initial procession the Archbishop of Canterbury, Primate of All England, officiating, addresses the congregation on the east, south, west and north sides (in that order) with the traditional words: "Sirs, I here present unto you King [Charles], your undoubted King: Wherefore All you who are come this day to do your Homage and Service, Are you willing to do the same?" At each point there is loud acclamation: "God save King [Charles]." This part of the service originally represented recognition by the aristocracy, who would have had the right to elect a new monarch.

Traditionally, this same theme was repeated after the crowning itself when a long line of hereditary peers knelt and paid homage to the monarch. This has now been replaced by "Homage of the People," when the Archbishop of Canterbury calls on "all persons of goodwill in the United Kingdom ... and of the other realms and the territories to make their homage, in heart and voice, to their undoubted King, defender of all." The injection of this pseudo-democratic element into the coronation service is slightly incongru-ous, as it may give the false impression that people can appeal directly to the king if they have a grievance.

Next after the acclamation comes the oath. The Archbishop of Canterbury addresses the king directly: "Sir, is your Majesty willing to take the oath?" The king replies: "I am willing." The oath is in three parts: political, judicial, and religious. First: "Will you solemnly promise and swear to govern the Peoples of the United Kingdom [and the other realms of which the King is the sovereign] according to their respective Laws and Customs?" King: "I solemnly promise so to do."

The judicial part of the oath is short: "Will you to your power cause Law and Justice, in Mercy, to be executed in all your Judgments?" King: "I will." The religious part of the oath is the most controversial, promising as it does "to maintain in the United Kingdom the Protestant Reformed Religion estab-lished by Law?"

On the face of it, this gives the impression of great monarchical power. First of all, the king does not actually "govern," but has to act in accordance with the "advice" he receives from his ministers. The king *reigns* but does not *rule*. In other words, the role of the monarchy is essentially ceremonial—or a "dignified" part of the constitution rather than an "efficient" part (but see Chapter 9).

The reference in the judicial part of the oath to the king's "judgments" is even more fictitious. The king has no say on the appointment of judges, and the prerogative of mercy, or the granting of a "royal pardon," as it is commonly known, has long been exercised by the government in the monarch's name and not directly by the monarch. One of the best known such pardons in recent years was that of Alan Turing, the famous cryptog-rapher and computer trailblazer, regarding a conviction for homosexual "gross indecency" in 1952. After an inconclusive series of votes in Par-liament, the Cameron administration decided to have the queen grant Turing a royal pardon through the royal prerogative, which was signed in December 2013.

Until Henry VIII's break with Rome in 1534 over his desired divorce from Catherine of Aragon, England was a Catholic country. The first Protestant coro-nation was that of Henry's son and successor, the boy-king Edward VI, in 1547. His half-sister and successor, Mary I, tried to turn the clock back and had a full-scale Roman Catholic coronation in 1553. Though her half-sister and successor, Elizabeth I, was actually crowned by a Catholic bishop in 1559, the coronation oath and service was decidedly Protestant. Under the Act of Supremacy of 1558 Elizabeth became Supreme Governor of the Church of England, a title borne by all her successors down to the present day—but, again, one that has become largely nominal.

"Zadok the Priest"

The anthem "Zadok the Priest" has been recited at every English coronation since that of King Edgar in the year 973. It is sung just prior to the anointing of the monarch with oil. The words, adapted from the Bible, were set to glorious music by the composer George Frederick Handel for the coronation of George II in 1727, and this setting has been used at every British coronation since then.

The lyrics read:

> *Zadok the priest and Nathan the prophet anointed Solomon king.*
> *And all the people rejoiced and said:*
> *God save the King! Long live the King! God save the King!*
> *May the King live for ever. Amen. Hallelujah.* (Based on 1 Kings 1:31–45)

The first three lines refer to the coronation in 970 BCE of Solomon, who was not yet king, but the last line refers to his father, King David, who was on his deathbed and wanted to ensure Solomon's succession. Bathsheba was David's then wife and Solomon's mother:

> *Then Bath-sheba bowed her face to the earth, and did reverence to the king, and said, Let my lord king David live for ever.* (1 Kings 1:31)

The historical anointing of Solomon is significant in several ways:

- Solomon's accession is assured not by a crown but by anointing with oil, making him "God's anointed," or in Hebrew, *mashiach,* or "messiah." The whole concept of the Jewish messiah is of a king descended from David. Hence the genealogies produced for Jesus in the New Testament books of Matthew (1:1–16) and Luke (3:23–38) to attempt to prove that he met this criterion. But, the very fact that the two genealogies are so different from each other indicates that there is no basis to that claim (see M. Arnheim *Is Christianity True?* 1984, and *The God Book,* 2015). Oil was used in the ancient world for cleansing and purification, much as soap is used today.
- Though we are not told specifically that Solomon was chosen by God, the fact that he was anointed by two major religious figures, Zadok the High Priest and Nathan the prophet, was enough to secure his accession. According to the Bible, Saul, the first Jewish king, is anointed (in about 1030 BCE) by the prophet Samuel, after which he is referred to as *nagid,* "commander" or "leader," and only comes to be called *melech,* "king," after a popular gathering at Gilgal, to which Samuel extends a general invitation. But all that is said of the ceremony is: "And all the people went to Gilgal; and there they made Saul king before the Lord in Gilgal" (1 Samuel 11:15). So, Saul's accession to

the throne was evidently by way of public acclamation with divine approbation. However, some years later, after a victory against the Philistines and one against the Amalekites, which does not go quite to plan, Samuel informs Saul that God has deposed him as king, and Samuel then anoints David to take over from him.

- So closely was the concept of monarchy tied to religion that all future coronations in the Judaeo-Christian tradition were conducted by priests.

Charlemagne

After the fall of the Roman Empire in the West in or around 476, the fiction was preserved of a single Christian emperor based in Constantinople. But, using the excuse that the imperial throne was vacant because it happened to be occupied by a woman (the vicious and bloodthirsty Irene), on Christmas Day 800 Pope Leo III crowned Emperor Charlemagne, the ruler of modern-day France plus large parts of Germany and the northern half of Italy. Garbed as a Roman emperor sporting a laurel wreath and a traditional military cloak, Charlemagne styled himself on coins "Karolus Imperator Augustus." Though Charlemagne is sometimes credited with founding the so-called Holy Roman Empire, it is more accurately attributed to the Saxon ruler Otto I, crowned as emperor by Pope John XII in 962.

The Holy Roman Empire

Though it lasted until 1806, by the time it was dissolved, the Holy Roman Empire was correctly described by Voltaire as "neither holy, nor Roman, nor an empire." Starting out as a genuinely powerful super-monarchy, it morphed into an umbrella body chiefly covering a multiplicity of effectively independent mostly German states.

In keeping with the original concept of Augustus's principate, the position of Holy Roman emperor was in theory elective, not hereditary, though Augustus and his successors had soon realized the attraction of hereditary succession to the masses. The emperor of the Holy Roman Empire was in theory elected by a college of "electors," restricted from the thirteenth century to the rulers of just seven German states and Bohemia. Between 1438 and 1806 (with one exception) all Holy Roman emperors were members of the Austrian House of Habsburg.

The Last Contested Election: 1519

The last contested election of a Holy Roman emperor took place on the death of the Emperor Maximilian I in 1519. His grandson, the future Emperor Charles V, was his obvious successor, who was already king of Spain as Charles (Carlos) I.

Despite his impeccable claim based on heredity, so closely had the Holy Roman Empire come to be identified with Germany that Charles was felt not to be "German" enough, as he was born in present-day Belgium, had grown up speaking French and Dutch, was in Spain at the time of Maximilian's death, could speak no German, and had never yet set foot on German soil. But his main competitors had even less of a German connection and were rulers of states that were not even part of the Holy Roman Empire. These were Francis I of France and, amazingly, England's Henry VIII. After successfully bribing his way on to the imperial throne, Charles V (as he became) retained a disdainful attitude toward the German language. He is said to have remarked that he prayed in Spanish, spoke to women in Italian, and to men in French, while German was relegated to addressing his horse.

"England Is an Empire"

The 1519 election is significant as a symbol of the old belief, rooted in the Roman Empire, that there could be only one emperor in Europe. What was unique about 1519 was that candidates who threw their hat in the ring included two monarchs from countries well outside the Holy Roman Empire itself. This same concept was turned on its head when, after breaking with the Papacy in order to divorce his wife, in 1532 Henry VIII had Parliament pass an Act in Restraint of Appeals, which proclaimed: "This realm of England is an Empire . . . governed by one Supreme Head and King having the dignity and royal estate of the Imperial Crown of the same." This bold statement effectively cut England's ties with the Papacy and also made England a separate "empire" from the Holy Roman Empire, without daring to go quite so far as to claim the title of "emperor" for Henry VIII. It is this concept of English independence from mainland Europe that gave the Imperial State Crown its name, though a crown of that designation was already in evidence in the reign of Henry V (r. 1413–22) as indicative of English political independence even while still under Rome in regard to religion.

Napoleon: From First Consul to Emperor

Despite the long-term use of the title "emperor" chiefly by hereditary Holy Roman emperors of the House of Habsburg, the original, non-monarchical, Roman origin of the title was not entirely lost (see below). When the frenzy of the French Revolution was finally quelled by Napoleon Bonaparte, he first established a monarchy under the misleading title of "Consulate," with himself as First Consul, but then, on the strength of a supposed "yes" vote of 99.93% in a plebiscite (on a turnout of only 47.2%), declared himself not king but emperor. When Napoleon promoted himself to emperor, it was as "emperor of the French" (that is, of the people), *not* "emperor of France" (the country). He went one better than the old royal coronations from before the Revolution by actually inviting not a mere French bishop but the Pope himself to officiate, but, not wanting to owe his throne to the Church, he famously snatched the crown from the Pope and crowned himself (though some writers make the unlikely suggestion that the Pope had agreed to this in advance).

Britain is now the only western European monarchy to have a coronation. In Spain the last coronation was held in 1494, in Denmark in 1840, and in Sweden in 1873. The Netherlands, Belgium, and Luxembourg have never had a coronation. Instead of a coronation, in all these European monarchies there is a simple swearing-in ceremony, usually held not in a church but in the parliament or legislature, in which the new monarch swears to abide by the constitution. In most cases the crown is no longer ever worn by the monarch but may be seen discreetly placed to the side during the oath-taking. The absence of a coronation, inevitably involving the church and therefore God, is also a way of counteracting any claim of divine right.

Though on the one hand the heir to the French Revolution, Napoleon at the same time tried to start his own royal dynasty, naming several of his brothers as "kings" of conquered territories and, after divorcing his first wife, Joséphine, marrying Marie-Louise, daughter of the Holy Roman Emperor Francis (Franz) II, whom Napoleon persuaded to dissolve the Holy Roman Empire, after which his new father-in-law, anxious to cling to the title of *kaiser* (emperor) became Emperor Francis (Franz) I of Austria, even though as a constituent state of the Holy Roman Empire, Austria had only had the rank of an Archduchy. After his marriage to Marie-Louise, Napoleon would refer to France's guillotined Louis XVI (Marie-Louise's great-uncle by marriage) as *mon oncle* ("my uncle").

Napoleon's nephew, Louis Napoleon Bonaparte, followed his uncle's example. Elected as president of the Second French Republic in 1848, he staged a coup d'état three years later, followed by a plebiscite in which he obtained 97% support to reinvent himself as Emperor Napoleon III.

Victoria Regina Imperatrix

One of my favorite *Punch* cartoons shows British Prime Minister Benjamin Disraeli on bended knee accepting an earl's coronet from Queen Victoria, who is depicted sporting an imaginary oriental-looking crown. Published in August 1876, it is titled "Empress and Earl, or One Good Turn Deserves Another." It is a reference to Disraeli's acquisition for Queen Victoria of the title Empress of India, in return for which he was invested with the noble title of Earl.

Queen Victoria had long hankered after the title of "empress," especially after her own daughter and daughter-in-law's sister had or were in line to succeed to that title, which was seen to outrank that of a mere "queen." Queen

Victoria's daughter, also called Victoria, was married to the future German Kaiser Friedrich III, the title "kaiser" (from Latin *Caesar*) being the German equivalent of "emperor." And "Minnie," a sister of Alexandra, wife of Queen Victoria's son and heir, the future Edward VII, was married to the future Russian Tsar (or Czar) Alexander III—tsar or czar being the Russian equivalent of Emperor, also from *Caesar*.

Why does an emperor outrank a king? The label "empire" and "emperor" is now largely reserved to large, often multinational states such as Tsarist Russia, Imperial Germany (from 1871 to 1918), Imperial China, Japan, and Mughal-ruled India, to which Queen Victoria was essentially the heir. "King" and "emperor" have very different origins.

In the West "king" is by far the older term, represented by *rex* in Latin and *basileus* in Greek. In Rome the last king, Tarquinius Superbus, was deposed in 509 BCE and replaced with an oligarchy known as the "Republic," which had a visceral fear of one-man rule. That fear was realized and the oligarchy was toppled when Julius Caesar was named "dictator perpetuo" in 49 BCE, leading to his assassination by a group of oligarchs on the Ides of March 44 BCE. This sparked off a catenation of two civil wars. When the dust settled in 31 BCE, Caesar's great-nephew and adoptive son emerged victorious as sole ruler of the Roman world, reinventing himself in 27 BCE as *Imperator Caesar Augustus*. One title that he was careful to avoid was *rex*. Though Augustus and a number of his successors used "Imperator" (literally, "commander") as a *praenomen* (forename), it originated during the Republic as a title by which a successful general was hailed by his troops on the field of battle. It is not hard to see how in time it came to mean "emperor," and of course the English word *emperor* is derived from it. And, as the Roman emperor was superior to any king, the concept arose that an emperor was a higher type of king (see Chapter 6).

It was the Roman Republic rather than the Roman Principate or Empire that was particularly revered by the French revolutionaries, who failed to notice its oligarchic nature but took it at its word as a bastion of "liberty." Hence Napoleon's first government, which he called the "Consulate," a name taken straight from the Roman Republic, except that while Rome had two equal consuls who checked and balanced each other to prevent one-man rule, Napoleon's Consulate consisted of three consuls, of whom only the First Consul, Bonaparte himself, had any real power. The next step entailed coming out openly as a monarch. But for Napoleon, the heir of the Revolution, to assume the title of "king" would have been seen by former revolutionaries as a betrayal, while for monarchists it would have been the most flagrant insult. How could this Corsican upstart presume to restore the monarchy, which, after all, still existed in the person of the late Louis XVI's brother?—who, as it happens would ascend his ancestral throne as Louis XVIII once "the little corporal" was disposed of.

Napoleon combined in his own person two opposite features of the title of "emperor": its Republican and non-monarchical origin together with a claim that France could now replace the Holy Roman Empire (which Napoleon was instrumental in dissolving) as *the* European Empire par excellence.

Conclusion

Combining as it does three very different historic traditions, the British coronation is an impressive spectacle that projects an image of a powerful ruler. The truth is very different. But does the pomp and ceremony, played out in a heavy religious setting, have any practical significance? Considering that the English monarchy was abolished and a king executed in 1649 after nearly 600 years of genuine monarchy coupled with the same sort of display as there is now, the pomp probably contributes very little to the stability of the system or even the security of the monarchy itself. The ruling power elites in Britain and the other "constitutional monarchies" in western Europe are now more varied than even a century ago, but it remains in their interests to retain a titular monarch as head of state while the real work of government goes on behind the scenes.

Chapter 6
Legal Framework

Many monarchs throughout history have claimed to wield supreme power untrammelled by any restrictions. In practice it is well-nigh impossible for one person to keep direct control over a state of any size. That one person would need to rely to some extent on others. The crucial questions are: First, who has the whip hand? In other words, what is the power structure of that regime? And second, how true a reflection of the power structure is given by its legal framework?

Case Study: Rome

This is an analysis of the power structure of the Roman state from its inception.

- **753(?)–509** BCE: A monarchy, probably elective to begin with and possibly under aristocratic control in its latter years.
- **509–49** BCE: The Roman Republic: a largely hereditary oligarchy with a visceral fear of one-man rule.
- **31** BCE–**180** CE: The Augustan "Principate": a popular monarchy with power concentrated in the hands of the *princeps,* or emperor, but disguised so as to placate the senatorial elite.
- **180–284:** Descent "from a kingdom of gold to one of iron and rust" (Cassius Dio 71.36.3–4), followed by the "Crisis of the Third Century."
- **284–395:** The Dominate.
- **395–476:** Death-throes of the Roman Empire in the West.
- **395–1453:** Eastern Roman or Byzantine Empire.

Five Thousand Years of Monarchy, First Edition. Michael Arnheim.
© 2026 John Wiley & Sons, Inc. Published 2026 by John Wiley & Sons, Inc.

Rome: From Monarchy to Monarchy

In the beginning, Rome was a monarchy, which, according to tradition, lasted from 753 to 509 BCE. The monarchy appears initially to have been not hereditary but elective, with the king being chosen by the Senate, an aristocratic council, and confirmed by the citizens meeting together in the assembly known as the *Comitia Curiata*. According to tradition, the last three kings, Tarquinius Priscus, Servius Tullius, and Tarquinius Superbus ("Tarquin the Proud"), were Etruscans and the monarchy seems to have become hereditary at that time, as the two Tarquins were either father and son or grandfather and grandson, and Servius Tullius was supposedly the younger Tarquin's father-in-law.

Livy's account of the last period of the monarchy paints a very confused picture, with Tarquinius Superbus initially cultivating the support of the Senate against Servius Tullius, his father-in-law, portrayed as a populist king, distributing conquered lands to the whole populace and enjoying widespread popular support (Livy 1.46.1). Servius Tullius is even said to have been physically attacked by his son-in-law and murdered by Tarquin's entourage (Livy 1.48). Once ensconced in power, we are told, Tarquin "killed the leading senators who he believed had favored the cause of Servius" (Livy 1.49.2.1). This may indicate aristocratic opposition to his rule, which rather contradicts his earlier stance.

What, then, was the formal power structure under the Roman monarchy? If the earlier kings really owed their position to election by the Senate, an aristocratic body, that may point to an aristocratic regime from the start, with the king as essentially *primus inter pares*, or first among equals. The last three kings, however, may possibly represent a period of Etruscan domination over Rome. So the uprising that ended the monarchy may then be interpreted as the reclaiming by the indigenous Roman aristocracy of their previous pre-eminence against foreign domination. The only thing that appears to contradict this interpretation is the tradition that Lucius Junius Brutus and his co-conspirator Lucius Tarquinius Collatinus, who were chiefly instrumental in overthrowing the last king, Tarquinius Superbus, in 509 BCE and would become the first two consuls of the new Republic, were both related to the king, and that Brutus had two of his sons put to death for siding with the ousted king. If there is any truth in this picture of a family feud, then it may be that Tarquin's overthrow was the result of internecine conflict within the Roman aristocracy.

"Republic" and Democracy

The word "republic" is a translation of the Latin *res publica* or *respublica*, literally "the public thing, public matter, public business." The Latin adjective *publica* is a contraction of the non-existent **populicus*, from *populus,* "the people." So *res publica* or *respublica* means "the people's thing, the people's business," hence "public or civil affairs, public or civil administration, public or civil power," and hence "the state, commonwealth, republic" (Lewis and Short 1879). It generally refers to the Roman state, as against foreign states, for which the word *civitas* was preferred, and from which (via the French) we have the English word "city."

It is important to note that, in referring to the Roman state, *res publica* or *respublica* did not identify any particular form of government, and was still used to refer to the Roman state long after the Roman Republic had ceased to exist and when Rome was ruled by emperors. For example, in the dedication by Pliny the Elder (23–79 CE) of his *Natural History* to the future Emperor Titus, he congratulates Titus on his service to *the state*, this term being expressed by *res publica*—written in 77 CE, more than a century after the end of the Roman Republic (Plin. *H.N.* 3).

The term *res publica* or *respublica* clearly, therefore, carries no implication of democracy, even though it is based on the word *populus,* meaning "the people." The acronym SPQR, for Senatus Populusque Romanus ("The Roman Senate and People"), a corporate designation of the Roman state, likewise carries no implication of democracy and is also not associated with a republican form of government. In fact, it is first encountered only in the late Republic and continued to be used well into imperial times. Both the arch of Titus, dating from 81 CE (CIL VI 945), and the Arch of Septimius Severus, constructed in 203 CE (CIL VI 1033) were dedicated to the memory of these emperors by "The Roman Senate and People"—the latter well over two centuries after the demise of the Roman Republic.

From One Brutus to Another

Whatever the precise explanation may be for the overthrow of the monarchy, there can be no doubt about the nature of the "republic" which replaced it. Far from being a democracy, it was an oligarchy. Based on detailed prosopographical evidence we read: "In any age of the history of Republican Rome about twenty or thirty men, drawn from a dozen dominant families, hold a monopoly of office and power" (Syme 1939, p. 124). Similarly, Ernst Badian found that "the proportion of consuls who came from families that had already produced at least one consul never fell below 70 percent in the whole period between 179 and 49 BCE" (Badian 1990, pp. 371–413).

According to our sources, the Latin word *rex*, meaning "king," and the whole idea of monarchy was taboo in the Roman Republic (and long afterwards)—which makes perfect sense, as what an oligarchy dreads most is a strong ruler supported by the masses. But, as the history of the late Republic demonstrates, it would be a mistake to assume that this fear of monarchy was shared by the populace at large. Indeed, in times of crisis, the ordinary people would look to a strong leader to champion their cause against the oligarchy.

The Republican constitution, the creation of the ruling oligarchy, was carefully constructed so as to prevent power from being concentrated in the hands of any one person. One of its main features was collegiality, or shared power, together with short terms of office, and rotation.

The only exception to the rule of shared power was the appointment of a *dictator* in an emergency—which was strictly limited to a tenure of six months. The Senate had to pass a decree (*senatus consultum*) instructing the consuls to nominate a dictator. The dictator would then appoint a *magister equitum* ("master of the horse") to assist him and act as his deputy when necessary. Once appointed, the dictator had absolute power over the Roman state, superseding that of the consuls. The most admired type of Republican hero was someone like Cincinnatus, who, after resolving the immediate emergency in a fortnight, at once gave up his dictatorship and returned to his plough and to obscurity. The reason that Cincinnatus was fêted as an ideal Republican was that he had no interest in gaining personal power. After 202 BCE, the Senate would issue an emergency decree, labeled by modern historians *senatus consultum ultimum,* instead of appointing a dictator. The dictatorship was only revived much later on, in 82 BCE, first for L. Cornelius Sulla and then again for Julius Caesar in 46 BCE—but, so far from preventing one-man rule, it was now used as a vehicle to achieve just that, bringing down the Republic.

"In the Consulship of Julius and Caesar"

A visceral fear of one-man rule is characteristic of oligarchies and aristocracies, not least in the case of the Roman Republic, where, as mentioned above, this fear was kept in check by collegiality and rotation of office. However, a less than persuasive argument is put forward against this view by Lintott, who opines that, "We would be wrong ... to see collegiality in principle as a form of constitutional check: the multiplicity of magistrates was perhaps in origin intended rather as cover for a multiplicity of functions and insurance against the sudden death or disability of a magistrate" (Lintott 2003, loc 1250). There is no evidence for this. A key fact is that the consuls, who did *not* have "separate functions," had a veto power over each other. The use of the auspices to block a colleague's actions was a well-known political ploy to prevent an individual from becoming too powerful. An extreme example of this (not mentioned by Lintott) was the attempt in 59 BCE by Julius Caesar's conservative co-consul, Marcus Calpurnius Bibulus, to block Caesar's populist legislation by closeting himself at home and issuing proclamations announcing bad omens, of which no proof was required (Suet., *Julius*, 20.1). As a result, Bibulus was sidelined, and some wags signed mock-formal documents dated "Done in the consulship of Julius and Caesar" instead of "Bibulus and Caesar" (ibid., p. 20).

The Fall of the Republic

The last century of the Roman Republic was marked by confrontations between two groupings within the ruling oligarchy, one of which, the *Populares,* championed the cause, and depended on the support, of the lower classes, and the other, the *Optimates* (literally, "the best men"), of a more "conservative" mind-set, bent on the continued dominance of the senatorial elite.

Julius Caesar

The lineup for the final dénouement of the Republic took shape in 60 BCE, when the state was hijacked by an alliance between three strongmen in the so-called but unofficial First Triumvirate: Pompey, Crassus, and Caesar.

Gaius Julius Caesar was a nephew of the general and politician Gaius Marius (157–86 BCE), and he remained true to his uncle's populist politics. In Sulla's final purge of Marian partisans in 83 BCE, the 17-year-old Caesar was spared only through the intervention of his mother's family, which included supporters of Sulla, and the Vestal Virgins, because the young Caesar had been nominated as *flamen Dialis* (the high priest of Jupiter). In reluctantly sparing Caesar's life, Sulla is said to have predicted that Caesar would prove the ruin of the aristocracy, "for in that Caesar there are many Mariuses" (Suet, *Julius*, 1; Plut, *Caesar*, 1).

Caesar early on showed his mettle. When captured by pirates, who demanded a ransom of 20 talents of silver, the young Caesar insisted that he was worth at least 50. When released, he promised to return and crucify them all, which is exactly what he did. In 63 BCE Caesar was elected against great odds to the prestigious position of Pontifex Maximus, or chief priest of the Roman state religion. After serving as praetor in 62 BCE he was allotted the province of Hispania Ulterior (modern south-eastern Spain), where he conquered two local tribes and in 60 BCE was hailed as *imperator* (literally, "commander") by his troops on the field of battle.

With the support of his partners, Pompey and Crassus, in the (unofficial) First Triumvirate, Caesar was elected consul in 59 BCE and successfully proposed a popular law redistributing public lands (*ager publicus*) to the poor. He also managed, in the face of "conservative" opposition, to be allotted as his proconsular command (the command that an ex-consul was given after his term of office) not one but three provinces: Illyricum (the Balkans), Cisalpine Gaul (northern Italy), and later also Transalpine Gaul (southern France) (Suet., *Julius*, 19.2).

Caesar expanded Roman territory by his conquest of what was known as Gallia Comata (literally, "long-haired Gaul," northern France), which he publicized himself in his book *De Bello Gallico* (*The Gallic War*), inflicted on generations of schoolchildren right up to the present day.

Caesar's command had been extended to 50 BCE, by which time the Triumvirate had collapsed. Crassus had been killed in battle against the Parthians in 53 BCE; and Pompey had changed sides and become the champion of the *Optimates*, who now controlled the Senate and, unprecedentedly, made Pompey sole consul in 52 BCE. When Caesar's command ended in 50 BCE, he was ordered to disband his army and return to Rome as a private citizen, exposing him to possible prosecution. Instead, on 10 January 49 BCE, he chose to cross the Rubicon (the boundary between Cisalpine Gaul and Italy) with an armed legion, famously remarking (apparently in Greek) "the die is cast" (Plut, *Pompey,* 60.2; Plut, *Caesar*, 32.8.4; Suet, *Juius,* 33).

Caesar was now at war with the Republic, which had entrusted its fortunes to Pompey. After Caesar's decisive victory over Pompey at Pharsalus, in Greece, in July 48 BCE, Caesar entered Rome as a conquering hero. He was named dictator, then won a second consulship in an election presided over by himself, and resigned his dictatorship after 11 days. In 48 BCE he was named dictator again, this time for a year. Then in 46 BCE, after a few foreign interludes, he was named dictator for a year yet again, and was designated as dictator for nine further years. As if this were not enough, Caesar was also elected to serve as consul (simultaneously with his dictatorship) three more times, for 46, 45 and 44 BCE. Julius Caesar was now king in all but name. To drive the point home, in early 44 BCE he was named *dictator perpetuo* or *dictator in perpetuum* ("dictator in perpetuity"). In accepting this title Caesar effectively signed his own death warrant. Caesar was seen by the *Optimates* as threatening to bring to an end the 450-year-old Republic, and about 60 of them conspired to assassinate him, which occurred on the Ides of March (15 March) 44 BCE, one of the best-known dates in history.

It was Caesar's undoubted popularity with the masses, coupled with his arrogance and habit of plain speaking, that caused his downfall. He is said, for example, to have remarked "that the Republic was nothing but a name, without substance or form; that Sulla had acted like an idiot by laying down the dictatorship; and that people ought to be more careful when speaking with him, and should take what he says as law" (Suetonius, ibid., p. 77). Above all, not only was he unable to resist accepting most of the exceptional honors that were showered upon him, but he also does not seem to have recognized the likely backlash from the *Optimates*. According to Suetonius, among other honors accorded to him was the title *Pater Patriae* ("Father of the Nation"); several statues of himself, including one next to those of the seven kings of Rome; and a college of priests dedicated to himself. When, "amidst the immoderate and unusual acclamations of the people" (ibid., p. 79), a man in the adulating throng placed on one of Caesar's statues a laurel crown encircled with a white fillet, a symbol of royalty, and two tribunes ordered the fillet to be removed and the man responsible for placing it there to be imprisoned, Caesar reprimanded the tribunes and dismissed them from office. This gave the impression—welcomed by the populace and feared by the *Optimates*—that he aspired to make himself king, although when hailed by the people as *rex* (king), he responded jocularly, "I am Caesar, not Rex"—Rex being a name as well as a title. And when his staunch supporter Mark Antony, as consul, on several occasions placed a laurel crown on Caesar's head, Caesar waved it aside, and ordered it to be taken to the temple of Jupiter (ibid., p. 79).

When stabbed by his protégé Marcus Junius Brutus, Caesar probably did not cry "*Et tu, Brute?*" ("You too, Brutus?"), as suggested by Shakespeare, nor even, in Greek, "*Kai su, teknon?*" ("You too, my child?"), as rather sceptically suggested by Suetonius and Cassius Dio (Suet, *Julius*, 84; Cassius Dio 44.19).

So out of touch with reality were Caesar's assassins that, according to Plutarch, they marched to the Capitol, proudly brandishing their daggers full of confidence, and fondly imagining that they would be fêted for saving the Republic and restoring "liberty" (Plutarch, *Caesar*, 67.3).

In the immediate aftermath of the assassination, even Caesar's close friend, Mark Antony, was apparently unsure which way the wind was blowing. Plutarch, in his *Life of Antony*, says that Antony even gave the conspirators his son as a hostage, and entertained a leading conspirator, Cassius, to dinner, while Lepidus, Caesar's master of the horse (lieutenant to Caesar as dictator), did the same for Brutus (Plutarch, *Antony*, 13). As consul, Antony convened the Senate, spoke in favour of an amnesty and of allotting provincial commands to both Brutus and Cassius, and proposed a law abolishing the position of dictator forever. The Senate ratified these proposals, while voting to honor Caesar by giving him the posthumous title *divus* ("the divine Julius"), making him a minor deity, and confirming all Caesar's reforms (Plutarch, *Caesar*, 67.7; *Antony*, 14).

Armed with his new command, Brutus issued coins with the motto LEIBERTAS, the old-fashioned spelling of *libertas* ("liberty"), and others with the legend EID MAR, an abbreviation for (the once again intentionally archaic spelling of) *Idibus Martiis,* meaning "on the Ides of March," together with a *pileus* (cap of liberty given to newly enfranchised slaves), and two daggers, celebrating Caesar's assassination. On the obverse was a portrait of Brutus described as *imp(erator),* general (British Museum number 1860,0328.124).

A modern writer opines: "The portrayal of a living person on a Roman coin was taken as a sign of autocratic power" (Beard 2016, p. 295). Brutus certainly did not have "autocratic power," but is that what he was aiming at? Almost certainly not. The portrait of a living person on a coin *was* decidedly rare, but the name Brutus was closely identified in the Roman psyche with a fervent anti-monarchical tradition. Marcus Brutus himself claimed descent from the founder of the Republic, Lucius Junius Brutus, who, according to persistent tradition, had been instrumental in ending the monarchy in 509 BCE, some 450 years earlier, and whose portrait had appeared on coins minted by Marcus Brutus as moneyer at some time between 59 and 54 BCE. With the legends EID MAR, the date of Caesar's assassination, and LEIBERTAS, the watchword of the oligarchic Republic, the message conveyed by Brutus's coins was *not* that he was aiming at "autocratic power," but that he had emulated his iconic ancestor by liberating Rome from a tyrant who had enslaved it.

The populace, however, were incensed at the murder of their idol, as the assassins soon learned, when an unruly crowd descended on their houses intent on burning them down. As part of his lifelong devotion to the popular cause, in his will Caesar bequeathed to the Roman people his gardens near the Tiber, and left every Roman man 300 sesterces.

Caesar's Heir

Probably the most significant provision of Caesar's will was his adoption of his 19-year-old great-nephew, Gaius Octavius, known to his contemporaries as Caesar and to history as Augustus. But before he could take power he had to emerge victorious from a two-stage civil war, first against the conspirators, and then against Mark Antony.

Emerging victorious in 31 BCE from the Battle of Actium against Antony, the young Caesar established a new form of government, which, with modifications, was to last for three centuries, with repercussions down to the present day. But what sort of government was this to be? There is a great deal of confusion among modern writers about the nature, and even the name, of this new form of government. In common parlance, Augustus is generally referred to as the first Roman "emperor," and the system of government instituted by him as the "Roman Empire." But this is neither clear nor accurate. See the discussion below.

Avoiding Julius Caesar's Mistake

As an astute politician, Augustus took care not to make the same mistake as had cost Julius Caesar his life. Julius Caesar had ruled Rome as "dictator" for four years when he was appointed *dictator perpetuo* or *dictator in perpetuum* (literally, "dictator in perpetuity," commonly translated as "dictator for life" but more accurately "dictator for an indefinite period"). Acceptance of this title signaled the end of the Roman Republic, which had lasted for 450 years under an elite to whom one-man rule was carefully eschewed except for brief emergencies. Julius Caesar's position as *dictator perpetuo* posed a threat to this dominant minority, a number of whom therefore conspired to assassinate him on that fateful Ides of March, 44 BCE.

After his victory over Antony at Actium in 31 BCE, Augustus faced a serious dilemma. He was now master of the Roman world, but on what footing should his rule be placed? The title *rex*, or "king," which even Julius Caesar had refused, was anathema to the Republican aristocracy. But the title "dictator" was clearly also now off-limits. The common people, who adulated Julius Caesar, had no objection to one-man rule, as was made clear in their outpouring of grief on Caesar's assassination. Indeed, they wanted a strong leader to champion their cause. So the young Caesar's game plan was to retain the support of the masses without offending the aristocracy—a daunting balancing act.

The Transmogrification of an Equestrian

The historic figure who is usually referred to as "Augustus" was born in 63 BCE into an equestrian family (i.e. the second rank, below that of senator), with the undistinguished name *Gaius Octavius*. In 44 BCE, on adoption in his great-uncle Julius Caesar's will, he immediately took his adoptive father's name: *Gaius Julius Caesar*. It was usual for an adoptive son to tack his own original *nomen,* in this case "Octavius," on to his new name as an additional *cognomen,* "surname," often in adjectival form, so: "Octavianus." That is why he is generally referred to by modern historians during this period of his life as "Octavian," but he is not known ever to have used the name "Octavianus" himself. To his contemporaries he was known simply as "Caesar," and this was his greatest asset with the masses, as it enabled him to capitalize on his adoptive father's popularity, Moreover, besides having been a charismatic champion of the people, Julius Caesar was now a divinity, having been deified shortly after his death. So in 42 BCE, the next step in Augustus's transmogrification was to add *Divi Filius* ("son of a god" or "son of the divine (Julius)") to his name, which now became: *Gaius Julius Caesar Divi Filius*. In 38 BCE, in a masterstroke, both his forename "Gaius" and his family name (*nomen gentilicium)* "Julius" were ditched and replaced by *imperator* ("commander"), the victory title by which a successful general was hailed by his troops on the field of battle. This gave him a new identity: *Imperator Caesar Divi Filius*. But the culmination of his reinvention of himself came in 27 BCE, when he was accorded by the Senate the title *Augustus* ("the Sublime" or "the Revered"), a sobriquet associated with Romulus, Rome's mythical founder, so he emerged in his full glory as: *Imperator Caesar Divi Filius Augustus*.

Taking each component of this nomenclature separately:

Imperator: As Augustus tells us in his masterly autobiography, which came to be known as the *Res Gestae Divi Augusti*, he was hailed as *imperator* 21 times (Aug. *R.G.*, *§4*). This was the traditional way in which a successful general was honored by his troops on the field of battle. But, in a masterstroke, he now adopted it as a forename. This designation, which came later to be used to mean "emperor" (and has given us the English word "emperor"), is the reason that the whole regime instituted by Augustus came to be known in English (and similarly in the Romance languages) as the "Roman Empire." Because Roman emperors had never had the title of "king," when Napoleon Bonaparte assumed monarchical powers, he chose to call himself not "king" but "emperor," which did not offend against his Republican sensibilities as heir to the French Revolution.

Caesar: This is the only part of Augustus's final designation that was an actual name—Julius Caesar's *cognomen*. But it also became a title, later accorded to the emperor-designate and later still to a "junior" emperor, with the title *Augustus* reserved for "senior" emperors. It is the origin of the Russian imperial title *tsar* or *czar*, and German *Kaiser*, and hence *Kaiserzeit* for the whole period ushered in by Augustus's accession to power.

***Divi Filius*:** Being the son of a god was no mean feat—but Julius Caesar was reputedly already of divine stock before his deification, as a descendant of the goddess Venus Genetrix, whose image accordingly appears on coins issued by earlier members of the Julian *gens* ("clan"). The Julii traced their descent from Venus through Iulus, the son of Aeneas, the mythical Trojan prince who was an ancestor of Romulus, the eponymous legendary founder of Rome. It was partly to celebrate this tradition that Vergil wrote his *Aeneid*.

Augustus: This designation, meaning "the sublime one" or "the revered one," associated as it was with Romulus, gave the whole carefully crafted new self-image an aura of sanctity, and hinted at Augustus's claim to be the second founder of Rome. Augustus himself was to be deified on his death, as were most of his successors. The deification of the emperor became the basis of the Imperial Cult, which was eventually extended to worship of the *genius,* or "attendant spirit," of the living emperor, and especially in the Eastern provinces, of the living emperor himself as well.

Augustus's Autobiography (*Res Gestae Divi Augusti*)

In his carefully crafted autobiography, Augustus manages to paint a composite picture of himself as a powerful populist leader and at the same time as the restorer of the Republic—in order to win the support of the *plebs urbana* while conciliating the senatorial aristocracy at the same time. Here are a few choice extracts:

Victorious but merciful general: "I frequently waged civil and foreign wars by land and sea, and as victor I spared the lives of all citizens who sought pardon" (§3).

Recognition and modesty: "I twice celebrated a triumphal ovation and a curule triumph on three occasions, and was hailed as *imperator* 21 times, with the Senate decreeing more triumphs to me, all of which I refused" (§4.1).

Holder of Republican offices: "When I wrote this I had been consul 13 times, and was holding tribunician power for the 37th time" (§4.4). "When offered the consulship [in 22 BCE] every year for the rest of my life, I did not accept it" (§5.3).

"First settlement": In 27 BCE, "having come to be in complete charge of everything by universal consent, I transferred the state (*res publica*) from my power (*potestas*) to the control (*arbitrium*) of the Roman Senate and People." In return for this, he was named "Augustus" by the Senate. "After this time I surpassed everyone in influence (*auctoritas*), but had no more power (*potestas*) than the others who were my colleagues in each magistracy" (§34).

Dictatorship refused: "The dictatorship was offered to me by both the people and the Senate both when I was present and when I was absent from Rome in (22 BCE), but I did not accept it" (§5.1). In fact, in 22 BCE, there were food riots, with the urban masses calling on Augustus to become dictator to solve the problem. That was also the first year when Augustus declined the consulship, which so worried his loyal *plebs* that they refused to elect a second consul that year, ostensibly keeping the vacant seat open for Augustus. This concern erupted in riots in that year, and also in 21 and 19 BCE (Dio Cassius, 54.1, 54.6, 54.10).

Benefactor of the poor: Augustus contrasts his refusal of the dictatorship in 22 BCE with his acceptance of the task of saving the corn supply during the corn shortage in that year, which he achieved "within a few days" and "at my own expense and effort" (§5.2). Augustus proudly records his bounty to the *plebs urbana*, or ordinary people of the capital: 500 sestertii to each member of the *plebs* under Julius Caesar's will in 44 BCE; 400 each from the spoils of war in 29 BCE; and another 400 sestertii in 24 BCE, this time at his own expense; 12 rations of grain apiece at his own expense in 23 BCE; and 400 sestertii each for the third time in 11 BCE. The recipients of his bounty never numbered fewer than 250,000 people. But in 5 BCE he gave 240 sestertii apiece to 520,000 members of the urban *plebs*. At the time of his triumph in 29 BCE he gave 1,000 sestertii to 120,000 of his soldiers settled as *coloni* in Italy. And in 2 BCE he gave 60 denarii (240 sestertii) apiece to the more than 200,000 members of the *plebs* then in receipt of public grain (§15).

Figure 6 Augustus as Pontifex Maximus.
SOURCE: Prof. Mortel / flickr / CC BY 2.0.

Soldiers and veterans: Augustus paid out about 600 million sestertii for land in Italy to settle soldiers on as *coloni* there and 260 million for provincial land. And a further 400 million paid to soldiers on their retirement to their home towns (§16). Augustus founded colonies of soldiers in Africa, Sicily, Macedonia, and Spain, plus 28 colonies in Italy (§28).

Tribunician power: In 23 BCE Augustus was voted the tribunician power for life together with sacrosanctity of his person, which he had for some years and was a protection traditionally accorded tribunes of the *plebs* (§10.1).

For more on tribunician power, see under the discussion of the Republican constitution, earlier.

Pontifex Maximus: Augustus was offered by the people the position of *Pontifex Maximus*, chief priest of the Roman civic religion, which had been held by Julius Caesar, but he makes the point of stressing that he refused to accept it until the death of Lepidus (his former colleague in the Triumvirate), whom he studiously avoids naming but accuses of having taken the opportunity of civil war to "seize" the priesthood. Augustus's acceptance of the priesthood occurred in 12 BCE, "with such a multitude pouring in to my election from the whole of Italy as has never been said to have occurred before" (§10.2).

Pax Augusta: "During my principate the Senate decreed three times that the Temple of Janus should be shut" to signify the attainment of peace by victory throughout the Roman Empire, which had only occurred twice before since the foundation of Rome over seven hundred years earlier (§13). Augustus's rule did indeed usher in about two centuries of peace, which is therefore sometimes labelled the *Pax Augusta*, or more usually *Pax Romana*.

Public works: Augustus provides us with an impressive list of his public works, including his rebuilding of the Senate-house and his restoration of 82 temples in one year (28 BCE) together with several new temples, including one to the Divine Julius (Caesar). We also read of the repair of aqueducts, including the doubling of the supply to the Marcian aqueduct (§19–20).

Games: Augustus paid for 8 gladiatorial games, 3 athletics displays, 27 dramatic shows and 26 beast-hunts, and a massive mock sea-battle involving 3,000 men in addition to the rowers of ships involved. Above all, there were the Secular Games of 17 BCE, a magnificent religious festival (§22). The Roman satirist Juvenal, writing about a century after Augustus, famously remarked that the Roman populace were keenly desirous of only two things, "bread and circuses" (*panem et circenses*) (Juv. 10.81). Augustus's pandering to this desire is a mark of his populist side.

Pater Patriae: In 2 BCE "the Senate, the equestrian order and the entire Roman people" gave Augustus the title *Pater Patriae* ("Father of the Country")—the highest possible accolade that a Roman could be given.

Summary of bounty: Tacked on to the autobiography is an Appendix added after Augustus's death summarizing his bounty: 600 million denarii to the treasury, the Roman *plebs* and veterans; another impressive list of temples and other public works; an incalculable outlay (*impensa innumerabilis*) on games, dramatic shows, hunts, and the mock sea battle; donations to towns destroyed by earthquake or fire; and grants to individual friends and senators to make up their property qualification.

Did Augustus Wield Sole Power?

Constitutional position—"first settlement": Augustus is at pains to stress the constitutional nature of his rule. He admits that he had complete power until 27 BCE, but then claims to have handed back the *res publica,* the government of the state, to the Roman Senate and people—and thereby to have "restored the Republic," whose corporate designation was Senatus Populusque Romanus ("The Roman Senate and People") represented by the acronym SPQR. As mentioned earlier, there is no implication here of democracy. From 31 to 23 BCE Augustus was consul every year—the top Republican magistracy, which, however, it was un-Republican to hold so many times in succession. Under the so-called "first settlement" (a modern label) of 27 BCE, in return for "restoring the Republic" Augustus was accorded the title of "Augustus" borne as a name. Then comes the mock-modest boast, the most memorable phrase in the whole autobiography: "After this time I surpassed everyone in influence (*auctoritas*), but had no more power (*potestas*) than the others who were my colleagues in each magistracy" (§34). This is not a very reliable picture of the true position. For one thing, it omits Augustus's *imperium* ("command") over the provinces containing the greatest concentration of legions: Syria, Cilicia, Cyprus, Gaul, and Spain, together with Egypt, which, since the defeat of Antony and Cleopatra, had effectively become part of Augustus's personal patrimony. He governed all these provinces as consul, which was certainly not in keeping with Republican traditions. Even less so was the sheer magnitude of his vast *provincia.* As consul, he also had *imperium* in Rome and Italy and could override the governors of all the provinces which were not directly under his control. It is also worth noting that, even before his victory over Antony at Actium in 31 BCE, "the whole of Italy," together with the Gallic and Spanish provinces, Africa, Sicily, and Sardinia, swore a personal oath of allegiance to him (§25.2). Augustus does at least admit that he had more *auctoritas* ("influence") than anyone else. *Auctoritas* was an intangible quality which could not be made the subject of a formal grant but which enabled its holder to exert his will more subtly by suggestion, without force or even command—cf. some incorrect interpretations of *auctoritas,* like Michael Grant's theory that it "devolved" from the emperor to the *consilium principis,* the emperor's advisers (Grant 1971, pp. 130, 453). I agree with John Crook that *auctoritas* was not "the kind of thing that could "devolve" or "be transferred" at all" (Crook 1955, p. 17n). Another implausible interpretation tries to limit Augustus's *auctoritas* to a single incident in 28 BCE—on the ground that *auctoritas* is not mentioned anywhere other than in Augustus's autobiography (Rowe, 2013). But why would we expect *auctoritas* to be mentioned in the literary sources? It was not an official power but a nebulous quality, an aura of authority, which Augustus undoubtedly exuded in large measure. The language is not complex and clearly relates to a long period: "After this time. . ." The existence of Augustus's *auctoritas* over a long period is not in doubt. What is in doubt is Augustus's modest claim that it was *only* in respect of his *auctoritas* that he surpassed everyone else. The truth was that he surpassed everyone else not only in respect of his *auctoritas* but also in his formal *imperium.*

Constitutional position—"second settlement": In 23 BCE, after a life-threatening illness, Augustus's formal powers were placed on a slightly different footing from before (Dio Cassius 53.32). In particular, he no longer continued to hold the consulship year after year, thus freeing up one of the two "ordinary" consulships for someone else to hold. But he retained control of his provinces, which was renewed at regular intervals for the rest of his life. He was now given *maius imperium,* "greater command," proconsular (instead of consular) power not only over his provinces but also in Rome itself, with the right to override all other provincial governors. In 22 BCE Augustus handed back to the Senate the peaceful provinces of Gallia Narbonensis and Cyprus, but Illyricum was transferred to Augustus in 11 BCE and Sardinia in 6 CE; all new provinces were automatically entrusted to Augustus, and when the frontier was extended to the Danube, all troops in Macedonia were moved so as not to be under the control of the Senate. In the end, the only senatorial province with a garrison was Africa, with just one legion. Instead of the consulship, Augustus was now given *tribunicia potestas* ("tribunician power") on an annual and indefinite basis, and this became the way Augustus and all subsequent emperors counted the years of their "reign." So, coins would normally show a number after the tribunician power, thus: "TRIB. POT. IV." But, in fact, the emperors had more power than an actual *tribunus plebis* would have had during the Republic. One important power associated with tribunician power was the *ius auxilii,* or the right to come to the assistance of a citizen who complained of being oppressed by another magistrate. In Republican times, a tribune could exercise this power only in the city of Rome itself, but the imperial tribunician power extended throughout the Roman world. Augustus's tribunician power also gave him the right to submit legislative proposals to the *Concilium Plebis,* the popular assembly, and to summon the Senate and submit motions to it as well. Another important power included in the tribunician power was the *ius intercessionis,* the right to veto the acts of other magistrates, including the consuls, and of the Senate itself. In addition, tribunician power gave the emperor *coercitio,* the right enjoyed by all magistrates to compel a reluctant citizen to obey his orders, on pain of sanction. Above all, Augustus's *tribunicia potestas* carried with it *sacrosanctitas,* or inviolability, which meant that any assault on his person was prohibited by law. The position of tribune itself was low down on the traditional senatorial *cursus honorum,* or career structure, but, starting out as it did as a protection of the (original) plebeians against the patricians, the imperial tribunician power remained redolent of this ancient class struggle and enabled Augustus and his successors to stand as champions of the urban *plebs* against the senatorial aristocracy (see below).

Augustus and the urban *plebs*: Augustus established a bond with the urban *plebs* which his successors continued to maintain. In his important study titled *Plebs and Princeps*, Zvi Yavetz summed up the position in these words: "With the commencement of the Principate the emperors became in a sense *patroni* of the entire urban *plebs*. The *tribunicia potestas* was an important advantage, while generous *largitiones* and proper conduct helped in no small measure to this end" (Yavetz 1988, p. 152). However, a section of the *plebs* remained part of the *clientela* of major aristocratic houses. "Although the emperor was not officially referred to as *patronus* of all the *plebs*, there was a clear conflict between his influence and the patronage exercised by individual senators" (ibid., p. 97). Yavetz also plausibly suggests that "the laws limiting the emancipation of slaves were likewise passed for no other reason but to restrict the private *clientela* of the senatorial aristocracy" (ibid., p. 96f)—because a manumitted slave became a *libertus* or *libertinus* (in the later Roman Empire the two terms are used interchangeably), or "freedman," who would automatically become a *cliens* to his former master as *patronus*. "As a general principle he (Augustus) prevented anyone (Agrippa being the exception that proves the rule) from bestowing *beneficia* on the masses" (ibid., p. 97). Later emperors followed the same pattern, and it is worth noting that supposedly "bad" emperors got that reputation largely from their treatment of the upper echelons of society, while retaining the support of the *plebs* (see Yavetz on Nero, ibid., p. 153).

Augustus and the Senate: In his autobiography Augustus makes a point of stressing that all his honors and titles were granted to him by the Senate and people in time-honored Republican fashion—and that he refused the tainted title of dictator. The modest-sounding title *princeps*, or "first citizen," which is mentioned three times in the autobiography in a very matter-of-fact way, was intended to suggest that Augustus was merely "first among equals," although the reality was very different. It is this title which has given the whole period from Augustus to the accession of Diocletian in 284 CE the designation "the Principate," as it is usually termed by historians, although it is commonly referred to by the general public simply as "the Roman Empire," from the title *imperator*, which, as we have seen, was adopted by Augustus as a forename. Augustus made much of restoring the Republican constitution. Elections to the traditional Republican magistracies were put on a firm footing, and provincial commands were reserved for those who had reached the praetorship and the consulship. But Augustus did not want the old *nobiles*, the top echelon of the Senate, to continue to monopolize these commands. So he introduced into the Senate *novi homines*, "new men drawn from the length and breadth of Italy" (Jones 1955, p. 20). As we are told in the Appendix to his autobiography, he even gave some personal "grants to individual friends and senators to make up their property qualification"—a way of introducing hand-picked friends to high office. Augustus also used as a counter-measure against the nobility the "ingenious electoral machinery of the *Lex Valeria Cornelia* of 5 CE, whereby, although the freedom of the *comitia* (popular assembly) was theoretically left untrammeled, a strong lead was given to it by ten centuries composed in the main of the very class whom Augustus wished to see elected to praetorships and consulates. . . By the accession of Tiberius the monopoly of the *nobiles* had been broken, and a sufficient number of new men had been promoted to the higher ranks of the Senate to make it possible to entrust elections to the Senate itself" (ibid., p. 20f). It is important to realize, however, that being a member of the Senate was in itself no longer of great importance. Membership was only necessary in order to obtain appointment to provincial governorships—the overwhelming majority of which were in the gift of the emperor. Only the so-called senatorial provinces had governors allocated by the Senate. At the time of Augustus's death in 14 CE there were only 10 of these.

Augustus and the *equites*: Augustus tried to bolster the *equites* ("equestrians," literally "knights"), the second rank in the state, as a counterweight to senators, relying on them as military commanders, tax collectors, and in many other capacities. He broadened the scope of the equestrian class, encouraging the Italian towns to nominate suitable entrants into this order (Suetonius, Augustus, 46).

Augustus and the army: Important though the army was to Augustus, I agree with Brunt and Moore that it would be "a mistake to represent his power as depending mainly on the support of the army" (Brunt and Moore 1967, p. 15). Augustus went out of his way to reward his troops and veterans and to settle them in *coloniae* ("settlements") all around Italy and the provinces. Augustus made sure that the army was largely under his control, and by the end of his reign Africa was the only senatorial province with any troops at all (see above). And from the reign of the Emperor Gaius (Caligula) (37–41 CE) the whole army was commanded by the emperor. The praetorian guard under a praetorian prefect came to play an increasingly important role in the Roman Empire, especially after the time of Augustus. And the setting up of *cohortes urbanae* ("urban cohorts"), a sort of police force for Rome, which, together with the *vigiles*, or firemen, were important factors contributing to Rome's generally peaceful existence for the better part of four centuries.

***Consilium Principis*:** Augustus established the *Consilium Principis*, or emperor's advisory council, a semi-informal body drawn from his much larger body of *amici* ("friends"), which he consulted from time to time. This arrangement continued right throughout the Principate and ultimately became more formalized as the *consistorium,* a department of state, under Diocletian. John Crook's learned study of the *Consilium* does, however, appear to overestimate the influence of the *Consilium* on imperial decision-making. In the words of A.N. Sherwin-White: "It is by no means proved that the emperors regularly took the advice of a substantial body of *amici*, in any particular form, on most matters of high or low policy" (Sherwin-White 1957, p. 253).

Augustus: "Optimi Status Auctor"?

Suetonius quotes an edict in which Augustus expresses the hope that he will be remembered by posterity as *optimi status auctor* ("architect of the best state of affairs") (Suetonius, *Augustus*, 28.) In the *Aeneid*, similarly, Vergil correctly predicts that Augustus will usher in *aurea saecula* ("golden centuries") (Verg. *Aen.* VI.791–807).

But what was the nature of the regime that Augustus established? My own view is that Augustus was decidedly sole ruler of the Roman world. To sum up my findings, Augustus's position depended on the following factors:

- Duly authorized *maius imperium*—initially as a consul and then later as a proconsul—enabling Augustus to override any other magistrate, including a consul;
- Duly authorized tribunician power—with the wide powers described above.
- The support of the urban *plebs* as their effective patron.
- The support of the *equites*.
- *Auctoritas*, influence or esteem stemming from his connections and achievements;
- The support of the army, which, however, was *not* the mainstay of his power.
- *Amicitia*, a wide-ranging network of people linked to Augustus as their individual *patronus* or simply as *amici*, some of whom he would consult either formally, in the form of a *consilium* ("council") or informally, *inter amicos* ("among friends"), but who had no decision-making powers. Contrary to Syme (1939), this group did not constitute a "party" or an "oligarchy" of any kind (see below).
- *Money*: Augustus inherited Julius Caesar's fortune, to which he added the treasure of Egypt and other conquests. From this great fortune which had amassed he was able to make lavish gifts to the people of Rome and others, as is documented in the *Res Gestae* (see above).

From Tiberius to Diocletian

After the death of Augustus the trend was toward greater autocracy on the part of the emperor, together with a decline of the old aristocracy and recruitment to the Senate from an ever-widening circle both geographical and social. The ancient sources attribute the changes in the Senate to the deliberate policy of "bad" emperors like Tiberius, Domitian, Commodus, and Septimius Severus. Modern writers tend to stress demographic factors. Thus, Mason Hammond: "The chief and continuing factor which necessitated the introduction of fresh blood into the Senate must have been a failure on the part of the old senatorial families adequately to perpetuate themselves" (Hammond 1957, p. 75).

The low level of reproduction of the old senatorial families has probably been exaggerated, because we know that it was imperial policy from the start to broaden the scope of recruitment. The Emperor Claudius (r. 41–54), for example, forced the resignation of a number of senators who no longer met the property qualification and at the same time promoted the admission of senators from Gaul. In proposing the admission of Gallic senators in a famous speech to the Senate preserved in the bronze "Lyon Tablet," a different version of which was reported by Tacitus, Claudius made a point of mentioning that both Augustus and Tiberius had encouraged recruitment to the Senate of men of wealth and breeding from the provinces. Interestingly enough, Claudius's speech was interrupted with cries to the effect that "Italy is not so weak as to be unable to provide its own capital city with a senate." Yet the Senate nevertheless passed a decree approving the emperor's policy. (Tacitus, Annals, 11.23; `http://Sourcebooks. fordham.edu/ancient/48claudius.asp`) A number of detailed prosopographical researches were neatly summarized by Mason Hammond, showing that, of those senators whose origin is known, the proportion of provincials (i.e. non-Italians) increased steadily (with a couple of minor blips) as follows:

Vespasian (r. 69–79)—16.8%
Domitian (r. 81–96)—23.4%
Trajan (r. 98–117)—34.2%
Hadrian (r. 117–38)—43.6%
Antoninus Pius (r. 138–61)—42.5%
Marcus Aurelius (r. 161–80)—45.6%
Commodus (r. 180–92)—44.7%
Septimius Severus (r. 193–211) & Caracalla (r. 198–217)—57.4%
Elagabalus (r. 218–22) & Severus Alexander (r. 222–35)—52.5%
Third century—56% (Hammond 1957, ibid).

Under Vespasian, therefore, provincials made up only one-sixth of senators of known origin. There is a major jump under Trajan, and from the end of the second century provincials made up more than half the senators of known origin.

According to Lambrechts, as modified by Syme, in the period between 117 and 192 no fewer than 48% of *consulares* (ex-consuls)—and presumably an even higher proportion of senators of lower grades—were of non-senatorial and indeed provincial origin (Lambrechts 1936; review by Syme 1937, p. 271f). Vespasian was the first emperor of equestrian (or non-senatorial) origin. Trajan was himself a provincial, from Spain (albeit of Italian origin), and practically all subsequent emperors were also provincials.

The ever-widening circle of senators, from whom most provincial governors were drawn, was an important reason for the stability and general tranquility of the Roman Empire over a long period. In keeping with this trend, in the year 212 the Emperor Caracalla extended Roman citizenship to all inhabitants of the Roman world by means of the so-called *Constitutio Antoniniana* (see below).

Augustus himself was already clearly the sole ruler of the Roman Empire, as we have seen, although he was anxious not to make this fact too obvious, for fear of offending the element which had assassinated his adoptive father, Julius Caesar. Later emperors had no such qualms. The jurist Ulpian (170–228) famously declared: "*Princeps legibus solutus est*" ("the emperor is exempt from the laws" or "the emperor is not bound by the laws"), although this is sometimes interpreted to refer only to the marriage laws. That narrow interpretation is almost certainly wrong, because the historian Cassius Dio (155–235) makes it clear that the phrase "*legibus solutus*" exempts the emperor from *all* laws, but he dates this back to 24 BCE in the reign of Augustus—which, if true, is certainly not mentioned by either Tacitus or Suetonius.

Another similar and equally famous formulation of imperial power which is attributable to Ulpian is: "*Quod principi placuit legis habet vigorem*" ("What pleases the emperor has the force of law"), which is said to derive from the *Lex de Imperio,* the law defining an emperor's power on his accession.

Can such sweeping powers be traced back to the *Lex de Imperio Vespasiani,* the law defining the powers of Vespasian on his accession in the year 69? Unfortunately, only the latter part of the inscription promulgating this law has survived. This law provides that any candidate for a magistracy or other position of importance who is "commended" by the emperor shall be given "special consideration." There is also a blanket clause giving the emperor the "right and power" to execute anything that he considers to be "in accordance with the public advantage and the dignity of divine and human and public and private interests," just as Augustus, Tiberius, and Claudius had done. The exact scope of this power is not clear, but it is significant that it is said to have belonged to Augustus as well, and it would presumably have been granted to all subsequent emperors as well (*Ancient Roman Statutes*; Johnson et al. 1961, p. 149f).

The well-known story about how Claudius became emperor is instructive. On the assassination of Claudius's nephew, the Emperor Gaius Caligula in the year 41, Claudius was cowering behind a curtain, when a common soldier, seeing Claudius's feet protruding below the curtain, pulled him out and recognized him. Fearing the worst, Claudius fell at his feet in supplication, only to find himself hailed as emperor. This shows the deference and strong sense of loyalty of the ordinary people for their "betters" and for heredity, which was one of the reasons for the longevity of the Roman Empire. When the Julio-Claudian line ended with Nero, after a three-fold hiccup a new dynasty of the

Flavians was briefly established by Vespasian, and then from the accession of Nerva in 96 until the death of Marcus Aurelius in 180, a succession of "good emperors" was attainable thanks to adoption. None of these "good emperors" had sons of their own, but Marcus Aurelius was succeeded by his son Commodus, who unfortunately was not in his father's mould. Commodus's assassination in 192 was followed, after two more brief hiccups, by the Severan dynasty, which remained in power until 235. The next half century was turbulent until the accession of Diocletian in 284, which introduced what modern historians call the "strong e."

Here is a bird's-eye view of some major developments leading from the Principate to the Dominate (see Arnheim 1972, p. 21ff):

- Though in theory elected by the people, in practice consuls were nominated by the emperor.
- Starting in the early Principate, the Senate's financial control was gradually eliminated. As an institution the Senate was a mere cipher, happy to humour the emperor's every whim. But the same did not apply to senators as individuals. For, though *nobiles* (i.e. men whose ancestors included a consul) were excluded, the great majority of provincial governorships continued to be reserved for senators until the second half of the third century. But senatorial status was in the emperor's gift and emperors continually brought new blood into the Senate, as we have seen. Also, some government positions were reserved for equestrians and even freedmen (especially under Claudius).
- According to a well-known anecdote, after a petitioner was rebuffed by the Emperor Hadrian (r. 117–38) on his travels with the excuse that he had no time, she rounded on him with the taunt (in Greek): "Then don't be an emperor!" Hadrian relented. The point is that even the humblest subject could expect to have direct personal access to the emperor as of right.
- Asked for the password as he was dying, the Emperor Antoninus Pius (r. 138–61) responded *aequanimitas,* "tranquil stability," which could be taken as the motto for the whole Antonine period (96–180).
- The accession of Commodus on the death of Marcus Aurelius in 180 was described by the Roman historian and senator Cassius Dio as a descent "from a kingdom of gold to one of iron and rust" (Cassius Dio 71.36.3–4).
- Before his death in 211 the Emperor Septimius Severus is said to have advised his sons and successors: "Be harmonious, enrich the soldiers and scorn everyone else" (Cassius Dio 77.15).
- Caracalla's grant of Roman citizenship to all free adult males in 212 also had the negative effect of creating two classes of citizens, *honestiores* ("the more honorable," meaning men of senatorial and equestrian rank and decurions) and *humiliores* ("the more lowly"), comprising all free men below that level, who gradually lost some of the privileges previously attached to citizenship.

- In the course of the third century the old traditional framework was gradually abandoned, until by the end of the century only very few posts of importance were open to senators. The tendency now was to bypass the Senate by appointing non-senators directly to governorship without bothering to make them senators first.
- An ambiguous passage in *Aurelius Victor* has given rise to the belief that senators were deprived of military commands from the reign of Gallienus (260–68) onwards (Aurelius Victor, 33 f., 37.5–6).
- Be that as it may, a number of non-military provinces also experienced a change from senatorial to equestrian governors.
- But, while equestrians moved into the erstwhile preserves of senators, there was no movement the other way to produce Lambrechts's fabled "fusion" of the two orders (Lambrechts 1937, p. 107ff).
- This process culminated in the reign of Diocletian, who may justifiably lay claim to the title "Hammer of the Aristocracy," as I dubbed him in my book on the Later Roman Empire (Arnheim, 1972).
- The powers of the emperor were neatly summarized by Cassius Dio, who agreed with Ulpian that the emperor was above the law (Cassius Dio, 53.17.1, 18.1).
- Imperial trappings became increasingly grand. Nero was shown in his lifetime wearing the radiate crown of the sun—a symbol of divinity—on some of his coins. In the late third century this gave way to the jeweled diadem of the sun-god.
- By the third century an oath by the emperor's genius was considered more binding than one by the gods.
- From at least the reign of Diocletian (r. 284–305), anything connected with the emperor was given the epithet *sacrum* ("sacred," "holy").
- Under Diocletian the imperial court was well and truly decked out in oriental trappings, and an aura of cool aloofness, on the one hand, and abject self-abasement on the other pervaded everything.

Conclusion

The Augustan principate, a strong popular monarchy while placating the senatorial class, produced the justly famous *Pax Romana* (Roman peace), which lasted until at least the death of Marcus Aurelius in 180. In his inimitable rolling prose, Edward Gibbon (1737–94) described "the indissoluble union and easy obedience that pervaded the government of Augustus and the Antonines" (Gibbon 1776, Chapter 51). It is hard to disagree with Gibbon's characterization of the greatness of the Roman Empire built by Augustus: "The firm edifice of Roman power was raised and preserved by the wisdom of ages. The obedient provinces of Trajan and the Antonines were united by laws adorned by arts. They might occasionally suffer from the partial abuse of delegated authority; but the general principle of government was wise, simple, and beneficent. They enjoyed the religion of their ancestors, whilst in civil honors and advantages they were exalted, by just degrees, to an equality with their conquerors" (ibid., chapter 2). The secret of the success of the Augustan principate was to establish a strong monarchy with the support of the masses, both in Rome and in the provinces, while placating and, at the same time, diluting the senatorial aristocracy with new blood, and all the while disguising the true power structure under legal fictions.

From 180 until 284 the empire was dominated by the military, including the "The Crisis of the Third Century" from 235 to 284, during which time there were no fewer than 26 emperors recognized by the Senate. The "Dominate" established by Diocletian (r. 284–305) was an autocratic monarchy without specific support from any class, and Constantine I (r. 306–37), reversing Diocletian policy, initiated currying favour with the senatorial aristocracy in the West and did not cultivate lower-class support. From 395 the West was in its death-throes, while in the East a form of Caesaropapism dominated the so-called Byzantine Empire (a modern label) from 395 to 1453 (see Chapter 18).

Chapter 7
Social Mobility

In my Two Models of Government (Arnheim 2017a) I identified the two pure forms of government in terms of power structure as monarchy and oligarchy. But this is not just a matter of bottling and labeling regimes. The object of the exercise is to examine the effects (if any) and correlations of the power structure. A variable that correlates to some extent with power structure is social mobility. Oligarchies vary in the degree of "openness," or social mobility, that they allow. In an oligarchy based on birth, race, or ethnicity the elites will be closed, while those in a mixed oligarchy, as in most western European states, are more open. On the other hand, a popular monarch will benefit most from a general leveling of society—an application of the "tall poppy syndrome"—to prevent the resurgence of an elite that might threaten his position (see Chapter 15). Mao Zedong's "Cultural Revolution" belongs in this category (Chapter 8).

Oligarchy and Inequality

Inequality is the hallmark of oligarchy. In an oligarchy, with power in the hands of a minority, that minority will do all it can to retain power together with its wealth and status, and will therefore want to keep as big a gap as possible between itself and the masses. In order to maintain this gap, the oligarchy will tend to be opposed to too much social mobility, or, to put it another way, it will prefer the elites not to be too "open" (to use a sociological expression)—or, to put it yet another way, it will not want too much equality of opportunity. The oligarchy or the aristocracy of medieval Europe is a good example of this.

The inequality I am referring to, that between the ruling minority and the masses, may be called *external inequality*. However, for an oligarchy to thrive, prosper, and survive for a long time it is a good idea for it to be as close-knit as possible, and to achieve that it will help if there is a high degree of equality among its members—*internal equality*, which it is important not to confuse with *external* equality, i.e. equality between the ruling elite and the masses, which does not exist in any oligarchy. In fact, the more internal equality there is, the less external equality there is likely to be. It is in the interests of oligarchy to achieve and maintain as much *internal equality* as possible, meaning equality within the ranks of the oligarchy itself. *Internal equality* is a safeguard to protect the oligarchy against the rise to monarchical power of a single individual, especially one who might be propelled to power at the head of a popular movement.

A prime example of a close-knit oligarchy is Classical Sparta, where members of the oligarchy were known as "the Equals" (*hoi homoioi*), which of course refers purely to *internal* equality coupled with extreme external inequality between the ruling Spartiate minority and the Helots.

By definition, power in an oligarchy is in the hands of a minority, which, unless that minority is very small, will be self-reliant and inward-looking and will not need the support of the masses. This is another reason why there will tend to be a big gap between the ruling minority and those outside it—a gap not just in power and status but also in wealth and general well-being.

In sum, therefore, inequality will be found in any oligarchy, but there are of course degrees of inequality, depending on the degree of social mobility, or whether the elites are "open" or "closed," the latter meaning that there is little social mobility to enable outsiders to join the elite. In other words, in an oligarchy the elites will tend *not* to be very open.

The degree of *liberty* in such a society will depend on how open or closed the elites are, i.e. on how much social mobility is permitted by the system, which in turn depends on the degree of equality of opportunity (not to be confused with equality) that there is. A "night watchman" or libertarian state with minimal government restrictions on individual liberty would tend to result in a high degree of inequality, with comparatively easy access to the elite. This will tend to result in the enlargement of the elite, or the replacement of a monolithic, largely hereditary, elite with a proliferation of elites, as, for example, in eighteenth- and nineteenth-century Britian, and as identified in nineteenth- and twentieth-century America in Wright Mills's 1956 book, *The Power Elite,* discussed in Chapter 23.

Monarchy and Equality

In a true monarchy, where power is concentrated in the hands of a single person, the ruler needs support to maintain his position. He cannot obtain that support from the privileged classes, because they will want to rule the roost themselves as an oligarchy and will oppose the rise of any individual to power. So, monarchy must instead look to the masses for support.

If inequality between the ruling minority and the masses is a hallmark of oligarchy, monarchy exhibits the opposite tendency—a tendency to reduce the inequality gap between the (former) ruling oligarchy and the masses. This may be done in two different ways—either *positively* or negatively—or by a combination of the two. By a trend toward *negative equality* I mean reducing the privileges enjoyed by elite groups or former elite groups—as in the case of the ancient Greek tyrants, in the France of Louis XIV and XV, and also in Mao Zedong's China and in Cuba under Fidel Castro. The shorthand description of this is the "tall poppy syndrome," deriving from an incident in the sixth century BCE in which Thrasybulus, tyrant of Miletus, advises his fellow tyrant, Periander of Corinth, to crush the elite of his city and stop them from being a threat to his power. This message is conveyed by mime, with Thrasybulus taking Periander's messenger through a wheatfield, all the while lopping off the heads of any ears of wheat projecting above the others (see Chapter 15).

Positive equality, on the other hand, entails raising the level of the masses—as in Athenian "democracy" under Pericles or in the "Cultural Revolution" in Mao Zedong's China. The monarch may also be depicted stirring a huge pot of noodle soup, making all the noodles equal in size. This is a combination of positive and negative equality, with the monarch alone, of course, remaining outside the pot. Both these trends, toward positive and negative equality, are found only in genuinely monarchical regimes.

The association of this tendency with monarchy is not difficult to explain. The monarchical power of a king, a dictator, or any other kind of sole ruler can only be exercised at the expense of the oligarchy. Monarchy and oligarchy are at opposite ends of a seesaw—as the one goes up, the other inevitably goes down. Oligarchy is the default situation in any society. Monarchy can only come into existence by displacing this oligarchy. And for a monarchy to be maintained, it needs support—from the masses or common people, who, like the sole ruler, are also at loggerheads, or potentially at loggerheads, with the former ruling oligarchy or elite.

But, you may ask, why cannot the ruler or prospective ruler do a deal with the privileged element and reach a compromise in which power is shared between him and them—in, say, a constitutional monarchy? Yes, he can, but (except in rare *hybrid* cases, as discussed in Chapter 23), such a compromise will not result in shared power but in oligarchy. Why? Because the ruler in that arrangement will no longer have his own independent power base but will be reliant upon the support of the privileged element, the aristocracy or oligarchy, and will in effect be capitulating to them in the long run, if not immediately. Machiavelli was alive to this problem and warned "princes" (i.e. monarchs of all kinds) against having to depend for support on the nobility. Although Machiavelli speaks of the "nobility" (*li grandi*), what he says applies equally to a privileged elite in the form of a parliament, a judiciary, or any other vested interest (see Chapter 11).

But this kind of enforced equality is of course artificial, because it represses the natural innate competitive instinct not only to "keep up with the Joneses" but to surpass them. In other words, it puts an artificial lid on social mobility and will therefore inevitably be difficult to maintain for any length of time.

The remarkably durable Peronist monarchical regime in Argentina (dating from 1946, though under an anti-Peronist president since 2023) has resulted in an exceptional degree of equality (see Chapter 13). The position prior to the economic crisis of 2001 was described as follows: "An Argentine factory worker could reasonably aspire to live in a comfortable apartment, often with professionals as neighbors, eat meat every day, get competent medical care and, through his union, enjoy a couple of weeks' vacation each year at the beach. Argentines scorned what they saw as the individualistic dog-eat-dog, every-man-for-himself character of American capitalism and the chasm between rich and poor in nearby countries like Brazil, Chile and Peru" (Rohter 2006).

Figure 7 Juan and Eva Perón, official portrait, 1948.
SOURCE: Numa Ayrinhac / Pink House Museum / Public domain

Let us look at social mobility in a really long-lasting monarchy, the Roman Empire, as a case study.

Caution

In a 1970 paper titled "The Caste System in the Later Roman Empire," A.H.M. Jones claimed that "social mobility was greater in the Later Roman Empire than it had been in the Principate (Jones 1970). We know of a surprisingly large number of people of humble status, decurions (town councilors), *cohortales* (administrative assistants to provincial governors), and even urban workmen and peasants who rose through the law, the civil service, or the army into the upper grades of the imperial aristocracy and even to the imperial throne itself" (Jones 1974, p. 418). The article adopts a wide sweep down to the time of Justinian (r. 527–65), and these concluding remarks refer to the post-Constantinian East rather than the West.

This is the only place in Jones's article that the aristocracy is mentioned at all. What the article is actually about is the "hereditary classes" from much lower echelons of society. These, in Jones's words, fell into two main categories: "those whose personal service was required by the government, such as soldiers, agricultural laborers, and workers in the mints and the state factories and the public post, and those like the decurions [viz. municipal councilors] and also soldiers, agricultural laborers, the shippers (*navicularii*), and the guilds of Rome, who, though they might have to perform certain personal services, were mainly required to make a financial contribution to various essential activities" (ibid.). Focusing on these occupations, Jones declared his objective as endeavoring "to prove that in practice status and occupation were to a large extent hereditary under the Principate, and that the later emperors did little more than give legal sanction to a system which was, through various social and economic causes, beginning to break down" (Jones 1974, p. 396).

However, on the basis of the evidence assembled in my *Why Rome Fell* (2022), comparing the Principate with the Later Roman Empire, what we find is this:

- Under the Principate, increasingly, senatorial status was conferred on those whom the emperor wished to appoint to high office.
- The same is largely true of the Eastern Roman Empire, from Constantine onward.
- But in the West, from Constantine onward, the situation was exactly the opposite: appointment to high office was largely vouchsafed to those who already had senatorial status by birth.

Case Study: Roman Social Mobility

Social mobility fluctuated quite widely over the span of Roman history. The Roman Republic (509–49 BCE) is a case of oligarchy par excellence (see Chapter 6). This does not deny the existence of "new men," but it means that they were very much in the minority.

During the Principate (31 BCE–284 CE) the elites were more open. Detailed prosopographical research summarized by Mason Hammond (1957) shows that the proportion of provincial (i.e. non-Italian) senators of known origin increased steadily (with a couple of minor blips) from 16.8% under Vespasian (r. 69–79) to 56% in the third century (see Chapter 6).

Social mobility in the Later Roman Empire is more difficult to gauge. Under Diocletian (r. 284–305) senators were almost totally excluded from governorships, which became practically the exclusive preserve of equestrians. But, whereas senatorial rank, denoted by the title *vir clarissimus* (literally, "most distinguished man"), was hereditary, equestrian status was not hereditary but depended on the particular office held. By replacing senators with equestrians, and also relying to some extent on eunuchs, Diocletian clearly intended to enhance imperial power, which was demonstrated by his flamboyant dress and elaborate court ceremonial. Hence the modern label of "Dominate" attached to Diocletian's "tetrarchy."

Though the outward trappings of Diocletian's Dominate were perpetuated by his successors, the reality of power in the West underwent a major shift from the time of Constantine (r. 306–37), who brought members of the senatorial aristocracy back into high civil (but not military) government appointments, allowing them to combine office with local landholding. Constantine also began a long-continued process of inflation of titles of honor. For example, by the time of Valentinian I (r. 364–75) and Valens (r. 364–78) even the strictly equestrian post of *dux* (provincial military commander) carried the clarissimate, or senatorial status. According to A.H.M. Jones: "The new hierarchy effectively transformed the aristocracy from one of birth into one of office" (Jones 1964, p. 529). This was certainly true of the Eastern half of the empire, which lacked a traditional senatorial aristocracy like that of the West, and where the *clarissimi* of the new Senate of Constantinople were parvenus. But in the West, once high office, including the position of praetorian prefect, was opened up to senators, appointees tended to be men not just of senatorial rank but also of senatorial *birth*. As a result, in the West there was no real fusion or merger between the old senatorial aristocracy and new men, and nobles were very proud, and conscious of belonging to the old senatorial aristocracy. Social mobility in the West was, therefore, far more limited than in the Byzantine East, where there was no real hereditary aristocracy until the tenth or eleventh century. Until then, imperial power, though theoretically unlimited, was shared with bureaucrats, generals, the Church, and, to a very significant extent, eunuchs.

Chapter 8
Aristocratic Ethos

There is, and always has been, a deep-seated general belief that human beings are not all of equal worth. This, of course, flies in the face of the slogan "liberty, equality, fraternity," and also offends against "affirmative action" and "political correctness." Equality is much more often praised than practiced. This aristocratic ethos is prevalent not only, as expected, in societies ruled by an oligarchy but also in monarchies, though monarchs should beware of a power elite, which is likely to want to rule the roost itself and to reduce the power of the monarch or even to abolish the monarchy altogether.

Feudal Japan

Despite their divine status, Japanese emperors have had very little real power, which was instead vested in the military leader known as the *shogun*, who, appointed by and responsible to, the emperor, was the de facto ruler of Japan for most of the period between 1185 and 1868. The shogunate was in practice itself hereditary, though it was held by several different clans over time. Below the shogun came the *daimyo*, powerful feudal lords, beneath whom came the *samurai*, the Japanese aristocratic warrior class, who came to prominence in the twelfth century and, during the Tokugawa shogunate from 1603 to 1868, became the top class in the social hierarchy. With the Meiji "restoration" of 1868—in reality a shift to oligarchy—the *samurai* class was formally abolished and most *samurai* became members of the *shizoku* class between the *kazoku* (a merger between the *daimyo* with the former imperial nobility, the *kuge*) and the *heimin* (commoners).

Though in reality a monarchy during the shogunate, Japan's ethos remained firmly aristocratic. And the shoguns did their best to prevent the *daimyo* from

Figure 8   Coronation of Richard II, 1377.
SOURCE: Jean de Wavrin (Chroniques d'Angleterre) / Wikimedia Commons / Public domain

turning Japan into an oligarchy. This was done by the Tokugawa shogunate through the so-called *sankin-kotai* policy requiring the *daimyo* to alternate between living in their domain (*han*) and in the shogun's capital, Edo (Tokyo), every year, thus enabling the shogun to control them. However, the military aristocratic ethos continued unabated, and the glorification of the *samurai* persists to the present day in Japan and around the world.

The English Peasants' Revolt of 1381

The promotion of equality as a goal is surprisingly recent, though rare examples do pop up in earlier periods, as for example during the English Peasants' Revolt of 1381. The revolt, which broke out while King Richard II was only 14 years old, started as opposition to the poll tax combined with a demand for the removal of certain senior officials and law courts. The rebels also called for the end of serfdom, which had been greatly weakened by the Black Death of 1348–49 and 1361–62, which killed off about half the population, producing a labor shortage and giving the surviving serfs greater bargaining power. John Ball, a radical priest, gave the revolt its egalitarian tone: "When Adam delved and Eve span, who was then a gentleman?" The term "gentleman" meant nobleman, so what Ball was suggesting was that all people were originally equal and the gradations in society were an unacceptable novelty. Ball also composed the rebel slogan: "With King Richard and the true commons of England"—implying that, unlike the king's advisers, the rebels were loyal to the young king. At first Richard appeared to yield to the rebels' demands, issuing charters abolishing serfdom but refusing to hand over any of his officials and promising instead that he would personally dispense any disciplinary measures required (Dunn 2002, p. 96ff). The following day Richard went to meet the rebel leader, Wat Tyler, who, addressing the king over-familiarly as "brother" and "friend," got into an argument with William Walworth, Lord Mayor of London, who stabbed Tyler, followed by repeated sword blows from a royal squire, killing Tyler on the spot. With Tyler's head cut off and paraded on a pole, Richard knighted Walworth and some of his supporters. Ball and other rebel leaders were rounded up and executed, which put paid to any talk of equality and also of any chance of the king's reconciliation with the lower classes. Richard, who had never had a good relationship with the aristocracy, proceeded to appoint ministers opposed by Parliament, but the king replied that he would not dismiss a single scullion from his kitchen at the behest of Parliament. This dispute came to a head when a group of "Lords Appellant," seeking to impeach five of the king's non-noble favorites, effectively took over control of the government and reduced the king to a cipher. Richard did manage to claw back his authority briefly, but was deposed by one of the "Lords Appellant", his cousin Henry Bolingbroke, who ascended the throne as Henry IV (r. 1399–1413). Richard starved to death in captivity soon after. Richard II did recognize that the aristocracy were no friends of his as king, but his vacillations over the Peasants' Revolt destroyed his relationship with the lower classes as well, leaving him vulnerable to ambitious nobles, whose actions ultimately benefited Parliament in its conflict with the Crown.

Liberté, Égalité, Fraternité

This slogan of the French Revolution, which later became the national motto of France, is not actually a call for factual equality, or equality of outcome, but for equality of opportunity, which is really the exact opposite, meaning an equal chance to become unequal. This is clear from the wording of Article 6 of the "Declaration of the Rights of Man and of the Citizen" of 1789: "[The law] must be the same for all, whether it protects or punishes. All citizens, being equal in its eyes, shall be equally eligible to all high offices, public positions and employments, according to their ability, and without other distinction than that of their virtues and talents." There is a clear distinction here that people differ in their "ability," "virtues," and "talents." And Napoleon's ideal of *La carrière ouverte aux talents* ("the career open to the talents") is based on the same assumption, as is the remark attributed to him that every French soldier carries a marshal's baton in his knapsack, meaning that every soldier can reach high rank depending on merit.

"Some Animals Are More Equal than Others"

"All animals are equal, but some animals are more equal than others." This deliberately absurd spoof slogan is used in George Orwell's *Animal Farm*, published in 1945, to highlight the hypocrisy of a purported belief in equality. As a democratic socialist, Orwell was highly critical of the way the Russian Bolshevik Revolution of 1917 had turned out, and himself specifically described *Animal Farm* as "a satirical tale against Stalin." In fact, even Stalin (in power 1924–53) did not claim that the Soviet Union was an egalitarian society. Article 12 of the "Stalin Constitution" of 1936 reads: "In the USSR work is a duty and a matter of honor for every able-bodied citizen, in accordance with the principle: "He who does not work, neither shall he eat." The principle applied in the USSR is that of socialism: "From each according to his ability, to each according to his work." According to this the Soviet Union was at the stage of socialism and had not yet reached the stage of communism, the principle of which was the egalitarian principle: "From each according to his ability, to each according to his needs." Why then was the Communist Party so called? Presumably because this was the ultimate goal according to Marxist theory. But in fact, everything else to do with what the West called the "communist" bloc is labeled not "communist" but "socialist", such as "the Union of Soviet Socialist Republics" (USSR).

Vladimir Lenin (1870–1924), the Bolshevik leader and first head of government of Soviet Russia and the Soviet Union, originally introduced a highly egalitarian system. When told that everyone's wages were to be equalized, the famous Russian bass opera singer Feodor Chaliapin replied that, in that case, he would rather just be a stage-hand (cited in Chapter 2.) With the failure of the egalitarian policy, Lenin introduced a "New Economic Policy" (NEP), which he described as including "a free market and capitalism, both subject to state control" together with state enterprises operating on a "profit basis" (Lenin 1965). Peasants and others who profited from NEP were ridiculed as "NEPmen," meaning essentially *nouveaux riches*.

Stalin abandoned NEP in 1928, replacing it with a more "socialist" policy of forced collective farming. When this also proved unsuccessful, the "Stakhanovite" Program was introduced in 1935, under which, thanks to the progressive piece-rate system, workers who exceeded the norm in production were rewarded with a higher rate of pay. It is important to note that this overt abandonment of any semblance of egalitarianism, which was echoed, as mentioned above, in the "Stalin Constitution" of 1936, occurred under Joseph Stalin, a strong monarchical ruler. Anyone who expressed criticism of the system was branded a "Trotskyist saboteur" and could be sent to a labor camp. However, although Stakhanovite workers were held in great esteem and honored accordingly, they remained mere workers and never came to resemble any form of "power elite," and so posed no threat to Stalin, but, on the contrary, boosted his popularity by improving the economy.

Chinese Cultural Revolution

A monarchical ruler very conscious of the danger to his position from established elites was China's Mao Zedong (in power 1949–76), who, in order to safeguard his own position, turned Chinese society upside down in the name of equality in his "Great Proletarian Cultural Revolution" of 1966–76. If represented in a cartoon, Mao would be seen vigorously stirring with a huge ladle a cauldron of noodle soup labelled "Chinese society," and homogenizing all the noodles to a uniform consistency. The only person standing outside this homogenized noodle soup is, of course, Mao himself! But, so disruptive and destructive was this egalitarian process, that it was swept away after little more than a decade, and in 1981 the Chinese Communist Party passed a resolution declaring that the Cultural Revolution "was responsible for the most severe setback and the heaviest losses suffered by the Party, the country and the people since the founding of the People's Republic" (Digital Archive, 1981, Wilson Center, June 27, 1981). This reaction against Mao's egalitarianism has continued until the time of this writing, under the monarchical regime established in 2012 by Xi Jinping, whose "Fourteen Principles," written into the Party's constitution in 2017, lack any mention of the word "equality."

Athenian "Democracy"

It is no surprise that supporters of oligarchy should believe in inequality. Yet we find the same belief among those opposed to oligarchy as well, like supporters of Athenian "democracy" (see Arnheim 1977, p. 158ff). Some modern academics, including Professor A.H.M. Jones, have suggested that

"Democrats in general approved of the egalitarian principle," though he also concedes that the Athenians were "snobbish" in their choice of elected leaders, such as Pericles, who was an aristocrat (Jones 1957, p. 45). Josiah Ober opined that there was a democratic "ideology" to which Athenians subscribed (Ober 1989, p. 124). But the evidence does not support this view. Even (Thucydides' report of) Pericles's famous Funeral Oration, which is a defense of Athenian democracy, at the same time betrays a belief in the inherent *inequality* of human beings: "Our constitution is accorded the title of democracy, because it is governed not in the interest of the few but in that of the many. All are on an equal footing before the law in regard to private disputes; and, as regards esteem, as each man is distinguished in every way, so is he preferred in public life, not because of his membership of a particular class but rather because of his merit; again, no man able to do something for the benefit of the state is debarred through poverty or obscurity of rank" (Thuc. 2:37). Pericles makes it clear that though there is equality before the law, there is no equality "as regards esteem" (*kata axiōsin*) or "merit." He also does not claim that it is government *by* the many, only that it is "in the interest" of the many (*es pleionas*). This is a classic statement of populist monarchy, echoing Thucydides's famous characterization of Periclean Athens as "in name a democracy, but in reality rule by the first citizen" (Thuc. 2:65).

The belief in the inherent inequality of people that Thucydides (probably quite reliably) puts into Pericles's mouth in the Funeral Oration ties in with the age-old Greek concept of "giving each his worth" or "giving each his due," which is the key to the central Greek concept of "justice" (*dikaiosynē*), because it is based on the assumption that people are of different degrees of worth and that this is essentially hereditary (see Arnheim 1977, p.158ff). Aristotle summed it up like this: "It is reasonable to conclude that it is not the rich or the good who are well-born but those descended from ancestors who have long been rich or good" (Aristotle fragment 94 [Rose 1886]).

The ancient Greeks generally believed that it was "just (*dikaion*) to render each man his due," a view that can be traced back as far as Homer (see Arnheim 1977, p. 117ff). The implication is that different people should be treated differently in accordance with their merits. The Greek philosopher Aristotle (384–22 BCE) expressed the same concept like this: "It is thought that justice is equality, and so it is, though not for everybody but only for those who are equals; and it is thought that inequality is just, for so indeed it is, though not for everybody, but for those who are unequal" (Aristotle, *Politics* 3.1280a10). This concept can be restated more simply in a form sometimes misattributed to Thomas Jefferson: "The assumption is that people are unequal and must be treated accordingly. There is nothing more unequal than the equal treatment of unequal people."

Table of Ranks

So deep-seated is the aristocratic ethos that even monarchs who are conscious of the danger to themselves of a hereditary aristocracy have difficulty combating this ethos.

China

From 134 BCE under the Han Emperor Wu, appointment to government service was based on nomination by local nobles and officials, which reinforced not only the aristocratic ethos but also aristocratic power. As a corrective of this, in 220 CE, in the Three Kingdoms period, a new system was introduced called the "nine-rank method of recruiting men for office," which was modified in the Song dynasty (960–1279) to the "system of nine ranks and impartial judges." The system (applied to existing officials as well as to candidates for office) employed a scale of nine ranks to evaluate a person's merit, but in practice descent and an applicant's father's grade also played a role, thus defeating the object of the exercise. The "controllers" appointed to operate the system also tended to promote their own powerful families. In practice the system tended to favor hereditary and largely military aristocrats (Hook 1991). Hence the saying: "There are no poor people in the upper ranks and no powerful families in the lower ones" (Wilkinson 2012, p. 265).

Competitive written civil service examinations to aid the centralization of power in the hands of the emperor and the reduction of aristocratic influence were employed in earnest by the Sui (581–618) and Tang (618–907) dynasties, and had become the norm by the time of the Song dynasty (960–1279), ending only in 1905.

But the aristocratic ethos was difficult to combat: "Despite the rise in importance of the examination system, the Tang society was still heavily influenced by aristocratic ideals, and it was only after the ninth century that the situation changed. As a result, it was common for candidates to visit examiners before the examinations to win approval. The aristocratic influence declined after the ninth century when the examination degree holders also increased in numbers" (Lee 1985).

Japan

For the same purpose, namely of centralizing power in the hands of the emperor and reducing aristocratic influence, the Taika Reforms were introduced in Japan starting in 645. An important part of the reforms was the introduction of the *Ritsuryo* legal system based on Confucianism and Chinese Legalism, which established a centralized administration with the emperor at its head.

The reforms also included the nationalization of all land, to be distributed equally among all farmers, but the system gradually fell out of use. From 723, newly developed land could be inherited for three generations. From 743, reclaimed land could be transmitted by inheritance in perpetuity; and by 800 the land distribution system had effectively been abandoned. The reforms of 723 and 743 allowed the growth of private estates (*shoen*), building up the power of local clans, which weakened imperial power.

Another aspect of the Taika Reforms was a modification of the traditional *Kabane* system of hereditary noble titles, which from now on would no longer be linked to a particular political position but merely indicated a family's aristocratic lineage and social status, and the families were reorganized into a graded eight-*kabane* system. The original *kabane* system, which was hereditary, was replaced by the "Twelve Level Cap and Rank System," which was based on merit and individual achievement, though in practice the highest ranks were reserved to the aristocracy, and, contrary to China, Japan never introduced a competitive examination system for appointment to government service.

In the ninth century, the *Ritsuryo* system began to break down and farmers started giving their land to the aristocracy to avoid taxes, in return for which they received payment in rice. This had a negative impact on the emperor's wealth, as he had no land and was dependent on tax revenues. Civil government was primarily exercised from Kyoto by the emperor and his court, made up of members of the hereditary aristocracy (*kuge*), who were given grants of tax-free land. This remained the case until the rise of the Kamakura shogunate in 1192, when they were eclipsed by the *samurai* or *bushi*.

After general conscription was abolished in 780, the emperor and *kuge* had to rely on a new class of warriors for hire, who developed into the *samurai* and eventually turned against the aristocracy. The conflict between the Taira and Minamoto aristocratic clans, both of imperial lineage, fought out in the *Genpei War* of 1180–85, ended with the establishment of the Kamakura shogunate under Minamoto no Yoritomo, which marks the beginning of nearly 700 years, ending in 1868, during which Japan was under the military rule of a shogun, a hereditary position itself, supposedly under the emperor, who was reduced to a figurehead. During that whole period, no shogun ever tried to usurp the throne, chiefly because the emperor was revered by the populace as a direct descendant of the sun goddess, Amaterasu, and as the head of Shinto, the state religion.

Chapter 9
Equality, Equality of Opportunity and Privilege

rue equality, or equality of outcomes, which is virtually impossible to achieve, is encountered as a goal only in certain popular monarchies, starting with the "tall poppy syndrome" of the ancient Greek tyrants and emulated by Periclean Athens and modern regimes like Maoist China and Fidel Castro's Cuba. "For King Richard and the true commons of England," the rallying cry of the Peasants' Revolt of 1381, went hand in hand with the egalitarian slogan: "When Adam delved and Eve span, who was then the gentleman?" But Richard II soon switched sides (see Chapter 8). The "self-evident" truth "that all men are created equal," proclaimed in the U.S. Declaration of Independence, did not preclude an acceptance of slavery together with gradations among white men, only a minority of whom initially had the right to vote. In most oligarchies, the ideal of equality, or "equality of outcomes," is replaced in practice by its opposite, a belief in equality of opportunity—meaning an equal opportunity to become unequal, manifesting itself in a "rat race" and resulting in a stratified society marked by privilege.

"The Worst of All Governments"

In Chapter 7 of this book I posed the question: Why can there not be an accommodation between a monarch and the power elite under which they share power? A true hybrid form of government is decidedly rare. The United States is a possible example and is therefore discussed in Chapter 23.

But any agreement between a monarch and a power elite is likely to end up as an oligarchy, with the monarch reduced to an essentially ceremonial role. The reason for this is that a monarch attempting to share power with an elite will

Five Thousand Years of Monarchy, First Edition. Michael Arnheim.
© 2026 John Wiley & Sons, Inc. Published 2026 by John Wiley & Sons, Inc.

be dependent for support and advice on that very elite, which in its turn will be anxious to retain the whip hand.

A good example of this is the British "constitutional monarchy" established by the "Glorious Revolution" of 1688–89, which deposed James II and replaced him with his daughter and son-in-law, reigning jointly as William III and Mary II. Owing his throne to Parliament, William expressed the fear that he would have no more power than the doge of Venice, a byword for a purely ceremonial head of state. When Parliament initially voted William revenue for only three months (instead of for life, as had initially been provided for James II), William felt "tricked," and objected that "The worst of all governments is that of a king without treasure and without power" (Troost 2005, p. 214). To make up for this, William made full use of his veto power on legislation, withholding his assent from no fewer than five Bills passed by Parliament, including the Qualifications Bill, which would have laid down a property qualification for members of Parliament and would therefore have precluded anyone outside the landed gentry from becoming a member of Parliament. The king's "populist" veto actually made little difference, as members of Parliament were unpaid until 1911. William's successor, Queen Anne, vetoed only one Bill (on her ministers' advice), which was the last time that that power was exercised. It is now, in practice, dead.

Although the new dispensation after 1689 left the king with control over foreign affairs and an unrestricted right to appoint whatever ministers he liked, this power was illusory, as it depended on control of the purse strings, which was firmly in the grip of Parliament. As a result, the Hanoverian monarchs, who occupied the throne from 1714 onward, eventually found themselves having to appoint ministers who could command a majority in the House of Commons, which reduced the power of the king still further.

William IV (r. 1830–37) was the last king to appoint as prime minister someone who did not have a majority in the Commons. In so doing, the king persuaded himself that he was in charge, as he had now rid himself of the reform-minded Whigs, including "that dangerous little radical" (as the king called him), Lord John Russell. But William IV's new prime minister, the Tory leader Sir Robert Peel, was unable to deliver a majority and his administration was therefore hamstrung. Peel was anxious to resign but his resignation was repeatedly refused by the king before it was finally accepted. From commentators who did not know of his frantic attempts to resign, Peel earned the witty taunt that he had all the virtues of a prime minister except the virtue of resignation. But the lesson was not lost on Queen Victoria (r. 1837–1901), reluctant though she was to appoint prime ministers whom she disliked, such as Peel and Gladstone.

In fact, until 1965 the Conservative Party did not have an elected leader, so, when for some reason a vacancy at 10 Downing Street occurred while the Conservatives still had a parliamentary majority, the monarch had the power, and indeed the duty, to appoint a new prime minister. This was done with the aid of "soundings" taken by the monarch from leading Conservative politicians. When Sir Anthony Eden resigned as Prime Minister in 1957, Queen Elizabeth II appointed Harold Macmillan to succeed him. This was done largely on the strength of advice received from former Prime Minister Winston Churchill, who was opposed to front-runner "Rab" Butler, an "appeasement" supporter in 1938. When Macmillan in turn resigned in 1963 (ostensibly for health reasons, though he lived on for another 23 years, to the age of 92), he left nothing to chance in picking his own successor, as is discussed in Chapter 22 of this book. Sir Alec Douglas-Home, Macmillan's successor, himself strongly urged the party to give up the "soundings" system and set up a procedure for an elected leader, which was done in 1965. The result, which is still the position today, is that when there is a vacancy for prime minister, the monarch has to offer the position to the leader of whichever party has a majority in the House of Commons.

Equality vs. Equality of Opportunity

Egalitarian ideals are essentially of two types: belief in "equality of outcomes" (whether political or economic, or both) and belief in "equality of opportunity." Although very different, both types of equality depend on a belief in entitlement to equal rights, and especially equal political rights. But this belief in entitlement to equal rights itself derives from a more basic belief in equality of worth. Thus, the belief that everyone should enjoy equal political rights rests upon the belief that everyone is of equal political worth and that no man's political opinion is worth more than anyone else's. It is upon this ideological foundation that the sanctity of the modern concept of "majority rule" is based. Even that great Liberal prime minister, William Gladstone (1809–98), regarded majority rule with a certain amount of scepticism. "Decision by majorities," he remarked in Parliament in 1858, "is as much an expedient as lighting by gas." The example is instructive, as lighting by gas is now largely obsolete. Decision by majorities has nevertheless become more sacred than ever, because the concept of equality underpinning it has become so iconic.

Equality of opportunity really means that everyone must have an equal opportunity to become *unequal*. The idea is that this resulting inequality would depend solely on the "ability" or "merit" of the individual concerned without any of the advantages or disadvantages of birth, wealth, or environment. But why must everyone have equal opportunity in the first place? This can only be based on the assumption that everyone is of equal worth.

This is a logical conundrum. The whole idea of equality of opportunity is based on the concept of life as a competition between people, as a "meritocracy," or as a "rat race," to give it its modern pejorative label. For the competition to be fair, everyone must start from the same starting post, which alone will give each competitor an equal chance, an equal opportunity, to become a winner. So, upon examination, what equality of opportunity envisages is lining everybody up on level starting blocks and then firing a starting pistol and letting them compete to differentiate winners from losers. To repeat, therefore, equality of opportunity is equality to become unequal.

But how can a truly equal starting line be achieved? It is clearly a practical impossibility, as it would mean that everyone would have to be completely equal *before* the race begins. This is a paradox. It shows that the ideal of equality of opportunity really means that you have to have initial *equality* in order to achieve eventual *inequality*. So, though it appears at first sight to be a far more attainable objective than absolute equality or equality of outcomes, equality of opportunity is almost as difficult to achieve

"Rat Race"

Modern "democracies" therefore set people up—first making everyone believe that they are all equal and then dashing the hopes of many in the "rat race" without justification. Can this Gordian knot be untangled, or does it have to be cut? And, if so, how? The social and political system pre-eminent in the Western world today, "representative democracy," is a hypocrisy. What goes by the name of "democracy" is, in reality, oligarchy, and the ruling egalitarian ideology is belied by the reality of inequality—and the underlying general belief that people are *not* all equal (see Chapter 8). All the while the dominant minority holds on to power without genuine "merit" (whatever that means), and the "losers," those left behind in the rat race, are made to feel inferior and resentful.

Phony "Democracy"

In a meritocratic culture such as is dominant in the West today, failure cannot be explained by lack of intrinsic worth—because the dominant philosophy insists that everyone is of equal worth. It has to be blamed instead on such features as prejudice, favoritism or nepotism, or on the inherent unfairness of the system as a whole. All these factors are real enough, but they are cold comfort to the losers. Probably the chief refuge for the losers is mental illness. This is undoubtedly at least one of the causes of the alarmingly high incidence of mental illness in the West today. The British Mental Health Foundation says: "About a quarter of the population will experience some kind of mental health problem in the course of a year, with mixed anxiety and depression the most common mental disorder in Britain" (online: `www.mentalhealth.org.uk/help-information/mental-health-statistics/`).

In short, the real problem with modern "democracy" is that it is phony. It pretends to be what it's not: a system in which everyone is of equal worth and has an equal chance to succeed. Instead, it is an oligarchy in which the idea that everyone is of equal worth is not actually believed by the majority, and the promise of equal opportunity is a myth.

The actual hierarchical societies in history have generally been much more natural and genuine than the fake "democracy" that is held up as the modern ideal. Medieval western Europe provides us with a good example of a highly stratified society, in which, with the exception of occasional peasants' revolts (like the English Peasants' Revolt of 1381, sparked off by the imposition of a poll tax), people were for the most part content with their lot, which they accepted as the will of God. In fact, even in medieval Europe there was a certain amount of social mobility, and the Catholic Church provided an escape hatch for ambitious young men from an impoverished background. According to Gregory Clark's intriguing book, *The Son Also Rises*, there was actually more social mobility in

Figure 9 Writing the Declaration of Independence.
SOURCE: Jean Leon Gerome Ferris / Library of Congress / Public domain.

medieval England than there is today (Clark 2014)! Without necessarily accepting that, the point is that in the Middle Ages there was no rat race and people did not generally feel aggrieved because they were of lowly status.

As late as the mid-nineteenth century there was still a generally automatic acceptance of the idea of a divinely ordained stratified society, as reflected in the popular children's hymn "All Things Bright and Beautiful," composed by Mrs Cecil Alexander in 1848, the third verse of which reads:

> The rich man in his castle,
> The poor man at his gate,
> God made them high and lowly,
> And ordered their estate.
> (*Hymns for Little Children* 1848;
>   Cecil Frances Alexander.)

Equality vs. Liberty

"Liberté, égalité, fraternité" is a slogan associated with the French Revolution. After a speech of December 1790 by the radical revolutionary Maximilien Robespierre, this slogan was emblazoned on the tricolor flag and the National Guard uniform, although it was only during the Third Republic (1870–1940) that it became the official national motto of France. "Liberty and equality" was a slogan already encountered earlier in the eighteenth century and the two concepts are also to be found combined in the United States' Declaration of Independence of 1776: "We hold these truths to be self-evident, that all men are created equal, that they are endowed by their Creator with certain unalienable Rights, that among these are Life, Liberty and the pursuit of Happiness."

Besides the hypocrisy of this declaration in the face of slavery, there is a serious potential contradiction between liberty and equality.

Liberty Inversely Proportional to Equality

At its simplest, liberty, may be defined the way John Locke (1632–1704) defines "freedom under government," which is: "to have a standing rule to live by, common to every one of that society, and made by the legislative power erected in it; a liberty to follow my own will in all things, where the rule prescribes not; and not to be subject to the inconstant, uncertain, unknown, arbitrary will of another man" (Locke 1689, Chapter IV, §22, p. 10). In short, liberty by this definition gives everyone the right to do anything they like as long as it is not contrary to law, and also the right not to be subject to the arbitrary will of others.

Of course, the degree of freedom or liberty that this concept confers will depend on the constraints of the particular "standing rule" and of the laws of the state in question.

For convenience, let us posit a *laissez-faire* or "night watchman" state, or what the libertarian Robert Nozick termed "the minimal state," i.e. a state with powers limited to keeping order and protecting its borders. In a state like that, with minimal restrictions on enterprise, profit or the amassing and transmission of wealth—in other words, with maximum liberty—there will inevitably be a high degree of inequality. This is because human beings are naturally competitive and acquisitive, so that, with maximum liberty, the more ambitious, enterprising, and industrious among them are likely to become richer and more prosperous than their fellows and will also attain higher status. Evidence from all parts of the world and all periods of history points to inequality as what we may call the "default" situation for this reason.

Britain in the eighteenth and nineteenth centuries is a good example of this sort of society, as is the United States from its foundation until the presidency of Franklin Roosevelt (1933–45)—with few restrictions on liberty and high inequality. Liberty and equality are essentially inversely proportional to each other—the more liberty, the less equality, and vice versa.

At the opposite end of the spectrum is the case of Cuba under Fidel Castro, who, soon after seizing power as a dictator in 1959, expropriated the large landowners (including his own mother) and reduced wage inequality, so that, for example, a medical practitioner received only 700 pesos a month as against 400 pesos for an industrial worker. This was a deliberate policy of pandering to the workers, peasants, and students and showing them that he championed their interests against the previous elite groups, including middle-class professionals, large numbers of whom emigrated to Florida, while Castro cracked down on "counter-revolutionaries," many of whom were summarily executed (see Chapter 15).

"A Theory of Justice"

John Rawls's *Theory of Justice* (Rawls 1971) has been widely hailed as the best thing since sliced bread, or its philosophical equivalent. I have to confess that I am not particularly partial to sliced bread. More than that, as I am both a classicist and a barrister, the word "justice" sticks in my craw when it is used neither in its original Greek sense, *dikaiosynē*, nor in its legal courtroom sense. The problem—or rather, one of the many problems—with Rawls's rather pompous theory is that it falls between these two meanings of "justice."

The legal concept of justice sees justice as blind, or at least blindfolded, so as not to be able to favor one party over another. The key concept is therefore "equality before the law," which, however, is a chimera, because, as Lord Chief Justice Hewart (1870–1943) put it: "The courts are open to all, just like the Ritz Hotel." In other words, equality before the law simply does not exist.

The Greek word *dikaiosynē* can be translated as "justice" or "righteousness," which gives one some idea of its wide scope. It means essentially "doing the right thing." Rawls says that he is following Aristotle's understanding of "justice" as refraining from *pleonexia*, meaning "greed," "covetousness," or "avarice." But this is not Aristotle's main definition of "justice," especially in a political context. Aristotle's definition in that regard is "to give each his due," or to give everyone what he deserves. But how is one to determine what each person deserves? Everybody surely deserves the same as everybody else? Not at all. Neither Aristotle nor any of the other Greek philosophers believed in equality. "The worst form of inequality," he said, "is to try to make unequal things equal." Ancient society, both Greek and Roman, had an aristocratic ethos: there was no belief that all people were equal. That is a modern idea, dating from the eighteenth century—and it is still not genuinely subscribed to by most people in their innermost beliefs (see Chapter 8). The ancient Greeks did not believe in equality, but in fairness. And, as they believed that people were intrinsically unequal, fairness meant treating people unequally in accordance with what they deserved. The reason Plato gives for disliking democracy is that it "distributed a kind of equality to the equal and the unequal alike" (Plato, *Republic* VIII. 558c).

Rawls's theory is essentially an attempt to reconcile liberty and equality, which, as we have already seen, is a chimera. He offers his theory as an alternative to utilitarianism and to right-libertarianism.

His starting point is the highly artificial "original position," a variant of the many versions of the "social contract." Rawls posits a situation in which every individual reaches "principles of justice" from behind a "veil of ignorance" which blinds them to any self-knowledge. "No one knows his place in society, his class position or social status, nor does anyone know his fortune in the distribution of natural assets and abilities, his intelligence, strength and the like." Rawls assumes that this ignorance will lead to everyone's choosing a "maximin" position which would most benefit the least well-off—a completely unrealistic assumption. Thomas Hobbes (1588–1679) had a far deeper insight into human nature: "I put for the general inclination of all mankind a perpetual and restless desire of power after power, that ceaseth only in death" (Hobbes 1651, chapter 11).

Rawls's flight of fancy propels him into positing that everyone would then embrace two "principles of justice":

- "First: each person is to have an equal right to the most extensive scheme of equal basic liberties compatible with a similar scheme of liberties for others" (Rawls 1971, p. 53).

- "Second: social and economic inequalities are to be arranged so that they are both (a) reasonably expected to be to everyone's advantage, and (b) attached to positions and offices open to all" (ibid.).

Rawls seems to have started with his desired conclusion and worked backwards to his "original position." Determined to conclude that everyone would agree to some vaguely egalitarian distribution of liberty, he placed everyone in a state of ignorance to begin with. His "principles of liberty" are hardly more realistic than his "original position."

The first of these "principles" initially looks unobjectionable, until it is realized that his "scheme of basic liberties" does not include the right to own the means of production or even freedom of contract on a *laissez-faire* basis. Yet, unless restrained by some superior power, people will naturally try to compete with their neighbours and amass as much wealth as they can. The second "principle" is equally unrealistic. The only way to achieve greater equality or to level inequalities so as to benefit the least well-off is by means of control by a strong popular monarchical government, like that of Fidel Castro in Cuba. I doubt that that is what Rawls had in mind in his rarefied imagination!

"Two Concepts of Liberty"

Sir Isaiah Berlin's "Two Concepts of Liberty" is another much vaunted theory, the significance of which I believe has been greatly overrated. Berlin (1909–97) divides "liberty" into two types, positive and negative. For "negative" liberty he essentially adopts Thomas Hobbes's definition of liberty in *Leviathan*: "Liberty, or Freedome, signifieth (properly) the absence of Opposition; (by Opposition, I mean externall Impediments of motion); and may be applied no lesse to Irrational. And Inanimate creatures, than to Rational" (Hobbes 1651, II., xxvi, 261). The point is that the "opposition" is external. So, following on from this, Hobbes defines a free man as "he, that in those things, which by his strength and wit he is able to do, is not hindered to doe what he has a will to" (ibid., II, xxi, 262).

Berlin puts it like this: "I am normally said to be free to the degree to which no man or body of men interferes with my activity. Political liberty in this sense is simply the area within which a man can act unobstructed by others" (Berlin 2002, p. 122). But liberty, opined Berlin, could not be unlimited: "The extent of a man's, or a people's, liberty to choose to live as they desire must be weighed against the claims of many other values, of which equality, or justice, or happiness, or security, or public order are perhaps the most obvious examples. For this reason, it cannot be unlimited.... [R]espect for the principles of justice, or shame at gross inequality of treatment, is as basic in men as the desire for liberty" (ibid., p. 70). Shame at gross inequality of treatment? It is simply naïve to expect to find any such feeling in the breast of those whose success has come at the expense of others. Berlin does not seem to have realized that the more liberty there is, the more inequality there will inevitably be (see discussion above).

Berlin's concept of "positive liberty" is even less clear, so much so that he was forced to explain that, contrary to the impression he had initially given, he was not opposed to it: "Positive liberty . . . is a valid universal goal. I do not know why I should have been held to doubt this, or, for that matter, the further proposition, that democratic self-government is a fundamental human need, something valuable in itself, whether or not it clashes with the claims of negative liberty or of any other goal. . . .. What I am mainly concerned to establish is that, whatever may be the common grounds between them, negative and positive liberty are not the same thing" (Berlin 2002, introduction). What then is "democratic self-government" if it clashes with "negative liberty"? A minor problem, as we have seen, is that "democratic self-government" has never actually existed. But, regardless of that inconvenient fact, "self-government" must surely entail freedom of action without let or hindrance, or without interference from outside. Without that it can have no meaning.

But what, in any event, is Berlin's "positive liberty"? Berlin explains it like this: "The 'positive' sense of the word 'liberty' derives from the wish on the part of the individual to be his own master.. . . The freedom which consists of being one's own master, and the freedom which consists in not being prevented from choosing as I do by other men, may, on the face of it, seem concepts at no great logical distance from each other – no more than negative and positive ways of saying much the same thing. Yet the 'positive' and 'negative' notions of freedom historically developed in divergent directions not always by logically reputable steps, until, in the end, they came into direct conflict with each other" (Berlin 1969, p. 131f). Berlin's explanation of this development is less than pellucid and unhelpfully lacks any historical examples.

But, what he appears to be referring to is the distortion of the concept of liberty by "totalitarian" regimes, as foreshadowed in Rousseau's concept of being "forced to be free." Rousseau draws a distinction between *la volonté de tous* ("the will of all") and *la volonté générale* ("the general will"). The "will of all" can easily be discovered by a head-count, but "the general will" is a more mystical and, for Rousseau, a far more powerful concept. As a supposedly consenting member of a society, a person is presumed to agree to the "general will" of that society, even though the individuals making up that society are not asked to vote on this mystical "general will." In Rousseau's words: "So long as several men together consider themselves to be a single body, they have but a single will." The "general will" emerges, according to Rousseau from his version of a "social contract." Rousseau defines the essence of his version of the "social contract" like this: *Chacun de nous met en commun sa personne et toute sa puissance sous la suprême direction de la volonté générale; et nous recevons en corps chaque membre comme partie indivisible du tout* ("Each of us places his person and all his power in common under the supreme control of the general will, and as a body we receive each member as an indivisible part of the whole"). "Whoever refuses to obey the general will," Rousseau continues, "will be forced to do so by the entire body. This means that he will be forced to be free" (Rousseau 1762, Bk I, Chapter vii). This is a paradox. One might expect to be punished for disobeying the "general will," but what does it mean to be "forced to be free"? This is often identified with such concepts as "re-education" imposed by totalitarian regimes, for example, by sending some 17 million urban youth during China's "Cultural Revolution" (between 1966 and 1976) to the countryside to be "re-educated" by the peasantry and to be required to undertake (sometimes backbreaking) manual labor. This is an example of Berlin's "positive liberty." The totalitarian use of the concept of "positive liberty" is the reason that Berlin was commonly believed to be opposed to it, but, as we have seen, he subsequently went out of his way to deny this.

The Right to Disobey the Law

"Written by the world's best-known political and legal theorist" is what it says in the blurb to Ronald Dworkin's (1996) book titled *Freedom's Law*. Dworkin (1931–2013) proposes that "the abstract language of the [United States] Constitution" be interpreted "by reference to moral principles about political decency and justice."

A good example of Dworkin's thinking is to be found in an (unintentionally) amusing essay on "Civil Disobedience" in his book *Taking Rights Seriously*, in which he opines: "If the law is doubtful, [everyone] may follow his own judgment, even after a contrary decision by the highest competent court" (Dworkin, 1977).

Dworkin explains his position with reference to the US judicial system: "Sometimes, even after a contrary Supreme Court decision, an individual may still reasonably believe that the law is on his side. . .. We cannot assume, in other words, that the Constitution is always what the Supreme Court says it is." He adds: "In the United States, at least, almost any law which a significant number of people would be tempted to disobey on moral grounds would be doubtful – if not clearly invalid – on constitutional grounds as well."

This raises more questions than it answers:

- What is meant by "a significant number of people"? A million, a thousand, a hundred, ten? Dworkin offers no guidance.
- How is one to *know* how many people are "tempted to disobey"? This too is uncertain.
- What is meant by "tempted to disobey"? Dworkin is careful not to require actual disobedience for a law to be characterized as "doubtful." But being "tempted" to disobey is a peculiarly private matter. There are probably many

people who at one time or another are tempted to disobey the law against murder but who get no further than sticking pins into their intended victim's effigy, if that.

- However, according to Dworkin the temptation to disobey has to be based "on moral grounds." What exactly does this mean? "Moral grounds" presumably means on the basis that the law in question is in some sense "wrong." This sounds straightforward enough—until one starts looking at actual examples. Was opposition to Prohibition in the 1920s based on moral grounds—or simply on the ground that it was an inconvenience not to be legally allowed to have a beer after work? But Prohibition could also be looked at as an infringement of individual liberty—a moral basis. If so, then what about laws against the possession of drugs? On Dworkin's argument, are these not "doubtful" as well?
- But Dworkin goes further by suggesting that "doubtful" laws may also be "clearly invalid on constitutional grounds." And what if this "doubtful" or "clearly invalid" law itself forms part of the US Constitution—like income tax, for example? If a "significant number" of people object to it on moral grounds—which is almost guaranteed—can they justifiably refuse to pay?
- Perhaps the key word in Dworkin's formulation is the word "almost." Dworkin does not say that *any* law would be "doubtful" if a "significant number of people" were "tempted to disobey" it "on moral grounds"—but only *almost* any law! Who decides which laws qualify for this treatment and which do not? This is essentially a political question. The example that Dworkin chooses is the draft law at the time of the Vietnam War. But what about, say, a law obliging businesses to ensure that at least 30% of their employees are black? This would be a form of compulsory discrimination against the majority of the population—so there would be a moral basis for opposing it. Would Dworkin have been prepared to treat this law as "doubtful" too? From his support for "affirmative action," it is clear that he would not regard the 30% law as "doubtful."

On reflection, the whole edifice of Dworkin's attempted justification of disobedience to the law crumbles to dust. It clearly has nothing whatsoever to do with either law or morality but solely with politics. "Right-wing" laws are "doubtful," while "left-wing" laws must be strictly obeyed! (See Arnheim 2004.)

Dworkin's is essentially an anarchical "solution" to the question of obedience to law. Far from bolstering the principle of the rule of law, his approach must be seen as essentially subverting it.

Not that the concept of "the rule of law" is any more real than Dworkin's "solution": "A government not of men but of laws"—a high-sounding but fictitious principle, as proclaimed, for example, by America's second president, who inserted it into the Constitution of Massachusetts of 1780. In response to which an anonymous wag retorted: "A government not of laws, but of lawyers." And so it has been ever since. US Chief Justice Charles Evans Hughes (1862–1948) appears to have agreed: "We are under a Constitution, but the Constitution is what the judges say it is." Had Hughes stopped there, we would have assumed that he disapproved of this judicial supremacism. But he went on: "and the judiciary is the safeguard of our liberty and our property under the Constitution." So, while recognizing the exorbitant power of the judiciary, he commended it.

The problem is that many decisions of the courts are essentially political—not in a party political sense nor in any overt sense at all but imperceptibly drawing on the judges' ingrained and deep-seated values, which cannot simply be put to one side while they are sitting on the bench. Alexander Hamilton (1755–1804) could not have been more wrong when he predicted in the *Federalist Papers* that the judiciary would be the weakest of the three branches of government. As a result of the "twistifications" (as Jefferson called them) of Chief Justice John Marshall (in office 1801–35), the US Supreme Court turned out to be the strongest and most powerful branch of government.

Judicial Supremacism

And the same development has taken place in the United Kingdom. "The proper constitutional relationship of the executive with the courts is that the courts will respect all acts of the executive within its lawful province, and the executive will respect all decisions of the courts as to what its lawful province is." This fallacious opinion comes from the judgement of Lord Justice Nolan (as he then was) in the case of *M v. Home Office* (1994). According to this, the judges have the right to decide what the "lawful province" of the executive is. Does this mean that it is for the judges to decide—and, presumably, also to change—what the executive is permitted or not permitted to do? If so, that is *legislation,* which is reserved to Parliament under the bedrock constitutional principle of the sovereignty of Parliament. *M v. Home Office* itself represents the practical application of Nolan LJ's fallacious constitutional formulation. A unanimous House of Lords there decided that a court could issue an injunction against the Crown (i.e. against a minister in his official capacity) and that if the Crown disobeyed such an order the Crown could be held in contempt of court. Both these propositions were unprecedented and flew in the face of the Crown Proceedings Act 1947, which was "virtually rewritten" by the court (Carol Harlow and Richard Rawlings (1997), p. 603f). So much so, indeed, that the Scottish Court of Session refused to follow the House of Lords' decision. Instead of Nolan LJ's formulation, an accurate description of the relationship between the executive and the judiciary is that enunciated by Lord Mustill in 1995: "It is a feature of the peculiarly British conception of the separation of powers that Parliament, the executive and the courts have each their distinct and largely exclusive domain. Parliament has a legally unchallengeable right to make whatever laws it thinks fit. The executive carries on the administration of the country in accordance with the powers conferred on it by law. The courts interpret the laws, and see that they are obeyed" (*R v. Secretary of State for the Home Department, ex parte Fire Brigades Union* [1995] 2 AC 513, 567).

The Constitutional Reform Act of 2005 amounted to a complete capitulation by the executive to the judiciary. And the majority UK Supreme Court decision in 2015 in the case of letters written by Prince Charles (as he then was) to the government went so far that two courageous justices of the Supreme Court were prepared to characterize the decision as overstepping the proper power of the judiciary. In his trenchant dissenting judgement, Lord Wilson said that the majority on the UK Supreme Court "did not interpret" the relevant statute, "It rewrote it" (*R (Evans) v.Attorney General* [2015] UKSC 21).

Revocation

Judicial supremacism, which above all makes a mockery of any claim of "democracy," is a serious problem. But the solution is not disobedience to the law, no matter how incorrectly it has been "interpreted." That way lies anarchy.

But there is a ready solution: revocation. In the words of Lord Neuberger, the then president of the UK Supreme Court: "Any judicial decision can be revoked by Parliament through a statute" (Neuberger 2017). This important power is not anything exceptional, but a natural corollary to the bedrock constitutional principle of the sovereignty of Parliament that gives Parliament legislative supremacy. If a court reaches a decision to which (for any reason at all) Parliament objects, Parliament has the power to revoke, i.e. cancel, annul, reverse, or overturn, that decision. The two best-known examples of this power are the Trade Union Act 1913 and the War Damage Act 1965, both of which were passed by Parliament to revoke a judicial decision of the House of Lords (then the highest court in the land).

Chapter 10
The Oligarchy Trap and Other Fallacies

*P*ower structures are studied chiefly by social scientists, many of whom, including *Mosca, Pareto, Robert Michels, C. Wright Mills, and Jeffrey A. Winters, have plumped for a one-size-fits-all solution in the form of oligarchy. Very few historians have taken any interest in power structures. One of these, Sir Ronald Syme, a distinguished Oxford professor, surprisingly, fell into the same oligarchy trap: "In all ages, whatever the form and name of government, be it monarchy, republic, or democracy, an oligarchy lurks behind the façade."*

This chapter discusses some of the many different approaches to the writing of history, with my own criteria summarized at the end. The issues dealt with are as follows:

- **The oligarchy trap:** The one-size-fits-all theory that forces all forms of government into the same oligarchic straitjacket, blunting any ability to draw any distinctions between them.
- **"A monarchy rules through an oligarchy"**: A curious example of "oligarchy club" thinking on the part of Sir Ronald Syme, resulting in a blurring of the dividing line between the Roman Republic and Augustus's Principate, which actually marked a sea-change in Roman history.
- **Seesaw:** Lumping all governments together in a pot labeled "oligarchy" is a failure to recognize that, though a hybrid is possible, the more monarchy there is, the less oligarchy, and vice versa.
- **"Proper historical writing"**: Moses Finley, who is credited with founding a new "school" for the writing of ancient history, defined "proper historical writing" as writing and teaching that are "morally and politically committed"

Figure 10   Coronation of Louis XV, 1722.
SOURCE: Pierre Subleyras / Augustiner Museum / Public domain.

and even "socially subversive"—in other words, left-wing (though, with some notable exceptions, Finley's own writings show little sign of this bias).

- **The sceptical tendency:** A tendency of some historians to dismiss evidence accepted by most others, to the point of throwing the baby out with the bathwater.
- **Baby and bathwater:** Taken to an extreme, this tendency can result in a distorted or erroneous impression of whole periods.
- **"Drowning the baby":** This is exactly the opposite fallacy, of credulously accepting weak or even non-existent evidence—perpetrated by some of the same writers engaged in throwing the baby out with the bathwater.

- **Ranke: "Wie es eigentlich gewesen ist."** The classic statement of the need for historians to stick to facts and eschew any "lessons" to be drawn from them.
- **History as "one damned fact after another":** A disparaging characterization of the Rankean approach, begging the question, "What is a fact?"
- **"Cleopatra's nose":** The accidental theory of history, a rather superficial approach.
- **"An art of writing history":** Emphasis on elegant narrative, sacrificing analysis to style—which does not necessarily prevent bias.
- **Torpedoing Torpor:** A case study of how an attempt at humor may backfire.
- **"Williamanmary was a good King":** The (all too common) danger for a historian to rate people, events, developments, or whole periods as "good" or "bad"—a blatant rejection of any attempt at objectivity.
- **Causation:** In his *What is History?*, E.H. Carr opined: "The historian, like any other scientist, is an animal who incessantly asks the question, Why?" (Carr 1961, p. 113). Not all historians would agree with this, though my own view is that, whether historians are regarded as "scientists" or not, E.H. Carr is correct.
- **So what?** This is the ultimate test of the value—and utility—of the historian's researches.

Folk etymology derives "history" from "His story," meaning God's story, which cannot of course be taken seriously. The true origin of "history" is from the Greek *historia*, meaning "inquiry, investigation, research." The word entered Latin with the same meaning, and in Late Latin was shortened to *storia*, from which we get "story." So here we already have the two main classifications of history: history as literature and history as science. The heroine of Jane Austen's *Northanger Abbey* (written in 1803) describes reading history as "very tiresome: and yet I often think it odd that it should be so dull, for a great deal of it must be invention." This is a lighthearted caricature of the dilemma of historical writing, going to the heart of the question: "What is history?"

No one claiming to be a serious historian today would be likely to admit to being purely in the entertainment business, though by no means all professional historians would claim that history is a science either. There are a number of historical "schools of thought," including the French *Annales* school as well as the so-called Frankfurt School, the Vienna School, the Toronto School, and a good many other more informal groupings, tendencies, or traditions, each with its own answer to the question, "What is history?" Or, "What is the proper purpose of the study of history?" This chapter is devoted to a critical consideration of a number of different approaches to history.

The Oligarchy Trap

There is no shortage of theories which lump all forms of government together as "oligarchies." The best-known of these are the theories associated with the names of Vilfredo Pareto, Gaetano Mosca, and Robert Michels. A recent recruit to this club is Jeffrey Winters, a political science professor at Northwestern University, with his 2011 book titled simply *Oligarchy,* who, however, is anxious to distinguish his theory from those of Pareto, Mosca, and Michels. "Oligarchy ranks among the most widely used yet poorly theorized concepts in the social sciences" (Winters 2011, p. 1). This opening sentence of Jeffrey Winters' book, *Oligarchy,* is surprising, to say the least. Winters is presumably familiar with the writings of Gaetano Mosca, Vilfredo Pareto, and Robert Michels. Or is an oligarchy a different animal from an elite? Winters quotes the definition of oligarchy from the *International Encyclopedia of the Social Sciences* as "a form of government in which political power is in the hands of a small minority." Elitist theorists like Mosca and Pareto would have no quarrel with this definition as applicable not only to oligarchies but also to what Pareto called a "governing elite" and Mosca labeled a "ruling class" or "political class." And Michels, a disciple of Mosca's, refers to *his* elitist theory as "the iron law of oligarchy."

Whether labeled oligarchy, aristocracy, ruling class, or elite, this is a one-size-fits-all theory that forces all forms of government into the same straitjacket, blunting any ability to draw any distinctions between different forms of government or different power structures.

"A Monarchy Rules through an Oligarchy"

A surprising member of the oligarchy club is Oxford's Sir Ronald Syme (1903–89), one of the most highly respected ancient historians of modern times. Syme does not mince his words. In *The Roman Revolution*, Syme's magnum opus, we come upon this categorical assertion: "In all ages, whatever the form and name of government, be it monarchy, republic, or democracy, an oligarchy lurks behind the façade" (Syme 1939, pp. 7, 15). Writing in 1939, Syme portrayed Augustus essentially as a prototype of a fascist dictator. Was Augustus's rule not monarchical, then? Syme certainly seemed to think it was. So how did he square this with his sweeping blanket theory of oligarchy? "A monarchy rules through an oligarchy" is Syme's baffling formula (ibid., p. 8).

In a purely banal sense, it is of course true that no individual can rule a state single-handed. The ruler will need the assistance and support of others in order to maintain power. But here we come to a crucial divide: between those who serve a ruler in an inferior capacity and are removable by the ruler at will, and those upon whose support the ruler *depends* to maintain his position and who *share* his power. Where a ruler is surrounded by purely inferior minions who do his bidding, that is not an oligarchy, because the minions have no independent power base of their own. In that scenario, power is concentrated in the hands of the ruler, who exercises sole power. It is therefore a monarchy. An "oligarchy," by contrast, is a form of government where power is shared by the members of an elite group.

The essential difference between monarchy and oligarchy is the whereabouts of power. It is not always obvious whether the entourage surrounding a ruler is beholden to him or whether he is beholden to them, or possibly whether they are mutually dependent on each other. The key question to ask is: Who has the whip hand?

Seesaw

Syme's bald assertion that "A monarchy rules through an oligarchy" is a contradiction in terms. Monarchy and oligarchy are opposites, although a hybrid combination between the two can sometimes exist. In other words, the relationship between monarchy and oligarchy is in the nature of a seesaw, in which the more power that is exercised by the one, the less is left to the other. But hybrid examples do not alter the fact that monarchy and oligarchy are diametric opposites (see Chapter 2). Lumping all governments together in a pot labeled "oligarchy" amounts to a failure to recognize that there are, in fact, two polarized forms of government, monarchy and oligarchy, which have opposite power structures, resulting in major practical differences.

Fifty years later, in 1989, Syme is still unrepentant. He describes the Augustan Principate as "autocratic government," adding; "The Princeps duly went on to exploit the "res publica," encroaching on the functions of Senate, of magistrates, of laws" (Syme 1989, p. 1f). But, at the same time Syme is still barking up the oligarchy tree: "Oligarchy is imposed as the guiding theme, the link from age to age whatever be the form and name of government" (ibid., p. 13).

The existence of a ruling party, especially in a one-party state, may sometimes give a clue to the whereabouts of power, but not always. So, for example, Adolf Hitler ruled Germany as "Führer" of the Nazi Party, but it would be a mistake to see power as vested in the party, or any members of the party, rather than in Hitler personally. The same applies to Communist Party leaders such as Joseph Stalin in the Soviet Union, Cuba's Fidel Castro, and Mao Zedong and Xi Jinping in China. As far as Rome is concerned, there was in fact no Augustan "party," although Syme evidently thought there was: "Without a party a statesman is nothing. He sometimes forgets that awkward fact" (Syme 1939, chapter 4).

Even if there had been an Augustan "party," that would not necessarily prove that the system was an oligarchy. Augustus's *Consilium Principis* (advisers to the emperor), drawn from his *amici* ("friends"), did not constitute a party in any sense. Nor was it a "council" or "cabinet" whose advice he was obliged to take. Indeed, certain important issues on which we might expect him to have taken advice do not appear to have been referred to the *Consilium* at all. Membership of the *Consilium* was not fixed, its meetings were irregular and the emperor was not obliged to accept its advice in any event. Informal chats *inter amicos*, "among friends," likewise, do not constitute any kind of oligarchy.

Like strong monarchs throughout history who understood the realities of power, Augustus clearly recognized that the old Republican aristocracy, and especially the *nobiles*—"descendants of consular houses, whether patrician or plebeian in origin" (Syme 1989, p. 10)—were foes or potential foes to his regime, just as they had been to Julius Caesar, but he recognized that Julius Caesar's blunt forthrightness was not the answer, so he developed much subtler tactics to neutralize potential enemies, which enabled him to establish one of the stablest and most durable regimes in history.

Syme recognized Augustus's defeat of the old nobility: "Not a mere faction of the nobility had been defeated, but a whole class" (Syme 1939, p. 490). And: "Power receding, aristocrats looked to priesthoods for "dignitas" and social eminence" (Syme 1989, p. 3f.)—recognition of the fact that the defeated aristocrats understood the need to look outside government appointments to achieve or maintain a position in society. And:

> Hostility to the *nobiles* was engrained in the Principate from its military and revolutionary origins. In the first decade of his constitutional rule, Augustus employed not a single *nobilis* among the legates who commanded the armies in his *provincia*, and only three men of consular standing. When his position becomes stronger, and a coalition government based largely on family ties has been built up, *nobiles* like Ahenobarbus, Piso and Paullus Fabius Maximus govern the military provinces, it is true. But a rational distrust persists, confirmed under his successors by certain disquieting incidents, and leads to the complete exclusion of the *nobiles*, the delayed but logical end of Revolution and Empire (Syme 1939, p. 502).

Except for the suggestion of a "coalition government," of which there is no evidence whatsoever, Syme correctly highlights Augustus's reluctance to give military commands to *nobiles*. And he also looks ahead, beyond Augustus, to "the complete exclusion of the *nobiles*." Yet Syme still fails to recognize that the regime established by Augustus was not an oligarchy at all but a different type or model of government altogether, a form of monarchy, in which power was concentrated in the hands of a single individual, and that this form of government would continue long after Augustus.

It is quite baffling to understand why Syme, while correctly holding that Augustus initiated a monarchy, would want to attempt to square the circle with the self-contradictory and erroneous oracular comment that "A monarchy rules through an oligarchy." In a word, Syme's one-size-fits-all oligarchic theory is just plain wrong, and never more so than when applied to the Augustan Principate.

"Proper Historical Writing"

Sir Moses Finley (1912–86), Cambridge Professor of Ancient History from 1970 to 1979, who had been highly critical of the state of ancient history writing, was asked in a 1985 interview by Keith Hopkins about his view of "proper historical writing." In the interview:

> [Finley] reflected on what he termed 'proper historical writing' and the part he had played in fostering it. He drew a contrast with the production of 'forty-page articles' on the detail of historical narrative: 'You offend nobody. You are acknowledged as a good scholar. It is easier.' He favoured instead the writing and teaching of history that was (as formulated by Hopkins) 'morally and politically committed' and even 'socially subversive.' He emphatically agreed that his own preferred way forward was harder and made more enemies (Jew et al. 2016, p. 57).

> 'Do you think that you and your followers have in any way managed to change the normal way in which Ancient History is practiced? You may not have been setting out to campaign against, but the impact was one of a campaign, wasn't it, setting up a new school?' To which Finley replied: 'Well, school, alright. [*sic*] The difficulty is that there are too many ancient historians, any statement saying ancient historians now do this is easily falsified. But I don't have any doubt that … there is now an increasing number of ancient historians who do more of what I call proper historical writing. Now I am not suggesting that I did it, because of me, but I am prepared to accept that I have some responsibility for it. Whether they represent more than a minority in the field I doubt—because it's a bit the hard way to do things' (ibid., p. 297).

Several important points emerge from this exchange:

- Finley is critical of the traditional type of academic article on some "detail of historical narrative" (see the discussion on Ranke, below).
- Finley's own definition of "proper historical writing" is writing that is "morally and politically committed" and even "socially subversive"—in other words, tendentious writing supporting or even promoting a particular political, moral, and social position. This is a far cry from the idea of the historian as a detached, neutral observer (see the discussion on Ranke, below).

- Finley claims some personal responsibility for increasing the number of ancient historians doing "proper historical writing."

These points are question-begging, in the following ways:

- Finley admits that what he calls "proper historical writing" is only his own personal preference, but at the same time he clearly takes pride in regarding it as superior to the conventional approach against which he had campaigned. There is no suggestion on Finley's part that there could be more than one type of "proper historical writing."
- The writing of politically motivated history—Finley's "proper historical writing"—is nothing new. A good example is the Whig interpretation of English history, which dominated the field for over two hundred years. But that would hardly have qualified as "morally and politically committed" or "socially subversive" writing. Finley's left-leaning political sympathies are well known, but it has to be said that, with some notable exceptions, there is little sign of an overtly left-wing bias in his writings.
- Finley's emphasis on how "hard" it was to write history in his preferred way may possibly explain his overly sceptical tendency to dismiss evidence that many other historians were prepared to accept.

The Sceptical Tendency

Here are just a few examples of Finley's scepticism:

Homer: In *The World of Odysseus,* first published in 1954, Finley categorically dismissed the idea that the Homeric epics threw any light on Troy or Mycenaean Greece: "the narrative is a collection of fictions from beginning to end" (Finley 1954/2002, p. vii). Finley essentially maintained this position for the rest of his life, for over thirty years—flying in the face of ever more impressive archaeological and linguistic evidence. The *Iliad* and the *Odyssey* make no claim to be historical records. They are epic poems reduced to writing probably between 800 and 700 BCE, but evidently based on much older oral traditions relating to a war between Greeks and Trojans hundreds of years earlier (see West 2011, pp. 383–93). The relevant evidence is threefold:

- First, Homer's Troy, or Ilium, has now been reliably located on what is now called the mound of Hisarlik in present-day Turkey—a site occupied by a number of successive civilizations, the ones favoured by archeology are Blegen's Troy VIIa or Manfred Korfmann's Troy Vii, dated to between 1260 and 1180 BCE (Blegen 1995, p. 164; Korfmann 2013, p. 110).
- This archaeological evidence is supplemented by archaeological evidence from Greece itself. Book II (lines 494–759) of the *Iliad* provides a "catalogue of

ships" listing 164 Greek cities that contributed men to the campaign against Troy, most of which have been identified with archaeological remains dating from before 1150 BCE, when the whole Mycenaean world collapsed. In Homer, the Greek world is united in a loose confederacy under Agamemnon, King of Mycenae, which is reflected in the archaeological remains of Mycenae, Tiryns, Pylos, and other sites.

- The third source of evidence is Linear B, Mycenaean Greek as deciphered by Michael Ventris and John Chadwick (Ventris and Chadwick 1958). This reveals a hierarchical society under a *wanax,* or "king" (before the loss of the digamma, making it *anax* in Homer, which explains some anomalies in Homeric scansion), as well as numerous other features, such as the appearance of a number of Homeric names like Hector and Achilles as the names of ordinary people in the Linear B tablets.
- Do the Homeric epics make some "mistakes" in representing Mycenaean society? Of course they do. The poems do not claim to be historical documents, and there was a long period of oral transmission before the traditions were eventually committed to writing. But the evidence of Mycenaean Greece reflected in the poems is so impressive as to make it counter-productive to simply discard it, as Finley did (Finley 1954/2002; cf. Arnheim 1977, p.13ff; Wood, 2015).

Economies of scale: Finley dismissed the notion that the Romans had any idea of the commercial exploitation of land. He largely based this on a single letter from Pliny the Younger (61–c. 113 CE) to a friend asking for advice on whether he should buy an estate adjacent to one he already owned. "Apart from the bailiffs," opines Finley, "there is not a whisper of possible economies of scale that could or would follow the consolidation of two adjoining estates..." (Finley 1973, p. 113). In fact, Pliny lists a number of potential economies of scale: "The same work could be carried on at both places, they could be visited at the same cost of traveling, they could be put under one steward and practically one set of managers... Moreover, one must take into account the cost of furniture and head-servants, besides gardeners, smiths and even the gamekeepers, and it makes a great difference whether you have all these in one place or have them distributed in several" (Plin. *Ep.* 3.19).

Latifundia: Finley pooh-poohed the famous stricture of Pliny the Elder (died 79 CE) on the rise of large estates: "*[L]atifundia perdidere Italiam vero et provincias*" ("Large estates have destroyed Italy and even the provinces") (Plin. *H.N* 18.7.35). Pliny's remark is unjustifiably dismissed by Finley (erroneously translating the perfect tense *perdidere,* short for *perdiderunt,* as present tense "are destroying") as "no more than moralizing archaism..., a lamentation for the lost Roman yeomanry and the simpler good old days" (Finley 1973, p. 202, n. 51). Yet, Pliny had clearly put his finger on a development which was ultimately to transform the whole nature of the Roman economy and society.

Cleon: One of Finley's more (unintentionally) amusing—and palpably partisan—enterprises was his spirited defense of Cleon, the Athenian demagogue who succeeded Pericles as the "champion of the people." Here, among other things, Finley omits any mention of the well-evidenced devious means employed by Cleon, notably his use of "sycophants," meaning deceitful or calumnious informers against the rich and noble, enabling Cleon to bring lawsuits to strip them of their wealth and undermine them (for more on this see Chapter 13).

Baby and Bathwater

A good example of the baby–bathwater fallacy is Fergus Millar's rejection of Sir Ronald Syme's laconic conclusion, which was based on solid prosopographical evidence of his own and other historians, like Ernst Badian, that: "In any age of the history of Republican Rome about twenty or thirty men, drawn from a dozen dominant families, hold a monopoly of office and power" (Syme 1939, p. 124). This picture of the Roman Republic as dominated by a small elite was shared by Matthias Gelzer and his school, among others. But the correct view of the Republic as a narrow oligarchy does not entitle one to conclude that *all* regimes have always been oligarchies, regardless of their façade. Syme's falling into this oligarchy trap is as surprising as it is wrong (see above).

"Drowning the Baby"

Fergus Millar was also guilty of exactly the opposite fallacy from that of throwing the baby out with the bathwater—namely, drowning the baby in an overflowing bathtub. This fallacy consists in the undue credulity of accepting weak or even non-existent evidence.

Though in a sense opposites, the two fallacies are actual correlative, or complementary, to each other. For, having thrown the baby out with the bathwater, Millar had to find a substitute for it. What he hit upon was a passage in Polybius that he misinterpreted as a description of the Roman Republic as a direct democracy: "Using 'democracy' in a strictly neutral sense, it is undeniable that the constitution of the Roman Republic was that of a direct democracy" (Millar 2002, p. 165). From a purely legalistic, constitutional point of view, the "people" would indeed appear to have held center-stage. But Millar was referring not only to the legal or constitutional position but also to political realities, as is stressed by Millar's staunch defender T.P. Wiseman: "Fergus Millar forcefully insisted on the centrality of the People's role in the political life of the republic" (Wiseman, loc 76. referring to Millar 2002, pp. 109–42). As is shown in Chapter 6, nothing could be further from the truth.

Ranke: "Wie es eigentlich gewesen ist"

It was in opposition to the idea of history as literature that Leopold von Ranke (1795–1886) famously characterized his approach to the writing of history as encapsulated in the phrase, *Wie es eigentlich gewesen ist,* normally translated as "How it actually happened," or "What actually happened." However, there is some doubt about what Ranke meant by this. A revisionist approach maintains:

> Ranke's oft-quoted dictum has generally been misunderstood in the English-speaking world as asking the historian to be satisfied with a purely factual recreation of the past. Ranke's writings make it clear that he did not mean this. In fact, the word *eigentlich,* which is the key to the phrase just quoted, has been poorly translated into English as 'really' or 'actually; 'essentially' would be a better rendition in this context. This gives the phrase an entirely different meaning, and one much more in keeping with Ranke's philosophical ideas. It is not factuality, but the emphasis on the essential that makes an account historical. 'To history has been given the function of judging the past, of instructing men for the profit of future years. The present attempt does not aspire to such a lofty undertaking. It merely wants to show how it essentially was.'—*blos zeigen, wie es eigentlich gewesen (ist)* (Iggers and von Moltke 1973/2010, pp. xix–xx).

Ranke is here drawing a contrast between history as a guide to the future and history simply as a straightforward factual account of the past—the latter being his approach. The revisionists may therefore be wrong to substitute "essentially" for "really" or "actually" in this context. But, either way, Ranke's emphasis is on the "facts" of history rather than on any "lessons" that may be drawn from them.

History as "One Damned Fact After Another"

So, is history just "one damned fact after another"?—a disparaging characterization of the orthodox Rankean approach sometimes attributed to Arnold Toynbee, whose 12-volume *A Study of History* (1934–1961) adopted a whole different philosophy of history, identifying five stages through which Toynbee claimed 19 world civilizations had passed or were passing.

This of course begs the questions: What is a historical fact? And is it possible for a historian to write purely factual history? In his well-known book, *What is History?* E.H. Carr remarks: "It used to be said that facts speak for themselves. This is, of course, untrue. The facts speak only when the historian calls on them: it is he who decides to which facts to give the floor, and in what order or context" (Carr 1961, p. 25).

Ranke himself, perhaps inadvertently, provides us with examples of this. For instance, in his six-volume *History of England Principally in the Seventeenth Century,* we read in some detail of William Penn's visit to the Hague in the summer of 1686 in a failed effort to reconcile William of Orange with his father-in-law, King James II (Ranke 1875/2018, IV 389ff). This visit is not even mentioned in Macaulay's five-volume *History of England from the Accession of James II,* covering the period 1685–1702 (Macaulay 1848). Why, then, did Ranke consider this abortive mission as a *historical fact* worth describing, and indeed highlighting? William of Orange was of course a staunch Protestant, while James II was a devout Catholic, which was one of the factors eventually resulting in his being ousted and replaced by William of Orange, reigning jointly with James's daughter, as William III and Mary II. A striking fact about James II—and treated as such by both Ranke and Macaulay—was his close friendship with William Penn, the founder of Pennsylvania, a member of the Society of Friends, or Quakers, the Christian denomination probably furthest removed from Catholicism. The king's "Declaration of Indulgence," seeking to institute a policy of religious toleration, is stigmatized as a fraud by Whig historians like Macaulay. But William Penn's evident acceptance of James's intentions as genuine must weigh in the balance—and this may possibly account for Ranke's decision to turn this otherwise insignificant and unsuccessful visit to the Hague into a *historical fact.*

Geoffrey Elton rejected Carr's distinctions between *facts* and *historical facts,* and Carr probably did make too much of this point (Elton 1967). Carr cites as a prime example the crossing of the Rubicon: "It is the historian who has decided for his own reasons that Caesar's crossing of that petty stream, the Rubicon, is a fact of history, whereas the crossing of the Rubicon by millions of other people before or since interests nobody at all" (Carr 1961, p. 27). This is not quite correct. The Rubicon marked the boundary between Italy and Cisalpine Gaul, and it was strictly forbidden for a general to enter Italy with his army. Julius Caesar's crossing of the Rubicon was recognized as a significant fact at the time, as it amounted to a declaration of war against the Roman state. Hence Caesar's remark, as reported by Suetonius, *iacta alea est* ("the die is cast") (Suet., *Jul.* 32), or "let the die be cast," supposedly loudly declared in Greek, as Plutarch would have us believe (Plut. *Pomp.* 60.2.9). The crossing of the Rubicon was a bad choice on the part of Carr, as it does not actually support his distinction between *facts* and *historical facts.* But there certainly is no shortage of examples to support his distinction—William Penn's visit to the Hague in 1686 being one.

"Cleopatra's Nose"

"If Cleopatra's nose had been shorter," opined the great French mathematician and writer Blaise Pascal, "the whole face of the world would have changed" (Pascal 1995, p. 162). This is what may be termed the accidental view of history.

Professor Sir Geoffrey Elton of Cambridge (1921–94), who championed traditional political history, went from one extreme to the other in this respect. He created a sensation in academic circles with his 1953 book *The Tudor Revolution in Government*, which sought to prove that a sea-change occurred in English history in the 1530s when medieval household government, centered on the king, was replaced by a more impersonal bureaucratic form of government. To this double whammy, consisting of the *nature* and *date* of the "revolution" in government, Elton added one more: that the architect and facilitator of this "revolution" was Henry VIII's chief minister, Thomas Cromwell, and not the king himself, who played only a minor role in it. So major was this "revolution," Elton believed, that it paved the way for England's future stability and greatness.

Before long Elton found his theory assailed from all sides, and it is no longer an icon of historical orthodoxy. For one thing, it turned out that incipient bureaucratic government could be traced back at least half a century before the 1530s. Elton's demotion of Henry VIII to a walk-on part in his own show was also plainly wrong.

Robbed of his place in the vanguard of the historical revolution, Elton went almost to the other extreme of accidental history, playing down the role of Parliament in the sixteenth and even the seventeenth century:

> Prolonged involvement with Parliament has in the end convinced me that the customary concentration on it as the center of public affairs, however traditional it may be, is entirely misleading. This is a message, it seems to me, that needs to be absorbed into the general history of England. We have been misled by the Victorians and their obedient successors who read the modern Parliament back into history; and I do not except the story of Parliament in the seventeenth century from these reservations. I now wonder whether the institution—one of the Crown's instruments of government—ever really mattered all that much in the politics of the nation, except perhaps as a stage sometimes used by the real contenders over government and policy (Elton, 1986, p. ix).

But, if Parliament was not a "real contender," then who or what was? Elton rejects as "old hat" the theories that attributed the English Civil War to either a "rising" or "declining" gentry—two favorite explanations for the English Civil War—and is equally dismissive of "Puritanism" as leading to an "irreconcilable conflict." He adds that "we are possibly ill-advised" to mistake (Sir Edward) Coke's personal battles with James I or Francis Bacon "for titanic conflicts of principle" over the common law. Professor Hugh Trevor-Roper's explanation in terms of the clash between "court" and "country" is equally curtly dismissed. Needless to say, Christopher Hill's Marxist interpretation gets short shrift, as does "a much subtler but essentially unchanged version of his earlier views concerning the bourgeois and urban revolutions against the economic and social structure of a gentry-run rural society."

Elton then rounds on the whole notion that the conflict was inevitable: "Most historians seem also convinced that there was something seriously wrong with the system of government inherited by the Stuarts: it is thought that when James I came to the throne nothing could have prevented conflicts with Parliament so serious as to call in doubt the whole survival of the structure. The Tudor constitution is considered ramshackle." "What these views have in common," opines Elton, referring to all the explanations that he has curtly rejected, "is a sense of inevitability, a feeling that so profound a disturbance as a civil war must have had roots so deep, causes so fundamental, that no analysis can be expected to discover them clearly enough. . ... The mistake is one of logic: to suppose that because the civil war happened therefore it was bound to happen, and that because the civil war gave arms and voice to rival groupings therefore rival groupings made the war inevitable." And finally: "Under James I and Charles I, says Mr Hill, the political nation "was rent by political disagreements which led to civil war". But is this strictly accurate? Assuredly, the nation was rent in those years, but in 1640 the one thing quite out of the question was a civil war. When the Long Parliament met, the gentry—the political nation—were remarkably united, and the king had no party to speak of" (Elton 2003, p. 164ff).

With this feast of negativism, Elton appears to be close to the school of thought that sees history as "just one damned fact after another." Elton is undoubtedly right to reject the assumption that just because something happened, it was bound to happen. But he is wrong to go to the other extreme and concentrate exclusively on the immediate run-up to the events in question. Could the English Civil War have been averted? Quite possibly. But that does not alter the fact that there was a history of longstanding tension and intermittent clashes between Crown and Parliament from the fourteenth century. There had always been two alternative paths ahead, leading to two opposite destinations: monarchy or oligarchy. The situation in England was by no means unique. Most states in western Europe reveal a similar clash between Crown and privileged classes. In most cases, as in France, Spain, and the German states, the Crown won—at least initially. But in England the Crown lost.

The reasons for this defeat are more immediate, but to ignore the longstanding and deep-seated forces leading to the outbreak of Civil War in the first place, as Elton does, is to substitute the historian's role as explainer and interpreter with that of narrator and storyteller.

"An Art of Writing History"

Harvard's Professor Samuel Eliot Morison (1887–1976), the author of numerous chiefly narrative histories, made a special plea for historians to pay more attention to style: "American historians, in their eagerness to present facts and their laudable concern to tell the truth, have neglected the literary aspects of their craft. They have forgotten that there is an art of writing history" (Morison 1946). But Morison's concern with literary style resulted in something of a superficial approach to historical developments and did not save him from espousing a partisan interpretation of history. In his presidential address to the American Historical Association in December 1950, he called for a history of the United States "written from a sanely conservative point of view," in reaction against what he called "the Jefferson-Jackson-F.D. Roosevelt line" (Morison 1951, pp. 272–3).

Torpedoing Torpor

History is replete with curious events and humorous anecdotes, but a forced attempt at humor on the part of a writer is likely to backfire. Here, for example, is a curious passage in Simon Schama's *A History of England* comparing Charles I (r. 1625–49) unfavorably with his father James I (r. 1603–25), and attributing James's greater success to "torpor":

> The problem with Charles Stuart was his good intentions, and the stubborn literalness with which he meant them to take effect. Conversely, in retrospect one can see quite clearly what enormous political assets his father's natural laziness and low threshold of distraction really were. (Uncannily, the same would be true of Louis XV and XVI. Benign torpor should perhaps have been on the list of recommended virtues for successful princes.) James I's tendency to leave government to others . . . was, since those others happened to be of the calibre of Robert Cecil and Francis Bacon and Lionel Cranfield, the best thing he could have done for the country. Charles I, on the other hand, was positively driven by the itch to govern. . . Just as it had for Augustus, for Constantine and, especially, for Alfred the Great, whose biography was commissioned by the king, Duty Called! (Schama 1992, loc 1092).

Is this intended to be some sort of joke? If so, it is not very funny. The point that Schama seems to be making is that "torpor" assists a monarch to become "successful," whereas conscientiousness and "the itch to govern" have the opposite effect. An amusing paradox? The only problem is that it simply has no basis. Louis XV is held up as a parallel example of "torpor" to James I, but it is not quite clear where Louis XVI fits in. Is he another example of "torpor," presumably because of his devotion to locksmithery and hunting? Or is he cited as an example of the opposite, because of his desire to be loved by his subjects? And what about Augustus, Constantine, and Alfred the Great, who, driven by the call of "duty," are presumably cited as parallels to Charles I. Yet, were they not "successful"—except perhaps for Alfred's burning of the cakes?

Here is the lowdown on these monarchs:

James I enjoyed the races and liked to lavish time and money on his favorites. But torpor? Certainly not. Robert Cecil, Francis Bacon, and Lionel Cranfield undoubtedly were able ministers, but both Bacon and Cranfield were publicly disgraced. As for James himself, his fervent belief in the divine right of kings found expression not only in his writings but also in his dealings with Parliament, which were less than harmonious and presaged Charles I's ultimately fatal clash with that body. But was James I a "successful" king, as Schama suggests? Only if escaping the fate of his mother, Mary Queen of Scots (beheaded), his son Charles I (beheaded), his grandson Charles II (in exile for 10 years), and his grandson James II (deposed) constitutes success!

Louis XV certainly liked to keep himself amused, and had no shortage of mistresses to this end, but he also understood that it was in the interests not only of the Crown but also of the ordinary people of France to keep the aristocracy in check, and his reign culminated in the complete victory achieved by his astute minister Maupeou over the *parlements*, the protagonists of the aristocratic interest.

Louis XVI on his accession senselessly gave up this hard-won victory and recalled the *parlements*, which led straight to the fateful summoning of the Estates General in 1789 and ultimately to the guillotine. Was Louis XVI an example of "torpor"? Quite possibly—but he can hardly be described as a success.

Augustus, the first Roman emperor, was without a doubt one of the most successful rulers of all time. As Schama admits, Augustus was driven by the call of duty, so it is hard to know why Schama even mentions him.

The same applies to **Constantine**, another largely successful Roman emperor who was anything but torpid.

As for **Alfred the Great**, he is the only English king to win the accolade of "the Great." Success but no torpor here!

The real point is that "successful" monarchy can be achieved only at the expense of the aristocracy, which simply cannot be done with torpor.

"Williamanmary was a Good King"

1066 And All That, published in 1930, a delightfully amusing spoof of English history as taught at the time, claimed to include "103 Good Things, 5 Bad Kings, and 2 Genuine Dates" (Sellar and Yeatman 1930). This is a parody of the highly subjective and moralizing tendency epitomized in the dominant Whig interpretation of English history, according to which King James II (r. 1685–89) was a "bad king" ousted in the "Glorious Revolution" and replaced by his daughter and son-in-law reigning jointly as William III and Mary II—converted in the parody into a composite "good king" called "Williamanmary."

On the other hand, there was a school of thought promoting objective history. A protagonist of this approach to history was Lord Acton (1834–1902), Regius Professor of Modern History at Cambridge. As prospective editor of the original *Cambridge Modern History,* Acton proclaimed that "our Waterloo must be one that satisfies French and English, German and Dutch alike; that nobody can tell, without examining the list of authors, where the Bishop of Oxford laid down the pen, and whether Fairbairn or Gasquet, Liebermann or Harrison took it up" (Acton 1906, p. 318). While enunciating the goal of objective history, Acton neglected to ask how that was to be achieved, or even whether it was feasible. As Acton himself wrote no history to speak of, except the text of a few lectures, he was unable to demonstrate how he would square his goal of objective history with the rather subjective aphorism for which he is best known—"Power tends to corrupt, and absolute power corrupts absolutely"—to which he added the even more subjective: "Great men are almost always bad men, even when they exercise influence and not authority: still more when you superadd the tendency or the certainty of corruption by authority" (Acton 1887/2011).

Sir George Clark, editor of the *New Cambridge Modern History* (1957), was not quite as ambitious as Acton, but refused to rule out objective history as an attainable goal, rejecting the view that "since all historical judgments involve persons and points of view, one is as good as another, and there is no "objective" historical truth" (Clark 1957, pp. xxiv–xxv).

The main problem with objective history is simply that historians, like everyone else, inevitably have their own predilections, tendencies, and biases, of which they may not even be aware. Many historians writing today are scrupulous in attempting to avoid overt bias of any kind, but the moment one allows oneself to characterize something or someone in history as "good" or "bad," one immediately falls prey to unconscious bias. "Democracy" is of course a particular buzzword at present. Any form of government labeled "democratic" is generally automatically considered "good," and, conversely, any government that is considered "good" is frequently labeled "democratic." Athenian "democracy" is a case in point, discussed in Chapter 13, and, more surprisingly, the Roman Republic, discussed in Chapters 1–6.

"Late Antiquity"

Despite the mockery, not unmingled with scorn, heaped by *1066 And All That* on overtly judgemental historical writing, that type of writing has surfaced with a vengeance in recent years, particularly in the area of "late antiquity." Here are a few such assertions picked almost at random:

- **"The unnerving but mercifully brief reign of Julian"** (Brown 1997a, p. 638): So, according to Brown, Julian presumably was "a bad emperor." The context makes it clear that this is simply because of Julian's paganism, and ties in with Brown's special pleading for Christianity with which his writings are shot through and through. Is this sort of language—and blatant prejudice—really befitting a work of academic history?
- **"The sheer success of the post-Constantinian state"** (ibid.): The word "sheer" turns what might otherwise have appeared to be a genuine assessment of the achievements of the regime into cheerleader hype. There is in fact no attempt at analysis here at all.
- **"No lip service paid to the widespread notion of decay"** (Brown 1997b, p. 124f): Looking back at his *World of Late Antiquity*, published in 1971, Brown opined that he had been able to write "the entire history of the religious and cultural revolution associated with the end of the ancient world without invoking an intervening catastrophe and without pausing, for a moment, to pay lip service to the widespread notion of decay" (ibid.). While limiting his claim to "religious and cultural" matters, Brown here manages to cast doubt on the very existence of any "catastrophe" or "decay."
- **"The barbarian invasions . . . brought no widespread destruction"** (Brown 2013, loc. 826): The detailed researches of Peter Heather, and other historians labeled "counter-revisionists" by some adherents of "Late Antiquity," provide us with a welcome corrective to Brown's rose-tinted view, revealing widespread "barbarian" destruction indeed in Italy, Gaul, Spain, and Africa: "Any attempt to reconstruct fifth-century events brings home just how violent the process was. In my view, it is impossible to escape the fact that the western Empire broke up because too many outside groups established themselves on its territories and expanded their holdings by warfare" (Heather 2006, p. 434ff).
- **"Correct religion was the glory of the empire"**: This is the ultimate "good/bad" judgment call. Is one religion—namely orthodox Nicene Christianity—not only "better" than all the others, but so much better that it alone is "correct," or, for "correct" read "true"? But Brown goes further: "Precisely because correct religion was the glory of the empire, it had to be imposed in a manner that reflected the overwhelming dignity of the imperial power" (Brown 1997a, p. 644). This is doubly self-contradictory. First, if

"correct religion" was the "glory of the empire," that could only have been because it suppressed all "incorrect" religions. What sort of "glory" is bigotry and persecution? This "correct religion" was so "glorious" that it "had to be imposed"! If one religion is really so much "better" than the rest, would it not attract adherents without having to be "imposed"? And, how is religion to be "imposed" on people in a way that reflects "the overwhelming dignity" of government power? There is a straight line from this to the burning at the stake of the Spanish Inquisition and of Mary Tudor of England (r. 1553–1558). But, is Brown here speaking in his own person, or simply relaying the views of people of the period? It would be hard to claim the latter, as there certainly was no agreed view on "correct religion" at the time. And the concept is just too redolent of other remarks of Brown's to be shrugged off.

- **"Awesome theologians"**—a gushing, overtly subjective characterization, with no attempt to attribute it to anyone but Brown himself (Brown 1971, p. 9).

Causation

"The historian, like any other scientist, is an animal who incessantly asks the question, Why?" (Carr 1961, p. 113). So E.H. Carr. Of course, not all historians regard themselves as scientists. In fact, the majority probably do not. And there also are historians who do not keep asking "Why?" but who belong to the "Cleopatra's nose" school of narrative historians discussed above.

But I agree with Carr that a historian *should* keep asking the question, "Why?" until it cannot be asked any more. I also agree with Neville Morley's "basic assumption that the historian's task is to explain past events, rather than simply to record them, and to understand past society in terms of the underlying structures that shaped people's lives rather than simply describing the diversity of their experiences" (Morley 2004, p. 6).

What exactly is the meaning of "causation" or "causality"? This is an important field of investigation not only in the study of history but also in science generally, medicine, philosophy, and law. Causes may be classified variously, for example as "necessary" and "sufficient" causes; or into the legal categories of proximate and remote cause, *causa causans* and *causa sine qua non*. A useful classification for historians—though rarely actually discussed by them— is the division suggested by the French historian Marc Bloch, one of the founders of the *Annales* school, into "general causes" and "exceptional causes."

As an example of this classification, one might take the English Reformation under Henry VIII (r. 1509–47). Henry was himself a staunch Catholic and the author of a theological treatise attacking Martin Luther, for which he was granted by the Pope the special title Fidei Defensor ("Defender of the Faith"). But, because his wife was unable to bear him a male heir he asked the Pope to annul the marriage, a request that was denied. So Henry cut the Gordian knot and broke with Rome, making the Church of England a Protestant Church with himself as its "Supreme Head." So, the "exceptional cause" of the English Reformation was Henry VIII's personal desire for a divorce. But that is hardly enough to explain it. One would also need to explain why the Pope refused Henry's request, which involves an analysis of international relations of the time. For Henry to have himself declared Supreme Head of the Church of England required the consent of Parliament, which opens up a whole new avenue of investigation into the relations between Crown and Parliament. And, not least, one would need to factor in an explanation of the rise of the Reformation movement that was already in full swing on the Continent and had attracted English converts independently of the king's machinations. These factors would constitute the "general causes" of the English Reformation.

And what does a historian do once answers to all the "Why?" questions have been exhausted? In other words, when your pursuit of causes, causes of causes, and causes of causes of causes finally either bears fruit or brings you up against a brick wall? The question to ask at that point is: So what? (More on that below.)

But this does not detract from the fact that some of the most enjoyable, entertaining, or informative works of history belong in the category of narrative history. Patricia Southern, for example, the author of a number of carefully researched and well-written books on Roman history, makes no greater claim than accuracy. Here is what she says in the introduction to *The Roman Empire from Severus to Constantine*: "This book attempts to document the changes in the Roman Empire between the end of the second century and the beginning of the fourth" (Southern 2001, p. xii).

A more ambitious writer is Mary Beard, who describes her *SPQR: A History of Ancient Rome,* as offering "my contribution of why it (viz. Roman history) matters" (Beard 2016, p. 16). Despite the word "why," the book is largely narrative, with very little that could be described as explanation. It certainly makes for a racy read, containing some quirky observations and emphases—like the half-serious but completely baseless claim of Pompey to be regarded as "the first emperor" of Rome (ibid., p. 273f.); and an equally groundless throw-away remark, based on a coin legend, implying that Caesar's assassin Marcus Brutus was aiming at "autocratic power" (ibid., p. 295).

It is also unhelpful to introduce Roman history to the general reader (to whom the book appears to be addressed) with a 32-page first chapter titled "Cicero's Finest Hour" focusing on the Catilinarian conspiracy of 63 BCE—by any account *not* a major event in Roman history except for Cicero, who was *not* a major player in Roman history but who owes his immortality to his loquaciousness in written form and to the longevity of his secretary, Tiro, who reputedly lived to the age of 99, and dedicated his life to editing and promoting his late master's works.

So What?

I agree with Moses Finley's disparagement of pedantic academic writings that concentrate on minor details of historical narrative, like, for example, the debate about the precise date of birth of the Emperor Diocletian (Barnes 1982, pp. 30, 46; Bowman 2005, p. 68; Williams 1997, pp. 237–8; Rees 2004, p. 86). The question that needs to be asked is: So what? What difference does it make whether he was born on December 22 (his official birthday) or any other date, and whether it was in the year 244 or some other year? This could only have any significance if, for example, he led an army to victory at the age of six, or, perhaps, if he had lived to the age of 120. But even that would be a curiosity rather than a matter of significance.

What I am concerned with, among other themes, is the relationship between causation, power structure, and ethos. But, once these issues have been analyzed, and changes explained, it is important to stand back, and throw down the challenge: So what? Why does it matter?

Conclusion: "Proper Historical Writing"

There is certainly no shortage of approaches to the writing of history. But is there such a thing as "proper historical writing?" My own criteria are as follows. I hasten to add that I do not claim that these are the *only* possible criteria for "proper historical writing":

- Pay close attention to factual accuracy, without allowing the tail to wag the dog, or, in other words, without allowing trivial factual points to overshadow more important issues.
- Do not be in too much of a hurry to dismiss evidence out of hand. If in doubt, accept evidence on the basis of probability. Otherwise you will be in danger of throwing the baby out with the bathwater, resulting in a misunderstanding or misinterpretation possibly even of a whole period. See above for some serious cases in point.
- But also do not be too uncritical of dubious sources, which can also have a serious impact on your understanding of an issue or period. See above for examples.
- There is nothing wrong with fine writing, but do not sacrifice a proper understanding of a topic or period to stylistic elegance.
- Carefully think through the conceptual framework of your study. The "oligarchy trap" is a case in point. But do not abandon a search for a conceptual frameworks on that account.

- Aim to be as objective as possible, trying to recognize and put your own preconceptions, prejudices, and beliefs to one side.
- Do not judge historical figures, institutions, or societies as either "good" or "bad," and stop well short of writing history committed to a particular political, social, or religious cause. Otherwise, what you will produce will not be history but partisanship, special pleading, and propaganda—not to mention distortion of the subject matter.
- Keep asking "Why?" until you cannot ask it any more.
- Then ask "So what?" Look back at your period, problem, or issue, and test to see whether you can gain insight from other periods or subject areas.
- If, for example, you are exploring the causes of a particular war, cast a comparative eye over other wars. The same applies to the causes of a revolution, of the rise or fall of an empire, or of an economic upturn or crisis.
- I particularly commend to you the analysis of the power relations in all societies developed by Machiavelli, as explained in Chapter 11. My own studies of very different societies over a period of five thousand years confirm my own acceptance of this model, of just two diametrically opposed power structures: monarchy and oligarchy (or aristocracy).
- As I try to illustrate in this book, there is a relationship between the power structure of a society and the liberty and equality within it, its values, its social and political ethos, and its foreign policy.

Chapter 11
Machiavelli, Historian Extraordinaire

Machiavelli's The Prince *is one of the most perceptive works of history and political science ever written, recognizing the perennial hostility in every society between the common people and the aristocracy or privileged elite. A champion of the common people against the elite is likely to become a strong monarch. Or, to put it another way, true monarchy depends on popular support against the aristocracy or privileged elite, whereas a monarch dependent on aristocratic support is not really a monarch at all but a mere cipher. These hypotheses of Machiavelli's, based on his analysis chiefly of Italian history, are remarkably similar to my own "two models of government" as developed in all my historical writings and expounded in detail in my book, actually titled* Two Models of Government, *first published in 2016.*

Thucydides (c. 460–400 BCE) confidently proclaimed that he was writing his *History of the Peloponnesian War* not just for the gratification of his contemporaries but as "a possession for all time." This boast turned out to be prophetic. Thucydides prided himself on his accuracy, which he regarded not as an end in itself but "as an aid to the interpretation of the future, which, in the nature of humankind, must resemble the past, even if it does not repeat it" (Thuc. 1.22).

Five Thousand Years of Monarchy, First Edition. Michael Arnheim.
© 2026 John Wiley & Sons, Inc. Published 2026 by John Wiley & Sons, Inc.

"Two Distinct Humors"

Thucydides had an unlikely acolyte in the shape of Niccolò Machiavelli (1469–1527), who is generally characterized as an advocate of political deceit, cunning, and duplicity rather than as a historian. But the historical analysis that he propounded in *Il Principe* ("The Prince") has stood the test of time: "In every society throughout history there has always been tension between the aristocracy and the ordinary people. The common people do not wish to be ruled or oppressed by the aristocracy, while the aristocracy wish to rule and oppress the common people." A monarch who has the support of the common people, Machiavelli contends, is likely to be a strong ruler, while one who depends on aristocratic support will prove weak, as his ostensible aristocratic supporters will be competing with him for power. The bottom line is therefore that monarchy and aristocracy are by their very nature diametrically opposed to each other.

This analysis of the power structure implicit in every state throughout the world and throughout time forms the basis for Machiavelli's frank advice to rulers—though it has been misunderstood, or completely overlooked, by most commentators, including vaunted Machiavelli "experts." But, based as it is on a hard-headed view of reality, his advice has more practical value than the empty

Figure 11 Niccolò Machiavelli.
SOURCE: Santi di Tito / Wikimedia Commons / Public domain.

flattery and affected high-minded idealism of the usual "mirrors for princes," a popular literary genre of the time.

More than that, Machiavelli's analysis unlocks a whole new dimension of historical insight into any period to which it is applied—and it is applicable to any and every time and place (see my *Senatorial Aristocracy in the Later Roman Empire,* 1972; *Aristocracy in Greek Society,* 1977; *Two Models of Government,* 2017a; and *Why Rome Fell: Decline and Fall, or Drift and Change?* 2022).

Devil or Diplomat?

The name Machiavelli has long been almost a synonym for the devil, and in modern English the word *Machiavellian* still means cunning, scheming, or unscrupulous, especially in reference to politics. Niccolò Machiavelli (1469–1527) gained this reputation from his book of advice to rulers, titled *Il Principe* ("The Prince"). Though this little treatise ostensibly belongs to the well-known genre of "mirrors for princes," self-help books addressed to new or young rulers, its content and tone are very different from other books of the same genre. Instead of proffering conventional words of wisdom and diplomatic conduct, Machiavelli provides hard-edged amoral advice based on clear-eyed historical case-studies.

Here is a key statement from chapter 9 of *The Prince,* embodying an important insight into realpolitik: "In every state two distinct tendencies (humors) are found, namely that of the common people and that of the aristocracy. The common people do not wish to be ruled or oppressed by the aristocracy, while the aristocracy wish to rule and oppress the common people" (Machiavelli 2019, chapter 9). This theme of the mutual hostility between what Machiavelli calls *li grandi* (the aristocracy, nobility or privileged elite) and *il populo* (literally "the people," referring to the rank and file of the population, or the common people) runs right through *Il Principe.* The universality of the statement is noteworthy. This hostility between the aristocracy and the common people, says Machiavelli, is found *in ogni città,* literally "in every city." The Italian word *città,* coming as it does from the Latin *civitas,* is used by Machiavelli to refer not only to the city-states into which the Italy of his day was divided but also to large states like France or Turkey, or to the Roman Empire of antiquity. Similarly, the word *principe,* or "prince," from the Latin *princeps,* is used for the ruler of any state, regardless of title or status, including kings and emperors. This usage was paralleled in sixteenth- and seventeenth-century English, as, for example, in the phrase "Put not your trust in princes," found in the 1611 King James Version translation of Psalm 146, line 3.

Machiavelli continues:

Monarchy is brought about either by the common people or by the aristocracy, according as one or the other of these parties has the opportunity. For, the aristocracy, seeing that they are unable to resist the common people, begin to escalate the reputation of one of their number and make him ruler, so that they can give vent to their ambitions under his protection. On the other hand, the people, finding themselves unable to resist the aristocracy, elevate the reputation of one man and make him ruler so as to be protected by his authority.

One who comes to power with the assistance of the aristocracy maintains himself with more difficulty than one who becomes a ruler with the assistance of the common people, because the former finds himself surrounded by many around him who consider themselves his equals, and because of this he can neither rule nor manage them to his liking.

But he who comes to power by popular favour, finds himself alone and has around him either none or very few who are not prepared to obey him....

A man who becomes ruler through popular favor, then, must keep the people well-disposed towards him. This will be easy, since they want only not to be oppressed. But a man who becomes ruler against the wishes of the people, and through the favour of the aristocracy, must above all else try to win over the people, which will be easy if he protects them....I shall affirm only that it is necessary for a ruler to have the people well disposed towards him; otherwise, in difficult times he will find himself in desperate straits (chapter 9).

Machiavelli rejects what he calls "the trite proverb that he who builds on the people builds on mud...":

A ruler who bases his power on the common people, who can command and is a man of courage undismayed in adversity and is not lacking in other preparations, and who keeps the whole citizen body inspired by his spirit and resolution, will never find himself deceived by them and it will be shown that he has laid his foundations well.... Therefore a wise ruler ought to consider a course such that his citizens will always and in every kind of circumstance have need of the state and of him, and then they will always be loyal to him (chapter 9).

...[R]ulers should worry little about being plotted against if their subjects are well disposed towards them, but if their subjects are hostile and hate them, they should be afraid of everything and everyone. Well-ordered states and wise rulers have taken care with every diligence not to exasperate the aristocracy while satisfying the people and keeping them content, for this is one of the most important tasks for a ruler to undertake (chapter 19).

I also conclude that a ruler ought to respect the aristocracy, but not so as to make himself hated by the people (chapter 19).

And again:

All recorded monarchies are found to be governed in two different ways: either: by a single ruler with a body of servants who as ministers by his grace and favour assist him to govern the kingdom; or by a single ruler and barons, who hold that rank not by the favour of the ruler but by the antiquity of their blood. Such barons have states and their own subjects, who recognize them as lords and hold them in natural affection. Those states that are governed by a ruler and his servants accord their ruler greater authority, because no one is recognized as superior to him in all his dominions; and if they obey any other they do so as to a minister or official and do not hold him in any particular affection (chapter 4).

Machiavelli's argument runs as follows:

- In every state there is hostility between the aristocracy or privileged elite and the common people.
- Both sides select a leader.
- A leader dependent on aristocratic support will prove a weak ruler.
- Such a ruler will be dependent on "barons" with their own power bases.
- The people's loyalties will then be to these "barons" rather than to the ruler.
- However, a ruler dependent on popular support will be a strong ruler.
- Such a ruler will govern through servants who are totally beholden to him, so that popular loyalty is to him alone.
- But, while nurturing popular support, a wise ruler will take care not to exasperate the aristocracy.

One type of government that is absent from Machiavelli's schema is oligarchy or aristocracy. The closest we get to this is a weak monarchy dependent on the aristocracy, but a monarchy nevertheless. The reason for this omission is not accidental. *The Prince* is a book of advice addressed to "princes," or monarchs. As Machiavelli makes clear right at the outset, it therefore deals only with "principalities," or monarchies. Republican forms of government are discussed in Machiavelli's *Discorsi,* a commentary on the first 10 books of Livy.

Although Machiavelli's examples are drawn chiefly from either contemporary Italy or classical antiquity, his theory applies to many societies throughout history. The Greek tyrants, whose heyday was the seventh and sixth centuries BCE, are good examples of strong popular monarchy, while the position of the British Crown after the "Glorious Revolution" of 1689 is that of a weak monarchy subordinate to a privileged elite represented in Parliament. The Roman Republic, on the other hand, is an exemplar of oligarchy in which power was shared by members of a privileged elite eschewing any semblance of monarchy.

Published posthumously in 1532, *Il Principe* has aroused great interest from that date to the present day, yet Machiavelli's analysis of monarchy as set out in the bullet-points above has been all but ignored. Discussion has largely focused instead on Machiavelli's personality. Was Machiavelli really as cold, calculating, and amoral as would appear to be the case from *The Prince*? Or is that book a tongue-in-cheek satire? Alternatively, was Machiavelli a republican, or even a democrat, as the *Discorsi* have sometimes been interpreted?

Sir Isaiah Berlin spent a whole essay debating these points, without apparently realizing just how irrelevant they were (Berlin 2002). The more hidden Machiavelli's personal opinions are, the more likely it is that the advice which he proffers is objective and unbiased; and the more valuable that advice then becomes.

As for Quentin Skinner, a vaunted authority on Machiavelli, I have encountered only one remotely relevant comment by him on the whole leitmotif of the hostility of people against aristocracy: "A ruler who wishes to hold on to power must ensure above all that the whole populace, nobles and ordinary citizens alike, remain respectful and content with his government." This is no doubt a sound, if bland, principle of government. It is supposedly a paraphrase of the remark of Machiavelli's, already quoted above, but taken completely out of context. Skinner continues: "Well-ordered states and wise rulers have always been very careful not to exasperate the nobles and also to satisfy the people and keep them contented; this is one of the most important things for a ruler to do" (Machiavelli 2019).

In fact, Machiavelli's actual point is very different from Skinner's insipid supposed paraphrase. What Machiavelli is talking about here is the danger of conspiracy, making the point that, while popular favor is essential for a wise ruler, he should not exasperate the aristocracy. And this harks back to the passages from Machiavelli's chapter 9, quoted earlier, about popular monarchy. It would, of course, be ideal for a ruler to be able to count on the support of all his subjects, or at least the lack of discontent among them. But this is not what Machiavelli says, because he knows just how difficult this is to achieve. That is why he couches the ruler's relationship with the two elements in quite different ways. He must "satisfy" the common people and "keep them content"—very positive demands—while just not "exasperating" the aristocracy, a purely negative desideratum. What Machiavelli has in mind here is a monarch who depends primarily on popular support, but recognizes that, in the interests of harmonious government, he should refrain from exasperating (the Italian is *desperare*) the aristocracy, meaning to avoid incensing the aristocracy so much as to spur them into resorting to desperate measures to overthrow the ruler's regime. Julius Caesar's disdainful treatment of the senatorial aristocracy is a case in point of how the aristocracy can be driven to desperation, leading to the Ides of March. Augustus represents the perfect statesmanlike antithesis to this, of a ruler dependent on popular support who went out of his way to avoid offending the aristocracy whom he had just defeated.

Machiavelli's Caveats

It is worth noting that Machiavelli (1469–1527) was writing in an Italy made up of numerous city-states, mostly dominated by oligarchies or aristocracies, whose members he refers to as *li grandi* ("the elite," "bigwigs," "fat cats"). But his caveats apply equally to anyone or any entity with enough power, authority, or influence to pose a potential threat to the power of the monarch. An elected parliament is automatically and inevitably going to pose such a threat.

Monarchical power is also quite likely to be challenged by the judiciary. By no means all monarchs have recognized just how deadly a threat to monarchical power such bodies represent. And Machiavelli sounds a special warning against a monarch's delegating too much authority to his own ministers or subordinates.

The Persian Empire

Chapter 4 of *Il Principe* is headed: "Why the Kingdom of Darius, Conquered by Alexander, Did Not Rebel Against the Successors of Alexander at His Death." Machiavelli is struck by the fact that the successors of Alexander the Great (356–323 BCE), notably the Ptolemies in Egypt and the Seleucids in Syria, took over the Persian Empire, which Alexander had conquered, and managed to rule their respective kingdoms without too much trouble for centuries (in the case of Egypt, until 30 BCE and in that of the Seleucids until 63 BCE). Machiavelli's explanation for this is in terms of the power structure inherited from the Achaemenid Persian Empire:

> I answer that the monarchies of which one has a record are found to be governed in two different ways; either by a prince, with a body of servants, who assist him to govern the kingdom as ministers by his favor and permission; or by a monarch and barons, who hold that dignity by antiquity of blood and not by the grace of the prince. Such barons have states and their own subjects, who recognize them as lords and hold them in natural affection. Those states that are governed by a monarch and his servants hold their prince in more consideration, because in all the country there is no one who is recognized as superior to him, and if they yield obedience to another they do it as to a minister and official, and they do not bear him any particular affection.

The Persian Empire, according to Machiavelli, belonged to the category of monarchies where the ministers or governors (satraps) were the king's servants without a power-base of their own. This centralization of power gave the Persian Empire great strength and made it difficult to conquer—but easy for Alexander and his successors to rule after conquest.

France and Turkey

Machiavelli then applies this hypothesis to two monarchies in his own day, namely the Ottoman Empire ("the Turk") and the kingdom of France:

> The examples of these two governments in our time are the Turk and the King of France. The entire monarchy of the Turk is governed by one lord, the others are his servants; and, dividing his kingdom into sanjaks, he sends there different administrators, and shifts and changes them as he chooses. But the King of

France is placed in the midst of an ancient body of lords, acknowledged by their own subjects, and beloved by them; they have their own prerogatives, nor can the king take these away except at his peril.

In Machiavelli's day the Ottoman Empire was in its prime, ruled by Selim I (r. 1512–20) and his son, Suleiman the Magnificent (r. 1520–66). It used to be thought that the Ottoman Empire entered a period of decline after this, which led to its being labeled "the sick man of Europe," ending with its defeat in World War I. The accepted view is now more nuanced, though the centralization of power, on which Machiavelli places great emphasis, undoubtedly did give way to a much more decentralized pattern in the eighteenth century. So, Machiavelli's equation of centralized power and strong monarchy with invincibility still holds good.

France

His analysis of the France of his day is equally perceptive. In Machiavelli's day the monarchy was already beleaguered by a powerful aristocracy, which was in the end to prove the undoing of the *ancien régime,* not by foreign conquest but through revolution fomented by the aristocratic *parlements*, equivalent to Machiavelli's *grandi* (see Chapter 17).

Part II

Accession

Chapter 12
Heredity

At the time of this writing, the concept of monarchy in the West is inextricably bound up with the idea of hereditary succession, to the extent that the niceties of the hereditary line of succession are considered a matter of great moment—even though the monarchies in question are not true monarchies at all. Britain, Sweden, Norway, Belgium, Denmark, the Netherlands, and Luxembourg are all non-monarchical monarchies. Yet all of them have in recent years gone to the trouble of changing their system of succession from male primogeniture to the more "politically correct" absolute primogeniture, meaning that, instead of giving priority to males, the eldest surviving child of the deceased monarch inherits the throne regardless of gender.

The comical way in which the Roman Emperor Claudius was plucked from obscurity and hailed as emperor is a good illustration of the natural human predilection for heredity. Thirty-three years after Waterloo, which had consigned Napoleon to ignominious exile, the name "Bonaparte" won Napoleon's nephew the presidency of France, which he used as a springboard to reinvent himself as Emperor Napoleon III. Emperor Naruhito of Japan, who ascended the Chrysanthemum Throne in 2019, can trace his direct descent back over 1,500 years. The American decision to shield his grandfather, Emperor Hirohito, from any blame over World War II while stripping him of all power, undoubtedly helped to cement Japan's alliance with the US. In a number of monarchies, including the Middle Kingdom and New Kingdom of ancient Egypt, and the Roman Empire, a monarch would elevate a son as co-regent to ensure a smooth hereditary succession. And, in the interests of achieving the same objective, in many monarchies, including England and France, the heir apparent to the throne would be given a special title, sometimes accompanied by a formal investiture ceremony. The fact that when deposed in 1688, England's James II had a male heir, styled in the conventional manner "Prince of Wales," only made Parliament all the more determined

Five Thousand Years of Monarchy, First Edition. Michael Arnheim.
© 2026 John Wiley & Sons, Inc. Published 2026 by John Wiley & Sons, Inc.

to exclude from the throne all James's Catholic progeny. Similarly, when France's Louis XVI was guillotined in 1793, his seven-year-old son and heir, previously styled "Dauphin" and, under the Constitution of 1791, accorded the new title of "Prince Royal," was not recognized by the Revolutionary Government as King Louis XVII, as the monarchy had been abolished, but was kept a prisoner until his death at the age of 10 in 1795.

"The King is dead, long live the King!" This proclamation encapsulates the whole seamless essence of hereditary succession. The deceased monarch is immediately and automatically replaced by their successor. It is a formula intended to prevent an interregnum, a disputed succession, or the fragmentation of a state. But it is not nearly as effective in achieving these objectives as is sometimes believed.

How Significant is Hereditary Succession?

What difference, if any, does the form of accession make? A commentator on Gordon Tullock's *Autocracy* offers the following suggestion: "The introduction of automatic hereditary succession in an autocracy provides stability and limits the number of coups" (Kurrild-Klitgaard 2000). This conclusion, supposedly based on a study of the Danish monarchy between 935 and 1849, is, to say the least, misleading.

It is no accident that there is a correlation between heredity and stability, and likewise between elective monarchy and instability, but correlation is not the same thing as causation. Elected monarchs generally owe their position to a small aristocratic elite—the enemy *par excellence* of strong monarchy, autocracy, and dictatorship. Owing their position to their natural enemy, elective monarchs tend to be subordinate to the aristocracy, while hereditary monarchs tend to be less shackled, especially if they also have an independent populist base of support. But this is not a hard-and-fast rule, as laws of heredity can lead to disputed successions and even wars of succession, and there has been no shortage of weak hereditary monarchs who, after growing up amongst the aristocracy, do not recognize the inherent incompatibility between the interests of the aristocracy and those of the crown.

Heredity is, so to speak, the "default" form of modern Western monarchical succession, with more advantages than disadvantages. Provided the line of succession is clear and undisputed, heredity provides instant succession without a gap or interregnum.

Popular affection and loyalty also potentially make for stability and are more likely to attach to the scion of a long line of hereditary monarchs than to an upstart, but that is not inevitable. For example, until the reign of Queen Victoria (r. 1837–1901) the British monarchy was shown little respect, and in the late eighteenth and early nineteenth centuries was mercilessly lambasted by cartoonists like James Gillray and Thomas Rowlandson. Victoria and her husband,

Prince Albert, made a determined effort to project the image of a happy and harmonious family life infused with highly moral and religious principles. Hence the reputed remark of the scandalized nineteenth-century matron after seeing a performance of Shakespeare's *Antony and Cleopatra:* "How different from the home life of our own dear Queen!"

Cain and Abel

On the other hand, heredity can also lead to contested successions or even to civil and international strife. Such conflicts go back a long way into the realms of myth and legend, as in the stories of the rivalry between Cain and Abel and that between Jacob and Esau in the Book of Genesis, and the tale of the conflict between Romulus and Remus in the founding of Rome. There is no shortage of examples of very real disputed successions throughout history, among the most notable being: Antony vs. Octavian (Augustus) as successors to Julius Caesar; the conflict between the sons of Constantine after his death in 337; the Hundred Years' War; the War of the Spanish Succession; and the War of the Austrian Succession.

Primogeniture

Jörgen Möller comments: "In this world (up to 1800) the monarch was normally a distant figure for the large majority of all men and women in society. But whether the monarch was young or old, in good health or ailing, lived or died, mattered for both the grand and mighty and for the common man. Between AD 1000 and 1800 political stability in Europe revolved around what my co-authors ... and I have termed 'the politics of succession'" (Kokkonen et al. 2022). According to that Scandinavian study, the solution to the quest for stability was found to be primogeniture, giving priority in succession to the eldest son.

My own view is that the real basis of stability is to be found, not in the rules of succession, which is a superficial and mechanistic explanation, but in the power structure of a particular society at the relevant time. The one exception is where primogeniture is coupled with co-regency. Where the incumbent monarch has his son and heir crowned as king while the father is still alive, that has tended to smooth the heir's accession to sole monarchy on the father's death.

- It was a device frequently employed in the Middle and New Kingdoms of Egypt, possibly including a co-regency between Amenhotep III and his son and successor, the later Akhenaten.

- The British coronation anthem *Zadok the Priest* celebrates Solomon's anointing as king of Israel while his father, David, was still alive, thus smoothing Solomon's accession on David's death shortly thereafter.
- In the Later Roman Empire, the title "Augustus" designated a senior emperor, while his junior emperor and heir presumptive, whether a blood relation or not, was "Caesar."
- A notorious case of the failure of co-regency occurred with the vicious Byzantine Empress Irene (750/756–803), who, after being regent for her young son Constantine VI, was made his co-regent when he reached maturity, for which favor Irene showed her gratitude by having him deposed, blinded, imprisoned, and probably killed in order to become sole ruler herself.
- Russia's Peter the Great (r. 1682–1725) owed his position to co-regency from the age of 10 with his physically and mentally infirm 16-year-old half-brother Ivan V, whose disability did not prevent him from producing five children, fortunately for Peter all girls, one of whom became Empress Anna of Russia (r. 1730–40). To his credit, Peter never tried to depose his half-brother, who, however, took no active part in government.

Primogeniture from Jacob and Esau Onward

Fixing their gaze on medieval Europe, the Scandinavian historians cited above are evidently under the impression that primogeniture arose only during the period between 1000 and 1800 CE. This is simply not the case. One need only cast one's mind back to the poignant Bible story recounting the conflict between Jacob and Esau in Genesis 27. The author made them not only brothers but indeed (non-identical, fraternal) twins, thereby sharpening their rivalry even more and intensifying the significance of primogeniture. Esau is the first-born, but he gives up his birthright to Jacob in return for the proverbial "mess of potage." When the twins' now-blind father, the patriarch Isaac, on his deathbed calls for Esau to receive his sacred blessing as first-born, Jacob obtains the blessing by deception, covering his arms in lamb skin so as to induce Isaac into thinking that Jacob was the hairy Esau.

The story of Jacob and Esau is quite likely fictitious, but it illustrates the importance of primogeniture in early Jewish society, as attested by Deuteronomy 21:15–17, which provides a similar example to that of Jacob and Esau but places it on a legal footing: "If a man have two wives, one beloved and one hated," and each bears him a son, the first-born being the son of the hated wife, the man is not allowed to favor the son of the beloved wife, "but he shall acknowledge the first-born, the son of the hated wife, by giving him a double portion of all that he hath; for he is the first-fruits of his strength, the right of the first-born is his."

This rule giving the eldest son double the inheritance of any other sons (while excluding daughters altogether) is also found in ancient Egypt (which is quite possibly where the Jews got it from), yet in even earlier times the eldest son was the sole heir (see Lippert 2013).

Male patrilineal primogeniture was the very earliest form of inheritance in China going back to the so-called Longshan culture period (3000–1900 BCE) and the period of the Three Dynasties (Xia, Shang, and Zhou), covering the period 2070 to 828 BCE. In Han Chinese tradition the eldest son has been specially privileged, becoming the head of the family or inheriting the largest share if the family split up, and also heading the family's ancestor worship.

The Scandinavian primogeniture hypothesis, as it may be termed, is wrong on two counts. First, primogeniture, and particularly patrilineal primogeniture, existed in Europe and elsewhere for many centuries before 1000 CE, and secondly, primogeniture did not create stability, but on occasion even imperiled it.

English Succession Problems

One situation where the absence of primogeniture has affected stability is where there is no agreed system of inheritance. This was the case, for example, in the "the Anarchy," a protracted conflict between Stephen and Matilda (or Maud) from 1138 to 1153 over the English throne. As the daughter and only surviving child of Henry I (r. 1100–35) Matilda may appear to have had a stronger claim than Stephen, the son of Henry's sister Adela. This destructive conflict occurred at a time when the right of a woman to be queen regnant of England was not generally accepted.

The next issue in English history was whether a male could inherit the throne through a female who was not herself entitled to occupy it. This came to a head in the so-called Hundred Years' War, the longest military conflict in European history, which rumbled on between England and France intermittently from 1337 until 1453. When Charles IV of France died in 1328 without male issue the direct line of the House of Capet, which had occupied the French throne since 987, died with him. His closest male relative was his nephew (his mother's sister's son) Edward III of England, who duly claimed the French throne. The French nobility rejected his claim on the basis of the legal principle, *Nemo dat quod non habet* ("Nobody can give what he does not have"). It was well established that no woman had the right to occupy the French throne. So how could she transmit such a right to anyone else? The throne was therefore offered to Philip of Valois, whose father, Charles, Count of Valois, was a younger brother of Philip IV of France (r. 1285–1314), Charles IV's father. So Philip VI, as he became (r. 1328–50), was a paternal first cousin to Charles IV and is counted as the founder of the House of Valois, a cadet (i.e. younger) line of the Capetian House.

Though England's Edward III first appears to have accepted Philip VI's succession, a dispute soon arose giving Edward an excuse to resuscitate his claim to the French throne, which triggered seesaw military engagements starting in 1337. Initial English victories were followed by reversals and a long dormant period, when England's Henry V (r. 1413–22) burst on the scene carrying all before him. But his premature death, followed by the unique phenomenon that was Joan of Arc, eventually enabled the French to drive the English out of France.

In the meantime a protracted internecine conflict over succession to the throne had been playing out in England. Now known as the Wars of the Roses, from the emblems of the two sides, the White Rose of York and the Red Rose of Lancaster, the conflict first manifested itself during the reign of the weak Richard II (r. 1377–99). Having come to the throne at the age of 10, he was beset by hostile powerful nobles, including family members. Most powerful among these was his paternal cousin, Henry Bolingbroke, who managed eventually to depose and imprison the king and have himself declared king as the first Lancastrian king, Henry IV (r. 1399–1413).

Thanks partly at least to Shakespeare, Henry IV's son and successor, Henry V (r. 1413–22), is now commonly regarded as a particularly successful king. His prowess in battle is indisputable, but his diplomatic skills should not be under-estimated either, not least as far as domestic disputes were concerned. But his death at the age of 35 left a nine-month-old child, Henry VI, nominally in charge of the kingdom, which turned out to be disastrous both for the country and for the boy-king himself, who, to make matters worse, was pathologically indecisive and suffered from intermittent feeblemindedness. This opened up a challenge to his throne from the Yorkists.

While Henry VI's Lancastrian claim to the throne was by male patrilineal primogeniture as a direct descendant of Edward III through Edward's eldest son, Edward the Black Prince, the Yorkist claim was inferior to it in two respects: first by being only through Edward III's *second* son, Lionel, Duke of Clarence, and then only through the female line from him. The Yorkists did also have direct male-line descent from Edward III, but that was only through a much younger son of his, Edmund Duke of York.

So the Lancastrian line had the stronger claim—at least in the person of Henry VI. But his death (in captivity) and that of his only son (supposedly in battle), both in 1471, left the Lancastrian standard in the hands of a much more remote relative, who would become King Henry VII on defeating and killing the Yorkist Richard III in the Battle of Bosworth Field in 1485, which finally put paid to the Wars of the Roses.

Primogeniture was not in issue in this bloody war, which took a toll of the flower (no pun intended!) of the English aristocracy. It was agreed on all hands that, though females could not themselves occupy the English throne, a claim to the throne could be made through them by their male heirs. This left the sword as the only way to settle the dispute, which would probably not have arisen at all had Henry VI shown the same strength of character as his father, Henry V. As a result of his vacillations and mental instability he became an easy target. The Wars of the Roses was a military game of chequers, with Henry deposed by the Yorkist Edward IV in 1461, imprisoned in the Tower of London in 1465, restored to the throne in 1470, and finally imprisoned again and probably murdered in 1471.

Allegations of illegitimacy now became the weapon of choice in disputed successions. On Edward IV's death in 1483 the throne passed automatically to his 12-year-old son under the title of Edward V. But before the boy-king could be crowned, the deceased king's brother Richard quickly had both Edward V and his nine-year-old brother declared illegitimate and, as their closest relative, ascended the throne himself as Richard III. The two boys, known to history as "the Princes in the Tower," were probably subsequently murdered.

The question of legitimacy reared its head again after the feverish quest for a male heir by Henry VIII (r. 1485–1509). After the birth of his son in 1537, who would succeed him as Edward VI, Henry proceeded to have both his daughters (Mary, b. 1516, and Elizabeth, b. 1533) declared illegitimate—while still naming them in the line of succession to the throne after Edward and his putative heirs.

But there still seems to have been some doubt about whether females could inherit the throne. As a zealous Protestant, the young King Edward VI (1547–53) tried his best to block the succession of his fanatically Catholic half-sister Mary. But the attempt to place Lady Jane Grey on the throne fizzled out within a few days.

In the event, on Edward's death at the age of 15, Mary swept into London on a wave of public support. She initially issued a proclamation of religious toleration but within a few months she became transformed into the "Bloody Mary" of the history books, having at least 280 Protestants burnt at the stake.

Mary's marriage in 1554 to Prince Philip (the future King Philip II) of Spain, is the only case in English history of a royal husband ever being recognized as king *jure uxore* ("by right of his wife"). As if to emphasize their equal status, the coins of Philip and Mary show them facing each other, and all official documents, including Acts of Parliament passed during their joint reign, are in both names, with Philip's first (e.g. "In the third year of the reign of Philip and Mary"). However, unlike in the more usual arrangements of this kind found on the Continent, it was stipulated that Philip's position as King of England would end on Mary's death.

The closest case to the Philip–Mary co-rule was the joint monarchy of William III and Mary II established in the wake of the so-called "Glorious Revolution" of 1688/89 (see Chapter 14).

The Jacobite risings only go to show how wrong it is to place undue emphasis on primogeniture as the basis for stability. There had been some early attempts to allege that James II's son, James the Old Pretender, was illegitimate, but the broad opposition to his claim to the throne was not based on such imputations. It was widely, if tacitly, admitted that in terms of blood and the rules of primogeniture the Stuarts had a superior claim to the throne than the incumbent Hanoverians. The reason for the overwhelming rejection of the Jacobites was rather the opposition by the ruling classes to Catholicism and to anything smacking of monarchical "absolutism," as James II was believed to have attempted to impose and which the Young Pretender actually promised to introduce, which would of course greatly have reduced the power of Parliament. In other words, the key to this conflict over the succession was really simply competition for power. The elite had won power in 1689 and were not going to give it up without a struggle.

When George Louis, Elector of Hanover, succeeded to the British throne in 1714 he retained the throne of Hanover. There was then a "personal union" or "union of crowns" between Britain and Hanover, which continued until the death of William IV in 1837.

But when Queen Victoria succeeded William IV, she ascended the British throne, while the throne of Hanover went to her uncle, the Duke of Cumberland, because succession to the throne of Hanover was governed by the so-called Salic Law, or, to be precise, the semi-Salic Law, under which women were debarred.

In Britain there was male primogeniture, meaning that the eldest son of the deceased king was first in line of succession. Females could succeed, but only if there were no eligible males ahead of them. George III (r. 1760–1820) was succeeded by his eldest son, George IV (who was Prince Regent at the time). George IV had a daughter, who would have succeeded him had she not predeceased him without any children of her own. So the crown went to George III's next son, William IV, who also had no (legitimate) heir. George III's fourth son, Edward Duke of Kent, would then have acceded to the throne except for the fact that he was already dead, so the crown went to his only child, Victoria.

European Wars of Succession

An analysis of the European wars of succession points to the same conclusion as for Britain: it is not the rules of succession but the struggle for power that really matters.

War of the Spanish Succession

Urraca "the Reckless" of Castile and Leon (r. 1109–26) is thought to have been the first queen regnant in European history. Because of the novelty of her position, she was forced to marry Alfonso I of Aragon, who became co-ruler and king regnant in her domains while she only became queen consort in his. The marriage was extremely unhappy from the start and was annulled by the Church because the couple were first cousins.

There were seven other queens regnant in one or other Spanish kingdom until the accession of Isabella I "the Catholic" to the thrones of Castile and Leon (r. 1474–1504). On her marriage to Ferdinand of Aragon in 1475 he became co-ruler and king regnant (*jure uxoris*) of Castile and Leon while Isabella only became queen consort of Aragon. Ferdinand and Isabella, the "Catholic Monarchs," were thought of even in their own time as rulers of Spain, though there was no such legal entity until 1701. Thanks to the skilful Habsburg marriage politics devised by the Emperor Maximilian I (r. 1508–19), who married his son Philip I "the Fair" to the Catholic Monarchs' daughter Joanna "the Mad," Spain fell into the Habsburg column with the succession to all the Spanish kingdoms by Philip and Joanna's son, Charles I of Spain, the future Emperor Charles V of the Holy Roman Empire (King of Spain, r. 1516–56; Emperor, Holy Roman Empire, r. 1519–56).

Figure 12 Maria Theresa with her family, 1754.
SOURCE: Martin van Meytens / Wikimedia Commons / Public domain.

Habsburg fertility ensured direct patrilineal succession until the reign of the childless Charles II (r. 1665–1700). In his will Charles named as his heir his French nephew Philip of Anjou (grandson of Louis XIV of France and his first wife Maria Theresa, Charles's half-sister), who was probably his closest male relative, though there was a rival claim made by the Habsburg Archduke Charles of Austria, the future Emperor Charles VI.

Louis XIV lost no time in claiming the Spanish throne for his grandson. Charles II died on 1 November 1700. On 9 November the Spanish ambassador formally offered the throne to the French prince. On 16 November 1700, sweeping down a grand staircase at Versailles with his 16-year-old grandson on his arm, Louis XIV proudly announced to an assembly of ambassadors and dignitaries: *"Seigneurs, voici le roi d'Espagne"* ("Gentlemen, behold the King of Spain.")

Louis XIV's diplomatic advantage was soon lost by registering with the Parlement of Paris his grandson's claim to the *French* throne—raising the possibility of a union between France and Spain at some time in the future. This prospect so alarmed the so-called "Grand Alliance" led by Austria, Britain, and the Dutch Republic as to spark off the War of the Spanish Succession, which lasted from 1701 to 1714.

The outcome confirmed Louis XIV's grandson as king of Spain under the title of Philip V—subject to his renunciation of any right to the French throne for himself or any of his descendants. Had this limitation been accepted at the outset, there would probably never have been a War of the Spanish Succession. With this restriction in place, France did not really benefit from the presence of a Bourbon king next door. And, with a few interruptions along the way, the Spanish Bourbons would outlast their French cousins and retain their throne to the time of this writing.

Probably the biggest, though least recognized, beneficiaries of this bloody war (costing about 400,000 killed in combat on both sides) were the pirates. With many of the sailors enlisted in the navies of the warring powers now unemployed, they became pirates, contributing to the so-called "Golden Age of Piracy."

This war was probably even more senseless than most.

> *Now tell us all about the war,*
> *And what they fought each other for.*

These lines occur in a 1796 poem by Robert Southey, titled "After Blenheim". The Battle of Blenheim, fought in 1704, was a major battle in the War. Two little children ask their grandfather, Kaspar, living on the site of the battle, what it was all about. Kaspar has no idea, other than the meaningless "'twas a famous victory," which is the refrain at the end of each verse.

> *"It was the English," Kaspar cried,*
> *"Who put the French to rout;*
> *But what they fought each other for,*
> *I could not well make out,*
> *But everybody said," quoth he,*
> *"That 'twas a famous victory."*

War of Austrian Succession

The War of the Austrian Succession (1740–48) was triggered by the death in 1740 of Emperor Charles VI of the Holy Roman Empire without any male heirs. In 1713 Charles had issued an edict known as the Pragmatic Sanction to break the Salic Law in force up to that time which excluded women from the throne. As there were no male heirs at the time, the choice was between the daughters of Charles VI's older brother, the Emperor Joseph I (r. 1705–11), and Charles's own (as yet unborn) daughters. The Pragmatic Sanction gave priority to Charles's eldest daughter, Maria Theresa, who would be born in 1717, superseding the so-called Mutual Pact of Succession of 1703, which had given priority to Joseph's two daughters.

The Pragmatic Sanction applied only to the Habsburg *Erblande,* or (hereditary lands), or, more widely, the Habsburg monarchy, including Austria, Bohemia, Croatia, the Austrian Netherlands, the Kingdom of Naples and also Hungary, but not the imperial throne, which was elective and restricted to males.

Charles VI died on 20 October 1740, and on that very day Maria Theresa became ruler in her own right of the various component parts of the Habsburg monarchy. Joseph I's daughters opposed this as contrary to the 1704 pact and were supported by France and Prussia, triggering the War of the Austrian Succession. They were too late to stop Maria Theresa from gaining control of the Habsburg monarchy, but they did manage to get the one daughter's Bavarian husband elected to the imperial throne as Charles VII (r. 1742–45), after whose death Maria Theresa engineered the election of her own husband, Francis of Lorraine, as Emperor Francis I (r. 1745–65). Though known to history as an empress, Maria Theresa held that title only as a consort. By this time, however, the Holy Roman Empire was, as described by Voltaire, neither holy, nor Roman nor an Empire. And the position of emperor was largely nominal. Real power lay in ruling the individual member states, and Maria Theresa exercised that power herself over the territories making up the Habsburg monarchy, with only a "co-regency" accorded to her husband.

Sweden: Quirky Succession

A particularly strange example comes from Scandinavia itself. Sweden switched from elective to hereditary monarchy in 1544. Unlike his contemporary, Louis XVI of France, King Gustav III of Sweden (r. 1771–92) recognized the pernicious nature of aristocratic power concentrated in the Riksdag of the Estates (Parliament) and instituted what is sometimes misleadingly termed a "self-coup" or "auto-coup." In 1772 Gustav III summoned the Stockholm garrison and arrested the members of the so-called "Council of the Realm," which had effectively had supreme executive power for the previous half-century. The king made a tour of Stockholm and was widely received by enthusiastic crowds hailing him as a savior. Two days later the king convened the Riksdag and delivered a famous speech in which he attacked what he called what had become "an unbearable aristocratic despotism." He then put forward a new constitution that he had drawn up, which was unanimously adopted. This new "Instrument of Government," augmented by the 1789 Act of Union and Security, greatly increased the power of the Crown over that of the Riksdag, abolished most noble privileges, threw all public offices open to all (males) regardless of rank, and gave all citizens the right to petition the king directly. Gustav also extended freedom of religion to Roman Catholics and Jews. The popularity of this new "enlightened despotism" is indicated by the fact that three of the four "estates" represented in the Riksdag (clergy, burghers, and peasants) voted in favor of it, with only the nobility predictably voting against. Gustav implemented the new constitution with gusto, attacking corruption to the point where he put a whole supreme court of justice on trial.

Although Gustav III's attack on the aristocracy was exactly the opposite of the position adopted by Louis XVI, he took a leading role in putting together a military alliance of European rulers to crush the French Revolution and restore the imprisoned French king.

The Swedish aristocracy nevertheless remained implacably opposed to him and took the opportunity to launch a conspiracy against him, in which he was fatally shot in the back at a masked ball in 1792, leaving a 13-year-old son, known as Gustav IV Adolf, as his successor. For four years the assassinated king's brother Carl acted as regent, after which the young king pursued an active but disastrous foreign policy, leading to the loss of Finland to Russia. In 1809 an aristocratic conspiracy staged a coup in which the king was arrested and forced to abdicate, which he did in the hope of securing the throne for his son. But the Riksdag called by the conspirators declared not only Gustav IV Adolf deposed but also all his descendants. The king, who died in 1837, spent the rest of his life in an impoverished and miserable exile in Switzerland.

Meanwhile the Riksdag offered the throne to the king's uncle, his erstwhile regent, who ascended the throne as Carl (Charles) XIII (r. 1809–18) and immediately accepted a new "liberal" (i.e. anti-monarchical) constitution.

As Carl XIII was prematurely senile, infirm and childless, the French Emperor Napoleon was approached to recommend an heir, and he eventually reluctantly endorsed one of his marshals, Jean-Baptiste Bernadotte, whose wife, Désirée Clary, had once been engaged to Napoleon and had a sister married to Napoleon's brother Joseph. Bernadotte was duly adopted by Carl XIII.

Adoption is still recognized as equivalent to biological succession but, compared to Roman times, is seldom used—possibly because fertility is less of a problem among the royal houses of today than among Roman emperors. Sweden provides us with the best-known case of adoption in modern times. Though Napoleon's recommendation was acted upon, Bernadotte's wife, Désirée, detested anything to do with Sweden and never managed to learn the language. Bernadotte became King Carl XIV John of Sweden (r. 1818–44).

But why was there a need for adoption in the first place? Carl XIII was childless, but he only became king because of the deposition in a military coup of his nephew and predecessor, Gustav IV Adolf, who not only outlived him but also had a son, who was excluded from the throne as well. Gustav IV Adolf's daughter, Princess Sofia Wilhelmina, married Grand Duke Leopold of Baden and their granddaughter Victoria of Baden married the (Bernadotte) King Gustav V of Sweden (r. 1907–50), whose great-grandson is the present king of Sweden, Carl XVI Gustaf, who ascended the throne in 1973. So, ironically, adoption and biology eventually converged.

Sweden has outdone most other monarchies in clipping its monarch's wings. Not only has the king lost any say in the selection of the prime minister, but he is not even involved in the prime minister's formal appointment. There is nothing like the British virtual "kissing of hands." And not only has the Swedish monarch lost the power to veto legislation: bills passed by the Riksdag (Parliament) do not even require formal royal assent to become law.

In 1980 Sweden became the first country to adopt the principle of absolute primogeniture, meaning that the eldest child of the reigning monarch succeeds to the throne regardless of gender. Under this law the existing Crown Prince, Carl Philip, was replaced as heir apparent by his elder sister Victoria. King Carl Gustaf himself objected to the cruelty with which the title of Crown Prince, which Carl Philip had had from birth, was wrenched from him.

The Bernadotte Paradox

From the moment of his arrival in Sweden in 1810, Bernadotte took charge, becoming, first, regent to the decrepit Carl XIII and then succeeding him as Carl XIV Johan in 1818 and reigning until his own death in 1844.

There are a number of paradoxes surrounding Bernadotte. First, though he owed his elevation to kingship to his connection with Napoleon, he soon steered Sweden into an anti-French foreign policy, which also gave him the windfall of the throne of Norway (which had been under Danish control between 1397 and 1814!). Secondly, though invited to Sweden by those who had opposed royal power under Gustav III and Gustav IV Adolf, he himself came to adopt a more autocratic stance. Thirdly, the existence of primogeniture did not prevent the assassination of one king, Gustav III, and the violent deposition of his son, Gustav IV Adolf and all his descendants, and their replacement by someone who was not only not royal but who had no connection with Sweden whatsoever.

The key factor in this saga is therefore not primogeniture, which is simply a plaything in the hands of those controlling the levers of political power, but rather the power structure at any given time. Gustav III recognized that the ordinary people of Sweden and himself as king had a common enemy in the aristocracy, and he set himself the task of destroying their power base, the Riksdag. But he failed, and the fact that he had an undisputed male heir, his son Gustav IV Adolf, did not deter the aristocracy from destroying him also, albeit not by assassination but by deposition and exclusion of his line from the throne forever.

"Something is Rotten in the State of Denmark?"

Until 1665 the Danish throne was elective in theory but hereditary in practice. Particularly between 1282 and 1665 the power of the Crown was restricted by a "Coronation Charter." So, to compare the period before 1665 with that after 1665 on the basis of heredity is unhelpful, because in that respect there was practically no difference between the two periods. Our focus should rather be on the power structure.

The Danish monarchy probably dates back at least to the eighth century, with the earliest historically authenticated Danish king being Gorm "the Old" (r. c. 936–958). Originally elective but in practice hereditary by male primogeniture with the election of the eldest son of the deceased monarch, from the time of Frederik III (r. 1648–70) the Danish throne became hereditary in theory as well as practice. Frederik X, the current king of Denmark, can trace his descent back more than a thousand years (with a few twists and turns) to Gorm "the Old." It was during the reign of Gorm's son and successor, Harald "Bluetooth" (r. c. 958–86), that Denmark was Christianized, which may have assisted the king to establish a more centralized administration. But the introduction of the feudal system by Valdemar II (r. 1202–41), who gave land to members of the nobility in return for military service, only increased the power of the aristocracy at the expense of the crown and also deprived free peasants of the traditional rights and privileges that they had enjoyed for hundreds of years. Clashes with the Papacy, known as the "archiepiscopal conflicts," reduced royal power still further, giving the aristocracy the opportunity to impose a document known as the *Haandfaestning* ("Hand binding") on all Danish kings starting in 1282 and becoming a regular "Coronation Charter" administered as an oath at the coronation of every king from 1320 onward. This oath amounted to a complete capitulation of the king to the aristocracy. The king had to swear to co-operate with the aristocracy and reserve to them all ministerial posts and senior positions in local administration, and even to allow the aristocracy the say-so on questions of war and peace.

On the death of Christian IV after the longest reign in Scandinavian history (1588–1648), his son and successor Fredrik III found himself excluded from the negotiations leading to the Peace of Westphalia that brought the Thirty Years' War to an end, under which Denmark had to cede some territory to Sweden. Even Frederik's election as king in 1648 was blocked by the aristocratically controlled *Rigsraad* (Council of State) until he had made certain concessions to the aristocracy. Successfully repulsing a Swedish assault on Copenhagen in 1658/59, which brought Frederik great popular acclaim, enabled him to enhance royal power at the expense of the aristocracy. In this major political coup the king was ably assisted by Hans Nansen, the populist and pro-royal burgomaster of Copenhagen. Originally elected with the enthusiastic support of Christian IV in 1644, Nansen induced the burgesses of Copenhagen to accede to Frederik III's proposal to make the monarchy purely hereditary, to eliminate all aristocratic privileges, and to allow the middle classes access to all offices and dignities. Armed with this, Frederik was able to have the *Haandfaestning* of 1282 finally set aside and replaced by the so-called *Lex Regia* ("King's Law"), which established what, according to Danish Professor Jens Chr. V. Johanssen, "may be considered the most absolute of all the absolute European monarchies" and, which indeed, was the only formal constitution of any absolute monarchy. The law provided that the king was to be "the supreme head of and judge of the people" and independent of all laws other than the King's Law itself and respect for the rights of property. It was treason for anyone to suggest a change in the law.

After almost two centuries the system established under the King's Law was replaced in 1849 by a typical "liberal" constitution, which was slightly amended in 1953. The monarch remains the nominal head of state but has no more than a ceremonial role. The Danish constitutional website is quite frank: "Although the King is Sovereign, he has no independent power" (ch. 1.01). By "sovereign" is meant nominal head of state:

The King and Parliament jointly have the power to legislate. However, this is not quite the case in reality. In practice, the Government and Parliament define acts. The King only signs them. The King has to implement the Acts—he has the executive power. Today, this simply means that he only formally appoints the Ministers of a Government. In practice, it is the Ministers and their Ministries that subsequently make sure the laws are complied with (ch 1.03).

The King has no real influence on who will be Minister or who will be dismissed. The King appoints the Ministers recommended by the Prime Minister... The person in question may never have a majority against him or her. The King then appoints that person to be the new Prime Minister. The King must sign all Acts and important resolutions passed by the Government. However, the Acts and resolutions are valid only when one or more Ministers have also signed them (ch 3.14).

However:

The King can have Bills and proposals for other resolutions submitted to Parliament (ch. 3.21).

A Bill passed by Parliament has legal force when it is affirmed by the King no later than 30 days after it has been passed (ch. 22).

A Sovereign has not refused to sign a Bill since 1865. The Constitutional Act is interpreted today in such a way that the Sovereign is not entitled to refuse to sign.

Frederik III of Denmark stands in marked contrast to Louis XVI of France (r. 1774–92). While Frederik, working with Hans Nansen, identified himself with the interests of the middle and lower classes against the aristocracy and established a form of popular monarchy, Louis XVI ignored the advice of Mirabeau to place himself at the head of the Revolution rather than opposing it. Instead, in the hope of joining the anti-revolutionary and indeed anti-French forces launched by Austria, he fled to the frontier, from which he was ignominiously dragged back to Paris a prisoner in his own realm and was soon deposed and executed. Frederik III, by contrast, established a genuinely popular monarchy, as illustrated, for example, by the motto adopted by Christian VI (r. 1730–46): *Deo et populo* ("for God and the people"). The Struensee "coup" of 1770–72 is easy to misunderstand, when Johann Friedrich Struensee, the German personal physician to the mentally unstable Christian VII (r. 1766–1808), took virtual sole control of the government and introduced sweeping populist reforms, including abolition of noble privileges, abolition of the *corvée* (forced labor), abolition of press censorship, grants of farmland to peasants, and the introduction of state-owned grain storage. The problem with Struensee, who was hanged for his pains, was not so much his reforms as his arrogant attitude, the fact that he never learned to speak Danish, his alleged affair with the queen, and his apparent disrespect of the popular king, who, however, later wrote of the executed Struensee and his sidekick Brandt: *"Ich hätte gern beide gerettet"* ("I would fain have saved them both") (Lagen 2008, p. 450ff). This view of the Struensee reforms is confirmed by the fact that a similar reform program was instituted by Christian VII's son and successor, Frederik VI, as regent to his father (1784–1808), including the abolition of serfdom, the abolition of hanging and the abolition of the slave trade, though he adopted a more autocratic stance as king (r. 1808–39).

What then was it that eventually brought Frederik III's enlightened despotism to an end in 1849? King Frederik VII (r. 1848–63) evidently shared the same populist mindset as Frederik III and Frederik VI, as indicated by the motto he adopted on accession: *Folkets Kærlighed, min Styrke* ("The People's Love, my Strength"). The replacement of the 1665 "Royal Law" with a "liberal" constitution in 1849 was not a rejection by Danes of the 1665 regime but was really the result of the impact of the so-called Schleswig-Holstein question on Danish domestic affairs. Schleswig, Holstein, and Lauenburg were duchies under the Danish crown that were administered separately from Denmark proper. From 1815 Holstein and Lauenburg were part of the German Confederation, while Schleswig despite its German majority, was more closely tied to Denmark. The German majority in Schleswig wanted that duchy also to join the German Confederation. In 1848 King Frederik VII proposed integrating the administration of Schleswig into that of the rest of Denmark, which led to an uprising by the duchy's German population, demanding independence from Denmark and membership of the German Confederation. Frederik's rejection of this ultimatum sparked off the so-called First Schleswig War and also spurred the Danish king into authorising the drafting of a typical "liberal" constitution along the lines of the Norwegian Constitution of 1814 and that of Belgium of 1831. The importance of the Schleswig-Holstein question to Denmark can be seen from the fact that the loss of the duchies in 1864 reduced the physical size of the Kingdom of Denmark by 40%.

Chapter 13
Election

Monarchy is most closely associated with hereditary succession. But this can be misleading. As was shown in Chapter 1, most modern European hereditary "monarchies" are not real monarchies at all, and conversely, a number of elected heads of state or heads of government of "republics" are actual monarchs in disguise. In some cases the elections concerned are rigged, and in many others what began as an elective system morphed into hereditary succession. Less commonly, a leader who came to power by violent means has continued as the head of a political party seeking the voters' approval in elections, the genuineness of which, however, may be open to suspicion. Or, ironically, a leader generally believed to have seized power turns out to have come to power by election, albeit against a backdrop of violence.

"In Name a Democracy..."

There is no society in history that attracts more adulation among modern writers than Athenian "democracy." Athens is still fêted as the mother of modern democracy, but upon closer scrutiny the democratic credentials of Athenian democracy quickly unravel. The key feature of Athenian democracy is that it was a "direct democracy," in which all citizens were entitled to attend sessions of the *ekklēsia* (assembly). Yet the ancient sources, including the great philosopher Aristotle (384–322 BCE), lump popular Athenian leaders together with tyrants as "champions of the people." This use by Aristotle of the same designation for tyrants and democratic leaders alike is extremely significant. What it appears to mean is that Aristotle recognized that the power structure of Athenian democracy was essentially the same as that of tyranny. In the famous Funeral Oration

Figure 13 Pericles.
SOURCE: Copy of Kresilas / Wikimedia Commons / Public domain.

in praise of Athens, Pericles (according to Thucydides) makes the interesting observation that the Athenian form of government "is known as a democracy because it is administered not *in the interests of* the few but in the interests of the many" (*dia to mē es oligous all' es pleionas oikein dēmokratia keklētai*)—government therefore not *by* the many but only in the interests of the many (Thuc. 2.37). Did Pericles really say this? Though Thucydides does not claim that he was quoting the speech verbatim, A.B. Bosworth is probably justified in describing the Funeral Oration in Thucydides as a "potent distillation of the speech Pericles actually delivered" (Bosworth 2000, p. 16). To cap this important observation, we have Thucydides' own famous description of Periclean Athens: "In name a democracy, it became in fact rule by the first citizen" (Thuc. 2.65; see Chapter 13).

Populist Generals

Selection by lot was the hallmark of Athenian democracy—election being considered a feature of oligarchical government because it played into the hands of aristocratic factions. Yet the most important office in the state remained elective. This was the position of *stratēgos*, or general. There were 10 *stratēgoi*, elected for a year at a time but with no restriction on the number of times they could be re-elected—unlike the huge number of officials chosen by lot, who could serve only a single one-year term. Not surprisingly, the "champions of the people" tended to be elected as generals. Pericles is, of course, the best-known of these to be elected a general, but Themistocles, Ephialtes, and Cleon were also elected to that position at one time or another.

In 461 BCE, Ephialtes, the father of "radical democracy," was assassinated after meeting with strong opposition from Cimon, the leader of the aristocratic party. Ephialtes was succeeded as "champion of the people" by Pericles (c. 495–429 BCE), a member of the noble Alcmaeonid family on his mother's side, who was elected as a general 15 times between 445 BCE and his death from the plague in 429 BCE. Pericles' pre-eminence in Athenian politics lasted from at least 461 until 429 BCE and was marked by the implementation of an ambitious Program favorable to the masses.

Who Had the Whip Hand?

The central question is: Who had the whip hand in fifth-century Athens—the masses in the assembly or their demagogic leaders? Thucydides gave his assessment of Pericles in these words:

> [Pericles], deriving authority from his capacity and acknowledged worth, being also a man of transparent integrity, was able to control the multitude in a free spirit; he led them rather than was led by them; for, not seeking power by dishonest arts, he had no need to say pleasant things, but, on the strength of his own high character, could venture to oppose and even to anger them. When he saw them unseasonably elated and arrogant, his words humbled and awed them; and, when they were depressed by groundless fears, he sought to reanimate their confidence (Thuc. 2.65).

The historian, a younger contemporary of Pericles', clearly was a great admirer of his, and his description of Pericles as actually "ruling" a supposed democracy is not meant as criticism. The biographer Plutarch (45–120 CE), writing in Roman times, cites some examples of attacks on Pericles as a "tyrant," but makes it clear that what underlay both these gibes and Thucydides' favorable judgment was a common truth, namely that Pericles really did rule the roost:

> He made the city, great as it was when he took it, the greatest and richest of all cities, and grew to be superior in power to kings and tyrants. Of his power there can be no doubt, since Thucydides gives so clear an exposition of it, and the comic poets unwittingly reveal it in their malicious gibes, calling him and his associates "new Peisistratidae" [that is "sons of Peisistratus," i.e. tyrants] and urging him to take a solemn oath not to make himself a tyrant, on the plea that his pre-eminence was incommensurate with a democracy and too oppressive. Telecleides says that the Athenians had handed over to him lock, stock

and barrel. And this was not the fruit of a golden moment, nor the culminating popularity of an administration that bloomed but for a season; no, rather he stood first for forty years among such men as Ephialtes, Leocrates, Myronides, Cimon, Tolmides and Thucydides (Plut., *Pericles*, 16.5).

Pericles and the Aristocracy

A modern writer has mistakenly suggested that because Pericles was of aristocratic birth he must have engaged in politics as a member of an aristocratic elite: "The political machine of Pericles in fact drew from all elements of Athenian society, but predominantly from those very *chrēstoi* in whom we are supposed to see a party of the opposition" (Frost, 1964). This is incorrect for at least three reasons.

First, to speak of organized "parties" in ancient Athens is anachronistic and misleading. But, more important, it is plainly wrong to see Pericles as relying for his support on members of his own class, the *chrēstoi* (literally, "the good," i.e. the aristocracy). On the contrary, he was an anti-aristocratic aristocrat and a "champion of the people," as we know from Thucydides, Plutarch, and other ancient sources. Plutarch significantly tells us that Pericles refused all invitations to dinner and turned down all hospitality "so that in the long time that he was engaged in politics he did not go to a single one of his friends for dinner, except that, when his cousin Euryptolemus got married he stayed until the libations were poured and then immediately got up and left" (ibid., p. 7.4). In other words, Pericles deliberately eschewed the company of his own class. How convincing a champion of the poor would he have been if he was seen hobnobbing with the rich and noble, eating their food and quaffing their wine? We can draw a parallel with his successor Cleon's dramatic renunciation of his friendships. The anti-aristocratic aristocrat or anti-wealthy millionaire is still with us today in the shape of the Roosevelts and the Kennedys, not to mention Donald Trump.

Secondly, the fact that the "champions of the people" in the Athenian democracy included aristocrats like Pericles should not be dismissed with the remark that "the Athenian people were rather snobbish in their choice of leaders" (Jones 1957, p. 49). The question is: Why was this the case? The answer is that, though the regime was anti-aristocratic, the whole ethos of society remained aristocratic: the Athenian democracy—in common with ancient society in general—simply did not believe in equality (see Arnheim 1977, p. 158ff).

Thirdly, it is a fallacy to think of the dominant minority in any society as monolithic. Besides maverick members of the privileged minority who identify with the interests of "the many," there will always be factions and fissures within any dominant minority. In seventeenth-century England, for example, the propertied classes, which alone were represented in Parliament, were divided into those supporting the Crown and those wishing to subject the monarch to Parliament. A bloody civil war, followed by the execution of one king and, 50 years later, by the deposition of another, decided the matter in favor of parliamentary power (for more on this, see below).

The history of the United States provides further examples of this. Populist presidents like Thomas Jefferson (1801–09), Andrew Jackson (1829–37), Theodore Roosevelt (1901–09), Franklin D. Roosevelt (1933–45), Ronald Reagan (1981–89), and Donald Trump (2017–21 and 2025-) all combined support from disaffected anti-elite elements of the population with the backing of portions of the elites themselves (see Osnos, 2020).

Beneath the Surface of the Athenian Democracy

The comfortable, gentlemanly idea of "government by discussion" applied to fifth-century Athens by some of its adulators like A.W. Gomme and Moses Finley is totally misleading, especially in the period after the death of Pericles in 429 BCE. We must now explore what lies beneath the surface of that government. It will be found that the policies adopted by Athens in the latter half of the fifth century BCE had very little to do with the cut and thrust of debate in the assembly but a lot to do with certain underlying factors, including populism, charismatic leadership, and crowd psychology, aided by manipulation of the judicial system and bully-boy tactics.

Thucydides's respect and admiration for Pericles did not extend to Pericles's successors as "champions of the people" (*prostatai tou dēmou*). Cleon, who became the chief champion of the people after Pericles's death by plague in 429 BCE, was a charismatic leader with a booming voice, who knew how to whip up the passions of the Athenian masses. He increased the pay for service on the massive political juries favored by the Athenians, which, to prevent bribery, were made up of between 201 and 5001 jurors selected by lot every day.

The ancient sources generally portray Cleon in a very negative light. It is easy to wave these aside as prejudiced, because most Athenian intellectuals were conservatives hostile to the "democratic" regime, and Thucydides and Aristophanes also had personal grudges of their own against Cleon. Yet the picture of Cleon that emerges from the sources, including Thucydides's paraphrases of some of Cleon's speeches, has a ring of truth about it, which chimes in with the general pattern of popular dictatorship. Thucydides describes Cleon as "the most violent man in Athens" (Thuc., 3.36) and as "a popular leader of the time and very powerful with the multitude" (Thuc., 4.21). Aristophanes's portrayal of Cleon is much more vitriolic, especially in *the Knights* and *the Wasps*.

The comic dramatist Aristophanes (c. 446–386 BCE) made no bones about his hostility to the Athenian democracy, and he had a personal run-in with Cleon (died 422 BCE). At one point in the *Knights*, the chorus addresses "Demos" ("the people") with these words: "Demos, the rule that you possess is lovely, since everyone fears you like (*hōsper*) a tyrant. But you are easily led, enjoy being flattered and fooled, and you listen to the orators with mouth agape, and your mind is befuddled" (Aristoph., *Knights,* 111–119). Demos is said here to have "rule," but it would be a mistake to interpret this as meaning that Demos is a tyrant. What the chorus is saying is that Demos is feared *as if* he were a tyrant. Does that mean that power in Athens was in the hands of the people? Clearly not, because Demos is told that he is under the thumb of the "orators," who are identified elsewhere in the same play as demagogues, notably Cleon. The question is: Who has the whip hand, Demos or the demagogue? The answer is clear: it is the demagogue. To clarify this point further, we might look at a passage from another of Aristophanes's plays, *The Wasps,* where the anti-Cleon son chides his pro-Cleon father for allowing someone like Cleon to rule (*archein*) over him (Aristoph., *Wasps*, 666) Here there can be no doubt: rule is in the hands of the demagogues and not of the people.

Whisper vs. Shout

The attacks in the ancient sources on Cleon and his demagogic successors touched off a belated rearguard action mounted from the mid-twentieth century onward to "rehabilitate" these demagogues. One of the more amusing non-arguments advanced in this cause is to be found in Moses Finley's article on demagogues, in which he dismisses the Aristotelian remark about Cleon being the first man to "shout and rail" as "obviously a frivolous approach, nothing more than the expression of class prejudice and snobbishness." Finley poses a rhetorical question as his knock-out blow: "Are we to imagine that Thucydides the son of Melesias (and kinsman of the historian) and Nicias whispered when they addressed the Assembly in opposition to Pericles and Cleon, respectively?" (Finley 1962, p. 16). Finley's point is completely illogical. He assumes that whispering is the only alternative to shouting, which is arrant nonsense. Not all politicians shout and rail—and those who do are more likely to be radical demagogues rather than conservative leaders. The most obvious example is the rantings of Adolf Hitler, whose strident tones were not matched, for example, by the rousing yet subdued fervor of Winston Churchill. So desperate is Finley to rehabilitate Cleon that he ultimately resorts to tarring all leaders with the same brush: "the term [demagogue] is equally applicable to all leaders, regardless of class or point of view" (ibid., p. 19). This completely obliterates the clear distinction drawn in the ancient sources between the conservative oligarchic leaders and the demagogic "champions of the people."

"All Leaders were Demagogues"

Finley's bad point about Cleon's rants is part of a more general, and equally fallacious, attempt on his part to tar all Athenian leaders with the brush of demagogy. This is based on Finley's mistaken belief that the system was one of rational discussion, debate, and deliberation:

> A man was a leader solely as a function of his personal, and in the literal sense, unofficial status within the Assembly itself. The test of whether or not he held that status was simply whether the Assembly did or did not vote as he wished, and therefore the test was repeated with each proposal. These were the conditions which faced all leaders in Athens, not merely those whom Thucydides and Plato dismissed as 'demagogues,' not merely those whom some modern historians mis-call "radical democrats," but everyone, aristocrat or commoner, altruist or self-seeker, able or incompetent, who, in George Grote's phrase, 'stood forward prominently to advise' the Athenians (ibid., pp. 15–16).

This picture of the Athenian Assembly as a sedate debating society is yet another example of Finley's getting hold of the wrong end of the stick. It is negated by (a) the whole new style of politics which came in with Pericles and was amplified by Cleon; (b) the use of bully-boy tactics by Cleon and others; (c) the citizens' lack of interest in participating in this supposed exercise of power on their part; (d) the existence of charismatic leadership on one side only, namely, the populist side; (e) the fact that there was very little real disagreement in the assembly—with the majority simply endorsing their radical demagogic leaders' proposals; (f) crowd psychology; and (g) the highly irrational decisions taken by Athens under the leadership of the radical demagogues. [It is perhaps no surprise that Finley, pooh-poohing the ancient evidence, had to resort to George Grote (1794–1871), an activist radical British politician who never went to university and whose *History of Greece* was published between 1846 and 1856.]

"The New Politicians"

The radical demagogues undoubtedly *did* belong to a different leadership type from their conservative, oligarchic opponents like Cimon, Thucydides, son of Melesias, and Nicias. W. Robert Connor pointed out in *The New Politicians of Fifth-Century Athens* (Connor 1971) that these "new politicians" broke away from the traditional model of political support centred on a group of *philoi*, "friends," which were based on family connections and aristocratic clubs known as *hetaireiai*. The new model of politics was based instead on a direct personal relationship between the demagogues and the mass of lower-class citizens who attended the assembly and served in the law courts as jurors on the enormous juries introduced to prevent bribery.

To symbolize this personal bond with the masses, Cleon, we are told by Plutarch, renounced his friends, declaring himself to be more deeply in love with the assembly than with his friends. Thucydides and Aristophanes give further support to this picture. This model of politics rings true of charismatic populist demagogues in other societies and other periods as well, such as Benito Mussolini, Adolf Hitler, Fidel Castro, and Mao Zedong. Despite the "major doubts about Connor's presentation of the "new style" in politics" expressed by a nitpicking reviewer (Davies, 1975), Connor would actually have been justified by the evidence to take his theory of "the new politicians" even further. What there was in late fifth-century Athens was not just a "new style" of politics but a new form of government, with power in the hands of a populist charismatic leader of the masses against the interests of the rich and noble.

Cleon and the Sycophants

Not surprisingly, in his discussion of the radical demagogues, Finley omits any mention of the devious means employed by Cleon, notably his use of "sycophants," meaning deceitful or calumnious informers against the rich and noble, enabling Cleon to bring lawsuits to strip them of their wealth and undermine them. The comic dramatist Aristophanes and other comic poets lost no opportunity to expose the nefarious practices of these informers and their links to Cleon and other populist demagogues. Some of the fragments of the Attic orators also throw some light on the sycophants. And we learn from Plutarch of the intimidation of the conservative leader Nicias by Cleon and Hyperbolus, another radical demagogue. The system was wide open to this kind of abuse, because any Athenian could launch a prosecution against any other for alleged crimes against the state—and collect a reward if his victim was convicted. As a result, the "profession" of sycophancy attracted a lot of dubious characters, whose unjustified threatened lawsuits against the rich amounted to blackmail, which could pay off twice over, once with a payout from their intended victim and possibly also a gratuity for their good work from the radical demagogue on whose behalf they had set the whole process in motion in the first place. It was possible, though, for two to play at the same game. In Xenophon's *Memorabilia of Socrates* (2.9.1–6) there is an amusing passage recording a conversation between Socrates and his friend Criton, who is at his wits' end being harassed by sycophants who believe that he would bow to their threats rather than go to court to face their untrue allegations. On Socrates' advice, Criton engages Archedemus as a sort of private investigator, who brings (justified) charges against the sycophant and only drops those charges in return for the sycophant's withdrawing his charges against Criton and rewarding Archedemus.

Rome: Sham Elections

Roman history is shot through and through with the concept of election, though it would be a mistake (made by some modern writers) to regard this as at any time or in any sense democratic (see Chapter 6). Rome began as an elective monarchy, which evidently morphed into a hereditary one. In 509 BCE the monarchy was overthrown and replaced by a "republic," an oligarchy with a visceral fear of one-man rule and a constitution dominated by short-term shared elected office-holders, from the two consuls at its head down to the lowest magistracies. The one exception was the position of dictator, intended to be limited to emergencies, and appointment to which was made by the Senate. Julius Caesar's appointment as *dictator perpetuo* ("dictator for life") triggered his assassination by leading oligarchs, followed by civil war and the end of the Republic.

Caesar's heir, known to history as Augustus, who emerged as sole ruler in 31 BCE, replaced the Republican oligarchy with a thinly disguised elective monarchy which morphed into a hereditary monarchy and provided a stable form of government that lasted for over three centuries, though the basic framework of the Augustan "Principate," including the sham Republican relics, survived much longer (see Chapter 6).

Augustus himself had wanted to establish a dynasty by grooming his two grandsons, Gaius and Lucius Caesar, to take over from him. But both died very young, Lucius of illness in 2 CE at the age of 19 and Gaius two years later at the age of 23, supposedly from the after-effects of a battle wound. They are portrayed in a touching coin design wearing togas but each with a spear and shield propped up beside him. Augustus's actual successor was his stepson Tiberius (r. 14–37 CE), not a blood relation of his, whom Augustus adopted, probably under pressure from Tiberius's mother and Augustus's third wife, Livia.

The message that the elective nature of the principate was a sham was brought home by the surprise accession of the Emperor Claudius in 41 CE. On the assassination of the Emperor Gaius (Caligula) in 41 CE, his uncle Claudius, who had been excluded from public life, was spotted hiding behind a curtain and, instead of being put to death, as he expected, was raised on military shields and declared emperor purely because of his membership of the Julio-Claudian family.

The "five good emperors" came to power for precisely the opposite reason, namely the absence of a biological heir. Each of these emperors, namely Nerva, Trajan, Hadrian, Antoninus Pius, and Marcus Aurelius, whose joint reigns span the period 96–180 CE, was forced to adopt a non-relative as his heir. This was a blessing in disguise, as it enabled a combination between the constitutional fiction of election and the legal fiction of heredity, giving Rome five of its best emperors. But the spell was broken by Marcus Aurelius's son and heir, Commodus (r. 180–192 CE), who preferred performing as a gladiator in the Colosseum to serious administrative work. The historian and senator Cassius Dio described his accession as marking the descent "from a kingdom of gold to one of iron and rust" (Cassius Dio 72.36.4. Loeb edition, tr. E. Cary).

The last Roman "consul," Anicius Faustus Albinus Basilius—not coincidentally the scion of a great Roman aristocratic house—who held office in Constantinople in 541 CE, was not elected but appointed by the Emperor Justinian I and held the office without a colleague. The idea that the position of emperor was elective died hard, surviving in the Holy Roman Empire, where the emperor was always formally chosen by a number of Prince-electors, even though the position was in practice hereditary in the House of Habsburg from 1440 (with one gap of 25 years) until the dissolution of the empire in 1806. In the meantime, the Germanic successor states to the Roman Empire in the West after 476 CE were mostly at least partly or nominally elective, and the British coronation service still shows traces of the elective pre-Conquest Anglo-Saxon monarchy.

The Venetian Republic

For the whole period from at least 1172 until the dissolution of the Venetian Republic in 1797, the doge of Venice was a byword for an elected monarch with a purely ceremonial role (see Chapter 1). Other elected monarchs generally had at least some power, but subordinate to those, usually nobles, to whom the elected king was beholden. After some intermittent royal elections in Poland, the newly formed Polish-Lithuanian Commonwealth committed itself to an elected monarchy in 1573, when the future French King Henry III was elected. All male members of the very large Polish nobility were eligible to vote. Voting was in person, and it is estimated that the number of nobles who actually turned out to vote varied between 10,000 and 15,000. Once elected, a king was crowned and held office for life, sometimes combining it with a position in another state, like Elector of Saxony. Grand Royal Chancellor Jan Zamoyski clarified the position in a speech in 1605: "The king reigns but does not govern." The king shared power with the *Sejm* (Parliament) and the *Senat*. The *Sejm* could veto the king's decisions not only in legislation, including taxation, but also in foreign affairs, including matters of war and peace. According to the "liberum veto," any member of the *Sejm*, which was restricted to nobles, could stop the session and nullify any legislation passed, simply by calling out *Sisto activitatem* ("I stop the activity"). The system was labeled "Golden Liberty." The elected monarchy came to an end in 1791 and was replaced by the famous "Constitution of 3 May 1791," which aimed to turn the Commonwealth into the sort of constitutional monarchy that already existed in Britain. It was never implemented, however, because in 1795 the Commonwealth was finally swallowed up in the Third Partition of Poland between Russia, Austria, and Prussia.

The moral of the story is that elective monarchy, which tends to result in oligarchy, weakens not only the monarchy but the whole state. This does not of course apply to the regime established by Augustus in Rome, because that was not an elective monarchy at all but a real monarchy masquerading as an elective republic.

One Empire?

During the fourth century CE the Roman Empire was sometimes shared between two or more emperors, and in 395 the empire, still nominally one, was formally split into two halves, which ended in 476, when the last Western emperor, a young boy symbolically named Romulus Augustus, was deposed. The West was subdivided into a patchwork quilt of "barbarian" kingdoms, while the East, nowadays commonly referred to as the Byzantine Empire, continued a lengthy but largely inglorious existence until swallowed up by the Ottoman Turks in 1453.

The Holy Roman Empire

Though sometimes dated to Charlemagne's coronation in 800, the Holy Roman Empire is more accurately considered to have come into existence only on the coronation of Otto I in 962. Lasting until 1806, the Holy Roman Empire was described by Voltaire (1694–1778) as "neither holy, nor Roman, nor an empire." This was true of Voltaire's own day, when it was essentially an umbrella body chiefly covering a multiplicity of effectively independent (mostly German) states. But in the Middle Ages it had been a genuinely powerful state. In keeping with the original concept of Augustus's principate, the position of Holy Roman emperor was in theory elective, not hereditary, though Augustus and his successors had soon realized the attraction of hereditary succession to the masses. The emperor of the Holy Roman Empire was in theory elected by a college of "electors," restricted from the thirteenth century to the rulers of just seven German states and Bohemia. Between 1438 and 1806 (with one exception) all Holy Roman emperors were members of the Austrian House of Habsburg.

Henry VIII Duped

Despite his arrogance and high-handed treatment of his ministers and wives, Henry VIII failed to recognize the potential danger of Parliament to the Crown. Instead, he used the so-called "Reformation Parliament" (which sat in eight sessions between

1529 and 1536) to put through a major series of statutes breaking with Rome, making himself the head of a breakaway Church of England, dissolving the monasteries, and much else besides. As this suited Henry's egocentric purpose, it left him vulnerable to hypocritical flattery, which he lapped up unthinkingly. As Henry VIII himself told the Parliament: "We be informed by our judges that we at no time stand so highly in our estate royal as in the time of Parliament." Nothing could have been further from the truth. In placing such great reliance on Parliament, Henry greatly increased the power and prestige of Parliament, which, less than a century after his death, would result in a bloody civil war and the execution of a king, followed half a century later by the deposition of another king and the reduction of the monarch to a largely ceremonial cipher.

A "Democratically Elected" King

One of the strangest elected monarchs in history was the short-lived King Amadeo of Spain (r. 1870–73).

From the accession to the Spanish throne of the Bourbon King Philip V (a grandson of Louis XIV of France) in 1700, succession to the Spanish throne was governed by a form of the so-called Salic Law based on agnatic or male-preference primogeniture, or patrilineal succession, which restricted the succession to males. In 1830, King Ferdinand VII of Spain, who had no male heirs, issued a "Pragmatic Sanction" (ratifying a 1789 decree by his father, Charles IV), replaced Ferdinand's brother Carlos as his heir with Ferdinand's daughter, Isabella, who accordingly succeeded to the throne on Ferdinand's death in 1833, sparking off the so-called "Carlist Wars," a series of civil wars in 1833–40, a more minor episode in 1846–49, and another major flare-up in 1872–76. The Carlists never managed to gain the upper hand.

The absolutist monarchy was converted into a constitutional monarchy by the Royal Statute of 1834 and the Constitution of 1837, which was replaced by the 1845 Constitution, restricting the franchise to about 1% of the male population.

If you have ever been a stamp collector, you may have been struck by the proliferation of early Spanish postage stamps. Starting in 1850, a new stamp was issued practically every year until 1867. There was a different portrait of Queen Isabella each time, with alternating left- and right-facing profiles and even one full-face portrait, and constantly changing hairstyles. By contrast, British stamps used the same demure portrait of Queen Victoria from their invention with the "Penny Black" in 1840 until 1879, by which time Victoria was 60 years old.

But Isabella's unprepossessing appearance on the stamps was not her only problem, and the political turbulence was exacerbated by rumors of the queen's infidelities, including the allegation that her son and eventual successor, Alfonso XII, was fathered by a paramour.

In 1868 Isabella was ousted by a military coup and the new prime minister, General Prim, set out to find a democratic king, with the remark, "Looking for a democratic monarch in Europe is like trying to find an atheist in heaven." The throne was eventually offered to the second son of the king of Italy, Amadeo, in November 1870. While Amadeo was on his way to Spain, his sponsor, General Prim, was assassinated in Madrid, and the new king was sworn in in the presence of Prim's corpse. After a turbulent reign, marked by internal political squabbles, a failed assassination attempt against Amadeo, and a recrudescence of the Carlist War, Amadeo, declaring the Spanish people to be ungovernable, abdicated and returned to Italy in February 1873.

For the first time in its history, Spain was now proclaimed a Republic, which, however, was brought down by a military *pronunciamiento* in December 1874, and led to a restoration of the Bourbon monarchy under Isabella's 17-year-old son, Alfonso XII (r. 1874–85), the great-great-grandfather of Felipe VI, the king of Spain at the time of this writing.

Mussolini

Two things that everyone knows about the Italian dictator Benito Mussolini (1883–1945) are that he came to power with a "March on Rome" and that he got the trains to run on time. Apparently, it was only the express tourist trains that were punctual, not the little local lines. And, as for the March on Rome, which did actually take place, though with less than 30,000 men, Mussolini did not take part in it himself but instead took the train from Milan to Rome.

Mussolini began life as a socialist journalist and politician, who was expelled from the Italian Socialist Party (of the directorate of which he had been a member) for advocating Italian military involvement in World War I. When Italy did join the alliance against Austria and Germany, Mussolini served in the Italian army and was invalided out after being wounded in 1917.

Promoting "revolutionary nationalism," Mussolini started a new "fascist" party, named after the bundle of rods with an axe originally symbolizing the authority of the ancient Roman Republic. He was one of 35 members of his party to be elected to the Italian Parliament in 1921—out of a total of 535 seats—as part of Prime Minister Giovanni Giolitti's anti-Socialist "National Bloc," a coalition of liberals and conservatives.

With Italy descending into a spiral of left–right violence, with strikes and the occupation of factories by Socialists responded to by Fascist violence, the new liberal prime minister, Luigi Facta, tried to persuade King Victor Emmanuel III to declare a state of emergency to repress Fascist violence. When the king refused, Facta resigned, and the king then, on 31 October 1922, invited Mussolini to form a government. So, Mussolini did not seize power by force, though his appointment as prime minister was made with the threat of violence looming in the background. And in Mussolini's first governments the Fascists made up only a small minority, with the rest being nationalists and liberals, with even two Catholic priests from the People's Party.

The Acerbo Laws of June 1923 gave two-thirds of the seats in the Chamber of Deputies to any party or group of parties that garnered at least 25% of the vote, though it was not needed in the 1924 election, when the alliance of Fascists, liberals, Christian democrats and others actually won 64.94% of the vote, which gave them 355 of the 535 seats.

In December 1924, leading militant Fascists met with Mussolini and threatened to crush all opposition if he did not do so. To avoid a revolt by his own militants, Mussolini henceforth dropped the democratic façade. Accordingly, Mussolini now proceeded to turn Italy into a legal dictatorship and a police state. After an assassination attempt on Mussolini in 1926, all other parties were banned. In 1928 parliamentary elections were abolished. Voters were presented instead with a single list of Fascists which they could either accept or reject. In 1929 the list was supposedly approved by 98.43% of the voters.

Economic policy was generally anti-Socialist, including the closing down of labor unions. But he also nationalized business, claiming in 1935 that three-quarters of businesses were state control, and in 1936 he imposed price controls. After Italian Fascists attacked some left-wing autarkic projects at the behest of large landowners, in the 1930s Mussolini himself embraced the goal of autarky ("self-sufficiency"), raising high tariff barriers on trade with most countries except Nazi Germany.

The corporatist Labor Charter of 1927 implemented a collective agreement system between employers and employees, envisaged as a form of class collaboration. A popular slogan was: "Everything within the state, nothing outside the state, nothing against the state." In 1936 the "National Council of Corporations" actually replaced the Chamber of Deputies as Italy's "parliament." Of its 823 members, 66 represented the Fascist Party, with the rest split among 22 "corporations," each made up of employer and employee representatives.

Styling himself *Il Duce* ("the Leader"), Mussolini recreated himself as a powerful, omniscient, and omnipotent leader. His rhetoric was loud, long, melodramatic, and bombastic, with exaggerated hand movements and his chest (sometimes bare) thrust out in a defiant posture. While Mussolini wanted to appear internationally as a man of peace, such references were sometimes deleted for Italian consumption, where war was glorified, though there, too, he sometimes posed as a peacemaker, as the occasion demanded. "The crowd does not have to know," Mussolini is quoted as saying. "It must believe."

Mussolini broke the longstanding stalemate with the Catholic Church by signing a concordat with the Vatican in 1929, the Lateran Treaty, which entailed mutual recognition. The Italian state was finally recognized by the Church, and the Papacy was given Vatican City as a completely independent state, which, though a fraction of the size of the old Papal States that cut a diagonal swathe across central Italy, settled a long dispute, and was so greatly appreciated that Pope Pius XI declared Mussolini to be "The Man of Providence." This action on Mussolini's part undoubtedly won him many recruits to his movement.

In keeping with his image of recreating the Roman greatness of Italy with himself cast in the role of the Emperor Augustus, Mussolini embarked on an aggressive foreign policy, notably the invasion of Ethiopia in 1935, which cost 12,000 Italian lives and drained the Italian coffers. Between 1936 and 1939 Mussolini gave crucial support to Francisco Franco in the Spanish Civil War. In 1936 the Rome–Berlin Axis was formed, which became a full military alliance with Germany in 1939. In April 1939 Italy occupied Albania. King Victor Emmanuel wanted Italy to remain neutral in the spiraling conflict, and when Hitler invaded Poland in September 1939 Italy remained on the sidelines. However, after some dithering, Italy declared war on Britain and France on 10 June 1940. After some initial successes against Britain in Africa, Axis forces were defeated in the Tunisia Campaign in early 1943 and Italy suffered other major reverses on the Eastern Front. Allied bombings in Italy itself caused food shortages, and the Italian people lost faith in Mussolini, leading to major strikes. The Allied invasion of Italy was welcomed by the people, and, after a blistering attack on Mussolini and a 19-8 vote of no confidence in him in the Fascist Grand Council, on 25 July 1943 the king sent for Mussolini and formally dismissed him as prime minister. Rescued by Germany, Mussolini was given the headship of a doomed puppet regime known as the Italian Social Republic, covering the whole of northern Italy. As they were scrambling to get to Switzerland, Mussolini and his mistress Clara Petacci were intercepted by Italian communist partisans and summarily executed and their bodies hung upside down from the roof of a service station in Milan.

Throughout the period of Mussolini's dictatorship Italy was a monarchy under King Victor Emmanuel III. Does this indicate that Mussolini did not have complete power? Not at all. Victor Emmanuel III was a constitutional monarch who well understood the restrictions on his power, though the constitution, dating back to 1848, before there even was a united Italy, actually allowed him wider decision-making power than is normal in a constitutional monarchy, For example, he had the right to pick whoever he liked as prime minister, regardless whether or not they commanded a majority in the Chamber of Deputies. During the Fascist "March on Rome" 400 lightly armed policemen were enough to stop the "march." It was the king's realization that the Fascists were essentially loyal to himself that made him appoint Mussolini as prime minister in the first place in 1922 and then to remain in the background, allowing the whole state to be transformed, and even the calendar to be changed, with 1922 becoming the Year I. The king could have dismissed Mussolini after the brutal assassination of the Socialist leader, Giacomo Matteotti in 1924, for which Mussolini virtually accepted responsibility. But Victor Emmanuel made it clear that he would not dismiss Mussolini even if he lost a no-confidence vote in the chamber of deputies, though in fact Mussolini won the vote by 314 to 6. Even in November 1926 when Mussolini arbitrarily barred all opposition parliamentarians from taking their seats, which he declared forfeited, the king did nothing. The king did, however, veto Mussolini's proposal to add the *fasces* symbol in the center of the Italian flag next to the coat of arms of the royal House of Savoy. By 1928 even the king's right to dismiss Mussolini from office could be exercised only on the advice of the Fascist Grand Council, which however could only be convened by Mussolini. But the real reason Victor Emmanuel allowed Mussolini to take over the state as completely as he did was simply that he regarded him as a safeguard against socialism, communism, and anarchism. So he just allowed Mussolini to do more or less as he pleased and even returned the Fascist salute when the Fascist blackshirts saluted him. Yet, most importantly of all, the king stopped Mussolini from joining Hitler in his attack on Poland in 1939. The king had the advantage of being commander-in-chief, so that all military oaths of loyalty were to him, not Mussolini. It was only after Germany's successful sweep into the Low Countries and France that Mussolini managed to persuade the king to agree to allow Italy to enter the war, but the king insisted on remaining commander-in-chief, though Mussolini did manage to get the king to give him certain operational command powers. Though the king recognized in 1941 that the war was not going well for Italy, he was afraid that sacking Mussolini would rebound on himself, as all the anti-Fascist parties were republican and would abolish the monarchy if given the chance. When the king did finally dismiss Mussolini in July 1943, he was still hoping to retain a Fascist government (under Marshal Pietro Badoglio) in order to safeguard his throne, and he signed an armistice with the Allies. Desperation prompted Victor Emmanuel to abdicate in favor of his son the crown prince, who ascended the throne as Umberto II on 9 May 1946. In the referendum held a month later 54% opted for a republic, bringing to an end the new king's reign after 34 days and with it the Italian monarchy, which had lasted only 85 years.

Adolf Hitler

"The Nazi seizure of power" is a phrase commonly bandied about and is the title of at least one book. In fact, however, Adolf Hitler (1889–1945) came to power legally, albeit with the threat of violence in the background. Unlike Mussolini, Hitler had actually attempted to take power in a coup, which however was a dismal failure and cost Hitler a short spell in prison.

Though an Austrian citizen, at the outbreak of World War I in August 1914, Hitler voluntarily enlisted in the Bavarian army, part of the German army, instead of the Austro-Hungarian army, for which he had no respect. Hitler turned out to be an enthusiastic and brave fighter and was awarded the Iron Cross, Second Class and later First Class, on the recommendation of his Jewish commanding officer, who, probably through Hitler's intervention, received a pension from the Nazi government while living in the US throughout World War II. Hitler wore this decoration for the rest of his life.

Though temporarily blinded by a mustard gas attack in October 1918, Hitler would recall his service in the war as "the greatest of all experiences." After the war, he was sent by the army to infiltrate the fledgling right-wing German Workers' Party, which, on orders of his army bosses, he joined in 1920. Hitler now worked full-time for the party, under its new name, the National Socialist German Workers' Party, or "Nazi Party" for short, and created its banner by skilfully adapting the colors of the old German imperial flag to his design: a black swastika in a white circle against a red background. As a powerful demagogic orator Hitler became party leader, or Führer, with absolute power.

In November 1923, with the assistance of World War I hero General Erich Ludendorff, Hitler attempted to overthrow the Bavarian government in a coup, to be followed by a challenge to the national government in Berlin. The "Beer Hall Putsch," as it came to be called, was a fiasco, in which 15 Nazis and four police officers lost their lives. At their trials Ludendorff was acquitted while Hitler was sentenced to five years' imprisonment, of which he served altogether just over a year and took the opportunity to write the first volume of his book, *Mein Kampf* ("My Struggle").

In the Reichstag election of May 1924, with the Nazi Party banned, Nazis won 32 seats out of 472 under the name National Socialist Freedom Movement. Their support dropped to 14 seats out of 493 in December 1924, and, under the Nazi Party label, dropped to 12 seats out of 491 in May 1928. In September 1930 the Nazis were the second biggest party with 107 seats out of 577.

In March 1932 Hitler had the temerity to challenge the incumbent president, the 84-year-old hero of World War I, Field Marshal Paul von Hindenburg, who was reluctantly running for a second term. Hitler lost to Hindenburg in both rounds, scoring 30% in round one and 37% in round two, to Hindenburg's 49% and 53%. After Hitler's surprisingly good showing, the Nazis moved into top position in the Reichstag election of July 1932, with 230 seats out of 608, and, despite a slight drop in support, retained the top spot in November 1932 with 196 seats out of 584, reflecting 33.09% of the vote.

President von Hindenburg had wide powers under the then German Constitution, and the proliferation of parties in the Reichstag made the formation of a workable coalition well-nigh impossible. Under the influence of the so-called "Camarilla," a small cabal of politicians, army officers, and others close to him, on 30 January 1933 the president appointed Hitler as chancellor (prime minister), with only two other Nazis in the Cabinet.

But Hitler wasted no time in gaining a stranglehold over the government and the state. On 27 February 1933 the Reichstag building was set on fire. A young Dutch Communist, Marinus van der Lubbe, was arrested, tried, convicted, and executed for arson and high treason. He readily confessed, to being solely responsible, though his confession was called into question from the start, as the only tinder he had was his shirt. Yet, according to expert evidence at the trial, the main fires (there were several) had been set with quantities of chemicals and petrol that van der Lubbe could not have carried on his own. Even the Berlin fire chief, Walter Gempp, who personally directed the operations to contain the fire, testified to Nazi involvement in the fire, for which he was dismissed. In 1937 he was convicted of abuse of office and imprisoned, and in 1939, while awaiting an appeal decision, he was mysteriously found dead in his cell. Despite all this, academic opinion has shifted from believing van der Lubbe was framed by the real perpetrators, the Nazis, to acceptance of van der Lubbe's confession. Nevertheless, van der Lubbe was exculpated and given a posthumous pardon by the German government in 2007.

Be that as it may, Hitler took the opportunity of the fire to get President von Hindeburg to issue the Reichstag Fire Decree, which suspended habeas corpus, freedom of speech, and most other civil liberties. In the ensuing Reichstag election of 5 March1933, the Nazis improved their position by winning 43.01% of the vote, giving them 288 of the 647 seats, which still fell short of an absolute majority. The Enabling Act, which required a two-thirds majority, still passed, by 444 to 94, with the support of all parties except the Communists (whose 81 members were arrested) and the Social Democrats. This Act gave Hitler the power to rule by decree. And on 14 July 1933, less than six months since coming to power, the Nazi Party was declared the only legal political party, leaving Hitler with only a little internal housekeeping to do, by removing all internal opposition even from some formerly close associates like Ernst Röhm and Gregor Strasser, by means of murder in the "Night of the Long Knives."

As chancellor of Germany, Hitler now had his hands on all the levers of government, and as Führer he was the head of a powerful paramilitary organization with mass popular support. The cherry on the top was the headship of state, which fell fortuitously into Hitler's lap with the death of the 86-year-old President von Hindenburg on 2 August 1934. The post of president was now merged in that of chancellor, and Hitler effectively combined both offices in his own person, not omitting to help himself to the presidential salary as well as that of the chancellor. The most important power he gained from this was that of commander-in-chief, which he used by requiring the military oath of loyalty to be taken to himself personally. The merger of the presidency with the chancellorship was approved in a plebiscite by 89.93% of those voting, with a turnout of 95.65% of the electorate. Hitler was anxious to appear to have a "democratic" mandate, so storm troopers were stationed at polling stations and voters were discouraged from entering a polling booth to vote "no." The irony is that the law merging presidential powers with the chancellorship was itself illegal under Hitler's own "Enabling Act."

Hjalmar Schacht, who, as president of the Reichsbank, had defeated the hyperinflation of 1923 with the creation of the *Rentenmark,* a new currency based on a notional mortgage of all German property, was appointed by Hitler as minister of economics in 1934. He developed public works programs, notably the construction of the *Autobahnen,* to alleviate unemployment, which by 1938 was almost eliminated, He also introduced the "New Plan," an attempt to achieve German economic autarky, or self-reliance. He also tackled the government deficit with "Mefo bills," promissory notes used for deferred payment to finance the Nazi government's program of rearmament without breaking the Versailles Treaty. Disgusted at the anti-Semitic violence of *Kristallnacht* in 1938, Schacht suggested an alternative policy, under which Jewish property in Germany would be held in trust and used as security for loans raised abroad, which would also be guaranteed by the German government. Funds would be made available for Jewish emigration. Though accepted by Hitler and even by some prominent British Jews, it was rejected by Chaim Weizmann, on behalf of the British Zionist Federation.

Though Hitler was born and brought up as a Catholic, he found the German Protestant churches more pliable to his wishes. The overtly anti-Semitic German Christian Faith Movement was started in 1932, and in 1933 the "German Evangelical Church," a federation of Lutheran, Reformed, and United territorial churches, fell under the control of the so-called "German Christians," a Nazi organization, and proceeded to elect Ludwig Müller, a military pastor and Hitler's confidant on Church matters, as *Reichsbischof* ("State Bishop"). Besides opposition to the whole idea of Nazi Christianity, Müller also faced a good deal of criticism from within the Nazi Party, and he was effectively sidelined, though as late as 1944 he evidently received a grant of 500,000 Reichsmarks, largely "to pay off his debts."

Was Hitler to blame for World War II? *Lebensraum* ("living space") and *Drang nach Osten* ("Push to the East") were certainly two of his aims. But did he set out in power with a view to an aggressive policy of expansion? He was probably more of an opportunist. US President Woodrow Wilson had enunciated his "14 points" as a program for peace after World War I in 1918. He idealistically believed that his 14-point plan was the answer to "autocracy" in Europe. Above all, his plan involved dismantling the two major multinational empires, Austria-Hungary and the Ottoman Empire, and the grant of "self-determination" and "autonomous development" for each of the many nationalities involved.

Taking this concept to its logical conclusion, Hitler pointed out that ethnic Germans caught in a non-German state should likewise be given autonomy, and ideally the right to become part of Germany. He identified three such areas. First, the Sudetenland, a largely German-speaking area in Czechoslovakia; secondly, the largely German-speaking "Free City" of Danzig, in an imposed union with Poland; and thirdly, Memel, a German-speaking enclave within Lithuania. This last was the first to be conceded, without a shot being fired, in March 1939.

British Prime Minister Neville Chamberlain granted Hitler's demand for the Sudetenland, believing he had achieved "peace for our time." Instead, this led to the dismemberment of the rest of Czechoslovakia as well, and only whetted Hitler's appetite for more *Lebensraum*. The German foreign minister and former ambassador to London, Joachim von Ribbentrop, assured Hitler that neither Britain nor France would honor their commitments to Poland, on the strength of which, on 22 August 1939, Hitler ordered mobilization against Poland. On the very next day the Molotov–Ribbentrop Pact was signed between Germany and the Soviet Union, according to which Poland was to be shared while Lithuania, Latvia, Estonia, Finland, and Bessarabia were to go to the Soviet Union. A week later, on 1 September 1939, reassured that he would not be facing war on two fronts, on the pretext of not having been given Danzig, Hitler ordered the invasion of Poland. And on 17 September 1939, the Soviet Union invaded Poland as well. But, Ribbentrop was wrong: Britain and France did keep their commitment to Poland, and actually declared war on Germany two days after the German invasion of Poland. Nevertheless, tearing up his pact with the Soviets, on 22 June 1941 Hitler launched "Operation Barbarossa," a full-scale invasion of the Soviet Union by over three million Axis troops, which contributed largely to Germany's losing the war.

That Hitler was a dictator with supreme power from 1933 to 1945 puts him in the category of strong monarchy. He had no shortage of enemies, mostly created by himself, including communists, socialists, Jews, Roma (gypsies), and homosexuals. But he clearly also was genuinely popular with large elements of the German population, notably farmers, especially in the poorer areas of the north and east of the country, together with many middle-class people who were afraid of a communist takeover. Industrial workers who were members of labor unions were strongly opposed to him, however, and he took the earliest opportunity to close down the unions. Financially, he was backed by some wealthy businessmen, including both the steel moguls Fritz Thyssen and Gustav Krupp as well as the Bechstein family who made grand pianos, and even foreign admirers like the anti-Semitic car manufacturer Henry Ford. In addition, he received many thousands of small donations from supporters, for which special badges were issued. After the war, Hitler's erstwhile supporters in Germany always denied any knowledge of his inhuman and barbaric policies, but it is by no means certain that they would have withdrawn their support had they known. In *Mein Kampf*, without admitting that he himself was a liar, Hitler made the point that a big lie—especially if used repeatedly—is more readily believed by the masses than a small lie: "In the primitive simplicity of their minds they more readily fall victims to the big lie than the small lie, since they themselves often tell small lies in little matters but would be ashamed to resort to large-scale falsehoods" (Hitler 2008).

Hitler's persuasiveness and popularity were the product of several forces. First, there was his undoubted charisma, though his strident shrieking, coupled with his harsh Austrian accent and his exaggerated hand gestures, could also make him appear a figure of fun, as he does in Charlie Chaplin's 1939 movie, *The Great Dictator*. Secondly, there was the heightened emotive tone of the occasion, whipped up to fever pitch by the parading troops, the music, the impressive architecture (as at the Nuremberg party rallies), and the climactic warm-up to the Führer's speech by (in the early days) Rudolf Hess or Joseph Goebbels. Thirdly, Hitler's propaganda struck a chord with a large swathe of Germans, who shared Hitler's concept of a *Volksgemeinschaft* ("people's community") of "Aryan" blood against Jews, communists, war profiteers and others who had supposedly stabbed Germany in the back in World War I.

The reason Hitler is in this chapter is that, though his stormtroopers were engaged in street violence, chiefly against communists, his accession to power was as the result of a decision taken by President von Hindenburg. Had he not been appointed Chancellor at that time, could the Nazis have seized power by force? It is probably unlikely, especially if Hindenburg had instead reappointed Brüning, who had banned both Nazi paramilitary organizations, the SA and the SS, whom he blamed for the political violence and whose ban successfully caused a big drop in street violence. And his government had also banned the wearing of party uniforms in public, which likewise lowered the political temperature. But Brüning's request to Hindenburg in 1932 for an emergency decree giving financial relief to Junkers (Prussian aristocrats) with bankrupt estates, breaking them up into small farms and redistributing them to unemployed workers, was the last straw as far as Hindenburg was concerned, who was himself a Junker caught up in a scandal relating to this. Brüning's resignation was probably the last nail in the coffin of the Weimar Republic.

Juan Perón

A truly unique figure in world history was the Argentinian politician Juan Perón (1895–1974), who entered public life, unremarkably enough, as a participant in a military coup, but who, thanks in no small measure to his second wife, Eva ("Evita") Perón (1919–52), became a hugely successful populist politician, elected president of Argentina on three occasions, and founder of a major political movement that is still alive and well nearly 80 years later.

As a colonel, Perón took a leading part in the military coup of 1943 against the conservative President Ramón Castillo. Heading up the Department of

Labor, which he had upgraded to a Cabinet-level ministry, he forged an alliance with socialist labor unions and introduced a wide range of social welfare benefits for unionized workers. Forced to resign as a result of in-fighting within the ruling junta, he was arrested, but released after four days of mass demonstrations on his behalf organized by the unions and by his new partner, "Evita," whom he married shortly after.

Perón's opponents in the junta called elections for February 1946. Though facing a loose alliance of socialists, communists, centrists, and conservatives, and despite accusations of being a fascist sympathizer, Perón won with 53.71% of the vote, which translated into 304 electoral votes out of 376, together with 109 of the 158 seats in the Chamber of Deputies for his Justicialist Party. Thanks to the efforts of Evita Perón, women were given the right to vote in 1947. The Eva Perón Foundation established hundreds of new schools, clinics, old-age homes, and holiday facilities, and the planned community called *Ciudad Evita* just south of Buenos Aires.

Though thwarted in having Evita as his running mate in the 1951 election, Perón was re-elected with 62.49% and a margin of over 30% (the highest in Argentine history) and remained in power until he was removed by a military coup in 1955. His heavy-handed crackdown on intellectuals during this period aroused a huge amount of opposition. He fired over 2,000 university professors, and reassigned some of them to demeaning positions. For example, the well-known author Jorge Luis Borges was removed as head of the National Library of Buenos Aires and offered instead the position of "poultry inspector" at the meat market, an offer which he declined. Anti-Perón graffiti proclaimed *Haga patria, mate a un estudiante* ("Build the fatherland, kill a student"). The refusal of the 1943–46 junta to declare war on the Axis powers in World War II, together with his repression of opposition, often assisted by torture, gave Perón the reputation of being a fascist himself, while conservative critics opposed him for planning to legalize divorce and prostitution and his stripping the Catholic Church of its privileges, leading to a rift with this powerful organization and also alienating a good deal of support in the military.

Perón's uncanny ability to combine left- and right-wing features in his program had the unfortunate result of making enemies against himself of left- and right-wing organizations outside his party as well, as was demonstrated by the terrorist attack on a Peronist rally at Buenos Aires's *Plaza de Mayo* square on 15 April 1953, in which seven people were killed and 95 injured. Instigated by Perón to take reprisals, the crowd attacked both the Socialist Party headquarters and the elite Jockey Club, burning both buildings to the ground.

In September 1955 Perón was ousted by a military coup, and his party was banned. A number of Peronist leaders were charged with corruption, but none were convicted. Meanwhile Perón was in exile, escaping first to Venezuela and then to Spain, where he was granted political asylum by Francisco Franco.

Perón's deputy and a leading member of the left wing of the Peronist party, Dr. Héctor Cámpora, was eventually allowed to run in a presidential election held in March 1973, though Perón was still barred. Cámpora won with 49.53% of the vote. The way was now clear for Perón's return from exile. On the day of his return in June 1973, a crowd of 3.5 million (police estimate) left-wing supporters were waiting to welcome him, when some right-wing Peronist snipers opened fire on the crowd, killing 13 people and injuring 365. This so-called Ezeiza Massacre marks a final rift between the left and right wings of the Peronist movement. Cámpora resigned the presidency after just a few weeks, and in the ensuing election Perón swept back to power with 61.86% of the vote, but died less than a year later, in July 1974. His funeral procession drew a crowd of over a million, chanting "Perón! Perón! Perón!"

When first elected in 1946, Perón embarked on a populist program inspired by Evita, favoring workers and labor unions, nationalizing the Central Bank, the railroad, the merchant marine, public utilities, public transport, health care, the universities, the broadcasting system, and the labor unions. Perón attracted support—and opposition—from both left and right. Freedom of speech was stifled and dissidents imprisoned. That Perón was a dictator is not in doubt, but there is an ongoing debate on whether he was a fascist or more of a socialist. His admiration for Mussolini and Hitler was not a secret, and he would later be given asylum in Franco's Spain. In the years immediately after World War II, Perón welcomed to Argentina a number of Nazis accused of war crimes, including Adolf Eichmann and Dr. Josef Mengele. But in 1949 Perón's Argentina was the first country in Latin America to establish diplomatic relations with Israel while also allowing more Jewish immigrants than any other Latin American country.

Perón and Che Guevara were on good terms, sharing a common enemy in the United States. Perón described Che as *"un utópico inmaduro—pero entre nosotros—me alegra que sea así porque a los "yankees" les está dando flor de dolor de cabeza."* ("An immature utopian—but one of us—I am happy that it is so because he is giving the yankees a real headache") (O'Donnell 2011).

What are we to make of all these paradoxes? Was Perón left-wing or right-wing? In fact, he was both—or neither. He was a populist in the best "tall poppies" tradition, lopping off the poppies projecting above the rest with the active support of the generality of ordinary folk. Remarkably, three-quarters of a century since its inception, Peronism is still alive and well in Argentina and still drawing support from both left and right, though the two wings of the movement have drifted apart to some extent. But the essential "populist" nature of the movement comes out particularly in the second "principle" of Peronism: "Peronism is essentially of the common people. Any political elite is anti-people, and thus, not Peronist" (Perón 2015).

Perón was succeeded after his death in 1973 by the vice-president, his third wife, Isabel Perón, who was ousted by yet another military junta in 1976, the head of which, Jorge Rafael Videla, remained in charge on his own until 1981, when, after three further military presidents, he was succeeded by Leopoldo Galtieri, best known for unsuccessfully fighting the Falklands War with Britain, after which he was ousted. Carlos Menem, a conservative Peronist who privatized a number of industries nationalized by Perón, was president from 1989 to 1999. Adolfo Rodriguez Saá and Eduardo Duhalde were Peronists who served briefly as interim president followed by Néstor Kirchner, a left-wing Peronist, who held office from 2003 to 2007, who was succeeded in turn by his wife, Cristina Kirchner, who served two terms as president spanning the period 2007–2015, leaving office with an approval rating of more than 50%. Between 2019 and 2023 she served as vice-president under another left-wing Peronist president, Alberto Fernández, but in 2022 was convicted on corruption charges and sentenced to six years' imprisonment and a lifetime ban on holding public office. In the 2023 presidential election, the left-wing Peronist candidate Sergio Massa won the first round with 36% of the vote, but in the runoff lost to the right-wing-libertarian candidate, Javier Milei, who garnered 55.7% of the vote. A professed admirer of the US's Donald Trump and Brazil's Jair Bolsonaro, Milei was sworn in as president of Argentina on 10 December 2023.

Chapter 14
Marriage

Marital politics have played an important role in monarchical decision-making—at the expense of what might be thought much more important considerations, such as nationality, ethnicity, linguistic identity, or contiguity. Pursuit of marital politics might leave a monarch or a royal house with fragmented domains separated not only geographically but also linguistically, ethnically, and in terms of national identity. The Peace of Versailles that concluded World War I in 1919 dismembered both the Habsburg and Ottoman empires and gave rise to a number of new or revived independent states based on "national self-determination," together with a number of League of Nations "mandates," which merely exchanged one imperial power for another. And, far from being "the war to end all wars," a common catchphrase at the time, World War I—and the Versailles Peace Treaty itself—led straight to World War II. These wars have largely put paid to marital politics, which is really an extension of the principle of heredity, in favor of oligarchy under the guise of "democracy." But one principle that has been completely ignored is that of genuine popular monarchy, the only real alternative to oligarchy.

"Let Others Wage War……"

Bella gerant alii, tu felix Austria nube! ("Let others wage war, but you, blessed Austria, marry!") This slogan, attributed to Emperor Maximilian I of the Holy Roman Empire (r. 1508–19) became the unofficial motto of the House of Habsburg, though members of that family were in practice not averse to resorting to warfare when it suited them. The Latin word *nube* means "marry" viewed from the bride's vantage point, but the policy was practiced from the husband's viewpoint as well, as in Maximilian's own marriage to Mary Duchess of Burgundy in 1477. As a result

Five Thousand Years of Monarchy, First Edition. Michael Arnheim.
© 2026 John Wiley & Sons, Inc. Published 2026 by John Wiley & Sons, Inc.

of that marriage Maximilian became Duke of Burgundy *jure uxoris* ("by right of his wife"), meaning that, though she was duchess regnant, her husband shared this status with her, but lost it on her death in 1482. (Men gaining rights through marriage was a fairly standard practice in medieval Europe.) When Maximilian and Mary had a son, Philip, Louis XI of France spread a rumor that the child was a girl, so, to dispel doubts, at his baptism the unfortunate baby was displayed naked. Known as Philip the Fair, he married Joanna "the Mad" (*Juana La Loca)*, daughter of Spain's Isabella of Castile and Ferdinand of Aragon. As Isabella had died in 1504, Philip became king of Castile and León, again *jure uxoris*, but died shortly after, evidently of typhoid, in 1506. Distraught over her husband's death and not allowing her husband's corpse out of her sight, Joanna was plunged into depression, declared insane and confined to the Palace in Tordesillas for the rest of her life, dying in 1555. After the death of Ferdinand of Aragon in 1516, Joanna inherited that throne as well. Though now legally queen regnant of both Castile and Aragon (which would remain technically separate until 1707), Joanna was precluded from exercising any power, which went instead to her son as co-ruler, Charles I of Spain, who in 1519 added to his Spanish dominions the position of Holy Roman emperor and is accordingly known to history as the Emperor Charles V. Thanks to Charles's grandfather's marital politics, the Habsburgs were now firmly in control of Spain— which they would retain until 1700, when the death of Charles II would spark off the War of the Spanish Succession (1701–14).

Upon arrival in Spain in 1517 at the age of 17 to take up the crowns of Castile and Aragon, Charles could speak no Spanish, and the main objection to his election as Holy Roman emperor on the death of his grandfather in 1519 was that he was not sufficiently "German." His jocular ranking of languages was: "I speak Spanish to God, Italian to women, French to men, and German to my horse." Strangely, there was no rating either for Latin or Flemish, the language with which he had grown up. Though both his position as king of Spain and Holy Roman emperor came to him without firing a shot, his reign was dominated by warfare, against the German Protestants, against France, and of course, in his name though not personally, in the conquest of Mexico and Peru. He viewed the situation with sardonic humor, referring to his battle with France for control of northern Italy: "My cousin Francis and I are in perfect accord—he wants Milan, and so do I."

"Bloody Mary"

On the death of Henry VIII in 1547 there still seems to have been some doubt about whether females could inherit the throne. Up to that time the only female claimant had been Matilda (1102–67), daughter of Henry I, who lost out to her cousin Stephen during the civil war known as "The Anarchy" (1138–53), but did

Figure 14   Sixpence of Philip and Mary, 1554.
SOURCE: The Portable Antiquities Scheme / The Trustees of the British Museum / CC BY SA 4.0.

manage to secure the throne for her son, Henry II (r. 1154–89), the founder of
the Plantagenet line of kings, which lasted until 1485.

Henry VIII (r. 1509–47) finally obtained the male heir that he had gone to
such great lengths to achieve, but the young Edward VI, who succeeded to the
throne at the age of nine, would die before his 16th birthday in 1553. As a zealous Protestant, sensing his half-sister Mary's determination to turn the religious
clock back, Edward tried his best to block her succession to the throne. The
young king backed the attempt by his chief minister, the Duke of Northumberland, to remove both his half-sisters Mary and Elizabeth from the line of
succession and to champion the alternative cause of Lady Jane Grey, a committed Protestant conveniently married to Northumberland's son. Her claim to the
throne was based on the fact that she was a direct descendant of King Henry
VII and a cousin to Edward, Mary, and Elizabeth, but the only basis for her
being preferred to Mary and Elizabeth was their continuing legal classification
as "bastards." In a will amended in Edward's own hand, the throne is at first left
to "Lady Jane's male heirs" (of whom there were none) before being altered to
"Lady Jane and her male heirs." Initially, therefore, it was not envisaged that
Jane herself (aged 15) would become queen. The reason for the change may
have been the realization by Edward that he was dying and that naming only
putative heirs would have left the throne in limbo on his death.

In the event, on Edward's death Mary swept into London on a wave of public support, while Lady Jane Grey and her husband were lodged in the Tower
of London awaiting trial, and would later be beheaded. Mary initially issued a
proclamation of religious toleration, but within a few months she became transformed into the "Bloody Mary" of the history books, determined to extirpate

the "heresy" of Protestantism from her domain. Her fury knew no bounds. But before it reached fever pitch she decided to gain herself an illustrious partner in crime, the son and heir of none other than the great Emperor Charles V, himself a champion of the Catholic cause.

In 1554, Charles V was about to abdicate and retire to a monastery, dividing his dominions into two parts, with his brother Ferdinand becoming Holy Roman emperor and his Spanish crown going to his son, who would reign as Philip II from 1556 until his death in 1598. Having ascended the English throne in 1553, the 38-year-old Mary married the 27-year-old Philip, who had not yet ascended the Spanish throne. Though nowadays usually omitted from lists of British monarchs, Philip was not a consort but joint king regnant of England *jure uxoris* ("by right of his wife"), co-ruler with Mary. Laws were dated by joint regnal years, e.g. "In the third year of Philip and Mary" (his name first), the odd couple appeared facing each other on coins, and, had Mary not proved barren, Britain might today still have a Habsburg sovereign. The match was not popular in England, and a few restrictions were introduced into the marriage contract, notably the provision that Philip would lose his position on Mary's death. This occurred in 1558, though not before a burning spree in which she executed 283 Protestants as "heretics," including Bishops Ridley and Latimer, burnt at the stake together in Oxford, and Thomas Cranmer, archbishop of Canterbury, who, forced to watch his fellow bishops' ordeal, recanted his "heresy" but was himself burnt at the stake as well anyway. It is not known what Philip thought of these ruthless and obsessive burnings, but even Alfonso de Castro, a Catholic priest and theologian on Philip's staff, was appalled by them, though the Spanish Inquisition, with its own predilection for burning at the stake, was in its heyday during Philip's reign in Spain.

Mary's reign was unique in at least two respects. First, despite her barbarism, she was the first woman to be crowned queen regnant of England. [As mentioned above, the twelfth-century Matilda/Maud, who vied for the throne in a bitter civil war with her cousin Stephen (r. 1135–54), achieved very little recognition and was never crowned.] Mary was succeeded by her half-sister Elizabeth I (r. 1558–1603), who turned out to be one of the ablest and most successful British rulers of all time and established the right once and for all of females to succeed to the throne.

Secondly, Mary's marriage in 1554 to the future King Philip II of Spain is the only case in English history of a royal husband ever being recognized as king *jure uxore* ("by right of his wife"). All but one other British queens' husbands were mere consorts and were not even granted the courtesy title of "king." Prince George of Denmark, husband to Queen Anne (r. 1702–14), is hardly even a footnote in the history books. Queen Victoria's Prince Albert is of course a different case altogether, in terms both of his political and of his family role. Yet, he never had more than the title of "prince consort," and even that only after 17 years of marriage. Victoria had wanted to give him the title of "king consort," but the British government refused to put that proposal to Parliament—ostensibly on the ground that Albert was "foreign"! Yet he did at least speak English, which Philip of Spain did not—and even "king consort" is a far cry from a fully fledged king regnant, which is what Philip was. The 2013 replacement of male-preference primogeniture with absolute primogeniture—meaning that the eldest surviving child of the deceased monarch, regardless of gender, would inherit the throne—was done in conformity to "political correctness." But it has not been taken to its logical conclusion by giving the husband of a queen regnant the title of king consort, let alone that of co-equal king regnant! In fact, the position of the husband of a queen regnant has actually been reduced even below that held by Queen Victoria's husband, Prince Albert. Philip, Duke of Edinburgh (1921–2021), was not even accorded the demeaning title of prince consort, which Albert had been given in 1857 (see above). And, unlike Queen Victoria, who on her marriage to Albert adopted his family name, Saxe-Coburg-Gotha, Elizabeth II retained the (made-up) family name of Windsor after her marriage, provoking Philip to complain privately, "I am nothing but a bloody amoeba. I am the only man in the country not allowed to give his name to his own children." Philip was slightly mollified by the minor concession made in 1960 (after 13 years of marriage) of giving junior members of the royal family (those not styled "Royal Highness" or "prince/ss") the surname "Mountbatten-Windsor." The only public criticism of the plainly unfair treatment accorded to royal male consorts was expressed by Prince Henrik (1934–2018), husband of Queen Margrethe II of Denmark, who, objecting that he ought to have had the title of king, in 2016 indignantly renounced the title of prince consort that he had been accorded in 2005 (33 years after his wife's accession to the Danish throne).

"Bloody Mary" was the first British monarch whose accession was established by Parliament. Though Edward VI was much younger than his sister Mary, his succession to the throne after the death of his father Henry VIII was not in doubt. Under patrilineal primogeniture, which was well established, a male heir always took precedence over a female regardless of age. But Mary's position was much more tenuous. With the exception of the dubious claim of Matilda/Maud in the twelfth century, no woman had ever sat on the English throne, and it was by no means certain that that was permissible under the system of patrilineal primogeniture. It certainly was not allowed in France nor in any German state. But Henry VIII, who had used Parliament to break with the Papacy and make himself head of the Church of England, relied on Parliament also to regulate the succession to the throne. The first Act of Succession, passed in 1534, declared Mary illegitimate and disinherited her. Under the second Act of Succession, passed in 1537, both Mary and Elizabeth were declared illegitimate and both were disinherited, with the succession vested in any future offspring of Henry's third wife, Jane Seymour, who, however, would die in childbirth shortly after giving birth to the future Edward

VI later in 1537. In 1544 a third Succession Act, which superseded the two earlier statutes, without bothering to cancel their illegitimacy, restored Mary and Elizabeth to the line of succession, after Edward. And, if needed, this was the legal basis for Mary's succession to the throne after Edward VI's death in 1553 and for Elizabeth's succession on Mary's death five years later.

The closest case to the Philip–Mary co-rule was the joint monarchy of William III and Mary II established in the wake of the so-called "Glorious Revolution" of 1688/89. Both Philip and William were kings regnant and not consorts. Both marriages were essentially political and both were childless. Mary II and her sister, the future Queen Anne, were brought up in the Protestant faith of their mother, Anne Hyde, but their father, James II, converted to Catholicism when Mary was about seven years old and had a Catholic son, also called James, by his second wife in 1685. Though much younger than his sisters, this infant James, being male, took priority over them under patrilineal primogeniture, which was the undisputed system of succession in force at the time. However, the dominant elite as represented in Parliament was dead set against a Catholic succession and invited Mary's husband (King James's son-in-law) to invade England and depose James. Having achieved this, William refused to accept anything less than full and joint kingship with his wife continuing even after her death, and he threatened to go back to Holland if this was not granted. Faced with this ultimatum, Parliament acceded to this unprecedented demand, and in fact William did outlive Mary by a few years. But, as he died without issue, the Crown then passed to his sister-in-law Anne, who had a whole brood of children, all of whom predeceased her.

Setting their faces implacably against succession of the true heir, James II's son, commonly called "the Old Pretender," who was living abroad, the British ruling elite were now confronted with the serious problem of finding a Protestant heir. This was done by going all the way back to King James I (r. 1603–25) and tracing the line out to his great-grandson, the Elector George Louis of Hanover, who became King George I of Great Britain (r. 1714–27), whose direct descendants have occupied the British throne ever since.

The Hanoverian succession did not go unchallenged. In 1715 and again in 1745 there were Jacobite risings or rebellions—so called from the Latin of "James"—to regain the British throne for the ousted Stuarts. "The Forty-Five," as it is sometimes known, was the more serious of the two, with a Jacobite army under James II's grandson, the Young Pretender "Bonnie Prince Charlie," reaching as far south as Derby. But insufficient French assistance, lack of the expected support from Jacobites in England, and disagreements between the Young Pretender and his chief advisers resulted in an ignominious defeat at Culloden in April 1746.

The Jacobite risings only go to show how wrong it is to place undue emphasis on primogeniture as the basis for stability (see Chapter 12). The reason the

Jacobites lost out was simply a matter of power. The elite had won power in 1689 and were not going to give it up without a struggle.

Heir and Spare

Besides being his wife, "Bloody Mary" was actually Philip of Spain's first cousin once removed: Philip's grandmother was Joanna "the Mad" and Mary was the daughter of Joanna's younger sister, Catherine of Aragon, and Henry VIII of England. Joanna and Catherine were both pawns in the matrimonial chess game played by their father, Ferdinand of Aragon. But Ferdinand met his match (no pun intended) in England's Henry VII (r. 1485–1509). It was originally to Henry VII's son and heir, Arthur, Prince of Wales, that Catherine of Aragon was married. That was in 1501, when Arthur was 15 years old, but he died a few months later. Henry VII accordingly offered his "spare" son, the young Prince Henry, as a substitute for the deceased Arthur. So, a few days before her 18th birthday in 1503, Catherine was formally betrothed to the 12-year-old Henry, who rejected the marriage once he turned 14, but suddenly changed his mind and went ahead with the marriage after ascending the throne as Henry VIII in 1509. The only living offspring born to him by Catherine being a girl, Mary, Henry began to tire of her and tried to find ways of having their marriage annulled by the Pope. When this failed, Henry appointed the Protestant Thomas Cranmer as archbishop of Canterbury, who had no trouble declaring Henry's marriage to Catherine of Aragon null and void and against the law of God on the ground that she was previously married to Henry's brother Arthur. The biblical text relied upon by Cranmer was Leviticus 20:21: "And if a man shall take his brother's wife, it is impurity: he hath uncovered his brother's nakedness." But this was a blatant misinterpretation of the scriptural text, which is simply a condemnation of *adultery*—not marriage—between a man and his brother's wife. This biblical chapter contains a list of forbidden sexual acts, including a man's adultery with another man's wife, with his father's wife, with his daughter-in-law, his mother-in-law, his sister, and his aunt—and also strong condemnation of bestiality and homosexuality. There is no mention of marriage to the widow of a *deceased* brother, which in fact is not only allowed but even made obligatory (with some comical exceptions), by the biblical law of *Levirate marriage* in Deuteronomy 25:5: "If brethren dwell together, and one of them die, and have no child, the wife of the dead shall not be married abroad unto one not of his kin; her husband's brother shall go in unto her, and take her to him to wife; and perform the duty of a husband's brother unto her." Unlike Leviticus 20:21, this very precise text refers specifically to *marriage* and to a *dead* brother.

Of course, Henry's "divorce"—and the whole English Reformation that flowed from it—had nothing to do with the Bible (or even the allegation that

Catherine's marriage to Arthur had never been consummated), but was motivated purely and simply by Henry's consuming desire for a male heir.

"Perpetual Peace"

But Henry VII's dabbling in matrimonial politics was not confined to his marrying off his sons. To seal the "Treaty of Perpetual Peace" with Scotland in 1502, he arranged for his daughter Margaret to marry the Scottish King James IV (r. 1488–1513) in 1503. The peace was intended to end the intermittent border wars that had plagued relations between the two countries for at least two centuries. As a bad omen, the oath-taking ceremony had to be repeated as the word "England" in the text of James's oath had been accidentally(?) replaced by "France." And sure enough, after the 1513 attack on France as part of the "Holy League" by Henry VIII, who had ascended the English throne in 1509, James chose to side with France, with which Scotland had an "Auld Alliance" going back to 1295, thereby breaking the "Perpetual Peace" with England, and actually led a large army across the border into England, where he was defeated and killed in the Battle of Flodden together with the flower of the Scottish aristocracy. This entirely avoidable catastrophe is commemorated in the haunting bagpipe dirge, "The Flowers of the Forest."

But the short-lived Anglo-Scottish pact had an unforeseen long-term result. James IV had himself succeeded to the Scottish throne in 1488 at the age of 15, after his father, James III, had been killed in battle against a noble rebellion—under the nominal headship of the future James IV himself. So much for idea that primogeniture ensures stability! On James IV's demise at 40, his infant son, James V, was crowned king at the age of 17 months. And when he too died prematurely in 1542, this time from illness, the Crown passed to his six-day-old daughter, Mary Queen of Scots (1542–87), a devout Catholic, who fell foul of the influential Scottish Protestant nobles and the fiery Calvinist preacher John Knox.

The "Auld Alliance" with France came to her rescue, as, with a view to uniting France and Scotland, King Henry II of France (r. 1547–59) proposed marrying Mary to the three-year-old dauphin (heir to the French throne) Francis. Mary was duly bundled off to France. The ambitions of her father-in-law Henry II of France were heightened in 1558 by the accession to the English throne of the 25-year-old Elizabeth, the last of Henry VIII's offspring, who, as a Protestant, was considered illegitimate and not recognized as queen by many Catholics, including some in England itself. Taking advantage of this, Henry II of France proclaimed Mary of Scots not just as heir presumptive to the English throne (which she was), but as queen of England, and she was given a coat of arms reflecting this claim. On the death of Henry II in a jousting tournament in 1559, the 16-year-old Mary became queen consort to the 15-year-old Francis II of France, as the dauphin was now known.

In 1560 a brain abscess carried off the young Francis II, and the following year returned to Scotland to find it in religious and political turmoil. Mary gave way to the ascendancy of the Protestant nobles whom she found running the show. It never occurred to her to appeal to the people, the majority of whom were probably still Catholic.

In her search for a new husband, several potential royal matches were rejected by one side or the other, and a noble French poet who was an ardent admirer of hers was beheaded for treason after being caught hiding under her bed. In the end, in 1565 she married her English-born but Catholic half-cousin Henry Stuart, Lord Darnley, who had a claim to the English throne himself. Given the title of king consort, he demanded the "Crown Matrimonial" instead, the Scottish equivalent of the usual European position of king *juris uxoris,* which would not only have made him co-ruler with Mary but would also have entitled him to remain as king regnant for life if he outlived her, and leave the throne even to offspring with a new wife. However, Mary was not prepared to entertain any such demand. And in March 1566 Darnley was instrumental in arranging the murder of Mary's Catholic secretary and close personal friend David Rizzio right in front of Mary at a dinner party at Holyrood Palace. Though Darnley was probably gay, he gave Mary a son, James, who was born in June 1566. In February 1567 Darnley himself was murdered, probably with Mary's acquiescence, by James Hepburn, Earl of Bothwell, whom Mary married in a Protestant service in May of that year.

Twenty-six Scottish nobles, banded together as the "confederate lords," raised an army against Mary and Bothwell. While Bothwell was allowed safe passage to leave the country, Mary was detained and forced to abdicate in favor of her one-year-old son James, who was crowned as King James VI of Scots in July 1567. Mary had last seen James when he was 10 months old and would never see him again.

Escaping from her captivity, Mary managed to raise an army of 6,000 men, which was defeated by a smaller force under her illegitimate half-brother, the Earl of Moray, who had been appointed regent for the young king. Then, instead of making for France, where she was still recognized as queen dowager, Mary unwisely sought asylum in England. Never a particularly good judge of character, she was evidently expecting Elizabeth to assist her to regain her throne. Instead, the cunning, distrustful, and ever-vigilant Elizabeth kept Mary prisoner for 19 years, moving her from castle to castle, being careful to pick locations neither too close to the Scottish border nor to London or to the sea. Mary was allowed to have her own staff, who never numbered fewer than sixteen, and her chefs prepared sumptuous dinners for her with a choice of 32 dishes served on silver platters. But Elizabeth's fears were justified, as Mary was involved in plots against Elizabeth's life, which would have placed Mary on the English throne. When eventually put on trial for treason before a court of 36 English noblemen, Mary correctly pointed out that as a foreign queen she was not and never had been an English subject and could not therefore be guilty of treason. Needless to say, this plea fell on deaf ears and Mary was convicted by 35 votes to one and sentenced to death. Fearful of setting a precedent of regicide and afraid also of the possibility of revenge, Elizabeth only signed Mary's death warrant when it was presented to her in the midst of other papers requiring her signature, pretending afterwards that she had been tricked into signing it by her minister William Davison, who was lodged temporarily in the Tower of London for his pains.

But, once the warrant had been signed, Elizabeth's chief adviser, William Cecil, Lord Burghley, made sure the execution took place with no further ado, on 7 February 1587. Mary's cheerful disposition as she faced death was not justified by the botched job done by the executioner, who took two blows to behead her. Her long auburn hair turned out to be a wig, with short grey hair underneath. And, as the last pathetic touch, her little dog emerged from her petticoats.

James VI of Scots now became James I of England as well, ascending the English throne without incident on the death of Elizabeth in 1603. But the history of his Stuart successors would prove to be anything but a bed of roses.

Hundred Years' War

The underlying issue was whether a male could inherit the throne through a female who was not herself entitled to occupy it. This came to a head in the so-called Hundred Years' War, the longest military conflict in European history, which rumbled on between England and France intermittently from 1337 until 1453. When Charles IV of France died in 1328 without male issue, the direct line of the House of Capet, which had occupied the French throne since 987, died with him. His closest male relative was his nephew (his mother's sister's son) Edward III of England, who duly claimed the French throne. The French nobility rejected his claim on the basis of the legal principle, *Nemo dat quod non habet* ("Nobody can give what he does not have"). It was well established that no woman had the right to occupy the French throne. So how could she transmit such a right to anyone else? The throne was therefore offered to Philip of Valois, whose father, Charles, Count of Valois, was a younger brother of Philip IV of France (r. 1285–1314), Charles IV's father. So Philip VI, as he became (r. 1328–50), was a paternal first cousin to Charles IV and is counted as the founder of the House of Valois, a cadet (i.e. younger) line of the Capetian House. Though England's Edward III first appears to have accepted Philip VI's succession, a dispute soon arose giving Edward an excuse to resuscitate his clam to the French throne, which triggered seesaw military engagements starting in 1337. Initial

English victories were followed by reversals and a long dormant period, when England's Henry V (r. 1413–22) burst on the scene carrying all before him. But his premature death, followed by the unique phenomenon that was Joan of Arc, eventually enabled the French to drive the English out of France.

War of the Roses

In the meantime a protracted internecine conflict over succession to the throne had been playing out in England. Now known as the Wars of the Roses, from the emblems of the two sides, the White Rose of York and the Red Rose of Lancaster, the conflict first manifested itself during the reign of the weak Richard II (r. 1377–99). Having come to the throne at the age of 10, he was beset by hostile powerful nobles, including family members. Most powerful among these was his paternal cousin, Henry Bolingbroke, who managed eventually to depose and imprison the king and have himself declared king as the first Lancastrian king, Henry IV (r. 1399–1413).

Thanks partly at least to Shakespeare, Henry IV's son and successor, Henry V (r. 1413–22), is now commonly regarded as a particularly successful king. His prowess in battle is indisputable, but his diplomatic skills should not be underestimated either, not least as far as domestic disputes were concerned. But his death at the age of 35 left a nine-month-old child, Henry VI, nominally in charge of the kingdom, which turned out to be disastrous both for the country and for the boy-king himself, who, to make matters worse, was pathologically indecisive and suffered from intermittent feeblemindedness. This opened up a challenge to his throne from the Yorkists.

While Henry VI's Lancastrian claim to the throne was by male patrilineal primogeniture as a direct descendant of Edward III through Edward's eldest son, Edward the Black Prince, the Yorkist claim was inferior to it in two respects: first by being only through Edward III's *second* son, Lionel, Duke of Clarence, and then only through the female line from him, The Yorkists did also have direct male-line descent from Edward III, but that was only through a much younger son of his, Edmund Duke of York.

So the Lancastrian line had the stronger claim—at least in the person of Henry VI. But his death (in captivity) and that of his only son (supposedly in battle), both in 1471, left the Lancastrian standard in the hands of a much more remote relative, who would become King Henry VII on defeating and killing the Yorkist Richard III in the Battle of Bosworth Field in 1485, which finally put paid to the Wars of the Roses.

Primogeniture was not in issue in this bloody war, which took a toll of the flower (no pun intended!) of the English aristocracy. It was agreed on all hands that, though females could not themselves occupy the English throne, a claim to the throne could be made through them by their male heirs. This left the sword as the only way to settle the dispute, which would probably not have arisen at all had Henry VI shown the same strength of character as his father, Henry V. As a result of his vacillations and mental instability he became an easy target. The Wars of the Roses were a military game of chequers, with Henry deposed by the Yorkist Edward IV in 1461, imprisoned in the Tower of London in 1465, restored to the throne in 1470, and finally imprisoned again and probably murdered in 1471.

Allegations of illegitimacy now became the weapon of choice in disputed successions. On Edward IV's death in 1483, the throne passed automatically to his 12-year-old son under the title of Edward V. But before the boy-king could be crowned, the deceased king's brother Richard quickly had both Edward V and his nine-year-old brother declared illegitimate and, as their closest relative, ascended the throne himself as Richard III. The two boys, known to history as "the Princes in the Tower," were probably subsequently murdered.

The question of legitimacy reared its head again after the feverish quest for a male heir by Henry VIII (r. 1485–1509). After the birth of his son in 1537, who would succeed him as Edward VI, Henry proceeded to have both his daughters (Mary, b. 1516, and Elizabeth, b. 1533) declared illegitimate—while still naming them in the line of succession to the throne after Edward and his putative heirs (see above).

Chapter 15
Coup and Usurpation

*A*s shown in Chapter 2, true monarchy is essentially anti-aristocratic, and often populist. Such monarchs are quite likely to have come to power violently, in a coup or revolution, or by usurpation, sometimes with active or passive popular support. One of the most lasting usurpations was that by Gyges in Lydia (in modern Turkey) in about 680 BCE, who established a dynasty of direct descendants that lasted until the defeat of his great-grandson Croesus in 546 BCE. On Croesus's consulting the oracle at Delphi on whether he should attack the Persian King Cyrus, Croesus was told that if he did so he would destroy a great empire. The oracle was right—but the empire that Croesus destroyed was his own.

The Ancient Greek Tyrants

Ancient Greece provides us with a good example of populist monarchy by coup in the shape of the so-called *tyrants*, whose heyday was from 650 to 550 BCE, though tyrants pop up in later periods of Greek history as well. Tyrannies mostly arose on the overthrow of aristocratic (or oligarchic) governments. Today the word "tyrant" has pejorative connotations, but these bad associations date only from the fifth century BCE. Before that the word had simply been a neutral synonym for "king," and there is strong evidence that in their own day the tyrants were genuinely popular leaders of anti-aristocratic movements.

Aristotle put the tyrants' typical power base in a nutshell: "The majority of tyrants have generally developed out of demagogues who have gained the confidence of the people through their attacks upon the nobles" (Aristot. *Pol.* 1310b 8ff = V.8.2–3).

The tyrants' approach to the rich and noble is graphically illustrated by an anecdote related by Herodotus concerning Periander, tyrant of Corinth

Five Thousand Years of Monarchy, First Edition. Michael Arnheim.
© 2026 John Wiley & Sons, Inc. Published 2026 by John Wiley & Sons, Inc.

(r. 627–585), and his fellow tyrant, Thrasybulus of Miletus. Aristotle tells the same story, with roles reversed (Aristot. *Pol.* 3.1284a and 5.1311a). The story as told by Herodotus is that Periander sent a herald to Thrasybulus to ask his advice on the conduct of government. His advice was lost on the messenger, because it was mimed rather than spoken and amounted in fact to a graphic demonstration of the policy he was recommending:

> Thrasybulus led the man who had come from Periander outside the city and, entering a sown field, he walked through the corn questioning and interrogating the herald about his voyage from Corinth, and all the time he was lopping off any ears of corn that he saw projecting above the others, and he cast them aside as he cut them down until he had destroyed the best and richest portion of the crop by this means (Hdt. 5.92f).

Though this charade may have been wasted on the servant, it was certainly not lost on his master. This graphic demonstration epitomizes in itself the role of the tyrant as the enemy of the rich and noble and as a leveler.

Is this charming anecdote historical? Most probably. Not only does it ring true, but, in view of the reversal of roles, Aristotle's version would appear to derive from a different source from Herodotus's. But it really makes no difference whether it is true or not. As they say in Italian: *se non è vero, è ben trovato* ("if it's not true, it's plausible"). It neatly encapsulates the secret of monarchical power—sometimes labeled the "tall poppy syndrome"—well understood by many strong rulers throughout history, though, with a few notable exceptions, rarely by historians.

In a book specifically titled *The Greek Tyrants* by Anthony Andrewes, an Oxford professor, there is no mention at all of the famous anecdote. Even more disquieting, the book shows no sign of understanding the point made by Aristotle about the general anti-aristocratic basis of the tyrants' power (Andrewes 1956). The closest that Andrewes gets to any kind of general conclusion on the nature of Greek tyranny is in these vague remarks in the epilog (there is no "conclusion"):

> [The early tyrants] were a product of the instability of their times, in their case of the breakdown of archaic aristocratic government. . .. The basic cause was a change in the conditions, above all the economic conditions, of Greek life, and the symptom of trouble was the incompetence or mere anarchy of the aristocrats. When the trouble came to a head, the immediate need of the city concerned was for strong government to repair the damage and pull the state together, and the tyrant's unfettered executive power answered this need (Andrewes 1956, p. 147).

There is no sign here of any awareness of the dominant thread of populism running through Greek tyranny. Instead, the rise of tyrants is confusingly associated with "the incompetence or mere anarchy of the aristocrats." The term "mere anarchy" contradicts the very existence of aristocratic (or any other kind of) government, meaning as it does "no government." And the phrase "mere anarchy" makes about as much sense as "slight chaos" or "minor catastrophe." More important, if it means anything at all, the "mere anarchy of the aristocrats" should mean that aristocratic government had already broken down before the tyrant took power. Yet there is no evidence of that in any Greek state.

By contrast, Moses Finley, to his credit, drew a parallel between the tyrant Peisistratus and Pericles, the personification of Athenian democracy, recognizing the important truth that both were essentially "champions of the people" against the rich and noble:

> It is significant that of the few innovations by Pisistratus that have survived in the historical record, two were obviously designed to weaken the local power of the richer landowners by undermining major devices that fostered patron-client relations. . ... In that respect, Pericles was a direct heir of Pisistratus: he reestablished the apparently defunct board of deme judges and he instituted a long series of measures giving financial assistance to the poor from state funds... (Finley 1983, p. 47).

Tyranny and Democracy

In his *Rhetoric*, Aristotle names three demagogic tyrants—Theagenes of Megara (seventh century BCE), Peisistratus of Athens (died 527 BCE), and Dionysius I of Syracuse (c. 432–367 BCE)—who are said to have won the confidence of the people by their "enmity toward the rich." All three came to power by means of a coup. The same three names recur in Aristotle's *Politics* as tyrants who were "the champions of the people" (*hoi prostatai tou dēmou*) (Aristot. *Rh.* 1305a 18ff = V.4.5)—significantly, exactly the same phrase as used for Athenian democratic leaders.

The leveling regarded as most typical of tyranny was thought by Aristotle to have been invented by Periander, tyrant of Corinth (died 587 BCE). These measures included: "The cutting down of the illustrious and the destruction of the proud, and also the prohibition of dining clubs, social clubs, education or anything of that sort" (Aristot. *Rh.* 1313a 38ff = V.9.2). All these measures were directed against the activities of the rich. The poor were not much given to joining dining clubs or cultural societies—and would not have been able to afford that lifestyle in any case.

Athens: From Tyranny to Democracy

Referring to Athens, Plutarch remarks that: "From the beginning there had been a sort of hidden seam, as in iron, marking the difference between the popular and aristocratic parties" (Plut., *Pericles,* 11.3). The Aristotelian *Athenian Constitution* (*Athenaiōn Politeia [AP],* probably written by Aristotle himself or by one of his students) singles out two politicians in every generation, one billed as "the people's champion" (*prostatēs tou dēmou)* and the other as leader of the "notables" (*gnōrimoi)* or aristocracy (Aristot. *AP* 28). The popular leaders are identified in chronological order as Solon, Peisistratus, Cleisthenes, Themistocles, Ephialtes, Pericles, Cleon, and Cleophon. Significantly, Peisistratus, a tyrant, is here lumped together with the popular leaders of the democracy, including Pericles.

Solon, the earliest of Aristotle's "people's champions," came to power in 594 BCE in the wake of an economic crisis, but, when called upon by the masses to become a tyrant, he demurred. The masses found a more reliable champion in Peisistratus, who first came to power in about 561 BCE and did not let them down. It is significant that the people were not seeking to take power into their own hands: they were looking for a champion to take power on their behalf.

Aristotle's *Athenian Constitution* rounds off its assessment of Peisistratus's long rule by describing him as popular (*dēmotikos)* and humane (*philanthrōpos)*, ruling in accordance with the law and not favoring his own interests—even to the point of appearing in person to defend himself against a murder charge, whereupon his accuser took fright and fled. Though deposed twice, we are told, he easily got back into power because most of the nobles (*gnōrimoi)* as well as the people were well disposed toward him, the former by his social interaction and the latter by his assistance to them in their personal affairs, and he "behaved impeccably (*kalōs)* to both" (Aristot. *AP* 9). Adding aristocratic support to his original populist power base was an unusual—and far from easy—achievement for a tyrant, which presumably contributed to his resilience.

Peisistratus died in his bed in 527 BCE and was succeeded as tyrant by his son Hippias. The assassination of Hippias's brother Hipparchus in 514 BCE seems to have had more to do with a homosexual love triangle than with politics, and his aristocratic murderers, Harmodius and his lover Aristogeiton, later fêted as "tyrannicides" and even as "liberators," were actually neither. Hippias's tyranny lasted another four years, until 510 BCE, when he was ousted by an aristocratic coup—and then only with the help of a Spartan army on its second attempt, under the personal command of King Cleomenes I (Aristot. *AP* 19.4). The two aristocratic factions behind Hippias's ouster then fell out, and when Cleomenes took the Acropolis together with Isagoras and his aristocratic faction, "the rest of the Athenians united and besieged them for two days," resulting in the surrender of the Spartan army (Hdt. 5.72; Aristot. *AP* 20.3). This remarkable achievement, the overpowering of the mighty Spartan army by a motley host of Athenians, is yet further testimony to the popularity of the tyranny.

Cleisthenes, a member of the noble Alcmaeonid family, now moved into the vacuum left by the tyrant, and, according to Herodotus, "added the common people to his faction." (Hdt. 5.66) Aristotle, as we have seen, similarly lumped Cleisthenes together with Peisistratus as a "champion of the people" (Aristot. *AP* 28). But, where Peisistratus's demagogy took the form of one-man rule, Cleisthenes' was translated into a major reform of the Athenian constitution, which established what later came to be labeled democracy but which Cleisthenes himself called *isonomia*, or "legal equality," the hallmark of which was sortition, i.e. selection by lot—as distinct from election—of most official positions.

Modern Coups

The Greek Colonels' Coup

A coup d'état is by definition the illegal seizure of power, which in practice is generally military, which does not preclude popular support, as illustrated by some modern cases. The Greek colonels' "junta" of 1967–73 was essentially dictatorial rule by Colonel Georgios Papadopoulos, who always described the coup as a revolution. This was certainly not the case, though the regime was welcomed by large sectors of Greek society—92% of those voting in a referendum held in 1968 agreed to ratify a new constitution to be prepared by the regime, but this result cannot be relied upon, as voting was compulsory, though over 22% still abstained. Farmers, called by Papadopoulos "the backbone of the people," were encouraged to support the regime by canceling all agricultural loans and promoting rural economic development, which had been neglected before. There was widespread approval of the regime's economic policies, including the large-scale development of infrastructure and the promotion of tourism.

King Constantine II vacillated in the face of the coup, at first reluctantly endorsing it, then planning an abortive counter-coup, and then fleeing into exile. In 1973 Papadopoulos deposed the king and declared Greece a presidential republic with himself as president. This was approved in a referendum by 78.57% of those voting. Ironically, when initiating a policy of liberalization, the regime was toppled in a counter-coup by a disgruntled junta hardliner and head of the military police, Brigadier Dimitrios Ioannidis, as the "invisible dictator," who engineered a coup against President (Archbishop) Makarios of Cyprus, which resulted in a Turkish invasion of that island, leading to the loss of Northern Cyprus to Turkey and the collapse of Ioannidis's short-lived regime in Greece in 1974.

Fidel Castro

Another modern regime that always described its seizure of power as a revolution was that of the Cuban dictator Fidel Castro (in power 1959–2008). By contrast with the Greek "junta," which was decidedly right-wing, Fidel Castro's regime was left-wing, though he only admitted to being a "Marxist-Leninist" in

December 1961. But my analysis of regimes in terms of power structure demonstrates the irrelevance of terms like "left" and "right."

By the time he came to power in 1959 he had been fighting a guerrilla war against the regime of Fulgencio Batista since 1953, yet his assumption of power was really more in the nature of a coup. Despite his reputation for corruption, Batista was endorsed in 1940 by the Cuban Communist Party, and during his 1940–44 term in office Batista actually introduced some major social reforms and pro-union policies. Ironically, in his oft-quoted 1953 two-hour courtroom defense speech titled "History will absolve me," Castro attacked Batista for taking power by coup in 1933 and suspending the 1940 constitution, which Castro vowed to restore (but never did). And in fact in 1952 Batista returned to power by means of another (military) coup.

In 1954 Castro admitted his own lack of support:

I would honestly love to revolutionize this country from one end to the other! I am sure this would bring happiness to the Cuban people. I would not be stopped by the hatred and ill will of a few thousand people, including some of my relatives, half the people I know, two-thirds of my fellow professionals, and four-fifths of my schoolmates (Coltman 2003).

Figure 15 Fidel Castro with Che Guevara, 1961.
SOURCE: Unknown author / Wikimedia Commons / Public Domain.

As late as November 1956 Castro's supporters only numbered 82, of whom 21 survived a crash-landing of their yacht (farcically named the *Granma*) and an ambush by Batista troops. And even in August 1958 Castro had no more than 300 men under him, though by guerrilla tactics they managed to gain control of most of Oriente and Las Villas provinces. It was at this point that US President Eisenhower pulled the rug from under Batista and switched America's support to a right-wing military junta under the senior army general, Eulogio Cantillo. With the threat of a criminal indictment hanging over him, Batista announced his resignation to his associates at a New Year's Eve party on 31 December 1958 and scuttled into exile armed with a cache of more than US$300 million. General Eulogio Cantillo, Chief of the Joint Staff, then moved into the presidential palace, appointed Supreme Court judge Carlos Piedra as the new president and establishing a military junta. Setting up his base in the penthouse of the Havana Hilton hotel, Castro had Cantillo and his junta arrested and proclaimed Manuel Urrutia, a lawyer, provisional president, falsely declaring that Urrutia had been selected by "popular election." To curb corruption, Urrutia immediately started closing down all brothels, gambling outlets, and even the national lottery. This naturally aroused fierce opposition among the workers involved, supported by Castro, who, on the resignation of José Miró Cardona after six weeks in office, assumed the position of prime minister. This was Castro's first official appointment, in which his clash with Urrutia became final when Castro refused to hold elections. After being publicly denounced by Castro on television, Urrutia resigned as president and went into exile, at first seeking asylum in the Venezuelan embassy and then emigrating to New York, where he worked as a university professor.

Castro took to heart the lesson of the "tall poppy syndrome," as discussed in Chapter 15, to eliminate the opposition, thereby consolidating his own position while supposedly favoring the masses and creating a more egalitarian society.

Rounding up anyone suspected of having been a supporter of Batista's, he arranged show trials, the first of which was held at the Havana Sports Palace stadium before an audience of 17,000. In response to criticism of his mass executions, Castro remarked: "We are not executing innocent people or political opponents. We are executing murderers and they deserve it" (Coltman 2003, pp. 110–112).

Castro's "First Agrarian Reform," enacted just five months after his assumption of power in 1959, broke up large estates, confiscated the land and redistributed it to about 200,000 peasants. "[T]he first property he seized was his own family's farm. Castro's mother . . . never forgave her son" (Robinson 2005, p. Y07). "[T]he revolution," Castro is quoted as proclaiming, "is the dictatorship of the exploited against the exploiters" (Mankiewicz 1976, p. 83). Within a year, it is estimated, the Castro regime redistributed around 15% of the nation's wealth. Cubans who were paid less than $100 a month had their rents halved. Judges' and politicians' salaries were reduced, while low-level civil servants received a pay rise. Sugar production, the mainstay of the Cuban economy, was nationalized, together with the oil industry. In time, over 90% of the economy came under government control, and wages averaged less than $20 a month (Sanchez 2010). Education was greatly expanded and a free healthcare system was established. The flip side of the coin was the abolition of elections, the arrest of hundreds of "counter-revolutionaries," and the suppression of freedom of speech and of the press (Quirk 1993).

Under the slogan *¡En cada barrio, Revolución!* ("In every neighborhood, Revolution!"), Castro set up what he called "a collective system of revolutionary vigilance, so that everybody knows who lives on every block, what they do, what relations they have had with the tyranny [viz. the previous regime, under Fulgencio Batista], in what activities they are involved, and with whom they meet." This system involved a "Big Brother" type network of thousands of *Comités de Defensa de la Revolución* ("Committees for the Defence of the Revolution," or CDR), charged with spying on everyone living in every apartment block in the country and reporting back to the police. In their defense, these "committees" also had a role in "vaccination campaigns, blood banks, recycling, practicing evacuations for hurricanes. . ." (Sanchez 2010).

The most prominent and enduring symbol of the Cuban "revolution" is the iconic image, not of Fidel Castro but of Ernesto "Che" Guevara, emblazoned on T-shirts still proudly worn by thousands of admirers around the world. An Argentinian by birth, second-in-command to Castro in the fight against the Batista regime, and then a key member of Castro's government for a few years, Guevara left Cuba in 1965 to foment revolution in Africa and later in Bolivia, where he was captured and summarily executed by firing squad at the age of 39 in 1967. What is not quite so well known is that Che's departure from Cuba and his doomed mission to Bolivia were encouraged by Castro, who evidently felt threatened by Che. And, though "there was a guerrilla unit in Havana ready to deploy and rescue Guevara, Fidel never authorized the mission", abandoning Che to his fate (Müller 2015).

Castro's treatment of Che Guevara is of a piece with the "tall poppy syndrome." Not only did Castro cut the former elite down to size, but he also could not brook sharing power even with his closest and most fervent supporters.

Chapter 16
Conquest

*T*here are essentially two main types of accession: internal and external, with several subdivisions within each. Internal accession may be either by heredity, election, coup, or revolution. External accession is usually by conquest, and, in rare cases, by marriage. Conquest itself may be divided into foreign conquest and conquest by a related state or entity. All these varieties are in evidence from the earliest recorded time.

There are several possible motives for conquest: economic, political, or dynastic probably being the main ones. The conquests of Alexander the Great not only catapulted him into semi-divine status, but also enabled him to bequeath his short-lived power to long-lasting monarchical regimes, notably in Syria and Egypt. The Achaemenid Persian Empire conquered by Alexander was itself the product of conquest by Cyrus the Great two hundred years earlier, and was the heir to a succession of empires established by conquest, going back to the Neo-Babylonian, Neo-Assyrian, Old Babylonian, Old Assyrian, Neo-Sumerian, and Akkadian empires, taking us back to around 2330 BCE, when Sargon of Akkad established what is commonly regarded as the first empire properly so called.

Alexander vs. Augustus

Hearing that, after accomplishing most of his conquests by the age of 32, Alexander was at a loss what to do for the rest of his life, Augustus expressed surprise that Alexander did not regard it as a greater achievement to stabilize the empire which he had won than to win it (Plutarch 1931, p. 235).

This contrast between Alexander the Great and Augustus underlines the difference between the conqueror and the consolidator. Legend has it that on surveying the extent of his conquests Alexander the Great wept, lamenting that there were no more worlds to conquer. His empire was one of the largest in history, and he never lost a battle even when outnumbered.

Augustus's conquests came to an abrupt end with the loss of three legions under Publius Quintilius Varus in 9 CE to an alliance of Germanic tribes under Arminius. So distraught was Augustus at this humiliating defeat that, according to Suetonius, he stood butting his head against the wall and crying out: "Quintilius Varus, give me back my legions!" (Suet., *Vita Divi Augusti,* 23). Prior to this, Augustus had expanded the Roman Empire considerably, including the annexation of Egypt as part of his own patrimony. But his real achievement was to establish a new lasting form of government, a strong monarchy with popular support while also managing to placate the senatorial aristocracy.

It took some hard-fought battles to build up the Roman Empire, which reached its greatest extent under Trajan (98–117). "Where they make a desert, they call it 'peace'" is the bitter taunt cast in the teeth of Roman conquest by a probably fictitious Scottish chieftain in a certainly fictitious speech attributed to him by the Roman historian Tacitus (Tac. *Agric.,* 30). As was usual among ancient historians, Tacitus is here imagining how a Scottish chieftain might conceivably have felt about the Romans. This passage appears in a complimentary biography of Agricola, Tacitus's father-in-law, who was governor of Britannia. And there is no suggestion that the accusations hurled at the Romans in this made-up speech were true.

The Romans treated conquered peoples well, unless they rose up in revolt against Roman rule, in which case the rebellion was put down sharply, as happened with the Jews in 66–70 CE, when the Temple in Jerusalem was destroyed, and again in the case of the Bar Kokhba revolt of 132 CE. But, in 69 CE, just 55 years after the death of Augustus, the first emperor of equestrian (i.e. non-senatorial) origin came to power in the shape of Vespasian, and the Emperor Trajan (r. 98–117) was from Spain, after which the emperors were drawn from an ever-widening circle of provinces. Before long it became a proud boast for a member of a conquered nation, like, for example, Paul of Tarsus, to say: *Civis Romanus sum* ("I am a Roman citizen").

Increasingly over time, more and more provincials entered the senatorial aristocracy, which had the dual effect of empowering the provincials to identify with Rome and at the same time diluting the aristocracy with new blood and thereby making it less of a potential threat to the monarchy. And in 212 the Emperor Caracalla extended Roman citizenship to all free adult males throughout the empire. To this day, the Western provinces of the Roman Empire mostly speak languages derived from Latin, have Roman-based law, and have even transmitted these features to their own former colonies in the Americas.

Machiavelli's Hypothesis

In *The Prince,* written in 1513, Machiavelli cogently argues that a strong, centralized monarchy like the Achaemenid Persian Empire, administered by "servants" who can be hired and fired by the monarch, is harder to conquer than a weak, decentralized monarchy in which "barons" have their own independent regional power bases. The reason for this is that where the monarch is strong and all loyalties are focused on him, a prospective conqueror will be unable to find allies to help him topple the regime, whereas in the case of a weak, decentralized monarchy, a prospective conqueror would more readily find allies who would assist him for their own selfish purposes. However, Machiavelli continues, by the same token, once conquered, it is the strong, centralized monarchies that are easier to control, because the conqueror has replaced the conquered as the sole focus of loyalty. Therefore, says Machiavelli, it was with difficulty that Alexander conquered the Persian Empire, but, once conquered, it was ruled with comparative ease by his successors, the Ptolemies in Egypt and the Seleucids in Syria (see Chapter 11).

Alexander and After

On his death at the age of 33, Alexander's empire stretched from Greece to Egypt and as far east as the Indus River, an area of about 5.2 million square kilometers. Probably Alexander's most important achievement was his conquest of the great Achaemenid Persian Empire under Darius III. Alexander claimed at times to be taking his revenge on the Persians under Xerxes for burning of the Acropolis of Athens. Yet, Alexander also laid claim to be a worthier successor than Darius to the Achaemenid throne and appropriated the Achaemenid claim to be the protector of the peasantry. On Darius's assassination by Bessus, a leading satrap and relative of his, Alexander even claimed to have been named by the dying Darius as his heir, and in keeping with this, not only gave Darius an elaborate regal funeral and had him buried with his Achaemenid predecessors in the royal crypt in Persepolis, but also perpetuated the general structure of government and society under his own rule and even introduced the Persian custom of *proskynesis,* or prostration of his subjects before him, which, however, he abandoned when it was rejected by his Macedonian troops as overweening and pretentious. But Alexander's attempt to win the support of his subjects in the Persian Empire as the avenger of Darius III's death against Bessus, who had proclaimed himself king as Artaxerxes V, rang rather hollow against Alexander's brutal destruction of the ceremonial capital of Persepolis.

Persia was not the only part of his empire where Alexander decided to "go native." To be recognized as the legitimate heir to the long line of pharaohs or

Figure 16 Alexander the Great, tetradrachm.
SOURCE: Unknown author / Wikimedia Commons / Public domain.

kings going back to around 3100 BCE, Alexander sacrificed to the gods at Memphis and even consulted the famous oracle in the desert at Siwa, which declared him to be the son of Amun-Ra, and on the coinage minted after his death he is always portrayed with the horns of Amun. As Amun was the traditional head of the Egyptian pantheon, this tied in with his mother's belief that he was the son of Zeus, the chief god among the Greeks.

Alexander belonged to the Argead (or Temenid) dynasty of Dorian Greek origin, which had been the royal house of the kingdom of Macedon since around 700 BCE, though only reliably attested from the reign of Amyntas, who reigned from 512 until his death in 498/7 BCE as a vassal of the Achaemenid Persian Empire. Independence from Persia was achieved by Alexander I in 479 BCE. The history of the Argead family after that was punctuated by assassination and usurpation until the reign of Philip II (r. 359–336 BCE), who had himself usurped the throne from his young nephew Amyntas IV. Unlike other similar usurpations (such as Richard III's notorious usurpation of the English throne from his young nephew in 1483), Philip did not have Amyntas killed, but on Philip's assassination (by his own bodyguard), his son and successor, the future Alexander the Great, soon disposed of his cousin. His own family's turbulent history can only have left Alexander with a desire for a smoother succession in the future. Instead, leaving no clear successor, Alexander's own death at the age of 33 resulted in a protracted series of Wars of the *Diadochoi* ("Successors") which lasted from 322 to 281 BCE.

When the smoke cleared after this long period, Alexander's huge empire was shared out between three dynasties, each descended from one of Alexander's generals. The Antigonid dynasty, descended from Antigonus, controlled Macedon and much of Greece until the Roman conquest of 168 BCE. The Seleucids, from Seleucus "Nikator" ("the Victorious"), had an empire stretching at its height from present-day Syria to Pakistan. After considerable shrinkage it began to crumble after about 100 BCE, and finally succumbed to the Romans in 63 BCE.

After Alexander's death Egypt, together with Libya, Cyprus (and for a time Coele-Syria including Judea) fell to Ptolemy and his successors, which continued until 30 BCE, when it became part of the *patrocinium* ("personal domain") of the Roman ruler Augustus and his successors. The Ptolemies were the only *Diadochoi* who followed Alexander's example and "went native." styling themselves "pharaoh." appearing on coins and public monuments in this guise; and even going so far as to adopt the pre-Alexandrian custom of incestuous brother–sister marriage, which resulted in some genetic degeneration. It also led to a number of female pharaohs, mostly as co-rulers with their brother but also in a few cases as sole monarchs.

Besides the Ptolemies, the *Diadochoi* contented themselves with the ordinary Greek title for king, *basileus*, and did not ape local traditions. The Seleucids, in particular, were great Hellenizers, which brought them into conflict with their Jewish subjects, who successfully rebelled against them and established their own kingdom of Judea under the Hasmonean dynasty, which lasted from 104 until it too was swallowed up by Rome in 63 BCE.

Egypt—Previous Conquests

Before Alexander, Egypt had been conquered a number of times. The first real and complete foreign conquest of Egypt was achieved by the Kushite Piye, king of Nubia, in 744 BCE, and thereby establishing the Twenty-fifth Dynasty, which lasted till 656 BCE. The conquest was facilitated by Egypt's weakness and fragmentation at the time.

Egypt was reunited under Psamtik (Psammetichus) I, who established the Twenty-sixth Dynasty, which came to an end with the conquest by the Achaemenid Cambyses II of Persia in 525 BCE. From then until 404 BCE, Egypt was a constituent satrapy of the Persian Empire and the Persian *shahanshah* ("king of kings") adopted the title of pharaoh in Egypt.

This period is designated by Manetho (the third-century BCE Egyptian historian) the Twenty-seventh Dynasty, which was brought to an end by a rebellion under Amyrtaeus, the only Pharaoh of the Twenty-eighth Dynasty, who is thought to have been related to the Twenty-sixth Dynasty (664–525 BCE). But Amyrtaeus was himself defeated and executed by Nepherites, a general, who established the Twenty-ninth Dynasty, the last pharaoh from which, Nepherites II, was deposed and probably killed by Nectanebo I, establishing the

30th Dynasty. His grandson, Nectanebo II, is the last native pharaoh recognized by Manetho. He was defeated by the Persian King Artaxerxes III reconquering Egypt with difficulty in 340 or 339 BCE.

The Middle East before Alexander

From the beginning of recorded history we encounter conquests both vertical and horizontal. By horizontal conquest is meant the conquest of one city-state or nation by another, while a vertical conquest is more accurately termed a coup or revolution within a single city-state.

From an early but indeterminate date the Middle East was inhabited by Sumerians, Elamites, Akkadians, and Gutians. The Sumerians and Elamites were both non-Indo-European and non-Semitic peoples, though probably not related to each other, while the Akkadians were Semites. Both the Sumerian language and that of the Elamites are believed to have been "language isolates." meaning that they are not known to have been related to any other languages, so indicating separate demographic origins.

By the time of Alexander, the Middle East had already had a very long tradition of monarchy, going back to the Sumerians, who are often regarded as the earliest known civilization in the world. Situated in southern Mesopotamia (what is now south-central Iraq) the Sumerian civilization took the form of a number of independent city-states, each with its own god or goddess and ruled over by its own *lugal* ("king") or *ensi* (originally designated an independent ruler but later represented someone subordinate to a *lugal*). This hierarchy of rulers is reflected in the Sumerian King List, which begins with the words: "after the kingship descended from heaven the kingship was in Eridu," with Eridu being situated near the modern Iraqi city of Basra. The Sumerian King List describes the period as one where there was only one legitimate king at any one time, and kingship was transferred from city to city, but this "proto-federal" structure is doubted by some modern historians, who believe that there were often, in reality, a number of parallel rulers at any one time.

Sargon established what is commonly thought of as the earliest empire—in the modern sense of a state made up of a number of diverse nations. He also founded a hereditary dynasty of seven successive kings (including himself) that lasted for about 180 years (2334–2164 BCE), and his conquest of Sumer represented a Semitic victory over a non-Semitic nation—and its gods.

One of the most remarkable Sumerian rulers was of Lagash (fl. twenty-fourth century BCE), who assumed the title of *lugal* after ousting his supposedly corrupt predecessor Lugalanda. Urukagina attributed his victory to "Ningirsu, warrior of (the chief god) Enlil." which points to a coup or a revolution of some kind. Judging by Lugalanda's evident association with the aristocracy and

Urukagina's reforms, Urukagina's rise to power may well have been achieved with popular support. He clearly exercised his power in the interests of the lower classes, as can be seen from his legal code, probably the earliest such document known to history.

Urukagina stands out both in terms of his accession and in the nature of his regime. Lugalanda, the predecessor whom he deposed, had evidently inherited his throne from two successive father-and-son priestly rulers—possibly a sign of the preponderance of the priestly aristocracy at this time. Urukagina's accession may then represent a popular victory over a priestly aristocracy, or *mashkim* ("priest-judges").

Here are some extracts from his inscriptions: "Urukagina freed the inhabitants from usury, burdensome controls, hunger, theft, murder, and seizure (of their property and persons). He established freedom (of a type). The widow and orphan were no longer at the mercy of the powerful. It was for them that Urukagina made his covenant with Ningirsu (god of agriculture, son of the chief god, Enlil)."

More particularly:

> If a good ass is born to a client and his overseer says to him, "I will buy it from you," then if he wishes to sell it he will say, "Pay me what pleases me"; but if he does not wish to sell, the overseer must not force him. If the house of a powerful man is next to the house of a client, and if the powerful man says to him, "I wish to buy it," then if he wishes to sell he will say, "Pay me in silver as much as suits me," or "Reimburse me with an equivalent amount of barley."; but if he does not wish to sell, the powerful man must not force him (online: `web.archive.org/web/20181117032013/http://history-world.org/reforms_of_urukagina.htm`).

Urukagina's reforms were not enough to save his city, Lagash, from conquest at the hands of Lugal-Zage-Si (r. c. 2358–2334 BCE), *ensi* of the neighboring city-state of Umma, with which there had been long-running rivalry over the fertile plain of Gu-Edin. Lugal-Zage-Si's victory enabled him to unite the whole of Sumer under his control. He later overthrew Ur-Zababa, Ur, Nippur, Larsa, and Uruk, which he made his new capital. He claimed all the land between the Mediterranean and the Persian Gulf, and, after a reign of between 25 and 34 years, Lugal-Zage-Si himself met his comeuppance at the hands of Sargon of Akkad.

Although Sargon (r. c. 2334–2279 BCE) is often credited with being the creator of the earliest empire, that achievement is sometimes attributed to the much earlier Sumerian *ensi* Eannatum of Lagash, (fl c. 2500–2400 BCE) and who appears to have exercised control over the whole of Sumer, Elam, and Akkad.

Sargon's son and successor Rimush (r. c. 2279–2270 BCE) spent most of his short reign consolidating his father's empire by reconquering and destroying a number of major Sumerian cities by putting down widespread revolts against his rule. He also added Elam and Marhashi (Parahshum) to his empire, which his brother and successor, Manishtushu, placed under Akkadian military governors. Lagash was yet another addition to the empire, accompanied by a great deal of slaughter, probably also under Rimush. Sargon's grandson Naram-Sin (c. 2254–2218 BCE) kept control over the numerous city-states that comprised his empire by appointing some of his many sons as provincial governors and his daughters as high priestesses. Thanks to his conquests the empire reached its greatest extent under his rule. Though a shrunken Akkadian empire fell to the Gutians only in 2154, about 64 years after his death, he was retrospectively blamed for the defeat. In a poem written hundreds of years later, titled "The Curse of Akkad." the destruction of the Akkadian Empire and of the city of Akkad itself is blamed on Naram-Sin for angering the chief god Enlil and eight other gods. Though Naram-Sin's self-deification as "God of Akkad" is not alluded to, it may well have been relevant, as the respect and loyalty of the masses toward a king were closely tied to that ruler's devotion to the gods. A king who appeared to his subjects to have a good relationship with the gods was much more likely to receive the same devotion from them as he gave to the gods. By deifying himself Naram-Sin fell foul of this important practical rule of ancient kingship, because his self-deification amounted to neglecting his devotion to the traditional gods.

The Middle East would go from conquest to conquest for almost another two millennia until the conquests of Alexander the Great (356–323 BCE), who put his indelible stamp on at least part of it.

"England has been conquered many times, Scotland never"

"England has been conquered many times, Scotland never"—these words, with which King James VI of Scots introduced himself to his new English subjects in his first address to the English Parliament in 1604 were not calculated to endear him to his new subjects as James I of England.

This union of crowns was the result of marital politics gone wrong. Inheritance of the English throne by a Scottish king was probably the very opposite of what England's Henry VII Tudor had in mind when marrying his daughter Margaret off to James IV of Scots in 1503 to cement the "Treaty of Perpetual Peace" between the two former enemies. When James IV's brother-in-law, Henry VIII, who had succeeded Henry VII as king of England, declared war on France in 1513, James IV had to choose between his treaty with England and Scotland's "Auld Alliance" with France dating back to 1295. He chose France and actually invaded England, losing the war and his life at the Battle of

Flodden, which is still memorialized in the haunting Scottish lament, "Flowers of the Forest."

Though no doubt gratifying to Scottish pride, James VI's succession to the English throne in 1603 in a union of crowns was not in any sense a Scottish victory over England. What then was James thinking of as England's military defeats? Presumably, at least the Roman conquest, the Anglo-Saxon invasion, and of course 1066. But none of these was a pure conquest.

Roman Britain

Julius Caesar's invasions of Britain in 55 and 54 BCE were part of his conquest of Gaul, as some anti-Roman Gallic tribes were receiving assistance from Britain. Caesar satisfied himself by coercing a number of Celtic tribes into paying tribute and giving hostages in return for peace, but no British territory was annexed to Rome. Following the principle of *chequer-board politics* ("the enemy of my enemy is my friend"), Caesar defeated Cassivellaunus, the head of an anti-Roman alliance, and installed Mandubracius, who had sought Caesar's protection in Gaul, as king of the Trinovantes.

When Britain was finally conquered under the Emperor Claudius nearly a century later, this was done in aid of another fugitive British ruler, Verica of the Atrebates. Roman Britain lasted for about four centuries, but, as something of an outpost with an uninviting climate, it never attracted large-scale migration from other parts of the Roman world and was quickly abandoned around 410 CE when the grip of Rome on the Western provinces started to slip. By 430 CE, coinage had evidently ceased to be used as a medium of exchange. In fact, Britain was never thoroughly Romanized: by comparison with most of Western Europe, the Latin language did not take root in Britain during the four centuries of Roman rule.

"Not Angles But Angels!"

The next "conquest" of England was more in the nature of an influx rather than of a military operation. The identification of the migrants as the Germanic Angles, Saxons, and Jutes originated with Bede's *Ecclesiastical History of the Nation of the Angles*, written around 731. By that time the newcomers were well established, having come in waves from the mid-fifth to early seventh centuries. Wandering around Rome's slave market in the late sixth century, the future Pope Gregory I ("the Great") (in office 590–604) spotted a couple of blond young boys. On asking where they were from, he was told that they were Angles. *Non Angli sed angeli*, quipped Gregory ("Not Angles but angels"). Whether by pressure of numbers or military force, or a combination of the two, the Germanic settlers pushed the underlying Celtic population to the West, which is where their greatest concentration still is.

1066 and All That

The best known of all conquests of England is of course the Norman Conquest of 1066 under William "the Conqueror." The Norman Conquest is one of the most complex cases of conquest coupled with heredity and with an added dash of election.

Though William became king of England by defeating and killing Harold Godwinson in the Battle of Hastings, this was by no means a straightforward military victory. The childless King Edward the Confessor (r. 1042–66) had evidently named William as his heir quite some time before. William's grandfather was Edward's mother's brother, meaning that William was Edward's second cousin once removed. But there were several other claimants to the English Crown after Edward's death, including above all King Edward's wife's brother, Harold Godwinson and Edward's young great-nephew Edgar Aetheling.

The Confessor seems to have vacillated on the succession. Norman sources claimed that, in around 1064, Edward even sent Harold to Normandy to confirm his promise of the succession to William. And, if the Bayeux Tapestry is to be believed, William even supplied Harold with weapons and Harold swore a sacred oath to support William's claim to the English throne. Yet on Edward's deathbed he evidently named Harold as his heir. And, according to a Norman apologist, shortly before the Battle of Hastings, Harold sent an envoy to William claiming that this deathbed promise overrode Edward's earlier promise to William. William insisted that Edward's promise to him took precedence.

By this time Harold had already taken several decisive steps to claim the throne for himself. Edward the Confessor died on 5 January 1066. On the very next day the *Witan* (King's Council) met and named Harold as king, and this was followed by his coronation on the same day. Besides discounting Harold's deathbed nomination by the Confessor, Norman sources also called Harold's coronation into question by claiming that he was crowned by the "uncanonical" Archbishop of Canterbury Stigand rather than by Ealdred, archbishop of York, as claimed by the English sources. William was careful to make sure that at his coronation held on Christmas Day 1066 it was Ealdred who officiated, and he even arranged a separate coronation, also by Ealdred, of William's wife Matilda in 1068—only the second time an English king's consort had been crowned. An interesting and lasting innovation introduced by Ealdred into the coronation service was what is now called the "recognition." where the congregation is asked to confirm the enthroned monarch as their rightful sovereign. The reason for this addition was probably William's lack of endorsement by the *Witan* or *Witenagemot*—by contrast with Harold on the day after Edward's death and of Edgar Aetheling after Harold's death at Hastings.

Conquest Conspectus

What happened to the 10 Lost Tribes of Israel? These were the tribes that made up the northern Jewish Kingdom of Israel, with its capital in Samaria, as distinct from the southern Jewish Kingdom of Judah, with its capital and the Jewish Temple in Jerusalem. They disappear from view with the conquest of the Kingdom of Israel by King Shalmaneser V and Sargon II of the Neo-Assyrian Empire in around 722 BCE. According to the Bible: "In the ninth year of Hoshea, the king of Assyria took Samaria and carried Israel away to Assyria, and placed them in Halah, and in Habor, on the river of Gozan, and in the cities of the Medes" (2 Kings 17:6). The Assyrian records themselves claim that 27,290 inhabitants of the Kingdom of Israel (probably accounting for about a fifth of the population) were captured and resettled in Assyria. This was the second Assyrian attack on Israel, the first being in 732 BCE, when several cities other than Samaria were captured and an unspecified number of inhabitants were deported (2 Kings 15:29, 732 BCE). Unlike other conquerors, who killed or enslaved conquered populations, the Assyrians had a specific policy of assimilation and integration. Special treatment was reserved for urban elites, professional people, craftsmen, and scholars, who were resettled in the major Assyrian cities, where they were employed in the construction of temples and palaces and with the contents of the Royal Library of Ashurbanipal. Other less trained or skilled people were scattered widely over the Assyrian Empire. The object of the exercise was to prevent conquered peoples from rising in revolt and trying to throw off the Assyrian yoke, but were instead forced to give up their national, linguistic, and religious identity in favor of a new Assyrian one. But it was not all bad for the conquered populations, particularly the farmers among them, who were assigned a plot of land and similar status to native Assyrian peasants.

Most conquests have not involved deportation or resettlement. The Roman conquests, discussed above, did not involve enforced Romanization but allowed the conquered peoples to continue to worship their ancestral religions, which could easily be combined with the traditional gods of Rome, "oriental mystery cults." and the imperial cult—until Christianity became the official religion of the Empire in the fourth century CE, when freedom of religion was replaced by persecution of "pagans." Jews, and "heretics" alike (see Chapter 26).

Dynastic conquests, like those of the Franks, the Normans, the Slavs, and the Turks, followed by the colonial empires of the Portuguese, Spanish, Dutch, and British, resulted in a number of multi-ethnic empires in which the conquerors' dominant position was based on race, religion, or national identity, even where the conquered nations were ostensibly allowed independence, as in the twentieth-century cases of the Soviet Union's conquest of eastern Europe and Afghanistan and the United States' conquest of Iraq and Afghanistan. It is important to add Xi Jinping's China's "Belt and Road Initiative." adopted in 2013, involving investment in more than 140 countries, comprising almost 75% of the world's population and more than half of the world's GDP. The initiative has been criticized as "debt-trap diplomacy." a form of neo-colonialism. Brahma Chelaney, who is credited with coining the term "debt trap diplomacy" in 2017, describes China's aim as "to saddle small nations with debt that they could not hope to repay, leaving them ever more firmly under China's thumb" (Chelaney 2017).

Chapter 17
Revolution

"Is it a revolt?" asked the perplexed Louis XVI on hearing of the storming of the Bastille on 14 July 1789. "No, sire," replied the Duc de la Rochefoucauld, "it's a revolution." What exactly differentiates a revolution from a revolt or a rebellion? There have been numerous definitions, mostly unhelpful verbose sociological compilations. Etymologically, "revolution" just means "a rolling around," as in the speed of an old-fashioned gramophone record, expressed as, say, 78 rpm (revolutions per minute), a pretty peaceful occurrence. But my definition of "revolution" would be a violent mass rising aiming to overthrow the government.

Labeling some event or series of events as a revolution gives it a certain cachet, placing it above other events in terms of seriousness. As this book is concerned with monarchy, the question is whether, or in what circumstances, a monarchy has arisen out of revolution. The answer is, very seldom. One possible case is that of the ancient Greek tyrants, many of whom evidently came to power through a popular toppling of the previous oligarchy and who ruled with popular support (see Chapter 15). However, revolutions are not usually spearheaded by a successful new ruler. More often, such leaders emerge only later. Oliver Cromwell came to power in England at the head of his victorious New Model Army in the Civil War, or English Revolution, against King Charles I. Napoleon was the ultimate heir of the French Revolution, but only after it had run out of steam. Lenin's pre-eminence in Russia was achieved by the so-called October Revolution, which, however, was really a coup d'état. Besides the Greek tyrants, we shall just take a glance at the English, French, and American revolutions.

Five Thousand Years of Monarchy, First Edition. Michael Arnheim.
© 2026 John Wiley & Sons, Inc. Published 2026 by John Wiley & Sons, Inc.

England

The Norman kings of England were in a stronger position than their French counterparts. After the conquest of 1066, the king of England was able to wipe the slate clean and start from scratch, which the kings of France were never able to do. The Norman and Plantagenet kings did promise to honor the promises made to the aristocracy by their Anglo-Saxon predecessors, but they mostly ignored such undertakings. All land belonged to the king, who would distribute it to his followers as "barons" on feudal tenure, often in small, scattered parcels to prevent the barons from developing strong local power centers rivaling that of the king. Initially this gave the king great power. In time, however, the barons started ganging up on the king and forcing him to give them certain concessions. This is how Magna Carta came about. Contrary to all the ballyhoo surrounding it, Magna Carta has nothing to do with "democracy" and everything to do with the ding-dong battle between the aristocracy and the Crown. And one of the reasons why the barons disliked King John (r. 1199–1216) was that he (quite rightly) distrusted them and, in certain important respects, favored the common people. It cannot be stressed enough that strong monarchy is not the enemy of the ordinary people, but aristocracy or oligarchy is.

The rise of Parliament in the thirteenth century and its increasing control over grants of taxation weakened the English Crown further, while the French Crown gained the right to raise taxes without the consent of the Estates General, the equivalent of the English Parliament.

The Rise of Parliament

Magna Carta, including the final definitive version of 1297 ratified by Edward I (r. 1272–1307), is chiefly concerned with the relationship between the Crown and the barons, which continued to fester. But before long Parliament took over from the barons the role of chief obstacle to royal power, especially in regard to finance. Strong kings like Edward I (r. 1272–1307) were able to use Parliament for their own ends, as a way of uniting the country under the Crown and allowing Parliament to air their grievances in return for supply. A weak king, like Edward II (r. 1307–27), could find himself actually forced to abdicate by Parliament, under the leadership of the barons.

Henry VIII (r. 1509–47)

Henry VIII's chief preoccupation was to obtain a male heir, which led to his reliance on Parliament in order to allow him to divorce his first wife, Catherine of Aragon. But in order to do so he had to break with the Roman Catholic

Church and have himself declared "Supreme Head" (changed under Elizabeth I to "Supreme Governor") of the Church of England.

Though as ruthless and power-hungry as the image that he projected, Henry was gullible enough to be taken in by flattery, declaring to Parliament: "We be informed by our judges that we at no time stand so highly in our estate royal as in the time of Parliament." Yet, on his accession at the age of 17 he had shown himself much more vigilant, actually personally amending his coronation oath to limit him to "grant to hold the laws and *approved* customs of the realm *lawful and not prejudicial to his Crown and Imperial duty*," adding that these laws have been made with the king's consent. (Henry's amendments in italics; see Dudley, 1948) Henry's amendments were clearly intended to prevent the passing of any legislation that was at all likely to have a negative impact on royal power. The word "imperial" is significant.

Professor Geoffrey Elton's *The Tudor Revolution in Government*, which placed not the king himself but his minister Thomas Cromwell (1485–1540) in the driving seat of this development together with a shift from "household government" centered on the person of the king to a modern bureaucratic form of government, has now been consigned to the history of historiography (Elton 1953).

But the very fact that Henry VIII only had to snap his fingers to destroy Cromwell shows just how much personal control the king exercised. Further examples are not hard to find, such as the king's dismissal of Cardinal Wolsey, who was on his way to certain execution when he died of natural causes in 1530, and the downfall of Sir Thomas More in 1535—not to mention Henry's matrimonial antics, divorcing two wives and executing two more. Hans Holbein's iconic portrait of Henry VIII shows him as a masterful Renaissance ruler—especially when seen side by side with his father, Henry VII, who has instead the air of a conniving merchant.

Nevertheless, Henry VIII cannot be said to have exercised singlehanded autocratic power. For his extremely ambitious program of religious reform he needed—and, with Cromwell's help, managed to obtain—parliamentary support. In 1523 Parliament had already refused to agree fully to Henry's request for money. And the king's reliance on Parliament to implement his far-reaching legislative program only strengthened Parliament's hand for the future.

Elizabeth I (1558–1603)

Elizabeth I's Parliaments were not only comparatively few and far between but mostly also of very short duration: the days making up their sittings totalled less than three years of her 44-year reign. The queen simply did not trust Parliament and wanted to curtail its discussion of sensitive topics such as the royal succession, her possible marriage, the problem posed by Mary Queen of Scots (1542–87), and religion. So Elizabeth would try to get Parliament to vote supply as soon as possible and then send it packing. She was not averse to lecturing a Parliament in hectoring tones on the permitted limits of their deliberations: "For it is monstrous that the feet should direct the head" (online: www.elizabethfiles.com). And the queen had no compunction about lodging members of Parliament in the Tower of London for raising touchy issues in the House of Commons.

James I (r. 1603–25)

James I lacked Elizabeth's tact and finesse and made no secret of his belief in the divine right of kings, on which he had already written two treatises before his accession to the English throne (he had been James VI, king of Scots, since 1567, when he was only one year old).

James's well-known sobriquet, "the wisest fool in Christendom," given to him by Henry IV of France, was intended as a compliment, not an insult. And James was under no illusion about the proper relationship between a king and the different categories of his subjects. Here are some of his views as expressed in his two treatises on monarchy:

- **On the nobility:** "the nobility, although second in rank yet over-far first in greatness and power to do good or evil, as they are inclined" (James VI and I 2010, p. 124). "The natural sickness that I have perceived this estate subject to in my time hath been a feckless, arrogant conceit of their greatness and power...." [From *Basilikon Doron* ("Royal Gift") addressed to his eldest son, Prince Henry: "To remeid to these evils in their estate, teach your nobility to keep your laws as precisely as the meanest; fear not their orping or being discontented, as long as ye rule well."]
- **On cultivating the lower orders:** "and weary not to hear the complaints of the oppressed, *aut ne rex sis*" ("or you should not be a king") (James I 1996, p. 149). Note also James's expansion and support of the Court of Requests under Sir Julius Caesar. The court offered redress to the lower classes, whom it attracted away from the common law courts in great numbers thanks to its low charge for filing a complaint and its quick turnaround time—both resented by the common law judges, whose courts had neither of these advantages. With their characteristic lack of interest in justice, the common law judges went on a rampage against the Court of Requests.
- **On a king's superiority to the law:** kings existed "before any estates or ranks of men, before any parliaments were holden, or laws made, and by them was the land distributed, which at first was wholly theirs. And so it follows of necessity that kings were the authors and makers of the laws, and not the laws of the kings" (ibid.).

James I was not content to assert these views in writing. He also acted upon them in practice. To his first Parliament in 1604 he declared, in a remark not calculated to endear him to his new subjects: "England has been conquered many times, Scotland never." Not surprisingly, James's relationship with his Parliaments was less than cordial. Nor was his relationship with the judiciary any more harmonious. When James asserted his right to try cases himself as king, he was rudely rebuffed by Sir Edward Coke (1552–1634), who claimed that this power belonged solely to legally trained judges (*Case of Prohibitions* [1607] EWHC J23 (KB)). But the king's rejoinder proved prophetic: "If the judges interpret the laws themselves and suffer none else to interpret, they may easily make, of the laws, shipmen's hose!"—meaning that judge-made law would come to resemble the tattered and frayed stockings worn by sailors (quoted by Hamburger 2008, p. 223; Bowen 1957, p. 304).

Charles I (r. 1625–49)

If James's problems with Parliament appear serious, they were dwarfed by the clash with Parliament under his son, which ultimately escalated into civil war and brought the king to the scaffold. After four years of unproductive Parliaments, Charles ruled for 11 years (1629–40) without calling a Parliament.

This period is labeled by historians either as the "Eleven Years' Tyranny" or as a period of halcyon peace. Charles's loyal lieutenants, Thomas Wentworth, Earl of Strafford, and Archbishop William Laud, ably pursued their policy of "Thorough" to enhance the king's power by winning over the lower orders, offering them in the Court of Star Chamber genuine redress for their grievances against the privileged classes and checking the "enclosure movement," the appropriation or privatization of "commons" (i.e. common agricultural land) by wealthy landowners. The agrarian historian W.E. Tate (1967, p.124–127) called Charles I "the one English monarch of outstanding importance as an agrarian reformer." But Charles characteristically blotted his copybook by indulging in some enclosure of his own—in particular, by continuing his father's policy of draining the fenland commons to provide the Crown with additional revenue.

Finally forced in 1640 to call another Parliament by a need for money to finance a war against the Scottish Covenanters, Charles was rebuffed yet again and dissolved this "Short Parliament" after only three weeks.

Reluctant to call another Parliament, Charles then took the exceptional step of calling a *Magnum Concilium*, or Great Council of Peers, an assembly of the nobility established in Norman times but which had not met since the reign of Henry VII (1485–1509). While offering the king a loan of £200,000 to pay the army, the council advised him to call Parliament. In a remarkable parallel, Louis XVI of France—another king who did not properly understand the danger to monarchy posed by the aristocracy—was to make a similar mistake by calling an Assembly of Notables, which gave him the ill-fated advice to call the Estates General.

The "Long Parliament," summoned in 1640, was hostile to the king from the beginning. More than 350 of the 493 members of the House of Commons elected were opposed to the king. The Parliament lost no time in taking action against the king's most trusted and loyal advisers: Strafford, Archbishop Laud, and John Finch, the former Speaker who was now Lord Keeper of the Great Seal. When Strafford's impeachment failed, the Commons passed a Bill of Attainder against him, which was approved by the Lords—and, after a good deal of prevarication, signed by the king. After this, Charles showed himself by turns weakly conciliatory and blusteringly bullying, a combination which ultimately undermined his position.

The most notable event was the king's unwise personal appearance in the Commons chamber on 3 January 1642, accompanied by an armed guard, in a vain attempt to arrest five members for high treason. "I see the birds have flown," remarked the king, and, seated in the Speaker's chair, asked Speaker Lenthall to reveal the whereabouts of the five men. On bended knees, the Speaker famously pleaded, "May it please your Majesty, I have neither eyes to see nor tongue to speak in this place but as the House is pleased to direct me, whose servant I am here." So strongly is this incident embedded in the national psyche, that to this day the monarch's representative, known as (the Gentleman Usher of the) Black Rod, has the doors of the House of Commons ceremonially slammed in his face and has then to rap on the door three times before being admitted.

The incident regarding the five absent members of Parliament marks the beginning of open hostilities between the king and Parliament, which erupted into full-scale war at the Battle of Edgehill on 23 October 1642. After more than four years of a bloody civil war costing approximately 300,000 lives (amounting to 6% of the population of the country), Charles became a prisoner of Parliament in January 1647. At a show trial lasting a week on charges of high treason, 30 witnesses were called to testify against "Charles Stuart," as he was now referred to, in his enforced absence. Charles defended himself doughtily, claiming that the trial was illegal because the law was "that the King can do no wrong" and that "the arms I took up were only to defend the fundamental laws of this kingdom against those who have supposed my power hath totally changed the ancient government" (Wedgwood 1983).

The outcome of the king's "trial" was never in doubt, and neither was the sentence: death by beheading. Charles faced death with great composure, dignity, and fortitude, which redounded to the royalist cause in the long run. The day of the execution, 30 January 1649, was a cold winter's day, and Charles made a point of wearing two shirts, so that his shivering would not be mistaken for fear (official website of British monarchy—www.royal.gov.uk). Most remarkably, humbly, and perspicaciously, he attributed his fate to his failure to stand by

Strafford in his hour of need: "An unjust sentence that I suffered to take effect, is punished now by an unjust sentence on me." And:

> For the people. And truly I desire their Liberty and Freedom as much as any Body whomsoever. But I must tell you, That their Liberty and Freedom, consists in having of Government; those Laws, by which their Life and their goods may be most their own. It is not for having share in government (Sir) that is nothing pertaining to them. A subject and a soveraign are clean different things, and therefore until they do that, I mean, that you do put the people in that liberty as I say, certainly they will never enjoy themselves ... Sirs, ...I tell you (and I pray God it be not laid to your charge) That I Am the Martyr of the People (*Trial of Charles I*, 1963).

Had Charles come to a belated realization that Strafford and Laud were right and that true monarchy entailed a bond between the king and the ordinary people for the benefit of both against the interests of the privileged classes?

There is an indication also of the residual affection felt by ordinary people for their king. In the eyewitness account of Charles's execution by the young Philip Henry, a future nonconformist clergyman, we read: "At the instant when the blow was given, there was such a dismal universal groan among the thousands of people that were in sight of it, as it were with one consent" (quoted by Henry 1822).

Archbishop Laud's comment about Charles I quoted above was only too apt: "A mild and gracious prince, that knows not how to be, or to be made, great" (Trevor-Roper 2000, p. 409). Allowing Strafford and Laud to follow through on their policy of "Thorough" might have produced a popular monarchy, but Charles obviously did not understand the realities of politics. For example, he even allowed himself to be persuaded by Thomas Howard, Earl of Arundel, to cultivate the aristocracy as the main bulwark of royal authority, which led to his misguidedly relying on them in his war against the Scottish Covenanters in 1639, then after his defeat in his senseless summoning of a "Great Council of Peers" in 1640, and then finally in creating a royalist party of "Cavaliers" based on aristocratic support to counter Parliament in 1642, an image that did not do Charles any good in the Civil War (see Cust 2013).

Oliver Cromwell (1559–1658)—"Warts and All"[1]

Oliver Cromwell, member of Parliament for Cambridge, who became the commander of the parliamentary army in the Civil War, emerged from the war as "Lord Protector" of the "Commonwealth" (i.e. Republic), a position which he held from 1653 until his death in 1658.

---

[1] Note: When sitting for a portrait by Sir Peter Lely, Cromwell is reputed to have instructed the artist to paint him "warts and all."

Cromwell rode roughshod over Parliament in a way that Charles I would never have dared. Even before his installation as Lord Protector, on 20 April 1653, Cromwell, accompanied by about 40 musketeers, marched into Parliament (the "Rump" of the Long Parliament, elected in 1640) and closed it down after hurling some choice insults at it: "Is there a single virtue now remaining amongst you? Is there one vice you do not possess? Ye have no more religion than my horse." Addressing his men in reference to the mace, the symbol of the authority of Parliament, he ordered: "Take away that fool's bauble there, and lock up the doors" (online: `http://en.wikisource.org/wiki/Dissolution_of_the_Long_Parliament`).

According to another source, turning to the assembled members, he barked, "Depart, I say, and let us have done with you. In the name of God, go!" (Chambers 1832). The dismissed Parliament was briefly replaced by a nominated assembly sometimes called Barebone's Parliament. Then, on 16 December 1653, under a written constitution—the only one in British history—known as the Instrument of Government, Cromwell was sworn in as Lord Protector of the Commonwealth for life. The form of government established by this very short document vested executive power in the Lord Protector and legislative power in the Protector in Parliament—not unlike the constitutional settlement that was to be introduced as part of the so-called "Glorious Revolution" of 1688–89. Cromwell was now addressed as "Your Highness" and he starting signing his name "Oliver P" (P for "Protector"), copied from the royal style of signing "Charles R" (R for Rex). After reluctantly turning down the offer of the crown with expanded powers, he was re-installed as Lord Protector in a ceremony resembling a coronation, dressed in an ermine-trimmed purple robe seated on King Edward's Coronation Chair (dating back to 1296) and invested with all the trappings of monarchy except the crown itself and the orb. The coinage portrays him in the guise of a Roman emperor, complete with laurel wreath and the legend OLIVAR DG RP ANG SCO ET HIB ("Oliver, by the Grace of God of the Republic of England, Scotland and Ireland, Protector").

Was Cromwell a Dictator?

Was Oliver Cromwell a dictator? Ironically, Oliver Cromwell probably came closer than any English king to exercising sole power. But his power was based on a standing army, which was disbanded only after the Restoration of the monarchy in 1660. The army's loyalty to the Protectorate was based on a combination of discipline and radical Protestant religious belief. Cromwell famously declared that he would "rather have a plain, russet-coated Captain, that knows what he fights for, and loves what he knows, than what you call a Gentleman and nothing else." Does this mean that he ruled by "repression"? Not really. The army was indeed called upon to put down a number of opponents in what were essentially policing actions, but the only serious rising during the Protectorate was the

Penruddock royalist uprising of 1655, which was, however, put down by a single troop of horse. The army could hardly be regarded as an oligarchy, because it did not share power with Cromwell but did his bidding.

Cromwell, being himself of gentry stock, attended a grammar school and Sidney Sussex College, Cambridge. He certainly was no social revolutionary. Here is what he said at the opening of Parliament in 1654: "A nobleman, a gentleman, a yeoman; the distinction of these: that is a good interest of the nation, and a great one!" (online: `https://www.olivercromwell.org/Letters_and_speeches/speeches/Speech_4.pdf`). Cromwell goes on to attack the Levelers, posing the rhetorical question, "Did not that leveling principle tend to the reducing of all to an equality?" Cromwell had clearly been afraid of this tendency, although the Levelers were no longer a force to be reckoned with by 1654. Yet Cromwell still paints their egalitarian tendency in lurid colors: "And that the thing did and might well extend far is manifest; because it was a pleasing voice to all poor men, and truly not unwelcome to all bad men."

On Oliver Cromwell's death in September 1658, his son Richard Cromwell was appointed Lord Protector, but he proved ineffectual and was removed by the army seven months later. Amazingly, on 16 March 1660 the Rump Parliament, which had been resuscitated, together with the addition of the members "purged" from it in 1648, finally dissolved itself after preparing the way for the Restoration of the monarchy under Charles I's son, Charles II (r. 1660–85).

French Revolution

For an analysis of the long-term lead-up to the Revolution, see Chapter 19.

When I was 10 years old, a good deal of classroom time was devoted to a study of the French Revolution. As a lover of the eighteenth century, my illustration of the Estates General of 1789 portrayed deputies of the Third Estate complete with wig, frilled jabot, and knee-breeches, which earned a reprimand from my teacher: "These were common people. They couldn't afford to dress like that." Needless to say, the teacher was wrong.

The Estates General was the ancient parliament of France, which, however, was summoned by the king only when needed. The last time before 1789 that it had been called was in 1614 in the reign of Louis XIII. It was made up of three "estates," the clergy (First Estate), the nobility (Second Estate), and the commons (Third Estate). The right to vote was restricted to males of at least 25 who owned property and paid taxes. Of the 578 deputies elected for the Third Estate, half were lawyers or local officials, almost a third were businessmen, and 51 were large landowners. So much for my teacher's idea that the Third Estate was represented by poor peasants!

In preparation for the meeting of the Estates General, every voting district was asked to submit a *cahier de doléances* (notebook of complaints). Those of the Third Estate vary a good deal. But there are a few common themes that reappear in the complaints of one district after another, and they are chiefly about the aristocracy, who paid practically no taxes, and to a lesser extent about the Church, which also enjoyed considerable privileges. There were very few complaints about the king. Here is an extract from one of the more eloquent of the *cahiers*, from Provence:

> The nobility enjoys and owns everything, and would like to free itself from everything. However, if the nobility commands the army, the Third Estate makes it up. If nobility pours a drop of blood, the Third Estate spreads rivers of it. The nobility empties the royal treasury, the Third Estate fills it up. Finally, the Third Estate pays everything and does not enjoy anything (*Cahiers de doléances,* Lauris (sénéchaussée Aix): https://revolution.chnm.org/items/show/482).

In his speech welcoming the deputies, King Louis XVI declared himself "the people's greatest friend," which he no doubt sincerely believed. But, lacking an education in history or statecraft, the king did not understand that the aristocracy posed the chief threat to the monarchy. His predecessors, Louis XIII, XIV, and XV, were only too well aware of it, and so were some of Louis XVI's own ministers.

Charles Alexandre de Calonne, who served as Controller-General of Finances from 1783 to 1787, tried repeatedly to introduce a *subvention territoriale,* a universal land tax that would be levied on all property without distinction, abolishing the tax exemption enjoyed by the aristocracy and the Church, and in so doing solving the two main problems confronting the regime, namely the huge deficit of 110 million livres and the general grievance felt by the Third Estate against unfair privileges. Had this land tax been introduced, the king would have reaped the reward of gratitude and support from the Third Estate.

Calonne knew that this reform would never be accepted by the *Parlement de Paris*, a superior court made up of aristocrats which had arrogated to itself the right to register all royal decrees. So he tried to bypass this bugbear by calling a handpicked Assembly of Notables, an aristocratic body which had not been summoned since 1626 but which turned out to be no more favorable to the proposed reform (Calonne, nicknamed *Monsieur Déficit,* was blamed for the country's parlous financial state, because Jacques Necker, finance minister 1777–81, had published a *Compte Rendu,* or "Statement of Account," purporting to show a huge surplus in the national coffers in 1781). Calonne hit back with a direct appeal to the people in which he accused the Assembly of Notables of simply trying to defend their privileges at the expense of the people. Stung by this, the "Notables" plotted to turn the king against Calonne, who was duly dismissed by the king in 1787. And the "notables" then came out openly in favor

Figure 17   "Third Estate carrying First Estate (clergy) and Second Estate (nobility) on his back," 1789.
SOURCE: Gallica Digital Library / Wikimedia Commons / public domain.

of placing more checks on royal power. In exile, Calonne lamented, "The King, who assured me a hundred times that he would support me with unshakable firmness, abandoned me, and I succumbed" (Hardman 2016).

Yet, in 1771, under Louis XV, his minister, Chancellor of France René de Maupeou, successfully ended the long struggle of the monarchy against the *parlements* by abolishing them, but, instead of showing gratitude for this hard-fought victory, on his accession in 1774 Louis XVI summarily dismissed Maupeou and restored the *parlements*. This decision turned out to be a fatal error on the part of the feckless 19-year-old king, who had lived his whole life among aristocrats at Versailles. His lame explanation at the time was: "It may be considered politically unwise, but it seems to me to be the general wish, and I want to be loved." Yet he would have been "loved" far more if he had he allowed the victory to stand and take shape. Then he could have implemented Calonne's tax reform without needing to have it "registered" by a self-serving aristocratic *parlement*. And the whole history of France might have been very different.

The deputies of the Third Estate in the Estates General, who declared themselves a National Assembly in June 1789, did not labor under any such misapprehensions. In August, the National Assembly abolished once and for all the aristocratic *parlements*, that Louis XVI had unwisely restored. And during the "Reign of Terror" of 1793–94 the label *aristo* became not just an insult but also a death sentence.

The most perspicacious of the new names brought to the fore by the Revolution was Mirabeau, who, though a noble, was elected as a deputy for the Third Estate to the Estates General in 1789 and soon became prominent. As a monarchist he advised the king not to oppose the Revolution but to embrace it and place himself at the head of it. Had Louis XVI really understood his own sentiment of being "the people's greatest friend," he would have followed Mirabeau's advice. Instead, he ran away to the frontier, probably intending to join France's enemies massed on the border. This "Flight to Varennes" of June 1791 was not only the wrong thing to do but proved disastrous for the king, who was recognized, ironically from his faint embossed portrait on a Revolutionary *assignat* (paper money), and hauled back to Paris as a prisoner. Mirabeau, whose advice had been spurned, had meanwhile died of pericarditis. The king, stripped of his crown, was guillotined on 21 January 1793 as *citoyen* Louis Capet.

The Revolution raged on, in 1793–94 under the sanctimonious radical Maximilien Robespierre as leading member of the "Committee of Public Safety," who met his quietus by guillotine in July 1794. Besides (apparently) coining the slogan *Liberté, Égalité, Fraternité,* Robespierre opposed declaring war on Austria, warning quite correctly that, while defeat would mean restoration of the monarchy, victory would create a dictatorship. And it was precisely by a military route that dictatorship came to France in the shape of Napoleon Bonaparte, the ultimate beneficiary of the Revolution (see Chapter 19).

American Revolution

The American Revolution is a term used to refer to the long struggle (1765–83) for independence from Britain of the 13 colonies on the Atlantic coast of North America, which erupted into a hard-fought War of Independence in 1775, which was declared in 1776 and finally recognized by Britain in the Treaty of Paris of 1783.

It is estimated that "Patriots," or those in favor of independence from Britain, numbered 40–45% of the white population, with 15–20% being pro-British "Loyalists" or "Tories" and the rest being neutral. Between 80,000 and 100,000 "Tories" fled in the face of the "Patriot" victory, about half of them to Canada. Most were comparatively poor farmers.

The Patriot cause included many yeoman farmers, craftsmen, and small businessmen, but its leaders were generally well-educated and wealthy. George Washington, the commander in chief of the revolutionary "Continental Army," who emerged as the first (unopposed) president of the United States (in office

1789–97), was one of the richest men in Virginia, thanks largely to his wife Martha's inheritance from her first husband.

But the conflict even divided families: William Franklin, son of Benjamin Franklin, whose portrait still graces the $100 bill, was a stalwart Loyalist, serving as the last British governor of New Jersey, and spent two years behind bars for his pains. Father and son were never reconciled.

Though the political party founded in 1792 by Thomas Jefferson (president 1801–1809) and James Madison (president 1809–17) is commonly referred to by modern historians as the "Democratic-Republican" party, its actual name was simply the "Republican Party" (not to be confused with today's Republican Party, which, despite its nickname of "Grand Old Party," was only established in 1854). Madison excoriated democracy. And even Jefferson, a great believer in majority decisions, evidently thought it right to restrict the franchise to yeoman farmers, i.e. property owners.

At the time of the first presidential election of 1788–89, the electorate was limited to white, male property owners, making up 6% of the population. The right to vote is not mentioned in the US Constitution, and was left from the beginning to the individual states to determine. Between 1800 and 1830 the right to vote gradually expanded until it included most males over 21. By 1860 only five states still had a tax-paying qualification for voting. By contrast with the somewhat selective concept of "Jeffersonian Democracy," "Jacksonian Democracy," named for Andrew Jackson (president 1829–37), who, with the help of Martin van Buren (president 1837–41), established a party in 1834 specifically named the Democratic Party, relied on support from poor farmers, urban industrial workers, and Irish Catholics.

George Washington had all but one of the qualities of a dictator. He was a successful military leader who had just won a war of independence for his country. He was widely popular and was elected his nation's first president by acclamation. When selected by the Virginia state legislature as a delegate to the Constitutional Convention of 1787, he declined, only to be unanimously drafted as president of the Convention. In that capacity he could easily have steered it toward a monarchical style of government, but instead he chose to act more as a facilitator and a chairman of debate. What was lacking was any desire on his part to possess dictatorial power. He eschewed all honorific forms of address suggested by Vice President John Adams, such as "His Elective Majesty," "His Mightiness," or "His Highness," settling for the description, "The President of the United States," and with it the simple form of address, "Mr President," which remains the norm today.

Part III

Varieties of Monarchy

Chapter 18
Autocratic Monarchy

*T*he labels "autocracy," "despotism," and "absolutism" tend to be treated as *synonyms and applied to monarchies where the ruler has unbridled power, while "benevolent despotism" and "enlightened absolutism" are applied to rulers who used their power to improve the lot of their subjects—from the ruler's point of view. Frederick II "the Great" of Prussia (1740–86), one of the main exemplars of "enlightened despotism," believed that a ruler should be the "first servant" of the state.*

These labels are often misapplied, however. Another leading proponent of "enlightened despotism," Joseph II, Holy Roman emperor from 1765 to 1790, aroused so much opposition to his reforms that the epitaph that he despondently composed for himself read as follows (translated from the German): "Here lies a prince who, in spite of his best intentions, was unable to accomplish any of his plans." One of the main reasons for this negative result was that Joseph's reforms were all top-down policies imposed by him without gauging public opinion in advance. Trying to make German the official language throughout his very diverse realms was bound to raise widespread opposition. While realizing that the influential Hungarian aristocracy would oppose his reforms, he adopted a heavy-handed approach to them without winning the support of the peasantry. The Hungarian Diet was stripped of its ancient prerogatives, thus offending the aristocracy, who numbered forty thousand out of a total population of five million, while the "magnates," who made up 10% of the nobility and controlled most of the land, resisted Joseph's reforms of the feudal system, which emancipated the peasantry without giving them ownership of land or even freedom from dues owed to the landowning aristocracy.

Russia

A third member of the "enlightened despotism" club was Catherine II "the Great" of Russia (r. 1762–96)—who, however, was much less committed to the ideas of the "Enlightenment" than either Frederick the Great or Joseph II, and actually annulled an edict freeing Orthodox serfs, issued by her husband, Peter III, whom she overthrew and probably had murdered. On her accession, Catherine had five hundred thousand serfs, and a further 2.8 million were attached to the Russian state. Whether Catherine can be regarded as an autocrat at all is unclear, as she relied heavily on her noble favorites like Count Grigory Orlov and Prince Grigory Potemkin, to whom she may actually have been secretly married. The government of Tsarist Russia was jocularly described as "absolutism tempered by assassination," and no fewer than five tsars were assassinated between 1762 and 1918. Catherine's son and successor, Paul I (r. 1796–1801), was assassinated by a group of dismissed army officers. Paul's son and successor, Alexander I (r. 1801–25), began his reign with the intention of becoming a constitutional monarch, but after the defeat of Napoleon, who had tried unsuccessfully to invade Russia, his views became more conservative. "Liberty should be confined within just limits," he asserted. "And the limits of liberty are the principles of order."

Alexander's successor was his younger brother, Nicholas I (r. 1825–55), who was greeted on his accession by the "Decembrist Revolt" of some 3,000 young army officers demanding a constitutional monarchy. Though the revolt was easily crushed, it involved some loss of life, and several Decembrists were executed, with many more being imprisoned or exiled to Siberia. Nicholas I's motto was "Orthodoxy, Autocracy and Nationality."

Before writing *War and Peace*, as it happens, Leo Tolstoy was planning to write a novel about the fate of Decembrists on their return from Siberia. Besides restrictions on the monarchy, the Decembrists had demanded the abolition of serfdom, which was eventually ordered by Tsar Alexander II in 1861, who would be assassinated for his pains by a young socialist revolutionary.

By this time the Russian monarchy had been in conflict with the aristocracy for a long time. The so-called "Time of Troubles," which had lasted from 1598 to 1613, ended with the election by the Zemsky Sobor (a parliament made up of the estates of the realm) of Michael Romanov, who initiated major reforms, depriving the boyars (the old feudal aristocracy) of their independent principalities. Peter the Great (r. 1682–1725) abolished the advisory council of boyars and replaced it with a senate of his own choosing. He also introduced the "Table of Ranks," a formal list of positions and ranks for the aristocracy in the military, government, and court. Every noble was expected to start at the bottom rank and work his way up on the basis of merit. The object of the exercise was to deprive the aristocracy of an independent power-base and to make them dependent on, and therefore loyal to, the tsar. This rather backfired when in 1767 Catherine the

Great made promotion up the 14 grades automatic after seven years regardless of merit. Appointment to the entry-level 14th grade gave an official personal nobility, with hereditary nobility once he reached the eighth grade, which was raised by Nicholas I in 1845 to the fifth grade and by Alexander II in 1856 to the fourth grade for civil service appointments and the sixth grade for military ones. This elaborate system was the exact opposite of what was required for a strong centralized monarchy, as it not only kept the aristocracy in government but even made them hereditary, thus posing an even greater threat to the tsar. By 1914 the Russian aristocracy numbered about 1.9 million members out of a total population of 138 million, and most important government posts were staffed by nobles, who also had their own self-governing body, the Assembly of the Nobility, unwisely created by Catherine the Great in 1766. The emancipation of the serfs in 1861 did weaken the aristocracy, with the setting up of *zemstvo*, elected local self-government councils, reducing aristocratic influence in local government. Nevertheless, the nobles kept almost all the meadows and forests and had their debts paid by the state, while the emancipated serfs had to pay a third over market price for the small plots of land that they were allowed to retain.

Imperial China

By contrast with Russia, instead of trying to co-opt the aristocracy, the emperors of China established a completely novel system of competitive examinations for government officials known to the West as "mandarins," who, lacking an independent powerbase of their own and coming from many diverse areas and social and economic backgrounds, were neither willing nor able to pose a threat to the regime. By the same token, from the T'ang (618–907), when competitive examinations were introduced, the emperor had no need to depend on the traditional Chinese aristocracy, which therefore lost a good deal of its power.

It was an ancient Confucian principle that membership of the ruling class should be based on merit, through equal educational opportunity for all. This was put into practice by the T'ang dynasty in the seventh century by the introduction of a system of competitive written civil service examinations (upon which the modern Western examination system was modeled over a thousand years later.) This reform gradually achieved its objective of breaking the long monopoly of political power by the hereditary aristocracy. The Sung dynasty (960–1279) likewise deliberately utilized the examination system to counter the authority of regional military governors, and to enhance social mobility—and thereby increase imperial power.

According to Ho Ping-Ti's detailed study of Chinese social mobility, "The fact that there was more social circulation during the T'ang than during the previous three centuries cannot be much doubted, although it is difficult to

say whether the truly humble and poor had much chance of social success."
Adding that if "the hereditary aristocratic clans were no longer able to monopolize political power from the mid-seventh century onward, [they] remained
the dominant political factor and enjoyed unrivaled social prestige down to
the very end of the T'ang period." However, in the early Sung dynasty (960–
1126), 46.1% of recorded officials came from *han-tsu*, or "humble," clans or
families, as against only 13.8% in the late T'ang period (756–906.) "The trend
of increasing mobility continued after the founding of the Ming dynasty
(1368), when the examination and academic degree system became more
elaborate and the school system nationwide." However, "The early Manchu
rulers (from 1644), unlike the Ming founder, who came from a poor peasant
family, were mainly concerned with winning the support of the key social
class in their conquered land, namely, the scholar-official class," resulting in
a "much curtailed opportunity structure for the humble and obscure."
(Ho, Ping-ti, 1976, p. 262.) "It was perhaps more than coincidental that the
Taiping Rebellion or Revolution (1850–64), the most massive civil war in
world history, was precipitated by Hong Xiuquan (Hung Hsiu-ch'üan), a
member of a small landowning peasant family who had repeatedly failed to
obtain his first degree" (ibid.).

In general:

> [T]he most striking characteristic of the post T'ang society was that, on one
> hand, social success depended more on individual merit than on family status,
> and that, on the other hand, high-status families had little means of perpetuat
> ing their success if their descendants were inept.... For during the Ming-Ch'ing
> period (1368–1911) there were various institutionalized and noninstitutional
> channels which promoted the upward mobility of successful families but there
> were few institutionalized means to prevent the long-range downward mobility
> of unsuccessful families. In this sense, Ming-Ch'ing society was highly competi
> tive in its peculiar ways (ibid., p. 257).

Case Study: The Later Roman Empire

The Emperor Septimius Severus (r. 193–211) is famously said to have advised
his two sons, Caracalla and Geta, shortly before his death: "Be harmonious (between yourselves), enrich the soldiers, scorn all others" (Cassius Dio
77.15). Caracalla soon got rid of his brother, and behaved arrogantly toward
most other people, though in 212, by the *Constitutio Antoniniana,* he extended
Roman citizenship to all free male inhabitants of the empire. As his father
had advised, his main concern was the army, though his extension of citizenship actually had a detrimental effect on military recruitment. The army

was made up of legions, recruited from Roman citizens, and *auxilia,* drawn from *peregrini,* non-citizen provincials, who became citizens automatically after 25 years' service. After 212, however, there was no longer any incentive for *peregrini* to enlist, and more "barbarians" were recruited than ever before.

Between Caracalla's assassination in 217 and the accession of Diocletian in 284, a succession of emperors met a similar fate. The period from 235 to 284 is known as the Crisis of the Third Century, when the Roman Empire's very existence was threatened by a combination of threats, foreign and domestic, military, political, and economic.

Diocletian's solution stabilized the empire, at least temporarily. As a military man, his focus was primarily on defense, and security. By sharing his power with three other emperors in the so-called tetrarchy ("rule of four"), and by greatly increasing the number of provinces, and separating military and civil commands, he secured the frontiers while tightening up the administration of the empire. The Christian writer Lactantius (c. 250–c. 325) went so far as to claim that under Diocletian there were more men on the government's payroll than taxpayers (Lactantius, *Mort. Pers.,* 7.3)! This was an exaggeration, but modern estimates still suggest that Diocletian doubled the size of the civil service from about fifteen to thirty thousand (Treadgold 1997, p. 19). On the basis of a population of between fifty and sixty-five million, this averages out at about one official per two thousand inhabitants (Jones, 1964, p. 594; cf. Bagnall 1987, p. 66).

The corollary to this was the compilation of the Gregorian and Hermogenian codes under Diocletian's direction—codification being a novelty at the time, which was to burgeon greatly in the future, right up to the present day. Diocletian took very seriously his responsibility as the fount of all law, and there are about 1,200 rescripts still surviving—probably only a fraction of those issued—chiefly from the period 293-4 alone (see Connolly 2010). Rescripts are legal responses, probably drafted by professional government lawyers in the *scrinium a libellis,* or imperial secretariat, to petitions from people of varying degrees all around the empire (see Honoré 1979, pp. 51–64).

Men of senatorial origin had a monopoly on provincial governorships under Augustus. This was one of the chief ways that this master politician was able to placate this important class—leading members of which had been responsible for that cataclysmic event on the Ides of March 44 BCE. But, as time went by, emperor after emperor continued to dilute the senatorial order with men of their own choosing from outside the order, and, increasingly, from outside Italy. In the third century, emperors started appointing non-senators to governorships without even bothering to dunk them in the *curia* (Senate-house) first. Diocletian completed this process, largely eliminating members of the senatorial order from positions of any importance.

Principate to Dominate

Diocletian's accession to power in 284 is an important watershed in the conventional chronology of the Roman Empire, marking the end of the Augustan "Principate" and the beginning of a new form of autocratic monarchy labeled by modern historians the "Dominate," or simply as the beginning of the "Later Roman Empire," or in French, the transition from "Le Haut-Empire" to "Le Bas-Empire," while adherents of the "World of Late Antiquity" school trace "Late Antiquity" as far back as to the period around the year 150. Oxford University in its wisdom also used to designate 284 as marking the beginning of its "Modern History Schools" syllabus!

Imperial Power

The emperor's relationship with the senatorial aristocracy is of central importance. Diocletian had a visceral dislike of, or at least total disdain for, the traditional senatorial aristocracy of the West, and he completed the job begun by previous emperors of practically eliminating them from all offices of any importance. This distinction between Diocletian and Constantine is crucial. But Diocletian's dislike of the senatorial aristocracy did not impel him to cultivate the support of the lower classes, as had been done under the Principate. He hardly ever set foot in Rome, which he clearly regarded as the capital of the empire in name only. He came to power through the army, and any threat to his position would come from that quarter.

By contrast, for their own reasons, Constantine (r. 306–37) and his successors pandered to the senatorial aristocracy in the West, and like Diocletian, but unlike Augustus and his successors up to Marcus Aurelius, the late Roman emperors showed no interest in courting the support of the lower orders. As a result, the population in the West was demoralized and showed no enthusiasm to prop up the regime when assailed by "barbarians." This helps us to understand the "decline and fall" of the Roman Empire in the West (see Arnheim, 2022).

Constantine and Christianity

Though Constantine only formally converted to Christianity on his deathbed in 337, he is commonly represented as being favorably disposed toward it from a much earlier date. Constantine was, of course, the first Roman emperor to embrace Christianity, but he did so stealthily—and with good reason. The old idea is quite wrong that Christianity must already have been strong in terms both of numbers and influence in order to attract as cold and calculating a ruler as Constantine (see Arnheim, 1972, p 73n). With all its splits, it appears to have

Figure 18 Constantine with the god Sol Invictus.
SOURCE: Gallica Digital Library / Wikimedia Commons / Public domain.

accounted for only about 10% of the population of the empire in Constantine's time, and that concentrated in the East, which did not form part of Constantine's empire until 324.

If any god was specially favored by Constantine it was the pagan sun god, *Sol Invictus* ("the Unconquered Sun"), whose image appears repeatedly on Constantine's coinage until 324, including the magnificent gold single *solidus* and multiple *solidi* coins, showing jugate busts of Constantine and Sol in lock-step, minted in Ticinum as late as 316.

Constantine first came out openly as a Christian by summoning the ecumenical Council of Nicaea in 325, hard on the heels of Constantine's defeat of his co-ruler Licinius in 324, which, significantly, for the first time gave Constantine rule over the Eastern provinces, the stronghold of Christianity.

Constantine hedged his bets on Christianity. If the evidence about 312 has any validity—and there is something of a question mark over it—Constantine was obviously not ready to "come out" openly in favor of Christianity at that point. The absence of Christian symbolism on his victory arch erected in 315 is telling. This may well be explained by the religious preferences of the Senate, but that must mean that the Senate either did not know about Constantine's Christian leanings or wanted to make clear its opposition to them.

Constantine's role in the Council of Nicaea is also not quite clear. That he convened the Council, presided over the opening session, and took part in the discussions is not in doubt, but after acting in accordance with its rejection of Arianism, he switched sides. For, though the assembled bishops resoundingly rejected Arianism (a non-trinitarian version of Christianity), Constantine, hav-ing banished its founder, Arius, eventually recalled him from exile and banished his nemesis, Athanasius of Alexandria, to Trier. And Constantine's confessor, by whom he was baptized, was in fact an Arian-leaning bishop who also happened to be a distant relative of his, Eusebius of Nicomedia, and who also enjoyed the confidence of Constantius II (r. 337–61), an Arian, or at least a pro-Arian emperor (as would be the Emperor Valens, r. 364–78.)

Even as late as 333, Constantine instituted the position of *Pontifex Flavialis* in Hispellum (modern Spello, in Umbria), a pagan priesthood specifically named after himself and part, therefore, of the imperial cult, with the one proviso that there should be no sacrifices. This is a good example of Constantine's hedging of his bets. The ban on sacrifice no doubt salved Constantine's conscience, though it would not have gone far enough to satisfy Christians, who would not have been in favor of any kind of imperial cult.

The Religion of the Senatorial Aristocracy

Constantine's policy of appointing members of the senatorial aristocracy again to high office was a major concession to this class. But what was his motive for doing so? Among other possible reasons, it could have been a counter-intuitive response by a pro-Christian emperor to a staunchly pagan class, with a view to winning their support, or at least their neutrality. But it is not certain how staunchly pagan the aristocracy was, though they continued to hold traditional pagan priesthoods, and their stronghold in the West was much less Christian than the East in any case. The strength of the senatorial aristocracy evidently correlates with weak imperial power in the West under Constantine's successors.

Constantinople: The "New Rome"

One of Constantine's best known achievements was his establishment of a new capital—later unofficially known as the "New Rome"—in the old Greek city of Byzantium, which he renamed Constantinople. Rome itself was too far West, and too far from the frontier. It also happened to be the stronghold of the senatorial aristocracy, which Constantine favored in civil appointments, as was shown above, but which he probably never entirely trusted. Such was the strength of the senatorial aristocracy in Rome that as late as 392, when a grammarian and rhetorician called Eugenius (Eugenius 6—PLRE; Jones et al. 1971–1992), who had served as *magister scrinii* (in one of the imperial secretariats), was raised to the purple by the Frankish-born *magister militum* ("general") Arbogast, the senatorial aristocracy persuaded the nominally Christian Eugenius to support the old pagan religion with public funding, notably by restoring the Altar of Victory (removed by the Emperor Gratian) and rededicating the Temple of Venus and Rome. Eugenius appointed senatorial aristocrats to high office, notably

(Virius) Nicomachus Flavianus and his namesake son (Flavianus 15 and 14—PLRE; Jones et al. 1971–1992).

Constantinople had no such associations. Constantine established a separate Senate in Constantinople, made up largely of new men, who were later held up to ridicule by Libanius for their lowly origins. (Libanius, *Or.* 42.22–26; cf. Chastagnol, 1992, pp. 354–56; Jones, 1964, pp. 538, 546.) However, large landowners from the Eastern half of the Empire were also attracted into the new Senate, not least in order to mitigate their tax burden (see Moser 2019, pp. 436–61).

Constantine the Reformer

Though Constantine followed the example set by Diocletian in some ways, he broke with him in two crucial respects: provincial administration and religion. After Diocletian axed the senatorial aristocracy from all positions of power, Constantine welcomed them back even to the top position of praetorian prefect—but only in the West. In so doing, Constantine weakened his own position and that of his successors in the West, which goes some way to explaining why the West fell to the "barbarians" while the East survived. The powerful aristocrats of the West simply had no interest in propping up the Emperor and the central imperial government. This is also relevant to the issue of Christianity, because the Western aristocrats were evidently still largely pagan and were not going to shore up a Christian emperor—which is why Constantine hedged his Christian leanings until the end. (For more on the Later Roman Empire, see Arnheim, 2022.)

Chapter 19
Dynastic

*T*he term "dynasty," from the Greek dynasteia, *meaning "power," "domin-ion," "overlordship," usually represents a series of rulers from the same family, and "dynastic politics" refers to policies designed to further the interests of a particular dynasty. But what relationship (if any) is there between dynastic rule and the power structure? The fewer dynastic changes that a state undergoes, the greater its stability—or so one might expect.*

China

This is true to some extent of China, where the dynasties were not only mostly quite long-lived, but there was continuity across them. One of the most important aspects of this was the sidelining of the major aristocratic families in favor of the competitive imperial examination system to select scholar-officials, which lasted for close on two thousand years, starting during the Han dynasty (206 BCE–220 CE) and being abolished only in 1905, just before the imperial system as a whole was swept away. Though the expense of the tuition involved gave the wealthier classes an advantage in the examinations, the rank of scholar-official was not hereditary. So, though these highly educated and intelligent officials enjoyed high status and prestige, they never posed a threat to imperial power. Interestingly, a partial recrudescence of the old imperial examination system has been in evidence in Communist China since 1993.

Another important bastion of imperial power against the aristocracy was the eunuchs, from at least around 146 CE until the end of the Qing dynasty in 1912. Some eunuchs exerted great power, which was facilitated by their closeness to the emperor. The reason they were entrusted with such responsibility

Figure 19   Chinese emperor receiving a candidate during the Palace Examination, Song Dynasty (960–1279).
SOURCE: Ming Dynasty Painting / Wikimedia Commons / Public domain.

was that, as they could not have children and start a dynasty, they would not be tempted to seize the throne, and they could easily be demoted or disposed of. In his memoirs, Puyi, the last emperor of China, tells with some embarrassment of the relish with which he had punished his eunuchs while he was a young boy. The tension between the eunuchs and the scholar-officials or mandarins also redounded to the benefit of imperial power. It has been plausibly suggested that, while the eunuchs represented the personal views of the emperor, the mandarins represented the viewpoint of the bureaucracy (Huang 1981).

Here is a conspectus of the dynasties into which Chinese history is conventionally divided between 2070 BCE and 1912 CE:

- The Zhou dynasty (1046–256 BCE), which originated the concept of the "Mandate of Heaven" to legitimize their rule. According to this doctrine, virtuous, just, and able rulers had a divine "mandate" to rule, which was withdrawn if the ruler proved unworthy. The doctrine could be a double-edged sword, as it could also be used to justify rebellion. In fact, the Zhou rulers used it to justify their overthrow of the Shang dynasty on the ground that it had lost the Mandate of Heaven.

- The Qin dynasty (221–206 BCE), best known for the Terracotta Army of Qin Shi Huang, who first united China as a single imperial state under the so-called Legalist system. It was during this dynasty that feudalism was abolished and replaced with a centralized bureaucratic administration. It was also in this period that eunuchs are first in evidence as civil servants.
- The Han dynasty (206 BCE–220 CE), which made Confucianism the official philosophy of China, emphasizing stability and order. In 165 BCE, Emperor Wen first introduced the system of competitive written examinations for the selection of officials. In 134 BCE, Emperor Wu (r. 141–87 BCE) introduced the *Xiaolian* recommendatory system for the appointment of officials. Though there were already eunuchs employed as civil servants, Emperor Huan of Han (r. 146–68) is sometimes credited with first making systematic use of them.
- Sui dynasty (581–618). The "nine-rank system," supposedly based on merit, was introduced for appointing high officials. Though intended to centralize selection and thereby imperial power, in practice it played into the hands of the aristocracy, as the so-called Controllers, whose job it was to nominate and evaluate candidates, abused their position to promote the interests of their own family members. As a result, the saying arose: "There are no poor people in the upper ranks, and no powerful families in the lower ones" (Wilkinson, 2012, p. 265) (see Chapter 8). To replace these recommendatory systems, the competitive written examination system to select civil servants began in earnest.
- The Tang dynasty (618–907). Besides seeing the adoption of Buddhism, this dynasty also intensified the use of the imperial examination selection system as a way of enhancing the power of the emperor at the expense of the aristocracy. The examinations were open to all males other than those whose fathers were artisans or merchants. Because of the expense of the training required for these examinations, a disproportionate number of civil servants came from aristocratic backgrounds. Nevertheless, the late Tang and early Song period saw the disappearance of the great aristocratic clans, some of which had enjoyed even more prestige than the emperor. This was facilitated by the establishment of state-run schools to enable non-aristocratic candidates to enter for the competitive examinations. "By the late Tang the Chinese state had largely succeeded in dominating society everywhere and in supplanting the locally-based magnates who had held sway in the provinces since the fall of the Han" (Tackett, 2006, p. 217).
- The Song dynasty (960–1279), responsible for making the imperial competitive examination system obligatory for officials, who became known as scholar-officials, scholar-bureaucrats, or "mandarins." The widespread use of printing helped to prepare a wider class of candidates for the examinations. The number of candidates for the low-level prefectural examinations

grew from 30,000 a year in the early eleventh century to 400,000 by the late thirteenth century. Besides scholar-officials actually in office, a large educated non-hereditary elite social class grew up who supervised local affairs on behalf of the central government.

- The Yuan dynasty (1271–1368), established by Kublai Khan, who brought China under Mongol rule. As the civil service examinations favored Han Chinese and the Chinese language, they were initially discontinued, but restored in modified form in 1315.
- The Ming dynasty (1368–1644), during which the content of the imperial examination was narrowed down mostly to Neo-Confucian texts. The highest degree, in the imperial examination system, the *jinshi,* became a prerequisite for the top positions, while there was an oversupply of the holders of the basic *shengyuan* degree, leaving a number of unemployed "graduates."
- The Qing (or Manchu) dynasty (1644–1912). In the nineteenth century, the training needed for the imperial examinations became too expensive, except for the rich, who could also buy office directly for their sons. The examination system was abolished in 1905. In general, this was a troubled period punctuated by rebellions and war and culminating in a revolution that forced the abdication of the last emperor, Puyi.
- Maoist Communism, starting with the proclamation of the Chinese People's Republic in 1949 and under the strong monarchy of Mao Zedong from 1949 to 1976, and Xi Jinping since 2012. Mao rejected the examination system in favor of a system based on loyalty to the Communist Party. However, under the "Provisional Regulations on State Civil Servants" of 1993, a competitive examination system was reintroduced, which was still in force at the time of this writing, attracting over a million candidates every year, with a 2% success rate. An alternative and easier route to a civil service appointment is through membership or probationary membership of the Chinese Communist Party.

Japan

Since 539 CE there has been a single dynasty on the Japanese "Chrysanthemum Throne" which has produced an unbroken succession of emperors, who, however, hardly ever exercised great power. During the Heian period (794–1185) power was largely in the hands of the Fujiwara aristocratic clan, related to the imperial house by marriage, through the position of regent, *Sessho,* vizier, *Kampaku,* or *Sekkan* (the collective term for both positions together), and they continued to be very influential right up until the twentieth century, when two of their members served as prime minister, one in 1937–39 and

1940–41, and the other in 1993–94. Tokugawa Ieyasu, the founder of the Tokugawa shogunate (1603–1868) was related by marriage to the Fujiwara clan, and a daughter of the last shogun was married to a second cousin of Emperor Hirohito (r. 1926–89).

Between 1192 and 1868, with brief interludes, the real rulers of Japan were the military *shoguns,* nominally appointed by the emperor but in practice members of largely hereditary dynasties of their own, notably that of the house of Tokugawa, which was in power from 1616 to 1868. The shogunate was akin to a feudal system. At the top was the shogun, below whom came the *daimyo,* hereditary landholding magnates, who arose out of the *shugo,* or military governors appointed by the shogun to oversee one or more of the provinces. In the mid-fourteenth century there arose the so-called *shugo-daimyo,* who turned into *daimyo* in the late fifteenth century. Below them came the large class of samurai, comparable to medieval European knights, but without landowning. At the bottom of the pile, which was cemented by ties of loyalty all the way up and down, were the peasants.

The shogunate was brought to an end by the so-called *Meiji Restoration* of 1868, which, despite its name, handed power not to the emperor but rather to a Meiji oligarchy under the leadership of a small select group of informal extraconstitutional advisers to the emperor known as *Genro* ("original elder"), up to the early 1930s. In 1947, under American occupation after Japan's defeat in World War II, Japan adopted a new constitution, which stripped the emperor of all power and reduced him into a constitutional monarch (see Chapter 22).

Egypt

Ancient Egyptian history, spanning the period from 3100 to 30 BCE, is still divided into "dynasties," based on the *Aegyptiaca (History of Egypt)* compiled by Manetho, an Egyptian priest of the third century BCE. Manetho identified 30 dynasties, to which three have been added. Manetho's concept of "dynasty" was not automatically equated with heredity but only with continuity. Whenever he detected some break in continuity, whether related to heredity or not, he would signal a new dynasty.

This gives Egyptian history a more disjointed appearance than it deserves. So, for example, Ahmose I (r. c. 1550–1525 BCE), listed as the first member of the Eighteenth Dynasty, was the brother and successor to Kamose (r. 1554–1549 BCE) of the Seventeenth Dynasty. The reason that Ahmose I is treated as founding a new dynasty is that he reconquered Lower Egypt from the Hyksos (designated the Fifteenth Dynasty), who had been dominant there for about a century.

The pharaoh derived a good deal of his power from the belief in his divine status, discussed in Chapter 4 of this book. The cataclysmic short-lived religious revolution associated with the name of Akhenaten (r. 1351–1334 BCE) of the Eighteenth Dynasty has probably got a good deal to do with his desire to strip the priesthood of Amun of their power and prestige. Although he correctly understood just how major a threat the priesthood posed to his position as pharaoh, he did not know how to cultivate popular support for the monarchy against the priesthood. And he was evidently unaware that the widespread popular devotion and idolization enjoyed by an Egyptian pharaoh was inseparable from the people's devotion and idolization of the traditional gods channeled through the priesthood. Asked to choose between the pharaoh and the traditional gods, the people evidently chose to remain true to the age-old religion and gods of Egypt. And this lesson was not lost on subsequent pharaohs. The economy was a "command" economy in which all major activities, such as agriculture, mining, and trade, were under the pharaoh's control.

The transition between the Eighteenth and Nineteenth Dynasties is marked by three non-royal pharaohs in succession: Ay II, grand vizier under Tutankhamun; Horemheb, a former general; and Ramesses I, a former grand vizier, who established a new hereditary line reigning from 1292 to 1186 BCE. Ramesses I is rightly considered the founder of a new dynasty, the Nineteenth, as he was of non-royal birth, and served as grand vizier under the Horemheb Dynasty.

The Hyksos (probably of Semitic origin) were the first foreign pharaohs of Egypt and their control of Lower (northern) Egypt coexisted with the Sixteenth and Seventeenth Thebes-based (Upper Egypt) Dynasties. Manetho's depiction of the Hyksos as oppressive invaders is no longer universally accepted. An alternative modern view associates the Hyksos with the peaceful settlement of the Nile delta by Canaanite people over a long period starting as early as the late Twelfth Dynasty (1991–1802 BCE) and breaking away from native Egyptian rule during the weak Thirteenth Dynasty (1802–c. 1649 BCE).

In keeping with the prevailing view in Roman times, the Jewish historian Josephus associated the Hyksos with the Hebrews or Jews of the Old Testament. Josephus goes so far as to claim that, when expelled from Egypt, the Hyksos founded Jerusalem (Josephus, *Contra Apion* I. 90). Modern scholarly opinion is very divided on the nature and provenance of the Hyksos and their connection, if any, with the biblical Exodus tradition.

The two leading figures in the biblical account both have Egyptian associations. Joseph's "coat of many colors" is reminiscent of the portrayal of some foreigners in Egyptian pyramid art. His position as vizier, or chief minister, is consistent with what we know of the role of historically authenticated viziers or grand viziers. And his building of public granaries or storehouses chimes in with what we know about the central control of the economy of ancient Egypt generally. But, if Charles F. Aling is right, which seems likely, Joseph lived in the Middle Kingdom and served under a pharaoh in the Twelfth Dynasty (1991–1802 BCE) (Aling 1981). Among other reasons, Joseph's position as second only to the pharaoh himself according to the Bible, accords with the period when power was being centralized in the hands of the pharaoh and taken away from the nomarchs, provincial governors, whose power had grown when the administration of Egypt was decentralized under Djedkare Isesi, who reigned in the late twenty-fifth to mid-twenty-fourth century BCE. After this, the post of nomarch became hereditary, giving its holders even greater power. But the Twelfth Dynasty saw royal power enhanced at the expense of the nomarchs.

The name of the leading figure in the Exodus story, Moses—*Moshe* in Hebrew—has clear Egyptian associations. It may be a shortened version of an Egyptian name. The latter part of pharaonic names such as "Thut*mose*" or "Ra*messes*" means "son of." So Thutmose means "Son of (the god) Thoth," Ramesses means "Son of (the god) Ra," and Ahmose means "Son of the Moon." This ties in with the Biblical tradition that Moses was adopted as a foundling by pharaoh's daughter and brought up in the royal palace. In these circumstances the baby Moses would have been given an Egyptian name such as "Son of [a named god]." The Book of Exodus provides a completely different, Hebrew, etymology for Moses's name. This was presumably in order to distance him from his adoption by the Egyptian royal family while retaining the traditional foundling folk-tale—as in the story of Romulus and Remus and Hansel and Gretel in *Grimm's Fairy Tales* (which were not inventions created by the Brothers Grimm but a compilation of painstakingly collected traditional folktales).

The first real and complete foreign conquest of Egypt was achieved by the Kushite Piye, king of Nubia, in 744 BCE, and thereby establishing the Twenty-fifth Dynasty, which lasted till 656 BCE. The conquest was facilitated by Egypt's weakness and fragmentation at the time.

Egypt was reunited under Psamtik (Psammetichus) I, who established the Twenty-sixth Dynasty, which came to an end with the conquest by the Achaemenid Cambyses II of Persia in 525 BCE. From then until 404 BCE Egypt was a constituent satrapy of the Persian Empire and the Persian shahanshah ("king of kings") adopted the title of pharaoh in Egypt.

This period is designated the Twenty-seventh Dynasty, which was brought to an end by a rebellion under Amyrtaeus, the only Pharaoh of the Twenty-eighth Dynasty, who is thought to have been related to the Twenty-sixth Dynasty (664–525 BCE). But Amyrtaeus was himself defeated and executed by Nepherites, a general, who established the Twenty-ninth Dynasty, the last pharaoh from which, Nepherites II, was deposed and probably killed by Nectanebo I, establishing the Thirtieth Dynasty. His grandson Nectanebo II is the last native pharaoh recognized by Manetho. He was defeated by the Persian King Artaxerxes III reconquering Egypt with difficulty in 340 or 339 BCE.

Case Study: France

When King Louis XVI faced the guillotine in 1793 he was addressed neither as "king of France," nor even as "king of the French" (referring to the people rather than the territory), but simply by his name as an ordinary citizen, yet, surprisingly, not as "citizen Louis Bourbon" but as "citizen Louis Capet." Louis belonged to the House of Bourbon, a dynasty which had occupied the French throne since the accession of Henry IV in 1589 as a cadet branch (i.e. junior branch) of the Capetian dynasty founded by Hugh Capet, king of the Franks from 987 to 996, whose male-line descendants from Philip II reigned as kings of France from 1190 onward. By addressing their deposed king as "Louis Capet," the radical revolutionaries were unwittingly recognizing the antiquity of his dynastic descent, or possibly deliberately mocking it.

After the abolition of the monarchy and Louis XVI's execution, France went on a roller-coaster journey, through a bloody "Reign of Terror," a conservative *Directoire,* Napoleon's autocratic *Consulat,* his even more autocratic but (until his undoing in Russia) phenomenally successful French Empire, and then the restoration of the Bourbon monarchy under two of Louis XVI's brothers, first Louis XVIII, who, with greatly reduced powers, nevertheless made a point of restoring a hereditary aristocracy, and then Charles X, who was said to have "learned nothing and forgotten nothing." Charles X's ousting in 1830 marked the end of the direct Capetian line, which still occupies the throne of Spain in the person of Philip VI, a direct descendant of the first Bourbon king of Spain, Philip V (r. 1700–24 and 1724–46), a grandson of Louis XIV of France, who was prepared to expend blood and treasure that he could ill afford in the 13-year-long War of the Spanish Succession in order to place his grandson on the Spanish throne. This was all part of dynastic politics, which, however, did not pay off on this occasion, as Philip V had to renounce the French throne for himself and his heirs in perpetuity.

France was a monarchy continuously until 1792 and then intermittently until 1870, when it finally committed itself to a republican form of government. Until the mid-nineteenth century, conflict between monarchy and aristocracy was a leitmotif of French history. A hard-fought victory over the self-important aristocratic *parlements* was won by the monarchy under Louis XIV and Louis XV, only to be thrown away by Louis XVI on his accession in 1774. Monarchy did, however, stage a spectacular comeback under the Bonapartes in the nineteenth century. But at no time would I describe the French monarchy as "absolute," a term that is all too freely bandied about by protagonists on both sides. Absolute power means, literally, autocratic, arbitrary power untrammeled by limitations of any kind—which is virtually impossible.

(continued)

(continued)

"L'état c'est moi" ("I am the state") is a boast commonly attributed to King Louis XIV (r. 1643–1715), but it has been plausibly suggested that what Louis XIV meant was something rather less dramatic than it sounds, to the effect that his interests as king should be identified with the interests of the state (Mettam, 1988). Louis XIV cultivated the image of himself as "The Sun King" (*Le Roi Soleil*). The portrayal of Louis XIV as an absolute monarch by historians goes back at least to Voltaire (1694–1778), who, though celebrated as a father of the French Revolution, was also a great admirer of Louis XIV—and not in spite of his putative absolutism but because of it. In recent years, however, this image of Louis XIV as an absolute monarch has been disputed. So, we have to ask: How powerful was Louis XIV actually in practice? And what about his predecessors and successors?

With the notable exception of Louis XI (r. 1461–83), until the accession of the first Bourbon king, Henry (Henri) IV (r. 1589–1610), the French monarchy was generally quite weak, and the country was dominated by the aristocracy. Henry IV and Louis XIII (r. 1610–43) were fortunate enough to have very able ministers who understood the fundamental truth that strong monarchy could only be established at the expense of the aristocracy. Early on in his long reign, Louis XIV had to contend with a serious aristocratic rising, the Fronde, which was successfully put down, after which the power of the monarchy was enhanced, a process culminating in the last few years of Louis XV's reign (1715–74) with the utter defeat of the *parlements*, the major thorn in the side of the Crown—only to have this great victory thrown away by Louis XVI (r. 1774–92) on his accession.

It is important to note that the *parlements* were not "parliaments" in the English sense but superior courts of law of appellate jurisdiction with a wide remit, especially in regard to taxation. The most important of these was the *Parlement de Paris*, but by 1789 there were 12 other provincial *parlements*, with a total of over a thousand members in the country at large, with 12 or more councilors sitting at any one time. One particularly important power exercised by the *parlements* was their control over legislation, whereby no royal decree had the force of law in any province until it was approved and published by the *parlement* of that area.

Henry IV: "A Chicken in Every Pot"

It is really only from the time of Henry (Henri) IV that a policy of establishing a strong monarchy at the expense of the aristocracy was pursued with any degree of consistency. Henry IV is also credited with the populist promise that there would be a chicken in every peasant's pot every Sunday. However, the introduction by Henry's otherwise very astute minister, Sully, of the Paulette tax in 1604, allowing office-holders to pass their offices on to their heirs or even sell them, antagonized the *noblesse d'épée* (literally, the "aristocracy of the sword," the traditional hereditary aristocracy) while creating a formidable new aristocracy, the *noblesse de robe* (the "aristocracy of office-holders"), which eventually joined the traditional aristocracy in opposition to the Crown. Henry's assassination in 1610 handed the throne to his not quite nine-year-old son Louis XIII.

Louis XIII (r. 1610–43)

The accession of a minor and the existence of a regency was a signal to the aristocracy to rise up in revolt. Some groups within the aristocracy even went so far as to raise private armies and conspire with foreign states against the French Crown. This opposition was successfully crushed during Louis's reign, especially after the appointment of Cardinal Richelieu (1585–1642) as chief minister in 1624, which turned out to be a great boon to the monarchy, for, while Richelieu was intent on safeguarding his own position, he remained loyal to the king (contrary to the picture painted of him in the fictitious *Three Musketeers*) and to the task of aggrandizing the power of the monarchy and reducing that of the aristocracy. The means that he employed to this end included the demolition of all aristocratic fortified castles (unless needed for national defense); restricting the *Parlement de Paris* to judicial matters and prohibiting it from involvement in politics; and the setting up of an unofficial secret service, plus the imposition of press censorship. Richelieu was intent on creating in France a powerful nation state under a strong centralized monarchy. On Richelieu's death, he was succeeded by his hand-picked successor, Cardinal Mazarin, who was of Italian origin (under the name Mazzarino), and who served as chief minister of France from 1642 until his death in 1661.

Louis XIV (r. 1643–1715)

Louis XIV was only five years old when he ascended the throne. Once again, there was a regency, which once again was taken advantage of by the aristocracy to raise the banner of revolt in the so-called Fronde, in which they were joined by the *parlements* and also enjoyed a certain amount of popular support, especially in Paris. The Fronde is usually divided into two stages: first, the *Fronde Parlementaire* (1648–49), sparked off by the Crown's shortage of money, leading to Mazarin's proposed suspension of judges' salaries for a few years, and his attempt to create new posts to subvert the position of the *Parlement de Paris*, which demanded the right to give consent to new taxes. Secondly, the *Fronde des Nobles* (1650–53), which ended with the bourgeoisie of Paris turning against the *frondeurs*. With remarkable foresight, Cardinal de Retz, himself a leading *frondeur*, predicted in 1649: "*Les parlements, qui soufflaient sur le feu, en seraient, un jour, consumés*" ("The *parlements*, which fanned the flames, will one day be consumed by them") (Cobban, 1950, p. 64). This prediction was realized 150 years later!

The lesson of the Fronde was not lost on the young Louis XIV, who, following on from the policy of Richelieu, ordered the demolition of aristocratic castles, and required nobles to spend at least part of the year at Versailles, a huge palatial complex which was constructed for this purpose among others. Nobles here would be granted honors and favors in accordance with their closeness to the royal person. Only those deemed the most important personalities, numbering about a 100, would be admitted every morning to the *Grande Levée* (following an even more intimate *Petit Levée*, to which only a select few were admitted), during which the king was dressed and given breakfast (a bowl of broth), and a shorter version of the same ceremony took place when the king retired at night (Saint-Simon, 2007).

After Mazarin's death in 1661, Louis XIV effectively became his own chief minister. He deprived the *parlements* of their right to decide on the validity of laws, and he streamlined both criminal and civil procedure with the introduction in 1667 of the *Grande Ordonnance de Procédure Civile*, nicknamed the *Code Louis*—foreshadowing Napoleon in this respect. And law enforcement in Paris, and later in other cities, was placed under a lieutenant general of police. But French law in general still remained a patchwork quilt of different jurisdictions.

Louis XIV understood only too well the need to reduce the power of the aristocracy, and, besides the measures already mentioned, he deliberately chose as his ministers men of ability of non-noble backgrounds, like Jean-Baptiste Colbert, or from newly ennobled families, as in the cases of Michel Le Tellier, Hugues de Lionne, and Nicolas Fouquet. Having no independent power base of their own, these ministers depended on royal favor, in return for which the king could count on their loyalty and obedience. He would not tolerate malpractice on the part of a minister, so, when Fouquet, superintendent of finances from 1653 to 1661, was revealed to have made huge amounts of money out of his government position, he was arrested and imprisoned for life.

It would be hard to disagree with these remarks of Roger Mettam's:

> The conflicts which troubled the internal history of France in the seventeenth century almost all had one element in common—they were caused, or were at least prolonged and invigorated, by the unceasing struggle of the crown against the independent power of the varied groups who formed the privileged orders in French society (Mettam 1977, p. ix).

And:

> Although most groups in French society—nobles of the sword and of the robe, clerics, municipal officials and the ordinary men of town and countryside— sometimes showed considerable hostility to each other, it was against the central government that their most vigorous protests were directed (ibid., p. xiv).

And again: "The result of this investigation may point to a degree of centralized control which, if it was on the increase, was far from absolute" (ibid., p. 16).

However, while rightly rejecting the "absolutist" label, Mettam ends up tilting against windmills: "The historians who have exaggerated the effectiveness of centralized government under Louis XIV have tended particularly to inflate the importance of the intendants, whom they have seen as the very basis of the absolutist regime they have described" (ibid., p. 16). Once it is recognized that, though not "absolute," Louis XIV was a strong monarch, Mettam's objections about the intendants fall away. These were royal officials with supervisory powers over finance, justice and police in the provinces or *généralités*:

- Mettam remarks that, like government ministers (secretaries of state), the intendants came from "established bureaucratic families." This objection will not stand up to scrutiny. The position of intendant was a high-level administrative office, which could hardly be entrusted to just anyone off the street.
- However, Mettam admits that the post of intendant was neither hereditary and was also "not a position that could be bought, and was therefore one from which the holder could easily be dismissed" (ibid.). In addition, "unlike all other bureaucratic offices," the position of intendant of a *généralité* "was always given to a man who was not a native of that generality and therefore had no personal vested interest in the life of the area." And: An intendant "would use every legitimate means, and sometimes others, to demonstrate the efficiency of his administration and his suitability for higher office in his home district."
- Moreover: "During the ministry of Colbert (1661–83) the intendants were used more extensively than ever before, not just to spy on the bureaucracy but to send in highly detailed reports about every aspect of provincial France. Throughout the kingdom they acted as the eyes and ears of the Paris ministers.... Sometimes the intendants were sent on general tours of inspection in their area, on other occasions they were asked to investigate specific problems" (ibid., p. 17).

Not surprisingly, the very existence of intendants had been a major grievance of the *frondeurs*, who, as we have seen, plagued Louis XIV's youth. Mettam grudgingly admits that under Colbert the intendants "did indeed improve the efficiency of the administration, but slowly and only to a partial degree.... Throughout France they did root out the worst examples of corrupt officialdom, though much sharp practice remained" (loc. cit.).

Louis XIV's France was divided into 34 *généralités*, most of which were so-called *pays d'élections*, where the royal government was dominant through intendants. But there were a few *généralités*, designated *pays d'états*, situated mostly around the perimeter of the country, where elected provincial estates still retained a certain amount of autonomy. Here the intendants were less effective, and the king was forced to rely on aristocratic provincial governors, who existed in all provinces but mostly with only nominal powers. But Louis XIV changed the system so that appointment to a governorship was initially for only three years and no longer depended on any hereditary or social right, but on royal favor alone.

Another important area of royal power was religion. By the Concordant of Bologna of 1516, Pope Leo X granted King Francis (François) I (r. 1515–47) the right, known as the *droit de régale,* which had been claimed for several centuries before, to nominate bishops, archbishops, abbots, and priors in certain parts of France. In 1673 Louis XIV issued a declaration extending the *régale* to the whole country. When Bishop François-Étienne Caulet of Montauban refused to recognize the *régale* in 1679, Colbert sent in the intendant Nicolas-Joseph Foucault, who annulled the bishop's administrative acts, "and took control of the diocese's finances, leaving the bishop nearly starving." Caulet published a scathing attack on the *régale,* and then died. Foucault arrested the printers and clergy loyal to Caulet with *lettres de cachet* ("an order signed by the king, generally ordering imprisonment without trial") (Soll 2009, p. 140). Though this is just one case, it reveals Louis XIV's determination to rule the roost in as many different policy areas as possible. And in 1681 Louis XIV convoked a church assembly in Paris presided over by the archbishops of Paris and Reims, which had no trouble in siding with the king against papal authority on the question of the *régale.*

But Louis's best known religious move proved ultimately to be a costly mistake: the revocation of the Edict of Nantes in 1685, promulgated in 1598 by Louis's grandfather, Henry IV, which had extended religious toleration to Protestants, (of whom Henry had been one before converting to Catholicism, reputedly with the famous words, *Paris vaut bien une messe* ["Paris is well worth a Mass"]).

Though not "absolute," Louis XIV was undoubtedly a strong king who from his earliest youth understood the danger to the French Crown posed by the aristocracy and the *parlements*—and greatly strengthened the monarchy in response. Though taking no active steps to woo the support of the lower classes, Louis XIV's self-aggrandizement, and the cultivation of the image of himself as *Le Roi Soleil* ("The Sun King") seems to have impressed the lower orders, who generally had little love for the aristocracy. In 1698 the perspicacious British diplomat and man of letters (and Fellow of my Cambridge college, St John's), Matthew Prior, observed of the French that: "The common people of this nation have a strange veneration for their king" (Mansel 2019, p. 447).

In rejecting the "absolutist" label traditionally attached to Louis XIV, Mettam argued that Louis XIV ruled traditionally and respected local privileges (Mettam 1988). This is an over-reaction to the "absolutist" label, as is shown by the facts assembled above. In the *pays d'états,* as we have seen, Louis was constrained to rely on provincial governors, who, though drawn from the local aristocracy, were appointed not on the basis of birth and heredity but on merit, and only for three years at a time. As for the *pays d'élections,* which made up the majority of the *généralités*, here royal power was exercised through hand-picked intendants from outside their administrative areas, and who were closely controlled by the central government. Colbert (whose long period in office, 1661–83, was only terminated by his untimely death from untreated kidney stones) was indefatigable in instructing intendants and other officials directly and in great detail. Torn between starting work early in the morning and retiring late after a full day's labor, Colbert decided to do both. Totally loyal and trusted though he was, Colbert himself received instructions directly from the king.

Another modern writer, who mistakenly classified Louis XIV's post-Fronde reign as a "success" amounting to a "class alliance" between king and aristocracy, compounded his error by labeling this as "absolutism," which he defined as "the political manifestation of a system of domination protecting the interests of a privileged class of officers and landed lords" (Beik 1985, loc. 4506, 4449). It is disquieting to find this kind of muddled thinking relied upon by historians.

Roger Mettam at least recognized that seventeenth-century French history was marked (as quoted above) by "the unceasing struggle of the crown against the independent power of the varied groups who formed the privileged orders in French society," and that, although royal power increased at the expense of these privileged groups, it did not reach the height entitling it to be labeled as "absolute," which would mean (contrary to Beik's idiosyncratic definition of the term) untrammeled autocratic royal power.

A welcome corrective to Beik and other "revisionists" is John Hurt's *Louis XIV and the Parlements* (Hurt 2002)—which was unpersuasively attacked by Beik in his article "The absolutism of Louis XIV as social collaboration" (Beik 2005). Hurt argues with great force that Louis XIV's "political subjugation (not too strong a word) of the parlements should bulk larger in our assessments of the Sun King's reign. All the current general treatments, along with recent biographies, have underestimated the depth and significance of this achievement. It is time to give it due interpretative weight. Arguably, the victory won by Louis XIV was of such consequence that it influenced the government's relations with the tribunals into the middle of the eighteenth century" (Hurt 2002, loc. 4840–46). The crucial importance of the relationship between the Crown and the *parlements* right up to 1789 is discussed above.

Louis XV (r. 1715–74)

The death of Louis XIV in 1715 after a reign of 72 years plunged France into yet another minority—the third in succession—with the accession of his five-year-old great-grandson, Louis XV. Louis XIV's putative advice to the new king from the grave was sound, and succinctly sums up Louis XIV's own philosophy of government: "Listen to the people, seek advice from your Council, but decide alone."

The regent, the duc d'Orléans, perpetuated Louis XIV's assertion of royal power, though it is just as wrong to refer to his rule as "absolutist" as it is to Louis's. But Orleans made it clear that he was determined to pass on to the young king royal authority in its entirety, as he had received it, and to stop the *parlements* from meddling in affairs that were none of their business (Mansel 2019, p. 448.)

In 1726, Louis XV appointed as chief minister his former tutor, Cardinal Fleury, who remained in office until his death in 1743. With the assistance of two successive controllers-general of finances, Fleury managed to balance the budget for a time and to stabilize the currency. He also instituted a major road-building program, including the construction of major highways, some of which are still in use today. The power of the *parlements* was curbed by dismissing 139 members of provincial *parlements* and removing the right of the *Parlement de Paris* to deal with religious matters.

On Fleury's death in 1743, Louis XV effectively became his own chief minister, chairing meetings of the *Conseil d'en haut* (High Council) consisting solely of the three most important ministers plus the dauphin, or heir to the throne; and he delegated most other decisions to ministerial committees.

Louis XV understood the need to stand up to the aristocracy, but lacked the will to do so, so that the attempt, for example, to impose a new *vingtième* (twentieth) tax on nobles as well as commoners was abandoned in the face of vocal opposition from the *parlements*, the clergy, and those aristocratically controlled provincial estates which still existed and retained rights over taxation. In 1753 the *Parlement de Paris* was sufficiently emboldened to proclaim itself the "natural defender of the fundamental laws of the kingdom," which really meant the protector of feudal rights against the monarchy. The king's resolve was also sapped by the influence exerted over him by the aristocratic courtiers who surrounded him at Versailles.

The duc de Choiseul, Louis XV's influential foreign minister from 1758 to 1761 and again from 1766 to 1770, involved France in a number of mostly unsuccessful foreign wars, which did not assist the position of the Crown. Professor Alfred Cobban's comment is apt: "Under Choiseul it is almost true to say that capitulation to the *parlements* became official policy" (Cobban, 1950, p. 75).

Maupeou (1714–92)

However, everything changed with Choiseul's dismissal and the appointment of René de Maupeou as chancellor of France in 1770. Having himself served briefly as president of the *Parlement de Paris*, Maupeou understood only too well the fundamental opposition between monarchy and aristocracy. Once ensconced in his new position, he devoted himself wholeheartedly to administering a knockout blow against the *Parlement* on behalf of the Crown. In January 1771, Maupeou had the members of the *Parlement de Paris* exiled and their offices confiscated, replacing them with a royal court operating under the same name. Maupeou then took similar action against the provincial *parlements*. The practice of buying and selling offices was banned in the new *parlements*. These were intended as merely the first steps in a wholesale reform of the judicial system, but the whole enterprise was abruptly cut short by Louis XV's death and Maupeou's dismissal by the new king, Louis XV's grandson, Louis XVI (Echeverria, 1985). The overhaul of the judicial system had to wait until Maupeou's secretary, Charles-François Lebrun, held office as Third Consul under Napoleon Bonaparte between 1799 and 1804.

Lebrun (1739–1824)

The drawn-out struggle between the Crown and the aristocracy centered on finance, with the aristocracy clinging to their privileges, including exemption from taxation, which it was in the interest of the Crown to abolish—an interest which the Crown shared with the ordinary people of France. It was Maupeou's secretary and right-hand man, Charles-François Lebrun, who first formulated the policy that came to be called the "Maupeou Revolution." "The Third Estate," he predicted, "would support the government against the views and interests of the nobility, the clergy and the parlements" (Echeverria 1985, p. 132). This vision of a monarchy standing at the head of a popular "revolution" against the privileged elements was put in hand in 1770 and was operational until the death of Louis XV in 1774, when the policy was reversed by Louis XV's feckless grandson, Louis XVI. Maupeou threw up his hands in despair at the way the new king discarded this hard-fought victory—*"J'avais fait gagner au roi un procès qui dure depuis trois cents ans. Il veut le reperdre, il en est le maître"* ("I had won for the king a case that has lasted 300 years. He wishes to lose it again. He is the master of it").

Maupeou's interrupted overhaul of the judicial system—including the introduction of a uniform national code of laws, as proposed by Lebrun and Maupeou in 1771—and the reorganization of the national finances were eventually completed under Napoleon Bonaparte 30 years later—with the active participation of none other than Charles-François Lebrun, in his capacity as Third Consul (1799–1804) and then as arch-treasurer of the French Empire (1804). Remembering the struggle of the Bourbon monarchy against the aristocracy, Lebrun advised Napoleon against the restoration of titles of nobility, though he himself was persuaded by the emperor to accept the hereditary title *duc de Plaisance*. If only Louis XVI had had the sense to allow Maupeou to bring his victory to completion instead of reversing it, perhaps the French Revolution would never have happened!

"The Inevitable Liquidation of an Exhausted Expedient"

Durand Echeverria, author of a book on the *Maupeou Revolution* (1985), characterized Maupeou's dismissal by Louis XVI as "the inevitable liquidation of an exhausted expedient." This is wrong on two counts. First, Maupeou's defeat of the *parlements* can hardly be called "an exhausted expedient," as no such complete victory over the *parlements* had ever previously been achieved. And secondly, why was its "liquidation" inevitable? Despite their pretences, the *parlements* represented the interests of the privileged orders. So, what was inevitable was the "liquidation" of the *parlements*, not of an attempt to abolish them— and this is demonstrated by the speed and ease with which the *parlements* were in fact "liquidated" by the National Assembly in the early days of the French Revolution.

"Constitutional Consensus"

Munro Price, in his book on the comte de Vergennes, likewise appears to misunderstand Maupeou's trouncing of the *parlements*, which he describes as follows: "This act, whose importance has recently been underlined by historians, dealt a major blow to the constitutional consensus on which the absolute monarchy rested" (Price 1995, p. 2). This opinion should also be rejected on two counts. First, the inflated claims of the *parlements* can hardly be regarded as any kind of "constitutional consensus." On the contrary, the exaggerated claims made by the *parlements* in the 1750s had never been accepted by the Crown. And secondly, to suggest that the "absolute monarchy" rested on such anti-monarchical claims is a contradiction in terms. A succession of royal ministers over three centuries recognized that the relationship between the Crown and the *parlements* was a zero-sum game: the greater the power of the *parlements*, the less was that of the Crown, and vice versa. Absolute monarchy could only be achieved by completely subordinating, or even abolishing, the *parlements*. Which is why the label "absolute monarchy" is probably inapplicable to the *ancien régime* as a whole, because the knock-out blow administered by Maupeou to the *parlements* was so short-lived.

"Could Not Have Been Undone"

Professor Alfred Cobban's view of the subject is preferable. In his article on "The parlements of France in the eighteenth century," he remarks: "Freed from the opposition of the parlements .... Terray [Controller General of Finances] was able to introduce important financial reforms. By 1774 he had reduced the debt to manageable proportions" (Cobban 1950, p. 76).

And:

In spite of widespread agitation the new courts were functioning ... and the reform seemed to be definitive. There was no sign that Louis XV would desert the minister who had rid him of the turbulent parlements, when the whole situation was changed by the king's death. Whatever ill services Louis XV had done the French monarchy by his life, the greatest was in the moment of his death, when, if he had lived a few more years, time would have been gained for the new courts set up by Maupeou to consolidate themselves and his work could not have been undone (ibid.).

Run-Up to Revolution

Louis XVI, who succeeded his grandfather in 1774 at the age of 19, was indecisive and lacked Louis XV's perspicacity and cynicism. The reinstatement of the *parlements* was one of his earliest acts, undoing centuries of painstaking work (see above). When asked to explain his decision, he said: "It may be considered politically unwise, but it seems to me to be the general wish and I want to be loved" (Hardman 1993). The trouble was that the *parlements* spared no effort or expense in portraying themselves as intermediaries between the Crown and the people. In the *Grandes Remonstrances* of 1753, for example, they had claimed that "if subjects owe obedience to kings, kings for their part owe obedience to the laws," of which the *parlements* regarded themselves as the guardians. Alfred Cobban puts it like this: "As the last relic of the medieval constitution left at the center of government, the parlement of Paris, though no more in fact than a small, selfish, proud and venal oligarchy, regarded itself, and was regarded by public opinion, as the guardian of the constitutional liberties of France" (Cobban 1965, vol. I, p. 67). The *parlements* certainly knew how to manipulate public opinion, and a loose coalition of "patriots" put out more than 500 books and pamphlets, or *maupeouana*, appealing to the "nation" against Maupeou's "despotism." But even these "patriots" eventually saw through the pretensions of the *parlements*: "For it was the faithful remnants of the patriot party who, still under that banner, led the prerevolutionary charge in 1787–88 against the "despotism" of the royal ministers Alexandre de Calonne and Lomenie de Brienne, who in turn followed Maupeou's example in subsidizing pamphlets that renewed the charge of "aristocracy" against the parlements and their partisans" (Van Kley 1999, p. 252). The clearest indication of the *lack* of popular support for the *parlements* is the fact that the *parlements* were suspended as early on in the Revolution as November 1789, with their formal abolition following in September 1790.

After several unsuccessful controllers-general of finance, Louis XVI appointed Lomenie de Brienne, who had just been named president of the Assembly of Notables. After an initial success by Brienne against the *Parlement de Paris*, that body finally consented to its own abolition, on condition that the

Estates General were summoned to tackle the national crisis. Brienne resigned his post in August 1788, and on 24 January 1789 the king reluctantly summoned the Estates General to meet on 1 May 1789.

Estates General to Guillotine

This august body, the equivalent of the English Parliament, had last met in 1614. It was made up of representatives of the three estates: the clergy, the nobility, and the commons. Though some representatives arrived late in Paris (some only in 1791), the clergy initially had 303 representatives, the nobles 282, and the Third Estate, making up 95% of the population, was allowed a double representation of 578, drawn largely from the bourgeoisie together with a number of nobles, as there was no restriction on their standing for election by the Third Estate instead of by their own class. The franchise for the Third Estate was made up of property-owning males of at least 25 years of age. The double representation accorded the Third Estate by Louis XVI in response to a demand made in the press was an empty gesture, as the king also went along with the requirement of the *Parlement de Paris* that the three estates sit and vote "by orders," i.e. separately, with each estate having an equal vote (as had been done in 1614), thus enabling the first two estates to outvote the Third Estate.

In practice, however, things worked out very differently. After a plenary session presided over by the king on 5 May 1789, the representatives got bogged down in a debate on "verification," including whether the three orders should vote together or separately as ordered by the king. On 27 May, the nobles voted to confirm separate "voting by orders." On 17 June the Third Estate renamed themselves the "National Assembly" and invited the other two orders to join them. Under the influence of his Council, the king made another blunder by ordering the hall where the Third Estate had been meeting to be locked and guarded by troops. Undaunted, on 20 June the representatives simply moved to the royal indoor tennis court (*jeu de paume*), where they took the famous "Tennis Court Oath," swearing not to disband until there was a national constitution. After the majority of the clergy, followed by some nobles, had joined the Third Estate, the king, making a virtue of necessity, asked all three orders to meet together. On 9 July the National Assembly recreated itself once again, this time as the "National Constituent Assembly," thereby arrogating to itself not only the right to speak in the name of the French nation as a whole but even to frame a new constitution for it—something that was not even mooted in the *cahiers de doléances* ("lists of grievances"), which, on the contrary, had largely expressed loyalty to the king and the monarchy in its traditional form.

Just five days later, on 14 July 1789, came the storming of the Bastille, a medieval fortress and prison in the center of Paris, which was known to have held political prisoners incarcerated purely on the basis of *lettres de cachet*. One of its most high-profile inmates was the eccentric Marquis de Sade, who, how-ever, had been transferred to an insane asylum on 2 July. On 14 July only seven old men were left in the Bastille, none of whom were of any political impor-tance. Nevertheless, the significance of the event cannot be denied. The governor of the Bastille, the marquis de Launay, was savagely murdered and his head paraded around the streets mounted on a pike, but what the fall of the Bastille really represented was an attack on royal authority.

In the four months before the fall of the Bastille it is estimated that there were more than 300 peasant riots in a number of provinces (Lefebvre 1973). Interest-ingly enough, as testified to by a M. Conard of Dauphiné, "On the 29th [of July] the peasants everywhere believed that the pillage was ordered by the king; ... that Louis XVI had taken the side of the peasants against their feudal oppressors" (op. cit.., p. 99). This shows that for the king to have adopted an anti-aristocratic stance, as indeed a number of his predecessors had done, was not beyond the bounds of belief, even in July 1789. Alas for Louis XVI, he lacked the imagina-tion and political nous to follow this path. On the contrary, when the Assembly, impelled by the peasant riots, decided on that fateful night of 4 August 1789 to abolish "feudalism" root and branch (though mostly only in return for compen-sation to the feudal seigneurs and the church), Louis XVI demurred. "I will never consent," he naïvely wrote to the Archbishop of Arles, "to despoil my clergy and *noblesse* ... I will not give my sanction to decrees which would despoil them, for then the French people might some day accuse me of injustice or weakness" (ibid., p. 108). When the decree was presented to him for the royal assent, Louis procrastinated and finally signed it into law only on 3 November 1789 under pressure from unrest in Paris. After this, the Revolution continued to spiral out of control.

Mirabeau (1749–91): "L'indivisibilité du Monarque et du Peuple"

In 1791 Honoré Gabriel Riqueti, comte de Mirabeau, a reprobate aristocrat who was at once a leading revolutionary and a staunch royalist, advised Louis XVI in a secret *mémoire* to move to Rouen or some other provincial capital, appeal to the people, summon a great convention, and effectively place him-self at the head of the Revolution rather than impotently stand against it. Like some of Louis's more politically savvy predecessors and their ministers, Mira-beau recognized that there was a natural close reciprocal symbiotic or visceral bond between king and people which already existed beneath the surface but needed to be kick-started into action and power: *"L'indivisibilité du monarque et du peuple est dans le coeur de tous les Français; il faut qu'elle existe dans l'action et le pouvoir"* ("The indivisibility of the monarch and the people is in the heart of all French people; it is necessary for it to exist in action and in power") (*Mémoire* to the comte de la Marck and presented to the King by the comte de Provence, the future Louis XVIII; quoted in Stephens 1911). Mirabeau's sudden (but probably natural) death on 2 April 1791 robbed the king of what was probably his last chance to save himself and the monarchy, and the royal family were then confined as virtual prisoners in the Tuileries Palace in Paris.

The king's attempt in June 1791 to flee to the royalist town of Montmedy (on the border of the Austrian Netherlands, modern Belgium) and seek the protection of Austria, which was ruled by Queen Marie Antoinette's brother, the Emperor Leopold II, was exactly the sort of thing that Mirabeau had counseled against. Ironically, the king was recognized from his embossed portrait on a revolutionary *assignat* banknote in the small town of Varennes-en-Argonne. The royal family were then ignominiously hauled back to Paris as traitors and prisoners. This episode dealt a fatal blow to the monarchy, leading to Louis XVI's deposition in 1792 and his beheading in January 1793, followed by that of Marie Antoinette in October of the same year.

Mirabeau's *cri de coeur*, quoted above, was actually an echo of what Maupeou and other astute ministers of the monarchy had been urging for generations, namely the common interest of the Crown and the people in abolishing or at least reducing the privileges of the aristocracy.

What Mirabeau was proposing was that, instead of cowering in the face of the Revolution, the king should place himself at the head of it. Could this possibly have worked? Possibly, but as Charles F. Warwick put it: "[I]t is really not a question whether Mirabeau could have saved the monarchy, but rather a question whether Louis would have let him" (Warwick 2005, location 49; 32). The lessons of the *ancien régime* were finally learnt and put into effect by Napoleon, who established, albeit briefly, a popular monarchy with an efficient administration and a fair tax policy.

Alfred Cobban put the situation in a nutshell:

> If we compare the French monarchy in the eighteenth century with practically any other European monarchy of the same period, the striking fact that emerges is the comparative effectiveness of the limitations on royal power in France, and this in spite of the fact that, in the absence of other checks, organized opposition to the crown was concentrated in a single institution (Cobban 1950, p. 64).

Referring to the final abolition of the *parlements* by the Revolution in 1790, Cobban remarked: "The last stage in their history is the story of their unresisted elimination by the National Assembly, which thus achieved, almost without effort, what the monarchy had struggled so long to do in vain" (ibid., p. 80). "And thus was consummated the prophecy of the Cardinal de Retz in 1649.... *'Les parlements. qui soufflainent sur le fleu, en seraient, un jour, consumés'* (*'The parlements, which fanned the flames, will one day be sonsumed by them')*" (ibid., p. 64).

As noted above, this remark, dates from the Fronde, of which Cardinal de Retz was a leader, 150 years before the Revolution.

Napoleon Bonaparte (1769–1821)

Napoleon Bonaparte (1769–1821) ruled France, initially as First Consul from 1799 to 1804 and then as emperor from 1804 until 1814 and finally for a 100 days in 1815. In spite of the shortness of his rule and his final defeat at Waterloo, Napoleon made an indelible mark on history, not least by means of the Code Napoléon, which still forms the basis of codes of law in many countries around the world.

Napoleon is usually seen as heir to the French Revolution, in terms of both ideology and nationalism, which developed into imperialism. He was not only one of the most gifted generals in history but also an extremely adroit politician. Napoleon clearly understood the lessons of ministers of the *ancien régime* like Sully, Richelieu, Mazarin, Colbert, Fleury, Maupeou, Terray—and, not least, Lebrun—and their masters, Kings Henry IV, Louis XIII, Louis XIV, and Louis XV. So Napoleon's rule also marks the fulfillment of the elusive goal of these astute monarchs and ministers, namely the establishment of a popular monarchy by means of a streamlined administration, overhaul of the financial system and reorganization of the legal system.

Napoleon's defeat at Waterloo put an end to his career, but not to his fame. Despite his defeat and ignominious last years as a prisoner of the British on the remote island of St Helena, Napoleon continued to be revered by the French as a heroic figure. Before the adoption of the euro, the highest denomination French banknote proudly displayed a youthful Napoleon Bonaparte against a backdrop of victorious legionary standards. And anyone unfamiliar with French history who has attended the *son et lumière* show at the Invalides in Paris, where Napoleon is buried, may be forgiven for being unaware of his inglorious end.

From Napoleon to Napoleon and Beyond

The Bourbon Restoration lasted only 15 years, first under Louis XVI's brother, the conservative Louis XVIII, who died in 1824, and then under another brother, the reactionary Charles X (r. 1824–30), who was said to have "learned nothing and forgotten nothing." He in fact completely failed to learn the crucial lesson that the aristocracy was no friend of strong monarchy, and he was overthrown in 1830 by a popular rising known as the July Revolution.

He was succeeded by his cousin Louis Philippe, who reigned as a constitutional monarch until he, too, was overthrown in 1848. He cultivated an unpretentious style, adopted the image of "citizen king," and was nicknamed the "bourgeois monarch." To demonstrate his acceptance of popular sovereignty, he was styled "king of the French," in other words, king of the people, as against "king of France," the traditional title. However, this populist tone rang rather hollow. For example, only about two million of the nine million adult French males of voting age had the right to vote. To demands for universal suffrage, Louis Philippe's last prime minister, François Guizot, responded with a challenge: *"Eclairez-vous, enrichissez-vous, améliorez la condition morale et matérielle de notre France: voilà les vraies innovations"* ("Have the sense to enrich yourselves, improving the moral and physical condition of our France: that is true progress") (*Le Moniteur*, 2 March 1843. Quoted in "Guizot and Representative Government"; Guizot 2002). The famous cartoon of 1831, showing Louis Philippe gradually turning into a pear, was prophetic. By 1848 the pear was so rotten that a whiff of popular discontent was enough to dislodge it. Within three days, fearing for his life, the citizen king fled to England unimaginatively disguised as "Mr Smith."

The ensuing election—under universal manhood suffrage—swept Napoleon's nephew, Louis Napoleon Bonaparte, to power. Despite his unprepossessing appearance and monotonous speeches delivered with a slight German accent, he won the presidency of the short-lived Second Republic with 74.2% of the votes cast. His program was unabashedly populist, but success was vouchsafed to him by one thing alone: the name Bonaparte. His endorsement by Victor Hugo's newspaper, *L'Evénement,* encapsulated his appeal: "We have confidence in him: he carries a great name." Debarred by the Constitution from re-election, the "prince-president," as he styled himself, resorted to a coup d'état to perpetuate his position. His action was approved in a plebiscite held in 1851 by 92% of the votes cast on a turnout of over 80%. The path was now cleared for him to follow in his late uncle's footsteps and declare himself emperor as Napoleon III, which occurred a year later on the strength of a 97% majority in another referendum.

France's defeat in the Franco-Prussian War of 1870 resulted in the emperor's humiliating capitulation and brief captivity in Germany, followed by exile in England. But the ignominious collapse of the Second Empire, as it was called, did not put an end to the French love affair with monarchy. After the establishment of the Third Republic in 1870, Henri, comte de Chambord (1820–83), grandson of Charles X (r. 1824–30), and a direct descendant of the first Bourbon king of France, Henry IV (r. 1589–1610), made a bid for the throne, which was seriously entertained by the royalist-dominated National Assembly. Had it not been for the comte de Chambord's insistence on the pre-revolutionary *fleur-de-lys drapeau blanc* (a white flag emblazoned with numerous fleur de lis) as the national flag instead of the red-white-and-blue tricolor, France may well have had yet another flirtation with monarchy.

Yet the fact that France has been a republic since 1870 has not prevented it from hankering after strong leadership, as personified particularly by President

Charles de Gaulle, leader of the "Free French" resistance to Germany during World War II, who subsequently served as prime minister (1958–59) and then, from 1959 to 1969, as the first president of the Fifth French Republic, which was largely his creation. De Gaulle's leadership was summed up by the phrase used by his successor, Georges Pompidou, in announcing de Gaulle's death to the French nation: *"Le general de Gaulle est mort; la France est veuve"* ("General de Gaulle is dead; France is a widow").

At the time of this writing, France appears to be torn between extreme right-wing populism represented by Marine Le Pen's *Rassemblement National* (National Rally), formerly known as the National Front, on the one hand, and a broad-spectrum socialist "New Popular Front" on the other. Marine Le Pen obtained 41.45% of the vote in the second round of the 2022 presidential election, and her "National Rally" has been the single largest party in the National Assembly since 2022, polling 37.06% of the vote in the second round of the legislative election of 2024. Emmanuel Macron owed his re-election as president in 2022 to a left-wing grouping that was only intent on keeping Le Pen out, but in 2024 a similar broad left-wing alliance joined Le Pen to bring down Macron's conservative prime minister, Michel Barnier. While Le Pen's supporters appear to form a solid block, the same cannot be said for the left-wing alliance, which is made up of a number of mutually hostile strands.

Binary Power Structure

The key to a true understanding of the binary power structure of French history is the obscure figure of Charles-François Lebrun (1739–1824). We first meet him as Maupeou's perspicacious assistant in the victory over the aristocratic and anti-monarchical *parlements* in the reign of Louis XV. That victory was senselessly discarded by Louis XVI on his accession in 1774, with disastrous consequences for the monarchy—and for France. But Lebrun never lost sight of the fact that there was a natural alliance between the people and a strong monarchical government against their common enemy, the aristocracy. And he was able to bring this alliance to fruition 30 years later under a new ruler with the same perceptive insight: Napoleon Bonaparte.

Chapter 20
Military

*I*s there a correlation between the power structure of a society and its foreign policy? Above all, is a state likely to be more or less aggressive on the basis of its domestic power structure? The oligarchic Roman Republic (509–49 BCE) was much more aggressive in its foreign policy than the Principate (27 BCE–284 CE), a strong monarchy. What happened was that, without actually setting out to build a huge empire, the Republic, which lacked a strong central government, found itself embroiled in foreign disputes, which (because of its efficient army, originally developed for self-preservation), resulted in more and more annexations. The Cambridge historian Sir John Seeley famously remarked in 1883 that the British Empire had come about "in a fit of absence of mind" (Seeley, 1883, p. 12). This obvious exaggeration nevertheless contains a kernel of truth, which may be applicable to the Roman Republic as well. Like the Roman Republic, Victorian Britain was an oligarchy which, feeling vulnerable, had developed into a formidable fighting force.

But militarism may also have a more deliberate, personal origin, three of the best examples of which are the strong monarchical figures of Alexander the Great (356–323 BCE), Napoleon Bonaparte (1769–1821), and Adolf Hitler (1889–1945). In all three cases their military adventurism, launched in pursuit of an inherited goal, was driven well beyond that goal by an "outsider" inferiority complex.

Classical Sparta was probably the most highly militarized state in history, but it was an oligarchy (headed up by two joint kings), which depended for its survival on an elite perpetually on a war footing against internal enemies. By contrast, the fact that Cypselus, tyrant of Corinth in the seventh century BCE, ruled without a bodyguard was justifiably taken as a sign of his popularity. The military activities

Five Thousand Years of Monarchy, First Edition. Michael Arnheim.
© 2026 John Wiley & Sons, Inc. Published 2026 by John Wiley & Sons, Inc.

of popular monarchies tend to be directed outwards, often in the form of expansionism. Alexander the Great, Napoleon, Hitler, Stalin, and even Fidel Castro are examples of this.

Alexander: Though Greek-speaking, the Macedonians were scorned by the Greeks as "barbarians." Alexander's father, Philip II of Macedon, sought to overcome this slur by competing in the Olympic games, which were exclusively for Greeks. By defeating Athens, Philip managed to become the head of a Panhellenic alliance intended to defeat the Greeks' traditional foe, Persia. In taking on his father's mantle, Alexander achieved this goal and went well beyond it, not only defeating the Persians but also taking over their empire as a conquering colossus and putting his stamp on it for hundreds of years to come.

Napoleon: As a Corsican, Napoleon was ridiculed for his Italian accent, sallow complexion, lank hair and short stature. But, thanks to the lax Corsican social structure in which the undistinguished Bonaparte (originally Buonaparte) family was classified as noble, he was able to gain admission to the prestigious royal military school that was intended exclusively for the scions of the French aristocracy. To add to this complex picture, he emerged as the heir to the French Revolution, while his wife, Josephine de Beauharnais, was the widow of an aristocrat who had been guillotined by the revolutionaries during the "Reign of Terror." Napoleon's first major military assignment was to disperse counter-revolutionary royalist forces in Paris in 1795, which he did with "a whiff of grape-shot," leaving between 100 and 300 royalists dead on the streets of Paris.

The French Revolution had unleashed an alliance against it of several European powers, but by 1795 France had captured the Austrian Netherlands (modern Belgium) and the Dutch Republic (modern Netherlands). Once Napoleon assumed power in 1799 and then as emperor in 1804, he took the war to the enemy, which succeeded spectacularly until the notoriously catastrophic invasion of Russia in 1812. He made a point of placing three of his brothers as kings over conquered states: his brother Joseph as king first of Naples and then of Spain, Jérome as king of Westphalia, and Louis as King of Holland. After marrying Marie-Louise, daughter of the Austrian Emperor Francis I (nephew of Marie Antoinette, the wife of Louis XVI), he would refer to the guillotined Louis XVI as *mon oncle* ("my uncle")—all creating the spectacle of the heir to the Revolution trying to start his own imperial and royal dynasty!

Hitler: As an Austrian by birth, Hitler was another outsider. In fact, he would only become a German citizen in 1932, just a year before his appointment as German chancellor (prime minister). On the outbreak of World War I in 1914, instead of joining the Austrian army, as he should have done, he decided to sign up to the Bavarian part of the German Imperial Army. For bravery in battle he was awarded the German Iron Cross on the recommendation of his Jewish commanding officer, Hugo Gutmann. This did not prevent Hitler from blaming the Jews for Germany's defeat. His failed "Beer Hall Putsch" (military coup) in 1923 earned him about a year in a luxury prison and he then went on to win power as chancellor through the ballot box (with the help of some street violence) in 1933. With watchwords *Lebensraum* ("living space") and *Drang nach Osten* ("push to the east"), after annexing his Austria to form *Grossdeutschland* ("Greater Germany"), he turned US President Woodrow Wilson's doctrine of national self-determination to claim for Germany the German-speaking enclaves of the Sudetenland (in Czechoslovakia), Danzig (a "free city"), and Memel (in Lithuania). After Britain and France capitulated to him over the Sudetenland, Hitler invaded and annexed the rest of Czechoslovakia as well. When the Polish government refused Hitler's demand to become a German satellite state, Hitler expected Poland's allies, Britain and France, to sell it down the river as they had done with Czechoslovakia. When they unexpectedly stood firm, Hitler invaded Poland, thus initiating World War II. Ditching the Molotov–Ribbentrop Pact, which included an agreement to partition Poland between Russia and Germany, in 1941 Hitler sent three million troops to invade Russia in the doomed Operation Barbarossa. From there to the Berlin bunker in which Hitler killed himself and his new bride, the ever-faithful Eva Braun (not to mention his German shepherd dog, Blondi), was just a matter of time.

The three outsiders: Alexander, Napoleon, and Hitler were all strong monarchical rulers who managed to inspire great trust and adulation in their followers. What connection, if any, does this have with their military careerism? Just this—that without a solid domestic power base, their military ambitions would not have had sufficient force behind them to develop. And it is not entirely coincidental that possession of a strong domestic power base should find expression in military expansion. The strong underlying support enabled rulers like Alexander and Napoleon to achieve, in a remarkably short time, much that was positive and lasting as well, and even Hitler's legacy was not entirely negative. Alexander Hellenized a large part of the eastern Mediterranean and he bequeathed a model of strong monarchy that was followed by his successors for centuries. Napoleon spread some of the more positive values of the French Revolution and freedom of religion, together with Roman law, throughout western Europe. As for Hitler, besides the terrible loss of life in the Holocaust and the war itself, and the enslavement of most of eastern Europe to Soviet communism, he bequeathed the efficient *Autobahn* system and the Volkswagen "Beetle," not to mention "Operation Paperclip," in which more than 1,600 German scientists, engineers, and technicians were taken into US government service after World War II, including Wernher van Braun, a Nazi Party member and SS officer, who became a pioneer of rocket and space technology in the United States.

Some Correlations

Before Christianity became the official religion of the Roman Empire in 380 CE, there were no religious wars, but since that time religious persecution and religious wars have been endemic. The reason for this sea-change is explained in Chapter 26 of this book.

After a series of civil wars, the Roman Emperor Augustus on three occasions ceremoniously shut the gates of the Temple of Janus to symbolize the bringing of peace to the Roman world. From 27 BCE, when the name "Augustus" was bestowed on him until the death of Marcus Aurelius in 180 CE, the gates of Janus were mostly shut, marking this period as the *Pax Romana* ("Roman Peace"). By the death of Trajan in 117 the Roman Empire had reached its greatest territorial extent, with a population of some 70 million, accounting for about a third of the world's population, and by the edict known as the *Constitutio Antoniniana* issued in 212 the Emperor Caracalla granted Roman citizenship to all free male inhabitants of the empire.

In the ancient Persian empires, Ptolemaic Egypt and Seleucid Syria, subject nations, once pacified, mostly reconciled themselves to the new situation, and in the Roman Empire they actually merged with their erstwhile conquerors. By contrast, modern colonial empires have been confronted with sporadic resistance to their rule, leading in most cases to protracted and ultimately successful demands for independence. How can this major difference be accounted for? It is no accident that the successful ancient empires were strong centralized monarchies.

Figure 20 Helmeted Hoplite, Sparta. de:Benutzer.
SOURCE: Ticinese / Wikimedia Commons / CC BY SA 3.0.

For example, after Cyrus the Great of Persia conquered the Medes in 550 BCE, he replaced client kings with satraps, or governors, who were directly answerable to and removable by himself. The difference was that kings, even when they were subordinate to a higher king or emperor, would be protected by divine right, or *Khvarenah* ("glory," "splendor"), enabling them to build a local power-base for themselves, which would have been more difficult for a satrap or governor to do, especially when his power was checked and controlled by the "eye of the king," who reported directly to the great king. Other checks on the satrap's power included the secretarial scribe, the chief provincial financial controller (*ganzabara*), and the general in charge of the army units posted to his provinces and its fortresses, not to mention the tendency to switch satraps from one province to another. Freedom of religion was another key to the success of the Achaemenid Empire, leading to a cultural and religious merger of subject nations with the conquerors. Cyrus's successors were not all as sagacious in the art of statecraft, and unwisely allowed satrapies to become hereditary, spelling danger to the regime (see Olmstead 1948).

Sparta

Though Sparta had a king, or actually two kings, it was not in any sense a monarchy or even a dyarchy, but a tightly knit oligarchy that was on a permanent war footing. Sparta had a dual hereditary monarchy, with two kings of equal status, drawn from two separate families, the Agiads and the Eurypontids. Whatever the origin of this system may have been, it served the useful purpose of not allowing any one person to become too powerful, but, so anxious was Sparta to prevent one-man rule, that the kings' few powers were whittled down as time went by. The kings' functions were chiefly military. The Athenian orator Isocrates (436–338 BCE) described the Spartans as "under oligarchy at home and monarchy in war" (Isocrates iii:24). But the individual king who was commander-in-chief in a particular campaign was accompanied in the field by one or two "minders" in the shape of ephors (see below). And in the fifth century BCE the kings appear to have lost the right to declare war.

- **Homoioi.** One of the main thrusts of the Spartan, so-called Lycurgan, system was to create as much equality among the Spartiate citizenry as possible, which was achieved by a thoroughgoing reform of society. First, there was what Polybius described as "an equal share of civic land" (Polybius 6:45). Every newborn Spartiate male was officially examined by the elders of his tribe, and, if declared healthy, was assigned an allotment (*klēros* or, in Doric, *klāros*), which could never be sold. Hence the description of the Spartiates as *hoi homoioi* ("the peers" or "the equals"), although it was possible for Spartiates to own land other than their allotment and complete economic equality was never achieved.

- **Agōgē.** After the initial physical inspection by his tribal authorities, a new-born Spartiate boy was returned to the care of his parents until the age of 6, and from 7 to 16 he was educated by the state. Sparta was the only Greek state to have a nationalized educational system, under a magistrate known as the *paidonomos,* or "pastor." Until the age of 30, every Spartiate male lived in barracks together with others of the same age, took his meals in a communal mess (*syssition*), and was subjected to a strict regimen of discipline and military training known as the agōgē. Only then was he allowed to set up house on his own (Plut., *Lycurgus,* 16). But this by no means marked the end of his public service. Until the age of 60 he could be called upon to lay down his life for the state in battle, and he would remain a member of his *syssition* for the rest of his life (ibid., p. 10ff).

- **Krypteia.** Those young Spartiates who graduated from their military training with the best grades, so to speak, were allowed to serve in the *Krypteia* (literally, "secret matters"), a cross between secret police and a "special forces" military unit, whose special mission was to seek and destroy any helots they encountered.

- **The boy with the fox.** The tough code of discipline included training in secretly scrounging for food, with a beating for anyone who was caught. A well-known story tells of a Spartan boy who captured a live fox, intending to slaughter and eat it later on. Just then he spotted some other Spartan boys approaching, and, in keeping with his training, hid the fox under his tunic. While engaged in conversation with the other boys, the fox gnawed into his stomach without his betraying any sign of pain, preferring to drop dead from his wounds rather than to be disgraced (ibid., 8.1).

- **Women.** Although Spartiate women had no political rights as such, they were the only women in any Greek state to be allowed to own property in their own name. There was even a form of state education for girls, involving gymnastics—performed naked, like the boys—as well as dance, music, and poetry.

- **Ephors.** The five ephors, who were elected by the citizens for a year at a time, were effectively the chief magistrates of Sparta. The title literally means "overseer" or "supervisor," possibly because one of the ephors' main functions was to check the power of the kings. Every month the kings and ephors swore a mutual oath, the ephors agreeing to preserve the kingship provided the kings respected the laws of the state (Xenophon, *Constitution of Sparta,* 15.7). The ephors alone had the right to remain seated in the presence of a king, and if summoned by the ephors the king, was obliged to obey—at least at the third attempt (Xenophon, *Constitution of Sparta,* 15.6; Plut., *Cleomenes,* 10). The ephors could arrest or fine a king—as when King Archidamos was fined for marrying too short a wife—or even depose him, but only if the ephors saw a shooting star on a specific night set aside for watching the heavens every ninth year (see Arnheim 1977, p. 201, n. 120). Every autumn the ephors would formally declare war on the helots, which allowed any Spartan citizen to kill a helot with impunity (Xenophon, *Constitution of Sparta*, 15:6).

- **Apella**. Full Spartan citizenship was reserved to Spartiate males, who, once they reached the age of 30, were entitled to meet together in the assembly, known as the *Apella*. Meetings may originally have been presided over by the kings, but in classical times this function was exercised by the ephors. Hence the formula for decisions of the Apella: "It was resolved by the ephors and the assembly" (Xenophon, *Hellenica III*, 2.23, IV.6.3). The Lycurgan constitution, or *Rhetra*, declared that "Sovereignty and power are to belong to the people" (Plut., *Lycurgus*, 6.1). However, a rider to the *Rhetra* provided: "But if the people should make a crooked decision, the council of elders and the kings shall set it aside" (Plut., *Lycurgus*, 6.4). But who had the whip hand: the council, the ephors, or the assembly? Probably the best evidence is to be found in Xenophon's *Hellenica*, which includes no fewer than eight reports of meetings of the assembly, in six of which definite decisions are recorded, all on matters of considerable moment—usually after genuine debate (see Arnheim, 1977, p. 200, n. 101). The famous debate of 432 BCE leading to the outbreak of the Peloponnesian War provides further support for the leading role of the assembly. On that occasion the assembly was addressed by envoys from some Spartan allies and then by an Athenian envoy. It is significant that the assembly deliberated upon the addresses right away and, having reached the conclusion that the Athenians were in the wrong, decided to go to war with Athens at once. King Archidamos then got up in the assembly and tried to exercise a restraining influence, but it was the rousing speech of the ephor Sthenelaidas, agreeing with the original consensus, that carried the day. Not only, therefore, was the final decision taken in the assembly, but it was there and there alone, so far as we know, that the question was discussed from the beginning (Thuc. 1:79). Several similar examples are to be found in Xenophon (see Arnheim 1977, p. 201n. 110). How does all this square with the statements of Aristotle and Plutarch to the effect that the council had the sole right to initiate legislation—or with the rider to the *Rhetra* about "crooked decisions"? In practice, it seems, the assembly had the whip hand in decision-making—which is more in keeping with the Lycurgan reforms aimed at achieving as much equality among the citizens as possible.
- **Gerousia**. The *gerousia*, or council of elders, which also supposedly owed its origin to the Lycurgan reforms of the seventh century BCE but probably long predated them, was an elective body of 28 citizens of at least 60 years of age plus the two kings. If a king was absent from a council member, his nearest

relation could take his place, with two votes for the absent king plus his own vote, but if a king was present, he had just one vote. For the relationship between the *gerousia* and the *apella*, see under "*Apella*" above.

From a modern perspective there can be no doubt that Sparta was an oligarchy or an aristocracy of the most extreme kind. It is estimated that in about 480 BCE, the ruling Spartiate population numbered only about 32,000, as against approximately 170,000 helots and 50,000 *perioikoi*, making a total population of about 252,000.

The tight-knit egalitarianism of the Spartiates was established and perpetuated against not one but two or even three dangers. First and foremost, the Spartiates were in a perpetual state of war against the helots, which kept them on a permanent state of high alert. Secondly, there was the danger of one-man rule, and thirdly the danger of divisions within the Spartiates themselves.

Whoever instituted the Lycurgan system understood the need for equality among the citizen body in order to perform a delicate balancing act: confronting the helot threat while preventing either the rise of one-man rule or the resurgence of the old aristocracy, a much smaller minority of birth and wealth within the Spartiate minority.

At its most rigorous, the Lycurgan system gave "the equals" an esprit de corps and a morale that made them the envy of the whole Greek world. Even in defeat, their patriotic devotion and camaraderie has echoed down the centuries, as in Simonides's poignant epitaph for the 300 Spartans who fell at Thermopylae in 480 BCE:

> ὦ ξεῖν᾽, ἀγγέλλειν Λακεδαιμονίοις ὅτι τῆδε
> κείμεθα τοῖς κείνων ῥήμασι πειθόμενοι.
> ("O stranger, go and tell the Spartans that here
> we lie obedient to the last to their orders.")
> (Simonides of Ceos c. 556–469 BCE;
> Hdt. vii.228)

It is worth noting that the Messenians were not the only helots. There also were Laconian helots, who do not appear to have joined the Messenian helots in their revolts. The reason for the difference is that the Messenian helots continued to regard themselves as a separate nation which had been unjustly subjugated, whereas the Laconian helots apparently simply accepted their lot like slaves in other Greek states. However, the helots—of both varieties—were *not* chattel slaves as were found everywhere else but had the superior status of state-owned serfs. Unlike slaves, they could not be bought and sold; they lived in their own family units and only had to contribute 50% of the produce of their land to the state, retaining the balance for their own consumption or sale on the open market.

Constant fear of a Messenian uprising informed the whole tenor of Spartiate society, including their tight-knit discipline, solidarity, and courage even in the face of impossible odds. But why did they never try to reach a compromise settlement with the Messenians? The difference between the Spartiates and the Messenians was probably less than that between Serbs and Croats today, who of course have had a history of serious conflict. The Spartiates and the Messenians spoke different but mutually intelligible dialects of Greek, the Spartiates Doric, and the Messenians the Mycenaean dialect as recorded in the Linear B tablets from Pylos. Unlike the Serbs and Croats, who belong to different branches of Christianity, there was no discernible religious difference between the Spartiates and the Messenians. Nevertheless, there was clearly a sense of ethnic pride on both sides. The contrast between the attitude of the Messenian helots and that of the Laconian helots is instructive. The seething discontent of the Messenian helots appears to have arisen not so much from absolute low status as from *relative deprivation*. The status of the Messenians was no worse than that of the Laconian helots, yet they felt more relatively deprived, because of their self-identity as a subjugated nation. Pylos, one of the main centers of Mycenaean civilization, was in Messenia, and had a huge palace attached to it, the ruins of which are still there. It is generally referred to as the Palace of Nestor, named after the king of Pylos in Homer's *Iliad*.

Chapter 21
Totalitarian

Totalitarianism is a twentieth-century concept generally defined as a repressive one-party regime under an autocratic charismatic leader controlling the population in every way possible and demanding absolute obedience to the leader's ideology. It is applied particularly to both Stalinist Russia and Nazi Germany as well as to Fascist Italy and is extended to other more recent regimes such as Maoist China and Fidel Castro's Cuba. Though the repressive nature of such regimes tends to be stressed by outside observers, they also evidently have some popular, albeit not universal, support. One good thing about the concept of totalitarianism is that it pays no attention to the concepts of "left wing" and "right wing" but recognizes the convergence of the two extremes in a similar form of regime. One criticism of it is that it is applied only to regimes that have arisen since World War I. This is understandable, because it was only in the twentieth century that technology became available that enabled a government to brainwash the population through mass media and, as "Big Brother," to monitor the activities of the population on a daily basis. However, there are some earlier examples, notably that of ancient Sparta, a tightly knit militaristic oligarchy of "Spartiate" homoioi ("equals") on a constant war footing against a suppressed majority population of "helots," which lasted for about four hundred years, discussed in Chapter 20 (see Arnheim 1977).

Mussolini

The first twentieth-century state to be labeled totalitarian was Fascist Italy (1922–43), which was established after the so-called but peaceful "March on Rome" under the leadership of *Il Duce* ("the Leader"), Benito Mussolini, as dictator with the title of prime minister. King Victor Emmanuel III remained as

Five Thousand Years of Monarchy, First Edition. Michael Arnheim.
© 2026 John Wiley & Sons, Inc. Published 2026 by John Wiley & Sons, Inc.

nominal head of state but retained the ultimate power (which was eventually used) of dismissing the prime minister.

In his early years Mussolini was widely praised for his efficient administration, epitomized by "getting the trains to run on time." But Mussolini, a former Socialist journalist, had a much more ambitious vision, of reviving the glories of ancient Rome through a policy of total control of the population, under the slogan: *Credere, Obeddire, Combattere* ("Believe, Obey, Fight"), which, however, coexisted with the much more conventional older conservative slogan of *Dio, Patria, Famiglia* ("God, Fatherland, Family") coined by Giuseppe Mazzini (1805–72), a founding father of the *Risorgimento* (Italian unification).

Fascist economic policy was generally anti-Socialist, including the closing down of labor unions. But he also nationalized business, claiming in 1935 that three-quarters of businesses were state control, and in 1936 he imposed price controls. After Italian Fascists attacked some left-wing autarkic projects at the behest of large landowners, in the 1930s Mussolini himself embraced the goal of autarky ("self-sufficiency"), raising high tariff barriers on trade with most countries except Nazi Germany.

The corporatist Labor Charter of 1927 implemented a collective agreement system between employers and employees, envisaged as a form of class collaboration. A popular slogan was: "Everything within the state, nothing outside the state, nothing against the state." In 1936 the "National Council of Corporations" actually replaced the Chamber of Deputies as Italy's "parliament." Of its 823 members, 66 represented the Fascist Party, with the rest split among 22 "corporations," each made up of employer and employee representatives.

Styling himself *Il Duce*, Mussolini recreated himself as a powerful, omniscient, and omnipotent leader. His rhetoric was loud, long, melodramatic, and bombastic, with exaggerated hand movements and his chest (sometimes bare) thrust out in a defiant posture. While Mussolini wanted to appear internationally as a man of peace, such references were sometimes deleted for Italian consumption, where war was glorified, though there too, he sometimes posed as a peacemaker, as the occasion demanded. "The crowd does not have to know," Mussolini is quoted as saying. "It must believe."

Mussolini broke the longstanding stalemate with the Catholic Church by signing a concordat with the Vatican in 1929, the Lateran Treaty, which entailed mutual recognition. The Italian state was finally recognized by the Church, and the papacy was given Vatican City as a completely independent state, which, though a fraction of the size of the old Papal States that cut a diagonal swathe across central Italy, settled a long dispute and was so greatly appreciated that Pope Pius XI declared Mussolini to be "The Man of Providence." This action on Mussolini's part, undoubtedly won him many recruits to his movement.

In keeping with his image of recreating the Roman greatness of Italy, with himself cast in the role of the Emperor Augustus, Mussolini embarked on an aggressive foreign policy, notably the invasion of Ethiopia in 1935, which cost 12,000 Italian lives and drained the Italian coffers. Between 1936 and 1939 Mussolini gave crucial support to Francisco Franco during the Spanish Civil War. In 1936 the Rome–Berlin Axis was formed, which became a full military alliance with Germany in 1939. In April 1939, Italy occupied Albania. King Victor Emmanuel wanted Italy to remain neutral in the spiraling conflict, and when Hitler invaded Poland in September 1939 Italy remained on the sidelines. However, after some dithering, Italy declared war on Britain and France on 10 June 1940. Following some initial successes against Britain in Africa, Axis forces were defeated in the Tunisia Campaign in early 1943 and Italy suffered other major reverses on the Eastern Front. Allied bombings in Italy itself caused food shortages, and the Italian people lost faith in Mussolini, leading to major strikes. The Allied invasion of Italy was welcomed by the people, and, after a blistering attack on Mussolini and a 19–8 vote of no confidence in him in the Fascist Grand Council, on 25 July 1943 the king sent for Mussolini and formally dismissed him as prime minister. Rescued by Germany, Mussolini was given the headship of a doomed puppet regime known as the Italian Social Republic, covering the whole of northern Italy. In April 1945, while scrambling to get to Switzerland, Mussolini and his mistress Clara Petacci were intercepted by Italian Communist partisans and summarily executed and their bodies were famously hung upside down from the roof of a service station in Milan.

The general disgust and contempt shown to Mussolini by his own people in the end is easily verifiable, but did he ever enjoy genuine popularity? In other words, was his populism really popular? Mussolini was shy of elections, the last one being held in the form of a referendum in 1934, in which voters (restricted to adult males who were members of a trade union, soldiers, or clergy) were asked to approve the candidates list of the Fascist Party, the only one allowed. Not surprisingly, 99.84% said "yes." Nevertheless, until Mussolini joined Nazi Germany to form the Axis in World War II, he does appear to have had genuine widespread support.

Hitler

Adolf Hitler's "Third Reich," the vaunted "Thousand-Year Reich," lasted only 12 years, from 1933 to 1945—a far cry from the "First Reich," the Holy Roman empire, which supposedly lasted from 800 (though actually only from 962) until 1806, and even from the "Second Reich," Imperial Germany (1871–1918). (On Hitler's rise to power, see Chapter 13.)

The term "the Nazi seizure of power" is not quite accurate. In fact, Hitler was appointed chancellor (prime minister) by a reluctant President Paul von Hindenburg in the wake of the Nazi victory in the 1932 election, from which it had emerged as the largest party in the Reichstag (Parliament), but with only

37.3% of the vote. Besides Hitler there were only two other Nazis in the Cabinet. But then came the Reichstag fire, supposedly set by Marinus van der Lubbe, a young Dutch Communist. This gave Hitler a pretext for getting Hindenburg to sign the Reichstag Fire decree of 28 February 1933, which suspended basic rights and allowed detention without trial. This enabled the Nazis to use street violence to put pressure on the electorate in the ensuing election in March 1933, in which the Nazis were the largest party, this time with 43.9% of the vote. All 81 Communist Party deputies were rounded up and arrested, and the Social Democratic Party was declared illegal, and on 14 July 1933 Germany officially became a one-party state.

The 86-year-old President von Hindenburg died on 2 August 1934. Seventeen days later Germans were again asked to vote, this time in a referendum in which 89.93% approved the amalgamation of the positions of president and chancellor in Adolf Hitler, who in practice used neither designation, preferring to be known as the *Führer*.

With the reins of power firmly in his grasp, Hitler proceeded with an energetic and ambitious economic program, while at the same time playing off different factions of the Nazi Party against one another, including the "Night of the Long Knives" in June/July 1934, in which 200 of Hitler's potential enemies were brutally murdered, including his former close associate Ernst Röhm.

But this did not halt Hitler's domestic and international agenda. May Day 1933 was declared a "Day of National Labor," and trade union delegates were invited to Berlin to celebrate it. The next day Nazi stormtroopers smashed up union premises around the country, all trade unions were dissolved, and their leaders arrested.

Hjalmar Schacht, who, as president of the Reichsbank, had defeated the hyperinflation of 1923 with the creation of the *Rentenmark,* a new currency based on a notional mortgage of all German property, was appointed by Hitler as minister of economics in 1934. He developed public works programs, notably the construction of the *Autobahnen,* to alleviate the high unemployment, which stood just below 30% in 1933 and was almost eliminated by 1938. Schacht also introduced the "New Plan," an attempt to achieve German economic autarky, or self-reliance. The high government deficit was reduced with "Mefo bills," promissory notes used for deferred payment to finance the Nazi government's program of rearmament without breaking the Treaty of Versailles. Disgusted at the anti-Semitic violence of *Kristallnacht* in 1938, Schacht suggested an alternative policy, under which Jewish property in Germany would be held in trust and used as security for loans raised abroad, which would also be guaranteed by the German government. Funds would be made available for Jewish emigration. Though accepted by Hitler and even by some prominent British Jews, it was rejected by Chaim Weizmann on behalf of the British Zionist Federation.

Though Hitler was born and brought up as a Catholic, he found the German Protestant churches more pliable to his wishes. The overtly anti-Semitic German Christian Faith Movement was started in 1932, and in 1933 the "German Evangelical Church," a federation of Lutheran, Reformed, and United territorial churches, fell under the control of the so-called "German Christians," a Nazi organization, and proceeded to elect Ludwig Müller, a military pastor and Hitler's confidant on Church matters, as *Reichsbischof* ("state bishop"). Besides opposition to the whole idea of Nazi Christianity, Müller also faced a good deal of criticism from within the Nazi Party, and he was effectively sidelined, though as late as 1944 he evidently received a grant of 500,000 Reichsmarks, largely "to pay off his debts."

Hitler's toothbrush mustache, his unprepossessing appearance and his ranting and raving, complete with elaborate arm gestures, make him appear today as a figure of fun—and the high volume of his delivery did in fact strain his vocal chords to the point where he developed a polyp that had to be surgically removed. But in his heyday Hitler does appear to have possessed genuine charisma and to have enjoyed a good deal of hero worship. The hysteria of the crowds who lined the streets on his triumphal tour of the Sudetenland after he had successfully persuaded Britain and France to let him have it looks genuine enough, as does the enthusiasm of the welcoming throng of people welcoming him to Vienna after the *Anschluss* (annexation) of Austria, both in 1938. The enthusiasm of the crowd apparent in film recordings of a Nuremberg *Parteitag* (rally) was artificially whipped up by the stirring music, marching, and speeches, but it would be a mistake to think that these people were play-acting.

This all ties in with the whole ethos of Nazi Germany, starting with the greeting *"heil Hitler!"* replacing all previously normal greetings. The Nazi Party swastika flag in the traditional old colors of black, white, and red became the national flag instead of the Weimar tricolor flag of black, red, and gold, which had left-wing connotations, arising as it did out of the revolution of 1848. *Ein Volk, Ein Reich, Ein Führer!* ("One People, One Realm, One Leader!") was a slogan that encapsulated the *Führerprinzip* ("leader principle"), the doctrine that the *Führer's* word was law, but it also radiated power downwards, so that the leader at each level could count on unswerving obedience from those below him, while he owed unconditional obedience to the leader above him. This principle was resorted to in the Nuremberg Trials of 1945–46. Nazi defendants charged, for example, with war crimes and crimes against humanity would plead not guilty on the ground that they were only "following orders," but this defense was not accepted, so a number of the leading Nazis who stood trial were sentenced to death, including Hermann Göring—though he "cheated the hangman" by biting into a potassium cyanide capsule the night before his scheduled execution.

Soviet Union

In his "Secret Speech" of March 1956, Nikita Khrushchev, the then leader of the Soviet Union, denounced Joseph Stalin, Soviet dictator from 1927 until his death in 1953, for his "despotism" and "personality cult," contrasting him with the founder of the Soviet state, Vladimir Lenin, who was in power from 1917 until 1923, dying in January 1924. It was in Khrushchev's own interest to portray Stalin as betraying Lenin's heritage, but it would be a mistake to think of Lenin as a peace-loving consensus politician.

The "October Revolution" itself (in November 1917) was really a coup, engineered primarily by Lenin. When Lenin's Bolsheviks lost the ensuing election to the Constituent Assembly, Lenin had the Assembly dissolved under the slogan "All power to the Soviets" (Soviets being workers' councils, dominated by the Bolsheviks). It was Lenin who instituted the "Red Terror" of 1918–22, in which there were probably at least 100,000 executions (with some much higher estimates) of *kulaks* (peasants owning more than eight acres of land) and political opponents of all shades of opinion. And it was Lenin who, banning internal divisions within the Bolshevik (Communist) Party, made Russia a one-party state in 1921. The infamous secret police, originally called the Cheka, was also established by Lenin. Lenin's principle of "democratic centralism" gave the illusion of genuine freedom of speech in the upper echelons of the party, supposedly combining "freedom of debate" with "unity of action."

Stalin greatly intensified all these negative features and the violent nature of the Soviet state generally. Many "Old Bolsheviks," who had joined the party before 1917, were purged by Stalin in a series of show trials in the 1930s. In 1932–33, about eleven million people died from famine as a result of the forced collectivization of agriculture. And Stalin promoted an energetic personality cult, with himself—a short, squat, pockmarked figure with a heavy Georgian accent—as an unlikely "father," "savior," or "warrior" icon. How genuine was the adulation that Stalin received during his lifetime? It is hard to tell, as, despite his disclaimers, the Stalin personality cult was energetically promoted by the party. But Russians were used to one-man rule, regardless of the cruelty. An apocryphal anecdote has a peasant, Ivan, rushing in to his village, shouting, "The tsar spoke to me! The tsar spoke to me!" "Well," urged his inquisitive neighbors, "What did he say?" "He said," uttered the breathless Ivan, "Get out of my way, you scum!"

Fidel Castro

"We are not executing innocent people or political opponents," was Fidel Castro's retort to critics of his mass executions soon after taking power in Cuba in 1959. "We are executing murderers and they deserve it" (Coltman 2003).

Castro's "First Agrarian Reform," enacted just five months after his assumption of power in 1959, broke up large estates, confiscated the land, and redistributed it to about 200,000 peasants. "[T]he first property he seized was his own family's farm. Castro's mother ... never forgave her son." (Robinson 2005, p. 107). "[T]he revolution," Castro is quoted as proclaiming, "is the dictatorship of the exploited against the exploiters" (Mankiewicz 1976, p. 83). Within a year, it is estimated, the Castro regime redistributed around 15% of the nation's wealth. Cubans who paid less than $100 a month had their rents halved. Judges' and politicians' salaries were reduced, while low-level civil servants received a pay rise. Sugar production, the mainstay of the Cuban economy, was nationalized, together with the oil industry. In time, over 90% of the economy came under government control, and wages averaged less than $20 a month (Sanchez 2010). Education was greatly expanded, and a free healthcare system was established. The flip side of the coin was the abolition of elections, the arrest of hundreds of "counter-revolutionaries," and the suppression of freedom of speech and of the press (Quirk 1993).

Under the slogan *¡En cada barrio, Revolución!* ("In every neighborhood, Revolution!"), Castro set up what he called "a collective system of revolutionary vigilance, so that everybody knows who lives on every block, what they do, what relations they have had with the tyranny [viz. the previous regime, under Fulgencio Batista], in what activities they are involved, and with whom they meet." This system involved a "Big Brother" type network of thousands of *Comités de Defensa de la Revolución* (*"Committees for the Defense of the Revolution,"* or CDR), charged with spying on everyone living in every apartment block in the country and reporting back to the police. In their defense, these "committees" also had a role in "vaccination campaigns, blood banks, recycling, practicing evacuations for hurricanes..." (Sanchez 2010).

Ever since Fidel Castro's seizure of power in 1959, Cuba has suffered a major brain drain. It is estimated that about half a million Cubans migrated to Miami, Florida, in the first 15 years of Castro's regime, and it was reported in 2012 that about 400,000 Cubans had arrived since 1980 (*The Economist* 2012).

But what of the bulk of the Cuban population who never left? How supportive are they of the regime? Since about 2011 Cuba has moved toward what they like to call "market socialism," meaning that a Cuban employed by a private company is still paid by the Cuban government (in Cuban pesos), and the government is paid by the employer firm. Ration books (*libretas*) are still in evidence, entitling everyone to a certain amount of food and other necessaries at nominal cost. There is practically no illiteracy in Cuba, and 85% of Cubans own their own homes and pay no property taxes or mortgage interest (*Los Angeles Times* 2017).

Maoist China

At dinner at St John's College, Cambridge, one evening in 1967, a young Chinese in a "Mao suit" came and sat next to me on the long student benches. He introduced himself as one of a small number of Chinese students who had just arrived in Cambridge. When I asked him why he was not wearing a student gown (then mandatory for dinner in "hall"), he explained that, as wearing a gown was a "class distinction," he and his colleagues had been given special dispensation from that obligation by the senior tutor. I pointed out that, if he looked around, he would find that *not* wearing a gown was a sign of class distinction. Within a few weeks my new-found friend was recalled to China to take part in the "Great Proletarian Cultural Revolution,"—an attempt by Mao Zedong, or "Chairman Mao" (1893–1976), to replace with his own personal power the new elite that had supplanted the old ruling elite since the Communist takeover in 1949.

The "Cultural Revolution," enforced by youthful Maoist "Red Guards," resulted in the destruction of much of traditional Chinese culture, the imprisonment and death of thousands of "class enemies," and the upheaval of society. Teachers and educational authorities were among the prime targets. One of the best-known features of this was the "barefoot doctors" program, which brought peasants with just a few months' training from the countryside to work in city hospitals, replacing university-trained doctors, who were sent to work in the countryside. New political slogans were everywhere, on posters, banners, newspapers, and even on bus tickets and cigarette packets. "Long live the red terror!" was one popular slogan. Mao's personality cult was at the center of the whole movement, and even incidental remarks of his became sacred writ: "Sweet potato tastes good; I like it." Some slogans frankly revealed the true purpose behind Mao's fomenting this "revolution": "Those who are against Chairman Mao will have their dog skulls smashed into pieces" (Huang 2001).

Mao's Cultural Revolution had two complementary sides. On the one hand, application of the "tall poppy syndrome" reduced everyone—except Mao himself—to the same level. But programs like that of the "barefoot doctors" opened an avenue of social advancement to some of the lowliest members of society while reducing the status of the newly emerging middle class. By contrast with Imperial China, which offered the prospect of advancement on the basis of merit as measured by competitive examinations, Mao's Cultural Revolution favored those with the least "merit" in any conventional sense. But that system proved short-lived. In due course China allowed social mobility through an economy best characterized as state capitalism, which has resulted in huge inequalities in Chinese society, while the Constitution of the People's Republic of China entrusts supreme political authority to the Communist Party. Since

Figure 21   Mao with US President Nixon, 1972.
SOURCE: The U.S. National Archives and Records Administration / Wikkimedia Commons / Public Domain.

2012 political power has been concentrated in the hands of a single ruling figure, Xi Jinping, who combines the posts of general secretary of the Communist Party and president with the unofficial designation of "paramount leader," without any term limit.

Chapter 22
Constitutional Monarchy

Constitutional monarchs are generally heads of state where someone else, usually a prime minister, is head of government. Constitutional monarchs range from pure figureheads to marginal decision-makers. The key feature of a constitutional monarchy, namely the separation between head of state and head of government, is also found in many modern republics, like Germany, Italy, Portugal, and India, where the president is a non-executive head of state, and the government is run by the prime minister. The chief difference between, say, the king of Sweden and the president of Germany is that the king is hereditary. Like most republics of that type, constitutional monarchies are not really monarchies at all but oligarchies.

Veto Power

Except for the prince of Liechtenstein, who is a true monarch, the crowned heads of Europe today are all so-called "constitutional monarchs," which really means that they are not monarchs at all but largely ceremonial heads of state with, at most, only a few so-called "reserve powers." Probably the most important of these "reserve powers" is the right to withhold the royal assent to legislation passed by the legislature, and thereby to veto it. However, in most constitutional monarchies this power has in practice been lost, though the formality of royal assent is generally required. And in some monarchies, to take effect legislation requires not only to be assented to by the monarch but also to be "promulgated" by them, meaning that the monarch formally orders the law to be officially published and executed.

Without the veto power, a monarch is essentially under the control of the executive government or the legislature, which amounts to being subordinate to an elite

Five Thousand Years of Monarchy, First Edition. Michael Arnheim.
© 2026 John Wiley & Sons, Inc. Published 2026 by John Wiley & Sons, Inc.

of one kind or another, and therefore in practice the figurehead or ceremonial head of state of what is actually an oligarchy, or, if hereditary, an aristocracy.

This is all part of the sham charade that lies at the heart of constitutional monarchy. For example, not only does the Norwegian constitution of 1814 (still in force) specifically give the king a "suspensive veto" (i.e. the right to hold up legislation temporarily) passed by the legislature, but it also goes into elaborate detail on how this tame veto can be overridden. In fact, however, the royal assent has never been withheld since the dissolution of Norway's personal union with Sweden in 1905.

A curious twist to the veto right was demonstrated by Belgium in 1990. The Belgian Constitution provides that, "the king sanctions and promulgates the laws." According to the Constitution, the royal assent is signified by the king's signature and a ministerial counter-signature—and the same procedure is laid down in the event of the king's refusal to assent to a law. In 1990, King Baudouin advised his cabinet that, as a devout Roman Catholic, he could not sign a law allowing abortion. A constitutional crisis was averted by the clumsy legal fiction of a declaration of the king's incapacity. With Baudouin temporarily out of the way, the offending law was then passed. And on the very next day, Parliament declared Baudouin to be capable of resuming his powers. This charade only demonstrated just how powerless the king was. Despite what the Constitution said, the king was unable to block a particular law, which went through without his consent.

The duty of promulgation is sometimes found without the power of assent. In Luxembourg, for example, until 2008 the grand duke was required to sanction and promulgate all new laws. When Grand Duke Henri refused to sanction (give has assent) to a law allowing euthanasia, the constitution was amended, depriving the grand duke of the power of assent and only requiring him to promulgate new laws by announcing that they had been enacted by the legislature, without the right to block them. The grand duke signed the Euthanasia Act 2009 under this new constitutional dispensation.

The US-influenced constitution of Japan of 1947, which is still in force, was "sanctioned and promulgated" by the emperor. The body of the constitution says nothing about "sanction," or the royal assent to legislation, but requires the emperor to promulgate amendments to the laws, without giving him the right to refuse to do so.

As was shown in Chapter 2 of this book, oligarchies are instinctively afraid of a single individual coming to power with the support of the masses, because that would threaten the oligarchy's very existence. The Roman Republic (509–49 BCE) was a tenacious oligarchy in its concern to prevent the rise a strongman, and its constitution was all geared to that. That is why even the very top position in government was shared between two equal consuls, who held office for only one year. Eventually, however, it was one-man rule that toppled the Republic.

Doge of Venice

But there has been no shortage over time of oligarchies with at least a nominal monarch at their head. A classic example of this is the Republic of Venice, which existed for a millennium before being dissolved under pressure from Napoleon in 1797. The Venetian head of state, known as the *doge,* was a byword for a powerless monarch. Elected for life in a complex process combining election and sortition, he was drawn from one of the inner circle of Venetian aristocratic houses and there were safeguards in place to prevent hereditary succession, though the same family names do recur from time to time on the list of doges. Instead of receiving payment for his service, on his election a *doge* was required to lay out a large sum of money as a bounty to his subjects when coins were thrown to the crowd thronging his coronation. Treated with the utmost dignity and respect both in Venice itself and internationally, the doge nevertheless had essentially a ceremonial role.

Figure 22   Caricature by James Gillray of the future King George IV as Prince of Wales, 1792.
SOURCE: James Gillray / Library of Congress / Public Domain.

Modern Britain

The monarchs of present-day western Europe, including Britain, may be described in much the same terms. They reign but do not rule. The king or queen is head of state, head of the nation, Supreme Governor of the Church of England, head of the Armed Forces, and head of the Commonwealth, all of which are largely ceremonial and symbolic roles. In his perceptive work titled *The English Constitution*, Walter Bagehot (1867) identified the British Constitution as comprising two parts, the "dignified" and the "efficient," the former including the Crown, endowed with "the right to be consulted, the right to encourage, the right to warn." An updated version of that is that the monarch must seek the advice of their ministers and must act on that advice. Whatever political opinions they may have they should keep to themselves.

The British "constitutional monarchy" of today was established by the "Glorious Revolution" of 1688–89, which deposed James II and replaced him with his daughter and son-in-law reigning jointly as William III and Mary II. Owing his throne to Parliament, William expressed the fear that he would have no more power than the doge of Venice, a mere ceremonial head of state. When Parliament initially voted him revenue for only three months (instead of for life, as Parliament had initially provided for James II), William felt "tricked" and objected that "the worst of all governments is that of a king without treasure and without power" (Wouter 2005, p. 214.) To make up for this, William made full use of his veto power on legislation, withholding his assent from no fewer than five Bills passed by Parliament, including the Qualifications Bill, which would have laid down a property qualification for members of Parliament and would therefore have precluded anyone outside the landed gentry from becoming a member of Parliament. The king's "populist" veto actually made little difference, as members of Parliament were unpaid until 1911. William's successor, Queen Anne (r. 1702–14), vetoed only one Bill (on her ministers' advice), which was the last time that that power was exercised. It is now, in practice, dead. If the king were to try it even once he would probably be found hitching a lift outside Buckingham Palace.

Although the new dispensation after 1689 left the king with control over foreign affairs and an unrestricted right to appoint whatever ministers he liked, this power was illusory, as it depended on control of the purse strings, which was firmly in the grip of Parliament. As a result, the Hanoverian kings eventually found themselves having to appoint ministers who could command a majority in the House of Commons. William IV (r. 1830–37) was the last king to dismiss the Whig prime minister, Lord Melbourne, who had a majority in the Commons, and appoint in his place someone who did not command a majority in the Commons and whose administration was therefore hamstrung. This was the Tory leader, Sir Robert Peel, who was anxious to resign but whose resignation was repeatedly refused by the king before it was finally accepted. From commentators who did not know of his frantic attempts to resign, Peel earned the witty taunt that he had all the virtues of a prime minister except the virtue of resignation. But the lesson was not lost on Queen Victoria (r. 1837–1901), reluctant though she was to appoint prime ministers whom she disliked, such as Peel and Gladstone. The result, which is still the position today, is that all the powers of the Crown are exercised by ministers, with the king or queen reduced to a cipher.

Queen Elizabeth II (r. 1952–2022) was very good at remaining tight-lipped on her political views. The only clear exception that I know of was in her opposition to Quebec's secession from Canada. Shortly before the 1995 referendum on the subject of Quebec's secession, the queen received a telephone call from someone pretending to be Jean Chrétien, the then Canadian prime minister. The caller was actually a Montreal disc jockey who was a dead ringer (in sound at least) for Chrétien. The pretend prime minister wasted no time in asking the queen to give a speech on television opposing Quebec's secession, and, after a brief chat with her private secretary, the queen agreed. Besides the fact that she had been scammed, what she did not realize was that she had already given the requested speech—as the whole conversation was broadcast live on radio. It was doubly wrong of the queen to give her opinion so openly. Not only was it on a highly sensitive political issue, but it was also constitutionally improper to bypass the Canadian governor-general, because although Elizabeth was queen of Canada, the functions of the Crown are exercised there through a governor-general, who was not even mentioned in the conversation with the "prime minister" (Transcript—*The Independent*, 28 October 1995).

The most important "prerogative power" held by the British Crown is the right to appoint the prime minister. In theory the monarch can pick whoever they like as prime minister, but in practice the Crown must appoint the leader of the majority party in the House of Commons. This became the rule in 1965, when the Conservative Party first had an elected leader, in the shape of Edward Heath. Prior to that, whenever the Conservatives had a majority in the Commons but for some reason the prime minister had to resign, it fell to the monarch to appoint a new one. In 1957 and again in 1963, the prime minister was picked by the queen on the basis of "soundings" taken from leading Conservatives. On the second of these occasions, when Harold Macmillan had to resign, ostensibly on grounds of ill-health (though he would live till 1986 at the age of 92), the queen was manipulated by the wily retiring prime minister. Two of Macmillan's acolytes were deputed to call every Conservative member of Parliament and ask them two questions. First: Who would you like to see as prime minister? Then, regardless of their answer: Would you accept Lord Home as prime minister? Some Conservative parliamentarians made the point that, though they had no objection to Lord Home, would he not be ruled out on the longstanding convention that the prime minister should always have a seat in the House of Commons?

Ignoring this, the result of the survey was misleadingly relayed to the queen as indicating solid support for Sir Alec Douglas-Home, as he became known on his appointment.

Australia

Though William IV was the last king to have dismissed a sitting British prime minister in 1834, a similar decision caused a constitutional crisis in Australia in 1975. Australia has a union of crowns with Britain, with a governor-general appointed by the Australian government acting on behalf of the monarch. In 1975 the then governor-general, Sir John Kerr, caused a constitutional crisis, straining the royal prerogative to breaking point, by dismissing the Labor prime minister, Gough Whitlam, who had a majority in the lower house of Parliament but whose administration was hamstrung by the opposition's control of the Senate. The governor-general (who, ironically, had been appointed on Whitlam's recommendation) chose to resort to this extreme measure instead of acceding to Whitlam's request to call a "half-Senate" election in an attempt to break the deadlock. Though Kerr was widely criticized for his high-handed action and resigned early as governor-general, his decision was justified by events. In the general election held a month after Whitlam's ouster, the Liberal–Country Party coalition was swept to power on a landslide victory under Malcolm Fraser, who had been appointed by Kerr to replace Whitlam.

Chapter 23
Hybrid

*I*s it possible to have a hybrid system of government, a composite between true monarchy and oligarchy? There is no shortage of parliamentary systems with a monarch as head of state. The western European "constitutional monarchies" belong to this model. These are not true monarchies at all but oligarchies. And the same applies to republics where the president is head of state but has practically no political power. So, where are hybrid monarchies to be found? The answer is that they are extremely rare.

What is probably the most famous hybrid in history did not exist at all. That is, Mommsen's dyarchy, supposedly shared rule between the Roman Emperor Augustus and the Senate. In fact, what Augustus established was very much a monarchy. One of the very few actual hybrid monarchies is a system that is not usually thought of as either a monarchy or an oligarchy, namely the United States of America, where power is shared between the president, Congress, the judiciary, and the "power elite."

Then there are a few shared systems, notably that of the current Fifth French Republic, which has both a president and a prime minister. But that alone does not make it a hybrid. In the French Fifth Republic established by Charles de Gaulle in 1958, both the president and the *Assemblée Nationale* are popularly elected, in separate elections held at different times. The president alone has the power to appoint the prime minister. And he can appoint anyone he likes. But if an opposition party has an absolute majority in the *Assemblée Nationale*, then the president is, in practice, constrained to appoint a prime minister from that party, because, if he does not do so, the prime minister and his government are likely to be brought down by a motion of no confidence passed by the *Assemblée Nationale*. If the president does appoint a prime minister from an opposition party—which is termed *cohabitation*—the president will find himself increasingly reduced to a cipher. So no hybrid

Five Thousand Years of Monarchy, First Edition. Michael Arnheim.
© 2026 John Wiley & Sons, Inc. Published 2026 by John Wiley & Sons, Inc.

there. This has happened a few times in recent French history: under President François Mitterrand between 1986 and 1988 and again from 1993 to 1995, and then under Jacques Chirac from 1997 to 2002. But what if the election to the *Assemblée Nationale* is deadlocked as in 2024, with no single party or group of parties able to command an absolute majority? President Macron's appointment of the conservative Michel Barnier in an attempt to bridge the gap between the extreme right "National Rally," which had a plurality of seats, and the left-wing "New Popular Front," backfired when these two opposing groups united to bring down the government, which Macron replaced with another minority government. At the time of this writing, it is too early to tell how this is likely to play out. But it is also not a hybrid situation, because, if he is brazen enough, the president can keep on trying different governments until his mandate runs out in 2027. The country is simply polarized beyond anything anticipated by Charles de Gaulle as the architect of the Constitution of the Fifth Republic. It may be necessary to go back to the drawing board to prevent a violent upheaval.

The United States

The United States of America is now generally regarded as a representative democracy, and it is certainly true that no single individual has ever quite managed to take sole power in America, the closest attempt probably being that of Franklin Delano Roosevelt ("FDR"), who was president from 1933 until his death in 1945.

A number of comparatively recent studies have come to the conclusion that the US is essentially ruled by a "power elite" or an oligarchy, and some of these studies are diametrically opposed to one another—for example, in identifying quite different and even mutually exclusive ruling elites. The solution probably lies in recognizing that present-day America really is a rare case of hybrid government, with power shared by at least three disparate elements:

- the president
- the US Supreme Court
- the "power elite" (however defined).

From Republic to "Democracy"

We here highly resolve ... that government of the people, by the people, for the people, shall not perish from the earth. These words come of course from the famous Gettysburg Address delivered by Abraham Lincoln on 19 November 1863. It is possible to dissect this now much-overworked threefold definition of democracy, but Lincoln appears to have treated the three variants as three facets of the same system of government—a form of government which he does not name but which is universally taken to be democracy. The phrase "shall not perish from the earth" implies that this form of government already existed.

But was Lincoln's America a democracy? And, for that matter, is the United States a democracy today? The answer to that depends to some extent on how "democracy" is defined, but, regardless of that, there are some serious question marks hanging over America's democratic credentials (see Arnheim 2018).

The American Revolution

For starters, the American Revolution was a rising not of the masses but of the wealthy elite of colonial society against British rule. The leading American revolutionaries were pillars of their communities. The US, of course, originated as thirteen British colonies. Although the colonies had elected assemblies, real power was in the hands of a governor appointed by the British government three thousand miles away. The colonists had no control over legislation, which was made by the British Parliament in London. The breaking point came with the imposition on the colonies of Stamp Duty, a tax on a wide range of purchases ranging from newspapers to playing cards. This sparked off the cry of "no taxation without representation."

Declaration of Independence

With the Declaration of Independence drafted by Thomas Jefferson in 1776, the American colonies threw off the British yoke in grandiloquent terms: "We hold these truths to be self-evident, that all men are created equal, that they are endowed by their Creator with certain unalienable Rights, that among these are Life, Liberty and the pursuit of Happiness." Was Jefferson being disingenuous in penning these words? When he drafted the Declaration he had one of the largest plantations in Virginia and 187 slaves. Although supposedly opposed to slavery, Jefferson freed no slaves except for the children of his mixed-race slave lover (and his wife's half-sister), Sally Hemings.

The phrase, "life, liberty and the pursuit of happiness" in the Declaration of Independence, it is worth noting, was a variation of "life, liberty and property," found in the Declaration and Resolves of Colonial Rights of 1774, a phrase which reappears in the Fifth and Fourteenth Amendments to the US Constitution, which prohibit the government from depriving anyone of "life, liberty, or property" without due process of law.

The Wealth of the Founding Fathers

America's founding fathers were indeed men of property. America's first president, George Washington, is reputed to have been one of the wealthiest men in America in his time. At his peak, his net worth (according to *Time* magazine) in 2010 dollars was $525 million, making him one of the wealthiest presidents (after John F. Kennedy and possibly Donald Trump) to date.

Washington's successor as president, John Adams, a member of one of Boston's leading patrician families, was a strong upholder of the privileges of property owners: "Property is surely a right of mankind as real as liberty." But, if democracy were to be introduced and power given to the majority without any property qualifications, then chaos would ensue: "Debts would be abolished first; taxes laid heavy on the rich, and not at all on the others; and at last a downright equal division of everything be demanded, and voted. ... The moment the idea is admitted into society, that property is not as sacred as the laws of God ... anarchy and tyranny commence."

Fear of Democracy

James Madison, the fourth president (1809–17), often described as "Father of the Constitution," whose net worth in 2010 dollars is estimated at $101 million, excoriated democracy:

> Democracy is the most vile form of government.... Democracies have ever been spectacles of turbulence and contention; have ever been found incompatible with personal security or the rights of property, and have in general been as short in their lives as they have been violent in their deaths (quoted in Arnheim 2018, p. 25).

If the founding fathers weren't democrats, what were they? The concept that they embraced was *republicanism*. John Adams—the same John Adams who attacked democracy—waxed lyrical in praise of republicanism. Here's how Adams defined it: "A government in which all men, rich and poor, magistrates and subjects, officers and people, masters and servants, the first citizen and the last, are equally subject to the laws" (Arnheim 2018, p. 26).

As you start reading this definition, you get the impression that it's going to be egalitarian—based on the equality of all people. But the last phrase gives the game away. Republicanism, according to this definition, isn't about any power that the people *have* but about a power that they are *under*. In a republic, says Adams, everybody is equal under the law. John Adams's ideal was not one of people power at all. Rather, his ideal was one in which the people were subservient to laws made by an elite group (of which he was a prominent member)—with the last word on the interpretation of those laws left to judges drawn from the same elite group.

The word "democracy" doesn't appear in the US Constitution at all—but "republic" certainly does. Article IV, Section 4 provides: "The United States shall guarantee to every State in this Union a Republican Form of Government." There is no precise definition of "republican," but Adams's views on the subject are a reflection of the framers' thinking (although Adams himself didn't attend the Constitutional Convention, as he was serving as US ambassador to Britain at the time).

"A Government Not of Laws but of Lawyers"

Adams's definition of republicanism ties in with his better-known statement of the goal aimed at by the newly independent states: "A government of laws and not of men." So important was this doctrine to John Adams that he introduced it into the Massachusetts Constitution of 1780.

But how can laws govern? They are, after all, just words on paper, and inevitably subject to interpretation—by courts, judges, and lawyers. An anonymous wag early on put his finger on this truth and retorted: "A government not of men but of laws? No, a government not of laws but of lawyers." Despite the obvious truth of this trenchant riposte, Adams's doctrine is still regularly trotted out, not only in America but also in Europe and elsewhere, in its shorthand form, "the rule of law," as a touchstone of democracy.

But the wag's throwaway line has proved prophetic, and even some Supreme Court justices have admitted that the meaning of the US Constitution changes in accordance with the changing views of the court. In the words of Chief Justice Charles Evans Hughes (1862–1948), "we are under a Constitution, but the Constitution is what the judges say it is," significantly adding, "and the judiciary is the safeguard of our liberty and our property under the Constitution." So, what starts out looking like a criticism ends up as an endorsement of judge-made law.

Judicial Review

The power of the US Supreme Court really began with the landmark decision in *Marbury v. Madison* (1803), in which Chief Justice John Marshall (1755–1835) declared in characteristically bombastic fashion: "It is emphatically the province and the duty of the judicial department to say what the law is." President Thomas Jefferson (1743–1826) objected strongly to the way the Supreme Court "usurped" the right "of exclusively explaining the Constitution," which, he correctly branded as an infringement of the important constitutional doctrine of the separation of powers, adding:

"The Constitution on this hypothesis is a mere thing of wax in the hands of the judiciary, which they may twist and shape into any form they please." A more accurate prediction about the US Constitution would be hard to find (see Arnheim 2018, p. 20f).

But Chief Justice Marshall went even further in *Marbury* and actually arrogated to the Court the power of judicial review, including the right to strike down any Act of Congress that the Court deemed "unconstitutional." This power does not figure in the Constitution at all and is essentially undemocratic. In addition, the *Marbury v. Madison* decision itself was almost certainly wrong and Marshall ought to have recused himself from sitting on the case because of a serious conflict of interest. The whole case arose out of the failure of President John Adams's secretary of state to deliver to Marbury his commission as justice of the peace. And who was that secretary of state? Why, none other than John Marshall himself! Marshall's ruling in *Marbury*, commented Jefferson, "would make the judiciary a despotic branch" (Arnheim, 2018, pp. 74, 166).

Marbury v. Madison

John Marshall should have recused himself from sitting on *Marbury v. Madison* because of a serious conflict of interest, and the legal reasoning that he used was well described by the "twistifications" applied to it by his distant cousin and personal foe, Thomas Jefferson. The case arose out of lame-duck President John Adams's last-minute attempt to appoint a whole raft of "midnight judges" the very day before his term was due to end. These were all political appointees. It rankled Adams, a Federalist, that he had been deprived of a second term by defeat in the 1800 election at the hands of his own vice-president, Thomas Jefferson of the Democratic Republican Party. Adams decided to take his revenge by ensuring that the judiciary remained Federalist-dominated well beyond his presidency.

All these "midnight" appointments were rushed through the Senate. But the commissions, or official letters of appointment, still had to be delivered to each of the new appointees. Time ran out on Adams's presidency before all the commissions had been delivered—and without an official commission, an appointment could not take effect.

William Marbury was one of Adams's "midnight" justices of the peace whose commission was not delivered in time. Thomas Jefferson, who was now president, ordered the new secretary of state, James Madison, to withhold the commissions that had not been delivered, including Marbury's. So Marbury petitioned the US Supreme Court to order Madison to deliver his commission to him.

Madison was the named defendant because delivering commissions to new appointees was one of the duties of the secretary of state. But the person who really let Marbury down was not Madison—it was Madison's predecessor as secretary of state, none other than one John Marshall—yes, the very same John Marshall who was presiding over the case as chief justice! If ever there was a blatant case of a conflict of interest, this had to be it.

But that did not deter Marshall from going on to expand the power of the Supreme Court—and of himself as chief justice—by what Jefferson called "the cunning and sophistry within which he is able to enshroud himself."

Writing for the Court, Chief Justice Marshall held that:

- Madison's refusal to deliver the commission to Marbury was unlawful. This was undoubtedly correct.
- But the Supreme Court did not have the power to order him to do so. This was not actually correct.
- Because the law that purportedly gave the Supreme Court this power was itself unconstitutional. This was also probably wrong.
- And the Supreme Court had the power to strike down unconstitutional laws. The Constitution certainly does not say so.

This last assertion is the most important of all and forms the basis of judicial review. But where does it come from? Marshall offered this curiously worded "explanation":

> Certainly all those who have framed written Constitutions contemplate them as forming the fundamental and paramount law of the nation, and consequently the theory of every such government must be that an act of the Legislature repugnant to the Constitution is void. This theory is essentially attached to a written Constitution, and is consequently to be considered by this Court as one of the fundamental principles of our society. It is not, therefore to be lost sight of in the further consideration of this subject [*Marbury v. Madison* (1803)].

The vague and oblique language of this "explanation" is hard to miss. Why does Marshall not come out directly and say: "The Constitution is the paramount law of the land, so any law repugnant to it is void"? Because the Constitution itself does not make this claim: it only asserts the superiority of federal over state law. So Marshall resorted to vague talk about "theory." But, having purportedly now established the paramountcy of the Constitution, he is ready to take the next step: "It is emphatically the province and duty of the Judicial Department to say what the law is." Here we do at least have a direct statement—but why "emphatically"? That word gives the game away. It is a sign of special pleading—"Methinks the lady doth protest too much!" Because, once again, the Constitution does not give the judiciary this power. This "emphatic" but baseless assertion enables Marshall finally to square the circle:

> So, if a law be in opposition to the Constitution ... the Court must determine which of these conflicting rules governs the case. This is of the very essence of judicial duty. If, then, the Courts are to regard the Constitution, and the Constitution is superior to any ordinary act of the Legislature, the Constitution, and not such ordinary act, must govern the case to which they both apply [*Marbury v. Madison* (1803)].

QED!

"A Despotic Branch"

Marbury v. Madison is trebly worrying in regard to the doctrine of the separation of powers:

- Not only did it give the judiciary the right to strike down Acts of Congress held to be unconstitutional.
- It also gave them the exclusive right to interpret the Constitution, a power that the Constitution itself does not confer on it, but which has become accepted as valid constitutional law.
- It gave the judiciary the ability to add to its own power simply by means of a Supreme Court decision—which is also nowhere to be found in the Constitution; and is in any case contrary to the whole principle of the separation of powers.

Jefferson's own take was quite different. This is what he said about Marbury's case:

> If this opinion be sound, then indeed is our Constitution a complete felo de se. (act of suicide).... The Constitution, on this hypothesis, is a mere thing of wax in the hands of the judiciary, which they may twist, and shape into any form they please. It should be remembered, as an axiom of eternal truth in politics, that whatever power in any government is independent, is absolute also; in theory only, at first, while the spirit of the people is up, but in practice, as fast as that relaxes. Independence can be trusted nowhere but with the people in mass. They are inherently independent of all but moral law. My construction of the Constitution is ... that each dept [or branch of government] is truly independent of the others and has an equal right to decide for itself what is the meaning of the Constitution in the cases submitted to its action; and especially where it is to act ultimately and without appeal.... In the case of Marbury and Madison, the

federal judges declared that commissions, signed and sealed by the President were valid, although not delivered. I deemed delivery essential to complete a deed, which, as long as it remains in the hands of the party, is as yet no deed, it is in *posse* only, but not in *esse*, and I withheld delivery of the commissions. They cannot issue a mandamus to the President or legislature, or to any of their officers (Thomas Jefferson to Spencer Roane, 6 September 1819—Jefferson 2019).

Above all, the effect of *Marbury* is to give a group of unelected justices the power to strike down as unconstitutional any laws passed by a democratically elected Congress that the unelected justices deem unconstitutional.

Here is what Jefferson wrote to Abigail Adams, John Adams's wife, who agreed with her husband and with John Marshall:

> You seem to think it devolved on the judges to decide on the validity of the sedition law. . . . But the opinion which gives to the judges the right to decide what laws are constitutional and what not, not only for themselves in their own sphere of action but for the Legislature and Executive also in their spheres, would make the judiciary a despotic branch (Thomas Jefferson to Abigail Adams, 11 September, 1804—Jefferson Works 12:135–38).

Despite Jefferson's visceral antipathy toward Marshall, he never felt able to take any action against him. It appears that he was hoping to have Marshall impeached, but after the failure of the impeachment of Justice Samuel Chase in 1804, he gave up that idea, remarking: "Impeachment is a farce which will not be tried again." Nevertheless, he did not hold back from attacking Marshall in his correspondence. Here is what Jefferson wrote about him in a letter to his friend and successor as president, James Madison:

> [A]nd infinitely the more from the want of any counterpoise to the rancorous hatred which Marshall bears to the government of his country, and from the cunning and sophistry within which he is able to enshroud himself. . .. His twistifications in the case of Marbury, in that of Burr, and the late Yazoo case, shew how dexterously he can reconcile law to his personal biases (Jefferson to James Madison, 25 May 1810; Jefferson 2019).

Judicial Review Today

Despite Jefferson's vehement opposition to Marshall's "twistifications," as he called them, he did nothing to counter the Court's "usurpations" (except for an abortive attempt to have Justice Samuel Chase impeached), and judicial review has remained the chief weapon in the Court's arsenal to this day, resulting in some quirky, not to say seriously aberrant, decisions, and some sharp changes in direction, including:

- *Roe v. Wade* (1973)—which deemed abortion a fundamental constitutional right, which in turn was loosely based on a right to privacy that was essentially plucked out of the air—was struck down by a 6–3 majority, in *Dobbs v. Jackson Women's Health Organization* (2022) on the ground that the right to abortion was not "deeply rooted in this nation's history or tradition," nor considered a right when the Due Process Clause of the Fourteenth Amendment was ratified in 1868 and formed no part of US law until *Roe*.
- *Citizens United v. Federal Election Commission* (2010), a 5–4 majority decision, which struck down the provision in the McCain-Feingold Act of 2002 prohibiting corporations and unions from making election campaign broadcasts within 60 days of a general election. This Supreme Court decision threw open the floodgates to special interest groups, allowing them to spend unlimited amounts of money in financing election campaigns in the media in the run-up to the election. The majority on the Court naïvely treated the issue as simply a matter of freedom of speech—election advertisements being characterized as "political speech." Justice Anthony Kennedy for the majority wrote: "If the First Amendment [guaranteeing freedom of speech] has any force, it prohibits Congress from fining or jailing citizens, or associations of citizens, for simply engaging in political speech." In his hard-hitting dissenting opinion, Justice John Paul Stevens argued that the vast sums of money that corporations are now allowed to spend on election campaigns will "unfairly influence" the electoral process. With characteristic wry humor he remarked: "While American democracy is imperfect, few outside the majority of this Court would have thought its flaws included a dearth of corporate money in politics." The effect of *Citizens United* (plus *Speechnow.org v. Federal Election Commission*) has been the proliferation of "super PACs" ("political action committees"), which, because they do not themselves make direct contributions to candidates or parties, are allowed to accept unlimited contributions, which are then used to finance political advertising campaigns.
- *Loper Bright Enterprises v. Raimondo* (2024), together with *Relentless Inc. v. Department of Commerce* (2024), overruled the principle of "Chevron deference" established in *Chevron USA Inc. v. Natural Resources Defence Council* (1984), under which a court had to defer to an agency's "reasonable interpretation" of an ambiguity in a law enforced by that agency. Now any issue of legislative ambiguity is determined primarily by the courts. So the 2024 decisions enhanced judicial power against that of the executive branch, interpreted as a conservative backlash against "big government."

FDR's "Court-Packing" Threat

The only president to seriously challenge the Court's exorbitant use of judicial review was Franklin Roosevelt (1882–1945), a number of whose "New Deal" programs were struck down as unconstitutional by the Supreme Court, despite having been signed into law and enjoying great popular support. Roosevelt retaliated against what he called the Court's "horse-and-buggy definition of interstate commerce." In his "fireside chat" on the radio on 9 March 1937, the first of his second term, which he had won by a landslide even bigger than in 1932, he described the American form of government as a three-horse team—the president, the Congress, and the courts. And he lashed out at the Supreme Court: "Two of the horses are pulling in unison today; the third is not." He outlined his plan "to infuse new blood" into the Supreme Court (and the other federal courts) by appointing an additional justice for every member of the Court over the age of 70. Six of the nine justices were already over 70. They were appointed for life (which is still the case today), so, if they chose to stay on, under Roosevelt's "court-packing" plan (as it was dubbed by its detractors) the president would have had the right to name an extra six justices, making a total of 15. In the event, however, Roosevelt did not have to resort to this drastic solution, as Justice Owen Roberts, who had previously voted consistently against New Deal

Figure 23   President Franklin Roosevelt and Winston Churchill, 1941.
SOURCE: US Navy / Wikimedia Commons / Public domain.

legislation, unexpectedly changed sides in the case of *West Coast Hotel v. Parrish*, in what was jocularly referred to as "the switch in time that saved nine" (i.e. the existing bench of nine justices). In a memorandum written 10 years later, Roberts strenuously denied that Roosevelt's threat to pack the Court "had any causal relation to my action in the Parrish case." However, there is evidence that, on the basis of the overwhelming support for Roosevelt's New Deal evinced by the 1936 election, Chief Justice Hughes persuaded Roberts to join him in henceforth supporting FDR's "New Deal."

The Right to Vote

In the new American Republic it was not only slaves who lacked rights. In most states the right to vote was restricted to men of property, which, it is estimated, left more than half of white men disfranchised (Thorpe 1898). It was only with the rise of "Jacksonian democracy" that the franchise was gradually extended, so that, as far as white men were concerned, by 1850 nearly all property qualifications had been lifted.

This development, followed by a bloody civil war (1861–65), ushering in egalitarian amendments to the Constitution, left the country still very much in the hands of the propertied classes—an oligarchy. The Supreme Court's 1954 egalitarian decision in *Brown v. Board of Education*, followed by President Lyndon Johnson's Civil Rights Act of 1964 and Voting Rights Act of 1965 finally gave African Americans the practical right to vote.

Yet the system of government still contains some essentially undemocratic features:

- **Presidential elections.** The electoral college system coupled with "winner-take-all" voting. In every state (except Nebraska and Maine), the candidate with the most votes automatically receives *all* that state's electoral votes, and the candidate with an absolute majority of *electoral* votes (*not* popular votes) becomes president. So, even if candidate P receives just one more vote than candidate Q in, say, Florida, candidate P takes all 30 of Florida's electoral votes. Nebraska and Maine are the only states to partition their electoral vote between the candidates using the so-called "district method."
- **Congress.** The first-past-the-post or winner-take-all system applies to Congressional elections too. Unlike a proportional representation system, in which a party's proportion of the vote determines its proportion of seats, in the first-past-the-post system a party could poll 40% of the vote across the country without winning a single seat in the House of Representatives or the Senate. As a result, only large parties survive in America, and there has been a two-party system throughout its history, the two parties since 1854

being known as the Democrats and the Republicans. This system also results in a large number of "safe" seats, where there is virtually no contest. In the 2014 Congressional elections, for example, five major polling organizations identified no fewer than 354 of the 435 seats in the House of Representatives as "safe" seats.

- **Gerrymandering.** When in 1812 Governor Elbridge Gerry of Massachusetts signed a Bill redistricting the state senate election districts to favor his own party, a map of the new districts was hit upon by a cartoonist, who noticed that the elongated shape of one such district resembled a salamander. "Salamander?" went the quip. "No, Gerrymander" (a combination of "Gerry" and "salamander"). In a series of recent cases, culminating in *Alexander v. South Carolina NAACP* (2024), the US Supreme Court has, by a majority, ruled that, except in cases of "racial gerrymandering" (which this was not), claims against "partisan gerrymandering," which had previously been declared unconstitutional, were political questions beyond the reach of the federal courts.
- **Judicial review.** This power, discussed above, which gives the US Supreme Court the power to strike down any Act of Congress which the Court deems to be "unconstitutional," flies in the face of the constitutional principle of the separation of powers and is essentially undemocratic.
- **Campaign finance.** See the *Citizens United* case discussed above.

Mount Rushmore

It is no accident that the four presidents honored with gigantic sculptures on Mount Rushmore were all "strong" presidents, though the power of the presidency has increased considerably since the project was initiated in 1927. The four figures carved into the mountain are George Washington, Thomas Jefferson, Abraham Lincoln, and Theodore Roosevelt. These four were selected by the sculptor, Gutzon Borglum, an American of Danish origin, supposedly to represent the America's birth, growth, preservation, and development, respectively, but that is a rather superficial way of classifying the four presidents.

George Washington

The first president, George Washington (in office 1789–97), was evidently an impressive leader, though not much of an orator and not an intellectual or thinker. Standing well over six foot tall with his natural long hair curled and powdered in the style of a fashionable wig, he had a reserved personality but commanded widespread respect. Unanimously appointed commander-in-chief of the "Continental Army" to lead the fight against Great Britain for the independence of the 13 North American colonies, he went on to be elected twice as president, both times unanimously again, but chose not to serve a third term, thus creating an unofficial precedent, which (after being broken by Franklin Roosevelt) was made official by the Twenty-second Amendment to the US Constitution, ratified in 1951. Though hailed as the "father of his country" from well before his presidency, he eschewed honorific forms of address such as "Your Highness" or "Your Excellency," asking to be called simply "Mr President," which has remained the form of address ever since. When a "federal district" was selected as the capital in 1789, it was named after him, and, confusingly, when, a century later, a "territory" on the Pacific coast was admitted as the 42nd state in 1889, that too was named "Washington." Washington has pride of place on the currency, appearing on the one-dollar bill and the 25-cent coin ("quarter"). Even the stars and stripes on the "star-spangled banner" have a Washington connection—taken from the coat of arms of George Washington's ancestors in the old country.

Though a natural leader, Washington was not power-hungry, had no interest in becoming a dictator, and made sparing use of his veto power over legislation, remarking candidly: "I give my Signature to many Bills with which my Judgment is at variance" (quoted in Ellis 1999, p. 133).

It is important to note that the American Revolution was a demand by the elite of the colonial population for self-government in the form of an oligarchy. As discussed above, they were averse to the very idea of democracy, and it is estimated that the poorest colonial settlers, amounting to about 40% of the free population, moved to Canada to remain under British rule. Washington was a slave owner, and at his death in 1799 there were 317 slaves on his estate. Among others, his personal slave, Hercules Posey, had escaped to a "free" northern state and was never found. Washington never responded to any of the anti-slavery petitions that he received, and slavery is not mentioned in his Farewell Address.

"Imperial Presidency"

In a 1973 book titled *The Imperial Presidency,* historian and Democratic party activist Arthur M. Schlesinger Jr held that presidential power had been extended unofficially during wartime (Schlesinger 1973). The first example of this that he identified was the deployment of troops to the disputed area between Texas and Mexico by President **James K. Polk** (in office 1845–49), leading to the Mexican-American War. But the driving force behind this was the belief in America's "manifest destiny," a slogan first coined in the 1844 presidential election won by Polk and essentially representing a thinly disguised form of American imperialism, which was still in evidence in the twenty-first century.

Schlesinger next cited the suspension of *habeas corpus* by **Abraham Lincoln** (in office 1861–65), where the president ignored a ruling by Chief Justice Roger

Taney (sitting as a circuit judge) in *Ex parte Merryman* (1861). John Merryman had been arrested for destroying railroad bridges in Maryland on which Union troops were traveling during the American Civil War. Merriman's lawyers petitioned the chief justice for *habeas corpus,* an order to release Merriman. Taney promptly ordered the Union Army general in charge to produce Merriman before Taney the next day. Lincoln ordered the general to ignore the judge's order and to continue holding Merriman in custody. Taney came out strongly against Lincoln's abuse of power, as Taney saw it, pointing out that according to Article I, Section 9 of the US Constitution, *habeas corpus* could be suspended only by Congress, not the president. Congress subsequently validated Lincoln's position, and the matter still remains moot today. But it was certainly a stretch of presidential power to ignore a judicial grant of *habeas corpus.* In public opinion surveys since 1948, Lincoln has consistently been ranked number one, which seems strange for someone who presided over the deadliest military conflict in American history, an avoidable civil war accounting for the slaughter of at least 620,000 men under arms plus an unaccountable number of civilian deaths; who initiated the long-term humiliation and subjugation of the defeated Confederacy in the euphemistically named "Reconstruction"; and whose solution to the slavery question was to deport the freed slaves to Africa—and whose hubris was so great and common sense so low that he took no proper precautions sitting in an open theater box just a few miles from the North–South border just five days after the Union victory.

But the conflict between the president and the unelected US Supreme Court appointed for life goes back much further, to **Thomas Jefferson's** bridling at Chief Justice John Marshall's "twistifications" and pontifications in *Marbury v. Madison* (1803) and generally, as discussed above. But, though itching to cut Marshall down to size, Jefferson never plucked up enough courage to even attempt to do so, fulminating instead in private for the rest of his life.

One of the strongest presidents was **Andrew Jackson** (in office 1829–37), who showed his populist tendencies against the elitist President John Quincy Adams (in office 1825–29) by declaring that "the voice of the people ... must be heard." At his inauguration in 1829 he threw the White House open to allcomers, earning him the nickname "King Mob." Believing that government officials should be responsible to the popular will, he introduced "rotation in office," giving each new president the right to replace incumbent office-holders with his own supporters—which came to be known as the "spoils system"—though some degree of patronage had already been introduced by earlier presidents, including Washington himself. Though reduced under the Pendleton Act of 1883, 150 years later the spoils system is far from dead—especially in appointments to high-level domestic positions and sensitive diplomatic postings.

"Jacksonian democracy" saw a great expansion of the franchise to cover most white men over 21. Jackson and his loyal subordinate, Martin van Buren, who succeeded him as president, were instrumental into developing the Democratic Party as a loose coalition of poor farmers, the urban working class, and Irish Catholics, leading to the beginnings of a genuine two-party system, with the Democrats being opposed first by the Whigs, and then, from 1854 onwards, by the new Republican Party, misleadingly labeled "Grand Old Party."

Jackson's populism gave him the sobriquet "the People's President," but it also earned him denunciation by left- and right-wing opponents as a tyrant. Never one to give up a fight, Jackson resisted Chief Justice Marshall's ruling in *Worcester v. Georgia* (1832) to the effect that the Cherokee Nation was sovereign and that the state of Georgia had no right to enforce state laws in its territory. Jackson's response to this ruling, as roughly summarized 20 years later, was to throw down this challenge: "Well, John Marshall has made his decision, now let him enforce it." The Court, of course, had no way of doing this. The ultimate losers were the Cherokees. In 1830 Jackson had signed into law the Indian Removal Act, giving the president the right to negotiate treaties to purchase tribal lands to relocate Native Americans to reserves west of the Mississippi, but agreement was often reached by exerting undue pressure. The policy enhanced Jackson's popularity, because the additional 170,000 square miles of land that it added to the public domain was redistributed to small farmers, who were given the opportunity to purchase land at low prices. This policy is now the basis of attacks on Jackson's memory, coupled with demands for the removal, for example, of his image from the 20-dollar bill.

Thanks largely to Jackson, the power of the presidency had expanded greatly since the days of George Washington. Thereafter, the expansion of presidential power was largely the product of war, which in turn was driven by the concept, often unspoken, of "manifest destiny."

The presidency of **William McKinley** (1897–1901) is sometimes said to mark a transition from congressional domination of the government to the strong presidency of the twentieth century, and the successful Spanish-American War fought on his watch gave the United States control over Hawaii, Puerto Rico, Guam, the Philippines, and Cuba, all of which, except for the Philippines (which was granted independence in 1946) and Cuba (which threw off American domination under Fidel Castro in 1959), still remain under American rule, with Hawaii becoming a state in 1960. This amounted to a major extension of the "Monroe Doctrine." The doctrine, proposed by President **James Monroe** (in office 1817–25) is essentially a warning to European powers against interfering in the politics of the Americas. McKinley and later presidents extended the concept to allow United States interference.

McKinley's assassination in 1901 handed the presidency to **Theodore Roosevelt** (in office 1901–09), a much more aggressive leader, whose motto, likening America to the world's policeman, was "Speak softly and carry a big stick, and you will go far." Not surprisingly, he issued the "Roosevelt Corollary" to the Monroe Doctrine, which threatened not only Europe but Latin

America as well with America's "exercise of an international police power." His pet project was the Panama Canal, which enabled American ships to cross easily from the Pacific to the Atlantic Ocean. In domestic affairs as well, he used the "bully pulpit" of the presidency to hammer home his extensive "progressive" program.

Woodrow Wilson (in office 1913–21) was a strange bundle of contradictions. As an academic he wrote a book titled *Congressional Government*, which championed the cause of legislative power coupled with a weak executive, yet he was a strong president, going so far as to present Congress soon after inauguration with a comprehensive legislative program, being the first president ever to do this. He also revived the practice of giving an annual State of the Union address at a joint session of Congress—something that, since Jefferson's presidency (1801–09), had been done only by way of a written report.

Though World War I had been raging in Europe since 1914, Wilson won re-election in 1916 on an anti-war platform with slogans such as "America First" and "He kept us out of war." Less than two weeks after his second inauguration in 1917, he obtained Congressional consent for a declaration of war against Germany. After victory was achieved by the Allies (in no small measure through the American involvement) Wilson emerged as a "liberal" world statesman dictating the punitive terms of the disastrous Treaty of Versailles, which dismembered the multinational Austro-Hungarian and Ottoman empires, giving self-determination to numerous nations, imposed unrealistic swingeing "reparations" on Germany, and established the ill-fated League of Nations, of which, despite its being Wilson's brainchild, the United States never became a member.

By contrast with his image as a liberal, Wilson was a believer in racial segregation. As a young boy who sympathized with the defeated South in the Civil War, Wilson had actually witnessed the humiliation of the handcuffed Jefferson Davis, president of the defeated Confederacy, being carted off to prison. And his position had not changed by the time he became president. He segregated the federal bureaucracy, with separate lunchrooms and toilets, and gave a speech explaining to African Americans why segregation was in their interests, while making it harder for them to obtain appointment to a civil service post.

The greatest expansion of presidential power has occurred since the first election of FDR (in office 1933–45), the only president to break the then unofficial two-term limit by being elected four times (and then dying in office). Until his time the president had only a small staff, who operated not from the White House, as is now the case, but from the so-called "President's Room" in the Capitol building housing Congress. The Executive Office of the Presidency was established in 1939, now housed mostly in the Eisenhower Executive Office

Building adjoining the White House, which had begun life in 1888 as the "*State, War, and Navy* (SWAN) Building."

Though his power was already greatly enhanced through the introduction of the "New Deal" right at the beginning of his presidency, entry into World War II in 1941 expanded it yet further. Roosevelt's power did not go entirely unchallenged, particularly by the US Supreme Court, which struck down several major New Deal programs as unconstitutional. Not one to allow such a setback, Roosevelt labelled the court's majority position as belonging to the "horse and buggy" era and sought to counter it with a "court-packing" scheme, which in the end was not needed because of Justice Owen Roberts's "switch that saved nine" (see above).

President **Harry S. Truman's** use of the atomic bomb on Japan in 1945 to bring an end to World War II made the US the greatest power on earth, but the proliferation of nuclear technology and a lack of commitment on the part of the US troops since the Korean War of 1950–53 have weakened its position, especially after a series of unnecessary and unsuccessful wars, starting with President **John F. Kennedy's** disastrous "Bay of Pigs" invasion of Cuba in 1961; the catastrophic Vietnam War conducted under five US presidents from 1955 to 1975; and the senseless and failed wars against Iraq (2003–11) and Afghanistan (2001–21).

Domestically, the forced resignation of President **Richard Nixon** over the "Watergate" scandal greatly weakened the presidency, though Nixon himself, who had opened up China to America, remained a highly honoured guest there. Internal divisions between the two political parties widened, resulting in three failed presidential impeachments, that of **Bill Clinton** in 1998 (the first since the failed impeachment of **Andrew Johnson** in 1868) and those of **Donald Trump** in 2019 and 2021, together with civil and criminal prosecutions of Trump and a number of his associates, resulting in prison time for some of them. Such was the lack of trust in politics that the result of the 2020 election, in which **Joe Biden** was elected president over Trump, was disputed with force when on 6 January 2021 the Capitol Building was attacked by a mob of Trump supporters unsuccessfully attempting to prevent Biden from being declared president. Trump's unexpected but conclusive 2024 victory, in the popular vote as well as in the electoral college, made it clear that the allegiance of, in particular, male, blue-collar, manual, and non-college-educated workers had shifted significantly from the Democratic to the Republican column, and in particular to fervent personal loyalty to Donald Trump himself. Another big surprise was the switch in Latino votes in his direction, again especially the males, among whom he actually won a majority. Trump's promise of "mass deportations" of illegal migrants struck a chord with these voters. Another major policy announcement is an increase in tariffs, the likely effects of which are hotly debated. Trump's populism is likely to enhance his power in his second term, and, if Trump's successor as Republican leader can perpetuate the shift in party support, a more populist and more "imperial" presidency is likely to result.

Who Runs America?

In his "Farewell Address to the Nation" delivered on 17 January 1961, President Dwight D. Eisenhower, a former five-star general, gave a stern warning against "the military-industrial complex": "In the councils of government, we must guard against the acquisition of unwarranted influence, whether sought or unsought, by the military-industrial complex. We must never let the weight of this combination endanger our liberties or democratic processes."

The term "military-industrial complex" refers to the close relationship between the military and the defense industry that it supplies. It links up with the contention in the 1956 book, *The Power Elite,* by sociologist C. Wright Mills that an unelected class of military, business and political leaders, which he dubbed "the power elite," dominated power in America (Mills 1956). Mills identified six interlocking power elites:

- **"The metropolitan 400"**—"high society" families as listed in the *Social Register.*
- **"Celebrities"**—big names from the world of entertainment and sport.
- **"The corporate rich"**—those in control of major corporations, today including internet moguls.
- **"The warlords"**—the Joint Chiefs of Staff and other senior military officers.
- **"The political directorate"**—Mills described this as "fifty-odd men of the executive branch" of the US federal government. Today this group must include women as well as men.

Some More Recent Theories

"Who governs? Who really rules? To what extent is the broad body of US citizens sovereign, semi-sovereign or largely powerless?" These are the questions that Professors Martin Gilens and Benjamin I. Page set themselves in their 2012 study, under the ambitious title, *Testing Theories of American Politics: Elites, Interest Groups, and Average Citizens* (Gilens & Page, 2014). They identify four alternative "families of theories":

- **Electoral democracy**—these theories "attribute US government policies chiefly to the collective will of average citizens, who are seen as empowered by democratic elections. . ... A fair amount of empirical evidence has been adduced ... that seems to support the notion that the median voter determines the results of much or most policy making. This evidence indicates that US federal government policy is consistent with majority preferences roughly two-thirds of the time." However, "Recent research by Larry Bartels and by one of the present authors (Gilens), which explicitly brings the preferences of 'affluent' Americans into the analysis along with the preferences of those lower in the income distribution, indicates that the apparent connection between public policy and the preferences of the average citizen may indeed be largely or entirely spurious."

- **Economic-elite domination**—this theory argues that "US policy making is dominated by individuals who have substantial economic resources, i.e. high levels of income or wealth—including but not limited to, ownership of business firms." The authors cite G. William Domhoff's "landmark work in this tradition," which explains how elites "may dominate key issues in US policy making despite the existence of democratic elections."
- **Majoritarian pluralism**—this school can be traced back to (future President) James Madison's argument in *Federalist Papers* No. 10 that struggles between diverse factions (i.e. parties) "would lead to policies more or less representative of the needs and interests of the citizenry as a whole."
- **Biased pluralism**—"Numerous case studies have detailed instances in which all but the most dedicated sceptic is likely to perceive interest-group influence at work." They reject the efforts—particularly during the Cold War era, when unflattering depictions of US policies may have been thought unpatriotic—to demonstrate that interest groups have no influence on policy at all.

Conclusion

There is just far too much evidence against regarding America as a democracy. C. Wright Mills's *Power Elite* still probably provides a better answer to the question "Who runs America?" than any of these more recent theories—provided one adds to his six interlocking elites the US Supreme Court and of course the president, making the system a rare form of **hybrid** between monarchy and oligarchy.

Chapter 24
Theocracy and Caesaropapism

The word "theocracy" comes from the Greek theos *("god") plus* kratia *("rule"), so "the rule of God/a god/gods." As divinities can only exercise power through some human agency, what "theocracy" means in practice is a state ruled by religious authorities. Caesaropapism (from "Caesar" plus "pope") is the combination of political with religious power, under the secular authority. The German sociologist and historian Max Weber (1864–1920) defined it as "the complete subordination of priests to secular power."*

In both these theoretically opposite systems there is no separation between state and church. The difference is that caesaropapism represents the subordination of the church to the state, and, more particularly, to a king or emperor; a theocracy is just the opposite, where the state is under the control of the church.

The distinction between Mesopotamian and Egyptian kingship is worth highlighting. The Egyptian pharaoh was seen not only as the intermediary between the gods and mankind, and as responsible for maintaining Maat (cosmic order, balance, justice), but as being a god himself, the incarnation of Horus. The Mesopotamian king, or lugal, *by contrast, was not seen as a god himself but rather as "the head of a theocratic society who exists as a high priest and political ruler, responsible for interpreting the will and laws of the gods on earth and making offerings in their favor for the advancement of the city" (Giffen 2021). In theory this meant that, while the pharaoh was an absolute ruler who could make whatever laws he liked, the Mesopotamian king needed a divine mandate, as illustrated, for example, by the Babylonian King Hammurabi (r. 1792–1750 BCE) from the sun god Shamash. But how much difference did this distinction between Egyptian and Mesopotamian kingship make in practice? In respect of power structure, probably very little, if any. In the New Kingdom of Egypt (c. 1539–1077 BCE), for example, power was evidently in the hands of the priests of Amun until it was wrested from them by Akhenaten with his new "Aten" religion, only to be restored to them after his death. Similarly, the decisions in favor of Cyrus the Great by the Babylonian god Marduk were actually Cyrus's own decisions.*

The Byzantine Empire may be regarded as exemplifying caesaropapism because of the strong control exercised by the emperor over the church, but by the same token the church also exerted considerable influence over the emperor. The Iranian regime since 1979 is a good example of theocratic government, governed as it is by a clerical "supreme leader," who outranks the president (sometimes also a cleric) and has direct or indirect control over all branches of government. A number of states in history have had kings invested with divine status, like the Egyptian pharaohs and, until recently, the emperors of Japan.

Byzantine Empire: Caesaropapism or Theocracy?

In the Byzantine Empire there was a close, almost symbiotic relationship between church and state. Was this a form of caesaropapism, as has sometimes been suggested, or a theocracy? Emperors certainly lent their support to the church by outlawing heretics and persecuting non-Christians but would also occasionally issue their own ecclesiastical edicts without the approval of a church council. Emperors would also convoke church councils, over whom they could exert a certain amount of influence, and exercised control over church appointments, including that of the Patriarch of Constantinople and, indeed, even of the pope in Rome, though this latter power lasted only from 537 to 752. This nexus between church and state, beginning with Constantine's convocation of the Council of Nicaea in 325, lasted throughout Byzantine history, with very few exceptions, and effectively resulted in mutual dependence of the two institutions, very different from the West where, for example, the so-called Investiture Controversy pitted church against state in a long-running conflict from 1076 to 1122, which resulted in the decline in monarchical power and an increase in the power of local lords throughout the Holy Roman empire (chiefly Germany and part of Italy.)

The best examples of theocracy at the time of this writing are Vatican City and Iran.

Vatican City

By the Lateran Pacts between Fascist Italy and the Holy See under Pope Pius XI in 1929, Vatican City came into existence as an independent state under the sovereignty of the pope, who is elected for life, though a very small number of popes have resigned or abdicated. Besides the Lateran Treaty itself and a financial annex, there was a Concordat regulating relations between Italy and the Catholic Church.

Vatican City is the world's smallest state in area and population, with only 764 citizens as of 2023. The government of Vatican City is unique. The pope is the sovereign, with legislative authority exercised in his name by the Pontifical Commission, the president of which, until 2025 always male, has some executive power as well, delegated to him or her by the pope.

Despite this, the pope has absolute executive, legislative, and judicial power. He also has sole power to create new cardinals, who generally hold that title for life, and it is the College of Cardinals under the age of 80 who elect a new pope, which requires a two-thirds majority.

According to a Roman Catholic dogma finalized at the First Vatican Council of 1869–70, the pope is infallible when speaking *ex cathedra* ("from the throne"), referring to pronouncements made officially.

Islamic Republic of Iran

Since 1979 Iran, or Persia, has been under a theocratic government headed by a "supreme leader." This regime replaced a monarchy under Mohammad Reza Shah Pahlavi, discussed in Chapter 31. At the time of this writing, there had only been two "supreme leaders" of the Islamic Republic of Iran: Ayatolla Ruhollah Khomeini (1979–89) and Ayatolla Ali Hosseini Khamenei (since 1989).

On 28 September 1978 the US Defence Intelligence Agency reported that the shah "is expected to remain actively in power over the next ten years." Yet, on 16 January 1979, less than four months later, the shah of Iran, Mohammad Reza Pahlavi, fled Iran never to return, leaving the country in the hands of Shapour Bakhtiar as interim prime minister, who had warned of "the dangers of clerical despotism and how the fascism of the mullahs would be darker than any military junta" (Milani 2008, p. 109). Neither the Americans nor Bakhtiar, a social democrat who had actually been jailed a few times for "insulting the shah," realized just how widespread opposition to the regime was. On 11 February 1979, the army declared itself neutral and refused to shore up the government, causing Bakhtiar's administration to collapse. On the same day, the leader of the revolutionary movement, Shiite Islamic cleric Ayatollah Ruhollah Khomeini, named Mehdi Bazargan as his own interim prime minister and demanded obedience to him as "God's government." On 30/31 March 1979 a referendum was held, asking: "Should the monarchy be abolished in favor of an Islamic Government?" According to the official count, 98% said "yes." In a further referendum held on 2/3 December 1979, the Constitution of the Islamic Republic of Iran was ratified, according to official figures, by 99.5%, and in yet a further referendum, held in 1989, the constitution was amended.

Despite promises of democracy made by Khomeini before he took power, the constitution is overtly theocratic. The supreme leader, who has to be a Shia Islamic cleric, superintends the operation of the executive, legislature, and judiciary, and he is also commander-in-chief of the armed forces. The supreme leader is appointed for life by the Assembly of Experts made up of 88 *mujtahids* ("clerics") elected by direct public vote for an eight-year term from a strictly vetted list of candidates. (In 2016, of the 801 applicants only 166 candidates were approved.) The body that does the vetting is the Guardian Council of 12 members, six Islamic *faqihs* ("experts in Islamic law") selected by the supreme leader and six Islamic "jurists" elected by the *Majlis* ("Parliament") from among jurists nominated by the chief justice (also appointed by the supreme leader). The Guardian Council can decide who can run for national office and can veto laws passed by the *Majlis*. The *Majlis,* currently made up of 290 seats, 8% of whom are women, is a legislature (elected by citizens aged over 18) with very restricted powers, as all legislation is subject to a veto by the Guardian Council. And all candidates have likewise to be approved. Candidates must be between 30 and 75 and have at least a master's degree or Islamic seminary diploma. In the *Majlis* elected in 2024, 233 of the 290 seats were won by "Principlists," better described as religious fundamentalists. The president of Iran is also popularly elected for a four-year term (and a maximum of eight years), but, despite the title, is not head of state, a position occupied by the supreme leader. The judiciary is supposedly independent, but judges have to demonstrate a commitment to Islamic principles and are selected by the chief justice, who, as mentioned above, is himself appointed by the supreme leader.

The irony of this whole development is that it is the result of a historical accident. Until Shah Ismail I (r. 1501–24) switched to Shia, Iran was a Sunni state. His only reason for changing was evidently to be different from the Ottoman Empire, whose sultan claimed to be the caliph ("head") of Islam worldwide. Had Persia remained Sunni, a theocracy like the current one could never have come into existence, as Sunni Islam does not really have formal clergy like the Shia.

Priests and Rulers in Ancient Mesopotamia

Religion and government both go back to the earliest historic times, and beyond. In Sumeria, before there were empires there were city-states under a form of theocratic government, each with its own priest-king. Each city-state had its own tutelary god with their own temple. When a number of cities came together voluntarily to form a larger state, they would share the same gods, temples, and worship.

Sumerian civilization began between 4500 and 4000 BCE, though the earliest historical records in the form of cuneiform tablets date only from around 2900 BCE. The earliest documents contain myths and legends about the gods in a polytheistic anthropomorphic pantheon, the most notable gods including An(u), Enlil, and Enki, who are portrayed in very human terms. Scholarly opinion generally takes the view that, in the earliest records, the gods were each allocated a particular "portfolio" related to natural cosmic and terrestrial forces, and that it was only later on, with the development of urbanization from about 2,500 BCE, that gods came to be identified with a particular city-state. It is perhaps more likely that each god had a dual identity, in terms of natural phenomena and local allegiance at the same time.

Each patron or tutelary god had their own temple and a high priest known in Sumerian as *en* or *ensi,* who evidently ran the government of their state as well as officiating in the temple. Somewhat later on we come across the title *lugal* (Sumerian for "big man"), often translated as "king," evidently a higher title than *en* or *ensi,* though it is not clear what the relationship was between the titles *en, ensi,* and *lugal.* Even when replaced by kings (*lugal*), the priests continued to be influential, and the *lugal* clearly had a religious as well as a secular role.

Sargon of Akkad

Sargon of Akkad or Agade (c. 2334–2279 BCE), a leading claimant for the title of founder of the first "empire," proclaimed himself "king of Akkad, overseer of Inanna, king of Kish, anointed of Anu, king of the land, governor of Enlil: he defeated the city of Uruk and tore down its walls, in the battle of Uruk he won, captured Lugalzagesi king of Uruk in the course of the battle and led him in a collar to the gate of Enlil" (inscription, Schøyen Collection).

Sargon triumphed over 34 cities in all, notably Uruk, Ur, E-Ninmar, Lagash, and Umma, and made Mari and Elam tributary to himself (MS2814, Schøyen Collection).

And again: "The god Enlil gave to him [the Upper Sea and] the [Low]er Sea" (Sargon inscription, E2.1.1.1).

And yet again: "Sargon the King bowed down to Dagan in Tuttul. He (Dagan) gave to him (Sargon) the Upper Land: Mari, Iarmuti and Ebla, as far as the Cedar Forest and the Silver Mountains."

Sargon also claimed to have conquered Elam and Parahshum, the two leading states east of Sumer. He referred to himself as "anointed of Anu," which presumably means that Sargon claimed the approval of this important sky god, associated with Uruk, one of the cities that Sargon conquered.

Sargon claimed that "the god Enlil gave him the Lower Sea (Persian Gulf) and the Upper Sea (Mediterranean)" (inscription). Enlil, started out as chief god of Nippur, one of the Sumerian cities conquered by Sargon. So holy was he that no other god could so much as look at him. Sargon's self-abasement before Dagan is also significant, as that god, primarily worshipped in Tuttul (in present-day Syria), one of Sargon's conquests, was a leading source of royal legitimacy.

Sargon installed his daughter Enheduanna as priestess of the Sumerian moon god Nanna, equated with the Akkadian moon god Sin or Suen, whose main cult center was Ur. Enheduanna is identified as the author of a number of Sumerian hymns, which continued to be used in the temple for at least six centuries after her time. Her appointment to this important post may well have been intended to help to cement ties between the Semitic Akkadian religion of her father Sargon and the religion of the vanquished Sumerians.

With his conquests extending from the Persian Gulf to the Mediterranean, Sargon claimed to be the ruler of "all the lands under heaven" and "from sunrise to sunset." The ensis, the priestly rulers of the conquered city-states, generally retained their positions but their status was reduced to that of vassals or provincial governors under Sargon. By the time of Sargon's grandson Naram-Sin (r. c. 2254–2218 BCE), the king was not just "Lord of the four quarters (of the world)" but for the first time a living god (*dingir*) with his own temple and worship.

Up to that time, the closest a king got to divinity was after his death. At some time between 2900 and 2700 BCE, Gilgamesh, the hero of the epic poem bearing his name, who probably was a historic king of the Sumerian city-state of Uruk, emerged posthumously as a god worshipped in various locations across Sumer and later as a judge of the dead in the underworld.

Like Sargon, Naram-Sin made *his* daughter high priestess of the Sumerian moon god, Nanna-Sin in Ur; both grandfather and grandson appointed their sons as *ensi,* provincial governors; and both also married their daughters off to vassal rulers of remote parts of the empire, while they relied on local people as tax collectors.

Another way in which Sargon and his successors retained the loyalty of their Sumerian subjects was by making Sumerian the official language of religion, ceremonial and administration—a status which it continued to enjoy in Mesopotamia at large until the first century CE, even though it had been replaced as a spoken language by about 2000 BCE.

"The Seven Gods Who Decree"

At the head of the Sumerian pantheon were seven gods, sometimes referred to as "the seven gods who decree." The number seven was sacred to the Sumerians—hence the seven-day week, which even the French Revolution was unable to abolish. The seven gods were An(u), Enlil, Enki, Nanna, Inanna, Utu, and Ninhursag.

The Sumerians themselves, who were neither Semitic nor Indo-European, were conquered and absorbed by the Akkadians, later the Babylonians, still later the Assyrians, and later still the Persians—yet, as mentioned above, the Sumerian language survived for centuries as the language of religion and, with it, the Sumerian gods either under their original names or by becoming equated with gods of the conquerors.

Alternatively, a conqueror would either destroy the patron god of the conquered state and replace it with his own god or pay homage to the conquered god in the conquered state while still worshipping his own patron god in his home state.

Enki: The Sumerian god Enki was worshipped by the Babylonians and Assyrians under the name of Ea and possibly by the Canaanites as Ia. Originally associated with the city of Eridu (near modern Basra in Iraq), where there was a temple more than 6,500 years ago, which was only abandoned during the Persian period.

Enlil was the head of the Sumerian pantheon, later known as Ellil, whose chief seat of worship was his temple in the city of Nippur. Besides his association with Nippur, Enlil was chiefly a storm god, with very wide powers. He is credited with separating heaven from earth and thereby making the earth habitable, inventing the mattock and promoting agriculture. In the Sumerian creation myth, Enlil rewards King Ziusudra with immortality for having survived the flood, though in the Babylonian version of the flood myth Enlil caused the flood himself to exterminate the human race for disturbing his sleep. Enlil was also an earth god. According to one Sumerian hymn, such was the brightness of his glory that the other gods could not gaze at him. He rose to prominence with the rise of Nippur in the twenty-fourth century BCE and his cult declined after Nippur was sacked by the Elamites in 1230 BCE and he was replaced by Marduk as the chief Mesopotamian god.

Besides his cosmological associations, Enlil was seen as a just and moral ruler who was emulated by kings from the whole Sumerian region who traveled to Nippur in order to be legitimized by Enlil. Babylonian kings continued to offer Enlil this homage even after he had been replaced by Marduk as chief god.

Enlil was worshipped as Elil or Ellil by the Babylonians, whose first period of dominance, as the Amorite-controlled Old Babylonian Empire is generally dated from about 1894 BCE to about 1595 BCE. Babylon was then conquered by the Hittites, who handed it over to their allies the Kassites, who would control it for the next four centuries (c. 1592–1155 BCE), during which time Nippur regained importance, and Enlil with it. In the Middle Assyrian Empire covering an area from west of the Euphrates to east of the Tigris well north of Babylon from about 1363 to 912 BCE, the Assyrian national god Ashur merged with Enlil with titles such as "the Assyrian Enlil." However, the two gods were still treated as separate in the Tukulti-Ninurta Epic describing the war between the Assyrian King Tukulti-Ninurta I (r. c. 1243–1207 BCE) and the Kassite Babylonian King Kashtiliash IV (r. c. 1232–1225 BCE), which was something of a Pyrrhic victory for the Assyrians, who, though capturing Kashtiliash IV and carting him off in chains to Assyria, ordering a massacre of many inhabitants of Babylon, and abducting the image of the Babylonian god Marduk, were met with rebellion and the intervention of the Elamites, and had to return Babylon to the Kassites. The Tukulti-Ninurta Epic, written from the Assyrian point of view, portrays the Assyrian king as the innocent victim of the Babylonian king, who is accused of breaking a treaty between the two empires and making an unprovoked attack on Assyria, which so offended the Babylonians' own gods that they abandoned their sanctuaries.

El, the Hebrew version of **Enlil,** occurs numerous times in the Hebrew Bible, referring sometimes to the Jewish God, whose specific name was YHWH (the Hebrew alphabet lacks vowels), or translating the generic concept of "god." It still survives in numerous theophoric names, such as Daniel ("God is my judge"), Emmanuel ("God with us"), Israel ("God rules"), Michael ("Who is like unto God?"), and Samuel ("God heard"). The Jewish God is also repeatedly referred to in the Hebrew Bible as *Elohim,* the plural of *El,* but is treated as grammatically singular and takes a verb with a singular ending. The Arabic *Allah,* the Muslim word for God, has the same origin. The Jewish god is portrayed in the Jewish Bible as ruling the Jews in a type of theocracy through leaders such as Moses in the Exodus from Egypt, and Joshua in the occupation of the Holy Land, and then through the prophet Samuel up to the establishment of a monarchy, first under Saul, and then, when he proved unworthy, under David and Solomon (c. 970–831 BCE), who is directed to build the Temple, which was destroyed by the Neo-Babylonian King Nebuchadnezzar in 586 BCE and replaced by the Second Temple in about 516 BCE, which was destroyed by the Romans in 70 CE.

Shamash: In his counter-attack against Babylon, Tukulti-Ninurta (c. 1243–1207 BCE) is said to have had the support of the sun god Shamash, who had a wide remit, including the ability to monitor everyone's actions on earth and dispense justice accordingly. Shamash was the sixth god in the Early Dynastic god list from modern Fara after Anu, Enlil, Inanna, Enki, and Nanna, but his ranking seems to have slipped later. There are some isolated references to Shamash as the supreme god, but this never became general. Though known to the Babylonians and Akkadians by the name of Shamash, his Sumerian name was Utu, and he was also associated with the Hurrian sun god Shimige. Another name by which he is known is Amna, probably from the same Semitic root as the Hebrew word *amen,* which is of course still in daily use in Jewish, Christian, and Islamic worship, meaning originally "confirmed" or, in religious services and benedictions, "let it be so, it is true."

Shamash, or possibly Marduk, is portrayed on a stele showing him investing the Babylonian King Hammurabi (r. c.1792–c.1750 BCE) with his royal insignia. Probably the best known representation of Shamash is in the Louver stele showing Hammurabi receiving his famous law code from the god. In the lengthy prolog, Hammurabi pays respect to Shamash, but top billing goes to other gods: Anu, Bel, and Marduk.

Inanna: Known as "the queen of Heaven," this powerful Sumerian goddess, known to the Akkadians, Babylonians, and Assyrians as Ishtar, had her main cult center at Uruk, of which she was the patron goddess. Her husband was the Sumerian god Dumuzid, known to the Semites as Tammuz. Inanna was believed to have been given by Enki on behalf of Enlil the *mes,* divine decrees regulating

Sumerian social and religious institutions and conduct. She was the twin sister of Utu (Shamash). So close was the perceived relationship between gods and humans that this great goddess could actually be condemned to death by the seven judges of the underworld, though she is saved from this fate by Enki, who sends two sexless assistants to rescue her and her husband is then dragged down to the underworld to replace her. In the Early Dynastic period, Kish's tutelary god was Ishtar (Sumerian: Inanna) with her consort Ea, but by the Old Babylonian era, Ishtar had been joined by Zababa with his wife Bau. Ishtar was also the tutelary goddess of Uruk, which was in fact her main center of worship.

Gilgamesh

The Epic of Gilgamesh was an Akkadian compilation based on Sumerian poems some of which date back to about 2100 BCE in the Third Dynasty of Ur. The oldest surviving version of the composite epic, known as the "Old Babylonian" version, dates from the eighteenth century BCE and is titled "Surpassing All Other Kings." Although encrusted with many legendary and mythical elements, the epic seems to have been based on an actual King Gilgamesh of the Sumerian city-state of Uruk during the early part of the Early Dynastic period (c. 2900–2350 BCE). Inscription: "Gilgamesh is the one whom Utu has selected." He was evidently deified soon after his death, and in the twenty-first century BCE King Utu-hengal of Uruk worshipped Gilgamesh as his patron deity. And there are clay tablets inscribed with prayers addressed to Gilgamesh as a judge of the dead in the underworld.

Despite this tradition, the original story portrays Gilgamesh very differently, as a repressive king of Uruk, whom the gods wanted to stop oppressing the people of Uruk. To this end they created Enkidu, a wild man who challenges Gilgamesh to a test of strength, which Gilgamesh wins, but the two men become friends anyway and embark on a number of adventures together, including the slaying of the Bull of Heaven sent to attack the pair by the goddess Ishtar/Inanna after Gilgamesh spurns her proposal of marriage. Surprisingly, perhaps, it is Enkidu not Gilgamesh who is punished with death by the gods. After repeatedly failing the trials presented to him in his search for immortality, Gilgamesh eventually gives up on his quest for immortality and returns home to Uruk. In an early variant Sumerian version of the story, Gilgamesh is portrayed as a brother of the goddess Inanna (Ishtar) who saves a special tree and converts it into a throne for the goddess.

The main *Epic of Gilgamesh* contains some mixed messages about Gilgamesh as a king and about kingship in general. But the poem headed "Gilgamesh and Aga" dating from the Old Babylonian period (c. 1894–1595 BCE), the only Gilgamesh poem apparently lacking any mythical elements, is more informative on that score. Aga, king of Kish, exceeds his authority as Uruk's overlord by demanding that Uruk's inhabitants dig wells for Kish. As a leading citizen of Uruk, Gilgamesh advises his fellow citizens to refuse to comply, but

Uruk's "city fathers" advise submission to Aga's demands. Gilgamesh repeats his advice to refuse Ada's demeaning demand, and this time the city fathers accept his advice and appoint him as *lugal* (king). Aga then besieges Uruk with his army, and after some initial confusion is defeated, captured, and withdraws his demand, thus ending Kish's hegemony over Uruk.

The relevance of this poem to Sumerian kingship is four-fold. First, it reveals the original elective nature of Sumerian kingship and the importance of the "city fathers." Secondly, it reveals the power exerted by the king once elected, as Gilgamesh is shown here to be completely in charge of Uruk's military response to Aga's invasion and siege, emitting a divine radiance that cows the Kishite army though Aga himself remains immune to it.

Thirdly, it gives a picture of a hierarchy of city-states, with some subordinate to others and their kings in a similar relationship to one another. It appears that Kish exercised hegemony not only over Uruk but had at one time been dominant over all the Sumerian city-states. Such was the importance of Kish that control of it was taken as legitimizing dominance over northern Mesopotamia, much as control of Nippur legitimized dominance over the south. And later kings affected the style "King of Kish" even if they were rulers of other cities, not including Kish. The Sumerian King List claims that Kish was the first city to have a king after the flood, and its language appears to have been Sumerian, though some writers have identified it as a Semitic-speaking city, which would turn the Kish–Uruk conflict into a Sumerian–Semitic competition for supremacy. However, this seems unlikely. Kish was under Babylonian control under Sin-Muballit, his son Hammurabi, and his successor Samsu-Iluna who all did major construction work, including rebuilding the city walls. Kish loses its importance after the Achaemenid period but had a late blooming under Sassanian and Islamic rule before being completely abandoned during the later years of the Abbasid Caliphate (750–1258).

Fourthly and finally, while otherwise lacking in any mythical or legendary elements, the poem does specifically mention the god Utu (Shamash) as being instrumental in Gilgamesh's releasing Aga after defeating him.

Rulers and Religion in Ancient Egypt

The monarchy with religious associations par excellence was that of ancient Egypt. From the unification of Upper and Lower Egypt in around 3150 BCE, the monarch, known as pharaoh, was believed to be divine, as the incarnation of the god Horus, the Egyptian tutelary deity depicted as a falcon-headed man wearing the *pschent,* the double red and white crown (white for Upper Egypt and red for Lower Egypt). From the reign of Intef I (r. 2133–2117 BCE) the ruling pharaoh came to be regarded as a manifestation of Horus in his lifetime and as Osiris after his death. By the time of Pharaoh Djedefre in the twenty-sixth century BCE, the pharaoh's father was believed to be the sun god Ra (or Re), prior to which his father was Atum, the primordial god from whom all else arose.

The unification of Egypt was itself possibly the result of a religious conflict. Upper Egypt (the south), represented by Horus, conquered Lower Egypt (the north), associated with Set. Horus and Set are variously portrayed as brothers and as nephew and uncle, with Set being Osiris's hostile brother and Horus being the son of Isis ad Osiris. This linkage is highly dubious, but does at least give some idea of the centrality of religion to the Egyptian monarchy and to Egyptian life generally. Each new pharaoh was believed to renew *Maat*, (order, morality, harmony, balance, justice) on his accession, in emulation of Horus, and, as part of the royal coronation ceremony introduced by Pharaoh Pepi II Neferkare (r. 2278-c. 2216), the new pharaoh was represented by a naked infant being suckled by his mother Isis (which possibly inspired the Christian Madonna and child image).

Even from predynastic times there were 20 men, "the Great Ten of Upper Egypt" and "the Great Ten of Lower Egypt," of unknown origin, who appear to have formed a sort of *eminence grise*, exercising power behind the throne, possibly an indication of a powerful oligarchy or hereditary aristocratic cabal, though nothing is known of any religious connections of these powerful men.

Pepi II Neferkare's power appears to have been weakened by nomarchs, hereditary regional governors, who were exempt from taxation—together with priests. Pepi II's presumed grandfather, Pepi I, had already shown signs of weakness by marrying two sisters who were daughters of a nomarch and later appointed their brother a vizier. Pepi II was the son of one of these sisters. Pepi II evidently had trouble with his viziers. He split the role, separating the vizier of Upper Egypt from that of Lower Egypt, whose seat was moved several times. But again these viziers are not known to have had any religious connections or allies. Pepi II's reign was succeeded by decades of famine and civil strife.

Priests of Amun

The pharaoh had a more serious rival in power than the nomarchs, and that was the priests, and especially the priests of Amun, worshipped as one of the most powerful gods. The priests were not only exempt from taxation but were actually in receipt of tax revenues, which enabled them to amass great wealth, even rivaling that of the pharaoh. And the power of the Amun priesthood was about to burgeon even more. In about 1780 BCE, Lower Egypt was invaded and taken over by the so-called Hyksos, who were eventually driven out by Ahmose I (c. 1570–1544 BCE). This catapulted Amun, hitherto essentially a local Theban god, into the status of savior of Egypt through his servant Ahmose, which enriched the priests of Amun even more.

Amenhotep III

Amenhotep III (r. 1391-c 1351) inherited from his father, Tuthmose IV, an empire of prodigious size, wealth, power, and international influence. He celebrated "Sed" festivals marking, respectively, 30, 34, and 37 years of his reign, which, while nominally in honor of Amun, elevated the pharaoh himself being a near god to one divine. (Kozloff, 2012, p. 195.) While not challenging the priests of Amun directly, he was evidently aware of the danger that their wealth and power posed to the crown. He accordingly elevated to the position of his own personal tutelary deity the minor sun god Aten, hitherto subordinate to the chief sun god, Ra (or Re). Unlike Ra, who was represented as a human male with the head of a falcon, Aten was non-anthropomorphic, depicted simply as the disc of the sun, with which the pharaoh merged at death.

Akhenaten

Amenhotep III's son and successor, Amenhotep IV, took his father's tentative steps against the overmighty priests to unprecedented lengths. After making Aten the chief god and declaring himself the son of Aten, he changed his name to Akhenaten, made himself the sole intermediary between Aten and the Egyptian people, and moved the capital from Thebes to "Akhetaten," or Amarna, He then went so far as to ban the worship of all other gods and ordered the defacing of the temples of Amun throughout Egypt. The "Great Hymn to the Aten," possibly composed by Akhenaten himself, put the position quite squarely: "O Sole God beside whom there is none! You made the earth as you wished, you alone.... You are in my heart, and there is none who knows you except your son."

Akhenaten seems to have miscalculated the likely effect of his cataclysmic religious reforms. He was trying to strengthen his position as pharaoh against that of the priests, and the hymns to the Aten actually focus as much or even more on the pharaoh than on his chosen god. In the words of Prof John Baines: "Amarna religion was a religion of god and king, or even of king first and then god" (Baines 1997, p. 281).

However, if he was trying to deprive the priests of Amun of their great wealth and power, he failed, as his reforms were reversed soon after his death, in the reign of his young son and eventual successor, who changed his name from Tutankhaten back to Tutankhamen or Tutankhamun, meaning "Living Image of Amun." Akhenaten's name was erased from all monuments, so much so that his existence was effectively obliterated for well over two millennia until the discovery of Amarna in the late nineteenth century, The Egyptian religion before the reform was a polytheistic communal religion with which the people could identify and which gave worshippers a choice of a whole array of gods, some of whom were in conflict with one another. The religion of the Aten, by contrast, was exclusive and intolerant. It has been suggested by some Egyptologists that Akhenaten's experiment actually had the effect of lowering the pharaoh's position in relation to his people. Before Akhenaten the pharaoh was the son of Ra, the living incarnation of Horus, and the representative of the divine order on earth. Akhenaten did his best to subvert this relationship. In an important public speech given before his name-change, Akhenaten lashed out at the ancestral gods of Egypt that it should have been his duty to honor and protect: "The temples of the gods have fallen to ruin, their bodies do not endure.... I have watched as the gods have ceased their appearances, one after the other. All of them have stopped, except the god who gave birth to himself" (cited in van Dijk 1993). With the reversal of Akhenaten's reforms, in the words of a recent study, "The king was no longer a god, but god himself had become king. Once Amun had been recognized as the true king, the political power of the earthly rulers could be reduced to a minimum" (ibid., p. 307).

Priests of Amun Back

For at least two centuries before the death of Amenhotep III, the temple of Amun at Karnak was the largest in Egypt and its priests had become more powerful than ever. After the Amarna period, the priests of Amun were back in business and growing in importance. In the Leiden Hymns, dating from the reign of Ramesses II (c. 1279–1213 BCE), Amun, Ra (Re), and Ptah (the god of creation) are treated as a trinity.

From 1080 to about 943 BCE in the so-called Third Intermediate Period, the power of the priests of Amun practically eclipsed that of the pharaoh. Egypt was under non-native, mostly Libyan, pharaohs, the prestige of the crown declined together with that of Egypt itself, and Thebes was essentially ruled by the high priest of Amun. The god supposedly made political decisions through his statue, which communicated by nodding assent. High Priest Pinedjem I was the effective ruler of Upper Egypt from 1054 to 1032 BCE, and his son assumed the throne and ruled Egypt from the new northern capital of Tanis for almost half a century as Pharaoh Psusennes I (r. 1047–1001 BCE), and a relative of his would later combine at the same time the position of high priest of Amun at Thebes (in the south) with that of Pharaoh Psusennes II based in Tanis (in the north) (r. 967–943 BCE). This just shows the stranglehold that the priests of Amun had over Egypt at this time.

Perceiving the priests as a threat to his own position, the Libyan pharaoh Shoshenq I (942–922 BCE) abolished hereditary priesthoods and reserved to himself the appointment of "god's wives" (a highly prestigious honorary position occupied by women). He stopped well short of banning the cult of Amun, which had become immensely popular as well as inordinately rich and powerful, but he did curtail its power to some extent. In about 750 BCE the Nubian pharaoh Kashta appointed his daughter as "gods' wife of Amun," making her the most powerful woman and the effective ruler of Upper Egypt. Kashta's son, Piye (r. 767–731 BCE), followed suit by appointing *his* daughter as "god's wife" and left her in charge of Upper Egypt while on campaign against Lower Egypt. The same pattern was followed by the pharaohs who succeeded Piye until the Persian conquest of 525 BCE, when the power of the priests of Amun was curtailed and the position of "god's wife" was abolished. However, the cult of Amun continued to flourish at Meroe, the capital of the Nubian Kingdom of Kush, until it was finally given its quietus by King Ergamenes of Meroe in about 285 BCE. According to the Greek historian Diodorus Siculus of the first century BCE, such was the power of the priests that, through a supposed oracle, they could even order a king to kill himself. But Ergamenes, envying the power of his contemporary, the Egyptian pharaoh Ptolemy II, had all the priests massacred "and instituted himself a new religion" (Diod. Sic. 3.2.6).

Akhenaten was no doubt right in seeing the priesthood of Amun as representing a threat to royal power. However, he did nothing to attract popular support to himself and his god as an alternative. So deeply embedded in the Egyptian national psyche was trust and faith in the traditional gods of Egypt that, when Akhenaten's attempt to undermine the age-old Egyptian pantheon rebounded on him, it not only benefited the priests but also greatly reduced the standing of the monarchy. This lesson, which was to be learned by Alexander and the Ptolemies, was lost on the Persians.

Persian Rule

Though the Persian Cambyses II, who conquered Egypt in 525 BCE, was given an Egyptian pharaonic name and tried to show respect for Egyptian culture and traditions, he alienated the support of the Egyptian priesthood by stopping their access to tax revenue. But Cambyses's execution of two thousand sons of Egyptian noblemen, including the son of Pharaoh Psammetichus III, followed by the putting down of a revolt staged by the defeated pharaoh coupled with the destruction of a good number of temples, did nothing to endear him to his new Egyptian subjects. The long reign of Cambyses's son and successor Darius I (r. 522–486 BCE) was also punctuated by several unsuccessful attempts to overthrow the Persian yoke. In 460 BCE Inaros, grandson of Psammetichus III, led a partially successful rising against Persian rule with Athenian assistance. After depriving the Persians of control over part of Egypt he was eventually, in 454 BCE, carried off to the Persian capital, Susa, where he was crucified.

A successful rising under Amyrtaeous in 404 BCE (facilitated by a disputed succession to the Persian throne) brought Persian rule over Egypt to an end, but the Persians managed to regain control of Egypt by eventually defeating the beloved Pharaoh Nectanebo II, whose popularity was largely based on his devotion to the traditional gods of Egypt with elaborate building programs in honor of Khnum, the

Apis Bull, Buchis (the *ka* or life force of the war god Montu), Anhur (a war god), and, of course, Amun. The Persians tried unsuccessfully to reconquer Egypt in 385, 383, 373, and 351, meeting with a resounding defeat on that last occasion, on the basis of which Nectanebo was hailed by the Egyptian people as "Nectanebo the divine falcon" and had shrines established in his name.

However, in 340 or 339 BCE, Nectanebo was finally defeated by the Persian King Artaxerxes III, who proceeded to destroy city walls, loot temples, and increase taxation. Believers in the Egyptian religion were persecuted and Egyptian sacred books pillaged. But the Persians would not have long to enjoy their ill-gotten gains. In 338 BCE Artaxerxes III was poisoned by the court eunuch and vizier Bagoas, who then proceeded to poison the new king, Artaxerxes IV Arses.

Alexander the Great

Intent on conquering the Persian Empire, in 334 BCE Alexander the Great crossed the Hellespont with an army of about fifty-five thousand and a fleet of 120 ships manned by crews numbering some thirty-eight thousand. Throwing a spear into Asian soil, he announced his acceptance of Asia as a gift from the gods. Granting city after city autonomy as he cut along the coast, when he reached the Phrygian capital of Gordium he met the challenge of the Gordian knot by simply slicing through it with his sword, thereby fulfilling the prophecy that whoever succeeded in untying the knot would become the "king of Asia." Defeated by Alexander at the Battle of Issus in 333 BCE, Darius fled, leaving behind his wife, mother, two daughters and incalculable treasure—not to mention a thoroughly demoralized army. Rejecting Darius's peace overtures, Alexander proceeded to cut a victorious swathe to Egypt, where he was welcomed as a liberator from Persian rule. He restored temples that had been neglected or destroyed by the Persians, built new temples to the Egyptian gods, and was crowned as pharaoh in the temple of Ptah in Memphis. He deliberately took a trip to consult the oracle of Amun-Ra at the remote oasis at Siwah, which pronounced him the son of Amun (or Ammon), on the basis of which he was always thereafter portrayed on coins, with the ram's horns of Amun, symbolizing divinity, protruding from his head. Not least, during his brief stay in Egypt he founded the city of Alexandria, which would become the populous, prosperous, and influential capital of Ptolemaic Egypt.

Ptolemaic Egypt

On Alexander's sudden death in Babylon at the age of 32 in 323 BCE, there was a good deal of confusion and jockeying for position among his leading lieutenants. Intent on staking his claim to Egypt, Ptolemy, a Macedonian, one of Alexander's closest associates and one of his most trusted generals, intercepted Alexander's body and had it brought to Egypt, where it was buried initially in Memphis and later in Alexandria. After a long series of wars among the so-called *Diadochoi*, or "successors," Ptolemy eventually emerged victorious as far as Egypt was concerned, had himself crowned "King and Pharaoh Ptolemy Soter" ("Savior") in 305 BCE, and ruled Egypt until his death in 282 BCE, establishing a hereditary dynasty that would last for almost three centuries, until 30 BCE.

The Ptolemies kept a delicate balance between their unabashed Hellenism and their identification with Egyptian culture, tradition, and religion. From the very outset thousands of Greeks and Macedonians flocked to take up the land grants offered by the regime, which afforded them a privileged position in Egyptian society. Koine Greek became the main official language of Egypt, though Demotic (a popular version of the original Egyptian language) was used in a subordinate capacity. The Greeks retained the citizenship of their original home states, were subject to Greek, not Egyptian, law, lived in separate communities from the native Egyptians, and occupied most top administrative and military positions, though as time went by, intermarriage produced a new Greco-Egyptian educated class. The Library of Alexandria, and the Mouseion which housed it, opened its doors during the reign of Ptolemy II Philadelphos (r. 285–246 BCE) and would soon become a major cultural and intellectual center in the Greek world, complete with accommodation for a number of resident scholars. It lasted well into Roman times and was evidently finally destroyed around 270 CE.

Figure 24 Ptolemy II.
SOURCE: Naples National Archaeological Museum / Wikimedia Commons / CC BY SA 2.5.

While a keen champion of Greek culture and scholarship, Ptolemy II also went to the traditional Egyptian extreme of marrying his own sister and boasting about it by taking the sobriquet *Philadelphos* ("Sister-lover"), though the marriage may not have been consummated, as it produced no issue. When this incestuous marriage was mocked in an obscene satirical verse, the Greek poet concerned was cruelly punished by being sealed into a lead casket and dropped into the sea. Nevertheless, brother–sister marriages became common among the Ptolemies, resulting in a certain amount of degeneration of the stock. It is not known whether incestuous marriage, which revulsed Greek moral propriety, had the desired effect of gratifying Egyptian opinion.

Serapis

The Egyptian religion was a communal religion, and, like most other communal religions, it was tolerant of other religions. The Ptolemies were exemplary rulers in this respect, and they promoted a new syncretist Greco-Egyptian deity, Serapis—but not at the expense of the traditional Egyptian gods. His image was typically Greek in appearance, and his cult drew elements from the worship of Osiris and the Apis Bull, with the accretion of attributes associated with the Greek gods Pluto, Demeter, and Dionysus. Serapis became extremely popular, not only in Egypt but throughout the Greco-Roman world, and his image can even be found together with that of the reigning Roman emperor on coins from the time of Vespasian (r. 69–79 CE) on. Its success made the cult of Serapis a prime target for Christian persecution, and, when pagan worship was outlawed by the Emperor Theodosius I in 391, the huge and magnificent Serapeum, or temple of Serapis in Alexandria, was destroyed after a long siege by a Christian mob directed by Pope Theophilus of Alexandria.

But the Ptolemies' devotion to Serapis did not stop them from lavishing attention on the traditional gods of Egypt, thereby legitimizing themselves as genuine Egyptian pharaohs. Ptolemy II's Egyptian subjects cannot but have been impressed by the vast scale of his temple-building program, which was continued by his son and successor Ptolemy III Euergetes, including the Temple of Horus at Edfu in Upper Egypt. Such was the scale of this temple that, construction having begun in 237 BCE, it was not completed until 57 BCE.

Rosetta Stone

In 236 BCE Ptolemy III convoked a synod of all Egyptian priests, and his son Ptolemy IV Philopator followed this precedent with a synod of all priests held in Memphis in 217 BCE. A series of pharaonic decrees was issued reflecting the relationship between the Ptolemies and the Egyptian priesthood. The Ptolemies were only too well aware of their need for a good rapport with the priests, upon which, to some extent at least, the Ptolemies' legitimacy as rulers of Egypt depended. This is well illustrated by the Rosetta Stone, whose fame derives from its linguistic importance, written in hieroglyphics with a translation into Demotic and also into Greek, it proved to be the key to deciphering hieroglyphics, which had baffled scholars for centuries. But the content of the Rosetta Stone, which is largely ignored, has a significance of its own. It is a decree issued in 196 BCE, in which the assembled priests of Ptah proclaimed the anointing of the young Ptolemy V Epiphanes as pharaoh and celebrating the quelling of a very serious revolt against Ptolemaic rule led by Horwennefer or Ankhwennefer, which lasted from 205 BCE until it was finally put down in 186 BCE, during which time quite a large part of Egypt was under rebel control. The decree goes into detail on the tax breaks given to the priesthood, the temples, the army, and the general population. The decree also celebrates the bounty in silver and grain bestowed by the pharaoh on the temples and the restoration and reconstruction of temples throughout Egypt. In addition, temples throughout Egypt were ordered to erect a statue of the pharaoh "in the most conspicuous place in the temple" and this was to be attended by priests three times a day. Furthermore, the ordinary population was invited to have in their homes a gold shrine similar to that found in the temples containing a statue of the pharaoh. Ten copies of the decree survive, a sign of just how important it was to the government. Reliance on priestly support was clearly crucial to the regime, but the priests did not themselves pose a danger to the Ptolemies' control over the country. By contrast with the elaborate Greek and Macedonian bureaucracy that administered Ptolemaic Egypt, the priests were native Egyptians, and, though many of them were probably able to speak Greek, they did not have their hands on the levers of power. Where their support counted was in corralling the general population in support of the regime, and bringing the pharaonic cult into private homes cannot but have assisted in this regard. The Ptolemies were shrewd rulers, who carefully avoided making the mistakes of Akhenaten, who did not understand the need to attract the populace into supporting his revolutionary new religion. The Ptolemies also avoided the mistake of the Persians, who did nothing to win the support of the priests. How much individual power the Ptolemies themselves wielded, as distinct from the Greco-Macedonian elite, is hard to say, but their regime was for the most part stable, fair, and tolerant, and Egypt was extremely prosperous under their rule.

Alexandria

Alexandria, a major Hellenistic cultural center and one of the most populous and prosperous ports in the Mediterranean, was largely stable and peaceful under the Ptolemies. Its Egyptian, Greek, and Jewish populations were, sensibly, each allocated a separate sector of the city. The Ptolemies did not persecute anyone for their religion, and the Jewish population of Alexandria was large and flourishing under their rule, though there would be clashes between Greeks and Jews much later under Roman rule. So important was Alexandria as a Jewish center that the famous Septuagint, a translation of the Hebrew Bible into Koine Greek, was undertaken there at the behest of Ptolemy II and became the standard biblical text for Jews, for whom Greek was and remained the lingua franca in the eastern Mediterranean in Roman and into Byzantine times.

The Jews

The Ptolemies' toleration of the Jewish religion contrasted with the attitude to the Jews under another of the post-Alexandrian empires, that of the Seleucids of Syria, who appear to have pursued an active Hellenizing policy aimed, according to Josephus, at stamping out the Jewish religion.

But what about the treatment of the Jews in pre-Ptolemaic Egypt? The historicity of the biblical accounts of Joseph, Moses, and the Exodus is widely questioned. But there are some snippets of evidence that may be worth considering.

The earliest non-biblical account of the Exodus is that of the Greek historian Hecataeus of Abdera, who wrote in about 320 BCE (as preserved in *Against Apion*, by first century CE Jewish historian Josephus, and in a variant version by the Greek historian Diodorus Siculus), who tells how the Egyptians blamed a plague on foreigners and expelled them from the country, whereupon Moses, their leader, took them to Canaan. This is obviously written from an Egyptian perspective, but the story as a whole is surprisingly similar to the biblical account. We have *plague* here, which the Bible claims was visited on the Egyptians as punishment for their refusal to let the Jews leave. We have *expulsion* rather than escape—an easy switch to make in a tendentious account. And we have *Canaan*, which is spot-on.

We can go further and link Joseph's *coat of many colors* with the distinctive garb of "Abishu the Hyksos" leading a group of visitors to Egypt, four of whom are portrayed wearing what can only be described as a colorful coat—or a *coat of many colors*. This comes from the tomb of an official called Khnumhotep, dating from about 1900 BCE. The Hyksos, who are recorded as actually ruling part of Egypt for about a century between 1640 and 1550 BCE, are described as shepherds—precisely the description given in Genesis to Joseph's family. And there is a curious little incident, almost an aside, relating to this. In trying to persuade the Egyptians to allow his family to settle in Egypt, Joseph warns his family not to reveal that they were shepherds, "for every shepherd is an abomination to the Egyptians" (Genesis 46:31). Could that be because an admission of being shepherds would remind the Egyptians of the hated Hyksos?

There are just too many coincidences here to ignore. Could the Hyksos have been Hebrews, Israelites, or Jews—or related to them? And could Joseph, with his distinctive multi-colored coat, have been one of them? The fact that there was no love lost between the Egyptians and the Hyksos comes as no surprise. The Hyksos were, after all, invaders who had wrested part of Lower Egypt from its native rulers. And is it not true that the Hyksos were expelled rather than that they asked to be allowed to leave? And that their destination was indeed Canaan? I would not press the coincidences further by suggesting any link between Akhenaten's religious reform and the Jewish religion. That link is just too tenuous.

Rulers and Religion in Ancient India

In 1947 the British Raj of India was partitioned into two states, India and Pakistan, both of which were granted independence, and in 1971 East Pakistan seceded from Pakistan to become Bangladesh. All three states became "republics," a designation which, as is shown in Chapter I, is as meaningless as the designation "monarchy." As shown in Chapter 1, the designations "monarchy" and "republic" have no meaning. It is worth noting that, while all three states have suffered some political assassinations, both Pakistan and Bangladesh have experienced military coups and periods of authoritarian rule (none of which would qualify as genuine strong popular monarchies), while India, vaunted as the world's biggest democracy, is effectively an oligarchy.

What we are concerned with in this chapter is the relationship between kings and religion in the three thousand years predating the British Raj. Throughout that period the dominant religion of the Indian subcontinent was Hinduism, a communal religion at the center of which was a hereditary caste system, which determined everyone's social and economic status and occupation. The top position in the hierarchy was occupied by the priestly caste of Brahmins. Generally speaking, if a society is stratified and headed up by a hereditary aristocracy, that aristocracy will be opposed to one-person rule because they will want to rule the roost themselves. So, if there is a king in such a society, he is likely to be a figurehead or a ceremonial head of state— weak, at best, and owing his position to the aristocracy, who will have the whip hand.

However, a priestly aristocracy like the Brahmins are an exception to this. While steeped in Vedic learning and in temple ritual and sacrifice, they would be well qualified to advise the king on ethics and morality, and could assist with clerical tasks, but they were unarmed and had no military training, so they would be unlikely to pose a threat to the throne. The lower castes' veneration of the king would form an integral part of their inherent respect for and honor of the Brahmins and the caste system as a whole.

Hinduism as a Communal Religion

Hinduism, a communal religion, is the religion of India par excellence. It is a development of the so-called Vedic religion with the accretion of a number of other traditions. The Vedic religion was brought to India by the Indo-Aryans, who reached India from Central Asia at some time between about 1800 and 1600 BCE.

Dating is very imprecise, but is assisted by linguistic analysis. The languages of India belong to one of two distinct groups: native Dravidian languages, such as modern Tamil and Telugu, in South India; and Indo-Aryan languages, notably Sanskrit and its modern descendants—including Hindi, Urdu, Bengali, Marathi, Punjabi, and Gujarati—spoken in North India. The Indo-Aryan languages were brought to India by a migration of Indo-Aryan people from Central Asia, probably from about 1800 BCE. The Indo-Aryans brought with them not only their language but also their religion, a communal religion related to the religions of other Aryan nations, such as the Greeks and the Romans. With shared deities including the Indo-Aryan sky god Dyeus, whose name and functions are parallel to the Greek god Zeus and the Roman god Jupiter (Jove). The earliest form of this Indo-Aryan religion is the Vedic religion, so called from the Sanskrit word *veda* ("knowledge"), as reflected in the Vedas, the oldest Hindu sacred texts, which are estimated to date from between 1500 and 1000 BCE or possibly between 1900 and 1200 BCE. During the Kuru Kingdom, the earliest Indian state properly so called, which occupied the area around modern Delhi between the twelfth and fifth centuries BCE, the Vedic religion developed into Brahmanism, or Brahmanical Hinduism, centered on the Brahmin priestly caste with the emphasis on ritual. The Vedic tradition was carried on by the allied Panchala Kingdom, which was one of the most powerful states of ancient India between about 1100 and 350 BCE. It was swallowed up by the Mauryan Empire between 322 and 185 BCE, then regained its independence until it was conquered by the Gupta Empire, which was at its height between 319 and 467 CE. Hinduism emerged victorious in competition with Buddhism and Jainism, which, unlike Hinduism, are essentially creed religions. This competition resulted in a resurgence of Brahmanical influence, dominating Indian society since the classical age of Hinduism 1800 or 1900 years ago, which, with the accretion of a number of other religious traditions, eventually became fully-fledged Hinduism.

Caste system

A leading feature of Hinduism is the *caste system*, which is still very much in evidence at the time of this writing. The English term "caste" (from the Portuguese *casta*) can be used to apply to two overlapping aspects of the same system: either *jati* (Sanskrit: "birth") or *varna* (Sanskrit: "color"). There are at present about 3,000 *jatis* and 25,000 *sub-jatis* in India, closed hereditary groups with defined social and occupational roles. A key feature of a *jati* is endogamy, marriage where both husband and wife belong to the same *jati*. A wide-ranging 2016 DNA study of unrelated Indians conducted by the *National Institute of Biomedical Genomics* found that interbreeding across *jatis* dipped suddenly years during the latter half of the Gupta era, which lasted from about 240 to 550 CE (*Proceedings of the National Academy of Science,* 25 January 2016). The Guptas were not inventing a system out of whole cloth, but only enforcing traditional norms. *Jati* identity and endogamy must have had a long history before then.

The other aspect of the caste system, *varna* (Sanskrrit: "color"), can probably be traced back to at least between 1500 and 1000 BCE, during the Kuru Kingdom. According to the *Manusmriti, t*here were four castes, each with its own allocated vocation. [The final form of this document, part of the Daharmasastra, probably dates from the first to third century CE. But it was evidently "a crystallization of accumulated knowledge" over a long period (Olivelle, 2009, p. 41ff)]

The four castes were (and are) as follows:

- Brahmin—the top, priestly caste
- Kshatriya—warrior caste, including the king
- Vaishya—agriculture and trade
- Shudra—artisans, laborers.

The top three *varnas* were considered "twice-born," the second birth being a spiritual initiation, or *upanayana*. It is not shared by the Shudras. And those outside the four castes, now called Dalits, Harijans, or "Scheduled Castes," were considered "untouchable."

So deep-seated and ingrained is the caste system that even Gandhi (1869–1948), the father of Indian independence, who renamed the "untouchables" as *Harijan* ("children of god"), for most of his life accepted the caste system as "responsible for the durability of Hindu society, seed of swaraj (independence), unique power of organization, means of providing primary education and raising a defense force, means of self-restraint, natural order of society, and most important of all, the eternal principle of hereditary occupation for maintaining societal order" (1922, cited online: https://www.lawctopus.com/academike/mahatma-gandhi-on-caste-gender/).

The current (1950) Indian Constitution speaks with forked tongue over "untouchability," categorically abolishing it only to let it bounce back with the aid of positive discrimination under the title of "Scheduled Castes": 'Untouchability' is abolished and its practice in any form is forbidden" (Art. 17). But in Part XVI of the Constitution we encounter a long list of special privileges enjoyed by the "Scheduled Castes," including reserved seats in the Lokh Sabah (Parliament) together with special educational and occupational concessions.

The Indian government is anxious to parry the labeling of the caste system as racism. But a dermatological study conducted in Uttar Pradesh and Bihar in 2017 found a correlation between caste and skin color, with the top castes having the lightest skin and the Dalits, (the "untouchables"), on average, the darkest. And the very fact that *jati* means "birth" and *varna* "color" is itself indicative of the ethnic origins of the system.

Tradition

According to tradition, the king was not expected to be drawn from the Brahmin priestly aristocracy but from the Kshatriya, which is understandable in the sense that his prime task was seen as safeguarding his kingdom internally and protecting it from enemies. As the Brahmins were not armed or trained as soldiers, and the Kshatriya were not priests or versed in the holy texts of Hinduism, there was a natural alliance of mutual dependence between a Kshatriya king and the Brahmin priests, who were rewarded with privileges including landholding and exemption from taxation.

Before the Mauryan Empire

For probably at least a thousand years before the Mauryan Empire (322–185 BCE), which at its height extended over the greater part of modern India, the dominant religion was communal Vedic-Brahmanism, or proto-Hinduism, supported by a succession of Kshatriya kings in alliance with the Brahmin priesthood. The Mauryan conquests replaced a number of small regional kingdoms and kept other kings in place under ultimate central control. This greatly reduced the power, prestige, wealth, and influence of the Brahmins, which was further eroded by the Mauryas' approach to religion. Without actively suppressing the traditional communal Hindu religion, the Mauryas showed themselves inclined to promote the more recent ascetic religions of Jainism, Ajivikism, and Buddhism.

Arthrashastra

In the absence of detailed historical records, we have to rely on texts straddling religion, law, and statecraft. One such work, formulated as a treatise on statecraft, is the *Arthrashastra* ("Statecraft"). Couched as a debate about advice to the Mauryan emperor, Chandragupta Maurya (322–297 BCE), it was supposedly written by his mentor and chief minister, Chanakya, or by Vishnuguptu or Kautilya, all of which may be different names for the same person. There is a slight problem in that both the supposed author and the intended recipient of his pearls of wisdom had died a good century and a half before the book was written. Like so many other early Indian texts, this appears to have undergone a number of recensions. Patrick Olivelle (2009) dates the oldest layer of text to between 150 and 50 BCE, with the final version only emerging between 175 and 300 CE. But even the earliest version is a good 150 years after the reign of the Emperor Chandragupta Maurya (r. 322–297 BCE).

The problem with the dating of the *Arthrashastra* casts a long shadow over how its contents are to be understood. But, regardless of date, it is a curious document, to say the least. Though not a religious treatise, it is predicated on the *varna*-based caste system. "This people consisting of four castes and four orders of religious life, when governed by the king with his scepter, will keep to their respective paths" (*Arthrashastra*, Bk I, chapter 4). The list of suggested qualifications for a government minister is very long, beginning: "Native, born of high family, influential...." Though the *Arthrashastra* is sometimes compared to Machiavelli's *The Prince,* there is certainly no parallel in this regard. Machiavelli made it clear that the worst enemies a ruler could have was what he called *li grandi* ("the aristocracy, the elite"), the very element that the *Arthrashastra* advised the king to favor (ibid., chapter 9). It goes further and advises the king to delegate power to his ministers. Something that he says about the priesthood was a little more in keeping with Machiavelli's thinking: "The king shall dismiss a priest who, when ordered, refuses to teach the Vedas to an outcaste person or to officiate in a sacrificial performance (apparently) undertaken by an outcaste person (*ayajya*)" (ibid., chapter 10). Here we do at least have a glimmer of recognition that it was in the king's interest to win the support even of the lower orders. The word *ayajya* would cover the Shudras, the lowest of the four castes, but probably not the "untouchables," who were regarded as falling outside the caste system altogether.

As advice supposedly tendered to a king, we might have expected to find some historical examples. But there are none, unlike Machiavelli's *The Prince*, which is bristling with case studies drawn from ancient history as well as from recent Italian politics. And the hypothetical problems that are addressed are decidedly odd. In a chapter on punishment for "sedition" we read that the death penalty is to be imposed on "a seditious Parasava (one who is begotten by a Brahmin on Shudra wife)." This kind of "mixed marriage" was of course contrary to tradition and acceptable norms, and it is perhaps understandable that the issue of such a marriage might feel shunned and aggrieved. But to be guilty of sedition he must presumably have been placed in a responsible official position in the first place. Yet there is repeated advice on how to deal with "seditious ministers" rather than on how to prevent appointing such potential trouble-makers in the first place. And the advice offered is invariably to employ secretive and underhand methods. This advice can be extremely complex. For example, the king is advised to send a seditious minister to put down a rebellion with an army of inefficient soldiers in which "fiery spies" are secretly embedded. During the fighting, the spies "under the guise of robbers may murder the minister and declare that he was killed in the battle" (ibid., Book V, Chapter 1).

The *Arthrashastra* does also contain some advice which appears at first sight to be a bit more promising. This advice, titled *Matsya Nyaya* ("Law of the Fishes"), is simple enough: "In the absence of a ruler, the strong will swallow the weak, just as in periods of drought big fish eat little fish, but under his protection, the weak resist the strong" (ibid.). There is an assumption here that once there is a ruler in place, the weak will automatically be protected against the strong. This is simply naïve. There are all too many examples from all parts of the world of monarchs who are unaware of the danger posed to them by "the strong"—and of ordinary people who do not understand the need in their interests of a strong ruler. What is missing here is any suggestion of the mutual dependence of a strong ruler and the masses.

Mauryan Empire

Even though composed over 150 years after Chandragupta Maurya's reign, it is possible that the *Arthrashastra* still reflects some of that ruler's actual practice, notably reliance on ministers and officials of high birth, concern for the economic well-being of the population at large, and a predilection for secrecy and spying. A recent study characterizes the Mauryan Empire like this:

> The geography of the Mauryan Empire resembled a spider with a small dense body and long spindly legs. The highest echelons of imperial society lived in the inner circle composed of the ruler, his immediate family, other relatives, and close allies, who formed a dynastic core.... Outside the palace, in the capital cities, the highest ranks in the imperial elite were held by military commanders whose active loyalty and success in war determined imperial fortunes. Wherever these men failed or rebelled, dynastic power crumbled.... In provincial towns and cities, officials formed a top layer of royalty; under them, old conquered royal families were not removed, but rather subordinated. In most *janapadas* (territories), the Mauryan Empire consisted of strategic urban sites connected loosely to vast hinterlands through lineages and local elites who were there when the Mauryas arrived and were still in control when they left (Ludden 2013, p. 46 f).

The picture that emerges is of a sprawling decentralized state, with power concentrated not in the emperor but in two different elites: in the major centers a military elite appointed by the emperor, and in the provinces hereditary local elites made up of the pre-existing conquered rulers of those areas.

As explained in Chapter 2, a monarch's interests are generally at variance with those of elite groups. Strong monarchy is more likely to be achieved in alliance with the lower classes and in opposition to aristocracy or elite groups.

The Mauryas certainly appear to have eschewed any reliance on the most obvious elite group in Indian society, namely the Brahmin priesthood, but in doing so they evidently made themselves dependent on a military elite, on the one hand, and a local royal elite on the other, and possibly on a third elite group of "councilors" at various levels. We read in the *Ashokavadana* that Chandragupta's son and successor Bindusara (c. 297–273 BCE) consulted a council of 500 on the succession, but that may have been assembled specifically for that purpose. In addition to these elite groups was yet a fourth group, the so-called *dhamma-mahamattas* under Ashoka, Buddhist missionaries who developed into a type of powerful political priesthood.

Chandragupta Maurya

The first Maurya emperor, Chandragupta Maurya, hedged his bets as far as religious observance was concerned. He evidently performed regular Hindu rituals, including sacrifice, and hosted major festivals with processions of elephants and horses, which might have placated his lower-caste subjects, without however appeasing the excluded Brahmins. He also promoted Buddhism, Jainism, and the Adivikas. After a reign of about 25 years, he abdicated and ended his life by fasting to death as an ascetic Jain monk. His successor Bindusara is variously described as a devotee of Hinduism and a patron of Adivikas, an ascetic cult which had a strong belief in predestination.

Ashoka

The third and best-known Mauryan emperor was Chandragupta's grandson and (probably) Bindusara's son Asoka or Ashoka (r. c. 268–c. 232 BCE), whose empire covered a large part of the Indian subcontinent, from present-day Afghanistan to Bangladesh. According to his edicts, after conquering Kalinga (north-east India) in a brutal war he devoted himself to *dhamma* (the Pali equivalent of Sanskrit *dharma,* "righteous conduct"), meaning essentially Buddhism. He is credited with large-scale support for Buddhist activities, including financing numerous *stupras* ("meditation centeres"), the Third Buddhist Council, and the *sangha* ("assembly"), and promoting widespread Buddhist missionary activity. Though he describes himself in his many inscriptions by the traditional Hindu term, "Beloved of the gods," he was essentially a propagandist for Buddhism, a creed religion which does not really believe in any gods.

This heavy reliance on elite groups other than the Brahmins—and the displacement of the Brahmins by non-traditional elements—did not bode well for the stability of the power structure of the Mauryan Empire. Stripping the Brahmins of their power and privileges must have been deliberate policy on the part of the Mauryan emperors, and especially Ashoka. But was it really to the emperors' advantage? As a hereditary religious elite with a great deal of prestige and influence but without an army, the Brahmins could be very valuable allies to a ruler, and a strong ruler could likewise be greatly advantageous to the Brahmins. According to Hindu *dharma,* Brahmins were primarily priests (though they are known to have engaged in other occupations as well), while the monarch was meant to be drawn from the Kshatriya, or warrior caste. Brahmins were therefore unlikely to aspire to political power (though there were some exceptions), but besides being in keeping with *dharma,* a Brahmin–Kshatriya alliance could be both popular and powerful. As a communal religion, Hinduism was (and is) rooted in the home, with daily prayers and offerings to the thousands of deities being made at small shrines in private houses up and down the country. The caste system, as an integral part of the religion, likewise has deep roots. It is essentially an aristocratic hierarchy, with the Brahmins at the top followed by the Kshatriya. It was a force for stability, and kept all the castes, including those at the bottom of the social pyramid, content with their preordained lot.

Ashoka's promotion of Buddhism, which ultimately proved much more successful outside India than within it, must have caused great consternation among the Brahmins, spurring them on to retaliate in the only way they knew how and in which they were well versed, namely writing. Among other writings, we have the apocalyptic *Mahabharata* ("Great India") narrative. Depicting violent resistance to the kind of "illegitimate" political power that the Mauryas must have represented, and it depicted the restoration of proper, *brahmanya* kingship, which sees the protection of Brahmins as one of its most sacred obligations.

After half a century of weak rulers and family feuds, the Mauryan Empire gave way in 185 BCE to the Shunga Dynasty, the founder of which, Pushyamitra, was a Brahmin.

The threat to the Brahmins posed by Buddhism in the person of Ashoka is well represented by an early Buddhist text, dating probably from the fifth or fourth century BCE and couched in the form of a dialogue, in which Gautama Buddha (the founder of Buddhism) asks a Hindu Brahmin called Sonadanda for the qualities by which a Brahmin can be recognized. The Brahmin lists five qualities: "He is of pure descent on both his mother's and his father's side, he is well versed in mantras, he is of fair color handsome and pleasing, he is virtuous learned and wise, and he is the first or second to hold the sacrificial ladle." Though derived to some extent from Hinduism, Buddhism was a proselytising creed religion rejecting the whole communal ethos of Hinduism, and not least the caste system. So Buddha gets Sonadanda to eliminate all but one of the five Brahmanic qualities that he has identified. Two of these qualities are connected with heredity: "pure descent," code for upper-caste parentage; and "of fair color" meaning light-skinned. After these deletions, the only qualities left for a "true" Brahmin are that he be "virtuous, learned and wise," purely moral and intellectual qualities. This puts in a nutshell the attempt on the part of Buddha to tear the heart out of the communal religion of Hinduism and replace it with the ethical and philosophical spirit of Buddhism. In India at least, Hinduism won.

Manusmriti

An important Brahmin-oriented text is the *Manusmriti,* which, as mentioned above, in its present form dates from the third century CE but had deep roots. It is important to realize that though the *Manusmiriti* is normative or even prescriptive rather than descriptive of the actual situation on the ground, it would be a mistake to regard it as a work of pure fiction. Couched as a compilation of laws, it harks back to an earlier time when traditional *dharma* ("law, order, duty, custom") was followed, some of which might still have been practiced, or have been revived, at the time when the *Manusmiriti* was compiled.

The *Manusmriti* was written from a Brahmin point of view, setting out the criteria of traditional *dharma.* There is a strong emphasis on the close relationship between the Kshatriya king and the Brahmin priests (cited in Olivelle 2009):

7.35: "The king has been created (to be) the protector of the castes (varna) and orders, who, all according to their rank, discharge their several duties."

7.8. "Even an infant king must not be despised, (from an idea) that he is a (mere) mortal; for he is a great deity in human form."

7.32 "Let a king act with justice in his own domain, with rigor chastise his enemies, behave without duplicity toward his friends, and be lenient toward Brahmins."

7.58: The king's chief minister should be "a learned Brahmin."

7.82 "Let him honor those Brahmins who have returned from their teacher's house (after studying the Veda); for that money which is given to Brahmins is declared to be an imperishable treasure for kings."

7.88 "Not to turn back in battle, to protect the people, to honor the Brahmins, is the best means for a king to secure happiness."

7.136. "Whatever meritorious acts a Brahmin performs under the full protection of the king, thereby the King's length of life, wealth and kingdom increase."

8.21 "The kingdom of that monarch who looks on while a shudra settles the law, will sink (low), like a cow in a morass."

10.96 "A man of low caste who thru covetousness lives by the occupation of a higher one, the king shall deprive of his property and banish."

10.1 "Let the three twice-born castes (varna), discharging their (prescribed) duties, study (the Veda); but among them the Brahmin alone shall teach it. Not the other two; that is an established rule."

11.4 "But a king shall bestow, as is proper, jewels of all sorts, and presents for the sake of sacrifices on brahmins learned in the vedas."

11.31 "A Brahmin who knows the law need not bring any (offence) to the notice of the king; by his own power alone he can punish those men who injure him."

11.56 "Falsely attributing to oneself high birth, giving information to the king (regarding a crime) and falsely accusing one's teacher, (are offences) equal to slaying a brahmin."

11.84 "The Brahmin is declared to be the root of the sacred law, and the Kshatriya its top, hence he who has confessed his sin before an assembly of such men becomes pure."

Horse-Sacrifice Ceremony

Evidence of the genuine antiquity of Hinduism as a communal religion with close links to monarchy is contained in the extremely cruel but spectacular horse-sacrifice ceremony, *Ashvamedha*, an elaborate political ritual to establish a king's right to rule, enactment of which is displayed on gold coins issued by the Gupta kings Samudragupta (r. c. 350–70 CE) and Kumaragupta (r. c. 415–55 CE), showing the horse anointed and decorated for sacrifice, with the legend: "The king of kings who has performed the *Vajimedha* sacrifice wins heaven after protecting the earth." Performance of this sacrifice is documented as early as the Puru period (fourteenth century BCE); and, among others, under the Kuru Kingdom (c. 1200–900 BCE); in the Shunga period (c. 185–73 BCE, Ayodhya inscription of King "Dana"); under King Bhavanaga (r. 305–20 CE) and other Naga kings, credited with 10 horse-sacrifices; and as recently as under King Jai Singh II of what later became Jaipur (r. 1734–41 CE), who performed the horse-sacrifice ceremony to assert his independence after breaking free from Mughal suzerainty.

Mughal Empire

After seeing off the Buddhist challenge in the Gupta period, Hinduism was set fair to dominate the northern half of India until the time of the Islamic Mughal Empire (1526–1858), while the south never experienced either a Buddhist challenge or Muslim rule, but remained Hindu-dominated throughout.

Islam loomed large in Indian history with the advent of the Mughal Empire, which ruled over most of northern India from 1526 to 1858, after which the subcontinent fell under British control, until 1947. The Mughal rulers were Muslims descended from the Persianized Turco-Mongol conqueror Timur (or Tamerlane) (r. 1370–1405). Though nominally a Muslim, the Emperor Akbar (r. 1556–1605) was tolerant of Hinduism and all other religions, and even invented a syncretic monotheistic religion of his own based chiefly on Islam and Hinduism. It proved very short-lived and only ever had 21 adherents. Akbar's policy of toleration was reversed by his grandson, Shah Jahan of Taj Mahal fame (r. 1628–58), and this hostility to Hinduism was perpetuated in the long reign of Aurangzeb (1658–1707), which saw increased pressure on the population to convert to Islam, the reinstatement of the *jizya* tax on non-Muslims and the implementation of the *Fatawa Alamgir*, a Sharia-based compilation of Islamic law. Aurangzeb also came into conflict with the Sikhs, and had their leader, Guru Tegh Bahadur, beheaded because he had objected to Aurangzeb's forced conversions. Some modern writers, however, defend Aurangzeb, pointing out that he employed significantly more Hindus as officials than his predecessors had done. If true, these Hindus would have served, however, in the lower echelons of the bureaucracy.

Such was the strength of Hinduism as a communal religion and stratified social system that even three centuries of Islamic rule failed to dislodge its hold over the masses, which it retains to this day. Though the close bond between king, Brahman priesthood, and the masses was broken with the advent of the Mughals, it had already cast an indelible shadow that contributed to the stability, vigor and dynamism of Indian society that is still visible today, bolstered by the policies of Narendra Modi, who has exercised strong monarchical leadership as India's prime minister since 2014.

Part IV

Correlations and Contrasts

Chapter 25
Liberty vs. Equality

Liberté, Egalité, Fraternité! The standard combination of liberty with equality in this slogan (and others) conceals the fact that liberty and equality are in a very real sense polar opposite. Popular monarchy correlates well with equality (as in the "tall poppy syndrome"—see Chapter 15), but is inimical to liberty, which means freedom to become unequal. Fidel Castro's Cuba provides a good illustration of this.

Monarchy and Equality

In a monarchy where power is concentrated in the hands of a single person, the ruler needs support to maintain his position. He cannot obtain that support from the privileged classes, because they will want to rule the roost themselves as an oligarchy and will oppose the rise of any individual to power. So, if he is to exercise sole power, a monarch must look for support instead to the masses.

If inequality between the ruling minority and the masses is a hallmark of oligarchy, true monarchy exhibits the opposite tendency—a tendency to reduce the inequality gap between the (former) ruling oligarchy and the masses. This may be done in two different ways—either *positively* or *negatively*—or by a combination of the two. By *negative equality* I mean reducing the privileges enjoyed by elite groups—the "tall poppy syndrome" (as practiced, for example, by the Greek tyrants, and in the France of Louis XIV and XV—see Chapter 15). On the other hand, raising the level of the masses is a trend toward *positive equality*—as in Athenian "democracy."

The association of this tendency with popular monarchy is not difficult to explain. The autocratic power of a king, a dictator, or any other kind of sole ruler

Five Thousand Years of Monarchy, First Edition. Michael Arnheim.
© 2026 John Wiley & Sons, Inc. Published 2026 by John Wiley & Sons, Inc.

can only be exercised at the expense of the power of oligarchy. True monarchy and oligarchy are at opposite ends of a seesaw—as the one goes up the other inevitably goes down. Oligarchy is the default situation in any society. True monarchy can only come into existence by displacing this oligarchy. And for a true monarchy to be maintained, it needs support—from the masses or common people, who, like the sole ruler, are also at loggerheads, or potentially at loggerheads, with the former ruling elite.

But you may ask, why can't the ruler or prospective ruler do a deal with the privileged element and reach a compromise in which power is shared between him and them—in, say, a constitutional monarchy? Yes, he can, but such a compromise will not result in shared power but in oligarchy. Why? Because the ostensible monarch in that arrangement will no longer have his own independent power base but will be reliant upon the support of the privileged element, the oligarchy or aristocracy, and will in effect be capitulating to them in the long run if not immediately. Machiavelli was alive to this problem and warned "princes" (i.e. monarchs of all kinds) against having to depend for support on the nobility or the "big men" (*li grandi*). Although Machiavelli speaks of "big men," what he says applies equally to any privileged element, including one in the form of a Parliament.

Oligarchy and Inequality

Inequality is the hallmark of oligarchy. In an oligarchy, with power in the hands of a minority, that minority will do all it can to retain power together with its wealth and status, and will therefore want to keep as big a gap as possible between itself and the masses. In order to maintain this gap, the oligarchy will tend to be opposed to too much social mobility, or, to put it another way, will prefer the elites not to be too open, or, alternatively, it will not want too much equality of opportunity. The oligarchy of the feudal aristocracy of Mediaeval Europe is a good example of this.

The inequality I am referring to, that between the ruling minority and the masses, may be called *external inequality*. However, for an oligarchy to thrive, prosper, and survive for a long time, it is a good idea for it to be as close-knit as possible, and to achieve that it will help if there is a high degree of equality among its members—*internal equality*, which it is important not to confuse with *external equality*, i.e. equality between the ruling elite and the masses, which does not exist in any oligarchy. In fact, the more internal equality there is, the less external equality there is likely to be. It is in the interests of oligarchy to achieve and maintain as much *internal equality* as possible, meaning equality within the ranks of the oligarchy itself. Internal equality is a safeguard to protect the oligarchy against the rise to true monarchical power of a single individual, especially one who might be propelled to power at the head of a popular movement. A prime example of a close-knit oligarchy is Classical Sparta, where the oligarchy was so close-knit that they were known as "the Equals" (*hoi homoioi*), which of course refers purely to internal equality, which was coupled with extreme external inequality between the ruling Spartiate minority and the Helots.

Power in an oligarchy is in the hands of a minority, which, unless that minority is very small, will be self-reliant and inward-looking and will not need the support of the masses. This is another reason why there will tend to be a big gap between the ruling minority and those outside it—a gap not just in power and status but also in wealth and general well-being.

In sum, therefore, inequality is the hallmark of oligarchy, with as little social mobility as possible enabling outsiders access to the elite. In other words, in an oligarchy, the elites will tend *not* to be very open. Oligarchy is, by definition, a system in which power is exercised by a privileged minority, which therefore depends on the perpetuation of inequality between the elite and the rest of the population.

The degree of *liberty* in such a society will depend on how open or closed the elites are, i.e. on how much social mobility is permitted by the system, which in turn depends on the degree of equality of opportunity (not to be confused with equality of outcomes) that there is. A "night-watchman" or libertarian state with minimal government restrictions on individual liberty would tend to result in a high degree of inequality. Oligarchic eighteenth- and nineteenth-century Britain is a good example.

The Aristocratic/Oligarchic Ethos

Oligarchy is and always has been the "default" model of government in all parts of the world throughout history. But it is important to recognize that both oligarchy and its concomitant *factual* inequality rest on a pervasive aristocratic or oligarchic *ethos* of inequality. To put it at its simplest: *there has always been a general belief that people are not equal* (see Chapter 8). This, of course, flies in the face of the slogan "Liberty, Equality, Fraternity," "affirmative action," and "political correctness," but promotion of equality as a concept is surprisingly recent, though rare examples do pop up in earlier periods, as for example during the English Peasants' Revolt of 1381.

Athenian "Democracy"

Even Pericles, the personification of Athenian "democracy," evidently believed in the age-old Greek concept of "giving each his worth" or "giving each his due," which is the key to the central Greek concept of "justice" (*dikaiosynē*), which is based on the assumption that people are of different degrees of worth. The great Greek philosopher Aristotle goes further, and asserts and that this merit is

Figure 25   Plato and Aristotle in "The School of Athens." Web Gallery of Art / Wikimedia Commons / Public domain.

essentially hereditary: "It is reasonable to conclude that it is not the rich or the good who are well-born but those descended from ancestors who have long been rich or good" (Rose 1886, Aristotle fragment 94) (see Chapter 8).

The belief not only that people are unequal but also that inequality is inherent, innate, and hereditary correlates with preference for a closed society—a society in which social mobility is kept in check. In other words, the aristocratic or oligarchic ideal is at variance not only with egalitarian ideals but also with the modern idea of "meritocracy," which is invariably allied to a belief in "equality of opportunity."

Machiavelli

The only concepts which come anywhere near my "Two Models of Government" hypothesis (Arheim 2017) are to be found in Niccolò Machiavelli's *Il Principe* ("The Prince"), written in 1513 and published posthumously in 1532 (for a fuller discussion on Machiavelli, see Chapter 11).

There is a natural antipathy between the nobility and the common people and also between the ruler and the nobility. As a result, there is a natural bond between ruler and people, on the basis that "the enemy of my enemy is my friend." So, while the nobility are opposed to strong monarchy, strong monarchy is a bulwark of the common people against the nobility. But by no means all monarchs are aware of the danger posed to them by the nobility, and even fewer historians are conscious of this.

Evidence in Support

There is no shortage of evidence to support these insights. For example, Henri (Henry) IV, Louis XIII, Louis XIV, and Louis XV of France were only too well aware that the chief threat to the Crown came from the aristocracy. Louis XIII called the Estates General in 1614, which would be the last time for 175 years. After fighting off the deadly challenge from the aristocracy in the *Fronde* (1648–53), Louis XIV largely neutralized the traditional landed aristocracy (*noblesse d'épée)* and also kept in check the *parlements*, appellate courts whose members were drawn largely from the *noblesse de robe* ("nobility of the gown"), and which were completely defeated by Louis XV's astute minister—only to have this victory senselessly thrown away by Louis XVI on his accession in 1774.

Chapter 26
Religious Toleration

"Oh dear, I think I'm becoming a god." This deathbed quip by the irrepressible Roman Emperor Vespasian is a flippant reference to the Roman practice of deifying dead emperors (see Chapter 4). In making fun of it, Vespasian revealed the tolerant Roman attitude to religion, which translated into toleration, or rather freedom of religion and worship, for a whole slew of foreign cults and their gods. All this changed with the establishment of Christianity as the sole official religion of the Roman Empire under Theodosius I. But this has less to do with the nature of government than with the nature of the religions concerned. As a communal religion, Roman paganism was tolerant; as a creed religion, Christianity was intolerant.

Communal and Creed Religions

Most people are surprised to learn that there were no religious wars in the ancient world before the dominance of Christianity in 380 CE. That is not to say that the ancient world was a time of peace and harmony. No, wars were endemic then, just not *religious* wars. The reason for this is that, before 380, *communal religions* were practically universal. Christianity, however, and Islam (which dates from the year 610) are *creed religions*. (The terms "communal" and "creed" religions were coined by myself in my *Is Christianity True? —Arnheim 1984*.)

The chief features distinguishing communal from creed religions are the following:

- **Identity of religion and society.** By contrast with the two biggest religions in the world today, namely Christianity and Islam, both of which are *creed religions*, most religions in the ancient world, were *communal religions*. The largest surviving communal religions today are Hinduism, Japanese Shinto, and Judaism, (which, however, has become something of a hybrid between a communal and a creed religion). In a system of communal religions, every nation, society, or community has its own gods and religion, membership of which is an integral part of membership of the community. For this reason, most of these religions do not even have a specific name. The Sumerian religion has no name other than "the Sumerian religion," the Hittite religion is simply "the Hittite religion," and the ancient Roman "pagan" religion is just "the Roman religion." In a communal religion, membership of religion is not separate from membership of the community, state, nation, or society, but is an integral part of it. You are a member of the religion simply by virtue of your membership of the community concerned. The word "Hinduism" is a modern coinage formed from "Hindu," related to the words "India," "Indus," and "Hindi" (the language). Everyone born in India is automatically a Hindu unless they (or their parents or ancestors) have converted to Islam, Christianity, or some other religion. "Judaism," similarly, is a modern coinage from "Judah," the name of an ancient Jewish kingdom, from the name of one of the 12 tribes, which in turn derives from the name of one of the sons of the Jewish patriarch Jacob.

- **Polytheism.** Besides being communal, most of the religions of the ancient world were polytheistic, each with a pantheon of hundreds of gods. It is estimated, for example, that there were over two thousand Mesopotamian gods.
- **Dual function.** Each god combined a "portfolio," or cosmic or natural function or domain with a local association. So, for example, An or Anu, the chief Sumerian god, was a sky god, and his local association was with the city-state of Uruk, of which he was the tutelary or patron god and where his main temple was situated. Likewise, the Sumerian moon god Nanna was the patron god of Ur and, under the Akkadian name Sin or Suen, was tutelary god of Harran, with temples in both Ur and Harran. Marduk, the patron god of Babylon, was associated astrologically with the planet Jupiter. Shamash, whose worship was originally associated with the Sumerian cities of Larsa and Sippar, became the Mesopotamian sun god who was believed to monitor human activities on a daily basis and dispense justice accordingly, being shown, for example, handing the Code of Hammurabi to the Babylonian king of that name. The Egyptian goddess Isis was believed to be the mother of the pharaoh, who was the manifestation in life of her son, the falcon god Horus, and in death of her brother and husband Osiris. Though her Egyptian origins were never lost sight of, Isis became extremely popular in a Hellenized fashion in the Graeco-Roman world.
- **Syncretism.** A striking feature of ancient communal religion is the ease with which the gods of one culture merge or fuse with those of another, or come to be treated as equivalent. In some cases, the names of the merged gods are so similar that it is evident that they were actually the same, but in

others two or more separate deities have evidently been equated with one another. Inanna, the Sumerian goddess of love and war, the tutelary goddess of Uruk, was evidently originally quite separate from the tutelary goddess of Agade (Akkad), Ishtar, but they were already merged by the reign of Sargon of Akkad (2334–2279 BCE), and Ishtar was also equated with the Canaanite, Syrian, and Phoenician goddess Astarte, who also came to be identified with the Greek goddess Aphrodite, whose Roman equivalent was Venus. Sometimes, however, there is complete fusion, despite widely differing names. A prime example of this is the moon god, whose Sumerian name was Nanna but who was known to the Babylonians by the Akkadian name Sin or Suen. The Roman god Neptune was evidently originally a freshwater deity, similar to the Irish god Nechtan, whose name may be etymologically connected with his, and the expansion of his "portfolio" to sea god may be the result of his being equated with the Greek god Poseidon.

- **Toleration.** The combination of a polytheistic communal religion with syncretism made for religious toleration, or even religious freedom. Communal religions are strong on ritual, ceremonial, and sacrifice, but not on doctrine, creed, or belief, which are largely absent. In communal religions the concept of "heresy" is unknown, and proselytism is unheard of.
- Where different nationalities met, there was no need for one to try to convert another. Instead, gods in one pantheon would merge with gods with the same or similar attributes and powers in another pantheon.
- For a Hittite priest, for example, to go on a "mission" and try to convert Egyptians or Babylonians to his religion could simply not have happened. It was recognized on all sides that every society had its own religion, and it was taken for granted that everyone automatically belonged to their own national or communal religion. So the very idea of conversion was practically unheard of.

Conversion

There were only two circumstances where conversion could occur. One was the rare circumstance of someone actually moving to another country permanently, as in the biblical case of Ruth, who decided to follow her mother-in-law, Naomi, from the land of Moab, where she was from, to Naomi's homeland, Judah. Ruth's moving commitment to her new identity encapsulates the whole communal outlook on life. Addressing her mother-in-law, Ruth pledges: "Where you go, I will go; and where you stay I will stay. Your people will be my people and your God my God. Where you die I will die, and there I will be buried" (Ruth 1:16–18). The key is the complete identity of religion with community.

The only other circumstance when conversion could take place in a world of communal religions would have been in the event of conquest. So close was

Figure 26 Cyrus Cylinder in the British Museum.
SOURCE: Prioryman / Wikimedia Commons / CC BY-SA 3.0.

the identity between a nation and their god that their defeat was the god's defeat as well. The conquered people would therefore be likely to switch their allegiance to the victors' god, especially if the defeated people were transported to the conqueror's country. This is what evidently happened to the Ten Lost Tribes of Israel after their country was conquered by the Assyrians in 722 BCE.

But conquest did not have to have this result. Instead of assimilating a conquered nation to their religion and society, a conqueror could choose to allow the defeated people to retain their separate national and religious identity. This is what Persian King Cyrus the Great (550–530 BCE) did, as evidenced both by the so-called "Cyrus Cylinder" and the Bible.

"Cyrus Cylinder"

The Cyrus Cylinder is one of the most celebrated, controversial, and misunderstood documents from the ancient world, a small clay cylinder found in the ruins of the ancient city of Babylon. It is not an edict or law of any kind but a "foundation deposit" (the ancient equivalent of a modern "time capsule"), intended to be buried for all time under the foundation of the restored temple of Marduk. It bears a Persian royal inscription in Akkadian cuneiform script and dating from soon after the Persian conquest of the Neo-Babylonian Empire and its incorporation into the Persian Empire, which occurred in 539 BCE. The text reviles the defeated Babylonian King Nabonidus, whose son and heir was the ill-fated Belshazzar of biblical notoriety, and it claims that Nabonidus had oppressed the people of Babylon, which ties in with an actual recorded attempt by Nabonidus to replace Babylon's national god Marduk with the moon god Sin as chief god, reversing Marduk's original elevation under Nebuchadnezzar (r. c. 1125–1104 BCE). However, Nabonidus failed to achieve his objective, the main reason evidently being opposition by the Babylonian populace itself, who venerated Marduk as their national protector. The Cyrus Cylinder draws a sharp contrast between Nabonidus and Cyrus, who is described as owing to Marduk (not worshipped in Persia) his victory over Nabonidus, and also as being welcomed by the people of Babylon as their new ruler.

The picture throughout is one where Cyrus the conquering king and Marduk the god of the defeated Babylonians are in lockstep. Cyrus's benevolence is twofold, geared both to his new Babylonian subjects and to their gods. The conquered people brought to Babylon as captives by the Babylonian kings were repatriated. And their gods, whose images had likewise been brought to Babylon, were allowed to be returned to their local shrines. Cyrus is portrayed as a humane ruler who is concerned with the welfare of his subjects, which includes respect for their gods. And Marduk, as the supreme head of the Babylonian pantheon, presides over it all, promotes it, and commends Cyrus for it.

Though the Cyrus Cylinder itself was meant to be buried in the foundation of the temple of Marduk in Babylon and never seen again, the text that it bore has been found on 10 other documents that had been lurking unnoticed in the British Museum prior to the discovery of the Cyrus Cylinder in 1879. This only intensified the hysteria over the Cylinder, which was seized upon by Mohammed Reza Pahlavi, the last shah of Iran (r. 1941–79), who described the Cyrus Cylinder as "the first declaration of human rights," and the United Nations still exhibits a replica of the Cylinder at its New York headquarters as "an ancient declaration of human rights." Even the Islamic regime which overthrew and replaced the Shah has identified itself with the Cylinder, with former Iranian President Mahmoud Ahmadinejad calling it in 2010 the "First Charter of Human Rights."

The fervor aroused over the Cyrus Cylinder also resulted in the discovery of a number of other "foundation deposits" with similar inscriptions produced by earlier Babylonian and Assyrian kings. The reviled Nabonidus himself issued a self-glorifying statement inscribed on the so-called Harran Stela, dating from between 542 and 540 BCE, found in the ruins of Harran (in modern Turkey), in which Nabonidus is commanded by the moon god Sin, as the supreme god, to rebuild Sin's temple in Harran, of which Sin was the patron god. This ties in with Nabonidus's unpopular attempt to replace Babylon's patron god Marduk with Sin, with whose worship Nabonidus's mother was evidently associated, either as a priestess or at least as a devotee.

An inscription by a previous conqueror of Babylon that contrasts with the Cyrus Cylinder is the inscription by the Assyrian King Sennacherib crowing on his victory over Babylon after a long siege in 690 BCE. He revels in describing how he had the defeated Babylonian king trussed up like a pig in the center of the city and how he demolished temples and shattered the images of gods, as the defeat of a nation was viewed equally as a defeat of that nation's gods.

The modern scholarly literature on the Cyrus Cylinder is as contradictory and divergent as it is voluminous, with some writers waxing lyrical on Cyrus's supposedly unique humanitarianism, while others insist that the inscription is propaganda of a well-known type. A proper understanding of the nature of communal religion would indicate that the Cyrus Cylinder belongs to a recognizable genre of triumphant inscriptions, where, instead of destroying the god of the defeated enemy, the conqueror pays homage to that god, in this case Marduk, and attributes his victory to Marduk's favor. This was a particularly astute strategy in this case, as the defeated king, Nabonidus, was unpopular with his own people and had been plotting to replace the revered patron god with another, making it all the more likely that Marduk would turn against Nabonidus and give Cyrus victory.

Cyrus Cylinder: A Closer Look

The contents of the Cyrus Cylinder will repay more detailed examination. [What follows is based on a modified version of Mordechai Cogan's translation published in Hallo and Younger (2003), adapted to Schaudig's edition with the help of Bert van der Spek and M. Stolper (online: `https://www.livius.org/sources/content/cyrus-cylinder/`).]

1. Marduk is described as "king of the whole of heaven and earth."
7. Nabonidus is directly accused of doing away "with the worship of Marduk, the king of the gods."
8. "He continually did evil against Marduk's city. Daily, without interruption, he imposed the corvée upon its inhabitants, unrelentingly, ruining them all."
9. "Upon hearing their cries, the lord of the gods became so furiously angry and ... their borders; the gods who lived among them forsook their dwellings."
12. "[Marduk] searched everywhere and then took a righteous king. His favorite, by the hand, he called out his name: Cyrus, king of Anshan; he pronounced his name to be king all over the world."
18. "All the people of Babylon, all the land of Sumer and Akkad, princes and governors, bowed to him and kissed his feet. They rejoiced at his kingship and their faces shone."
22. Cyrus's royal pedigree: "of an eternal line of kingship, whose rule Bel and Nabu love, whose kingship they desire for their hearts' pleasure."
24. "My (Cyrus's) vast army marched into Babylon in peace; I did not permit anyone to frighten the people of Sumer or Akkad."
26. "I relieved the weariness of the people of Babylon and freed them from their service. Marduk, the great lord, rejoiced over my good deeds."

29. "Throughout the world, from the Upper Sea to the Lower Sea, who live in the districts far-off, the kings of the West, who dwell in tents, all of them,
30. brought their heavy tribute before me.
From Babylon to Ashur and from Susa,
31. Agade, Eshnunna, Zamban, Me-Turnu, Der, as far as the region of Gutium, the sacred centers on the other side of the Tigris, whose sanctuaries had been abandoned for a long time,
32. I returned the images of the gods who had resided there (i.e. in Babylon) to their places and I let them dwell in eternal abodes. I gathered all their inhabitants and returned to them their dwellings.
33. In addition, at the command of Marduk, the great lord, I settled in their habitations, in pleasing abodes, the gods of Sumer and Akkad, whom Nabonidus, to the anger of the lord of the gods, had brought into Babylon."
34. "May all the gods whom I settled in their sacred centers ask daily
35. of Bel and Nabu that my days be long and may they intercede for my welfare. May they say to Marduk, my lord: 'As for Cyrus, the king who reveres you, and Cambyses his son....'"
36. "The people of Babylon blessed my kingship, and I settled all the lands in peaceful abodes."
37–45. Cyrus's offerings to the gods and his reconstruction of the walls of Babylon.

As an alternative to smashing up a defeated nation's temples, a conqueror might plunder the temples of their valuables and transport the defeated gods together with their worshippers as captives to the conqueror's country. Successful rulers of Babylon had done this in the past, and lines 30–33 of the Cyrus Cylinder boast of the repatriation to their homelands of several captive nations together with their gods, who had been transported to Babylon during Babylon's heyday.

Cyrus in the Bible

The much-debated references to Cyrus in the Bible clearly tie in with this. In the Book of Chronicles we read of a proclamation issued by Cyrus in the first year of his reign, reading: "Thus saith Cyrus king of Persia: All the kingdoms of the earth hath the Lord, the God of heaven, given me; and he hath charged me to build Him a house in Jerusalem, which is in Judah. Whosoever there is among you of all His people—the Lord his God be with him—let him go up" (2 Chron. 36:22–23).

The Book of Ezra quotes a proclamation issued by Cyrus in almost identical terms, with the addition of this verse: "Also Cyrus the king brought forth the vessels of the house of the Lord, which Nebuchadnezzar had brought forth out of Jerusalem, and had put them in the house of his gods" (Ezra 1:1–7). Nebuchadnezzar's plundering of the temple in Jerusalem is also known from Chronicles (2 Chron. 36:18).

Did Cyrus issue a proclamation about the Temple in Jerusalem? Despite all the academic hair-splitting on the subject, it really does not matter, because there is absolutely no doubt that the original Temple in Jerusalem, destroyed by the Neo-Babylonian King Nebuchadnezzar in 586 BCE, was replaced by a Second Temple built after Cyrus's conquest of the Neo-Babylonian Empire, and was completed and consecrated in 516/15 BCE during the reign of Cyrus' great-great-nephew Darius the Great (r. 522–486 BCE), and was in continuous use until its destruction by the Romans in 70 CE.

If the rebuilding of the Temple in Jerusalem really was the subject of a proclamation, it certainly could not have been in the first year of Cyrus's reign, 550 BCE, because he only gained control of Jerusalem through his conquest of Babylon in 539 BCE. And the Jerusalem Temple was clearly not mentioned in the Cyrus Cylinder, which was not a proclamation and dealt only with Mesopotamia. But, like so many academic controversies, this is irrelevant, not only because of the fully documented history of the Second Temple but also because Persian policy in regard to Jerusalem is paralleled by their policy in regard to Egypt, for example, where we know Darius built temples dedicated to the Egyptian gods Amun, Ptah, and Nekhbet (Shahbazi, 1994, p. 41ff).

After his conquest of Babylon, did Cyrus switch his loyalty from the Persian god Ahuramazda to Babylon's patron god, Marduk? Not at all. We learn from the Greek historian Arrian that Cyrus's tomb was guarded by "Magians," or Zoroastrian priests (Arrian, *Anabasis* 6:29). Similarly, Darius's tomb is clearly dedicated to Ahuramazda with an inscription starting: "A great god is Ahuramazda, who created this earth, who created yonder sky, who created man, who created happiness for man, who made Darius king, one king of many, one lord of many" (Daiva inscription—online: `https://www.livius.org/sources/content/achaemenid-royal-inscriptions/xph`). Cyrus and Darius clearly worshipped their own national deity, Ahuramazda, when in Persia, but honored Marduk when in Babylon and presumably other local gods when they found themselves in their territory. This policy of "going native" was no doubt calculated to win the goodwill of the conquered nations, but it was potentially a double-edged sword, as, by leaving the conquered nations intact, it enabled them to rise up in revolt to reclaim their independence. Under Darius the conquered regions became provinces governed by satraps appointed by, and sometimes related to, Darius himself, and the satrap's power was checked by a separate military commander answerable directly to Darius. Imperial spies known as the "king's ears" monitored both the satrap and military commander in each area and reported back to Darius through the efficient postal service instituted by him. Such was the multicultural nature of the empire that, by about 500 BCE, Aramaic, a Semitic language, replaced Old Persian, an Aryan language, as the official language of the empire.

Though the empire had declined to some extent in the two centuries between the death of Darius and the empire's conquest by Alexander, revolts were mostly put down quite smartly. When tax increases led to riots in Babylon in 482 BCE, Xerxes went to far as to sack the city, destroy the temple of Marduk, and melt down the three-times life-size solid gold statue of the god. And even Egypt, which had successfully thrown off the Persian yoke in 404 BCE, was reconquered by 343 BCE.

Roman Freedom of Religion

A different style of freedom of religion is found in ancient Rome, spanning a period of over 800 years, covering the Republic, the Principate and Late Empire, and coming to an abrupt end with the dominance of Christianity, which was favored by Constantine from at least the Council of Nicea in 325 and became the official religion of the Roman Empire in 380.

During this 800-year period, and especially from the Late Republic onward, there was a proliferation of foreign cults which were allowed to live and thrive alongside the Roman "pagan" state religion.

Alongside the array of deities in the pantheon of traditional Roman and equivalent Greek gods, some of the most popular foreign religions worshipped in Rome itself include:

- **Cybele/*Magna Mater* ("Great Mother").** A Phrygian cult welcomed to Rome with great pomp during the Second Punic War (218–201 BCE), it was popular with the Roman upper classes. Under Augustus the *Magna Mater* came to be identified with the imperial order. When the temple burned down, Augustus restored it.
- **Isis and Serapis.** The worship of Isis goes back to well before 2000 BCE in Egypt and in Rome from the early first century BCE. After the shrines had been destroyed a few times in the late Republic, without the cult being banned, and after expulsion by the Emperor Tiberius in 19 CE following a sex scandal, Isis and the Graeco-Egyptian god Serapis went from strength to strength in Rome, counting the Emperor Vespasian and his successors as devotees. The imposing Serapeum in Alexandria, built by Ptolemy III (r. 246–222 BCE) was closed down by Constantine in 325 and finally destroyed (together with Alexandria's famous library) by a Christian mob in 391.
- **Mithras.** Of Persian origin, this all-male cult appealed particularly to the Roman army between the first and fourth centuries CE. Numerous temples

of Mithras, or Mithraea, are found scattered throughout the Roman Empire, especially in the Western provinces, including one in London. Like other pagan religions, Mithraism was not exclusive. Almost all Mithraea contain statues of other gods besides Mithras, and dedications to Mithras are also found in the shrines of other cults, such as those of Jupiter Dolichenus.

Was this religious proliferation of foreign religions an indication of religious toleration? Some modern writers deny this, claiming that what may appear to be toleration was actually subjugation, absorption and suppression. Peter Garnsey, for example, opines that the Roman state religion was "disposed to expand or absorb or at least neutralize" the foreign cults worshipped in Rome (Garnsey 1984, p. 9). If that were so, why were these religions allowed to flourish, with their own temples and own priests, at the heart of the Roman Empire? It was not under the Roman pagan religion but under Christianity that they were closed down, and, especially after 391, banned, with the destruction of many varied pagan temples, statues, and images and the murder of a number pagan priests.

In fact, the pagan Roman state extended more than toleration to other religions. The term "toleration" has something of a negative connotation, meaning as it does permitting a practice with which one disagrees. The Roman state religion did not just tolerate other religions: it extended freedom of religion to them. But, it may be objected, were some cults not banned? And what about persecution of Christians and Jews? Actually, as we shall see, there is no evidence of religious persecution as such under the pagan Roman Empire.

One exception, though not for religious reasons, was the treatment of the Bacchanalia. In 186 BCE during the Republic, the Senate decreed that Greek Bacchanalian cult should be "controlled," meaning that, without being banned, it was placed under certain constraints, which were later relaxed. The reason for taking this exceptional step on the part of the Senate was the "depravity" of the cult's practices together with the fear that its leaders were planning insurrection (Livy 39:1).

The only pagan cult to have been permanently banned by the Romans was that of the Druids in Gaul and Britain, on the grounds that they practiced human sacrifice (Plin. *H.N.* 30.13). There may well have been a political motive as well: "So long as Celtic religion wore an intolerant nationalistic shape, in the form of Druidism, Rome saw in it a danger to her own imperial policy" (Collingwood/ Myres 1936, p. 261) Again, not a case of religious persecution.

"Christians to the Lions!"

"'Christians to the Lions' was a powerful slogan" (Beard et al. 1998, p. 212). Yes, in Hollywood. But the suggestion that this was the long-term attitude of the Roman "élite" to Christianity will simply not stand up to scrutiny. In a thoroughly researched work of scholarship, Candida Moss brilliantly and wittily dispels the myth of widespread and persistent Roman persecution of Christianity (Moss 2013). She sums up her findings in a nutshell:

> Between the death of Jesus around 30 CE and the ascension of Constantine in 313, Christians died as the result of active measures by the imperial government only (1) immediately following the Great Fire of Rome in 64, (2) around 250, during the reign of Decius, (3) briefly during the reign of Valerian in 257–58, and (4) during the 'Great Persecution'; under the emperor Diocletian, which lasted from 303 to 305 and was renewed by Maximinus Daia between 311 and 313. These dates represent the largest time span before Constantine. As we shall see, not all these episodes can reasonably be called persecution, and their implementation was limited to specific regions and to months rather than years. Even putting these caveats aside, we are talking about fewer than 10 years out of nearly three hundred during which Christians were executed as the result of imperial initiatives (ibid., p. 127ff).

Moreover, these episodes were motivated by politics, not religious intolerance.

Roman Persecution of the Jews?

For the mass of inhabitants of the Roman Empire, there was no conflict between their own local communal religion and the Roman state religion. The Jews were an exception. Though Judea fell under Roman rule in 63 BC, it was at first allowed the luxury of having its own king, but then in 6 CE it became a Roman province under a governor sent from Rome but continued to be treated as a separate nation to the extent of having its own Temple. But, though the Jewish religion was a communal religion, its adherents were not allowed to combine its worship with any other religion, and there was a sizeable independence movement. During the Great Jewish Revolt of 66–73, the Romans destroyed the Temple in the year 70. And the Bar Kokhba revolt of 132–35, which was brutally put down by Hadrian, resulted in Jews being banned (except one day a year) from Jerusalem. The ban was essentially reversed by Hadrian's successor, Antoninus Pius (r. 138–61). Jews were still exempt from pagan sacrifice in return for the *fiscus judaicus*, and Jews were included in the extension of Roman citizenship to all free male inhabitants of the Roman Empire by Caracalla's *Constitutio Antoniniana* of 212 (see Chapter 6). Under the Christian emperors, however, Jews gradually found themselves reduced to second class citizenship.

Misunderstanding Religious Toleration

As a communal religion, the Roman pagan civic religion was part and parcel of being Roman. You were a member of the Roman religion by virtue of your membership of Roman society. The two were inextricably bound up together. There is, unfortunately, a great deal of misunderstanding of the nature of a communal religion. Here is an example from the pen of Peter Brown: "Emperors had always been expected to have a firm religious policy in order to be sure of the support of the gods" (Brown 2013, p. 73). In fact, emperors generally had no religious policy at all, because the Roman communal religion was not seen as separate from Roman society. The concept of religious toleration is evidently an embarrassment to writers like Brown, for whom the triumph of Christianity was clearly one of the greatest, if not *the* greatest, achievement of "late antiquity." "Precisely because correct religion was the glory of the empire," opines Brown, "it had to be imposed in a manner that reflected the overwhelming dignity of the imperial power" (Brown 1997a, p. 644). What exactly is "correct religion"? Presumably the creed of the dominant denomination of Christianity, which, to put it at its simplest, is completely unprovable. Moreover, even if a particular creed could be proved to be "correct" or "true," why should it have to be "imposed" on anyone? How do you "impose" something on someone in a dignified manner? Far from being "dignified," for a ruler to "impose" a creed on someone because the ruler believes it is "correct" or "true" is mindless persecution and certainly cannot redound to that ruler's "glory." A further remark of Brown's explains his misunderstanding and rejection of religious toleration: "Religious toleration was, at best, a fragile notion. It contributed little to the working-out of codes of coexistence between the adherents of different religions" (ibid., p. 643). This is a curious remark, to say the least, considering that religious toleration—and, indeed, even freedom of religion—had been successfully practiced in Rome for 800 years.

But it was the mindless intolerance of rulers who believed they had the "correct" or "true" religion which they felt impelled to impose on their subjects and others which plunged the world into 1,500 years of religious bigotry, religious wars, and persecution, which has still not ended. Here are just a few highlights. The "Great Schism" between Eastern and Western Christianity over the word *filioque* has still not been healed since 1054. The Crusades of between 1095 and 1291 overlapped with the "Albigensian Crusade" against Cathar "heretics" between 1209 and 1229. The Spanish Inquisition lasted from 1478 until it was finally abolished in 1834. In England "Bloody Mary" burned 280 "heretics" at the stake between 1553 and 1558, and the Papal Bull of 1521 excommunicating Martin Luther has never been retracted. But it would be a mistake to think that this extended campaign of persecution was practiced only by the Roman Catholic Church. Every Christian denomination still believes that it alone has a lock on "truth," and the schism within Islam, another creed religion, remains as stubborn as ever.

"Religious Concord"

What a relief it is to turn from the prevailing lack of understanding of the ancient world of religious freedom to the rolling prose, relaxed wit and broad Enlightenment spirit of Edward Gibbon's *Decline and Fall of the Roman Empire,* composed between 1776 and 1789:

> The various modes of worship which prevailed in the Roman world were all considered by the people as equally true, by the philosopher as equally false, and by the magistrate as equally useful. And this toleration produced not only mutual indulgence, but even religious concord.... Such was the mild spirit of antiquity that the nations were less attentive to the difference than to the resemblance of their religious worship (Gibbon, 1776, chapter 2).

Chapter 27
Foreign Policy

*T*here is some correlation between the power structure of a regime and its foreign policy. The motive for an aggressive foreign policy may be dynastic, territorial, economic, nationalistic, linguistic, ideological—or even religious. As was pointed out in Chapter 26, some of the most serious wars in history have been religious wars. But it cannot be stressed enough that there were no religious wars in the ancient world before 380 CE, when Christianity became the official religion of the Roman Empire. The reason for this is quite simply the intolerant nature of Christianity as a **creed religion,** which believes that it alone holds the key to "truth," "salvation," and "eternal life"—and, counterintuitively, that "nonbelievers" and "pagans" must be forced to be "saved" from their "false" faiths. Besides this intolerance toward other religions, every Christian denomination brands the members of many other Christian denominations as "heretics." Some ostensibly religious wars, like the Crusades, for example, may have had economic and political, as well as religious, motivations, but it was religion that gave them their driving force.*

*Before 380 there were plenty of wars, just no religious wars. It was a world of **communal religions,** in which every nation had its own religion, and membership of that nation meant that one automatically belonged to that nation's religion (see Chapter 26). When a nation was conquered by another nation, its gods were conquered too. Members of the defeated nation could simply continue to worship their own gods, or, if they were deported to the conqueror's country (like Assyria, for example), they might become assimilated to that nation and its religion. The Persian king and conqueror Cyrus the Great (550–530 BCE) actually promoted the worship by defeated nations of their own religion, notably in the cases of Babylon and Judah. Similarly, until the fourth century CE, Rome welcomed the worship of "oriental cults" alongside the traditional Roman national "pagan" religion,* *and the common belief in Roman persecution of Christians is largely a myth (see Chapter 26).*

Popular monarchy, imbuing its supporters with enthusiasm, has a tendency to overflow into an aggressive or expansionist foreign policy. Periclean Athens is a good example, as is the Mali Empire of West Africa, the Chinese Ming dynasty, the France of Louis XIV and of both Napoleon I and III, Fascist Italy, and even the puny island of Cuba under Fidel Castro. The correlation is not complete, however, as expansionist tendencies have also been manifested by some oligarchies, notably the Roman Republic and Victorian Britain.

Sargon of Akkad

Sargon (c. 2334–2279 BCE), possibly the earliest recorded ruler of an empire, had a very active, not to say aggressive, foreign policy, involving the claim of having conquered no fewer than 34 Sumerian city-states. According to a victory inscription (quoted by Liverani, 2013, p. 143), after defeating the city of Uruk, he tore down its walls and "took Lugalzagesi, king of Uruk, in the course of the battle, and led him in a collar to the gate of Enlil." Sargon then went on to conquer Ur and E-Ninmar and claimed to have "laid waste" to the whole area from Lagash to the sea, after which he conquered and destroyed Umma. He ultimately claimed to have ruled from the "upper sea" to the "lower sea," meaning from the Mediterranean to the Persian Gulf, though this may just have been a boast. And in the last five years of his reign he was evidently faced with widespread revolts. Sargon appears to have ruled the conquered city-states through vassals, which may account for the revolts. But it also raises questions about the motivation for such extensive conquests (Inscription quoted by Liverani, 2013, p. 143.).

Sargon's motive for his aggressive foreign policy is not known, though his birth legend may possibly provide a clue. It is a variant of the legend associated with Moses. Sargon's mother is said to have been a high priestess, who concealed his birth by placing the infant Sargon in a basket and casting it adrift in a river. Akki, the drawer of water, saved him and appointed him his gardener, where he was discovered by the goddess Ishtar, who made him a king. Could this imply that Sargon was of foreign origin? He was evidently of Semitic origin, while the Sumerians, whom he conquered, were non-Semitic and also non-Aryan. Sargon therefore represents the first of a series of Semitic empires, which (with a brief neo-Sumerian interlude in the twenty-first/twentieth centuries BCE) lasted for almost 1,500 years until the (Aryan) Persian defeat of the last Neo-Babylonian king, Nabonidus. It is this watershed defeat that is predicted in the well-known fictitious Bible story in the Book of Daniel about Belshazzar's feast and the writing on the wall, *mene mene tekel upharsin,* interpreted by Daniel as meaning that the days of Belshazzar's kingdom were numbered, that Belshazzar himself (wrongly referred to as king when he was in fact only the crown prince) had been weighed and found wanting, and that his kingdom was about to be given to the Medes and Persians (Daniel 5:30–31).

Was Sargon's conquest of the Sumerian city-states ethnically motivated? Probably not. Conquered peoples in the ancient world could be enslaved, but they were often simply assimilated into the conquering nation. This is what seems to have happened, for example, to the 10 "lost tribes" after the conquest of the Kingdom of Israel by the Assyrians in 734 and finally in 722 BCE. (2 Kings 15:29 and 18:11–12.) According to Assyrian records, after the fall of Samaria, 27,280 people were deported to various places throughout the Assyrian Empire.

This was part of a "resettlement" or deportation policy practiced by the Assyrians from the reign of Ashur-dan (934–912 BCE). The status of the deportees varied. Some are depicted shackled or tied up, probably indicative of slavery, while others are shown travelling with their families and possessions. Deported farmers were given land to work with the same status as indigenous agricultural workers, skilled craftsmen and scholars were given matching positions, those showing an aptitude for fighting were drafted into the Assyrian army, and those with the highest education or training were placed in royal service (Oded 1979.)

Though the pre-Christian ancient world saw many wars of conquest, dynastic wars, and wars fought for access to scarce raw materials, there were no religious wars. Every nation had its own communal religion, most of which were polytheistic. A person's membership of their nation made them automatic members of that nation's religion. So missionaries and proselytization were unknown. When a nation was conquered, its gods were defeated as well. The conqueror could either replace the defeated gods with their own or add them to their own pantheon. Most gods in one religion could either merge or be equated with gods in another religion. Every religion, for example, had a sky god, a moon god, and a god of war. It was only with the dominance of a creed religion, Christianity, in the fourth century CE, that religious persecution and religious warfare rear their ugly head (see Chapter 26).

"Conquered Greece"

Graecia capta ferum victorem cepit. ("Conquered Greece defeated her rough conqueror") (Hor., *Epistles II.1*, lines 156–57). Educated Romans steeped themselves in Greek literature and philosophy, and Roman art, architecture, literature, and philosophy grew up in the shadow of their Greek models. When crossing the Rubicon, Julius Caesar did not say *Alea jacta est* (or *Jacta alea est*, as Suetonius has it) for "The die is cast." The phrase was not his own but was from a play by Menander—in Greek. And that is how he quoted it. And even in his death-throes after being stabbed by Brutus, his protégé, he did not say, *Et tu, Brute?* ("You too, Brutus?"), as Shakespeare would have us believe, but the Greek words: *kai su, paidion?* ("You too, my child?"). The language of the Romans was of course Latin, yet the Roman Empire was bilingual. In a huge swathe of land area originally conquered by Alexander the Great in the Eastern Mediterranean and Egypt, Greek remained not only the lingua franca but also the official language under the Roman Empire and later under the shrinking Byzantine Empire.

"They make a desert and call it peace" (Tac. *Agric.* 30). This is how Calgacus, a Caledonian (Scottish) chieftain, supposedly characterized Roman imperialism in a speech to his men before the Battle of Mons Graupius in 83 or 84 CE. Both the speech and Calgacus himself are probably fictitious, though the battle was real enough. Tacitus was not sympathetic to the Caledonians, who lost to the Roman governor of Britannia, Tacitus's father-in-law, Gnaeus Julius Agricola. But the speech is intended to reflect the likely spirit of resistance to Roman imperialism among the native inhabitants of conquered territories. Unlike most modern colonial powers, the Romans were extremely successful in assimilating conquered peoples. The privilege of Roman citizenship was highly prized, and even the Christian apostle Paul availed himself of the legal protection that it afforded, with the plea: *Civis Romanus sum* ("I am a Roman citizen"). As discussed in Chapter 6, in the year 212 the Emperor Caracalla extended Roman citizenship to all free male inhabitants of the Roman Empire. From the accession in 98 of Trajan, who was born in Spain, the majority of Roman emperors originated from the provinces. Trajan's successor also came from Spain, Septimius Severus from North Africa, Elagabalus from modern Syria, Severus Alexander from modern Lebanon, Maximinus Thrax from modern Bulgaria, Gordian I from Phrygia in modern Turkey, Philip the Arab from modern Syria, and most of the later emperors from the Balkans, down to Theodosius I (r. 379–95), who came from Spain. In most of the Western half of the Empire the Latin language replaced the original local languages, so that the daughter languages of Latin, known as the Romance languages, have some 900 million native speakers in the world today, including not only Europe but also the Americas.

"We Have No Eternal Allies..."

"We have no eternal allies, and we have no perpetual enemies. Our interests are eternal and perpetual, and those interests it is our duty to follow" (*Parliamentary Debates [Hansard]*, 1 March 1848). Thus Lord Palmerston as British foreign secretary in 1848. He is drawing a distinction here between interests and alliances. Shifting alliances may be called for in pursuit of the nation's interests, which remain fixed. This riled Queen Victoria (r. 1837–1901), who believed that policy should take second place to royal family loyalties and traditional friendships and alliances, but above all took offence at Palmerston's monopoly of decision-making in foreign affairs without always consulting her. The effects of the so-called "Glorious Revolution" of 1688/89, which ultimately reduced the British monarch to little more than a cypher, initially left the monarch in charge of foreign policy. As Stadtholder of the Netherlands for 17 years before ascending the English throne jointly with his wife, Mary II, in 1689, William III was already a major player in international affairs and remained so as king of England. But the monarch's participation in decision-making was on the wane. The Hanoverian George I (r. 1714–27) did not speak English and could only communicate with the prime minister, Sir Robert Walpole, in "dog Latin." As a result the king stopped attending Cabinet meetings, and this practice became permanent, even though George II and all later monarchs had fluent English. Another feature that militated against royal decision-making was the rise of the two-party system. But it took a long time for the realization to sink in that the crown should not meddle in foreign policy any more than in domestic affairs.

Queen Victoria found this particularly difficult to accept, as she was related to so many of the crowned heads of Europe. Hence the need for Lord Palmerston as foreign secretary to rap her over the knuckles with the remark quoted at the head of this section: nations do not have eternal friends and allies but *interests,* which might necessitate switching alliances from time to time. In the Schleswig-Holstein dispute, which erupted into a war between Prussia and Denmark in 1864, Victoria sided with Prussia while Palmerston favoured Denmark. Victoria's eldest daughter, also called Victoria, was married to the Prussian crown prince, who would become the short-lived Kaiser Frederick III of Germany in 1888. In fact, however, Queen Victoria also had a family tie with Denmark, as her eldest son, the Prince of Wales, the future British King Edward VII, was married to Alexandra, the daughter of King Christian IX of Denmark (r. 1863–1906), who was known as the "father-in-law" of Europe. The story goes that when on a visit to Christian IX in Denmark several of his relations went out on a hike in the countryside when they came upon a Danish peasant. One introduced himself politely: "I am the Prince of Wales" (the future Edward VII); then the next, "I am the king of the Hellenes" (King George I of Greece); "And I am the tsar of all the Russias," boomed a great bear of a man, Tsar Alexander III of Russia, another of Christian IX's sons-in-law. Not believing any of this, the Danish peasant then doffed his hat and performed an exaggerated mock-obsequious low bow and scrape, and proclaimed: "And I am the emperor of China." The story may be apocryphal, but it brings home the close-knit nature of European royalty in the period just before World War I. The question is: What difference did this make, and why did it not prevent this era-shattering catastrophe?

"Hang The Kaiser!"

Was World War I inevitable? If so, when did it become so, and why? Or could it have been averted, or even prevented altogether by the related crowned heads involved on both sides? Approaching this fraught issue from a fresh perspective, my research suggests that, contrary to general belief, the war could have been averted had two of the crowned heads involved had *more* rather than less power over their own governments: the German Kaiser Wilhelm II and Tsar Nicholas II of Russia, both of whom were actually intent on avoiding war.

Cause and effect are the lifeblood of history, but there is still no consensus on the cause or causes of World War I. The verdict of British Prime Minister David Lloyd George was that, "The nations slithered over the brink into the boiling cauldron of war..." This may be labelled the accidental theory. Inevitability is another popular explanation—or non-explanation. Martin Wright put it like this: "War is inevitable, though particular wars can be avoided" (Hinsley 1995, p. 4). Professor Sir Harry Hinsley, for example, opined that "the First World War is far from being unique among the wars of modern history" since 1494 (ibid., p. 1). The nineteenth-century British prime minister, Lord Salisbury, opined that "Europe would avoid another great war only if it became a federation" (ibid., p. 5). For someone who had lived through the bloody American Civil War of 1861–65 this is a remarkably obtuse prediction. Why, after all, should a federal Europe be any more immune from war than a federal United States?

Harry Hinsley himself fastened on "wilfulness amounting to paranoia on the part of the men who governed Germany" (ibid., p. 7). A similar view was expressed on 6 November 1917, while the war was still raging, by former United States president Theodore Roosevelt, who placed the blame on the "diplomacy of despots," and, more particularly, on "the despotism of Germany," adding: "This war was made by the militaristic and capitalistic autocracy of Germany..." (Bernstein 1918).

This view, shared by many other commentators, both then and now, draws no distinction between the German government and the Kaiser, who is cast as the arch-villain. "We shall squeeze the German lemon until the pips squeak" was a popular election cry in the British general election of December 1918. But Prime Minister David Lloyd George had a more personal slant: "Hang the kaiser." Article 227 of the Versailles treaty of 1919 called for the kaiser to be tried by a "special tribunal" of five judges, one from each of the victorious Allies, "for a supreme offence against international morality and the sanctity of treaties." But the Netherlands, which had granted the kaiser asylum, refused to extradite him, so no trial ever took place.

Kaiser vs. Chancellor

"Dropping the Pilot," a famous *Punch* cartoon (drawn by Sir John Tenniel of *Alice in Wonderland* fame), shows Otto von Bismarck's forced resignation as German chancellor in 1890, after nearly 30 years of service to the Prussian and German crowns. Indeed, the unification of Germany under Prussia in 1871 was largely Bismarck's doing. With his characteristic eye for detail, Tenniel portrays Bismarck in the foreground as a no-nonsense professional old helmsman, while a diminutive crowned young Kaiser Wilhelm II looks on petulantly with folded arms. The message is clear: expert statecraft is being replaced by hot-headed youthful caprice.

In practice, however, the Kaiser's position was by no means omnipotent. Under the German Constitution of 1871 (drafted by Bismarck), the kaiser had the power to declare war, but only with the consent of the *Bundesrat* ("Federal Council"), the upper house of the legislature. He could hire and fire the chancellor, or first minister, but once in office the chancellor essentially ran the show. In his memoirs, published in 1922, Kaiser Wilhelm blamed this also

Figure 27 "Dropping the Pilot," 1890. Bismarck dismissed by Kaiser Wilhelm II.
SOURCE: John Tenniel / Wikimedia Commons / Public domain.

on the Constitution, according to which he claimed that "the Chancellor alone is responsible for foreign policy." And: "The Emperor has influence on foreign policy only in so far as the Chancellor grants it to him" (Wilhelm II 1922, location 150). In fact, the Constitution had nothing to say about control over foreign policy. But in practice the position was very much as the Kaiser described.

Assassination of Franz Ferdinand

The assassination in Sarajevo, Bosnia, of Archduke Franz Ferdinand on 28 June 1914 is commonly seen as the spark that ignited the conflagration of World War I. The archduke was heir to the Austro-Hungarian throne, and his assassin, Gavrilo Princip, was a Bosnian Serb with links to the "Black Hand," a Serbian secret society. In 1908 Bosnia had been annexed by Austria-Hungary, which blamed Serbia for the assassination. Serbia denied any involvement and appealed for help to its big Slavic brother Russia.

This crisis threatened the delicate European balance of power, which was controlled by two alliances glowering at each other. Russia was allied to France, and both were linked more informally to Britain in the so-called Triple Entente, which was confronted by the Triple Alliance of Germany, Austria-Hungary, and Italy. Besides Germany's formal alliance with Austria-Hungary, the German kaiser happened to be a personal friend of the murdered archduke.

The Austrian Ultimatum

In order to exert some influence at this critical time, the kaiser naturally wanted to remain in his capital, Berlin, but he was persuaded by his officials to go on his annual cruise of the North Sea, which effectively took him out of circulation from July 6 to 26. When he learned from the Norwegian press that Austria-Hungary had presented an ultimatum to Serbia, he rushed back to Berlin and was visibly relieved to read a copy of the conciliatory Serbian reply, which he excitedly annotated: "A brilliant solution—and in barely 48 hours! This is more than could have been expected. A great moral victory for Vienna; but with it every pretext falls to the ground, and Giesl [the Austrian ambassador to Serbia] had better have stayed quietly at Belgrade. On this document, I should never have given orders for mobilization" (Fromkin 2004, p. 218). Wilhelm added that Serbia had made "a capitulation of the most humiliating kind" (ibid.). In fact, the last point in Serbia's response went so far as to say that: "[If Austria is not satisfied with this reply], the Serbian government ... are ready ... to accept a pacific understanding, either by referring this question to the decision of the International Tribunal of the Hague, or to the Great Powers."

Wilhelm believed that a temporary occupation of Belgrade was required until Serbia kept its word—a condition that would also be proposed by British

Foreign Secretary Sir Edward Grey a few days later (ibid.). Grey's comment on Serbia's response was: "Any nation that accepted conditions like that would really cease to count as an independent nation" (Fromkin 2004, p. 189).

Wilhelm "The Pacifist"

Wilhelm's concern to prevent war was not shared by either his military or diplomatic advisers, who in fact went out of their way to sabotage his efforts. (Fischer 1967, p. 72.) When the German shipping magnate Albert Ballin suggested that Wilhelm end his North Sea cruise to deal with the crisis, he was rudely rebuffed by the German foreign ministry, which replied that "everything must be done to ensure that he [Wilhelm] does not interfere in things with his pacifist ideas" (Fromkin 2004, p. 197).

Wilhelm and his chancellor, Theobald von Bethmann Hollweg, had been in agreement about giving Austria-Hungary a "blank cheque" of support against Serbia on July 6 just over a week after the assassination. But, while the kaiser was determined to prevent a general war, the chancellor, without a majority in the Reichstag (Parliament), fell increasingly under the influence of the German military, who were impatient to flex their muscles.

Referring to Wilhelm's undisguised relief at Serbia's conciliatory response to the Austrian ultimatum, a German general wrote: "Unfortunately ... peaceful news. The Kaiser wants peace.... He even wants to influence Austria and to stop continuing further" (Fromkin 2004, p. 159f). Bethmann Hollweg deliberately sabotaged the kaiser's message to Austria-Hungary in his instructions to the German ambassador to Vienna, Tschirschky: "You must most carefully avoid giving any impression that we want to hold Austria back. We are concerned only to find a *modus* to enable the realization of Austria-Hungary's aim without at the same time unleashing a world war, and should this after all prove unavoidable, to improve as far as possible the conditions under which it is to be waged" (Fischer 1967, p. 72). In passing on Wilhelm's message, Bethmann Hollweg carefully omitted the kaiser's strong plea to Austria-Hungary not to go to war (Fromkin 2004, p. 219). The Prussian war minister, General Falkenhayn, even went so far as to threaten the kaiser with deposition in favor of his son, the hawkish Crown Prince Wilhelm (who would later become a Hitler supporter) (ibid.).

"You've Made This Stew"

On his hasty return from his North Sea cruise on 26 July 1914, Wilhelm was met at Potsdam station by a nervous Bethmann Hollweg, who realized that the kaiser had unmasked his duplicity. "How did it all happen?" demanded the irate monarch. Recognizing that he was trapped, the chancellor simply tendered his resignation by way of apology. But the kaiser was not mollified. "You've made this stew," he fumed. "Now you're going to eat it!" (Butler 2010, p. 103.)

But that did not stop the chancellor and his staff from continuing their duplicity. On 25 July Sir Edward Grey had suggested that Germany persuade Austria to accept the Serbian reply to their ultimatum as "satisfactory" (Fischer 1967, p. 66.)—exactly what Wlhelm himself was to say a day later. But on the same day, 25 July, Jagow sent another message to Vienna urging them to declare war on Serbia without delay (ibid., p. 69.) Meanwhile the French foreign minister informed the German ambassador to Paris that France was anxious to find a peaceful solution and would use his influence on Russia in the interests of peace if Germany should "counsel moderation in Vienna, since Serbia has fulfilled nearly every point" (ibid.).

On 27 July the Austro-Hungarian ambassador to Germany reported that he had been assured by German Secretary of State (Foreign Minister) Gottlieb von Jagow that Germany "in no way identifies with" the British offer of mediation received from Foreign Secretary Sir Edward Grey. Then, on instructions from Bethmann Hollweg, German Ambassador Tschirschky failed to present Wilhelm's "Stop in Begrade" proposal until noon on 28 July by which time Austria had already declared war on Serbia (ibid., p. 73.)

On 28 July a fourth British offer of mediation, this time from King George V himself as well as Sir Edward Grey was put to Germany through its ambassador to London, Lichnowsky, who commented that King George desired that "British-German joint participation, with the assistance of France and Italy, may be successful in mastering in the interest of peace the present extremely serious situation" (Kautsky 2020, p. 210).

But, without even consulting Wilhelm, Bethmann Hollweg simply refused this eminently sensible last-minute attempt to prevent a general European war (Fischer 1967, p. 67). The hawkish Falkenhayn, supported by Moltke (the Younger), Chief of the German General Staff, advised Bethmann Hollweg to order a German attack on France and Russia at the same time!

To ensure acceptance of his peace plan, Grey proposed a "Stop in Belgrade" offer, in which Austria would occupy Belgrade and go no further— precisely the same proposal already put forward by Wilhelm. On 29 July Grey repeated this plan and urged Germany to accept it (Fromkin 2004, p. 226.) As historian Fritz Fischer pointed out, it was only when Bethmann Hollweg received a clear warning that Britain would intervene in a war did he begin to apply pressure on Austria for peace. (Fischer 1967, p. 79.) But it came too late.

Cousin Nicky

Tsar Nicholas II did not want to go to war with Germany any more than Kaiser Wilhelm wanted to go to war with Russia. The two monarchs were cousins and knew each other well, chiefly from visits to their British relatives. Wilhelm was Queen Victoria's grandson, and was at her bedside at the time of her death in 1901. Cousin "Nicky" had a Danish mother whose sister was the future Queen Alexandra, wife of Victoria's son and successor, Edward VII.

Pan-Slavism is often suggested as the motive for Russia's support for Serbia against Austria, thus unleashing the war. But Slavs were regularly at one another's throats, and until 1903 Serbia had been pro-Austrian.

Nicholas II was certainly no lover of regicides, or of the assassins of Franz Ferdinand, the heir to an ancient and honourable throne. Regicide has a tendency to become infectious, as Nicholas would discover to his cost when he and his whole family were unceremoniously shot by the Bolsheviks in 1918. Even the Serbian monarch who appealed (through his son, the regent) for Russian support against the Austrian ultimatum had come to power through regicide. In June 1903 King Alexander Obrenović and his wife were brutally murdered and their mutilated bodies thrown from a second-floor window. Alexander was replaced as king by Peter I of the rival Karageorgević house, which had been traditionally pro-Russian. Despite this, the tsar simply refused to offer Serbia any assistance.

How then did it happen that Russia, in concert with Britain and France, ended up supporting Serbia against Austria and Germany? The answer is that, like Wilhelm, Nicholas II was the prisoner of his own officials, but not for want of trying to break free. His influence in favor of peace could be felt as late as 30 July when it was reported that Serbia was now ready "on condition of certain interpretations, to swallow even Articles 5 and 6, that is, the whole Austrian ultimatum." The suggestion of talks was simply rejected out of hand by Bethmann Hollweg (Fischer 1967, p. 75). Not knowing about his chancellor's continued machinations, on 29 July Wilhelm had telegraphed the tsar: "I think a direct understanding between your government and Vienna possible and desirable" (Fromkin 2004, p. 223).

Nicholas replied on the same day in a telegram that does not appear to have reached Wilhelm: "It would be right to give over the Austro-Serbian problem to the Hague Conference." This was no empty gesture. The first Hague Conference, called in 1899 at the instigation of Nicholas II, was a meeting of 26 states, which laid down rules for the resolution of international conflicts. A second Hague conference, also called by Nicholas, involved no fewer than 44 states, and reached agreement on banning certain armaments and on the rules of war. The two Hague Conferences already held were essentially geared to the peaceful resolution of international conflict. So the proposal of yet another Hague Conference was undoubtedly genuine.

Another indication of the genuine peaceful intentions of both Nicholas and Wilhelm may be found in Nicholas's cancellation of general mobilization after an appeal from Wilhelm. But, under pressure from his senior generals, general mobilization was reinstated on 30 July 1914. (ibid., p. 231.)

Franz Joseph

Kaiser Franz Joseph of Austria, who was 84 years old in 1914, was the head of the Habsburg Austro-Hungarian empire made up of over 10 nations. By the *Ausgleich* ("compromise") of 1867 the empire had been split in two, between German-speaking Austria in the west and Hungary in the east. Hence the term "dual monarchy" and, in German, "*kaiserlich und königlich*," meaning "imperial and royal," because in Austria Franz Joseph was emperor, but in Hungary he had the title of king. In both halves of the empire there were large numbers of Slavs, including Czechs, Slovaks, Poles, Croats, and Serbs, who were subordinated to the German-speaking Austrians in the west or the Hungarian-speaking Hungarians in the east. German is only remotely related to the Slavonic languages, which are all interrelated with one another, but Hungarian, which is not an Indo-European language at all, is quite alien to all of them. Needless to say, the dual monarchy was highly unstable, with a number of independence movements among the different populations, which became violent from time to time.

At the head of this ramshackle edifice, Franz Joseph largely left decision-making to his ministers, though not to the same extent as Wilhelm and Nicholas. The two most influential were Foreign Minister Leopold Berchtold, who had lately become fairly hawkish, and Army Chief of Staff Franz Conrad von Hötzendorf, who had long called for a pre-emptive strike against Serbia. By contrast, the Hungarian prime minister, István Tisza, was steadfastly against war (but, ironically, would be assassinated in 1918 for responsibility for the war).

Though Franz Joseph had not always seen eye to eye with his liberal-minded nephew and heir, the murdered Franz Ferdinand, in a letter addressed to Kaiser Wilhelm, Franz Joseph opined that the only way to prevent the disintegration of his multinational empire was "to eliminate Serbia" as a state (Fischer 1967, p. 53)—adding that the decision for war against Serbia had been taken even before the assassination, which had only confirmed the need for it (Fromkin 2004, p. 157). And the ultimatum finally handed to Serbia on 23 July was couched in such humiliating terms as to be guaranteed rejection—except, of course, as mentioned above, that it was largely accepted.

Besides being illogical and doomed to failure, Franz Joseph's anti-Serbian ferment also happened to conflict with his family's age-old strategy in international affairs, as encapsulated in the motto: *Bella gerant alii, tu felix Austria nube!* ("Let others wage war, but you, happy Austria, marry!") The Latin verb *nubo* refers to marriage specifically from the bride's point of view. So what this slogan suggests is that Austria should pursue a peaceful policy and achieve its objectives by marrying off its daughters to powerful or influential men. In fact, the House of Habsburg had practiced this policy with great success for centuries, even to the point of marrying their enemies, including, for example, Franz Joseph's aunt Marie Louise, who married Napoleon Bonaparte after he had defeated her father, the Emperor Franz I, in battle.

Why then did Franz Joseph depart from this well-trodden policy path? It is hard to say, but it means that, of all the crowned heads engaged in World War I, he was the most culpable.

"International Catastrophe"

As can be seen from their proposals, the British government was as anxious to avoid war as Wilhelm. On 30 July 1914 Britain's King George V sent a telegram to his cousin, Prince Heinrich, the Kaiser's brother, reading as follows (with original spelling and punctuation):

> Thanks for your telegram so pleased to hear of williams efforts to concert with nicky to maintain peace—indeed i am earnestly desirous that such an irreparable disaster as an european war should be averted—my government is doing its utmost suggesting to russia & france to suspend further military preparations if austria will consent to be satisfied with occupation of belgrade & neighbouring servian territory as a hostage for satisfactory settlement of her demands other countries meanwhile suspending their war preparations—trust william will use his great influence to induce austria to accept this proposal thus proving that germany & england are working together to prevent what would be an international catastrophe—pray assure william i am doing & shall continue to do all that lies in my power to preserve peace of europe = George =

"William" here refers to Kaiser Wilhelm and "Nicky" to Tsar Nicholas. This telegram gives the lie to the common belief that the European leaders sleepwalked into war. George is alert to the imminent danger of a European war, which he calls "an irreparable disaster" and "an international catastrophe."

As late as 1 August 1914, just four days before declaring war on Germany, King George V noted that British public opinion was against joining the war. And he privately remarked that he preferred the traditional British policy of "splendid isolation." Also on 1 August, British Prime Minister Asquith wrote: "The City, which is in a terrible state of depression and paralysis, is the time being all against English intervention" (Fromkin 2004, p. 233). And: "The general opinion at present—particularly strong in the City—is to keep out at all costs" (Fromkin 2004 p. 236).

On 31 July France's General Joseph Joffre was refused permission to order a general mobilization (Fromkin 2004, p. 236). And, when on 1 August Britain offered to guarantee French neutrality, thus limiting the war to the eastern front, Wilhelm promptly accepted. But when the Kaiser ordered his forces to concentrate on Russia alone, he was met with fierce resistance from his Chief of General Staff, Moltke the Younger, who protested that it was too late, as the bulk of the troops were already advancing into Luxembourg and Belgium (Fischer 1967, p. 86). Wilhelm angrily rounded on him, and, referring to Moltke's famous uncle, retorted, "Your uncle would have given me a different answer!" (Albertini 1953, vol III, p. 172, referencing *Die Deutschen Documente zum Kriegsausbruch,* vol. III, p. 562). Wilhelm, trapped by the military, feebly went along with most of Moltke's arrangements, though he was able to cancel the planned invasion of the Netherlands, leaving the incompetent warloving Moltke lamenting, "Now, it only remains for Russia to back out, too" (Fischer 1967, p. 86). Once war broke out, Wilhelm, sidelined by the military commanders Hindenburg and Ludendorff, became a "shadow-kaiser," confined to ceremonial duties.

Germany's violation of Belgian neutrality, guaranteed by the Treaty of London of 1839, changed everything. On 3 August Grey spoke in the House of Commons, calling for British action against Germany. Large crowds started gathering outside Buckingham Palace. On the following day, 4 August 1914, Asquith went to see King George and an ultimatum was issued demanding German withdrawal from Belgian soil by midnight Berlin time. Bethmann Hollweg dismissed the 1839 Treaty as "a scrap of paper." The most catastrophic war in history (up to that time) had begun.

Envoi

The description of Wilhelm by his own officials as a "pacifist"—intended as censure, not praise—illustrates just how wide the split was between the kaiser and those supposedly serving him. It also reveals a very different Wilhelm from the strutting young monarch who "dropped the pilot," Bismarck, and managed through his bluster to earn for Germany the unenviable label of "the Hun."

Why, you may well ask, did the kaiser not just accept Bethmann Hollweg's resignation after unmasking his duplicity? The chancellor's overweening power had long rankled the kaiser—hence, of course, his clash with Bismarck. Even Wilhelm's father, the liberal Kaiser Friedrich III, had during his brief 99-day reign drafted a decree limiting the chancellor's power, which, however, was never promulgated. In regard to Bethmann Hollweg, Wilhelm seems naïvely to have believed that the chastened Chancellor had learned his lesson.

The paradoxical conclusion is that *had* Kaiser Wilhelm and Tsar Nicholas had *more* power over their own governments, had they been true autocrats, as is still quite commonly believed, the general European war that broke out in August 1914 could have been averted.

But the international situation would still have been fraught with danger. So it is necessary to take a step back and ask whether that situation would itself have been enough to cause perhaps a *different* conflagration. And a closer examination of the relationship between the internal politics and foreign policy of each country is also called for. That will all have to be the subject of another study.

Part V
Exit

Chapter 28
Natural Death

Hereditary monarchs who die in their beds after a long reign are best placed to establish a dynasty or stabilize a regime. Examples include Ramesses II of Egypt, King David of Israel, the Roman emperors Augustus and Constantine, the Mayan King Pakal, Genghis Khan, Louis XIV of France, and Frederick the Great of Prussia. The natural death of a ruler who has had a long reign can also cause disruption if the succession is disputed. This applies whether the monarch in question has achieved much (positive or negative) or nothing at all.

The Russian dictator Stalin's death in 1953 after close on 30 years of brutal repressive totalitarianism not only left the succession in doubt but also threw the whole Soviet system of government into turmoil. The death of the effete Charles II, the last Habsburg king of Spain, after a reign of 35 years, unleashed the War of the Spanish Succession (1701–14). By contrast, the death of Alexander the Great at the age of 32 did not prevent his long shadow from falling on a large part of his empire, amassed in less than 12 years, and from remaining Hellenized for over a thousand years.

*Rulers who long survive their time in office are likely to be largely forgotten by the time of their death. **Mohammad Zahir Shah** (1914–2007), king of Afghanistan from 1933 to 1973, was ousted by a coup, returned aged 87 in 2002, but was pressured by the United States to renounce all monarchical ambitions, though most delegates to the Loya Jirga ("Grand Assembly") are understood to have preferred the king to the American-backed Hamid Karzai. The king was extremely flexible, saying: "I will accept the responsibility of head of state if that is what the Loya Jirga demands of me, but I have no intention to restore the monarchy. I do not care about the title of king. The people call me Baba and I prefer this title" (Bearak 2007). This offer was ignored, thereby missing a potentially valuable opportunity, and the king died aged 92 in 2007.*

Five Thousand Years of Monarchy, First Edition. Michael Arnheim.
© 2026 John Wiley & Sons, Inc. Published 2026 by John Wiley & Sons, Inc.

Figure 28   Antoninus Pius.
SOURCE: Unknown author / Wikimedia Commons / Public domain.

*Non-hereditary rulers are, of course, even more likely to survive their time in office, usually by sniping from the sidelines. US Presidents **John Adams** and **Thomas Jefferson** are prime examples. A more recent example is **Herbert Hoover**, US president 1929–33, who died at the age of 90 in 1964, 31 years after losing to Franklin Roosevelt in the famous election of 1932. **Jimmy Carter**, born in 1924 and serving as US president from 1977 to 1981, the first US president to reach the age of 100, founded the Carter Center to "advance human rights" in more than 80 countries, has been active in the "Habitat for Humanity" housing organization and has been engaged in a number of diplomatic outreaches.*

Alexander to Constantine

The more closely associated a ruler is with a regime, the longer their rule is likely to last and the more likely they are to die a natural death. But the succession can be problematic:

- **Alexander the great (356–323 BCE):** After carrying all before him in a phenomenally successful career of lightning conquests, at the age of 32 Alexander evidently contracted some fever which proved fatal after about a week, though the precise cause of death has been a subject of controversy for centuries, and there has also been a suggestion of poisoning. A recent medical study claimed that he probably died of typhoid fever, which was endemic in Babylon at the time (Cunha 2004). Without any clear heir, his death unleashed 40 years of warfare between the *Diadochoi* ("Successors"), but, surprisingly, after the dust settled, Alexander's empire split into two main kingdoms, Ptolemaic Egypt (which lasted until 30 BCE) and Seleucid Syria (until 63 BCE), which owed their stability in no small measure to the example set by Alexander.

- **Augustus (r. 31 BCE–14 CE):** In his *Annals* the Roman historian Tacitus (c. 56–120 CE) purports to recount both the positive and negative views of Augustus by Romans on his death. With the exception of a rather distorted view of the imperial cult, the negative criticisms are petty, while the positive points are true without undue flattery, with a recognition that, after the civil wars, "the sole remedy for his distracted country was government by one man. Yet he organized the state, not as a king or dictator but under the designation as first citizen. The empire was bounded by the ocean or distant rivers. The legions, the provinces, the fleets, were all interconnected; justice for the citizens, respect for the allies; the city of Rome itself magnificently refurbished; and a resort to force only in the interests of order" (Tac. *Ann.* 1:9; tr. M. Arnheim). Augustus's chosen heirs had all predeceased him, possibly through the machinations of his wife, Livia, who was determined to secure the succession for Tiberius, her son by a previous marriage. The uneventful handover to Tiberius at least ensured the continuity of the regime, the administration of which was placed on a firm footing by Claudius (r. 41–54). The idea of the restoration of the old oligarchic Republic was finally put paid when the childless Nerva (r. 96–98), the first emperor actually chosen by the Senate, was forced to adopt as his son and heir Marcus Ulpius Traianus, or Trajan, who combined military support with popular appeal—which, coupled with hereditary succession, whether natural or by adoption, was shown to be a winning formula and gave Rome a period of unprecedented peace and prosperity.
- **Vespasian (r. 69–79):** A Roman emperor who famously faced death, cheerfully remarking on his deathbed, at the age of 69: *"Vae, puto deus fio"* ("Gosh, I think I'm becoming a god")—a reference to the practice of deifying emperors on their death (Suet., *Vita Vespasiani* 23:4). (For the serious implications of this remark see Chapters 4 and 26 of this book.)
- **Antoninus Pius (r. 138–161):** Sensing that the end was near, the Roman Emperor Antoninus Pius entrusted the empire and his daughter to the safekeeping of his adoptive son and heir, Marcus Aurelius. Just then the tribune of the night-watch entered, requesting the password. *"Aequanimitas,"* came the reply, his last word—equanimity, signifying tranquility, balance, or stability, a fitting label for his reign and that of all five "good emperors," whose reigns spanned the period from 96 to 180.

- **Constantine I (r. 306–337):** He came to power as Roman emperor through the breakdown of Diocletian's "Tetrarchy" (four-emperor system), ruling at first in the West alone and then, after 324, over the whole Roman Empire. In 325 he summoned and presided over the first Church Council, held at Nicea, though he only converted to Christianity on his deathbed—baptized by an Arian "heretic" bishop. His restoration of power in the imperial administration in the West to members of the senatorial aristocracy contributed to the fall of the Western Empire in the fifth century. His death triggered a massacre of family members by his son Constantius II, who then divided up the empire with his brothers Constantine II and Constans, emerging as sole ruler in 350 and himself dying in 361.

Disputed Succession Leading to War

Disputed successions can actually lead to war, as in the case of Charles II of Spain, who, inheriting the throne at the age of three, died, after lifelong ill health, at 38, sparking off the War of the Spanish Succession (1701–14).

- **Charles (Carlos) II of Spain (r. 1665–1700):** His poor health may well have been the result of the fact that his father and mother were uncle and niece. King Louis XIV of France immediately proclaimed a grandson of his as Philip V of Spain, but Louis's plan of uniting Spain with France backfired, as the Peace of Utrecht of 1714 required Philip V to renounce the French throne for himself and his heirs forever. The irony is that, while the French Bourbons faced deposition and execution in the person of Louis XVI in 1793, a second deposition in the person of Charles X in 1830, and a final deposition in 1848 in the person of Louis-Philippe of the Orléans cadet line, the Spanish Bourbons (Borbónes) are still on the throne of Spain at the time of this writing in the person of the aptly named Philip (Felipe) VI, who ascended the throne in 2014.

American Presidents Who Died Naturally in Office

Non-hereditary leaders who are in power for a fixed term or terms do not usually die in office. Eight presidents of the United States, for example, died in office, four by assassination (dealt with in Chapter 30) and four by natural causes:

- **William Henry Harrison (in office 4 March to 4 April 1841):** His main claim to fame is the fact that he was the first US president to die in office after the shortest presidency in American history. But he deserves to be remembered for several other reasons as well. His grandson, Benjamin Harrison, was elected as president too, serving from 1889 to 1893. The Harrisons were a well-known political family, whose extensive branches included Abraham Lincoln and the "king" of rock "n" roll, Elvis Presley. Scorning the icy weather at his inauguration as president on 4 March 1841 by riding to the ceremony on horseback without an overcoat or hat, he caught a chill while delivering the longest (almost two hours) inaugural address in history. Most notably, he called for voting rights for inhabitants of the District of Columbia, which even now has only been partially realized. Three weeks later he took to his bed with pneumonia, or possibly typhoid fever, which, with the aid of a team of medical men, soon became fatal. He died at 68 just a month after taking the oath of office. His death is also memorable because the US Constitution was unclear whether the vice president who takes over after a presidential death is actually president or only acting president. This question was all the more controversial at the time, as the vice president, John Tyler, was a former Democrat who did not get on with the late president's Whig principles and colleagues. Tearing up every letter addressed to him as "acting president," Tyler insisted that he was now the president, which he managed to get the Whig-controlled Congress to accept. But, proceeding to veto some major Whig legislation, he was expelled from the Whig Party, who referred to him as "His Accidency." Tyler's bold insistence that he was the president and not just "acting president" would be confirmed by the Twenty-fifth Amendment ratified in 1967, but Tyler's assertion had already made that a reality for the future.

- **Zachary Taylor (in office 1848–50):** Like Harrison, the next Whig president, Zachary Taylor, was also something of a war hero. Despite some rumors of assassination, Taylor evidently died, at 65, of a form of gastroenteritis, and the medical treatment that he received only ensured that he would not recover. He was the last president to own slaves while in office. The succession to the presidency of Vice President Millard Filmore proved uneventful.

- **Warren Gamaliel Harding (1921–23):** If ever there was a US president who looked as though he was at death's door it was Democratic President (Thomas) Woodrow Wilson (in office 1913–21), who in October 1919 suffered a serious stroke that left him bedridden. His wife kept his disability a secret from the public and even from his Cabinet, and she in effect became acting president. Despite his poor health, he lived through his party's crushing defeat in the 1920 election, was well enough to accompany the incoming Republican president, Warren Harding, at his inauguration on 4 March 1921, and, amazingly, actually outlived Harding, who died unexpectedly in San Francisco from an apparent heart attack at the age of 57 on 2 August 1923. He is best known for (inadvertently) inventing the word "normalcy" (a misreading of "normality") and for his steadfast opposition to American membership of the League of Nations, (one of Wilson's favorite ideas), which in fact the US never joined. He was mourned by nine million people, lining the railroad route taken to transport his body from San Francisco to Washington DC. Honored with an imposing, unprecedented mourning postage stamp, all the praise heaped on Harding quickly turned to mud when the "Teapot Dome" scandal and other instances of corruption started coming to light, though his reputation has been slightly rehabilitated since then. His successor, Calvin Coolidge, after serving out the rest of Harding's term of office, was elected in 1924 to a full term of his own as president and left office with a high popularity rating. Famously taciturn, he was known as "Silent Cal," though he did not hold back when asked his opinion of his commerce secretary as the Republican presidential nominee in 1928: "For six years that man has given me unsolicited advice—all of it bad."

- **Franklin Delano Roosevelt "FDR" (in office 1933–45):** Probably the US president who has come closest to being an autocratic monarch, he was elected four times, breaking the then unofficial two-term presidential limit set by George Washington. He revolutionized the whole of American government and politics with his semi-socialist "New Deal" and made the Democratic Party the natural majority party (see Chapter 23). He won his first term with a landslide victory in 1932, polling 57.4% of the vote as against 39.6% for the incumbent Republican president, Herbert Hoover, and even in his last election, in 1944, he won 53.4% of the vote as against 45.9% for his Republican opponent, Thomas E. Dewey. It was a remarkable achievement by any standard, and all the more so as Roosevelt was confined to a wheelchair throughout his presidency, having been stricken down with polio in 1921 at the age of 39.

- At the Yalta Conference with Churchill and Stalin in February 1945, toward the end of World War II, he unwisely accepted Stalin's promises, including an undertaking to allow free elections in eastern Europe after the war, which enabled the Soviet Union to bring down an "iron curtain" cutting off eastern Europe from the west, which was not lifted until the collapse of the Soviet Union and its "Warsaw Pact" in 1991. The British prime minister, Winston Churchill, it has to be said, was equally gullible, writing: "Poor Neville Chamberlain believed he could trust Hitler. He was wrong. But I don't think I am wrong about Stalin" (Berthon and Potts 2007). At Yalta, FDR had just over two months to live, so his mental faculties may not have been at their sharpest by that time. The well-known group photograph taken at Yalta shows Roosevelt looking like a living skeleton. But, though much older than FDR, Churchill had no such excuse, as he would live for another 20 years.

- While sitting for a portrait on 12 April 1945, Roosevelt suddenly slumped forward in his chair with a "terrific headache" and died shortly afterward from what was diagnosed as a cerebral hemorrhage. He was 63 years of age.

Harry S. Truman, who had met with Roosevelt only twice since becoming vice president in January 1944, succeeded to the presidency without knowing of the Manhattan Project nuclear research program or the atomic bomb, which he would soon order to be dropped on Japan to end World War II.

Child-Kings

Some of the saddest cases are those of children who die as pawns in adult games of chess.

Louis XVII of France (1785–95) is one example, the son of Louis XVI and Marie Antoinette, both of whom were guillotined in 1793 during the "Reign of Terror" of the French Revolution, leaving him as a neglected prisoner in the "Temple." After his death at the age of 10 his heart was removed by one of the attending physicians, who kept it in his family. It eventually found its way to the royal necropolis in the Basilica of St Denis, where it is kept in a crystal urn. [**Puyi** (1906–67), the last emperor of China, who was forced to abdicate at the age of six and was later Emperor of Manchukuo under Japanese control, is discussed in Chapter 30.]

Probably the best-known child-king case is that of the "Princes in the Tower," which still exercises a certain fascination in the minds of film-makers and mystery writers:

- **Edward V (r. April to June 1483):** Edward V (aged 12) and his brother Richard (aged 9) were lodged in the Tower of London on the death of their father, Edward IV. Edward IV's sudden death on 9 April 1483, at the early age of 40, was explained by his physicians as the result of his practice of overeating, followed by the use of an emetic to induce vomiting and then going back to gorging himself again. This could have caused the apoplexy that he apparently suffered. A biographer remarks that Edward IV "remains the only king in English history since 1066 in active possession of the throne who failed to secure the safe succession of his son. His lack of political foresight is largely to blame for the unhappy aftermath of his early death" (Ross 1974, p. 451). This is probably too harsh. Evidently aware that he was dying, Edward added a codicil to his will naming his brother, the future Richard III, as Protector after his death. He ought perhaps to have known his brother better than to have trusted him, but he seems to have satisfied himself that he had safeguarded his young son's position. Dominic Mancini, an Italian friar visiting London, kept a close watch on the two young princes, who were initially seen playing in the grounds of the tower, but who then disappeared from view after the summer of 1483. On 6 July 1483, their uncle Richard was crowned as Richard III, and in 1484 an Act of Parliament was passed, known as *Titulus Regius* ("The Royal Title"), declaring the princes to be illegitimate.

There is little doubt that the princes were murdered on the orders of Richard III. Edward V is one of the only two English kings who were never crowned, the other being Edward VIII, who abdicated in 1936. Several people later claimed to be either Edward V or his brother. But two small human skeletons answering the description of the two princes in terms of size and likely ages were discovered in a wooden chest by workmen refurbishing the Tower of London.

- Richard III was killed in the Battle of Bosworth Field in 1485, which ended the Wars of the Roses with the victory of the Lancastrian claimant, who became Henry VII (r. 1485–1509). During his reign several people came forward claiming to be either Edward V or his brother Richard, notably Lambert Simnel, who was crowned "King Edward" in Dublin; and Perkin Warbeck, who managed to get King James IV of Scotland to accept him as "Prince Richard" and even to send an invasion force to England on his behalf. When the attempt failed, Perkin Warbeck was captured, and, despite renouncing his claim, was imprisoned and executed.

Chapter 29
Abdication

Diocletian (r. 284–305) was the first Roman emperor to abdicate. Abdication has become much more common in recent times, particularly among constitutional monarchs, including Queens Beatrix of the Netherlands and Margrethe II of Denmark, Kings Juan Carlos of Spain and Albert II of Belgium, and Emperor Akihito of Japan. In addition there was the abdication of the kings of Cambodia and Bhutan and the emirs of Kuwait and Qatar. Not to mention the abdication, or retirement, of Pope Benedict XVI in 2013. Abdication is not always entirely voluntary, as, for example, in the case of Britain's Edward VIII in 1936.

Netherlands

Having inherited the Dutch throne in 1890 at the age of 10, Queen Wilhelmina of the Netherlands abdicated in 1948, passing the throne to her daughter Juliana, who abdicated in 1980 at the age of 71, being succeeded by her daughter Beatrix, who in her turn abdicated in favor of her son Willem- Alexander in 2013 at the age of 75.

Wilhelmina was not the first Dutch monarch to abdicate. Her ancestor Willem I (r. 1815–40), the first member of the House of Orange-Nassau to bear the title of king, abdicated after the loss of Belgium and a reduction of his powers under a new Constitution.

Wilhelmina's abdication in 1948 came in the wake of the nationalist rebellion against Dutch rule in the oil-rich Dutch East Indies (mostly comprising Indonesia), which ended with the Dutch transferring sovereignty to Indonesia in 1949 after a bloody four-year war. Though a constitutional monarch with minimal power, Wilhelmina was heavily criticized by the Dutch economic elite for the loss of the East Indies.

Five Thousand Years of Monarchy, First Edition. Michael Arnheim.
© 2026 John Wiley & Sons, Inc. Published 2026 by John Wiley & Sons, Inc.

Figure 29 Charles IV of Spain and his family.
SOURCE: Museo del Prado / Wikimedia Commons / Public domain.

In 1983 the Dutch monarch lost the position of even the nominal head of the Dutch armed forces. The abdications of Queens Juliana and Beatrix were not in response to any pressure.

Spain

The abdication of King Juan Carlos in favor of his son Felipe (Philip) VI in 2014, after a reign of 39 years and under a certain amount of pressure, was only the most recent of a number of Spanish abdications. His grandfather, Alfonso XIII, who had been king since the day he was born in 1886 (as the posthumous son of Alfonso XII), fled Spain following his abdication after what was perceived as an anti-monarchist vote in the municipal elections of 1931. This was followed by the declaration of the Second Spanish Republic, which the ex-king accused of being "inspired and sponsored by communism, freemasonry and Judaism" (quoted in Gonzalez Calleja 2011, p. 77). Francisco Franco, the leader of the victorious Nationalists in the ensuing Spanish Civil War (1936–39), let it be known at the outset that he would not be restoring Alfonso XIII to the throne but ruled himself as *caudillo* ("leader") from 1936 until his death in 1975, with Juan Carlos groomed to take over as king—but he failed Franco by standing firm for the new parliamentary system when it was challenged in an attempted coup in 1981.

Alfonso XII's mother, Isabella II, had been forced to abdicate by a military *pronunciamiento* leading to a so-called "Glorious Revolution" in 1868, after which the Italian Prince Amadeo was invited to occupy the Spanish throne. While the new king was on his way to Spain, his sponsor, Prime Minister General Prim, was shot dead on the streets of Madrid. It did not take long before King Amadeo abdicated, finding the Spanish people, as he put it, to be "ungovernable." Spain now tried for the first time the alien format of a republic, but when that too failed they fell back on the Bourbons (or, in Spanish, Borbones), and it was then that they called upon Isabella's young son to take the throne as Alfonso XII.

Going a bit further back in Spanish history, we come to a game of musical chairs involving no fewer than three abdications. Faced with a serious riot in 1808, partly instigated by his son Ferdinand, King Charles IV of Spain abdicated in favor of Ferdinand (reigning as Ferdinand VII) and then sought the assistance of Emperor Napoleon of France to regain his throne. Instead, Napoleon summoned father and son to Bayonne, forced both to abdicate and kept Ferdinand as a prisoner in France for six years, meanwhile handing the Spanish throne to his own brother Joseph. Wrongly assuming that the Spanish people would welcome the blessings of the French Revolution personified by Napoleon and his brother, this only led to widespread revolts, turning into the protracted Peninsular War, with Britain supporting the anti-French Spanish guerrillas. Napoleon's defeat led to his brother's abdication and the restoration of Ferdinand VII.

The earliest abdication in Spanish history was that of Carlos I of Spain, better known as the Emperor Charles V of the Holy Roman Empire, who ruled Spain from 1516 till 1556, when he abdicated all his kingdoms and retired to a monastery. It was under his rule that Spain conquered Mexico and Peru, while in Europe he was faced with the Protestant Reformation in the person of Martin Luther. It is thought that the need to agree an accommodation with the Protestants in the Peace of Augsburg of 1555 was one of the main reasons for his decision to abdicate. The Peace hit upon the formula *Cuius regio, eius religio* ("Whose realm, his religion"), meaning that the ruler of each German state could choose the religion, Catholic or Protestant, of his state. The inhabitants of a Catholic state had to be Catholic and those in a Protestant state Protestant. Catholics who found themselves in a Protestant state had to move to a Catholic state, and Protestants living in a Catholic state had to move to a Protestant state. In only a few German cities were Catholics and Protestants allowed to coexist side by side.

China

One of the most pathetic cases of abdication is that of Puyi (1906–67), the last emperor of China of the Qing (Manchu) dynasty. In 1908, at the age of 2, he was selected by the Empress Dowager Cixi to succeed his half-uncle, the childless Guangxu emperor (r. 1875–1908). Without warning, he was forcibly whisked away to the Forbidden City in Beijing by a group of court eunuchs and guards. Though he cried his way through the deafening music and frightening ceremonial of his coronation on the Dragon Throne, he soon became used to being treated as a divine being with supreme power and everyone kowtowing before him and obeying his every whim. "Flogging eunuchs was part of my daily routine," he would write. "My cruelty and love of wielding power were already too firmly set for persuasion to have any effect on me" (Behr 1987, p. 74f). After his marriage, Puyi began to take control away from the traditional court aristocrats and the eunuchs, who, while supposedly attending to his every need, were stealing on a lavish scale. Instead he appointed able and responsible officials.

In October 1911 an army mutiny in Wuhan sparked off widespread demands for the overthrow of the Qing dynasty, which had ruled China since 1644. The dynasty was widely seen as having lost the "Mandate of Heaven" by its incompetent and corrupt rule. In 1912, with China now declared to be a republic, Puyi was forced to abdicate while being allowed to retain his title with the protocol applicable to a foreign monarch. For just 11 days in July 1917, Puyi was restored as emperor by General Zhang Xun in a move that failed to achieve any public or official recognition, so forcing Puyi to abdicate again. In a coup led by the warlord Feng Yuxiang in 1924, Puyi was expelled from the Forbidden City and reduced to the status of a private citizen. Then, taking refuge in the Japanese legation, he moved to the Japanese "concession" in Tianjin, where he remained until 1931.

From 1932 to 1945 Puyi was the nominal ruler of the Japanese-controlled Manchuria, renamed Manchukuo, first as "chief executive," then, from 1934, as "emperor," and from 1938 as a "god-emperor," a pale shadow of the emperor of Japan.

After Japan's defeat in World War II, Puyi abdicated yet again and was taken prisoner by Russian forces, who returned him to China after Mao Zedong's Communists had taken power there in 1949. After "remodeling" and "re-education" he was released in 1959 and given the job of a street-sweeper. Getting lost on his first day at work, he accosted astonished passers-by with the plea: "I'm Puyi, the last emperor of the Qing dynasty. I'm staying with relatives and can't find my way home." So contrite did he become for his supposed past crimes that he made a point, for example, of always boarding a bus last. On one occasion he missed his ride, because he mistook the bus conductor for a passenger.

Japan

The Taika reforms starting in 645 centralized the administration with the emperor at its head. The Emperor Tenmu (r. 673–686), who was the first to be accorded the title *tenno* in his own lifetime, renewed the *kabane* system of hereditary noble titles, which had been modified under the Taika reforms (see Chapter 8). Temnu reduced the influence of powerful aristocratic clans such as the Otomo and the Soga clans, and the previously powerful Omi and Muraji were reduced in status in the new eight-level *kabane*. He tried to keep his many feuding sons from making war on one another, but one of them was executed for treason after his death. He was succeeded on the throne by his widow, the Empress Jito, who also happened to be the daughter of Emperor Tenji (r. 668–672). Under her rule there was a *Kugyo,* or *Daijo-kan,* or "Great Council of State" of four men, headed by the *Daijo-daijin,* or "chancellor," who in Jito's case was the third son of Emperor Tenmu. This form of "cabinet government" declined with the rise of the Fujiwara clan (see Chapter 4). Besides the Empress Jito and two other empresses, over 60 Japanese emperors abdicated, mostly in favor of a son, the latest being Akihito, who abdicated in favor of his son Naruhito in 2019.

A more meaningful type of abdication is associated with the so-called "cloistered emperors." During the Heian period of Japanese history (794–1185), the last period before the emperor became eclipsed by the shogun, it was common for an emperor to retain power and influence after abdication and retirement to a Buddhist monastery, in order to counterbalance the influence of the Fujiwara regents. In the meantime the purported new emperor, the "cloistered emperor's" chosen successor, would carry out the ceremonial duties of the monarchy. A separate imperial court would develop around a cloistered emperor, who would also have his own troops, the so-called *Hokumen no Bushi,* which eventually led to the rise to power of the Taira clan, which was related to the imperial house. The Taira were opposed by the Minamoto clan in a war, in which the Taira were soundly beaten, enabling the Minamoto to establish the first shogunate in 1192, which lasted to 1333.

Interestingly, during the whole period from 1192 to the end of the last—Tokugawa—shogunate in 1868, no shogun tried to usurp the imperial throne, because the shogun had his authority from the emperor, who was not only the head of the Shinto state religion but could also trace his lineage from time immemorial and was believed to be a direct descendant of the sun goddess Amaterasu.

In 1868 the "Meiji Restoration" brought the shogunate to an end in the name of the emperor but actually gave power to an oligarchy. On only two prior occasions had the emperor tried to recover their lost power. In 1219 the Emperor Go-Toba engaged in such an attempt only to be defeated by a samurai army. And in 1333 the Emperor Go-Daigo overthrew the Kamakura shogunate in the so-called "Kenmu Restoration" of imperial power, which lasted only until 1336, when the Ashikaga shogunate was established. Go-Daigo rejected the shogun's attempt to alternate the imperial throne between two branches of the imperial house, and his son Go-Murakami emerged victorious in 1339, reigning until his death in 1368, with the Ashikaga shogunate in place.

Chapter 30
Assassination

When does a murder become an assassination? The word "assassin" comes from the drug "hashish" (cannabis) being originally applied to a group of Nizari Ismailis (a branch of Shia Islam under the spiritual leadership of the Aga Khan) known as the "Order of Assassins," who murdered certain leading political and religious figures between the eleventh and thirteenth centuries. The term "assassination" tends now to be confined to the murder of a prominent or powerful person, with "regicide" referring specifically to the murder of a king. "Execution," on the other hand, strictly refers to the carrying out of a death sentence after a trial, though the term is now commonly used for gangland murders as well. All these terms have some emotive overtones and there can be disputes as to which one is most appropriate in the circumstances. For example, the beheading of King Charles I of England in 1649 was deemed an "execution" by his enemies, while royalists regarded it as "regicide," with the late king even becoming "Charles the Martyr" to High Anglicans.

Causation

The recent academic theory seeking to establish a causal relationship between the incidence of regicide and the prevalence of primogeniture does not stand up to scrutiny. It is one of the many theories that try to base major developments on superficial causes. The reason why assassinations do or do not take place must be sought elsewhere in the power structure and forces at work in the societies in question.

If you are looking for superficial causes, the presence or absence of primogeniture is less significant than the degree of hubris of the victim. How else can one explain why, on 14 April 1865, Abraham Lincoln chose to attend a theatrical performance in Washington DC, right on the border with the Confederacy, which had surrendered just five days before? And, as if that were not enough, why was he seated in an unprotected box while his stand-in bodyguard was drinking in a nearby tavern? Besides Lincoln's hubris, security was sadly lacking. When the same negligent and probably drunk stand-in bodyguard was assigned as bodyguard to Lincoln's widow as she was moving out of the White House after the assassination, Mary Lincoln rounded on him yelling: "So you are on guard tonight, on guard in the White House after helping to murder the President" (Martin 2010, p. 2).

Similarly, why did Tsar Alexander II step out of his bulletproof carriage, contrary to his coachman's earnest entreaties, after a first bomb had left him unharmed? There was nothing he could have done to assist his fatally injured footman, and it was folly to try to confront the bomber, which he was also evidently planning to do when hit by the second bomb outside the coach. Similarly, why did John Kennedy choose to ride in an open convertible limousine through downtown Dallas on a visit to Texas in the hope of reconciling two hostile wings of the Texas Democratic Party? He ought to have known that his trip was fraught with danger, though, as it turned out, his assassination was unconnected with the intra-party feud. But the cheers of the crowd could have been acknowledged just as well, and without risk, from within a bulletproof car. Another key example of a wholly avoidable assassination was the murder of Archduke Franz Ferdinand, heir to the Austrian throne, in Sarajevo, the capital of Bosnia-Herzegovina, in 1914, which sparked off World War I. At the Congress of Berlin in 1878, Austria-Hungary had been given the right to occupy and administer Bosnia-Herzegovina, while that territory remained part of the Ottoman Empire, and in 1908 Austria-Hungary decided to annex it, which raised international objections and was particularly resented by Serbia and the Bosnian Muslims. For Austrian Kaiser Franz Joseph to send his heir Franz Ferdinand on a visit to Sarajevo in the midst of this ferment was asking for trouble. And annexing the territory in 1908 was foolhardy. The Habsburg empire of Austria-Hungary was already a bubbling cauldron of mutually hostile national, linguistic, and religious groups. But it would be a mistake to assume that the assassination of Archduke Franz Ferdinand was a real cause of World War I rather than simply a spark that lit an already existing fuse (see Chapter 27).

The Ides of March

The Ides of March, 44 BCE, is one of the best-known dates in history, marking as it does the assassination of Julius Caesar, which plunged Rome into civil war and ultimately resulted in a lasting new regime under Caesar's heir, Augustus.

Figure 30 Julius Caesar as "dictator perpetuo," 44 BCE.
SOURCE: Gallica Digital Library / Wikimedia Commons / Public domain.

The events leading up to this climactic event are discussed in Chapter 6 of this book. It is worth contemplating, however, the possible alternative scenarios confronting Rome at the time.

Pompey

Caesar's rise to power came about initially by defeating his erstwhile colleague in the so-called "First Triumvirate" of 60 BCE, Pompey (Gnaeus Pompeius; 106–48 BCE), who was given the *cognomen* ("surname," "sobriquet") Magnus ("the Great") on the strength of his glittering military career, including his spectacular success in clearing the Mediterranean of pirates in three months in 67 BCE. Though the senate was nervous of Pompey's potential power, he disbanded his army at Brundisium on his arrival back in Italy in 62 BCE. While Caesar was the leader of the *Populares,* the "party" within the ruling oligarchy that championed the cause, and depended on the support of the lower classes, Pompey threw in his lot with the more conservative *Optimates* (literally, "the best men"), bent on the continued dominance of the senatorial elite. During this time Caesar was finishing up the conquest of Gaul. If he were to disband his army and return to Rome as a private citizen, he would likely have been faced with prosecution. He chose instead to defy the Senate and cross into Italy with one armed legion, supposedly with the famous remark: "The die is cast."

Caesar was now at war with the Republic, which had entrusted its fortunes to Pompey, who was roundly defeated at Pharsalus in 48 BCE, leaving the way open to Caesar to enter Rome as a conquering hero, leading to a brief period of sole rule and then to his assassination.

The question is: What if Pompey had won? Would he have taken sole power too? A recent writer opines that that is exactly what would have happened. As "the rise of men such as Pompey was more or less unstoppable, ... Pompey has a good claim to be called the first Roman emperor" (Beard 2016, pp. 277, 273). Pompey was certainly ambitious, but more for fame and praise than for power. And, when he was in possession of political power as sole consul, Pompey showed himself politically inept. (See the discussion on this in Chapter 6.)

Brutus

An even more egregious error of the same type is made in regard to one of Caesar's leading assassins, Marcus Junius Brutus, who, during the civil war against Antony and the future Augustus, issued coins with his own likeness on the obverse and "Liberty" or "Ides of March" on the reverse. The whole basis of this second civil war was Brutus's desire (in the name of his putative ancestor, Lucius Junius Brutus, whose name was a byword for anti-monarchical republicanism) to restore the oligarchic Republic that Julius Caesar had destroyed. Had Brutus and the assassins won this civil war and Brutus then tried to assume sole power, his attempt would have been smartly nipped in the bud by his co-conspirators, who were dedicated *Optimates* to a man—not that Brutus had ever shown the slightest inclination to become sole master of Rome.

Antony

Instrumental in defeating the conspirators at Philippi in 42 BCE, Antony (Marcus Antonius) was given the Eastern half of the Roman world while his ally, the future Augustus, took charge of the West. But the two soon drifted apart, with Antony in thrall to the Egyptian Queen Cleopatra, and eventually Antony and the future Augustus came to blows in the Battle of Actium in 31 BCE, which Antony lost. What if he had won? He was already master of half the Roman world, which he had governed for more than a decade. But his behavior in the immediate aftermath of Caesar's assassination makes one wonder about his political nous. Despite being a loyal Caesarian, so poor was his reading of the political signs that he entertained to dinner one of the leading conspirators, Cassius, and even gave his son to the conspirators as a hostage (see Chapter 6).

Julius Caesar's assassination turned out to be a boon for Rome and the world—but only because it was ultimately succeeded by that signal product of ingenious statecraft, the Augustan Principate, which is hard to envisage with anyone else at the helm (see Chapter 6).

"Absolutism Tempered by Assassination"

It has been suggested that the incidence of regicide has been sharply reduced where succession to the throne is based on primogeniture, or the right to succeed of the eldest legitimate child or son (agnatic primogeniture) (Bagge 2019). This sounds plausible, as an assassin might be expected to have second thoughts if he knows to whom the succession is vouchsafed. In practice, this hypothesis does not hold up very well.

It may be worth testing this theory against the incidence of assassination in Tsarist Russia, whose constitution was cynically described as "absolutism tempered by assassination," a recognition of the pivotal role of the tsar, upon whose autocratic personal power the stability of the state depended. Five tsars were assassinated between 1762 and 1918.

A good example of the non-applicability of the theory about the incidence of regicide is the assassination of Tsar Alexander II in 1881, whose son and successor, Alexander III (r. 1881–94) would adopt a much more hardline policy generally than his "liberal" father. Though his political views would not have been widely known at the time, there certainly was no doubt about the succession. Would-be assassins would have been well aware of the fact that eliminating Alexander II was not going to topple the regime.

So, why *were* the revolutionaries so intent on assassinating Alexander II, who had in fact survived five attempts on his life before succumbing to the self-styled "intelligentsia" of *Narodnaya Volya* ("People's Will") in 1881? The second attempt was made while the tsar was riding in an open carriage, with his two sons and the French Emperor Napoleon III seated beside him, during the tsar's visit to the World Fair in Paris in 1867. The would-be assassin was Antoni Berezowski, the young son of an impoverished Polish nobleman, whose motive was the liberation of "Congress Poland" from Russian rule—an understandable but not very practical objective, as the death of Alexander II would have been unlikely to persuade his successor to relinquish his control, no matter what his views were. If the Berezowski family had been forced to free their serfs in Alexander II's abolition of serfdom, that might have been another motive for the attempted assassination. Alexander II was the most "liberal" of all Russia's rulers, and he was dubbed "Alexander the Liberator" for, in addition to freeing the serfs, he deprived the nobility of some privileges, abolished corporal punishment, reformed the judicial system by introducing elected local judges, and established the *zemstvo* system of local elected assemblies.

Radical revolutionaries, bent on toppling a regime as a whole, may be even more opposed to reforming rulers than they are to autocratic rulers, as reforming rulers may have a certain amount of moderate support, which the radical revolutionaries wish to eliminate together with the hated regime. Strangely, however, the self-styled *Narodnaya Volya* "intelligentsia" who assassinated

Alexander II had actually claimed that they would lay down their arms once political concessions were made (Offord 1986). But they later saw violence as the only way to overthrow the hated tsarist regime, imagining that the assassination of Alexander II would spark a revolution.

Some contemporary accounts portray Alexander II as being reduced to a nervous wreck by all the attempts on his life. Yet, his conduct during his assassination does not bear this out. For one thing, the assassination took place while the tsar was traveling along his accustomed Sunday route. Had he been afraid of assassination, he would surely have varied his route. And, once his carriage was struck by a bomb, despite the coachman's pleas for him to remain inside the bulletproof carriage (a thoughtful gift from Napoleon III), he emerged to assist his fatally injured footman, and in response to enquiries remarked, "Thank God, I'm untouched." Crying "It's too early to thank God," another assassin stepped forward and hurled a second bomb at the tsar, which proved fatal. Five revolutionaries actively engaged in the assassination plot were duly rounded up, tried, and hanged, while the second bomber died of wounds from his explosion. The reactionary Alexander III (r. 1881–94) reverted to the policy epitomized by his grandfather Nicholas I (r. 1825–55) in the slogan, "Orthodoxy, Autocracy and Nationality," this last component meaning Russification. Alexander III cracked down hard on all dissent, and revolutionary groups were driven underground. Alexander is said to have warned such groups: "Where two or three of you are gathered together, there I am among you" in the form of the *Okhrana,* or secret police. The plot by *Narodnaya Volya* to kill Alexander III on the sixth anniversary of his father's assassination was nipped in the bud, the ideologue and chief bombmaker being the older brother of Vladimir Lenin, the future Soviet leader, whose name was Aleksandr Ulyanov, and who was tried and hanged at the age of 21. Their father, Ilya Ulyanov, was a distinguished school inspector, who was promoted to "active state councilor," elevating him, in accordance with Peter the Great's "Table of Ranks," into the ranks of the hereditary aristocracy and gave him the right to be addressed as "Your Excellency."

Both Alexander II and Alexander III had an undisputed son and heir waiting in the wings, so this assassination and attempted assassinations have nothing to do with the presence or absence of primogeniture, but rather with the nature of the regime, which aroused a lot of opposition among the educated bourgeoisie, from which the assassins and would-be assassins were largely drawn. These revolutionaries, imbued with the idea of a widespread peasant revolution toppling the regime, were unable to interest the peasants in their vision, despite going to considerable lengths to do so, including deliberately taking menial jobs that would place them cheek by jowl with the peasantry. Yet, though respected or even revered by the peasantry as autocratic ruler by divine right and as head of the Orthodox Church, the tsar did not actively seek peasant support, and Alexander II's emancipation of the serfs actually backfired, because the arrangement was for the state to buy the land from the landowners in the form of a loan to the freed serfs, who were then required to pay it back to the state as "Redemption Payments." Not surprisingly, this hardship created a big dent in the gratitude felt by the peasants for their emancipation. In 1901, during the reign of Nicholas II (r. 1894–1918), there was widespread famine, and in the "Years of the Red Cockerel," 1903–04, much countryside land was simply seized by the peasants. And, besides reducing some aristocratic privileges, the tsars still relied far too much on aristocratic ministers and bureaucrats and a system of administration which actually increased the size of the aristocracy by rewarding good service with hereditary ennoblement.

Britain's Queen Victoria (r. 1837–1901) is another case which is clearly unconnected with the rules for succession, as her eldest son and successor, the future Edward VII (r. 1901–10), waited somewhat impatiently for over 60 years to ascend the throne, and, if he had predeceased his mother, she had a whole brood of younger children. Yet Victoria was the target of no less than eight assassination attempts, perhaps the most brazen of which was the attack by Robert Pate in 1850, who struck the Queen on the head with a metal-tipped cane. After several attempted shootings, Victoria quipped, "It is worth being shot at to learn how much one is loved." But this brave front was only a façade.

Most of Victoria's assailants had no known motive, but two were Irish nationalists of sorts and one was opposed to female rule. But none of the attempts was made because of a doubted succession!

"Unbearable Aristocratic Despotism"

One of the most perceptive of monarchs in regard to the danger to monarchy posed by the aristocracy was Gustav III of Sweden (r. 1771–92), discussed in Chapter 12. Accusing the aristocratic "Council of the Realm," which had controlled Sweden for the past half-century, of imposing an "unbearable aristocratic despotism," he introduced a new "Instrument of Government" greatly augmenting his own power, which was approved by three of the four "estates" (clergy, burghers, and peasants) represented in the Riksdag (Parliament), with only the aristocracy remaining implacably opposed—so much so, indeed, that they launched a conspiracy against him, shooting him in the back at a masked ball in 1792, leaving the throne to the 13-year-old Gustav IV Adolf.

There is no reason to think that the assassins would have held off if Gustav III's heir had been an adult, because they did, in fact, depose the heir some years later anyway, barring his descendants from the throne forever. The throne was then given to the deposed king's uncle, who became Carl (Charles) XIII (r. 1809–18) under a new "liberal" (i.e. anti-monarchical) constitution. And, in an unprecedented move, Napoleon's Marshal Jean-Baptiste Bernadotte, who had no connection with Sweden, was adopted as son and heir to the prematurely senile, infirm, and childless Carl XIII, whom he succeeded as Charles XIV John (r. 1818–44). The new king was no liberal, but exercised as much power as he could within the constraints of the "Instrument of Government" of 1809. From 1917 the king was obliged to select his ministers from the majority party in the Riksdag. The Instrument of Government of 1974 clipped the wings of the monarchy even more closely. In 1980 the Act of Succession replaced "agnatic primogeniture" (which gave precedence to a son over daughters, regardless of age) with "absolute primogeniture," which gives the succession to the eldest child regardless of gender. The Amendment of 2009 introduced some more "politically correct" measures.

A sidelight on the fate of Gustav III is provided by Giuseppe Verdi's opera *Un Ballo in Maschera* ("A Masked Ball"), composed in 1859. The original libretto was about the assassination of Gustav III, but such was the sensitivity of conservative governments at the time to the possibility of the assassination of a monarch, that the plot had to be changed to relate to the fictitious assassination of the governor of seventeenth-century colonial Massachusetts.

Chapter 31
Deposition

*D*eposition, *or dethronement, refers to the removal or ousting of a ruler from power. There is a fine line between deposition and abdication, similar to that between jumping and being pushed. A ruler may be removed for a variety of reasons, ranging from a family quarrel, to a coup d'état, to revolution, to civil war, to conquest. It has been suggested that: "Monarchies with a fixed succession rule [are] much less plagued by instability than less institutionalized autocracies." (Kurrild-Klitgaard 2004). It seems plausible that a planned deposition might be put on hold for fear that an heir might seek to avenge the deposition. However, this does not appear to be supported by evidence in some of the best-known cases of deposition. Britain's Charles I, Louis XVI of France, and Nicholas II of Russia, all of them with heirs under a "fixed succession rule," were deposed in a revolution and then brutally killed. In all three cases, the revolutionaries were bent on permanently abolishing the monarchy, though in Britain and France the monarchies were subsequently restored under an heir. A notoriously unstable monarchy which nevertheless had a "fixed succession rule" was that of modern Greece, which is discussed below. Few deposed rulers ever stage a comeback. The Athenian tyrant Peisistratus was one, together with the Byzantine emperor, Zeno, Henry VI of England, Ferdinand VII of Spain, and Constantine I and George II of Greece. One of the strangest cases was the deposition, under the guise of abdication, of Gustav IV Adolf of Sweden, who was forced to pass over his own son and renounce the throne in favor of his decrepit uncle, leading almost immediately to the throne being offered to a non-noble foreigner with no connection to Sweden and no experience of government of any kind (see Chapter 12). So much for the idea that a "fixed succession rule" makes for stable monarchies.*

Five Thousand Years of Monarchy, First Edition. Michael Arnheim.
© 2026 John Wiley & Sons, Inc. Published 2026 by John Wiley & Sons, Inc.

Peisistratus: "Champion of the People"

Aristotle names three demagogic tyrants including Peisistratus of Athens (died 527 BCE) as "champions of the people" who won the confidence of the people (*dēmos*) by their "enmity toward the rich." All three came to power by means of a coup.

Peisistratus first came to power in about 561 BCE and did not let the *dēmos* down. It is significant that the people were not seeking to take power into their own hands: they were looking for a champion to take power on their behalf. Aristotle's *Athenian Constitution* rounds off its assessment of Peisistratus's long rule by describing him as popular (*dēmotikos*) and humane (*philanthrōpos*), ruling in accordance with the law and not favouring his own interests—even to the point of appearing in person to defend himself against a murder charge, although his accuser then took fright and left.

Though deposed twice, we are told, he easily got back into power because most of the nobles (*gnōrimoi*), as well as the people, were well disposed toward him, the former by his social interaction and the latter by his assistance to them in their personal affairs, and he "behaved impeccably (*kalōs*) to both." (Aristot. *AP* 9). Adding aristocratic support to his original populist power base was an unusual—and far from easy—achievement for a tyrant, which presumably contributed to his resilience.

Peisistratus died in his bed in 527 BCE and was succeeded as tyrant by his son Hippias, who was ousted in an aristocratic coup (with the help of a Spartan army on its second attempt) in 510 BCE (for more on this, see Chapter 15).

Figure 31   William III and Mary II, 5 guineas, 1692.
SOURCE: Daderot / Wikimedia Commons / Public domain.

"The Glorious Revolution"

England's "Glorious Revolution," deposing King James II, was neither glorious nor a revolution. His father Charles I (r. 1625–49) had been beheaded in 1649 after losing a long and gruelling civil war, but 10 years as a "Commonwealth," mostly spent under the rule of Oliver Cromwell, left the people hankering for a restoration of the monarchy, which duly took place in 1660.

After spending long years in exile abroad, Charles I's son Charles II, known as "the Merry Monarch," adopted the watchword, "I will not go on my travels again." Accordingly, he was prepared to toe the line and accept the reduced role offered to him by Parliament, which gave him more time to devote to his numerous mistresses.

His brother and successor, James II (r. 1685–89), had a very different attitude to royal power. His conversion to Catholicism during Charles's reign led to the "Exclusion Crisis" of 1679–81, in which the Whig party in Parliament launched an (ultimately unsuccessful) attempt to exclude James from the throne. However, though he ascended the throne on Charles II's untimely death in 1685, James was ousted in the so-called "Glorious Revolution" of 1688–89—a misnomer, as it was in reality the recovery by Parliament of its pre-eminent position established by the civil war and the execution of Charles I.

Though James II is portrayed by his enemies and many modern historians as a power-hungry despot, probably the chief objection against him on the part of the parliamentary elite was his Declaration of Indulgence extending religious toleration to Catholics and Protestant Dissenters alike—including Quakers, a leading member of which, William Penn, founder of Pennsylvania, was a close friend of his. In his speaking tour to whip up support, James II struck a very modern note in a speech delivered in Chester: "Suppose ... there should be a law made that all black men should be imprisoned, it would be unreasonable and we had as little reason to quarrel with other men for being of different [religious] opinions as for being of different complexions" (Sowerby 2013, p. 42)

Was James genuine in wishing to extend toleration to all and sundry—or was this, as his detractors maintain, just a ruse to enable him to bring the country back into the fold of Rome? His Quaker friend William Penn certainly believed in his sincerity, but James's deposition deprived him of the opportunity of putting the policy into practice.

In June 1688, a group made up of six Protestant noblemen and a bishop actually invited William of Orange to invade England "to save the Protestant religion." William, a staunch Protestant, who was married to James's Protestant daughter Mary, obliged, landing at the head of a large army. Losing his nerve, James fled to France, dropping the Great Seal of England into the River Thames. Parliament, refusing to depose him, claimed that he had abdicated, leaving the throne vacant, and duly invited William and Mary to occupy it as joint monarchs

William III and Mary II. Despite his impulsive flight, James had not intended to abdicate and decided to put up a fight to reclaim his throne. When he landed in Ireland with French troops in March 1689, the Irish Parliament remained loyal to him and he raised an army made up largely of raw recruits. But William, pursuing him to Ireland, defeated James at the Battle of the Boyne in July 1690, sending James scuttling back to France.

James's Catholic son and rightful heir to the throne, known as the Old Pretender, made an unsuccessful attempt to claim the throne in 1715, and a more serious attempt was made on his behalf by his son, "Bonnie Prince Charlie," in 1745, who entered Edinburgh unopposed and penetrated as far south into England as Derby before retreating. The last direct heir to James II was Bonnie Prince Charlie's younger brother, Cardinal York, who died in 1807. Though the "Jacobite" claim (from *Jacobus,* the Latin for "James") continued to be passed to more distant relatives, no further attempt was made to claim the throne.

Was James II deposed or did he abdicate? He never accepted either scenario, but the "Glorious Revolution" turned out to be a major turning point in English history, handing the whip hand once and for all to Parliament—meaning, in practice, to the ministers of the Crown, who, among other things, gained full control of the succession to the throne.

With some difficulty, Parliament ensured a Protestant succession, passing over the "Old Pretender," who was the rightful heir to the throne. After Mary's death in 1694, William III occupied the throne on his own until his death in 1702 and was succeeded by James II's other Protestant daughter Anne (r. 1702–14), all of whose children predeceased her. By means of some highly convoluted genealogical acrobatics, Parliament then traced the Protestant line back to James I and out again to the safely Protestant Elector George Louis of Hanover, who was offered the throne as King George I (r. 1714–27), and the British throne has been occupied by a direct descendant of his to this day.

Though now stripped of practically all political power, the House of "Windsor" (reinventing itself in 1917 by naming itself after a castle), has shown little sensitivity to the very real claims of the Jacobites. Until 2022 the Hanoverian line avoided using names claimed by the Jacobites. But the king who ascended the throne in that year took the name Charles III, the very title used by the rightful Jacobite claimant to the throne, Bonnie Prince Charlie (1720–88). Similarly, on the accession of Elizabeth II (r. 1952–2022), pillar-boxes in Scotland were blown up for displaying the royal cypher EiiR ("Elizabeth II Regina"). The problem was that there had never been a Queen Elizabeth reigning in Scotland. "Elizabeth II" was simply not a genuine title. Elizabeth II of what? Supposedly of the United Kingdom. But that was incorrect, because there had never been an Elizabeth I of the United Kingdom. The only Queen Elizabeth regnant that there had ever been was queen of England alone, from 1558 to 1603, well before the existence of the United Kingdom, which only came into existence in 1707. The problem of the exploding pillar-boxes was finally solved by replacing the EiiR cypher in Scotland with just a crown—the Scottish crown.

Monkey Business

When Greece obtained its independence from Turkey, the 17-year-old Prince Otto of Bavaria was invited to ascend the throne, which he did as King Otto I in 1832. Trying to reign as an absolute monarch, Otto was forced to grant a constitution in 1843. As a newly independent state, Greece was by international agreement under the "protection," or really control, of the "Great Powers," Britain, France, and Russia, which only made Otto's position more difficult. In 1850 Otto was the victim of "gunboat diplomacy" when British Foreign Secretary Lord Palmerston sent the British navy to blockade the Greek port of Piraeus with warships to force Otto to agree to compensate a British subject, Don David Pacifico, for the alleged vandalization of his house by a Greek mob. Otto's great love for Greece and everything Greek was not reciprocated by his subjects, and in 1862, after reigning for 30 years, he was deposed in a bloodless rising, but he never agreed to abdicate.

Then, in a remarkable development, the Greek electorate was asked to pick a new king. Queen Victoria's second son, Prince Alfred, was the official favourite, and he received 95% approval in a referendum, but, under international pressure, declined the offer. The other "candidates" were all write-ins, the deposed Otto receiving one vote (out of 240,000) and Prince William of Denmark, who was eventually selected, six votes.

The seventeen-year-old William ascended the Greek throne in 1863 under the regnal name George I and reigned for 50 years until his assassination in 1913 by someone variously described as a socialist and an anarchist. George was not deposed, but his son and successor Constantine I made up for this by being ousted twice, the first time being in 1917 in the "National Schism," when the king favoured neutrality for Greece in World War I, while Prime Minister Eleftherios Venizelos established an alternative "provisional revolutionary government," which declared war against Germany. Constantine was forced to give up the throne in favour of his second son, Alexander, who was pressured to appoint Venizelos as prime minister. With Greece now allied to the West, it gained about a third more territory at the end of World War I and tried to make further territorial gains at Turkey's expense in the Greco-Turkish War of 1919–22. But, in a freak accident in October 1920, King Alexander died of sepsis from a monkey-bite.

With public opinion swinging decisively against Venizelos in the election of November 1920, in which Venizelos himself failed to win a seat, the scene was set for the return and reinstatement of King Constantine, which was opposed by Britain and France but supported by 98.97% of voters in a referendum held in December 1920. But, after defeat in the Greco-Turkish War, in which the over-extended Greek army ill-advisedly attempted to capture Turkey's new capital, Ankara, located deep in Anatolia, where there was no significant Greek population, in September 1922 an army rising forced Constantine to abdicate in favour of his eldest son, who became George II.

A failed royalist coup in 1923 forced George into exile while refusing to abdicate. The Greek Parliament declared the country a republic in 1924, approved in a referendum by 69.98% of the votes, and King George II was deposed and banished. But, after 23 governments, 13 coups, and one dictatorship over a decade, Greece was ready to restore the monarchy, which was done in 1935, with yet another referendum approving restoration by 97.87% of the votes. Voting was compulsory but it was not by secret ballot. "As a voter one could drop into the ballot box a blue vote for George II ... or one could cast a red ballot for the Republic and get roughed up." (*Time* Magazine 1935). The king backed an authoritarian, nationalist, and anti-communist regime under Ioannis Metaxas as prime minister, who died in January 1941. In April 1941 Germany invaded Greece as part of World War II, forcing George into exile again, this time in London, where he set up a government-in-exile. In 1946 yet another referendum reinstated the monarchy, though with only 68.4% of the vote, as there was a civil war going on between monarchists and communists. George did not live long enough to benefit from this result, as he died in April 1947 at the age of 56.

As he was childless, George II was succeeded by his brother Paul, whose reign, until his death in 1964, was uninterrupted by any deposition interludes. But his son and successor, Constantine II, was not quite so fortunate. In 1967 a junta of Greek colonels staged a coup. The king vacillated, at first reluctantly endorsing it, then planning an abortive counter-coup, and then fleeing into exile. This time there was no return to monarchy. In 1973 the king was deposed and Greece declared a presidential republic with Colonel Georgios Papadopoulos as president. This was approved in a referendum by 78.57%. After the overthrow of the junta and the collapse of the brief "invisible dictatorship" of Brigadier Dimitrios Ioannidis, the "Third Hellenic Republic" was established, with Konstantinos Karamanlis as prime minister, in 1974, following which yet another referendum on the monarchy was held, on 8 December 1974. The king was not allowed to return to Greece to campaign but was restricted to participating in televised debates and making televised broadcasts from London. In the result, on a 75.58% turnout, 69.18% voted in favour of a republic and 30.82% for a constitutional monarchy (see Chapter 15).

The notorious instability of the modern Greek monarchy cannot be explained by the lack of a "fixed succession rule." The line of succession was clear at all times, yet we find repeated depositions, a change of dynasty, and switches between monarchy and republic. Focusing on the rules of succession is not only unduly superficial and completely unhelpful, but it also diverts one's attention from the really important features, such as the power structure. Of all the kings of modern Greece, only Otto the Bavarian, who "went native," was really imbued with a love of all things Greek. But even he never made a connection with the ordinary people of Greece that would have been necessary for a successful reign. When he finally tried to reach out to them in 1862, it was too late. The kings of the Danish Glücksburg family never immersed themselves fully in Greek culture but always remained a bit aloof from it. They were also constrained by international pressures and by constitutional limitations, but, by entrusting power, whether willingly or not, to dictators like Venizelos and Metaxas, they compromised their own independence. Constantine II, who spent nearly fifty years in exile, admitted that his younger children did not even speak Greek.

Part VI

Conclusion

My analysis of the power structure of a number of societies spanning the past five thousand years reveals that, regardless of labels, there are and have always been essentially only two types of government: monarchy and oligarchy. It also reveals that in every society there will always be two opposing elements: an elite minority and the mass of ordinary people. The elite, seeking to retain power for itself as an oligarchy, will be averse to true monarchy, or one-person rule. By the same token, true monarchy will arise when the elite lose power to a popular leader.

- An early example is the twenty-fourth-century BCE Sumerian ruler Urukagina, who came to power with popular support by toppling an oligarchy.
- The Ancient Greek Tyrants owed power to popular risings against oligarchies.
- Athenian "democracy", under Pericles, and even more so under Cleon, is a further example of popular monarchy victimizing the former privileged elite. During his short reign, Alexander the Great sought to identify with his subjects in his widespread newly conquered empire.
- This mind-set was successfully emulated for three centuries by the Ptolemies, Alexander's successors in Egypt.
- Capitalizing on his popularity with the Roman masses, the Roman Emperor Augustus established a lasting stable monarchy, sidelining the senatorial aristocracy without exasperating them.

- Without appealing directly to the people, Chinese emperors hit upon an ingenious long-term counterblast to aristocratic power in the form of competitive civil service examinations.
- Kings Louis XIII, XIV, and XV of France and their adroit ministers kept the aristocratic threat in check and eventually managed to crush the overmighty aristocratic *parlements*—only to have that victory senselessly surrendered on his accession by the callow Louis XVI, thereby giving rise to the French Revolution, including the guillotine for the king, ironically alongside the "aristos".
- A more recent example of popular monarchy with active pandering to the masses is Peronist Argentina.
- Fidel Castro's Cuba is another modern example of a longstanding popular monarchy with the mass execution of opponents, expropriation of large landholdings, and nationalization of foreign assets.

By no means all monarchs have been conscious of the danger posed to them by the elite.

Even England's arrogant and ruthless Henry VIII, who had no qualms about executing ministers and two of his wives, was naïve enough to be taken in by flattery, remarking to Parliament: "We be informed by our judges that we at no time stand so highly in our estate royal as in the time of parliament." Nothing could have been further from the truth. Using Parliament for his own ends to break with the Catholic Church, Henry effectively built Parliament up into a potential threat to the monarchy, which resulted in the execution of one king, Charles I, the deposition of another, James II, and the ultimate reduction of the monarchy to a ceremonial cypher.

What is the significance, if any, of a society's power structure? Features discussed in the body of this work in terms of their relevance to power structure include stability and the degree of liberty and equality in a society.

Stability

The Persian Achaemenid Empire is an example of a monarchy that owed its longevity and stability in no small measure to its popular support. At its height the largest empire in history up to that time, it lasted from 550 to 330 BCE. Its founder, Cyrus the Great (r. 550–530 BCE), who conquered the Medes, the Babylonians, and the Lydians, organized his vast empire under a centralized bureaucratic multicultural system. And, though his varied domains were amassed by conquest, he recognized the need to win the support of his new subjects. His success in doing so was undoubted, notably through his veneration of the Babylonian god Marduk, his repatriation of other Mesopotamian gods, and, not least, his instrumentality in the building of the Second Temple in Jerusalem—while still remaining faithful to the Persian Zoroastrian religion and its god, Ahura Mazda.

"They make a desert and call it peace." This is the imagined taunt about the Roman Empire attributed to a fictitious Scottish chieftain by the Roman historian Tacitus (Tac. *Agric.* 30). The Romans certainly had to contend with local resistance while conquering their vast empire. Nobody likes losing their independence to a foreign invader. But, once an area was subdued and had tasted the benefits of Roman civilization, the local populace generally became reconciled to Roman rule. The elites were open, meaning that not only Roman citizenship but also advancement to senatorial status was open to provincials. And from Trajan (r. 98–117) onward the emperors themselves mostly came from the provinces. Romanization was not forced on anyone. Latin became the language of the Western Empire, while the East continued to speak Greek. And religion was another unifying force. Edward Gibbon captured its spirit in his inimitable rolling prose: "The various modes of worship which prevailed in the Roman world were all considered by the people as equally true, by the philosopher as equally false, and by the magistrate as equally useful. And thus toleration produced not only mutual indulgence, but even religious concord." (Gibbon 1776, chapter 2.) The only thing wrong with this description is that the concept of "truth" would have meant nothing to the polytheistic communal religions that produced this syncretist uniformity and created this climate of freedom of worship. These religions were concerned with ritual and devotion but lacked any creed or set of beliefs. (For the supposed exceptions of Judaism and Christianity, see Chapter 26.)

No modern colonial empire has been able to achieve anything like the stability, harmony, and equanimity of the Roman Empire. Instead, their history has mostly been marked by rebellion, revolution, or war, by which they were brought to an end. Even the most enduring of these, the Portuguese Empire, which lasted for over 450 years, is a case in point. *Assimilados* ("assimilated"), indigenous people who were Portuguese in language, dress, manners, and culture and Roman Catholic in religion, were given certain privileges. But this was a superficial veneer. The whole *assimilado* program only began in 1910, after 400 years of Portuguese rule, and even by 1958 there were only 4,353 *assimilados* in Mozambique out of a total population of 6,234,000, and in Angola 30,089 *assimilados* out of a total population of 4,392,000 (De Andrade 1951, p. 215).

The difference between Rome and these modern empires is in their power structure. While the Roman Empire was a popular monarchy, built on the support of the masses in both Italy and the conquered provinces alike, the modern empires made no attempt to win the support of their colonial subjects, and in the mother country power was mostly in the hands of an oligarchy. Between 1932 and 1968, Portugal was under the dictatorship of António de Oliveira Salazar and his *Estado Novo* ("New State"), an autocratic monarchy without active popular support.

The British Empire grew and declined in the two centuries after the so-called "Glorious Revolution" of 1688, which turned England (and later Britain) into an oligarchy, which it remains to the present day. Under the slogan "No taxation without representation" the 13 British colonies broke away in a War of Independence and became the United States of America. In reaction against this loss, Britain invented "dominion status", initially applied to Canada and then later also to the other "white dominions" of Australia, New Zealand, and South Africa, under which each dominion was given "representative government" and, later, "responsible government". This latter effectively made each dominion autonomous and, by the Statute of Westminster of 1931, completely independent of Britain—the British Empire was renamed the "British Commonwealth of Nations", or, later, simply "the Commonwealth". However, by the Immigration Act 1971, the status of "British citizen" with the right of abode in the United Kingdom was limited to people from the Commonwealth with "patriality", a specially made-up term largely restricted to those with a parent or grandparent born in Britain. This excluded not only the indigenous populations of the ex-colonies but even many "white" settlers. At the time of this writing the Commonwealth is largely a fiction, made up of all former dominions and colonies including some countries, like Mozambique, Togo, Rwanda, and Gabon, which had no connection with Britain whatsoever. Much of the time of the 2024 Commonwealth Heads of Government meeting was devoted to demands from a number of member states for "reparations" to be paid by Britain for slavery and the slave trade. Britain's closest neighbour, the Irish Republic, which declared independence from Britain after three centuries of strife, is not a member of the Commonwealth.

The key to the stability of a state or empire is power structure. Strong monarchy with popular support is probably more likely to create a stable regime than any other, particularly if it also succeeds in placating the elite. The prime example of this is the Roman Empire in its heyday from 27 BCE until at least 180 CE.

Liberty and Equality

The greatest degree of equality can be achieved by strong popular monarchy applying the "tall poppy syndrome", meaning that, in a field of poppies, any poppy heads projecting above the others are lopped off. All the poppies are then level—except for the monarchical ruler doing the lopping. Examples of this include the ancient Greek Tyrants, Athenian "democracy", and Mao Zedong's Chinese "Cultural Revolution".

This is actual equality, or "equality of outcomes", as distinct from "equality of opportunity" or "meritocracy", in which there is a "rat-race" to determine winners and losers. "Equality of opportunity" really then means lining everyone up on the same starting line, firing a starter pistol, and letting them compete against one another. Equal opportunity is therefore in a very real sense the opposite of actual equality, because equal opportunity means equal opportunity to become *unequal*. For this to work, everyone has to be equal in absolute terms before the race begins—which is an impossibility. So, though "equality of opportunity" is commonly seen as more attainable than equality of outcomes, it is actually just as unrealistic.

Liberty and equality are inversely proportional to each other. The more liberty there is, the less equality, and vice versa. They are at opposite ends of a seesaw: when the one is up, the other is down. Total liberty exists only in the hypothetical anarchic "state of nature", where everyone can do whatever they like, and, because human beings are by nature selfish and competitive, there is "a war of every man against every man", and life is "solitary, poor, nasty, brutish and short" (Hobbes 1651). The solution proposed by Thomas Hobbes (1588–1679) was a notional "social contract" in which everyone agreed to give up to a "sovereign" certain rights (like the right to kill) in return for law and order. Written in 1651, during the chaos of the English Civil War, this is Hobbes's justification for strong monarchy. But the version of the "social contract" that actually came into existence in Britain was based less on Hobbes's model than on that postulated by John Locke (1632–1704) with its emphasis on liberty rather than equality, thus effectively endorsing oligarchy, which has typified British government since the "Glorious Revolution" of 1688–89. A glaring recent example of just how remote Britain is from its vaunted democratic image is the "UK-Ukraine 100 Year Partnership Declaration" issued by the British Prime Minister's Office on 16 January 2025 committing the UK to 100 years of defense and financial support of Ukraine which, though terminable by either side on six months' notice, places a further burden on the far from healthy British Treasury in addition to the promise of military aid to Ukraine of £3 billion "every year for as long as it is needed". Though agreed to by the current Parliament, this flies in the face of the bedrock constitutional principle of the sovereignty of Parliament, meaning that no Parliament can bind any future Parliament.

The claim in the American Declaration of Independence composed by Thomas Jefferson, a slave-owner, "that all men are created equal" rings rather hollow, and the real emphasis should perhaps be on the claim to the possession of the "unalienable Rights" of "Life, Liberty and the pursuit of Happiness", amended from the more Lockean formulation of "Life, Liberty and Property". The "American dream" and the ideal of "From log cabin to White House" are actually just examples of meritocracy. But the "politically correct" or "woke" agenda applied in the US in recent years, by according special privileges to certain favoured categories, effectively cuts across any attempt to achieve equality of opportunity or meritocracy. The best known, most widespread, and oldest of such programs is "affirmative action", particularly as applied to education. US Supreme Court Justice Clarence Thomas, a beneficiary of such a program himself, through admission to Yale Law School in 1971, has been an indefatigable opponent of such programs. Affixing a 15-cent discount coupon to his diploma from Yale, he observed: "You had to prove yourself every day because the presumption was that you were dumb and didn't deserve to be there on merit." Forty-five years later, in 2025, the US Supreme Court finally came round to Clarence Thomas's view of a "colour-blind Constitution" as an approach to true equality of opportunity. In two cases brought by Students for Fair Admissions, one against Harvard and the other against the University of North Carolina, a 6–3 majority on the Court effectively overruled all previous decisions on race-based university admissions. In his concurring opinion Thomas put the Court's decision in a nutshell: "All forms of discrimination based on race—including so-called affirmative action—are prohibited under the Constitution." Donald Trump's re-election to the US presidency in 2024 was in no small measure owing to his promise to sweep away the "woke agenda" of the outgoing Biden administration. At the time of this writing it is too early to tell whether Trump's promise will be realized, and if so, for how long. But it is belief in the "American dream" that has converted the US from an oligarchy to a hybrid state between monarchy and oligarchy (see Chapter 23).

Part VII

Round-up

A checklist of some notable monarchs of the last 5,000 years.

KEY

A—An actual or true monarch exercising absolute, autocratic, or at least real power, regardless of title, but without specific popular support. Examples: Hammurabi of Babylon, Charlemagne, Henry VIII of England, Shogun Tokugawa Ieyasu of Japan, Francisco Franco of Spain, Xi Jinping of China.

A*—An actual or true monarch, regardless of title, exercising absolute, autocratic, or at least real power, ruling against the interests of the elite with active or passive popular support. Examples: Sumerian Urukagina, Cyrus the Great of Persia, Pericles of Athens, Alexander the Great, Roman Emperor Augustus, Juan Perón of Argentina.

H—Hybrid: monarch sharing power with an elite. Examples: Phraates of Parthia, Shapur I of the Persian Sasanian Empire, French President François Mitterand, US President Franklin D. Roosevelt, King Hussein of Jordan.

C—Constitutional monarch: head of state with little or no actual power. Examples: All doges of Venice between 1268 and 1797, all British monarchs since George I, all Danish monarchs since 1849, all Japanese emperors since 1947, all presidents of the German Federal Republic since 1949.

Five Thousand Years of Monarchy, First Edition. Michael Arnheim.
© 2026 John Wiley & Sons, Inc. Published 2026 by John Wiley & Sons, Inc.

- (A) Abdullah, king of Saudi Arabia (r. 1932–53)
- (A) Abdullah I, king of Jordan (r. 1921–1951)
- (H) Abdullah II, king of Jordan (r. 1999-)
- (A) Akbar, Mughal emperor, India (r. 1556–1605)
- (A) Akhenaten (Amenhotep IV), Egyptian pharaoh (1351–1334 BCE)
- (A*) Alexander the Great, king of Macedon (356–323 BCE)
- (A) Alexander I, tsar of Russia (r. 1801–1825)
- (A) Alexander II, tsar of Russia (r. 1855–1881)
- (A) Alexander III, tsar of Russia (r. 1881–1894)
- (A) Amenhotep III, Egyptian pharaoh (Eighteenth Dynasty) (r. c. 1386–1353 BCE)
- (A) Antiochus III, king of Seleucid Empire (Syria) (r. 222–187 BCE)
- (A*) Antoninus Pius, Roman emperor (r. 138–161)
- (A) Ardashir, Shahanshah, founder of Sasanian Empire (Persia) (r. 211–224)
- (A) Ashoka, Maurya emperor, India (c. 268–232 BCE)
- (A) Ashurbanipal, Assyrian king (Neo-Assyrian Empire) (669–631 BCE)
- (A) al-Assad, Bashar, president of Syria (2000–2024)
- (A) al-Assad, Hafez, president of Syria (in office 1971–2000)
- (A*) Augustus, Roman emperor (in power 43 BCE–14 CE)
- (A) Aurangzeb, Mughal emperor (Padishah), India (r. 1658–1707)
- (A*) Caesar, C. Julius, Roman dictator (100–44 BCE)
- (A*) Castro, Fidel, prime minister of Cuba (1959–1976), president of Cuba (1976–2008)
- (A) Catherine II ("the Great"), tsarina of Russia (r. 1762–1796)
- (A) Chandragupta, Maurya emperor, India (r. 321–297 BCE)
- (A) Charlemagne, king of the Franks (768–814), "emperor of the Romans" (800–814)
- (A) Charles V, Holy Roman emperor (1519–1556), as Charles I, king of Spain (1516–1556)
- (A) Charles III, king of Spain (r. 1759–1788)
- (A/A*) Charles I, king of England and Scotland (1600–1649)
- (A*) Claudius, Roman emperor (r. 41–54)
- (A*) Cleon, Athenian general and demagogue (died 422 BCE)
- (A) Cleopatra VII, queen of Egypt (r. 51–30 BCE)
- (A) Constantine I, Roman emperor (r. 36–337)
- (A) Croesus, king of Lydia (r. c. 585–546 BCE)
- (A) Cromwell, Oliver, Lord Protector of England, Scotland & Ireland (1599–1658)
- (A*) Cypselus, Tyrant of Corinth (r. 657–627 BCE)
- (A) Cyrus II ("the Great"), Persian king (Achaemenid dynasty) (r. 559–530 BCE)
- (A) David, king of Israel (r. c. 1010–970 BCE)

- (C) De Gaulle, Charles, president of France (in office 1959–1969)
- (A*) Diocletian, Roman emperor (r. 284–305)
- (A) Domitian, Roman emperor (r. 81–96)
- (A) Elizabeth I, queen of England (r. 1558–1603)
- (C) Elizabeth II, queen of United Kingdom (r. 1952-)
- (A?) Enkhelyawon, king of Mycenaean Pylos? (equivalent to mythical Homeric kings Agamemnon or Nestor?) (thirteenth century BCE)
- (A) Entemena (or Enmetena) Sumerian king (r. c. 2418–2391 BCE)
- (A) Farouk, king of Egypt (r. 1936–1952)
- (A) Franco, Francisco, caudillo of Spain (in office 1939–1975)
- (A) Franz Joseph I, emperor of the Austro-Hungarian Empire (r. 1848–1916)
- (A) Frederick II ("the Great"), Prussian king (r. 1740–1786)
- (A) Gaius ("Caligula"), Roman emperor (r. 37–41)
- (A*) Gaozu, Chinese emperor, Han dynasty (r. 202–195 BCE)
- (A) Genghis Khan, Mongol emperor (r. 1206–1227)
- (C) George III, king of the United Kingdom (r. 1760–1820)
- (A) Gregory VII, pope (r. 1073–1085)
- (A*) Guangwu, Chinese emperor, Han dynasty (r. 25–57)
- (A*) Gustav II Adolf, king of Sweden (r. 1611–1632)
- (A*) Gustav III, king of Sweden (r. 1771–1792)
- (A) Gyges, king of Lydia (r. c. 680–644 BCE)
- (A*) Hadrian, Roman emperor (r. 117–138)
- (A) Hammurabi, Babylonian king (r. c.1810-c. 1750 BCE)
- (A*) Hattušili III, Hittite king (New Kingdom) (r. c. 1267–1237 BCE)
- (A*) Henry (Henri) IV, king of France (r. 1589–1610)
- (A) Henry VII, king of England (r. 1485–1509)
- (A) Henry VIII, king of England (r. 1509–1547)
- (A) Herod ("the Great"), king of Judea (r.? 37–1 BCE)
- (A) Hiram I, king of Tyre, Phoenicia (r.? 980–947 BCE)
- (C) Hirohito, emperor of Japan (r. 1926–1989)
- (A*) Hitler, Adolf, German dictator (*Führer*) (in power, 1933–1945)
- (A*) Hongwu, Chinese emperor, Ming dynasty (r. 1368–1398)
- (C) Hussein, king of Jordan (r. 1952–1999)
- (A) Irene, Byzantine empress (r. 780–802)
- (A) James VI & I, king of Scots and England (1566–1625)
- (A) James II & VII, king of England and Scotland (r. 1685–1688)
- (A*) Jing ("Emperor Jing of Han"), Chinese emperor (r. 157–141 BCE)
- (A) Joseph II, Holy Roman emperor (r. 1780–1790)
- (A*) Kangxi, Chinese emperor, Qing dynasty (r. 1661–1722)
- (A) Khufu (Cheops), Egyptian pharaoh (Fourth Dynasty) (r. c. 2589–2566 BCE)
- (A) Kublai Khan, Mongol emperor (r. 1260–1294)
- (H) Lincoln, Abraham, US president (in office 1861–1865)

- (A*) Louis XIII, king of France (r. 1610–1643) All anti-aristocratic.
- (A*) Louis XIV, king of France (r. 1643–1715) but without active
- (A*) Louis XV, king of France (r. 1715–1774). popular support
- (A/C) Louis XVI, French king (e. 1774–1792)
- (A) Louis Philippe, king of the French (r. 1830–1848)
- (A*) LugalZageSi, Sumerian king (*lugal/ensi*) (r. c. 2375–2350 BCE)
- (A*) Mao Zedong (Mao Tse-tung), chairman of the Chinese Communist Party (in office 1943–1976)
- (A*) Marcus Aurelius, Roman emperor (r. 161–180)
- (C) Meiji, emperor of Japan (r. 1867–1912)
- (A) Mobutu Sese Seko, president of Zaire (in office 1965–1997)
- (A) Moctezuma (Montezuma), Aztec emperor, Mexico (r. 1502–1520)
- (A) Moshoeshoe I, king of Lesotho (r. 1822–1870)
- (C) Moshoeshoe II, king of Lesotho (1938–1996)
- (A*) Mugabe, Robert, prime minister (1980–1987) and president of Zimbabwe (1987–2017)
- (A) Muhammad, founder of Islam and Islamic caliphate and empire (570–632)
- (A) Mursili I, Hittite king (r.? c. 1620–1590 BCE)
- (A*) Mussolini, Benito, Italian prime minister and Fascist leader ("Il Duce") (in office 1922–1943)
- (A*) Muwatalli II, Hittite king (New Kingdom) (r. c. 1295–1272 BCE)
- (A) Nabonidus, king of neo-Babylonian Empire (r. 556–539 BCE)
- (A*) Napoleon I (Bonaparte), First Consul (1799–1804), emperor of the French (1804–1814, and March to June 1815)
- (A*) Napoleon III (Louis Napoleon Bonaparte), president of France (1848–1852), emperor of the French (1852–1870)
- (A) Nebuchadnezzar II, king of Neo-Babylonian Empire, r. 605–562 BCE.
- (A*) Nero, Roman emperor (r. 54–68)
- (A) Nicholas I, tsar of Russia (r. 1825–1855)
- (A) Nicholas II, tsar of Russia (r. 1894–1917)
- (A) Nicholas I, king of Montenegro (r. 1860–1918)
- (A*) Pakal (K'inich Janaab' Pakal), Mayan king of Palenque (603–683 CE)
- (A*) Peisistratus, Tyrant of Athens (r. 561, 559–556, 545–527 BCE)
- (A*) Periander, Tyrant of Corinth (r. 627–585 BCE)
- (A*) Pericles, Athenian general (c. 495–429 BCE)
- (A*) Perón, Juan, president of Argentina (in office 1946–1955 & 1973–1974)
- (A) Philip II of Macedon (r. 359–336 BCE)
- (A) Philip II of Spain (r. 1556–1598), king of England (r. 1554–1558)
- (A) Ptolemy II Philadelphus, pharaoh of Egypt (283–246 BCE)
- (A*) Qin Shi Huang, of Qin, Chinese emperor (r. 221–206 BCE)
- (A) Ramesses II (Ozymandias), Egyptian pharaoh (Nineteenth Dynasty) (r. 1279–1213 BCE)

- (A*/−) Richard II, king of England (r. 1377–1399)—at first championing the Peasants' Revolt, but later under control of "Lords Appellant" and finally deposed
- (A) Robespierre, Maximilien, member of Committee of Public Safety (1793–1794), president of National Convention (1794)
- (A*) Roosevelt, Franklin Delano, US president (in office 1933–1945)
- (A*) Roosevelt, Theodore, US president (in office 1901–1908)
- (A) Salazar, António de Oliveira, prime minister of Portugal (in office 1932–1968)
- (A*) Sargon, king of Akkad (r. c. 2350–2299 BCE)
- (A) Sennacherib, Assyrian king (Neo-Assyrian Empire) (r. 705–681 BCE)
- (A) Senusret I (Sesostris), Egyptian pharaoh (Twelfth Dynasty) (r. 1971–1926 BCE)
- (A) Shah Jahan, Mughal emperor, India (r. 1628–1658)
- (A) Shaka, founder of Zulu kingdom (r. 1816–1828)
- (A) Sneferu, Egyptian pharaoh (Fourth Dynasty) (r. long reign around 2600 BCE)
- (A) Solomon, king of Israel (r. c. 970–931 BCE)
- (C) Solon, Athenian statesman and lawmaker (c. 630- c. 560 BCE)
- (A) Stalin, Joseph, Russian dictator (in power, 1924–1953)
- (A) Suleiman I ("the Magnificent"), sultan of Ottoman Empire (r. 1520–1566)
- (A*) Taizu, Chinese emperor, Song dynasty (r. 960–976)
- (A*) Taizong, Chinese emperor, Tang dynasty (r.626–649)
- (A) Theodosius I, Roman emperor (r. 379 = 395)
- (A*) Thrasybulus, Tyrant of Miletus (r. seventh century BCE)
- (A) Tiberius, Roman emperor (r. 14–37)
- (A) Tiglath-Pileser III, Assyrian king (Neo-Assyrian Empire) (745–727 BCE)
- (H) Timur (Tamerlane), amir of Timurid Empire (r. 1370–1405)
- (A) Tito, Josip Broz, president of Yugoslavia (1892–1980)
- (A*) Tokugawa Ieyasu, Japanese shogun (1543–1616)
- (A*) Tokugawa Iemitsu, Japanese shogun (1604–51)
- (A*) Trajan, Roman emperor (r. 98–117)
- (A*) Trump, Donald, US president (in office 2017–2021 and 2025-)
- (A*) Urukagina, Sumerian king of Lagash (twenty-fourth century BCE)
- (A) Valentinian I, Roman emperor (r. 364–375)
- (A*) Vespasian, Roman emperor (r. 69–79)
- (C) Victoria, queen of United Kingdom (r. 1837–1901)
- (A*) Wen ("Emperor Wen of Han"), Chinese emperor (r. 180–157 BCE)
- (A*) Wu Zetian, Chinese empress (624–705)
- (A) Xi Jinping, president of China (1953-)
- (A*) Yongle, Chinese emperor, Ming dynasty (r. 1402–1424)
- (C) (Mohammed) Zahir Shah, king of Afghanistan (r. 1933–1973)

Primary Sources & Abbreviations

<u>Translations</u>: Where primary sources are quoted in translation, the translations are by myself unless otherwise indicated.

<u>Bible</u>: Unless otherwise indicated, biblical citations are from the King James Version, which is in the public domain in the United States.

<u>Inscriptions</u>: Inscriptions referred to by just a number are from CIL.

<u>Papyri</u>: Papyri are referred to in the text with an initial "P." E.g, P. Oxyrhynchus.

AE	*Année Épigraphique*
Amb. *Ep.*	Ambrose, *Epistulae*
Amm.	Ammianus Marcellinus
Anon. Val.	Anonymus Valesianus
Apuleius	Apuleius, *Metamorphoses*
Aristophanes	*Knights*
Aristophanes	*Wasps*
Aristoph.	**Aristophanes, *Knights***
Aristoph.	**Aristophanes, *Wasps***
Arist. *Fragmenta*	**Aristotle, *Fragmenta*, ed. V. Rose, 1886, Teubner**
Aristot. *AP.*	Aristotle, *Athenian Constitution*
Aristot. *Pol.*	Aristotle, *Politics*
Aristot. *Rh.*	Aristotle, *Rhetoric*
Arrian	Arrian, *Anabasis*

Aug. *Civ. Dei*	Augustine, *De Civitate Dei*
Aug. *R.G.*	Augustus, *Res Gestae Divi Augusti*
Aur. Victor	Aurelius Victor, *Liber de Caesaribus*
Ausonius	*Mosella, Ephemeris, Epigrammata, Caesares*
Boethius, *Consol.*	Boethius, *De Philosophiae Consolatione*
Cassiodorus	Cassiodorus, *Variae Epistolae*
Cassius Dio	Cassius Dio, *Historia Romana*
Cic. *Ad Fam.*	Cicero, *Epistulae ad Familiares*
Cic. *Pro Sestio*	Cicero, *Pro Sestio*
Cic. *De Nat Deorum*	Cicero, *De Natura Deorum*
CIL	*Corpus Inscriptionum Latinarum*
CJ	*Codex Justinianus* (Justinian's Code)
Claudian	Claudius Claudianus, *De Consulatu Stilichonis*
CTh	*Codex Theodosianus* (Theodosian Code)
Dig.	Justinian, Digest (Pandects)
Diod. Sic.	Diodorus Siculus, *Bibliotheca Historica*
Epit. Caes.	*Epitome de Caesaribus*
Eus. *HE*	Eusebius, *Historia Ecclesiastica*
Eus. *V. Const.*	Eusebius, *De Vita Constantini*
Eutrop.	Eutropius, *Breviarium*
Evagrius	Evagrius Scholasticus, *Historia Ecclesiastica*
Gregory of Tours	Gregorius Turonensis, *Historia Francorum*
Hdt.	Herodotus, *Histories.*
Hor., *Epistles*	Horace, *Epistles*
Hor. *Od.*	Horace, *Odes*
ILS	*Inscriptiones Latinae Selectae*, ed. H. Dessau
Isocrates	Isocrates, *Orations*
Jerome	Hieronymus, *Commentaria in Ezechielem*
Jerome, *Ep.*	Hieronymus, *Epistulae*
Joh. Eph.	John of Ephesus, *Historia Ecclesiastica*
Jordanes, *Get.*	Jordanes, *Getica*
Josephus	Josephus, *Contra Apion*
Julian, *Caes.*	Julian, *De Caesaribus*
Julian, *Ep.*	Julian, *Epistulae*
Julian, *Mis.*	Julian, *Misopogon*
Juv.	Decimus Junius Juvenalis, *Satires*
Lactantius, *Mort. Pers.*	Lactantius, *De Mortibus Persecutorum*
Libanius, *Ep.*	Libanius, *Epistulae*
Libanius, *Or.*	Libanius, *Orationes*
Livy	Titus Livius, *Ab Urbe Condita*
Lucr.	Titus Lucretius Carus, *De Rerum Natura*
Macrobius	Macrobius, *Saturnalia*

Mart.	M. Valerius Martialis, *Epigrams*
Not. Dig.	*Notitia Dignitatum Occidentalis/Orientalis*
Orosius	Orosius, *Historiarum adversus Paganos libri VII*
Petron.	C. Petronius Arbiter, *Satyricon*
Plautus	T. Maccius Plautus, *Miles Gloriosus, Stichus*
Plato,	Republic VIII. 558c
Plin. *Ep.*	Pliny the Younger, *Epistulae*
Plin. *H.N.*	Pliny the Elder, *Historia Naturalis* (Natural History)
Plut.	Plutarchus, *Parallel Lives*
Plut. *Apoph.*	Plutarchus, *Apophthegmata Laconica*
Plut. *Mor.*	Plutarchus, *Moralia*
Polybius	*Histories*
Procopius	Procopius, *Anecdota* (Secret History)
Rut. Nam.	Rutilius Namatianus, *De Reditu Suo*
Salvian	Salvianus, *De Gubernatione Dei*
SHA	*Scriptores Historiae Augustae* (Augustan History)
Sid. Ap. *Carm.*	Sidonius Apollinaris, *Carmina*
Sid Ap. *Ep.*	Sidonius Apollinaris, *Epistulae*
Socrates	Socrates, *Historia Ecclesiastica*
Soz.	Sozomen, *Historia Ecclesiastica*
Suet.	C. Suetonius Tranquillus, *De Vita Caesarum*
Symmachus, *Ep.*	Q. Aurelius Symmachus, *Epistulae*
Symmachus, *Panegyrics*	Q. Aurelius Symmachus, *Panegyrici*
Synesius	Synesius, *De Regno*
Tac. *Agric.*	Tacitus, *Agricola (De Vita et moribus Julii Agricolae)*
Tac. *Ann.*	P. Cornelius Tacitus, *Annals*
Tac. *Hist.*	P. Cornelius Tacitus, *Histories*
Themistius	Themistius, *Orationes*
Theodoret	Theodoret, *Historia Ecclesiastica*
Thuc.	Thucydides, *Peloponnesian War*
Verg. *Geo.*	P. Vergilius Maro, *Georgics*
Verg. *Aen.*	P. Vergilius Maro, *Aeneid*
V. Mel.	*Vita S. Melaniae Junioris*
Xenophon	Xenophon, *Constitution of Sparta*
Xenophon	Xenophon, *Hellenica*
Xenophon	Xenophon, *Memorabilia of Socrates*
Xenophon	Xenophon, *Memorabilia*
Zosimus	Zosimus, *Historia Nova*

Select Bibliography

This bibliography contains secondary sources referenced in the text.
See also PRIMARY SOURCES and GLOSSARY.

Bibliography

Abulafia, D. (2011). *The Great Sea: A Human History of the Mediterranean*. New York: Oxford University Press.

Acton, Lord (1887/2011). Acton-Creighton correspondence. `https://oll.libertyfund.org/titles/acton-acton-creighton-correspondence` (accessed 7 May 2025).

Acton, Lord (1906). *Lectures on Modern History*. Cambridge: Cambridge University Press.

Agache, R. (1973). La villa gallo-romaine dans les grandes plaines du nord de la France. *Archeologia* 55: 37–52.

Albertini, L. (1953/2005). *Origins of the War of 1914*, vol. 3. London: Enigma Books.

Alexander, C.F. (1848/2023). *Hymns for Little Children*. Legare Street Press.

Alföldi, A. (1948). *The Conversion of Constantine and Pagan Rome*. Oxford: Oxford University Press.

Aling, C.F. (1981). *Egypt and Bible History*. Grand Rapids: Baker Books.

American Psychological Association (1995). Intelligence: knowns and unknowns. *American Psychologist* 51 (2): 77–101.

Andrewes, A. (1956). *The Greek Tyrants*. London: Hutchinson.

Five Thousand Years of Monarchy, First Edition. Michael Arnheim.
© 2026 John Wiley & Sons, Inc. Published 2026 by John Wiley & Sons, Inc.

Angold, M. (1984). *The Byzantine Aristocracy: Ninth to Thirteenth Centuries*. British Archaeological Reports International Series.

Arlidge, A. and Judge, I. (2014). *Magna Carta Uncovered*. London: Hart Publishing.

Arnheim, M. (1972). *The Senatorial Aristocracy in the Later Roman Empire*. Oxford: Oxford University Press.

Arnheim, M. (1977). *Aristocracy in Greek Society*. London: Thames & Hudson.

Arnheim, M. (1984). *Is Christianity True?* London: Duckworth.

Arnheim, M. (2004). *Principles of the Common Law*. London: Duckworth.

Arnheim, M. (2015). *The God Book*. Exeter: Imprint Academic.

Arnheim, Michael (2016). *God Without Religion*. London: Black House Publishing.

Arnheim, M. (2017). *Two Models of Government*. Exeter: Imprint Academic.

Arnheim, M. (2018). *U.S. Constitution For Dummies*, 2e. Hoboken, NJ: John Wiley & Sons.

Arnheim, M. (2022). *Why Rome Fell: Decline and Fall, or Drift and Change?* New York: Wiley Blackwell.

Badian, E. (1958). Review of Louis Harmand (1957). *Latomus* 774–777.

Badian, E. (1990). The consuls, 179-49 BC. *Chiron* 20: 37.

Bagehot, W. (1867). *The English Constitution*. London: Chapman and Hall.

Bagge, S. (2019). The Decline of Regicide and the rise of European Monarchy from the Carolingians to the Early Modern Period. *Frühmittelalterliche Studien* 53 (1): 151–189.

Bagnall, R.S. (1982). Religious conversion and onomastic change in early Byzantine Egypt. *Bulletin of the American Society of Papyrologists* 19: 105–124.

Bagnall, R.S. (1987). Conversion and onomastics: a reply. *Zeitschrift für Papyrologie und Epigraphik* 69: 243–250.

Bagnall, R.S. (1993). *Egypt in Late Antiquity*. Princeton, NJ: Princeton University Press.

Baines, J. (1997). The Dawn of the Amarna age. In: *Amenhotep III: Perspectives on his Reign* (ed. D. O'Connor and E. Cline). University of Michigan Press.

Bardill, J. (2012). *Constantine: Divine Emperor of the Christian Golden Age*. New York: Cambridge Universiy Press.

Barnes, T.D. (1982). *The New Empire of Diocletian and Constantine*. Cambridge, MA: Harvard University Press.

Barnes, T.D. (1992). Praetorian prefects 337-361. *Zeitschrift für Papyrologie und Epigraphik* 94: 249–260.

Barnes, T.D. (1995). Statistics and the conversion of the Roman Aristocracy. *Journal of Romance Studies* 85: 135–147.

Barnes, T.D. and Westall, R.W. (1991). The conversion of the Roman Aristocracy in Prudentius' Contra Symmachum. *Phoenix* 45: 50–61.

Barnish, S.J.B. (1988). Transformation and survival of the Western Senatorial aristocracy, c.400-700. *Papers of the British School at Rome* 56 (1988): 120–155.

Barnish, S.J.B. (1989). A note on the collation glebalis. *Historia* 1989: 254–256.

Barone, M. (2015). *How America's Political Parties Change*. Encounter Books.

Baynes, N.H. (1929). Constantine the Great and the Christian Church. Raleigh Lecture. *Proceedings of the British Academy*, vol. XV. London: Humphrey Milford.

Bazzaz, S. et al. (2012). *Imperial Geographies in Byzantine and Ottoman Space*. Cambridge, MA: Harvard University Press.

Bearak, B. (2007). Former King of Afghanistan dies at 92. *New York Times* (23 July).

Beard, M. (2016). *SPQR: A History of Ancient Rome*. London: Profile Books.

Beard, M., North, J., and Price, S. (1998). *Religions of Rome*. Cambridge: Cambridge University Press.

Behr, E. (1987). *The Last Emperor*. Toronto: Futura.

Beik, W. (1985). *Absolutism and Society in Seventeenth Century France: State Power and Provincial Aristocracy in Languedoc*. Cambridge: Cambridge University Press.

Beik, W. (2005). The absolutism of Louis XIV as social collaboration. *Past & Present* 188: 195–224.

Beloch, K.J. (1886). *Die Bevölkerung der griechisch-römischen Welt*. Duncker & Humblot.

Benedictow, O. (2012). *The Black Death 1346–1353*. London: Boydell Press.

Ben-Ghiat, R. (2020). *Strongmen: How They Rise, Why They Succed, How They Fall*. London: Profile Books.

Berlin, I. (2002). *Four Essays on Liberty*. Oxford: Oxford University Press.

Bernstein, H. (ed.) (1918). *The Willy-Nicky Correspondence*. Toronto: S, B, Grundy.

Berthon, S. and Potts, J. (2007). *Warlords: An Extraordinary Re-creation of World War II through the Eyes and Minds of Hitler, Churchill, Roosevelt and Stalin*. Da Capo Press.

Bidez, J. and Cumont, F. (ed.) (1922). *Julian, Epistulae, leges, poemata, fragmenta varia*. Paris: Les Belles Lettres.

Blackstone, W. (1765). *Commentaries on the Laws of England*. Oxford: Clarendon Press.

Blegen, C. (1995). *Troy and the Trojans*. Gazelle Book Services.

Bloch, M. (1992). *The Historian's Craft*. Manchester: Manchester University Press.

Bodin, J. (1576). *Six Bookes of a Commonweal*. London: Impensis G. Bishop.

Bosworth, A.B. (2000). The historical context of Thucydides' funeral oration. *Journal of Hellenic Studies* 120 (2000): 1–16.

Bowen, C.D. (1957). *The Lion and the Throne*. Boson: Little Brown.

Bowman, A. (2005). *Diocletian and the First Tetrarchy. In: The Cambridge Ancient History: The Crisis of Empire, AD 193–337* (ed. A. Bowman, A. Cameron, and P. Garnsey), 67–89. Cambridge: Cambridge University Press.

Boyd, W.K. (1905). *The Ecclesiastical Edicts of the Theodosian Code*. New York: Columbia University Press.

Bradbury, S. (1994). Constantine and the problem of anti-pagan legislation in the fourth century. *Classical Philology* 89: 120–139.

Brown, P. (1961). Aspects of the Christianization of the Roman Aristocracy. *Journal of Romance Studies* 51 (1961): 1–11.

Brown, P. (1971). *The World of Late Antiquity*. London: Thames & Hudson.

Brown, P. (1973). A Dark-Age crisis: aspects of the iconoclastic controversy. *English Historical Review* 88 (346): 1–34.

Brown, E. (1974). The tyranny of a construct: feudalism and the historians of medieval Europe. *American Historical Review* 1063–1088.

Brown, P. (1987). *Late Antiquity*. Cambridge, MA: Harvard University Press.

Brown, P. (1992). *Power and Persuasion in Late Antiquity*. Madison: University of Wisconsin Press.

Brown, P. (1995). *Authority and the Sacred*. Cambridge: Cambridge University Press.

Brown, P. (1997a). Christianization and religious vonflict," Chapter 21. In: *Cambridge Ancient History*, vol. XIII, 337–425 (ed. A. Cameron and P. Garnsey), 632–664.

Brown, P. (1997b). The world of late antiquity revisited. *Symbolae Osloenses* 72: 5–30.

Brown, P. (2013). *The Rise of Western Christendom: Triumph and Diversity A.D. 200–1000*, 3e. London: Wiley-Blackwell.

Brubaker, R. (2006). *Ethnicity Without Groups*. Cambridge MA: Harvard University Press.

Brunt, P. (1988). *The Fall of the Roman Republic and Related Essays*. Oxford: Oxford University Press.

Brunt, P. and Moore, J.M. (ed.) (1967). *Res Gestae Divi Augusti*. Oxford: Oxford University Press.

Burckhardt, J. (1898). *Die Zeit Constantins des Grossen*. Leipzig: E.A. Seemann.

Burgess, G. (1992). The divine right of kings reconsidered. *English Historical Review* 425: 837ff.

Burgess, R.W. (ed.) (1993). *The Chronicle of Hydatius and the Consularia Constantinopolitana*. Oxford: Oxford University Press.

Bury, J.B. (1923). *History of the Later Roman Empire from the Death of Theodosius I to the Death of Justinian*. London: Macmillan.

Butler, A.J. (1978). *The Arab Conquest of Egypt*. Oxford: Oxford University Press.

Butler, D.A. (2010). *The Burden of Guilt*. Casemate.

Cameron, A. (2007). The Imperial Pontifex. *Harvard Studies in Classical Philology* 103: 341–384.

Cameron, A. (2013). *The Last Pagans of Rome*. New York: Oxford University Press.

Cameron, A. (2014). *Byzantine Matters*. Princeton, NJ: Princeton University Press.

Cameron, A. and Garnsey, P. (1998). *Cambridge Ancient History*, vol. XIII. Cambridge: Cambridge University Press.

Cameron, A. et al. (ed.) (1997). *Cambridge Ancient History*, vol. 13. Cambridge: Cambridge University Press.

Cameron, A. et al. (ed.) (2001). *Cambridge Ancient History*, vol. 14. Cambridge: Cambridge University Press.

Carr, E.H. (1961). *What is History?* Harmondsworth: Penguin Books.

Chambers, R. (1832). *The Book of Days*, vol. 2. W. & R. Chambers Limited.

Chastagnol, A. (1962). *Les Fastes de la Préfecture de Rome au Bas-Empire*. Paris: Nouvelles Éditions Latines.

Chastagnol, A. (1992). *Le Sénat Romain à L'Époque Impériale*. Paris: Les Belles Lettres.

Chelaney, B. (2017). China's debt-trap diplomacy. *Project Syndicate* (23 January). https://www.project-syndicate.org/commentary/china-one-belt-one-road-loans-debt-by-brahma-chellaney-2017-01 (accessed 7 May 2025).

Cheyette, F.L. (2008). Climate and the Early Medieval environment. *Early Medieval Europe* 16: 127–165.

Cheynet, J.-C. (2018). *The Byzantine Aristocracy and its Military Function*. London: Routledge.

Cilliers, L. and Retief, F.P. (2018). Lead poisoning and the downfall of Rome: Reality or myth? In: *Toxicology in Antiquity* (ed. P. Wexler), 221–229. London: Academic Press.

Clark, G.N. (1957). *New Cambridge Modern History*, vol. 1. Cambridge: Cambridge University Press.

Clark, G. (2014). *The Son Also Rises*. Princeton: Princeton University Press.

Claydon, T. (2002). *William III*. London: Routledge.

Cobban, A. (1950). The Parlements of France in the eighteenth century. *History* 35: 65–80.

Cobban, A. (1965). *A History of Modern France, 3 vols*. Harmondsorth: Penguin.

Collingwood, R.G. and Myres, J.N.L. (1936). *Roman Britain and the English Settlements*. Oxford: Oxford University Press.

Coltman, L. (2003). *The Real Fidel Castro*. New Haven: Yale University Press.

Connolly, S. (2010). *Lives behind the Laws: The World of the Codex Hermogenianus*. Bloomington: Indiana University Press.

Connor, W.R. (1971). *The New Politicians of Fifth-Century Athens*. Princeton: Princeton University Press.

Cornell, T. (1995). *The Beginnings of Rome*. London: Routledge.

Crook, J. (1955). *Consilium Principis*. Cambridge: Cambridge University Press.

Crouch, D. (2007). *The Normans: the history of a dynasty*. London: Continuum.

Cunha, B.A. (2004). The death of Alexander the Great: malaria or typhoid fever. *Infectious Disease Clinics of North America* 18 (1).

Cust, R. (2007). *Charles I: A Political Life*. London: Routledge.

Cust, R. (2013). *Charles I and the Aristocracy*. Cambridge: Cambridge University Press.

Dauzat, A. (1926). *Les noms de Lieux*. Paris: Librairie Delagrave.

Davies, J.K. (1975). Review of Connor (1971). *Gnomon* 47: 374–378.

De Andrade, M. (1951). Portuguese Colonialism---Myths and Realities. In: *The Crisis*, 215. Crisis Publishing Co.

De Zulueta, F. (1974). *Patronage in the Later Empire*. Oxford: Oxford University Press.

Dondin-Payre, M. (1993). *Exercice du Pouvoir et Continuité Gentilice: Les Aciliii Glabriones*. Rome: Collection de l'École Française de Rome, École Française de Rome `https://www.persee.fr/issue/efr_0000-0000_1993_mon_180_1` (accessed 7 May 2025).

Doom, E. (2016). Volcanoes and heresies: historiographical perspectives on the Byzantine iconoclastic controversy. *Fairmount Folio: Journal of History* 7: 1–8. `http://core.ac.uk/download/pdf/276620084.pdf` (accessed 7 May 2025)

Drake, H.A. (ed.) (2006). *Violence in Late Antiquity: Perceptions & Practices*. Abingdon, Oxfordshire: Ashgate Publishing.

Drake, H.A. (2011). Intolerance, religious violence, and political legitimacy in late antiquity. *Journal of the American Academy of Religion* 79 (1): 193–235.

Drijvers, J.W. (1997). *Helena Augusta: The mother of Constantine the Great and the legend of her finding the true Cross*. Leiden: Brill.

Dudley, E. (1948). *The Tree of Commonwealth*. Cambridge University Press.

Dunn, A. (2002). *The Great Rising of 1381: The Peasant's Revolt and England's Failed Revolution*. Stroud: Tempus Publishing.

Dworkin, R. (1977). *Taking Rights Seriously*. London: Bloomsbury.

Dworkin, R. (1996). *Freedom's Law*. Harvard University Press.

Echeverria, D. (1985). *The Maupeou Revolution*. Baton Rouge: Louisiana State University Press.

Eck, W. (1971). Das Eindringen des Christentums in den Senatorenstand biz zu Konstantin. *Chiron* I: 381–406.

The Economist. (2012). Cuban-Americans: The Miami Mirror. *The Economist* (24 March). `https://thecubaneconomy.com/articles/2012/03/the-economist-special-report-on-cuba-march-24-2012/` (accessed 21 April 2025).

Eduardo, G.C. (2011). *Contrarevolucionarios 1931–1936*. Madrid: Allianza Editorial.

Elena, D.P. and del Tindaro, M.R. (1909). *Santa Melania Giuniore*. Rome: Senatrice Romana.

Ellis, R. (1999). *Founding the American Presidency*, vol. 133. Rowman & Littlefield.

Elton, G.R. (1953). *The Tudor Revolution in Government*. Cambridge: Cambridge University Press.

Elton, G.R. (1967). *The Practice of History*. London: Fontana Press.

Elton, G.R. (1986). *The Parliament of England 1559–1581*. Cambridge: Cambridge University Press.

Elton, G.R. (2003). *Studies in Tudor and Stuart Politics and Government*, vol. II. Cambridge: Cambridge University Press.

Figgis, J.N. (1922). *The Divine Right of Kings*. Cambridge University Press.

Finley, M.I. (1954/2002). *The World of Odysseus*. New York: New York Review of Books.

Finley, M.I. (1962). The Athenian demagogues. *Past & Present* 21: 3–24.

Finley, M.I. (1973). *Aspects of Antiquity*. Harmondsworth: Pengiuin Books.

Finley, M.I. (1983). *Politics in the Ancient World*. Cambridge: Cambridge University Press.

Finley, M. (2010). *Politics in the Ancient World*. Cambridge: Cambridge University Press.

Fischer, F. (1967/2007). *Germany's Aims in the First World War*. W.W. Norton.

Flaig, E. (1995). Entscheidung und Konsensus. In: *Herrschaft ohne Integration?* (ed. M. Jehne), 77–127. Stuttgart: Verlag Franz Steiner.

Flaig, E. (2003). *Ritualisierte Politik*. Zeichen, Gesten under Herrschaft im Alten Rom: Göttingen.

Flower, R. (2013). The insanity of heretics must be restrained: heresiology in the Theodosian Code. In: *Theodosius II: Rethinking the Roman Empire in Late Antiquity* (ed. C. Kelly), 172–194. Cambridge: Cambridge University Press.

Flower, H. (2014). *The Cambridge Companion to the Roman Republic*. Cambridge: Cambridge University Press.

Forsythe, B. (2005). *A Critical History of Early Rome*. Berkeley & Los Angeles: University of California Press.

Fromkin, D. (2004). *Europe's Last Summer*. Alfred A. Knopf.

Frost, F.J. (1964). Pericles, Thucydides son of Melesias and Athenian politics before the war. *Historia* 13 (1964): 385–399.

Galvao-Sobrinho, C.R. (1995). Funerary Epigraphy and the Spread of Christianity in the West. *Athenaeum* 83: 431–466.

Garnsey, P. (1970). *Social Status and Legal Privilege in the Roman Empire*. Oxford: Oxford University Press.

Garnsey, P. (1984). Religious toleration in classical antiquity. *Studies in Church History* 21: 1–27.

Garnsey, P. (2010). Roman Patronage. In: *From the Tetrarchs to the Theodosians* (ed. S. McGill, C. Sogno, E. Watts, et al.), 33–54. Cambridge: Cambridge University Press.

Gelzer, M. (1975). *The Roman Nobility*. New York: Wiley-Blackwell.

Gibbon, E. (1776). *The Decline and Fall of the Roman Empire*. London.

Giffen, K.J. (2021). A brief comparison of the nature of kingship between ancient Egypt and Mesopotamia. https://www.academia.edu/70914880/A_brief_comparison_of_the_nature_of_kingship_between_ancient_Egypt_and_Mesopotamia (accessed 7 May 2025).

Gilens, M. and Page, B.I. (2014). *Testing Theories of American Politics: Elites, Interest Groups, and Average Citizens*. Chicago: University of Chicago Press.

Gilfilla, S.C. (1965). Lead Poisoning and the fall of Rome. *Journal of Occupational Medicine* 7: 53–60.

Gillett, A. (2012). Review Article: Rome's fall and Europe's rise. *The Medieval Review*. https://scholarworks.iu.edu/journals/index.php/tmr/article/view/16453 (accessed 7 May 2025).

Gilliard, F. (1979). The Senators of sixth-century Gaul. *Speculum* 54: 685–697.

Goffart, W. (1987). *Barbarians and Romans*. Princeton: Princton University Press.

Goffart, W. (2009). *Barbarian Tides*. Philadelphia: University of Pennsylvania Press.

Goldberg, E.J. (1995). *The Fall of the Roman Empire Revisited: Sidonius Apollinaris and his Crisis of Identity, Essays in History*. Corcoran, Dept. of History: University of Virginia.

Gomme, A.W. (1962). *More Essays in Geek History and Literature*. Oxford: Oxford University Press.

González Calleja, E. (2011). *Contrarevolucionarios. Radicalización violenta de las derechas durante la Segunda República 1931–1936*. Madrid: Allianza Editorial.

Grant, M. (1971). *From Imperium to Auctoritas*. Cambridge: Cambridge University Press.

Grant, M. (1986). *The History of Rome*. London: Faber & Faber.

Green, J.A. (2009). *Henry I: King of England and Duke of Normandy*. Cambridge: Cambridge University Press.

Grey, C. (2007). Revisiting the 'Problem' of agri deserti in the late Roman Empire. *Journal of Roman Archaeology* 20 (1): 362–376.

Grote, G. (1846–1856). *History of Greece*. Cambridge: Cambridge University Press.

Gruen, E. (1995). *The Last Generation of the Roman Republic*. Berkeley & Los Angeles: University of California Press.

Gruen, E. (1996). *Studies in Greek Culture and Roman Policy*. Berkeley & Los Angeles: University of California Press.

Guizot, F. (2002). *The History of the Origins of Representative Government in Europe*. Translated by Andrew R. Scoble. Indianapolis: Liberty Fund.

von Haehling, R. (1978). *Die Religionszugehörigkeit der hohen Amtsträger des Römischen Reiches seit Constantins Alleinherrschaft biz zum Ende der Theodosianischen Dynastie (324-450 bzw. 455 n. Chr.)*. Bonn: Habelt Verlag.

Hailsham, L. (1979). *The Dilemma of Democracy*. London: Harper Collins.

Haldon, J.f. (2008). *Social History of Byzantium*. New York: Wiley-Blackwell.

Hallo, W.H. and Younger, K.L. (ed.) *The Context of Scripture. Vol. II: Monumental Inscriptions from the Biblical World*. Leiden and Boston: Brill.

Hallo, W. and Younger, K. (2003). *The Context of Scripture*, 3 vols. (Open Source).

Halsall, G. (2007). *Barbarian Migrations and the Roman West, 376–568*. Cambridge: Cambridge University Press.

Halsall, G. (2014). Two Worlds become one. *German History* 32 (4): 515–532.

Hamburger, P. (2008). *Law and Judicial Duty*. Cambridge, MA: Harvard University Press.

Hammond, M. (1957). The Composition of the Senate, AD 68-235. *Journal of Romance Studies* 47: 74–81.

Harlow, C. and Rawlings, R. (1997). *Law and Administration*, Cambridge University Press.

Hardman, J. (1993). *Louis XVI: The Silent King*. New Haven: Yale University Press.

Hardman, J. (2016). *The Life of Louis XVI*. New Haven: Yale University Press.

Harmand, L. (1957). *Le patronat sur les collectivités publiques des origins au bas-Empire*. Paris: Presses Universitaires de France.

Harper, K. (2017). *The Fate of Rome*. Princeton, NJ: Princeton University Press.

Hayes, J. (1972). *Late Roman Pottery*. London: British School at Rome.

Heather, P. (2006). *The Fall of the Roman Empire: A New History of Rome and the Barbarians*. New York: Oxford University Press.

Heather, P. (2018). Race, migration, and national origins. In: *History, Memory and Public Life* (ed. A. Maerker, S. Sleight, and A. Sutcliffe), 80–100. London: Routledge.

Henry, P. (1882). *Diaries and Letters of Philip Henry* (ed. L.,.M. Henry). London: Kegan Paul, Trench & Co.

Herbert, S. (2015). *The Fall of Feudalism in France*. Miami: Hard Press Publishing.

Hernstein, R. and Murray, C. (1994). *The Bell Curve*. New York: Free Press.

Hinsley, F.H. and Wilson, K. (ed.) (1995/2016). *Decisions for War, 1914*. London: Routledge.

Hitler, A. (2008). *Mein Kampf*, vol. I, ch x, translated James Murphy. Project Gutenberg.

Ho, P.-t. (1976). *The Ladder of Success in Imperial China: Aspects of Social Mobility 1368–1911*. New York: De Capo Press.

Hobbes, T. (1651). *Leviathan, or The Matter, Forme and Power of a Commonwealth Ecclesiastical and Civil*. London: Andrew Crooke.

Hölkeskamp, K.-J. (1995). *Senatus Populusque Romanus: Die Politische Kultur der Republik*. Wiesbaden: Franz Steiner Verlag.

Hölkeskamp, K. (2010). *Reconstructing the Roman Republic*. Princeton: Princeton University Press.

Holmes, C. (2005). *Basil II and the Governance of Empire (976–1025)*. Oxford: Oxford University Press.

Holt, J.C. (1992). *Magna Carta*. Cambridge: Cambridge University Press.

Honoré, T. (1979). 'Imperial' rescripts 193-305: authorship and authenticity. *Journal of Romance Studies* 69: 51–64.

Hook, B. (1991). *The Cambridge Encyclopedia of China*, 2e. Cambridge University Press.

Hopkins, K. (1963). *Eunuchs in Politics in the Later Roma Empire*. Trübner.

Hopkins, K. (1978). *Conquerors and Slaves*. New York: Cambridge University Press.

Huang, R. (1981). *1587. A Year of No Significance: The Ming Dynasty in Decline*. New Haven: Yasle University Press.

Huang, S. (2001). The power of words: political slogans as leverage during China's Cultural Revolution. In: *Chinese Conflict Management and Resolution* (ed. G. Chen and R. Ma). Santa Barbara, CA: Greenwood Publishing Group.

Hurt, J. (2002). *Louis XIV and the Parlements*. Manchester: Manchester University Press.

Iggers, G.G. and von Moltke, K. (ed.) (1973/2010). *Ranke: The Theory and Practice of History*. London: Routledge.

Inge, W. (1929). *Assessments and Anticipations*. London: Cassell.

Innes, M. (2006). Land, freedom and the making of the medieval West. *Transactions of the Royal Historical Society* 16: 39–74.

James, I. (1996). *The True Law of Free Monarchies* (ed. D. Fischlin and M. Fortier). Toronto: Victoria University Press.

James, V.I. and King, I. (2010). *Political Writings*. Cambridge: Cambridge University Press.

Jefferson, T. (1785). *Notes on the State of Virginia*. Philadelphia: Prichard and Hall.

Jefferson, T. (2019). *Delphi Complete Works of Thomas Jefferson (Illustrated)*. Delphi Classics.

Jeffreys, E.M. (2006). *Byzantine Style, Religion and Civilization*. Cambridge: Cambridge University Press.

Jehne, M. (ed.) (1995). *Demokratie in Rom?* Stuttgart: Die Rolle des Volkes in der Politik der römischen Republik.

Jew, D., Osborne, R., and Scott, M. (ed.) (2016). *M.I. Finley: An Ancient Historian and his Impact*. Cambridge: Cambridge University Press.

Johnson, A.C., Coleman-Norton, P.R., and Bourne, F.C. (1961). *Ancient Roman Statutes*. Austin: University of Texas Press.

Jones, A.H.M. (1948). *Constantine and the Conversion of Europe*. London: Hodder & Stoughton.

Jones, A.H.M. (1955). Elections under Augustus. *Journal of Romance Studies* 45: 1955.

Jones, A.H.M. (1957). *Athenian Democracy*. Oxford: Basil Blackwell.

Jones, A.H.M. (1958). The Roman colonate. *Past and Present* 13: 1–13.

Jones, A.H.M. (1964). *The Later Roman Empire*. Oxford: Basil Blackwell.

Jones, A.H.M. (1970). "The Caste System In the Later Roman Empire", *Eirene* 8(1970) 79–96.

Jones, A.H.M. (1974). *The Roman Economy*. Oxford: Basil Blackwell.

Jones, A.H.M., Martindale, J.R., and Morris, J. (1971–1992). *PLRE: The Prosopography of the Later Roman Empire*, vol. 3. Cambridge: Cambridge University Press.

Kautsky, K. (2020). *Democracy and Republicanism*. Haymarket Books.

Kelly, C. (2004). *Ruling the Later Roman Empire*. Cambridge, MA: Harvard University Press.

Kendall, L., Murray, J.L., and Linden, R. (2000). *Sociology in Our Times*, 2e. Scarborough: Nelson.

Kenworthy, L. (1999). *Egalitarian Capitalism*. Russell Sage Foundation.

Kokkonen, A., Möller, J., and Sundell, A. (2022). *The Politics of Succession: Forging Stable Monarchies in Europe, AD 1000–1800*. Oxford University Press.

Korfmann, M. (2013). *Troia-Wilusa Guidebook*. Troia Vakfi.

Kouroumali, M. (2013). Byzantine aristocracy. In: *Encyclopedia of Ancient History* (ed. R. Bagnall). Oxford: Blackwell.

Kozloff, A. (2012). *Amenhotep III, Egypt's Radiant Pharaoh*. Cambridge University Press.

Kritsotakis, D. (2008). Hadrian and the Greek east. PhD dissertation. Ohio State University.

Kurland, P. and Lerner, R. (1987). *The Founders' Constitution*. Chicago: University of Chicago Press.

Kurrild-Klitgaard, P. (2000). The constitutional economics of autocratic succession. *Public Choice* 103: 63–84.

Kurrild-Klitgaard, P. (2004). Autocratic succession. *The Encyclopedia of Public Choice* 193: 358–362.

Lagen, U. (2008). *Den afmægtige – En biografi om Christian VII*. Jyllands-Postens Forlag.

Lambrechts, P. (1936). *La composition du sénat roman de l'Accession au Trône d'Hadrien à la Mort de Commode, 117–192*. Antwerp: De Sikkel.

Lambrechts, P. (1937). *La composition du sénat roman de Septime Sévère à Dioclétien (193–284)*. Budapest.

Lee, T.H.C. (1985). *Government Education and Examinations in Sung (Song) China*. Hong Kong: Chinese University Press.

Lefebvre, G. (1973). *The Great Fear of 1789: Rural Panic in Revolutionary France*. New York: Pantheon Books.

Lenin, V.I. (1965). *Collected Works (1965)*, vol. 33, 186. Moscow: Progress Publishers.

Lenski, N.E. (2006). *The Cambridge Companion to the Age of Constantine*. Cambridge: Cambridge University Press.

Lewis, C.T. and Short, C. (1879). *A Latin Dictionary*. Oxford: Oxford University Press.

Liebeschuetz, W. (1997). Cities, taxes, and the accommodation of the Barbarians. In: *From Roman Provinces to Medieval Kingdoms* (ed. W. Pohl), 135–151.

Liebeschuetz, W. (2001). *The Decline and Fall of the Roman City*. Oxford: Oxford University Press.

Liebeschuetz, W. (2004). The birth of late antiquity. *Antiquité Tardive* 12 (2004): 253–261.

Liebeschuetz, W. (2015). *East and West in Late Antiquity*. Leiden: Brill.

Lieu, J., North, J., and Rajak, T. (1992). *The Jews Among Pagans and Christians in the Roman Empire*. Abingdon: Routledge.

Lincoln, A. (2005). *Gospel According to St John: Black's New Testament Commentaries*. London: Bloomsbury Publishing.

Liverani, Mario (2013). *The Ancient Near East: History, Society and Economy*. London: Routledge

Lintott, A. (2003). *The Constitution of the Roman Republic*. Oxford: Oxford University Press.

Lippert, S. (2013). Inheritance. In: *UCLA Encyclopedia of Egyptology* (ed. E. Frood and W. Wendrich). Los Angeles: University of California.

Littman, R.J. and Littman, M.L. (1973). Galen and the Antonine Plague. *American Journal of Philology* 94: 254–255.

Locke, J. (1689). Second treatise of Government. In: *Democracy: A Reader* (ed. R. Blaug and J. Schwarzmantel), 120–123. Columbia University Press.

Los Angeles Times. (2017). 'Opinion: Universal healthcare, no illiteracy and other Cuban feats under a US embargo', *Los Angeles Times* (20 June 2017). https://www.latimes.com/opinion/readersreact/la-ol-le-cuba-us-embargo-trump-20170620-story.html (accessed 21 April 2025).

Ludden, D. (2013). *India and South Asia: A Short History*. Oneworld Publications.

Macaulay, T.B. (1848). *The History of England from the Accession of James II*. London: Longman, Brown, Green, and Longmans.

Machiavelli, N. (2019). *The Prince* (ed. Q. Skinner and R. Price). Cambridge: Cambridge University Press.

Time Magazine (1935). GREECE: By the Grace of God. *Time* (18 November). `https://time.com/archive/6754571/greece-by-the-grace-of-god/` (accessed 29 April 2025).

Malnati, T.P. (1987). Juvenal and Martial on social mobility. *The Classical Journal* 83: 133–141.

Mankiewicz, F.J. (1976). *With Fidel: A Portrait of Castro and Cuba*. New York: Ballantine Books.

Mansel, P. (2019). *King of the World: The Life of Louis XIV*. London: Allen Lane.

Martin, P. (2010). Lincoln's missing bodyguard. *Smithsonian Magazine* (8 April). `https://www.smithsonianmag.com/history/lincolns-missing-bodyguard-12932069/` (accessed 7 May 2025). `smithsonianmag.com`.

Marx, K. and Engels, F. (1848). *The Communist Manifesto*. London: Communist League.

Mathisen, R.W. (2009). Provinciales, gentiles, ands between Romans and Barbarians in the Late Roman Empire. *Journal of Romance Studies* 99: 140–155.

Mathisen, R.W. (2011a). *Roman Aristocrats in Barbarian Gaul*. Austin: University of Texas Press.

Mathisen, R. and Shanzer, D. (ed.) (2011b). *Romans, Barbarians, and the Transformation of the Roman World*. London: Routledge.

Mathisen, R. and Shanzer, D. (ed.) (2017). *Society and Culture in Late Antique Gaul*. London: Routledge.

Matthews, J.F. (1975). *Western Aristocracies and the Imperial Court 364–425*. Oxford: Oxford University Press.

Matthews, J.F. (1989). *The Roman Empire of Ammianus*. London: Duckworth.

Mattingly-Sydenham (1968). *Roman Imperial Coinage*, vol. 3, Antoninus Pius to Commodus. London: Spink & Son.

Meier, C. (2017). *Res Publica Amissa*. Wiesbaden: Franz Steiner Verlag.

Meier, C. (2018). *Caesar*. London: Fontana.

Mennen, I. (2011). *Power and Status in the Roman Empire, 193–284*. Leiden: Brill.

Merlin, A. (1921). La Mosaïque du seigneur Julius à Carthage. *Bulletin Archéologique du Comité des Travaux Historiques et Scientifiques* 95–114.

Merrills, A. (2017). *Vandals, Romans and Berbers*. London: Routledge.

Mettam, R. (1977). *Government and Society in Louis XIV's France*. London: Macmillan.

Mettam, R. (1988). *Power and Faction in Louis XIV's France*. Oxford: Basil Blackwell.

Milani, A. (2008). *Eminent Persians: The Men and Women Who Made Modern Iran, 1941–1979*, 109. Syracuse University Press and Persian World Press.

Millar, F. (1992). *The Emperor in the Roman World*. Bristol: Bristol Classical Press.

Millar, F. (2002). *Rome, the Greek World, and the East*. Chapel Hill: University of North Carolina Press.

Millar, F. (2006a). *The Roman Republic in Political Thought*. Boston: Brandeis University Press.

Millar, F. (2006b). *A Greek Roman Empire: Power and Belief under Theodosius II (408–450)*. University of California Press.

Mills, C.W. (1956). *The Power Elite*. Oxford: Oxford University Press.

Momigliano, A. (1987). *On Pagans, Jews, and Christians*. Middletown, CT: Wesleyan University Press.

Mommsen, T. (1876). *Römisches Staatsrecht*. Leipzig.: S. Hirzel Verlag.

Mordechai, L. and Eisenberg, M. (2019). Rejecting catastrophe: the case of the Justinianic Plague. *Past and Present* 244 (1): 3–50.

Morison, S.E. (1946). *History as a Literary Art: An Appeal to Young Historians*. Boston: Old South Association.

Morison, S.E. (1951). Presidential address. *American Historical Review* 56: 272–273.

Morley, N. (2004). *Theories, Models and Concepts in Ancient History*. London and New York: Routledge.

Morris, R. (1976). The powerful and the poor in tenth century Byzantium. *Past and Present* 3–27.

Moser, M. (2019). *Emperor and Senators in the Reign of Constantius II*. Cambridge: Cambridge University Press.

Moss, C. (2013). *The Myth of Persecution: How Early Christians Invented a Story of Martyrdom*. London: Harper Collins.

Mouritsen, H. (2008). *Plebs and Politics in the Late Roman Republic*. Cambridge: Cambridge University Press.

Mouritsen, H. (2011). *The Freedman in the Roman World*. Cambridge: Cambridge University Press.

Mouritsen, H. (2017). *Politics in the Roman Republic*. Cambridge: Cambridge University Press.

Mühlberger, S. (1986). Prosper's Epitoma chronicon. *Classical Philology* 1986: 240–244.

Müller, A. (2015). *Che Guevara*. Valgo más vivo que muerte. Kindle E-Books.

Murray, C. (1984). *Losing Ground: American Social Policy, 1950–1980*. New York: Basic Books.

Needleman, L. and Diane (1985). Lead poisoning and the decline of the Roman aristocracy. *Classical Views* 4 (1): 63–94.

Neuberger, D. (2017). Twenty years a judge: Reflections and refractions. Neill Lecture, Oxford Law Faculty (10 February). https://supremecourt.uk/uploads/speech_170210_ca41b88877.pdf (accessed 7 May 2025).

Nixey, C. (2018). *The Darkening Age: The Christian Destruction of the Classical World*. London: Pan.

Noble, T. (ed.) (2006). *From Roman Provinces to Medieval Kingdoms*. London: Routledge.

Nock, A.D. (1933). *Conversion*. Oxford: Oxford University Press.

North, J. (1989). Review of brunt (1988). *Journal of Romance Studies* 79: 151–156.

Norwich, J.J. (1997). *A Short History of Byzantium*. London.

Nriagu, J.O. (1983). Did lead poisoning contribute to the fall of the Empire? *New England Journal of Medicine* 308: 660–663.

Ober, J. (1989). *Mass and Elite in Democratic Athens*. Princeton: Princeton University Press.

Ober, J. (2009). *Mass & Elite in Democratic Athens*. Princeton University Press.

Obolensky, D. (1974). *The Byzantine Commonwealth: Eastern Europe 500–1453*. London: Weidenfeld and Nicolson.

Oded, B. (1979). *Mass deportations and deportees in the Neo-Assyrian empire*. Wiesbaden: Dr. Ludwig Reichert Verlag.

O'Donnell, P. (2011). Opiniones de Perón sobre el Che. *El Pais* (8 October).

Offord, D. (1986). *The Russian Revolutionary Movement in the 1889s*. Cambridge: Cambridge UP.

Olivelle, P. (2009). *Manu's Code of Laws*. Oxford University Press.

Olmstead, A.T. (1948). *History of the Persian Empire*. University of Chicago Press.

Orfield, G. (1992). *Diversity Challenged*. Harvard Education Press.

Osnos, E. (2020). How Greenwich Republicans learned to love Trump. *The New Yorker* (11 May).

Ostrogorsky, G. (1986). *History of the Byzantine State*. Rutgers University Press.

Paribeni, R. (1940). Le Dimore Potentiores nel Basso Impero. *MDAI (R)* 55: 131–148.

Pascal, B. (1995). *Pensées*. Harmondsworth: Penguin Books.

Patterson, O. (1982). *Slavery and Social Death*. Cambridge MA and London: Harvard University Press.

Percival, J. (1976). *The Roman Villa*. London: Batsford.

Percival, J. (1992). The fifth-century villa. In: *Fifth-Century Gaul: A Crisis of Identity?* (ed. J. Drinkwater and H. Elton), 156–165. Cambridge: Cambridge University Press.

Perkins, P. (1998). *The Cambridge Companion to Biblical Interpretation* (ed. J. Barton). Westminster: John Knox Press.

Perón, J.D. (2015). *Modelo Argentino para el Proyecto Nacional*. Buenos Aires: Biblioteca del Congreso de la Nación.

Piganiol, A. (1947). *L'Empire Chrétien: 325–395*. Paris: Presses Universitaires de Franc.

Piketty, T. (2013). *Capital in the Twenty-First Century*. Harvard University Press.

Pirenne, H. (1954). *Mohammed and Charlemagne*, tr. Bernard Miall. London: Allen & Unwin.

Pirenne, H. (2014). *Medieval Cities*, revised ed., tr. Frank H. Halsey. Princeton: Princeton University Press.

Plutarch (1931). Regum et imperatorum apothegmata. In: *Plutarch's Moralia, Vol. III* (trans. F.C. Babbitt), 172A–263C. Cambridge, MA: Harvard University Press.

Pohl, W. (ed.) (1997). *Kingdoms of the Empire: The Integration of Barbarians in Late Antiquity*. Leiden: Brill.

Price, M. (1995). *Preserving the Monarchy*. Cambridge: Cambridge University Press.

Quirk, R. (1993). *Fidel Castro*. New York: W.W. Norton & Co.

Rampolla, C. (1909). *Santa Melania Giuniore*. Senatrice: Romana.

Rawls, J. (1971). *A Theory of Justice*. Cambridge, MA: Belknap Press.

Rees, R. (2004). *Diocletian and the Tetrarchy*. Edinburgh: Edinburgh University Press.

Retief, F.P. and Cilliers, L. (2006). Lead poisoning in Ancient Rome. *Acta Theologica* 26 (2) Supp. 7: 147–164.

Reynolds, S. (1994). *Fiefs and Vassals: The Medieval Evidence Reinterpreted*. New York: Oxford University Press.

Richards, J. (1979). *The Popes and the Papacy in the Early Middle Ages, 476–752*. London: Routledge Kegan Paul.

Riggio, R. (2012). What is charisma and charismatic leadership? *Psychology Today* (7 October). https://www.psychologytoday.com/blog/cutting-edge-leadership/201210/what-is-charisma-and-charismatic-leadership (accessed 7 May 2025).

Robinson, E. (2005). The controversial, charismatic Castro. *Washington Post* (30 January).

Rohter, L. (2006). Despite recovery, inequality grows in Argentina. *New York Times* (25 December).

Rösch, G. (1978). *Onoma Basileias*. Vienna: Österreichische Akademie der Wissenschaft.

Rose, V. (1886). *Aristotelis qui ferebantur librorum fragmenta*. Leipzig: Teubner.

Rosenstein, N. (ed.) (2010). *A Companion to the Roman Republic*. London: Blackwell.

Ross, C. (1974). *Edward IV*. University of California Press.

Rostovtzeff, M.I. (1923). Commodus-hercules in Britain. *Journal of Romance Studies* 13: 91–109.

Rostovtzeff, M.I. (1926). *The Social and Economic History of the Roman Empire*, 2e. Oxford: Oxford University Press.

Rotunda, R.D. (2014). *Increasing Revenue by Lowering Taxes*. Verdict, Justia. https://verdict.justia.com/2014/06/23/increasing-revenue-lowering-taxes (accessed 3 May 2025).

Rousseau, J.-J. (1762). *Du Contrat Social ou Principes du Droit Politique*. Amsterdam: Marc Michel Rey.

Rowe, G. (2013). Reassessing the auctoritas of Augustus. *Journal of Romance Studies* 103: 1–15.

Royalty, R.M. (2013). *The Origin of Heresy*. London: Routledge.

Runciman, S. (1951). *History of the Crusades*, vol. I. Cambridge: Cambridge University Press.

Russell, J.C. (1958). Late ancient and medieval population. *American Philosophical Society* 48: 1–152.

Sachedina, A. (2001). *The Islamic Roots of Democratic Pluralism*. Oxford: Oxford University Press.

Sacks, J. (1993). *One People: Tradition, Modernity and Jewish Unity*. London: Littman Library of Jewish Civilization.

de Saint-Simon, L. (2007). *Anthologie des Mémoires de Saint-Simon*. Paris: Livre de Poche.

Sallares, R. (2002). *Malaria and Rome: A History of Malaria in Ancient Rome*. New York: Oxford University Press.

Sallares, R., Bouwman, A., and Anderung, C. (2004). The spread of malaria to Southern Europe in antiquity. *Medical History* 48 (3): 311–328.

Salzman, M.R. (2004). *The Making of a Christian Aristocracy: Social and Religious Change in the Western Roman Empire*. Cambridge: Harvard University Press.

Salzman, M.R. (2006a). Symmachus and the 'Barbarian' generals. *Historia* 55: 352–367.

Salzman, M.R. (2006b). Rethinking Pagan-Christian Violence," Chapter 22. In: *Violence in Late Antiquity* (ed. H.A. Drake). Routledge.

Sanchez, I. (2010). Fidel Castro marks 50 years of neighborhood watch group. *CNN World* (28 September). https://edition.cnn.com/2010/WORLD/americas/09/28/cuba.castro/index.html (7 May 2025).

Sarris, P. (2015). *Byzantium: A Very Short Introduction*. Oxford: Oxford University Press.

Scarborough, J. (1984). The Myth of lead poisoning among the Romans. *Journal of the History of Medicine* 39: 469–475.

Schama, S. (1992). *A History of Britain*, vol. 2. London: BBC.

Scheidel, W. (1999). Emperors, aristocrats, and the grim reaper: towards a demographic profile of the Roman elite. *The Classical Quarterly* 49 (1): 254–281.

Schlesinger, A.M. Jr. (1973). *The Imperial Presidency*. Boston: Houghton Mifflin.

Schwartz, E. (1913). *Kaiser Constantin und Die Christliche Kirche*. Leipzig: Teubner.

Scott, E. (2012). *Mohammed and Charlemagnr Revisited*. Nashville: New English Review Press.

Seaver, J.E. (1952). *Persecution of the Jews in the Roman Empire (300–438)*. Lawrence: University of Kansas Publications.

Seeley, J.R. (1883). *The Expansion of England*, 12. Cambridge: Cambridge University Press.

Sellar, W.C. and Yeatman, R.J. (1930). *1066 And All That*. London: Methuen.

Sen, R. (2006). Defining Religion: The Indian Supreme Court and Hinduism. *Heidelberg Papers in South Asian and Comparative Politics* 29. University of Heidelberg, Department of Political Science. https://archiv.ub.uni-heidelberg.de/volltextserver/6936/ (accessed 7 May 2025).

Shahbazi, S. (1994). Darius the Great. *Encyclopaedia Iranica*, vol. 7, fasc. 1, pp. 41–50. New York: Columbia University Press. https://iranicaonline.org/articles/darius-iii/ (accessed 7 May 2025).

Shaw, B.D. (2015). The myth of the Neronian persecution. *Journal of Romance Studies* 105: 73–100.

Sherwin-White, A.N. (1957). Review of John Crook (1955). *Journal of Romance Studies* 47: 252–254.

Sircar, D.C. (1979). *Asokan Studies*. Calcutta: Indian Museum.

Sivan, H. (1991). A late Gallic branch of the Acilii Glabriones? *Notes on Ausonius' Professores 24 (Peiper) Mnemosyne* 44: 435–439.

Soll, J. (2009). *The Information Minister: Jean-Baptiste Colbert's Secret State Intelligence System*. Ann Arbor: University of Michigan Press.

Soren, D. (2003). Can archaeologists excavate evidence of malaria? *World Archaeology* 35 (2): 193–209.

Soren, D. and Soren, N. (1999). *A Roman Villa and a Late Roman Infant Cemetery*. L'Erma di Bretschneider.

Soricelli, G. (2010). Agri deserti. *Encyclopedia of Ancient History* 1–2.

Southern, R. (1953). *The Making of the Middles Ages*. London: Hutchinson.

Southern, P. (2001). *The Roman Empire from Severus to Constantine*. London: Routledge.

Sowerby, S. (2013). *Making Toleration*. Cambridge: Harvard University Press.

Stark, R. (1996). *The Rise of Christianity*. New Haven: Princeton University Press.

Stark, R. (2011). *The Triumph of Christianity*. London: Harper Collins.

Staveley, S. (2014). The nature and aims of the patriciate. *Historia* 32: 1.

Ste, D., Croix, G., Whitby, M., and Streeter, J. (2006). *Christian Pesecution, Martyrdom, and Orthodoxy*. Oxford: Oxford University Press.

Stephens, H.M. (1911) "Mirabeau", article in *Encyclopaedia Britannica*, Vol. 18 (11th edition.), pp. 566–570, Cambridge University Press.

Stephenson, P. (2011). *Constantine: Unconquered Emperor, Christian Victor*. London: Quercus.

Stern, H. (1954). Remarks on the 'Adoratio' under Diocletian. *Journal of the Warburg and Courtauld Institutes* 17: 184–189.

Sumption, J. (2009). *Divided House: The Hundred Years War*, vol. III. London: Faber & Faber.

Syme, R. (1937). Review of Lambrechts (1936). *Journal of Romance Studies* 27: 271.

Syme, R. (1939). *The Roman Revolution*. Oxford: Oxford University Press.

Syme, R. (1989). *The Augustan Aristocracy*. Oxford: Oxford University Press.

Tackett, N.O. (2006). The transformation of medieval Chinese elites (850–1000 CE). PhD dissertation. Columbia University.

Takács, S. (2000). Politics and Religion in the Bacchanalian Affair of 186 BCE. *Harvard Studies in Classical Philology* 100 (2000): 301–310.

Tate, W.E. (1967). *The English Village and the Enclosure Movement*. London: Gollancz.

Teegarden, D. (2013). *Death to Tyrants!* Princeton: Princeton University Press.

Thackeray, W.M. (2017). *Four Georges*. London: Books on Demand A Word To The Wise.

Thomas, C. (2008). *My Grandfather's Son*. New York: Harper Perennial.

Thorpe, F.N. (1898). *The Constitutional History of the United States*. Chicago: Callaghan & Co.

Torelli, M. (1968). The cursus honorum of M. Hirrius Fronto Neratius Pansa. *Journal of Romance Studies* 58: 170–175.

Torey, C. and Stylites, S. (1899). The Letters of Simeon the stylite. *Journal of the American Oriental Society* 20 (1899): 253–276.

Tougher, S. (2008). *The Eunuch in Byzantine History and Society*. Abingdon: Routledge.

Toynbee, A.J. (1934–1961). *A Study of History*, vol. 12. Oxford: Oxford University Press.

Treadgold, W. (1997). *A History of the Byzantine State and Society*. Palo Alto: Stanford University Press.

Trevor-Roper, H. (2000). *Archbishop Laud*. London: Orion.

Troost, W. (2005). *William III, the Stadholder-King*. London: Routledge.

Tullock, G. (2012). *Autocracy*. Springer.

van Dijk, J. (1993). *The New Kingdom Necropolis of Memphis: Historical and Iconographical Studies*. Groningen: University of Groningen.

Van Kley, D. (1999). *The Religious Origins of the French Revolution*. New Haven: Yale University Press.

Ventris, M. and Chadwick, J. (1958). *The Decipherment of Linear B*. Cambridge: Cambridge University Press.

von Ranke, L. (1875/2018). *A History of England Principally in the Seventeenth Century*. Oxford: Clarendon Press.

Walsh, P.G. (1996). Making a drama out of a crisis: Livy on the Bacchanalia. *Greece & Rome* 43 (2): 188–203.

Ward-Perkins, B. (2006). *The Fall of Rome: And the End of Civilization*. Oxford: Oxford University Press.

Warwick, C.F. (2005). *Mirabeau and the French Revolution*. Whitefish, MT: Kessinger Publishing.

Warwick, C.F. (2018). *Mirabeau and the French Revolution*. Miami: HardPress.

Wedgwood, C.V. (1983). *The Trial of Charles I*. Harmondsworth: Penguin.

Werner, K.-F. (1998). *Naissance de la noblesse*. Paris: Fayard.

West, M.L. (2011). The Homeric question today. *Proceedings of the American Philosophical Society* 155: 383–393.

West, C. (2013). *Reframing the Feudal Revolution*. Cambridge: Cambridge University Press.

Wetzler, P. (1998). *Hirohito and War*. Honolulu: University of Hawaii Press.

Whitby, M. (1991). John of Ephesus and the pagans. In: *Paganism in the Later Roman Empire* (ed. M. Salamon), 111–131. Krakow.

Whitehouse, D. and Hodges, R. (1983). *Mohammed, Charlemagne and the Origins of Europe: The Pirenne Thesis in the Light of Archaeology*. London: Duckworth.

Wickham, C. (1984). The other transition: from the ancient world to Feudalism. *Past and Present* 103: 3–36.

Wickham, C. (2006). *Framing the Early Middle Ages*. Oxford: Oxford University Press.

Wickham, C. (2010). *The Inheritance of Rome*. Harmondsworth: Penguin.

Wickham, C. (2016). *Medieval Europe*. New Haven: Yale University Press.

Wilhelm, II (1922). *The Kaiser's Memoirs*. Translated by T.R. Ybarra. New York: Harper & Brothers.

Wilkinson, E. (2012). *Chinese History: A New Manual*. Harvard University Press.

Williams, S. (1997). *Diocletian and the Roman Recovery*. London: Routledge.

Winters, J. (2011). *Oligarchy*. Cambridge: Cambridge University Press.

Wiseman, T.P. (2009). *Remembering the Roman People*. Oxford: Oxford University Press.

Wood, M. (2015). *In Search of the Trojan War*. London: Random House.

Yavetz, Z. (1988). *Plebs and Princeps*. Oxford: Oxford University Press.

Ye'or, B. (2013). *Understanding Dhimmitude*. New York: RVP Press.

Zakaria, F. (2003). *The Future of Freedom*. New York: W.W. Norton.

Index

A

Five Thousand Years of Monarchy, First Edition. Michael Arnheim.
© 2026 John Wiley & Sons, Inc. Published 2026 by John Wiley & Sons, Inc.

Printed and bound by CPI Group (UK) Ltd, Croydon, CR0 4YY

27/08/2025

14725037-0001